MONEY
AND BANKING

MONEY AND BANKING

SIXTH EDITION

RAYMOND P. KENT

University of Notre Dame

HOLT, RINEHART AND WINSTON, INC.

NEW YORK   CHICAGO   SAN FRANCISCO   ATLANTA
DALLAS   MONTREAL   TORONTO   LONDON   SYDNEY

To my wife

PREFACE

Since the first edition of this textbook was published in 1947, this sixth edition could be called the silver anniversary edition. But, considering what has happened to silver as money in our system, I hastily conclude that giving that designation to the twenty-fifth anniversary of a textbook in money and banking is something to be zealously avoided.

A twenty-fifth anniversary does require some celebration, however, and the results of it are here. The present book has a new outline, and much of it has been entirely rewritten. In using the fifth edition in my own classes, I found myself jumping back and forth in making assignments, at the same time telling my students that some topics had greatly declined in importance, while others had greatly grown in importance, including, among the latter, some topics that were entirely new developments. Such an obvious demonstration of my own dissatisfaction with the book's outline and areas of emphasis became somewhat embarrassing. Accordingly, I gradually came to a realization that if the jumping around occurred in a logical sequence I could avoid it and the attendant embarrassment by rearranging the topics in the book itself. Hence the new outline. I also realized that my reevaluation in class of topics that deserved new or increased emphasis and those that needed deemphasis or even elimination also ought to be incorporated in the new edition. Hence the great amount of rewriting, with the introduction of many topics that have gained prominence only in the past few years, new stress on others that have grown in importance, the playing down of others that have declined in significance, the omission of some topics that, though still pertinent, do not appear to be essential for an understanding of what money and banking are all about, and the elimination of much material that had become, to put it frankly, deadwood.

In all editions of this textbook, I have sought to give primary emphasis to monetary control as a means of managing aggregate economic activity toward full employment, price-level stability, and achieving good rates of economic growth; but in this edition, for the first time, I get to this emphasis with minimum delay—with references to monetary control in Chapter 1 and with all of Chapter 2 devoted to it. The same theme is prominent in Chapter 3, with its explanation of what the various features of monetary systems are designed to achieve, and with its analysis of the features of older systems that endeavors to explain how the features of the present fused gold-fiat system evolved. I believe that the student should learn quite early in a course in money and banking how such a fused system works or is supposed to work, and that this requires a rather detailed knowledge of the setup, operations, and rules of the International Monetary Fund. Hence the two chapters on our own monetary system—Chapters 4 and 5—with its domestic and international features separately treated. As bank demand deposits are our most important kind of money in volume and use, and as they are the kind of money toward which control must necessarily be aimed, they surely deserve the extended analysis given them in Chapters 6 and 7, including the early treatment of the processes of their expansion and contraction. It is always good to know how our monetary system got to where it now is, but there should be a concurrent recognition that banks are and have long been the principal creators of money—hence Chapter 8 on monetary *and banking* history in this sixth edition in place of two widely separated chapters in earlier editions.

Most sweeping among the changes incorporated in this edition are the gathering together and telescoping in Chapters 9, 10, and 11 of a preliminary treatment of central and commercial banking, major details about the roles of the principal classes of nonbank financial institutions, and the structure of the financial markets in which all these institutions operate—materials formerly carried in one early chapter and five concluding chapters, with some, indeed, also scattered elsewhere. Also of sweeping proportions has been the rewriting of the two chapters on monetary theory—now Chapters 18 and 19—with recognition of the restored respectability of the quantity theory, a more detailed description of the structure of the national product-national income accounts and their tie-in with the income-expenditure theory, and the scope of the controversy between the "monetarists" and the "nonmonetarists." Comprehensive, too, has been the rewriting of the chapters on money and financial institutions in their international roles—now Chapters 23 through 26. In these chapters, new emphasis is given to our balance-of-payments difficulties, including the problem of their measurement; to the commanding role of the rules of the International Monetary Fund in the determination of exchange rates and the resulting problems of currency overvaluation and undervaluation; and in the final chapter—entirely rewitten—to the nature of and close interrelationships among the problems of exchange rate stability, the need of international monetary reserves, and balance-of-payments surpluses and deficits.

Elsewhere in this edition much rewriting and updating was necessitated by recent developments in institutional structures and operations; in legislation, rules, regulations, and practices; and, of course, in statistics. So extraordinary have been the developments in the field of money and banking in many directions in the past few years that much rewriting would have been unavoidable, even had I not decided to change the book's outline comprehensively and to rewrite much of the material that deserved to be upgraded or downgraded or modified in other ways.

As with earlier editions of this textbook, this one is designed primarily for the student's first course in the area of money and banking or financial institutions. I have striven to make it clear and understandable for students at the undergraduate level, and, if I have succeeded, it should be all the more so for students who take such a first course at the graduate level. As the book has been rather remarkably shortened, its complete coverage in a single semester or quarter should be possible without undue strain, even with some supplementary assigned readings. At the same time it should be readily adaptable for two-semester courses or two- or three-quarter courses, probably with a wider array of supplementary readings. As for such readings, I present quite a few suggestions in the Recommended Sources and Readings at the end of the book.

In the preparation of the original edition of this textbook and its several revisions over a long period of years, I have greatly benefited from the criticism and advice of many generous colleagues in the fields of economics and finance at Notre Dame and at other institutions. For this criticism and advice, I continue to be indebted to all the men whose names I have cited in earlier prefaces; and for excellent analyses and recommendations that were most helpful to me in preparing this sixth edition, I express sincere gratitude to Professor Arthur G. Billings of Indiana State University, Professor Umesh Gulati of East Carolina University, and Professor Charles E. Wade of Texas Technological University. For continual support and encouragement in numerous ways, as well as for specific suggestions and advice, I also express deep appreciation to my Notre Dame colleagues Dean Thomas T. Murphy, Professor Bernard J. Kilbride, the chairman of my department, and Professors Jae H. Cho, LeClair H. Eells, Herbert E. Sim, and Edward W. Trubac. As in earlier prefaces, I must reserve for Professor Eells a special place among those who so richly deserve my gratitude. From the beginning and through all editions, his advice and criticism have been invaluable, and equally helpful have been his many expressions of encouragement and confidence.

I am also deeply obligated to many of my students at Notre Dame, both recent and back through the years, who have served as the testing ground for my materials and who have shown me, in many instances, how they could be improved.

Finally, I want to say that Claudia, my wife, deserves the greatest share of my gratitude for her unfailing support, encouragement, and patience, and for much material assistance.

Notre Dame, Indiana   R. P. K.
April 1972

CONTENTS

I

MONEY

CHAPTER 1

THE NATURE OF MONEY

Money deserves to be ranked among man's outstanding inventions. By overcoming the difficulties of barter, man has made possible a tremendous saving of time and trouble in marshaling productive factors and distributing the output to ultimate users. The sweeping technological progress since the start of the industrial revolution, the specialization of industry, the organization of production on the basis of minute divisions of labor, the establishment of national and international markets—all would have been greatly impeded, if not precluded, had not reasonably adequate monetary facilities been available.

This is not to imply that money is directly responsible for the great productive efficiency and high standards of living that prevail in advanced nations, for much obviously depends on other factors, such as a country's natural resources, the composition, education, and skills of its people, and the availability of managerial talents. At the least, however, the use of money simplifies the bringing together of the factors of production and the organizing of markets through which goods can be distributed.

WHAT IS MONEY?

Though money is much in our thoughts and conditions many of our actions, we have difficulty in defining exactly what it is—in distinguishing it precisely from all other kinds of things. However, there appears to be a wide consensus that a definition of money can be truly meaningful only if it is functional, that is, a definition that distinguishes money from all other things in terms of its uses. And there is wide consensus, too, that service as a medium of exchange and service as a standard of value are the two principal distinguishing uses to which money is put.

Definition

With these ideas in mind, therefore, let us say that *money is anything that is commonly used and generally accepted as a medium of exchange or as a standard of value.*

The choice of a comprehensive word such as *anything* appears to be necessary because no single word of more restricted meaning is capable of including all the "things" that have been used as mediums of exchange and standards of value in the various epochs of human history. Allowance must be made not only for the innumerable kinds of commodities that have been used in these two capacities but also for many varieties of paper instruments and for certain kinds of intangible "rights," such as bank demand deposits.

Money is anything *commonly used* as a medium of exchange or as a standard of value. Many kinds of "things" are occasionally used as mediums of exchange or as means of measuring value, but occasional use does not justify the classification as money. If, for example, a person has a quantity of garden produce that he wants to exchange for sugar, he may exchange the produce for eggs which, in turn, he exchanges for sugar at a grocery store. In this instance, the eggs serve as a medium of exchange, but they are surely not money because they are not commonly used in this way.

Money is *generally accepted* in the sense that people collectively are willing (and often anxious) to give all kinds and great quantities of goods in exchange for it, or customarily value all kinds of goods in terms of it, or use it in both of these ways. All things that are scarce and that have utility or the capacity to satisfy human wants possess value and could conceivably be used as money, but there is usually only one "thing" that the people of a country employ to measure the economic values of everything else and only a few "things" that they are willing to take in unlimited quantities in exchange for their own goods.

Finally, a thing is money if it is commonly used and generally accepted as a medium of exchange, *or* if it is commonly used and generally accepted as a standard of value. Recognition is thus given to the fact that, in any country's monetary system, one kind of money may serve as the standard of value without being used as a medium of exchange, while other kinds satisfy the medium-of-exchange function. However, it is also to be recognized that a single kind of money may serve simultaneously as the medium of exchange and the standard of value, as has often happened.

Kinds of money

In applying the definition of money as the criterion for judgments concerning what is and what is not money, one should have no great difficulty in recognizing the principal kinds of money in use in any country at a given time. In the United States, for example, we immediately notice that there is, indeed, one kind of money that is the standard of value although it is not used as a domestic medium of exchange, and that there are three major kinds that are used as mediums of exchange but not as standards of value. Our standard of value is the gold dollar as established by Congress in the legislation of 1934 and 1972, yet obviously gold coins or gold bars are not employed as domestic mediums of exchange. When, therefore, we say that a car of a given make and model is worth $3000 or that a certain painting is worth $400, we mean 3000 *gold* dollars and 400 *gold* dollars, respectively —or, at least, that is what Congress says we mean. But if we are buying the car or the painting, we make payment in a different kind of money, most likely by means of a check drawn on a bank demand deposit.

At any rate, the different kinds of money used in our system as mediums of exchange but not (officially) as standards of value are chiefly paper instruments issued by the Federal Reserve banks called "Federal Reserve notes," coins manufactured and issued by the U.S. Treasury, and demand deposits recorded on the books of commercial banks. (Commercial banks are distinguished from all other classes of financial institutions by the very fact that the demand deposits, or "checking accounts," of the general public are held with them.)

Paper Money and Coins Paper money, such as the Federal Reserve notes, and coins are usually classified jointly as *hand-to-hand money*, or *currency*.[1] When silver comprised 90 percent of the weight of our half dollars, quarters, and dimes, these coins were often described as *subsidiary* coins, while the nickel and cent were classified as *minor* coins. The term *subsidiary* indicated that, although most of the content of the half dollar, quarter, and dime was precious metal, the stated monetary value of the coins was still greater than the market value of the silver they contained; these coins were not *full-bodied*, as another expression had it. However, with the elimination of silver from the quarter and dime according to the provisions of the Coinage Act of 1965, and from the half dollar by legislation adopted at the end of December 1970, the distinction between subsidiary and minor coins no longer seems to have much significance. It is probably most convenient to classify all these coins as *fractional* coins, because each is a fraction of the dollar.

Bank Demand Deposits It is so clearly observed day after day that coins and paper money are widely used and generally accepted as mediums of exchange that no argument is required to prove the observation. But some students may reject the idea that bank demand deposits or checking accounts also qualify as money. Common use is hardly to be disputed, since it is estimated that at least 90 percent of the monetary volume of transactions is settled by checks drawn on demand deposit accounts. But what about general acceptability? Checks tendered in payment are often refused, and others are accepted reluctantly. Nevertheless, a distinction must be made between bank demand deposits, as a medium of exchange, and checks

---

[1]In international finance, however, *all* the moneys of foreign countries are generally called their "currencies" even though holdings of these moneys by outsiders consist mostly of demand deposit balances rather than paper money and coins.

as instruments by which balances in demand deposit accounts are transferred. In our society, there is no reluctance in receiving such balances as means of payment when the receiver is confident that the balances are really existent and will continue to be available for transfer to him—that, in other words, the checks tendered are "good." While, therefore, there may be doubts about the goodness of individual checks as transfer instruments, there is little doubt about the goodness of bank demand deposits and their general acceptability when people are confident that transfers ordered from these deposits by means of checks will actually take place.

It is important to emphasize that bank demand deposits do not consist of paper money and coins held in the vaults of commercial banks—that, instead, they are obligations of these banks to pay out paper money and coins in compliance with orders written by their depositors, that is, checks. Thus demand deposits are quite intangible; on the one side, they are simply the rights of depositors to receive payment and to order payment to others, and on the other, the obligations of the banks to pay as directed. (As indicated previously, the intangibility of demand deposits is one reason why a rather vague word like "anything" must be used in a definition of money.)

A very great proportion of the checks drawn on bank demand deposits in the United States are not actually settled by payments of paper money and coins. For the individual commercial bank, checks ordering it to pay are rather closely matched in monetary value by the checks also received that are drawn on other banks—checks that the bank sends to the other banks for payment—so that, as a rule, only the net difference need be settled. And usually the settlement of the net difference is arranged by means of deposit-account entries among the commercial banks themselves or with the Federal Reserve banks. It is for this reason that we are able to say that bank demand deposits widely serve fully and finally as mediums of exchange—without, that is, a need of their conversion into something else such as paper money and coins. A person obviously uses his demand deposit account fully and finally as a medium of exchange if he deposits his payroll check in such an account and then draws checks against it in paying for rent, food, clothing, and other consumer commodities and services. Through the intermediary of the demand deposit, he exchanges his labor service for consumer goods without need of making any conversion at all into paper money and coins.

Near-moneys and liquid assets

Although the principal kinds of things that a country uses as money can usually be identified with ease, one quickly notices that in many countries there are many additional "things" that have strong resemblances to money. These are called *near-moneys*. In the United States, near-moneys include savings deposits at commercials banks, mutual savings banks, and savings and loan associations; other classes of time deposits at these same institutions; cash surrender values of life insurance policies; and U.S. savings bonds that have been outstanding for at least 2 months.[2] Because the institutions that are obligated on these deposits, policies, and bonds are generally willing to meet these obligations on demand by payments in paper money and coins or by transfers to demand deposits, the obligations themselves take on, as it were, major qualities of "moneyness." Indeed, any instrument or claim is a near-money if it is of the nature of a *demand obligation* of an individual or institution that is fully capable at all times of meeting the obligation.

In many countries, too, a group of short-term debt instruments have such significant degrees of "moneyness" that they are included with money and near-moneys in a general classification of *liquid assets.* In the United States, such short-term instruments include U.S. Treasury bills and other Treasury obligations that are closely approaching maturity, bonds and comparable obligations of high-rated state and local governments and high-rated business corporations that also are closely approaching maturity, promissory notes sold widely in the open market by high-rated business enterprises (known as "open-market commercial paper"), bankers' acceptances, and time certificates of deposit issued by commercial banks. These short-term instruments have strong characteristics of "moneyness" because they will soon be converted into money as their maturities arrive, and because, indeed, their holders can usually sell them before maturity at prices quite close to the face values.

In deciding how much money should be in circulation from time to time—a topic to be analyzed in Chapter 2—the monetary authorities must take into account the volume of near-moneys and short-term liquid assets outstanding in the economy, because this volume may have an important influence on people's spending decisions. Even though goods are attractively priced, many people may be reluctant to buy if their money holdings are moderate and they have no other liquid assets, but they may spend readily if their money holdings, though moderate, can be quickly replenished by the conversion of other liquid assets.

THE FUNCTIONS OF MONEY

The functions of money include all the work that money does for us as members of an economic society. The two fundamental, or primary, jobs it performs have been indicated in the definition already presented: its services as a medium of exchange and as a standard of value. Other services of money are described as secondary functions because they are dependent upon and clearly subordinate to the primary functions. In secondary capacities, money serves as a standard of deferred payments, as a store of purchasing power, and as a guarantor of solvency.

---

[2]This period can be as short as 29 days, because the savings bonds bear the month of issue but not the day. Accordingly, a savings bond sold on January 31 would be redeemable on March 1 at the amount paid for it.

Money as a medium of exchange

Difficulties of Barter The importance of money's service as a medium of exchange can be readily understood when one considers the difficulties of barter. *Barter* is the direct exchange of goods for goods without the use of money as a medium of exchange. In *indirect barter,* reference is made to money for value comparisons although it is not used as a medium of exchange; in *pure barter,* money does not come into use either as a medium of exchange or as a standard of value. An outstanding difficulty in transactions of pure barter is the need to establish a direct-value ratio between each pair of goods offered for exchange. If ten kinds of goods are to be exchanged, it is necessary to express the value of A in respect to B, of A in respect to C, of B in respect to C, of B in respect to D, and so on; in all, forty-five ratios are required. In a money economy, on the other hand, the value of each good is expressed in terms of money as a *price.* In the exchange of ten kinds of goods, only ten prices are required, for prices make possible easy comparisons of the value of any good with the values of all other goods.

In our day, transactions of the pure barter variety are exceedingly rare, but indirect barter is quite common; even in the most advanced monetary economies, much "swapping" of goods takes place. The difficulty of pure barter is avoided, because the goods can be priced in terms of money even though money is not actually transferred. Nevertheless, two important difficulties often remain: a lack of divisibility in the things to be exchanged and a lack of a double coincidence of wants on the part of those who want to make exchanges. A person who owns something that has considerable value as long as it is in one piece, such as a house, a dairy cow, or a fur coat, faces a sea of troubles if he sets out to exchange it for specific quantities of a dozen other things that he hopes to get in return; likewise the person who sets out to find somebody who has what he wants and who wants precisely what he has to offer.

Generalized Purchasing Power When money is used as a medium of exchange, an exchange of goods for goods is broken up into two transactions: goods are given for money, and the money, in turn, is used to acquire other goods. Purchases and sales are substituted for the direct exchange of a barter economy. A person who owns one kind of goods in a quantity beyond his needs and who wants to acquire goods of other kinds does not have to seek someone who owns the wanted goods and who is willing to take what he has to offer. By selling the excess portion of his goods, he acquires money or "generalized purchasing power" that gives him freedom to select the quantities and qualities of the goods he wants to buy, to set the time and place of his purchases, and to choose the people with whom he will deal.

Through the use of money as a medium of exchange in production, distribution, and consumption, very great advantages are gained by economic society. The use of money permits business managers to concentrate their energies upon the technical problems of their industries—a concentration that makes possible the development of new processes and the improvement of techniques, with a resulting expansion in output. Business enterprises need not build houses, accumulate stores of food, clothing, household furniture, and other consumption goods, and provide service facilities of many kinds to take care of the physical requirements of their employees; they need not barter their finished goods for new machinery, raw materials, and other supplies; and they need not negotiate contracts with landowners to give them portions of their output in return for the use of natural resources.

When business enterprises pay money wages to their employees, money rents to landowners, money as interest to capitalists, and as one may say, money profits to themselves, the shares of the factors of production in the output of industry are immediately determined. According to economic theory, each factor of production in a capitalistic society receives an amount of money income that measures its marginal productivity, but economists do not necessarily argue that full justice is served when shares are determined on the basis of marginal productivity. At any rate, the intricate problems concerned with the proper distribution of output are more easily dealt with when the shares of the factors are stated in monetary terms. Problems and decisions about "just wages," "reasonable" rewards to enterprisers, taxation according to the principle of ability to pay, and the like would be much more complex than at present if the output of industry were directly distributed among the factors of production.

Those who receive money as rent, wages, interest, and profits in return for their contributions to production have wide choices in its disposal. The wage earner, for example, is not assigned to a certain house, whether or not it suits his needs and his desires, nor is he allotted predetermined quantities of food, clothing, and other goods of given descriptions. He is free to determine how the money or "generalized purchasing power" he receives as wages is to be spent. Though he may have been spending a certain amount for food, another amount for clothing, and other amounts for other commodities and services, he can vary these proportions at any time at his discretion. Moreover, choices can easily be varied within each classification, as when he buys more of one kind of food and less of another.

Adequacy of the Medium-of-Exchange Service Although money has certain shortcomings in three of its functions, as we shall soon see, we must generally extol its service as a medium of exchange. In that capacity, it truly serves us very well. Sometimes one hears that we should have a coin or several coins of smaller value than the cent, so that we could pay the exact amount of retail-sales taxes when they are imposed, for example, at 4 percent on purchases that total 35 cents, or so that we could buy without loss one item of a pair selling at "two for a quarter." But matters of this kind concern shortcomings in the list of denominations that the federal government has provided in our monetary system; they actually have little to do with the adequacy of money's behavior as a medium of exchange. On the other hand, if counterfeiting were prevalent and quite difficult to detect, or if paper money were issued in such great quantities that large bundles of it had to be used to make simple purchases (as in "astronomical inflations" that have been all too common in the monetary histories of some countries), then we could truly say that the medium-of-exchange function was being fulfilled very poorly.

Money as a standard of value

Measurement of Economic Value Any standard is a means of measurement, and money as a standard of value is employed to measure and compare the *economic values* of all kinds of goods, just as gills, pints, quarts, and gallons are used to measure quantities of liquids and as inches, feet, yards, rods, and miles are used to measure distances. Economic values are the capabilities of goods to command other goods in exchange; as we know, they are stated in monetary terms as *prices*. We do not say that a bushel of wheat is equivalent to 2 pounds of butter, to 3 dozen eggs, to a necktie of a certain kind and quality, or to the privilege of riding in a bus for a given number of miles. Rather, we say that wheat is worth $1.50 a bushel; butter, 75 cents a pound, and so on. The relationship between the value of any good and of all other kinds of goods can be easily ascertained, just as the relationship between two distances can be readily understood if we say that one is 40 feet and another is 60 yards.

In frequency of use, money's service as a standard of value is much more important than its function as a medium of exchange. Every use of money as a medium of exchange is preceded or accompanied, as it were, by its use as a standard of value; goods are not exchanged by means of money as a medium of exchange until they have first been given prices, that is, evaluated in terms of money. But, in addition, goods are constantly being evaluated in terms of money even though their exchange for money is not taking place. If a farmer wants to exchange some eggs for sugar at a grocery store, the value of each commodity is expressed in terms of money and the exchange is made, although no money passes from hand to hand. Again, people continually evaluate goods in terms of money when there is no immediate interest in exchange. A home owner may say that his house is worth $15,000; yet he may have no intention of selling it at that or any other price.

Business organizations, governments, private nonprofit institutions, and individuals would be severely handicapped if a monetary unit were not available as a standard of value. In the balance sheet of a business firm, for example, the values of both tangible and intangible assets are expressed in terms of money. Land, building, machinery, and other fixed assets are declared to be worth so many dollars although the firm has no expectation of selling them, and also valued in money are the short-term, or current, assets, such as inventories. In this respect, money is frequently alluded to as a *unit of account*, but this term is synonymous with *standard of value*. In the absence of money as a standard of value, a business firm, in reporting the state of its affairs, would have to describe its assets in terms of quantities, composition, and other physical characteristics, and its report would be unintelligible to many.

Defective Character of the Standard of Value   Unlike measures of liquids, distances, areas, and the like, which fully satisfy their respective purposes, money as a standard of value is defective. An acre of land in Pennsylvania has the same dimensions as an acre in California, and a gallon of gasoline sold in New York is the same quantity as a gallon sold in Oregon. Not so with money. Although money is used as a "yardstick" to measure the value of all goods, the length of the yardstick itself varies from time to time. It is as if a true yardstick were at one time 36 inches in length; at another, 32 inches; and at another, 45 inches. Variations in the length of the money yardstick occur as prices in general, that is, "price levels," rise and fall.

The misbehavior of money as a standard of value and the frequent failure of people to recognize this misbehavior often lead to much confusion and many maladjustments in the economic system, as in periods of inflation as discussed in Chapter 2. In a system of free enterprise, the standard of value is supposed to supply a "language" of prices by which the multifarious activities of producers and consumers can be coordinated, but too often this language becomes a Babel, or "confusion of tongues." Thus a wage rate of $5 an hour at the present time is not five times as good as a wage rate of $1 an hour paid in 1939 for the same kind of work, nor is a given make and model of automobile selling at the present time at $3400 four times as good as the same make and model that sold in 1940 at $850. Also, houses do not magically escape wear and tear and, instead, accumulate additional want-satisfying qualities in a manner to give them a value two or three times as high today as the value they had when built in, say, 1938. Many erroneous notions originate because people confuse the concepts of price and value—because they fail to realize that while all prices can rise in a given period of time, that is, the value of money itself can fall, it is impossible for all values to rise simultaneously.[3] All this means that money serves quite satisfactorily as a standard of value at a given time and within a limited area, but that its service in this capacity becomes more and more

---

[3]If at a given time A is priced at 60 cents a unit, B at 40 cents, and C at 20 cents, and some years later the prices of the three commodities are $1.20, 80 cents, and 40 cents, respectively, we can say that all these prices have risen but that the comparative values are exactly as they were before; or if at the later date the price of A is 50 cents and that of B 25 cents, we can say that both these prices have fallen, but that the value of A in relation to B has risen, while, conversely, the value of B in relation to A has fallen.

inadequate as we extend the time or the area in which prices are used as a means of comparison.

The failure of money to serve as well as we would like as standard of value originates in the indissoluble union of the standard-of-value function, on the one hand, with the medium-of-exchange, the store-of-purchasing-power, and the guarantor-of-solvency functions, on the other. The standard of value does not remain an abstract concept as does a gallon, an acre, or a mile, but it takes concrete form as mediums of exchange or is firmly linked to the mediums of exchange. The concept of a dollar, for example, may in the first instance be abstract, but it becomes concrete when we say that a dollar is equal in value to 12.632 grains of fine gold, and when we turn out coins, print pieces of paper, and open balances in demand deposit accounts and call these things dollars and fractions and multiples of the dollar. Regardless of the number of containers for the holding of liquids that we manufacture or destroy, a gallon still designates a specific volume of liquid; but if we substantially increase or decrease the quantity of dollars in circulation, the importance, that is, the purchasing power of each dollar, may be materially changed. It follows, of course, that the greater the instability of the purchasing power of money—the greater the range of price-level fluctuations—the less adequate is money as a standard of value.

Secondary functions of money

Money as a Standard of Deferred Payments   As a standard of deferred payments, money is used to measure a wide array of obligations to make future payments. A corporation contracts to pay a certain number of dollars semi-annually as interest on its bonds and a certain additional number as principal at their maturity. A person who obtains a consumer loan promises to pay a certain number of dollars monthly over a specified period to cover both interest and principal repayment. In an agreement with a labor union, a corporation agrees to pay wages at certain dollar rates for each hour of employment over the next two or three years. In return for premium payments, a life insurance company commits itself to make a specified lump-sum dollar payment to the beneficiary of the insured at the time of his death, or specified monthly dollar payments for as long as the beneficiary lives. Merchants buy goods for their inventories "on account," and they and their suppliers measure these accounts as dollar obligations of specific amounts.

Not only is money defective as a standard of value; in many periods, it has shortcomings as a standard of deferred payments of many degrees of gravity. These shortcomings will be indicated in Chapter 2 in a discussion of the unmerited shifts in income and wealth that occur in periods of inflation and deflation—shifts that occur for the very reason that money is employed to measure obligations on almost all income-payment contracts and debts. The means of measurement is the dollar, but the purchasing power of the dollar may fluctuate widely.

Money as a Store of Purchasing Power When money is used as a medium of exchange, two steps, as we have seen, are involved: something is sold for money, and the money is then used to buy something else. All exchange is basically the "swapping" of goods, for only misers want money for its own sake. Because it is possible, nevertheless, to defer the second part of the transaction, that is, to retain the money itself for any desired period of time, money fulfills an additional function by serving as a store of purchasing power.

A farmer may want to exchange his wheat for a tractor. He sells his wheat for money in the autumn, and because he does not want the tractor until the spring, he retains the money—stores his purchasing power in the form of money—during the winter. Again, most working people receive their wages and salaries in lump sums weekly or biweekly. They do not immediately spend the money they receive for the goods that they expect to consume before the next payday; usually they spend a little at a time, retaining temporarily a portion of their purchasing power in the form of money.

At any time, a substantial proportion of money reported to be "in circulation"—both hand-to-hand money and bank demand deposits—is actually being held idle as a store of purchasing power. This is necessarily true in the sense that the money is not being transferred at the moment or on a particular day in the purchase and sale of goods. Much of it, however, is held for a day or a few days at the most, so that the "transactions motive" for holding money overshadows its role as a store of purchasing power. But there are times when large quantities of money are held for indefinite periods, with the result that the medium-of-exchange function of this money is subordinated. This occurs when people look upon their money holdings as an asset preferable to stocks, bonds, real property, and commodities. In periods of general business contraction when many prices are falling, people are likely to rush into the market to dispose of securities and physical assets in exchange for money that they plan to hold until recovery is well under way. Even in periods of prosperity when many prices are rising, some people will surely prefer holding money to buying bonds bearing given rates of interest, because they anticipate that rising market rates of interest will cause market prices of bonds to fall.

Money as a Guarantor of Solvency A large amount of money is held by individuals and organizations simply for assurance that they will be able to meet money obligations as they come due. They realize that insolvenc ability to meet obligations—may result in wholesale seizures of in satisfaction of judgments that creditors obtain or the freezir bankruptcy proceedings. They realize that a mere excess of bilities is not safe—that money itself must be availabl obligations. When, therefore, money is held to avoid t faults engender, it serves its holders as a guarantor of s

The service of money as a guarantor of solvency

services as a standard of deferred payments and as a store of purchasing power. Obligations to pay are generally measured in terms of money—this is the application of the standard-of-deferred-payments function; but quantities of money must actually be on hand if the obligations are to be settled when they come due, and this is holding money as a guarantor of solvency. When, on the other hand, money is held as a store of purchasing power, the intention of the holder is to use it sooner or later to acquire goods; but when it is held as a guarantor of solvency, the intention of the holder is to give it to his creditors only if it becomes absolutely necessary for him to do so. In a sense, money serves best as a guarantor of solvency when the holder does not have to part with it at all. The businessman who holds money to be sure that he will be able to meet his payroll, his tax liabilities, and his obligations to suppliers actually expects to meet these liabilities out of current sales and collections from his customers, but he has something to fall back on if his sales volume falls off or if his customers become slow in paying. Similarly, the officers of a commercial bank are quite content to keep bundles of paper money piled up year after year in dark recesses of its vault, and they may become somewhat disturbed should they have to encroach on this hoard to meet the withdrawal demands of depositors.

Although money is defective as a standard of deferred payments and as a store of purchasing power, it acquits itself well as a guarantor of solvency. A person who today incurs a debt of $5000 to be paid in 5 years may gain or lose purchasing power in the repayment of the principal if the price level has a net fall or rise within that period of time, but he can be quite sure of his solvency if, as the maturity of the debt approaches, he holds $5000 that he knows he can allocate to the repayment—and absolutely sure if the $5000 is legal tender, as described a little later.

Unitary and quantitative functions

The functions of money as a standard of value and as a standard of deferred payments are unitary functions, while its functions as a medium of exchange, as a store of purchasing power, and as a guarantor of solvency are quantitative functions.

Only one unit of money is needed to measure the economic values of everything else and all obligations to pay money in the future, just as one standard pound, as maintained by the U.S. Bureau of Standards, is sufficient to measure everything that one wants to measure in pounds. Congress says   r standard of value (and by implication, our standard of deferred   is the gold dollar of 12.632 grains of fine gold. All that we need,   e lump of gold of this weight, since in measuring values and   can fractionize and multiply it in countless ways. If we say   s worth $500 and that something else is worth 50 cents,   t the first thing is worth 500 times the lump of gold and   is worth one half the lump of gold.

      is needed for the quantitative functions of money,

and this is the area in which the monetary authorities encounter difficult problems of decision making. Because paper money and coins are easy to manufacture and bank demand deposits are easy to create, the monetary authorities might decide to provide an abundant supply of these moneys so that the people are sure to have enough as mediums of exchange, stores of purchasing power, and guarantors of solvency. But, on second thought, the authorities would surely decide that such a choice would be a bad one, even an unconscionable one. Prices would be expected to rise rapidly because of the abundance of the money stock, with all the evils of ensuing inflation—evils largely associated with the malfunctioning of money as a standard of value and as a standard of deferred payments. Because of the indissoluble union between the unitary and quantitative functions of money, and despite the fact that the unitary functions, by definition, require only one unit, maintaining the outstanding quantity of money at optimum levels can always be expected to be difficult to achieve.

MONEY AS LEGAL TENDER

Legal tender is any kind of money that a government officially designates as an adequate instrument for the discharge of obligations stated to be payable in domestic money. Governments declare certain kinds of money in circulation to be "legal tender," or "legal means of payment," as a way of preventing endless disputes and litigation between debtors and creditors concerning settlements of outstanding obligations. Legal tender laws are enacted especially for the benefit of debtors, for they protect debtors from harassment by creditors who may refuse to accept payment in one kind of money and insist upon payment in another kind. Even the government limits its own rights as a creditor when it makes money legal tender "for public purposes," for it then recognizes the legal tender as an adequate instrument for the payment of taxes, fees, fines, and assessments, and the satisfaction of judgments.

When a person has an obligation to pay a specified sum of domestic money and the kind of money has not been designated by contract, any legal tender will satisfy the obligation. The creditor is warned, in effect, that he may as well accept the legal tender for he can never enforce payment in anything else. He will have no standing in the courts to bring a lawsuit aginst the debtor if the debtor can simply show that he offered legal tender to settle the obligation. The refusal of the creditor to accept legal tender does not, as a rule, relieve the debtor of his obligation to pay, but the debtor's only duty is to remain ready to pay in the very same legal tender that was originally rejected. The creditor is disadvantaged in that no interest accumulates on the obligation from the date of refusal, and in that, should he persist in refusing the legal tender, the debt may be outlawed eventually by statutes of limitations.

Legal tender is not a cure-all for debtors. Many kinds of contracts cannot be satisfied by offers of legal tender. If a person contracts to deliver a carload of wheat, he cannot meet his obligation by offering legal tender equal to the market value of the wheat; nor can he fulfill an obligation to deliver a certain amount of Canadian dollars by offering an equivalent amount of American dollars that are legal tender. Even more important is the fact that merchants and others who have goods for sale cannot be forced to sell in exchange for legal tender. Because a contract of sale, like any other contract, is an *agreement* between competent parties, the seller can refuse to sell unless the buyer offers in return something that he is willing to take, whether or not it is legal tender.

FOR REVIEW

1. How has money as an "invention" contributed to economic progress? Does it continue this kind of contribution today? Discuss.
2. What is money? On the basis of what criteria do we distinguish it from everything else?
3. What is the distinction, if any, among coins described as full-bodied, subsidiary, minor, and fractional?
4. What is the nature of bank demand deposits? Is it logical to say that such deposits are money but that checks drawn on them are not money? Explain.
5. How are near-moneys distinguished from money itself? What kinds of assets, in addition to money and near-moneys, are described as liquid assets?
6. Explain how it is possible for a money to serve as a standard of value but not as a medium of exchange, and vice versa.
7. In the United States at the present time is money defective in any significant way as a standard of value? as a medium of exchange? Explain.
8. What is meant by the indissoluble union between the two primary functions of money? Why may this union be a source of economic difficulties?
9. Why is it said that money is generalized purchasing power? Is there any advantage in this for the economy? Explain.
10. Explain the distinction between the functions of money as a standard of deferred payments and as a guarantor of solvency.
11. Is money defective in any way in its services as a store of purchasing power and as a gurantor of solvency? Explain.
12. What is the relationship, if any, between the service of money as a guarantor of solvency and its designation by the government as legal tender?
13. Which of the functions of money are said to be unitary and which quantitative? From the standpoint of monetary control, what is the importance of this distinction?
14. What is legal tender? Why are some kinds of money said to be legal tender and others not? Of what advantage is it to the economic society to have some kinds of money designated as legal tender?

CHAPTER 2

MONETARY CONTROL

GOALS OF MONETARY CONTROL

Considering all that was said in the preceding chapter about defects in the services of money as a standard of value, a standard of deferred payments, and a store of purchasing power, and about changes in the value or purchasing power of money as the source of the defects, one would surely be inclined to conclude that controlling the quantity of money in circulation, or the "money stock," should be aimed directly and exclusively to achieving continual stability in the value of money. Such stability should apparently make money serve in an optimum way in all its functions.

Actually, however, we expect monetary control, or "monetary policy," to do more than this. We expect it to make a strong contribution to maintaining the full employment of the labor force and to achieving high rates of economic growth year after year. Indeed, full employment is usually ranked higher than stability in the value of money as a goal of monetary control, and sometimes, too, achieving high economic growth rates is given a superior ranking. Such superior rankings indicate an acceptance of the probability that some instability in the value of money may have to be tolerated in order to maintain full employment and high growth rates.

Even further, monetary control is expected to be directed in such manner that our financial relationships and transactions with other countries will be free of serious distortions and difficulties—that, in other words, we will be able to maintain year after year a "reasonable" position in our balance of international payments. This fourth goal is generally regarded as being less important than the other three, but highly desirable nevertheless.

Monetary and other controls

The concept is that wise control of the rate of expansion (and possibly contraction) in the total stock of money may be fruitful in pushing the economy closer and closer to the four goals, and that, contrariwise, mistaken monetary policy may be the source of disruptions throughout the economic system and in international economic relationships of many degrees of magnitude. While most economists conclude that monetary control may be fruitful, few hold that it alone is sufficient for the achievement of the four goals. The large majority believe that wise monetary policy must be joined with judicious governmental policies in many other directions, particularly with wise fiscal policies—decisions about taxation and government spending—but also with well-planned policies of enforcement of antitrust laws, promotion of competition, wider dissemination of information about markets and market conditions, job training for the unskilled, foreign trade and investment regulation, and so on.

Employment Act of 1946

A legislative foundation for the present-day interest in the probable effectiveness of monetary policy, fiscal policy, and other governmental policies as means of achieving full employment, a stable price level, and a continuing good rate of economic growth was constructed by Congress in February 1946 when it passed the Employment Act that states:

> The Congress hereby declares that it is the continuing policy and responsibility of the federal government to use all practicable means . . . to coordinate and utilize all its plans, functions, and resources for the purpose of creating and maintaining . . . conditions under which there will be afforded useful employment opportunities, including self-employment, for those able, willing, and seeking to work, and to promote maximum employment, production, and purchasing power.

Here maximum employment is generally interpreted to mean what is called "full employment"; maximum production, to mean a high rate of economic growth from year to year; and maximum purchasing power, a high degree of stability in the general level of prices.

At the time of its adoption, the Employment Act made no great stir. It was widely regarded as a "pious" statement of wishful thinking. But it has gained honor and respect with the passing years, and more and more do current Congresses seem to feel that the pledge of 1946 ought to be fulfilled, regardless of what the Congress of that year may have thought about it. At any rate, the machinery set up by the Employment Act has proved most useful, and it should be much more so with the passing years. By the terms of this legislation, the President is directed to submit to Congress an annual "economic report" (followed by as many supplementary reports as he cares to make) in which he reviews recent developments and current trends in employment, production, and purchasing power, forecasts future developments, reviews federal programs already in operation, and recommends further action. For the preparation of the "economic report," the President has the assistance of his Council of Economic Advisers, composed of three members appointed by himself with the advice and consent of the Senate. The report goes to Congress where it is referred to the Joint Economic Committee which has a membership of seven representatives and seven senators. The joint Committee analyzes the report and, in turn, may make specific recommendations for legislation to the regular committees of the House and Senate.

THE GOAL OF FULL EMPLOYMENT

Of the three major goals of monetary control (and other "practicable means" of control by the federal government), the goal of the full employment of the labor force is generally recognized to be the most important. The economic well-being of the great mass of people clearly and closely depends on the capacity of great numbers of individuals to sell their labor services continuously for a steady flow of money incomes as wages and salaries. A stable price level would be only of limited advantage if many millions of persons in the labor force could not find jobs. Nor would a high rate of economic growth be very attractive if it resulted from investment in machinery and equipment that displaced many workers who could not find jobs elsewhere.

As the primary goal of monetary control, full employment is generally defined tentatively as meaning that jobs are readily available on reasonable terms for all who are able and willing to work. Such a definition assumes, of course, that most able and willing members of the labor force actually have jobs at which they are working, but it also demands that jobs be available on reasonable terms to people who are not working, provided that they are able and willing. However, the definition is said to be "tentative" because allowance must be made for some slack in the economy—in recognition of the impossibility of perfection in economic performance and the inadvisability of setting perfection *as a goal*. Allowance must be made for some unemployment of labor—for a "tolerable" level about which we ought not to be much concerned. Moreover, when we try to apply the definition in counting who is employed and who is unemployed, we will surely conclude that it leaves many difficult questions unanswered.

"Tolerable" unemployment

Making allowance for "tolerable" unemployment gives recognition to the premise that no economic system can be expected to behave perfectly for an indefinite period, and to the premise, too, that no group of government authorities can work effectively if they know they are to be judged in terms of what would be a perfect accomplishment. A striving for perfection beyond a certain point might, indeed, prove to be more harmful than beneficial. One might ask, for example, whether vigorous use should be made of the instruments of monetary and fiscal policy if 200,000 persons, able and willing to work, are unemployed. The obvious answer must surely be:

certainly not. But once such a figure has been introduced, the logical procedure is to repeat the question with successively higher figures. Is unemployment of 500,000 persons tolerable, or a million, or 2 million, or 3 million? Where does unemployment reach a level at which the monetary and fiscal authorities should begin to make vigorous application of their instruments?

There appears to be a consensus in the United States that a level of unemployment not exceeding 3 percent of the civilian labor force is "tolerable." In this general view, pushing unemployment well below the level of 3 percent would be very good, indeed, but failure in this direction ought not to be a reason for great concern or for the launching of extensive government programs aimed at improvement. On the other hand, actions toward improvement should surely be taken when the level of unemployment goes above 3 percent, and the further above, the more vigorous the action.

Although the continual unemployment of 3 percent of the civilian labor force—about 2½ million persons in terms of the labor force in late 1971—might seem to be an unconscionable waste of manpower, such an allowance for "tolerable" unemployment can be justified on several grounds. For one thing, the same persons will not necessarily be unemployed month after month and year after year, for it is to be expected that people will be constantly moving into and out of the unemployment pool. Without doubt, an allowance must be made for seasonal unemployment in many industries, especially agriculture and the construction industry. Although much progress has been made in smoothing out seasonal peaks and troughs, as in the construction industry, one can hardly anticipate the complete elimination of the seasonal factor. Again, automation and other technological progress in specific industries must be expected to result in the displacement of some workers, with perhaps considerable delay in their finding jobs elsewhere. Likewise, the decline of some communities as more favorable locations for certain industries are developed elsewhere should be expected to add to the pool of unemployment, with much of the addition likely to be prolonged because of reluctance of many people to move to other localities. Still further, allowance must be made for people who voluntarily quit their jobs because of a dislike for their bosses, their fellow workmen, or working conditions, or for other reasons, and who remain in the labor force in the sense that, able and willing to work, they immediately begin to seek other employment.

Measurement of employment and unemployment

The many difficult questions of measurement left unanswered in the definition of employment given earlier must be answered in a manner generally recognized as sound and adequate if the monetary and fiscal authorities are to have proper data for policy decisions.[1] Who is in the labor force and

---

[1]This does not mean, of course, that the monetary and fiscal authorities are to be expected to take action or avoid it solely on the basis of employment and unemployment

out of it? Who is able to work? What degrees of mental and physical disabilities make people unable to work? Who is willing to work? Is an able person willing to work even though he is not looking for a job because he thinks that no jobs are available? Who is actually employed—a person who works only a few hours a week, a person who has a job far beneath his skills, or somebody who is working in a family enterprise without pay? Who is unemployed—the student who is seeking a part-time job during the school year to help to pay his tuition and living expenses, the housewife who would take a job outside the home if it were offered to her, or the farm worker who is out of a job in January for seasonal reasons? What are the "reasonable terms" upon which jobs should be available if the full-employment criterion is to be satisfied?

However the student might answer these questions, he should know how they are answered by the government agencies that collect, analyze, and publish statistics of employment and unemployment in the United States. He may then be able to judge whether or not these data give the monetary and fiscal authorities an adequate basis for policy decisions. The principal arrays of statistics are collected monthly by the U.S. Bureau of the Census for the Bureau of Labor Statistics based on household interviews. These data are published in much detail, with many breakdowns, such as the age, sex, color, and marital status of both employed and unemployed persons, full-time and part-time employment, and the length of unemployment.[2] In the compilation of these data, the questions posed before—or some of them —are answered as follows:

> *Data based on household interviews* are obtained from a sample survey of the population 16 years of age and over. . . . The information is collected by trained interviewers from a sample of about fifty thousand households, representing 449 areas in 863 counties and independent cities, with coverage in fifty states and the District of Columbia. The data collected were based on the activity or status reported for the calendar week including the twelfth of the month. . . .
>
> *Employed persons* comprise (a) all those who during the survey

---

figures, however accurate they may be considered. Rather, we expect these authorities to keep watch upon a great number of business "indicators" as guides to policy actions. At the least, however, accurate employment data will surely indicate how effective have been the policy actions already taken, as well as the urgency of the need of further action.

[2]The student will find it highly instructive to make a careful examination of all these data as published by the U.S. Department of Labor in each monthly issue of its *Employment and Earnings*. In this publication he will find two additional kinds of employment and unemployment statistics, also in considerable detail: employment in nonagricultural industries, compiled by the U.S. Bureau of Labor Statistics from employer reports, and unemployment subject to compensation under the state unemployment insurance systems, reported by state agencies. He will thus see that the monetary and fiscal authorities have available a large body of information for judging the employment and unemployment situation as it develops from month to month.

week did any work at all as paid employees, in their own business, profession, or farm, or who worked 15 hours or more as unpaid workers in an enterprise operated by a member of the family, and (b) all those who were not working but who had jobs or businesses from which they were temporarily absent because of illness, bad weather, vacation, labor-management dispute, or personal reasons, whether or not they were paid by their employers for the time off, and whether or not they were seeking other jobs.

Each employed person is counted only once. Those who held more than one job are counted in the job at which they worked the greatest number of hours during the survey week. . . .

Unemployed persons comprise all persons who did not work during the survey week, who made specific efforts to find a job within the past 4 weeks, and who were available for work during the survey week (except for temporary illness). Also included as unemployed are those who did not work at all, were available for work, and (a) were waiting to be called back to a job from which they had been laid off, or (b) waiting to report to a new wage or salary job within 30 days. . . .

Not in the labor force includes all civilians 16 years of age and over who are not classified as employed or unemployed. These persons are further classified as "engaged in own home housework," "in school," "unable to work" because of long-term physical or mental illness, and "other." The "other" group includes for the most part retired persons, those reported as too old to work, the voluntarily idle, and seasonal workers for whom the survey week fell in an "off" season and who were not reported as unemployed. Persons doing only incidental unpaid family work (less than 15 hours) are also classified as not in the labor force.[3]

To this official statement of standards may be added the observation that "reasonable terms" for available jobs is generally understood to mean that hours, wages, and other working conditions should be in keeping with the normal standards reached in specific kinds of occupations and in specific areas of the country. Work standards can be "reasonable" even though they differ materially from occupation to occupation and from area to area. It is possible that, at a given time, many more job opportunities would be created if, for example, wages were cut "across the board" 20 or 30 percent; nevertheless, an availibility of jobs dependent upon such a severe drop in wage standards would hardly satisfy the full-employment criterion.

THE GOAL OF PRICE-LEVEL STABILITY

As a major goal of monetary control, stability in the value or purchasing power of money means stability in the general level of prices, since the one is the reciprocal of the other. If prices in general rise by 20 percent, the value or purchasing power of money falls in inverse proportion by 16⅔ per-

---

[3]*Employment and Earnings,* September 1970, pp. 115, 117.

cent (1/1.2); and if the value of money rises by 25 percent, the price level falls in inverse proportion by 20 percent (1/1.25). In the first instance, the value of money is 83⅓ percent of what it was previously, and in the second, prices are at a level equal to 80 percent of the earlier level.

In realistic terms, a stable price level is understood to be one that fluctuates only within quite narrow limits from month to month and from year to year. An absolute lack of fluctuations must be ruled out as an impossible objective, as is an absolute level of full employment. At the same time, the freedom of individual prices to fluctuate, even over wider ranges, must be accepted for reasons such as changes in sources and costs of raw materials, variations in the efficiency of capital and labor, the introduction of new products, the swings of popular fancy from some products to others, and big shifts in the supplies of some goods because of weather conditions. But the idea is that fluctuations in individual prices, upward and downward, should be largely offsetting, so that when averages of these prices are taken from time to time *as the price level*—in the form of price index numbers— their fluctuations ought to be quite small.

Inflation and deflation

That substantial changes in the price level go hand in hand with much that is harmful in economic society is a proposition that is widely understood and accepted. This understanding and acceptance are continually indicated by widespread popular fears of "inflation" and "deflation." *Inflation* is a persistent upward movement in the price level at a substantial rate that typically continues for a period of years, and *deflation* is a persistent downward movement at a substantial rate typically continuing over a period of years. A rise in a country's price level of 0.3 percent or 0.4 percent a year for many years would hardly deserve to be called inflation because such a rate of increase is not a significant one. It would surely be within "tolerable" limits. Likewise, a period in which a price level rose by 3 percent in one year, fell by 2 percent in a second year, rose by 4 percent in a third, and fell by 3 percent in a fourth would hardly deserve to be described as a period of alternating inflation and deflation. Though the rates of these price movements could be said to be substantial, no persistence in one direction or the other is measured. The fluctuations of this 4-year period would be likely to be sources of some difficulties in the economic system, but those difficulties would be much less serious than those that result when all the fluctuations are in a single direction. Even when the price level rises or falls persistently at a substantial rate, the harm suffered by the economic society tends to be greater or less depending on the total movement of prices in a given period of years. "Creeping inflation," in which the price level rises by not more than, say, 3 percent a year, is surely much less disruptive to economic well-being than a "galloping inflation" in which it rises by perhaps 8 to 10 percent a year, and it certainly is much less disruptive than an "astronomical inflation" in which the price level may be doubled, tripled, or multiplied manifold in each of several years. The "persistent" price-level movement of inflation and deflation is not necessarily without interruption. If the price level rises persistently for 5 years, falls moderately in the sixth year, rises at a substantial rate for another 6 years, and then remains stable in the thirteenth year, the full period of 13 years—or, at least, the first 12—would surely deserve to be called one of inflation.

In the foregoing analysis of the meaning of inflation, no mention was made of the *causes* of price movements. For judgments about whether or not inflation is occurring, a consideration of causes is hardly required; it is the fluctuations of the price level that have meaning. Some people, for example, seem to think that almost any expansion in the money stock is "inflation" or that it is "inflationary." But if business activity is expanding, more money will generally be needed in the economic system, and supplying appropriate amounts will surely help to preserve economic balance rather than to disrupt it. One can inflate and deflate balloons, footballs and basketballs, price levels, and it is true, money stocks; but for precision in thought, it is always best to think of inflation and deflation in terms of what happens to the price level.

Harmful effects of inflation and deflation

The maladjustments that develop in economic systems in periods of inflation and deflation may be given a threefold classification: (1) comprehensive changes in total productive activity and therefore in total output and employment, (2) an arbitrary redistribution of real income among various classes of the people, and (3) an equally arbitrary redistribution of wealth.

Changes in the Tempo of Economic Activity   Comprehensive changes in the pace of economic activity go hand in hand with persistent substantial increases and decreases in the price level, chiefly because people expect a price movement upward or downward to continue in the same direction for months and years and make important economic decisions accordingly. Nowadays, indeed, people's expectations about price-level movements are almost entirely expectations that prices will rise if they change at all. It is obvious that a wide array of the prices of important commodities and services have a high degree of upward flexibility but that they are "sticky" in the opposite direction—that they are highly resistant to cutting. The probability of continuing strong inflationary pressures for many years are great, while the possibility of any substantial deflationary movement appears to be quite remote. In the following analysis, therefore, attention is given chiefly to what happens in periods of inflation, although some references to the harmful effects of deflation are included because it is desirable to see both sides of the picture.

In a period of inflation, a speculative fever takes hold. A "flight" from money to goods and property rights takes place, for it is anticipated that money balances will constantly lose purchasing power, and at the same time, it is anticipated that extraordinary "windfall" profits can be had by simply buying goods and other kinds of property, holding them for a while, and then selling them at the higher level of prices expected. Businessmen build up their inventories to extraordinary levels, and professional speculators negotiate future contracts for later deliveries of commodities that they expect to be able to sell at higher prices. Businessmen, too, may advance the dates of planned acquisitions of buildings, machinery, and equipment so as to avoid the higher costs they think will prevail later on; in this, they are likely to be encouraged by the ease with which they can sell new equity securities in a buoyant stock market. Wage earners arrive at decisions of a similar kind; as they, too, expect prices to continue to rise, they decide to buy today houses, automobiles, household appliances and furniture, and many other things that otherwise they would postpone buying for several months or even years. And state and local governments decide that this is a good time to make a vigorous attack on the backlog of much-needed schools, hospitals, and other public facilities now that both tax revenues and property valuations are up.

All this extraordinary demand for output feeds the fires of inflation, bringing about the very increase in the price level anticipated. Indeed, the situation looks very good. Jobs are plentiful, opportunities for overtime work abound, capital facilities are employed near capacity levels, wage rates rise, and profit margins rise even faster. But all is not well. Some prices are "sticky" in the upward direction—it is impossible to keep them moving up at the same rate as the general advance; thus the industries whose prices they are do not share at all or share only moderately in the over-all prosperity. Labor organizations decide that advances in wage rates are not keeping pace with the increasing cost of living, and numerous strikes occur. Income and wealth are shifted about haphazardly, as will be seen later on. Probably most serious of all is the fact that scarce resources are used wastefully in the anxiety of everyone to take advantage of immediate conditions and used uneconomically in the sense that they are drawn into areas of activity which, in other circumstances, could not capture or hold them. The whole price mechanism is distorted; money serves poorly as a standard of value.

What is more, very few people, whatever their economic roles may be, expect the "boom" in business activity to continue indefinitely, and signs of a slowdown will prompt many to take quick action to convert their paper profits to realized profits in cash or to avoid losses. And such action will surely tend to be depressive in its effects—tending to transform the slowdown into a genuine recession. Speculators will rush to unload their holdings. Businessmen will decide that their inventories are much too large and that they must cut their replenishment orders to suppliers, and they are likely to decide, also, that their capital expansion projects are much too grandiose and also must be cut back. More pressures will be added to make such decisions if there is a slump in the stock market and if interest rates on new borrowings are high, as they are likely to be in the later months of an inflationary period. As wage earners become anxious about their job prospects, they, too, can be expected to become much more cautious in their spending, especially for housing and consumer durable goods. Even as the inflation proceeds, industries that sell extensively in foreign markets are likely to find their export sales progressively falling as they are "priced out of" the foreign markets. Indeed, these and other industries are likely to experience drops in domestic sales because of the competition from lower-priced goods shipped in by foreign producers located in countries where inflation is not occurring or is more limited. All these developments mean reductions in demand for domestic output, with resulting curtailments of productive activities, increased idleness of factories, and a swelling of the ranks of the unemployed. As a further result, the inflationary pressures are likely to expire, and there may even be a modest downward movement in the price level, although a strong deflationary development is highly improbable. At any rate, the greatest probable evil of an inflationary boom is the "bust" that is likely to result.

Redistribution of Income   Not only does total output expand in periods of inflation and contract in periods of deflation, but the shares of output that go to various classes of the people shift about in a haphazard way. Rewards and punishments are meted out, as it were, without regard to the merits or lack of merits of those who receive them. The greater the degrees of inflation and deflation, the greater are the resulting injustices. In periods of inflation, some people gain purchasing power even though they have not increased their contribution to production, while others lose it even though their contribution to production has not been diminished; and in periods of deflation, those who previously gained are likely to lose purchasing power, and those who were previously disadvantaged are likely to enjoy unmerited advantages.

The effects of inflation and deflation on the real income of wage earners and salaried workers are of particular importance because these classes constitute the majority of the population. Since there is usually a lag in the movement of wages and particularly in salaries as the price level changes, those who work for wages and salaries are "pinched" in periods of rising prices because their money income will buy fewer goods. In periods of falling prices, they gain a temporary advantage because their unchanged money wages and salaries will buy more goods than before, but their joy in this situation is likely to be dampened by the fear that they will shortly lose their jobs.

People whose money income is derived entirely or largely from pensions, retirement allowances, annuities, and interest on government and corporation bonds and other debt instruments, all of which are usually fixed in money amount, are even more at the mercy of changing price levels. When the general price level rises, their fixed income buys fewer commdities and services—much as if the price level had remained the same and their money income had been reduced. Owners of land and buildings who lease these properties for long periods at fixed rentals are similarly situated.

Owners of business establishments, whether proprietors, partners, or stockholders of corporations, generally benefit from inflation and suffer a loss of real income in times of deflation. The chief reasons for this are that, as already indicated, wage and salary payments—the largest item of expense for many businesses—lag in their movements, while overhead expenses, such as property taxes, depreciation charges, maintenance costs, and interest costs on earlier borrowings, do not generally vary in proportion to changes in the price level, if they vary at all. Higher selling prices rapidly expand the margin of profit when costs rise more slowly, but the margin of profit is quickly dissipated when prices fall and costs remain swollen. It is to be recognized, nevertheless, that all kinds of businesses do not fare alike as price levels change, and this is all the more an unhappy consequence of inflation and deflation. Some selling prices are fixed or are supported by government regulations, some—"administered prices"—are subject to close management by the selling firms, and others have diverse degrees of flexibility depending upon the elasticities of the supply of and demand for the goods whose values they express.

Redistribution of Wealth Wealth, too, is haphazardly shifted about from person to person as a result of inflation and deflation. Shifts in real income, as just discussed, can result in shifts in wealth accumulations, but shifts in wealth can occur independently of income shifts.

Such an independent shift in wealth occurs chiefly in the payment of the principal of outstanding bonds and other debts. If a person receives $1000 at the maturity of a 10-year corporation bond in which he invested $1000 at the time of issuance, and if in the 10-year period the price level rose by 25 percent, he gets back only 80 percent of the purchasing power he originally gave to the corporation. Considering the great volume of bonds and other debts constantly being created and paid off in a country such as the United States, such redistributions of wealth can be, and often have been, of enormous proportions. Moreover, the shift in wealth can be much greater if the creditor is unable to await maturity for payment. Market rates of interest tend to rise markedly with strong and prolonged inflation, and this causes a fall in the market prices of outstanding lower-rate bonds and other interest-bearing obligations. Four or five years before maturity, the holder of the $1000 corporation bond might be able to get only $850 or $900 for it in the market. In June 1970, for example, U.S. Treasury 4-percent bonds

of $1000 denominations due in 1973 were selling in the market at about
$890, and 4-percent U.S. Treasury bonds due in 1993 were selling at about
$640.

The holding of wealth in the form of money can also result in substantial
shifts in purchasing power. As inflation progresses, money itself constantly
loses purchasing power, and as deflation progresses, it constantly gains
purchasing power. Here rewards and punishments appear to be especially
unmerited. By deferring their spending, hoarders of money doubtless contribute to the intensification of deflation and business recession; yet, as
prices fall, they are rewarded, as it were, by a constant gain in the purchasing power of their money balances. On the other hand, when restraint in
spending would contribute to stability in the economy, holders of money
are penalized for restraint, for the purchasing power of their balances constantly diminishes as prices advance.

Trade-offs

Although the goals of full employment and price-level stability are recognized as objectives to be striven for simultaneously, they are not necessarily
compatible in all circumstances. In a period of recession during which the
price level is relatively stable, monetary and other government actions
aimed at stimulating business activity will be likely to bring about a reduction in unemployment with relatively little upward pressure on the price
level. But as business activity continues to expand and as unemployment
gets down to around, perhaps, 3 or 4 percent of the labor force, further
stimulative action may have effects chiefly in the direction of price increases rather than further reductions in unemployment. As less efficient
workers are hired, less efficient machinery and equipment are returned to
production, and increased demand for raw materials causes increases in
their prices, costs go up and producers try to cover these increased costs—
and perhaps more—by raising their selling prices.

Accordingly, many economists hold that, at relatively high levels of business activity with relatively low levels of unemployment, government authorities who exercise controls must decide whether to accept inflation of
various degrees in exchange for further reductions in unemployment of various magnitudes. They must decide how much inflation they will "trade off"
for additional employment. Would a price-level increase of 3 percent a year
be a reasonable price to pay for getting unemployment down from 4 to 3
percent of the labor force and keeping it there, or would a price-level increase of 4.5 percent a year be acceptable as a result of actions to maintain
unemployment at a level of 2 percent?

The trade-off idea is well-illustrated by our experience in the decade of
the 1960s, for which some summary data are presented in Table 2-1. We
had a recession in business activity from May 1960 through February 1961,
after which business activity moved up persistently, with some minor interruptions, to the fall of 1969, when a downturn occurred. In February 1961,

unemployment was at the high level of 6.9 percent of the civilian labor force and a lot of idle capital resources were also available, so that it was possible to promote a rapid expansion in output for several years, with unemployment being steadily reduced and with the price level, as measured by consumer prices, rising only moderately. But in 1966 the annual rate of increase in the price level accelerated as the unemployment rate was further reduced, and further acceleration in price-level increases occurred in 1968 and 1969 as further decreases in the unemployment rate were achieved—decreases that were, indeed, quite modest.

Table 2-1   **Consumer Prices, Real GNP, and Unemployment, 1960–1969**

	ANNUAL RATE OF INCREASE IN		
YEAR	CONSUMER PRICES (PERCENT)	REAL GNP (PERCENT)	RANGE OF UNEMPLOYMENT[a] (PERCENT OF CIVILIAN LABOR FORCE)
1961	1.0	1.9	6.0–7.1
1962	1.1	6.6	5.4–5.8
1963	1.2	4.0	5.4–5.9
1964	1.3	5.5	4.8–5.5
1965	1.7	6.3	4.1–5.0
1966	2.9	6.5	3.5–3.9
1967	2.9	2.6	3.6–4.3
1968	4.2	4.7	3.3–3.7
1969	5.4	2.8	3.3–3.8

[a] Seasonally adjusted monthly rates.
Source: Unemployment rates from U.S. Department of Commerce, *Survey of Current Business,* various issues, and rates of increase in the U.S. Bureau of Labor Statistics consumer-price index and real GNP computed by the author from data presented in the same source.

While our experience in the 1960s illustrates the trade-off principle, it does not prove that the trade-offs that did occur were necessary. Since economics is concerned with optimum uses of *scarce* resources, it hardly seems fitting for economists to say that we must forgo the potential output of, say, 4 percent of the labor force in order to achieve price-level stability, or that forgoing the potential output of an additional 2 or 3 percent of the labor force above the ordinarily "tolerable" level is the price that must be paid in order to bring an inflationary movement to a halt. All the more unconvincing does the trade-off idea seem to be when one considers the experience of certain foreign countries that have succeeded in recent years in simultaneously maintaining lower rates of both unemployment and inflation than has the United States—even while, as in the case of West Germany, importing wage earners from Italy and soldiers from the United States. Perhaps it is only that our tools of monetary and fiscal policy are inadequate to do the job.

Measurement of price levels

If the money stock is to be controlled and other government actions are to be taken in order to maintain a high degree of stability in the price level, it must be possible to measure changes in the price level with a reasonable degree of accuracy—to determine how stable or unstable it has been recently. Fortunately, techniques of measurement by the construction of index numbers of prices are well-developed and are quite logical from the standpoint of mathematical theory. But there is still the question of which arrays of prices are to be included in index-number construction as representing *the* price level, and here judgments are less certain. At least, we can say that in the United States the index numbers that are widely recognized as the best measure of "general" price levels are the wholesale- and consumer-price indexes of the U.S. Bureau of Labor Statistics and the "implicit price deflators" of gross national product published by the Office of Business Economics of the U.S. Department of Commerce.

Index Numbers of Prices   A price index number is an average of numerous specific prices as they prevail in given markets in a designated week, month, or other period, with each price customarily weighted according to its relative importance and with the average usually expressed as a percentage of an average of the same scope computed for a selected "base period" that is given a value of 100 percent, or simply "100." Assume, for example, that we want to construct index numbers from the prices of five commodities whose unit prices were as follows in the base year 19xx and 2 years later in 19yy:

COMMODITY	19xx PRICE	19yy PRICE
A	$2.00	$2.10
B	0.10	0.12
C	0.40	0.38
D	6.00	6.60
E	0.05	0.07

We could add up the five 19xx prices and divide this total into the total of the 19yy prices, but the result would hardly be meaningful. A's price might be for a bushel, B's for a pound, C's for a quart, and so on, and in terms of the base year, we would be giving D's price a weight three times that of A, sixty times that of B, and so on. It would be unlikely that D as a commodity in the market would be three times as important as A and sixty times as important as B. To eliminate this kind of distorted weighting, a popular technique is to make all the prices of the base period 100 (percent) and to express the prices of subsequent periods as relatives (percentages) of the base-period prices. Applying this technique to the illustration, we get:

COMMODITY	19xx PRICE	19xx RELATIVE	19yy PRICE	19yy RELATIVE
A	$2.00	100	$2.10	105
B	0.10	100	0.12	120
C	0.40	100	0.38	95
D	6.00	100	6.60	110
E	0.05	100	0.07	140

No longer, then, does the 60-cent increase in the price of D swamp the 2-cent increase in the price of E. Simply as price changes, the increase in E is revealed as being four times the increase in D. Perhaps, however, E, as a commodity in the market, is not that important, or perhaps it is more important. Another adjustment needs to be made. Now all the prices are equally weighted, so that it would seem to be a step toward realism to give them the weights they deserve—precisely according to the respective market importance of each commodity. Such weighting is usually effected by multiplying each price relative by the total dollar sales of the commodity in the base year or some other selected year. If people spend $20 billion for C and $5 billion for D, it is surely realistic to say that C is four times as important as D and should have weight of that proportion in the index. Assuming certain value weights for the five commodities (in billions of dollars, let us say), we can complete the illustration as follows:

COM-MODITY	19xx PRICE	19xx RELA-TIVE	19xx WEIGHT	19xx WEIGHT × RELA-TIVE	19yy PRICE	19yy RELA-TIVE	19yy WEIGHT	19yy WEIGHT × RELA-TIVE
A	$2.00	100	$ 8	$ 800	$2.10	105	$ 8	$ 840
B	0.10	100	25	2500	0.12	120	25	3000
C	0.40	100	20	2000	0.38	95	20	1900
D	6.00	100	5	500	6.60	110	5	550
E	0.05	100	16	1600	0.07	140	16	2240
			74	7400			74	8530

By dividing 7400, the first sum of weights times relatives, by 74, the sum of the weights, we get a price index of 100 for 19xx; and by dividing 8530 by 74, we get a price index of 115 for 19yy. Our hypothetical price level for the five commodities has increased by 15 percent. But there still may be objection on the grounds that people are unlikely to spend year after year proportional dollar amounts for the various commodities equal to the proportions of the year from which weights were taken. As this objection is undoubtedly valid, it is generally admitted that uniform weighting from year to year makes many published price index numbers somewhat inaccurate, with the inaccuracy tending to increase the further given index numbers are from the year from which the weights were selected. If, however, weights are changed from year to year, the resulting index numbers are likely to be even more inaccurate, since they would reflect both changing prices and changing weights.

It should be understood that almost all published price index numbers are percentages. The index for 19yy is 115 *percent* of the index of the base year 19xx. Accordingly, the typical index number, standing by itself, indicates what change in average prices has taken place since the base period— an index of 82 indicates a decline of 18 percent, and one of 132 indicates an increase of 32 percent. When, however, one cites index numbers without reference to the base period, one must be careful to distinguish between percentage changes and changes in "percentage points." An increase in the price level from 120 in one year to 125 in the next year *is not* an increase of 5 percent; it is an increase of 5 percentage points, amounting to an increase of $5/120$, or about 4.2 percent.

BLS Index of Wholesale Prices　The index numbers of wholesale prices of the Bureau of Labor Statistics are constructed from the prices of about 2200 commodities produced by the domestic manufacturing, mining, agricultural, forestry, and fishing industries, and imported from foreign countries, with average prices that prevailed in the year 1967 serving as the base. The index numbers are weighted averages of price relatives (as in the foregoing hypothetical illustration) and the weight given to each commodity price is the dollar amount of the commodity's sales in 1958 plus, in some instances, the 1958 sales value of other commodities of which it is deemed to be representative but whose prices are not separately included. The 2200 commodities included are products at various stages of output, from raw materials to finished goods, and the prices compiled are prices paid in the first important commercial transactions in which the respective products are involved, but not including retail transactions. Hence one must not read too much into the term *wholesale*—by no means does the index simply measure prices charged by wholesalers to retailers.

In addition to the over-all index numbers, the BLS publishes many indexes for individual commodities and for various groupings of commodities. The latter include indexes for farm products, processed foods, all commodities other than farm products and processed foods (with additional indexes for thirteen major subdivisions of this category, such as chemicals and allied products and metals and metal products), raw materials, intermediate materials, finished goods, durable goods, and nondurable goods.

BLS Index of Consumer Prices　The consumer-price index numbers of the

BLS measure the "cost of living" of wage earners and salaried workers who dwell in "urban" areas, that is, in communities of 2500 persons or more. The BLS emphasizes that these index numbers do not measure the average cost of living of the whole population of the country, because its consumer price surveys are concentrated in the stores, shopping centers, hospitals, and other outlets of goods *and services* where urban wage earners and salaried workers do most of their buying. The prices of approximately 400 kinds of goods and services are included, and average prices for the year 1967 serve as the base. These prices are converted to price relatives, and each relative is weighted in proportion to the position it held in the "market baskets" of urban wage earners and salaried workers as surveyed in 1960 and 1961. For example, dairy products has a weight of 2.80; meat, poultry, and fish, one of 5.63; and food in general, a total weight of 22.43. Weights allocated to other important groupings of consumer goods and services are these: shelter, fuel and utilities, and household furnishing and operation, 33.23; apparel and upkeep, 10.63; transportation, 13.88; and health and recreation, 19.45.[4] Because these weights are proportions of total "market baskets," their sum is necessarily 100. Some additional weighting is used to allow for population differences in the cities in which price surveys are made.

In addition to the over-all index numbers, there are separate indexes for the major groupings mentioned above, and for thirty-four subgroups within the major expenditure groups, as for dairy products. Moreover, a separate array of index numbers is published for each metropolitan area that had a population of a million or more in 1960.

The consumer-price indexes of the BLS are generally thought to have an upward bias because of difficulties in making adjustments for improvements in the quality of consumer goods and services and for shifts in the contents of "market baskets" from month to month, especially shifts that result from shopping for "specials."

Implicit Price Deflators of GNP   The implicit price deflators of gross national product (GNP) as published by the U.S. Office of Business Economics are "implicit" because they are not index numbers constructed in the usual way, but are simply derived from the relationship between the values of total output in given years at the prices of those years and estimates of what these values would have been at the prices that prevailed in the base year 1958. For example, GNP in 1969 at 1969 prices was reported at $931.4 billion, and it was estimated that the same output would have cost $727.1 billion at 1958 prices.[5] Accordingly, the implicit price deflator for 1969 is 128.1, as found by dividing $931.4 billion by $727.1 billion, and indicating an average increase in the prices of all kinds of commodities and services

---

[4]*Monthly Labor Review,* April 1964, p. 386.
[5]*Survey of Current Business,* July 1970, p. 17.

included in GNP of 28.1 percent in the 11-year period. Although the deflators are derived in the manner indicated, the Office of Business Economics uses many price index numbers in estimating what given components of output would have cost at 1958 prices. It constructs some of these indexes itself, while receiving some from other agencies such as the BLS. If, for example, the output of a given component of GNP sold for $6 billion in 1969, and if the price index number for this component in 1969 on the 1958 base was 120, its estimate of what the component would have sold for at 1958 prices would be $5 billion, as found by dividing $6 billion by 1.20 (moving the decimal point two places to the left, because index numbers of this type are always percentages).

In addition to the implicit price deflators for GNP, the Office of Business Economics publishes deflators for the four major components of GNP, that is, personal consumption expenditures, gross private domestic investment, net exports of goods and services (actually separate deflators for exports and imports), and government purchases of goods and services, as well as deflators for many subcomponents, such as consumer durable goods in the personal consumption category and autos and parts in the category of consumer durable goods.

As index numbers, the GNP deflators are generally thought to have an upward bias, chiefly for three reasons: the substantial weight given to labor costs without adjustment for increases in labor productivity; the substantial weighting accorded material costs without sufficient adjustment for improvements in quality; and the weighting of the price index number of each year by the spending patterns of that year, rather than by the spending patterns of the base year (or of some other single year), as is the usual method of weighting in other index-number construction.

Which Index? Because the BLS indexes of wholesale and consumer prices and the GNP implicit price deflators do not always move in the same direction in a given period of time, and because they definitely do not vary at the same rates, they raise the interesting question of which of the indexes best measures changes in what we have been calling the "price level." It seems that there are at least three price levels, as in 1969 when, for the whole year, the wholesale index was reported at 106.5, the consumer index was at 109.8 and the GNP deflator (converted to the 1967 base year) was at 108.9. In order to attain stability in the "price level," which of these indexes should the monetary authorities and other control agencies of the government accept for judgments of success or failure? These people do not tell us which price level they want to stabilize, although it is a reasonable presumption that they would be happiest if able to stabilize all three simultaneously, without forgoing the additional goals of full employment and high rates of economic growth.

It is doubtless wise for the authorities to avoid reporting which price level as measured by a given series of index numbers they are trying to stabilize. They can reasonably say that each of the three means of measurement has certain merits and weaknesses that they must constantly take into account, each gives them different kinds of messages that they must carefully weigh one against the other, and most important of all, they must concentrate attention on the individual price series that make up the over-all totals before deciding what actions they should take or avoid. They are likely to conclude, for example, that no actions ordinarily available to them are likely to stop increases in the consumer index that result from rapidly rising costs of medical care or to stop increases in the GNP deflators that result from increases in the prices the federal government contracts to pay for military equipment and munitions and other war supplies. For the mass of people, however, there is little doubt that the BLS consumer-price index is most widely accepted as the best measure of changes in the price level. Changes in the index are given the widest publicity, and of course, the people readily notice changes in the prices that they pay for consumer goods. Since, indeed, the economic welfare of most of the population is more directly and immediately affected by changes in the prices of consumer goods than by changes in wholesale prices or in the GNP price deflators, it is surely realistic to argue that the level of consumer prices is the "price level" to which the monetary authorities and other controllers should give most attention in their stabilization efforts.

THE GOAL OF A HIGH RATE OF ECONOMIC GROWTH

It might appear that the continuous full employment of the available labor force should, of itself, provide a good rate of economic growth. If capital equipment and natural resources can be employed only to the extent that labor is available to work with them, output at full employment might seem to be at a maximum. And if new jobs can readily be found for people who come into the labor force from schools, colleges, households, and foreign countries, output must expand, so that economic growth should take place without control. Nevertheless, a distinction of character can readily be made between the two goals of "a high rate of economic growth year after year" and "full employment." Maximum output is not necessarily achieved by full employment, and finding jobs for additions to the labor force, although it undoubtedly results in expanding output, cannot be depended upon to improve output per capita. Even at a level of full employment, there must be means by which productive capacity can be increased.

Emphasis on improvements in capital facilities

The means to increase productive capacity surely include finding new sources of raw materials, upgrading labor skills, and improvements in many kinds of capital equipment. Improvements in capital equipment are especially emphasized as a means of accelerating growth rates. Every encouragement must be given to the replacement of inefficient and archaic capital facilities, liberal spending for new kinds of labor-saving equipment as well as for research and invention aimed at new "break-throughs" in this area, and quick acceptance and adoption of other improvements in technology.

In other words, "automation" must be hailed as a great blessing in whatever degree it may be attainable in various industries—as a means *par excellence* for increasing the productivity of labor. Automation, it is argued, is not a new invention of the 1950s (although it was much in the public mind in that decade as an explanation for high levels of unemployment); it has been proceeding since the dawn of the industrial revolution. And without this long development—with considerable acceleration, it is true, in the past 2 or 3 decades—standards of living in industrial countries would be far lower than they now are. Indeed, countries deserving to be called "industrial" in the modern sense would simply not exist.

More trade-offs

By definition, however, labor-saving machinery and equipment displace workers, so that the goals of maintaining full employment and sustaining a high rate of economic growth would appear to be incompatible. There is not much question that, in periods of rapid expansion in capital equipment, unemployment above what is ordinarily held to be the tolerable limit may have to be accepted. But one can argue that such excesses in unemployment should be of short duration. The very expansion in production with expanded flows of money income should give rise to new and greater demands for goods from other sources, particularly from the service industries, and therefore increased needs for workers in these areas. And extensive programs of job training and retraining should smooth the movement of workers from the displacing industries to the industries of new or higher demand.

An even greater degree of incompatibility is generally recognized as possible between the goals of price-level stability and sustaining a high rate of economic growth, and as especially probable in periods in which full employment is approached or is being achieved. In most periods in which unemployment is considerably above the tolerable limit, a high level of investment spending for new capital equipment can hardly be other than beneficial. It should promote reemployment while providing the means for subsequent expansion in growth rates, and at the same time, it should exert relatively little upward pressure on the price level. This was precisely our experience in the period 1961–1965 as indicated in Table 2-1. But when full employment is closely approached or is reached, a high level of investment spending coupled with high levels of consumer and government spending and spending by foreigners for exports may exert strong inflationary pressures. It largely depends on where business enterprises get the money for the spending for productive facilities. If consumers and governments are willing to limit their spending in order to provide sufficient savings to finance the investment spending, the inflationary pressures will be held in check. But if much of the investment spending is financed by newly created money, these pressures will be strong, and it is likely that the economy will quickly "overheat," as the popular expression has it.

According to most current estimates by economists, a GNP growth rate for the United States in the range from 4.0 to 4.5 percent, with full employment prevailing, should be sustainable year after year without serious inflationary pressures. However, some of the estimators appear to accept unemployment levels as high as 4 percent of the civilian labor force as being tolerable.

Measurement of economic growth

Almost everybody measures rates of economic growth in terms of the growth of *real* gross national product, that is, the growth of GNP adjusted for price-level changes. Since GNP is the output of all kinds of goods in a given period of time, its growth would seem to be the best possible measure of advances in economic well-being. But increases in GNP as a result of price-level increases must surely be regarded as disadvantageous rather than beneficial. Hence the need of adjustment for price-level changes. For example, the U.S. Department of Commerce reported a GNP level of $865.0 billion for 1968 and one of $931.4 billion for 1969 in 1968 and 1969 prices, respectively. Thus the growth rate in "current dollars" was $931.4 – $865.0/ $865.0, or 7.7 percent. But GNP implicit price deflators were reported at 122.3 for 1968 and at 128.1 for 1969, indicating that price increases were responsible for much of the increase in current-dollar GNP. To get GNP for the two years in "constant dollars," that is, dollars of the purchasing power of the base year 1958, we apply the following formula and make the divisions indicated:[6]

Current-dollar GNP ÷ implicit price deflator = constant-dollar GNP
For 1968: $865.0 billion ÷ 122.3 = $707.2 billion
For 1969: $931.4 billion ÷ 128.1 = $727.1 billion

We find that the year's rate of growth in real GNP was $727.1 – $707.2/ $707.2, or 2.8 percent.

Although widely accepted as the best measure of economic growth, the growth rate of real GNP is not without defects for judgments about improvements in economic well-being. An obvious way of making the measure more realistic would be to make a further adjustment for population growth in order to get growth rates of per capita real GNP. And this immediately suggests other considerations: how evenly or unevenly GNP is distributed among the whole population; what proportion is devoted to military purposes; what proportion consists of goods that are quite low in benefits or that are positively harmful; and what injury is done to the environment and

---

[6]The same formula can be used, of course, to convert any current-dollar component of GNP to a constant-dollar amount.

to the people as a result of the customary ways by which productive operations are carried on.

THE GOAL OF REASONABLE
BALANCE-OF-PAYMENTS POSITIONS

As a goal of monetary and fiscal controls, attaining a reasonable balance-
of-payments position from year to year means that our total spending in
foreign countries should not greatly exceed or greatly fall short of total
foreign spending in the United States. Excesses in our total spending abroad
in a given period of time are called "deficits" or "unfavorable balances,"
and shortfalls in our total spending abroad—which are, of course, excesses
in total foreign spending in the United States—are called "surpluses" or
"favorable balances." Accordingly, the goal can be restated as the avoidance
of large surpluses and deficits or, alternatively, the avoidance of large favorable and unfavorable balances in the totals of international spending in
which we participate. Especially do we want to avoid large surpluses and
deficits that persist chronically, that is, for several years.

For each quarter and year, the U.S. Department of Commerce reports
in great detail the kinds and magnitudes of the international spending transactions in which we participate. A brief summary of its report for the year
1970 is presented in Table 2-2 for analysis aimed at explaining what the
goal of a reasonable balance-of-payments position is all about.

In Table 2-2, we see that transactions that require payments by foreigners to Americans are classified by us as exports or credits and are indicated
by plus signs; and that transactions that require payments by Americans to
foreigners are classified by us as imports or debits and are indicated by
minus signs. We also see that the transactions that require payments between us and foreigners are chiefly purchases and sales of merchandise and
services and international lending and investing (capital flows), but include
some special classes such as the "unilateral transfers."

In 1970 we acquired claims for payment on foreigners of $41,980 million
by exports of merchandise of that value to them, and they acquired claims
on us of $39,870 million by our purchases of merchandise from them. On
merchandise transactions, therefore, we acquired net claims on foreigners
equal to the difference between these two figures, that is, $2110 million.
This was our "balance of trade," and it was "favorable." (Note that the
terms *favorable, unfavorable, deficit,* and *surplus* are often thus used de-
scriptively for certain "balances" in the balance of payments as well as for
the over-all totals.) The service transactions include most importantly the
expenditures of American tourists in foreign countries; expenditures of
foreign tourists in the United States; freight charges here and abroad for
international shipments of goods; charges for insurance, bank services, advertising, and so on; income earned by Americans on their investments in
foreign countries; income earned by foreigners on their investments here;

and military expenditures of the federal government in foreign countries. In 1970 foreigners purchased American services of these kinds (including the services of our foreign investments) at a cost of $20,923 million, while our purchases of foreign services amounted to $19,443 million, so that we had a "favorable" balance here of $1480 million. Combining this with the balance-of-trade surplus of $2110 million gave us a surplus in our "balance on merchandise and services" of $3592 million.

Table 2-2   **Balance of International Payments of the United States in 1970 (in millions of dollars)**

	EXPORTS (CREDITS)	IMPORTS (DEBITS)	NET EXPORTS (+) OR NET IMPORTS (−)a
Merchandiseb	+41,980	−39,870	+2110
Servicesc	+20,923	−19,443	+1480
	+62,903	−59,313	
Balance on merchandise and services			+3592
Unilateral transfers (net):			
Remittances, pensions, U.S. government grants,d and other transfers			−3149
Balance on current account			+444
Long-term capital flows (net):			
From the United States to foreign countries:			
U.S. Government		−2029	
Private		−5781	
		−7810	
From foreign countries to the United States		+4328	−3482
Balance on current account and long-term capital			−3038
Other transactions affecting the liquidity balance (net):			
Nonliquid short-term private capital flows		−548	
Allocation of special drawing rights (SDRs)e		+867	
Errors and omissions		−1132	−813
Net liquidity balance			−3852
Liquid private capital flows (net)			−5969
Official reserve transactions balance			−9821

ᵃ Some items do not add or subtract exactly to totals because of rounding.
ᵇ Excluding transfers under military grants and military agency sales contracts.
ᶜ Including military transactions (other than transfers under grants) comprising direct military expenditures abroad of $4851 million as a minus item, offset in part by exports under military agency sales contracts of $1480 million as a plus item.
ᵈ Excluding military grants.
ᵉ See Chapter 5.
Source: Survey of Current Business, June 1971, pp. 30, 32.

But in 1970 we gave away much purchasing power by donations to foreign charities, remittances to relatives dwelling in foreign countries, social security and other pension payments to Americans living abroad, government grants for economic development to poorer countries, and so on. Such give-aways or "unilateral transfers" amounted to $3149 million on a net basis (that is, with transfers of similiar kinds by foreigners to Americans subtracted), and this figure is shown with the minus sign because the give-aways, in effect, required payments to foreigners. Accordingly, the amount of the give-aways partially offset our net claims on foreigners from the merchandise and service transactions, leaving us with net claims of only $444 million, the "balance on current account."

In 1970, however, we spent much more than this current-account balance plus the amount of new foreign long-term investments in the United States in adding to our long-term investments in foreign countries. Thus the over-all result of all our merchandise and service transactions, the unilateral transfers, and the flows of long-term investment funds inward and outward gave foreigners net liquid claims on us of $3038 million, the "balance on current account and long-term capital," a balance that was liquid in the sense that foreigners could demand payment immediately or in short periods. By reason of certain net outflows of short-term investment funds amounting to $813 million (to be described in Chapter 23), these liquid claims of foreigners were increased from $3038 million to $3852 million, the "net liquidity balance."

Although our liquid liabilities to *all* foreigners increased by $3852 million in 1970, our net liquid liabilities to private foreigners—individuals, commercial banks, other private business enterprises, and so on—actually declined by $5969 million. As we did not pay off these liabilities, the only thing that could happen to them was their sale by the private foreigners to their central banks or other "official agencies." Thus if our liquid liabilities to all foreigners increased by $3852 million, and if our liquid liabilities to private foreigners decreased by $5969 million, our liquid liabilities to foreign "official agencies" must have increased by the sum of these figures, that is, by $9821 million, the amount of the "official reserve transactions balance."[7]

There is much uncertainty about which of the balances in our balance of payments best measures the performance of the American economy in its international economic transactions, although it is generally agreed that such a choice must be made among the balance on current account and

---

[7]That the official reserve transactions balance amounted to a deficit of $9821 million in 1970 is proved, as it were, by additional figures published by the Department of Commerce that show how this balance was "financed" or "settled"—the financing figures totaling $9821 million with the plus sign, because the balance of payments must balance. However, these additional figures and many other details about our balance of payments are omitted here, since its structure and meaning are treated at much greater length in Chapter 23.

long-term capital, the net liquidity balance, and the official reserve transactions balance. As all three of these balances were large negative or "unfavorable" ones in 1970, there was little doubt that our performance in that year was quite poor—that our balance-of-payments position was far from being "reasonable." Moreover, it could be argued that there must have been some serious failure in monetary and fiscal control (and possibly in other kinds of controls) to have permitted this.

FOR REVIEW

1. What is meant by monetary control or monetary policy? What are generally accepted as the major goals of monetary control?

2. Why is the Employment Act of 1946 cited in relation to the goals of monetary control?

3. What is meant by full employment as a goal of monetary control? In connection with a goal of full employment, is it not strange to allow for a level of "tolerable" unemployment? Is unemployment at 3 percent of the civilian labor force too high or too low as a "tolerable" level? Discuss.

4. Are the techniques and standards of the U.S. Bureau of the Census in counting the employed and the unemployed realistic and trustworthy? How would you change its definitions? For what reasons?

5. Is it realistic to allow for a "tolerable" degree of fluctuations in individual prices? in the price level? Discuss.

6. What is meant by inflation and deflation? What are the major reasons why inflation is held to be harmful to an economic society? Are these reasons valid for all degrees of inflation? Can you see any good in moderate inflation?

7. How well does money serve as a standard of value in periods of inflation? as a standard of deferred payments? as a store of purchasing power?

8. What is the relationship between the goal of full employment and the goal of price-level stability? Which of these goals is the more important? What do you think of the soundness of the trade-off idea?

9. Does the technique of index-number construction as described in this chapter appeal to you as mathematically sound and logical? Why or why not?

10. How do the BLS consumer- and wholesale-price indexes and the implicit price deflations of GNP differ among one another in that which they are designed to measure? Which of these is probably the best measure of *the* price level in the United States? Why do you think so?

11. What is indicated by price index numbers of, say, 82 and 115? Why is it important to distinguish between percentage changes in index numbers and changes in percentage points?

12. Is not the goal of a "high rate of economic growth" much the same as the goal of full employment? Explain.
13. What is the usual means by which economic growth is measured? Why must this means of measurement be "corrected" for changes in the price level? What is the technique for making such a correction?
14. What is meant by a reasonable balance-of-payments position as a goal of monetary policy? If the balance of payments balances, how can it be said to be favorable or unfavorable?

PROBLEMS

1. Compute a price index number as a weighted average of relative prices for the prices of the following six commodities, A–F, for the year 19yy, with 19xx = 100, assuming market prices in 19xx and 19yy and the weights to be applied as follows:

	PRICES		
COMMODITY	19xx	19yy	WEIGHTS
A	$0.08	$0.10	4
B	1.25	1.30	1
C	0.30	0.33	6
D	0.12	0.15	10
E	0.60	0.75	5
F	3.00	2.70	2

2. A rise in prices in general in a given period of time of 20 percent is equivalent to what percentage decline in the purchasing power of money?
3. A fall in the purchasing power of money in a given period of time of 25 percent is equivalent to what percentage rise in the general price level?
4. Between 1959 and 1969, the BLS consumer-price index (1967 = 100) rose from 87.3 to 109.8. What was the percentage rise in consumer prices in this 10-year period? the rise in percentage points? As measured by this index, what was the percentage decline in the purchasing power of the consumer dollar?
5. On the 1967 base, the BLS consumer-price index for 1963 was 91.7. As an index number on the same base, what was the purchasing power of the consumer dollar in 1963?
6. Between 1964 and 1970, the BLS index of wholesale prices (1967 = 100) rose from 94.7 to 110.4. What was the percentage rise in wholesale prices in this 6-year period? the rise in percentage points? As measured by this index, what was the percentage decline in the purchasing power of money?
7. At current prices, GNP amounted to $931.4 billion in 1969 and to $976.5

billion in 1970. But 1970 was a year of inflation as indicated by GNP implicit price deflators (1967 = 100) of 108.9 for 1969 and 114.7 for 1970. Determine, therefore, the percentage increase or decrease in *real* GNP in 1970, that is, GNP "corrected" for the price-level increase.

8. At current prices, the output of consumer goods amounted to $577.5 billion in 1969 and to $616.7 billion in 1970. But consumer prices rose in 1970 as measured by an implicit price deflator (1967 = 100) of 108.0 for 1969 and one of 113.0 for 1970. What, then, was the percentage increase in the output of consumer goods in 1970 after adjustment for the increase in prices?

CHAPTER 3

MONETARY SYSTEMS

A monetary system comprises all the kinds of money a country has outstanding, all the institutions that have powers and responsibilities for money creation and extinguishment, and all the laws, rules, regulations, and procedures that govern this creation and extinguishment. In modern monetary systems of advanced countries, the kinds of money are chiefly paper money, coins, and bank demand deposits; and the institutions are principally the national government, especially its treasury department, the central bank, such as the Federal Reserve System of the United States, and the commercial banks—the banks that hold the demand deposits of the general public. The laws, rules, regulations, and procedures are many, varied, and often complex, but all are generally aimed at making the money stock manageable in a manner that will advance the economy toward the goals of full employment, price-level stability, and sustained growth at high rates, while making money itself serve in an optimum way in the five capacities analyzed in Chapter 1.

QUALITIES OF GOOD MONETARY SYSTEMS

Manageability of the money stock

In the first place, then, the total quantity of money in circulation must be manageable by the monetary authorities who are exclusively or chiefly the officials of the central bank. Indeed, a *central bank* can be best defined as an institution that has exclusive or at least major responsibility for controlling the expansion and contraction of the volume of money in circulation in order to promote the general welfare. It should be well within the power of the monetary authorities to bring about substantial changes in the money stock and to accomplish this speedily.

Elasticity of the different kinds of money

In addition to manageability of the over-all money stock, the principal kinds of money that are used as mediums of exchange, stores of purchasing power, and guarantors of solvency should have high degrees of elasticity, that is, a capacity for easy and voluminous expansion and contraction. Given the decisions of the monetary authorities on the total quantity of money, the people, in turn, should have the right to hold this quantity in whatever forms they like. If they want to exchange paper money for coins, coins in sufficient quantities should be available; if they want to make withdrawals from demand deposits in the form of paper money, the banks should be in a position to meet these withdrawal demands; and if they want to increase their demand deposit balances by deposits of paper money and coins, the banks should stand ready to accept these deposits without hesitation.

Elasticity is especially important for paper money that is legal tender, since all persons who have claims to payments in domestic money can demand that these payments be made in legal tender. Such claims include rights to make withdrawals from demand deposits—because demand deposits themselves are not legal tender—rights to convert near-moneys, claims to payments at maturity of short-term liquid instruments, and indeed, claims to payments on all other kinds of obligations payable in domestic money. Ordinarily, claimants will not ask for payment in legal tender, but they are likely to do so in times of economic stress, and if legal tender is not forthcoming, panic ensues, as in the United States in 1893, 1907, and 1932–1933.

Equality of purchasing power of different kinds of money

Not only should people be free to exchange one kind of money for another easily; they should be able to do so without rewards or penalties, as by receiving premiums or paying discounts. For coins having a face value of $50, for example, a person should be able to get $50 in paper money or in a demand deposit account—not, say, $49 in paper money or $52 in the demand deposit. This means that the purchasing power of each kind of money in its various denominations should be equal to the purchasing power of other kinds in the same denominations. Four quarters should have the same purchasing power as a paper dollar or a dollar in a demand deposit.

Unequal purchasing power of different kinds of money in given denominations can cause serious disruptions in economic systems. In 1862 and 1863, for example, the federal government issued paper money called "United States notes" that were not redeemable in gold even though gold coins were then in general circulation. In effect, the government said that its "greenbacks" having a face value of $10 were equal in purchasing power to $10 in gold coins. But the people refused to believe this. They hoarded gold coins and spent greenbacks. The gold coins largely disappeared from circulation, as should have been expected from the operation of *Gresham's law*. The basic doctrine of Gresham's law is this: if two kinds of money in circulation are given equal face values by the government and if they actually have unequal purchasing power in the market, the kind that has less purchasing power in the market will tend to drive the other out of circulation. In the period of the Civil War, the greenbacks tended to drive gold coins out of circulation because the greenbacks in their various denominations (face values) as given by the government had less purchasing power than gold coins of equal denominations. A corollary doctrine of Gresham's law is this: to the extent that the money that has greater purchasing power in the market remains in circulation, it will circulate only at a premium. This kind of result also occurred during the period of the Civil War and subsequently. In 1864, for example, $39 in gold coins would buy about as much as $100 in greenbacks.

Stability in value

Stability in the value or purchasing power of the different kinds of money in circulation must surely be included among the qualities of a good monetary system. At this point, however, we should be ready to accept this as a highly desirable quality without question, considering all that was said about it in the preceding two chapters. In Chapter 1, we saw that money's services as a standard of value, as a standard of deferred payments, and as a store of purchasing power become defective as a result of price-level instability; and in Chapter 2, we saw that stability in the price level—which is simply another way of referring to stability in the value of money—is one of the three great objectives of monetary control.

Safety

For many generations before the early 1930s, it was generally believed that money could be safe only if it were full-bodied in itself or if it were readily redeemable in gold or silver coins having market value equal to its face value. But full-bodied coins and redeemability no longer have much meaning for the domestic operation of modern monetary systems in which such coins are not issued, and treasuries and central banks have no obligations to redeem paper money, coins, and bank demand deposits in something else.

Instead, from the standpoint of domestic operation, we must think of monetary safety in the sense that the different kinds of money in circulation will not be repudiated in whole or in part or lost in whole or in part through bankruptcies. Our federal government must not say that a new kind of paper money will be substituted for Federal Reserve notes at a ratio of 1 to 100 and that an outstanding debt of, say, $1000 can now be settled by payment of ten units of the new money. It must not say that Federal Reserve notes will no longer be accepted for tax payments, or that coins will be accepted only at the market values of their cupronickel or copper contents. Because we do not expect the federal government to take actions such as these, we are probably justified in holding that our paper money and coins are "safe." But we should recognize that bank demand deposits do not necessarily have safety of this character. The failure of an insured bank can result in the wiping out of all or a part of one's deposit balance in excess of

$20,000, and the failure of a noninsured bank, all or a part of one's whole deposit balance.

(We can also think of monetary safety in the sense of endowing a country's moneys with stable purchasing power. With stable purchasing power, money will be safe in the very important sense that when it is accepted in exchange for goods, it will be exchangeable, in turn, for other goods in reasonable quantities. But stability in value has already been separately treated as a desirable quality for the moneys of a good monetary system.)

Access to foreign markets

The moneys of a country that has a good monetary system should give its people easy access to foreign markets for buying and selling commodities and services, for making and receiving investments in physical facilities and securities, and even for gift giving and receiving. Foreign moneys needed for payments abroad should be obtainable in exchange for domestic money at reasonable rates, and foreign moneys received from abroad should be readily exchangeable for domestic money at reasonable rates.

Some countries have easy access to foreign markets because their moneys are widely accepted by foreigners in exchange for that which they want to sell. Such is the position of our dollar, which is accepted almost everywhere in the world, and which, in turn, is used by foreigners for payments to us as well as in transactions with other foreigners. For a money to be held in such high esteem by foreigners, it must generally have a quality of safety somewhat different in scope from that already described. The foreigners are likely to be much concerned about the *redeemability* of the highly regarded money. They will be willing to accept as much as they need for their own spending abroad and whatever amounts they want to hold as reserves but will want assurances that amounts they accept beyond these requirements will be redeemable in something eminently attractive, such as gold or drawing rights at the International Monetary Fund.

But countries whose moneys are not generally acceptable abroad need not be cut off from foreign markets. As long as their exporters are able to sell abroad for generally acceptable moneys, such as our dollar, the British pound, or the German mark, and as long as the exporters are willing to sell these moneys at home for domestic money, importers can buy these moneys for making payments abroad.

For easy access to foreign markets, rates of exchange need to be at reasonable levels. At the present official valuation of the British pound at $2.6057 in our money, it could be that the kinds of British goods that Americans are most interested in buying are unduly expensive or unduly cheap. And because the official valuation of the British pound obtains both in the United Kingdom and the United States, undue expensiveness of British goods would mean undue cheapness of American goods for British importers, with unfair competitive advantages for them and the American exporters and unfair competitive disadvantages for British exporters and

American importers. Likewise, undue cheapness of British goods would mean undue expensiveness of American goods for British importers, with unfair competitive advantages and disadvantages running in the opposite direction.

Both short-term and long-run stability in the rates of exchange among the moneys of many countries, especially the leading industrial nations, is also generally held to be highly desirable. If the British pound costs $2.60 in New York this week, it ought not to cost only $2.55 next week and only $2.50 in the following week; nor should it cost only $2.40 next year and only $2.20 in the following year. Probabilities of short-term and longer-term fluctuations of such wide ranges could be expected to greatly impede flows of goods and capital investment between the two countries.

Other qualities of good monetary systems

Other qualities of good monetary systems are usually so much taken for granted that we could easily forget to mention them. For completeness, however, they deserve to be mentioned.

Easy Recognition The different kinds of money should be readily recognizable with little or no possibility of error. For paper money and coins, this largely means that counterfeiting ought to be very, very difficult, but it also means that paper money and coins of the various denominations ought not to be easily confused even by people who are not very bright. Perhaps each denomination of our paper money should have a different color from the others, as has sometimes been suggested. For bank demand deposits, recognition has obvious difficulties. One wants to be sure that the drawer of a check is who he says he is and to be confident that he has and will continue to have a sufficient balance in his deposit account to cover the check.

Durability The different kinds of money should be durable. In this, coins and bank demand deposits easily qualify. Coins last a long time, and even when they become worn and abraded, it is not difficult to set up channels for their withdrawal from circulation, melting, and recoining. As book or tape entries, bank demand deposits can last indefinitely on cards in the drawers of bookkeeping machines or in the drums of computers. As for paper money, it ought not to disintegrate in your wallet or handbag like the wax-paper liners in some food cartons. Although its estimated life averages around 6 months, bank tellers can be alerted to sort out badly worn and tattered paper money—they call it "mute" for mutilated—for shipment to the Federal Reserve banks and the U.S. Treasury for destruction and replacement.

Convenient Denominations Money should be provided in convenient denominations. Think of the difficulty merchants would have in providing "change"—and our difficulty in carrying it around—should the lowest denomination of our paper money be $20. Think of the inconvenience we have endured—rather mild, it is true—because of difficulties in keeping half dollars in circulation. On the other hand, we have no occasion to worry about the denominations of bank demand deposits, since checks can be made out for any amounts ranging from fractions of a dollar to many millions of dollars.

CLASSES OF MONETARY SYSTEMS

The basic, unifying feature of any monetary system is the declared standard of value, and all other features of the system, as stated in the opening paragraph of this chapter, are closely tied to the standard of value. A country's monetary system is, therefore, all the kinds of money it employs and all the institutions, laws, rules, regulations, and procedures that are involved in money creation and extinguishment, all as related to a specific standard of value as foundation. So central, indeed, is the role of the standard of value that monetary systems are themselves often referred to as standards, as when we speak of the gold "standard" or the bimetallic "standard." Such references result, of course, in some confusion in terminology—the standard of value as the foundation, and the monetary standard as a system having this foundation—but the references are so common that we must learn to distinguish the connotation when the word *standard* is used.

Commodity and fiat systems

There are two classes of monetary systems or standards: commodity systems and fiat systems. A *commodity system* is one in which the standard of value is declared to be a designated quantity of a particular commodity or designated quantities of two or more commodities, and in which the purchasing power of each unit of money in circulation is kept equal to the purchasing power of the standard of value as thus designated. A *fiat system* is the opposite of a commodity system: there is no commodity designation for its standard of value, or if there is one, the purchasing power of moneys in circulation per unit is not kept equal to the purchasing power of the standard of value as thus designated.

In recent centuries, commodity monetary systems have almost invariably been built on standards of value designated as specific quantities of gold, of silver, or of both gold and silver at the same time. In the Coinage Act of 1792, for example, the United States established a bimetallic system with the dollar as the standard of value declared to be worth 24.75 grains of fine gold and simultaneously to be worth 371.25 grains of fine silver. From 1879 to 1933, however, the gold dollar of 23.22 grains of fine gold was the sole standard of value, so that we were said to have a gold standard or system. As gold coins were actually in circulation in this period, our system was often described as a "gold-coin standard" in recognition, as it were, of the existence of variants of the gold standard.

In a fiat monetary system, the standard of value may simply be declared to be the dollar, the franc, or the peso with nothing said about the worth of this monetary unit in gold or silver or any other commodity or group of commodities. More likely, however, the standard of value will be given a valuation in gold or silver, but everybody will know that this valuation is a fiction, because moneys in circulation obviously do not have purchasing power equal to the declared gold or silver value. Descriptions of standards of value as quantities of gold or silver are likely to be encountered in fiat systems because they have most commonly come into being as a result of the inability of governments to keep the purchasing power of circulating moneys equal to declared gold or silver values. So the declared values remain as before even though the equality in purchasing power is lost. In the United States, for example, the standard of value was still bimetallic in 1862 and 1863 when the greenbacks were issued, but because the greenbacks, bank notes, and bank demand deposits were not redeemable in gold or silver coins, their purchasing power soon fell below that of these coins. Thus the gold and silver values attributed to the dollar as the standard of value became fictitious. Our Civil War experience indicates why fiat monetary systems are often called "paper standards." The standard of value became the greenback paper dollar, and greenbacks were the only money a person could get when "redeeming" bank notes and bank demand deposits.

Choice of monetary systems

In deciding over the centuries what kinds of monetary systems to have, governments have had varying attitudes toward the "qualities of good monetary systems" as analyzed in the first division of this chapter. Their decisions and pronouncements have indicated that they cherished some of these qualities above others, that they regarded some as being more or less incompatible with others, and that they simply took some for granted. In many periods in many countries, governments have apparently given no serious thought to some aspects of some qualities. But to say this is not necessarily to criticize, for the student should keep in mind that the list of qualities is the author's—that it was not spelled out in the same context and sequence in pronouncements of governments or their central banks nor handed down from on high. Justifying criticism, however, are the claims that governments (and their apologists) have sometimes made that their monetary systems were endowed with certain good qualities when it was quite obvious that these virtues were absent. Anyway, thoughts of this kind should be kept in mind as we turn to an analysis of the principal classes and subclasses of monetary systems with which the world has had recent experiences. In this analysis, it will be convenient to start using the past tense, because we will be looking at older systems, how they worked, and how they were supposed to work, and then to change to the present tense as we try to understand how features of the older systems have been modified and substituted for in "modern" monetary systems.

THE GOLD STANDARD

For many decades before the early 1930s, the gold standard dominated the monetary arrangements of most of the world. It enjoyed a phenomenal growth in the latter part of the nineteenth century and in the early years of the present century until the outbreak of World War I, and its general acceptance meant the discarding of silver and bimetallic monetary systems. In that long period of growth, the fiat standard was not looked upon as an alternative to the gold standard but as a temporary substitute for it during periods of war and other great disturbances. In the latter decades of the last century and in the early years of the present one, the adoption of the gold standard by any nation was generally regarded as signaling the nation's arrival at monetary maturity, and economically weak, underdeveloped countries looked forward to the time when they, too, could achieve fellowship with the more progressive nations by establishing the standard. So great was the prestige of the gold standard that it was looked upon as the end product of a long process of monetary evolution—the end had been reached, and there was nothing to be gained by further change.

The gold standard suffered a general collapse during World War I, but that happening did little to injure its prestige. In the decade of the 1920s, the countries that had suspended it during the war period set to work to restore it, and most of them succeeded. But they encountered quite unexpected difficulties in achieving the restoration and even greater difficulties after the restoration had been effected. The standard became an object of suspicion; perhaps, after all, it was not to be espoused as a source of unmixed blessings. Much more serious troubles were incurred in efforts to maintain the standard in the Great Depression of the 1930s, and most countries came rather quickly to the decision that its benefits had been grossly overemphasized. Accordingly, they did not hesitate long before again suspending it. In terms of the broad ramifications and pervasive influence it used to have, it has remained in suspension to the present time, and prospects for its restoration are nil.

Qualities emphasized

The gold standard was held to be especially beneficial in giving moneys maximum safety, in giving individual countries easy access to foreign markets at stable exchange rates, and in having manageability of an extraordinary scope—but manageability of a peculiar character.

Safety   The moneys of a gold-standard country were expected to be safe because they were gold itself and moneys readily redeemable in gold. Gold was highly cherished for its own sake, and it was virtually unthinkable that it would ever be refused when offered as money. And as long as people had confidence that paper money, demand deposits, and fractional coins could easily be redeemed in gold, they were inclined to accept these moneys as being as safe as gold itself. The strange quality of the safety argument was that, in most countries at most times, the quantities of the moneys that were allegedly redeemable in gold—"credit moneys," they were called—far exceeded the amount of gold available for redemption. Such a situation seemed to justify critics' description of the gold standard as a "fair-weather standard"—a criticism that was sometimes validated by "suspensions of the gold standard," that is, suspensions of the redeemability of the credit moneys in times of war and severe economic stress.

Easy Access to Foreign Markets   As for easy access to foreign markets, gold was the international standard of value and was generally acceptable as an international medium of exchange. It was highly cherished everywhere. Accordingly, countries could buy and invest almost everywhere by using gold as the means of payment. Indeed, their credit moneys were generally accepted in payments to foreigners as long as the foreigners had confidence in the redeemability of these moneys.

As the international standard of value, gold was even more important. The values of goods wherever located could always be understood in terms of a country's domestic money as long as it and other countries set gold weights for their monetary units and maintained redeemability at the fixed weights. In the period 1925–1931, for example, Britain maintained redeemability of the pound at 113.0015 grains of fine gold, and the United States, the redeemability of the dollar at 23.22 grains, so that the *par of exchange* between the two monetary units was 113.0015 ÷ 23.22, or $4.8665. An American importer knew that something priced at £100 in Britain would cost him an amount quite close to $486.65. An amount quite close, but not necessarily exactly $486.65, because the importer also knew that the actual rate of exchange to be paid could vary within a range of about 2 cents above and below the par of exchange—by the costs of shipping 113.0015 grains of gold between the two countries. The stability of exchange rates among leading countries could be relied upon because these countries were expected to avoid changes in the gold weights of their monetary units and because costs of shipping gold were expected to vary very little from rather minute levels, such as 2 cents for a pound's worth of gold. And stability in exchange rates was thought to be tremendously beneficial in promoting world trade and investment, by giving importers and exporters confidence that payments to be made or received in foreign moneys in months or years would be convertible into domestic moneys at levels close to the unchanging pars of exchange.

It was recognized, of course, that some countries were not in a position to gain medium-of-exchange and standard-of-value benefits of the kinds described, especially countries that lacked sufficient gold reserves to make payments abroad and to maintain redeemability and countries that got themselves heavily in debt to foreigners. But the attractiveness of the benefits was expected to be a constant inducement to such countries to put their houses in order so as to be able to join the happy fellowship of the countries that had succeeded in gaining substantial economic strength.

Automatic Operation   In the matter of the manageability of the money stock in a gold monetary system, changes in the quantity of money in circulation were generally thought to be beautifully arranged. Expansion and contraction were to take place "automatically" in relation to the size of gold reserves. The gold-reserve requirements that applied to central and commercial banks were the key factor for automatic operation. If the gold reserves were increased, as by importation or domestic gold production, the banks could increase the volume of their outstanding notes and demand deposits by a multiple of the amount of additional gold, since the reserve requirements were usually set directly or indirectly as fractional percentages of notes and demand deposits; and if the reserves were reduced, as by exportation or withdrawals for domestic hoarding, the banks would reduce the volume of their outstanding notes and demand deposits by a multiple of the amount of the reserve loss.

There was no need for day-to-day decisions by central bankers or other monetary authorities who might make all kinds of mistakes in their decisions. Let the monetary system run itself. However, this was not really a wild idea, since it fitted in quite neatly with doctrines of *laissez faire* that were widely held simultaneously. If economic welfare could be maximized provided that government did not interfere with business activities and decisions, balanced the budget annually, and concentrated on chores of statecraft, military and police protection, and the like, it was not illogical to think that the monetary system, too, would work best without government interference.

Nevertheless, the government had to be called upon initially to set down certain "rules of the game" as the framework for automatic operation. It had these duties:

1.   To set the gold weight of the monetary unit.
2.   To provide for the redeemability of all units of credit money in gold at the established weight. Redemption could be provided for in three forms: in gold coins, in gold bars or bricks, (bullion), or in drafts that in turn were redeemable in gold coins or gold bullion. Thus three variants of the gold standard were recognized: the gold-coin standard, the gold-bullion standard, and the gold-exchange standard (the system with the draft arrangement). The government itself might promise redemption for all kinds of money, but the more common procedure was for it to commit itself to redeem some kinds of money and to require banks

to redeem other kinds. Moreover, redemption by way of bank obligations to redeem could be indirect, as for example, a requirement that commercial banks redeem demand deposits in notes of the central bank and a requirement that the central bank, in turn, redeem its notes in gold coin, bullion, or drafts.

3. To commit itself to buy and sell gold at the price equivalent of the fixed gold weight of the monetary unit (as at $20.67 an ounce when the gold weight of the dollar was 23.22 grains because a troy ounce is 480 grains). However, this chore could be turned over to the central bank. Moreover, slight variations in price were held to be tolerable, as for the costs of minting gold coins and for "handling" bullion.

4. To provide for free domestic and international markets in gold or in drafts payable in gold. The reason for this provision was that gold must be free to flow between the treasury or the central bank and domestic and foreign markets, so that the declared gold value of the monetary unit would not become fictitious as in some fiat systems. In the 1920s, for example, it would have been witless for the federal government to declare gold to be worth $20.67 an ounce if gold actually sold at $30 an ounce in New York or at the equivalent of $30 an ounce in London.

5. To have gold-reserve requirements apply to the creation and issuance of money by the central and commercial banks. Such requirements might be set by law, as in the United States, or by custom, as in England. Moreover, the requirements could be applied directly or indirectly, as in the United States where the Federal Reserve banks were required to hold gold reserves equal to fractional percentages of their outstanding notes and deposit liabilities and where these deposit liabilities, in turn, consisted very largely of reserves required of commercial banks against their own deposit liabilities.

International Aspects of Automatic Operation   Not only was the automatic operation of gold standards expected to "manage" the quantity of money in circulation at home in the best possible way, but great international benefits were claimed for strict adherence to the "rules of the game." Automatic international operation was expected to bring about a parity in the price levels of all gold-standard countries, so that none would for long be unduly benefitted or harmed if their price levels got out of line. According to the *theory of gold movements* (also called the "theory of the price-specie-flow mechanism"), forces would quickly go into action to correct such disparities. If a country's gold reserves increased by substantial amounts from, say, domestic gold production, more credit money would be created and the spending of this money would cause the price level to rise. Since exchange rates could fluctuate only within very narrow limits, the country's goods would now be more expensive to foreigners, while many kinds of foreign goods would be cheaper than goods available in the home market. The country's exports would fall off and imports would increase, and this shift in the balance of trade would be likely to require it to ship gold to foreign countries in order to pay for the net excess of imports. But the exportation of gold would reduce the monetary reserves, and this, in turn, would force the country to contract its domestic money stock in obedience to the rules of the game. The contraction should cause the price level to fall. At the same time, the importation of gold by other countries would result in expansions in their money stocks in accordance with the same rules of the game, and the spending of the newly created money would cause their price levels to rise. Thus the falling price level of the first country and the rising price levels of the others would restore parity among all, and presumably the direction of trade would resume its former course.

Price-Level Stability   No sweeping claims were made that the mechanisms of the gold standard resulted in a high degree of price-level stability. Such claims would have been in direct contradiction with the theory of gold movements, and indeed, substantial price-level fluctuations could be observed throughout the period in which the gold standard was in operation. Nevertheless, it was widely argued that price levels were much more stable than they would have been with any other kind of monetary system. The argument was stated in propositions concerning the relationship between gold production and price levels—propositions that, one may say, were extensions of the idea of automatic operation.

First of all, it was emphasized that the monetary gold stock of the world was stable, as accumulated over the centuries and as added to from current production only in modest proportions from year to year. At the same time, the gold-mining industry was (and is) one of diminishing returns or increasing costs, so that a rising price level would surely discourage expansion in mining activity and even reduce output from the mines already in operation. With costs increasing more or less in concert with the rising price level, the profit margins of the mining companies would narrow, and eventually they would find it unprofitable to work the less accessible areas of their mines and to process the inferior ores. Gold output would decrease. On the other hand, a declining price level would doubtless be accompanied by falling mining costs, and the resulting expansion in profit margins would prompt the mining companies to sink deeper shafts, to reopen poorer mines, and to resume processing of inferior ores, all of which would mean, of course, an increase in gold output. The inverse relationship between output and mining costs was expected to have a high degree of proportionality, since the mining companies knew that they had an unlimited market at a fixed selling price as set by the government.

Now, a rising price level indicated that the quantity of money in circulation was excessive, but the resulting decline in gold output, by reducing the rate of expansion in monetary reserves, would tend also to cause a reduction in the rate of further price-level increases. In a similar way, price-level falls would indicate an insufficiency in the money stock, but increases in the rate

of growth of monetary reserves resulting from newly encouraged gold production would tend to curb further falls. Even in this, however, defenders
of the gold standard generally admitted that price-level stabilization as a
result of shifts in gold production could be slow in coming, and that, meanwhile, substantial spurts of inflation and deflation could occur.

Variants of the gold standard

Gold-Coin Standard The principal distinguishing characteristics of the
gold-coin variant was a commitment by the government to provide gold
coins of relatively small denominations for general circulation. The denominations were typified by the $2.50, $5, $10, and $20 gold coins of the United
States before 1933, and the commitment itself was described as an establishment and application of the principle of *free coinage*. The free coinage of
gold was understood to be the right of the people to take unlimited quantities of unminted gold to the mints, to have it coined without profit to the
government, and to receive the coins in return. The "freedom" of free coinage thus did not necessarily mean an absence of mint charges. Under free
coinage, some governments did, indeed, absorb all costs of coinage, so that
their mint operations were said to be both free and "gratuitous." But some
governments charged a fee called "brassage" to cover the costs of coinage;
others, including the United States, absorbed the costs of mint operations
but charged for the alloys used in hardening coins; and still others, in making immediate exchanges of coins for unminted gold, charged interest for
the period expected to be required for minting. Nevertheless, the earning
of a profit by a government in turning out gold coins was understood to violate the principle of free coinage. (Profits derived by governments on coinage of any kind are known as "seigniorage.")

Provisions for free coinage were closely integrated, as it were, with provisions for free domestic and international markets in gold. As always, the
objective was to ensure that the official price and the market price of gold
would be equal. Accordingly, people were given privileges to buy gold at
home and abroad and to do with it as they pleased, including the privilege
of taking it to the mint to have it coined. Likewise, they were privileged
to melt down gold coins and sell the bullion at home and abroad or to use it
in other ways, as in the fabrication of jewelry. Such privileges meant that
discrepancies between the face value of gold coins and the market price
of equal amounts of gold bullion, aside from discrepancies resulting from
profitless mint charges, would be quickly corrected. Should market prices
rise above the face values of the coins, people would melt them down and
the increased market supply of bullion would bring down the market prices;
and should market prices fall below the coins' face values, people would
buy bullion in the market and take it to the mints to be coined.

Finally, the general availability of gold coins was meant to ensure that
almost everybody could redeem credit money in gold. In the United States,

as mentioned above, gold coins were available for the redemption of amounts of credit money as little as $2.50.

Gold-Bullion Standard   In each country that maintained the gold-bullion standard, regulations provided that the government or central bank would buy and sell unlimited quantities of gold at a fixed price as determined by the declared gold value of the monetary unit. Thus if a monetary unit were declared to be 20 grains of fine gold, the official price of a troy ounce of gold (480 grains) would be twenty-four monetary units. The willingness of the government or central bank to buy and sell unlimited quantities of gold, coupled with all the privileges of a free gold market, ensured an equality between the value of the monetary unit and the domestic and foreign market value of the same quantity of gold. Moreover, the redeemability of credit money in gold was routinely provided for, because the government or central bank, in selling gold, was willing to accept any kind of credit money in payment for it.

Beyond the benefits that were claimed for all three variants of the gold standard, two additional advantages were often claimed for the gold-bullion variant (as well as for the gold-exchange variant as subsequently discussed): (1) the self-evident avoidance of costs of coinage and of abrasion losses in circulation, and (2) the probability that each country's gold reserves would be held in bulk for the common good and not broken up into small private hoards. Proponents of the bullion standard believed that no useful purpose was served by the circulation of gold coins or by the hoarding that coin circulation made possible. They pointed out that people normally preferred to use credit money rather than gold coins, and argued that in times of economic stress it was better to conserve the gold reserves for the general welfare than to allow them to be drained off to serve the selfish interests of would-be hoarders. In line with this thinking, the monetary regulations adopted in countries that had the bullion standard generally provided for the sale of gold by the central authority only in relatively large quantities. The bar, or brick, most commonly made available for sale was one of 400 ounces, one that would be worth $15,200 in the United States at the present time. People who needed gold for "valid" purposes, as for jewelry manufacture or for payments to foreigners, would probably want to buy not less than that amount, while most would-be hoarders would be unable to amass sums such as $15,200 for buying a bar, or brick.

Gold-Exchange Standard   The gold-exchange variant was originally designed by mother countries to enable their colonies to maintain gold values for their monetary units and thereby to gain the alleged benefits of the gold standard, even when they had little or no gold reserves. Such was the arrangement that prevailed during most of the colonial period of India in its monetary connections with the British pound, and during most of the colonial period of the Philippines in its monetary connections with our dollar.

In the case of the Philippines, the monetary unit, the silver peso, was declared to be worth 50 cents in our money. Although the silver content of the peso had a market value much less than 50 cents, its *gold* value at this level was maintained because it was made redeemable in dollar drafts (checks) drawn by the Philippines treasury on United States banks—drafts that, in the United States, could be redeemed in gold coin or gold bullion. By exporting sugar and other commodities to the United States, the Philippines built up dollar deposits here that made redemption of silver pesos in gold dollars possible. But the redemption was indirect: silver pesos were *exchanged* for dollar drafts and the dollar drafts, in turn, were redeemable in gold because of the gold-standard rules of the United States—hence the "gold-exchange" concept. In effect, then, the physical gold reserves held by the United States served as reserves simultaneously for all credit moneys in circulation here and for all silver pesos and other credit moneys in circulation in the Philippines.

In the 1920s, it became increasingly popular for many countries to count as gold reserves whatever deposits their central banks held with banks in other countries that had gold-coin and gold-bullion standards, especially dollar deposits in the United States and sterling deposits in Britain. Even when these other countries held some of their reserves in gold at home and provided for the redemption of credit money in gold there, their monetary systems came to be called "gold-exchange standards" because large portions of their "gold reserves" were not really gold but moneys of foreign countries that promised redemption in gold. Because, indeed, this kind of counting of redeemable foreign moneys held by given countries as portions of their "gold reserves" continues to be widespread, and despite new means of international payment made available to these countries as members of the International Monetary Fund, their monetary systems are often described even now as "gold-exchange standards." At the present time, therefore, one must conclude that the term *gold-exchange standard* has no clearly defined meaning.

THE BIMETALLIC STANDARD

Safety for money in the redeemability sense can be said to have been even more emphasized in bimetallic monetary systems than in gold systems. Bimetallic systems were established because of convictions that money had to be full-bodied coins or redeemable in such coins, coupled with convictions that not enough money could be provided to do the work that money is supposed to do if gold only or silver only were selected for coinage and redemption. As gold and silver were not available in sufficient quantities separately to do the work of money, it seemed entirely logical to use the two metals jointly. Thus, bimetallic systems antedated gold systems, and when more gold became available as a result of new discoveries, such as that of California in 1848, bimetallic systems gradually gave way to gold systems.

It was not illogical for our Coinage Act of 1792 to make the dollar, as the standard of value, equal to 24.75 grains of fine gold and, at the same time, equal to 371.25 grains of fine silver; and it was not illogical for the Bank of the United States, established in 1791, to promise redemption of its bank notes in "specie," which meant gold or silver coins, whichever might be available to it for redemption from time to time. The mint ratio of 15 to 1 set for the value relationship of the two metals $(371.25 \div 24.75)$ appeared to be a wise selection, since their value ratios in the market had hovered in that vicinity for centuries—so closely, indeed, that a ratio of 15 to 1 seemed almost to be a natural law. Likewise, people had no reason to object to the redemption of bank notes in gold at the rate of 24.75 grains per dollar if they could use this amount of gold to buy 371.25 grains of fine silver in the market nor to object to redemption in silver at the rate of 371.25 grains per dollar if they could use this amount of silver to buy 24.75 grains of fine gold.

But the problem was that, while mint ratios were fixed for long periods of time, market ratios fluctuated, and disturbances in bimetallic systems resulted. Fluctuations in market ratios meant that governments, in maintaining their fixed mint ratios, overvalued one metal and undervalued the other, and this was the kind of circumstance that put Gresham's law into operation. Near the end of the 1790s, for example, the market ratio of silver to gold moved into the vicinity of 15½ to 1, so that the United States, by its official mint ratio of 15 to 1, was then overvaluing silver and undervaluing gold, and the overvalued silver tended to drive the undervalued gold out of circulation. The simple fact was that gold had greater value in the European market than it had as money in the United States, so that, despite the aim of bimetallism to have two precious metals for coinage and redemption, we quickly moved in the direction of having only silver for these purposes. In 1834, we changed the mint ratio to approximately 16 to 1, but we soon found that this did not solve the problem. Circulation trends went in the opposite direction. As the market ratio in Europe was still about 15½ to 1, the United States was overvaluing gold and undervaluing silver, and silver began to flow from our monetary system toward the European market. The flow eventually became extremely disadvantageous because it included fractional silver coins that were then full-bodied, so that difficulties in effecting small monetary transactions multiplied. As gold mining expanded, therefore, governments had good reasons to shift from the bimetallic standard to the gold standard in order to avoid difficulties of the types described.

THE FIAT STANDARD

Until the early 1930s, the fiat standard was not generally regarded as a kind of monetary system whose merits should even be considered as possibly rivaling the merits claimed for gold standards. It was regarded, rather, as a stop-gap kind of system necessitated in times of great economic stress and war because of the incapacity of governments and their central banks to maintain the unit purchasing power of credit moneys equal to that of the gold standard of value and to redeem them in gold itself. Fiat money was feared. The very thought of "irredeemable paper money" was frightening; there was much anxiety about excessive issues of such money made possible by suspensions of gold-reserve requirements and about disruptions in foreign trade and investment because of the freedom of exchange rates to fluctuate over wide ranges. The best thing to do with a fiat standard, it was generally thought, was to get rid of it as quickly as possible, that is, to "restore" the gold standard.

That *it was necessary* in many countries in many periods of stress and war to substitute the fiat standard for the gold standard might have been taken more widely as proof that the fiat standard had highly desirable elements of strength that the gold standard lacked. It was so taken by some thinkers. During the long period of the dominance of the gold standard, however, critical thought was chiefly directed to stressing the weaknesses of that standard rather than to making a positive case for the merits of the fiat standard. But with the faltering of the gold standard in the late 1920s and its complete breakdown in the early 1930s, the desirability of keeping the fiat standard permanently in place of the gold standard gained wider and wider attention and support.

Criticism of the gold standard

Redemption in Gold as a Fiction   The gold standard was criticized as being only a "fair-weather standard" that worked reasonably well only in times of prosperity, good wages and profits, and high-level employment. The people really lacked confidence in the redeemability of credit money in gold, and when economic stresses developed, the gold standard was immediately threatened. The individual was not much interested in the size of a country's gold reserves; he wanted to save himself although all else might be lost. Runs on the banks took place and large amounts of gold were withdrawn for hoarding. At the very time that confidence in the monetary system was most needed, the gold standard was suspended to "protect" the remaining gold reserves. Or at least, there were rumors of suspension—very credible rumors because it was obvious that the gold reserves were sufficient to redeem only a small fraction of all the outstanding promises to pay that were supposed to be ultimately payable in gold. The suspension or the rumors of suspension tended to lead to panic, thus aggravating a situation that might have been cleared up with much less difficulty had the *fiction* of gold redemption not obtained.

Harmful Effects of Automatic Operation   Another major line of criticism was that the vaunted automatic operation of the gold standard tended to be more harmful than beneficial. Almost necessarily, automatic operation had to be a poor arrangement for the management of the quantity of money in circulation, since a country's gold reserves were affected by many kinds of fortuitous circumstances, such as changes in the costs of gold mining, the discovery of new gold deposits, fluctuations in industrial demands for gold, hoarding and dishoarding, and importation and exportation. Importation and exportation were especially emphasized as likely sources of severe disturbances—not so much the international gold flows to be expected because of price-level disparities among countries as flows that were "flights of capital." Political agitation, labor unrest, civil strife, and other similar developments in any major country were likely to cause wholesale conversions of assets held in that country to the apparently safer money of other countries, with resulting massive "outflights" of gold. But the countries that received these gold flows, if they were operating their systems automatically, were forced, as it were, to share in the disturbances in whose origin they had no part.

Built-in Price-Level Instability The considerable ranges of price-level fluctuations that were observed to occur in gold-standard countries were also a basis for criticizing the gold standard. Here the critics had little opposition, since, as was mentioned previously, defenders of the standard admitted that it did not prevent substantial inflationary and deflationary movements. But the principle argument of the critics was that price-level instability was built into the system—that the very theory of the gold standard accepted price-level instability as the price to be paid for exchange-rate stability. According to the theory of international gold movements, as described earlier in this chapter, a significant rise or fall in the price level of a major country should result in its losing gold to other countries or gaining gold from them in such manner as to cause *their* price levels to move toward a new parity.

Case for the fiat standard

Money Stocks and Needs On the positive side, proponents of the fiat standard argued that the quantity of money in circulation in any country requires continuous management according to what is needed for the best fulfillment of its quantitative functions, and that this quantity is unlikely to be supplied by rigid and unthinking observance of gold-reserve requirements. They argued that if a larger supply of money is required to bring productive factors into operation, the supply should be created whether or not gold-reserve requirements can be met, and if the quantity of money needs to be reduced to halt inflation, the reduction should be effected even when gold reserves beyond requirements are held. They argued that the full utilization of manpower and other productive potentials has been precluded in many periods in many countries simply because their gold holdings and fixed reserve requirements did not permit sufficient amounts of credit money to be created.

Safety of Fiat Money Another positive argument is that fiat money can be safe in the sense of unlikelihood of repudiation or loss through bankruptcies and also in the sense of having stable purchasing power, and that safety in these senses is obviously much more realistic than safety in the sense of redeemability which repeatedly turns out to be a myth. Repudiation and loss are likely to be a result of abundant overissuance of money, but continuous management of the money stock without regard to gold reserves surely does not imply that the managers will be profligate or reckless. Their decisions may be unwise at times, but gold-standard rules also have significant elements of unwisdom. Moreover, continuous management can be directed to the prevention of inflation and deflation, as well as to other goals, and price-level fluctuations that would tend to result from international gold flows can be prevented by deliberate countervailing action.

Fiat Money and Exchange Rates   A further argument in favor of fiat monetary systems is that continuous monetary management aimed at price-level stability and other domestic goals can be quite compatible with high degrees of exchange-rate stability. The argument has been that the more successful fiat-standard countries are in achieving price-level stability at home, the less will exchange rates among them fluctuate, even when there are no par-of-exchange mechanisms to prevent wide fluctuations. And it has been further argued that even when a given country fails in its attempts to maintain price-level stability at home, it is likely that exchange-rate shifts to compensate for the resulting price-level disparities between it and other countries will be less disturbing than price-level adjustments in all these countries resulting from gold flows.

It has been emphasized that adjustments for price-level disparities among countries can be effected in either of two ways: by increases and decreases in price levels toward a new parity or by shifts in exchange rates. Assume, for example, that at a given time the exchange rate between the dollar and the British pound is $2.40 and that the price levels of the United States and England are at par in the ordinary sense that British goods are reasonably priced for American buyers and American goods are reasonably priced for British buyers, so that, for trade between the two countries, their price levels as index numbers can be said to be 100. Now, for reasons internal to Britain, its price level rises to 120 while the American price level remains unchanged. As a result, British goods become quite expensive for Americans and Amercian goods become quite cheap for the British. According to gold-standard theory and rules, the resulting shifts in buying and selling should cause gold to flow from Britain to the United States, and resulting changes in the money stocks of the two countries should cause the American price level to rise and the British price level to fall toward a new parity at, perhaps, 110. But this would be inflation in the United States and deflation in Britain with harmful effects on business activity and the distribution of wealth and income. It would be much better, according to proponents of the fiat standard, to let the price levels of the two countries stay at their respective positions of 100 and 120 and to achieve a new parity between them by simply permitting an exchange-rate shift to compensate for the disparity that had developed. A shift of the exchange rate to \$2.00 ($^{100}/_{120} \times \$2.40$) would eliminate the disparity. What had previously cost an American importer £10,000 would now cost £12,000, but the cost in dollars would be unchanged at \$24,000—previously 10,000 × \$2.40 but now 12,000 × \$2.00. And what had previously cost a British importer \$36,000, or £15,000, would now cost \$36,000, or £18,000, so that the decrease in the purchasing power of the pound would be as great in the United States as in England, and there would be no reason for the British to increase their buying of American goods.

It has been argued that exchange-rate fluctuation is to be much preferred to price-level fluctuation as a means of adjusting to price-level disparities, especially for a country such as the United States whose combined total of imports and exports of merchandise and services typically amounts to only about 10 percent of its gross national product.

THE GREAT COMPROMISE: THE FUSION OF GOLD AND FIAT STANDARDS

The theory, rules, arrangements, and procedures of the gold and fiat standards, as described in the preceding pages, would seem to make the two standards entirely irreconcilable. Nevertheless, important decisions have been made that the two standards can be harmoniously fused on what may be said to be a geographical basis. The harrowing experiences of the 1920s and especially of the 1930s convinced the monetary statesmen of most of the major countries that fiat-standard arrangements are far superior to gold-standard arrangements for internal monetary management, that gold-standard arrangements are far superior in the international sphere, and that monetary arrangements in the two spheres can be largely divorced from each other, although not entirely so. The conviction grew that, in managing its internal monetary affairs, a country can get along quite well on a fiat-standard basis: that it need not regulate the quantity of money in circulation in relation to the amount of its gold reserves; that it need not provide internal redeemability of credit money in gold or a free internal gold market; that it can achieve reasonable stability in its price level; and that it can retain the confidence of its people in its monetary system even when they are denied access to gold for uses other than industrial and ornamental. However, the conviction also grew that a continued application of fiat-standard principles and rules to international monetary affairs could only result in a continuation of the chaos of the 1930s. This was a conviction that gold is still eminently desirable as an international standard of value and medium of exchange, that each country's currency should be redeemable in gold at a fixed price for the settlement of international obligations, and that—much the same idea—a high degree of exchange-rate stability should be maintained.

The decisions for fusion were originally made at Bretton Woods, New Hampshire, in July 1944 at a conference of representatives of the United Nations that had assembled in order to plan for post-World War II reconstruction. They were principally embodied in an agreement for the establishment and operation of the International Monetary Fund, an agreement that the United States accepted by the adoption of the Bretton Woods Agreements[1] Act of July 31, 1945. The fused system is supposed to work as our own monetary system operates at the present time both internally and externally, a study to which the next two chapters are devoted. No better illustration of the characteristics of the fused system can be found than the features of our own system, since we were the prime mover in the formulation of the Bretton Woods Agreement, and since the dollar has had a key role in the structure and functions of the International Monetary Fund.

FOR REVIEW

1. What is included within the scope of what is called a "monetary system"?
2. Why is elasticity of the different kinds of money said to be a characteristic of a good monetary system? Why is the elasticity of legal tender said to be especially desirable?
3. How would it be possible to have two kinds of money of equal denominations with unequal purchasing power? In such a situation, why would Gresham's law be likely to "operate"? What would be the likely result?
4. What is meant by the safety of money? Are our Federal Reserve notes safe? our coins? our bank demand deposits? Discuss.
5. Although the Mexican peso is not widely used as an international medium of exchange, the Mexican people still have access to foreign markets. How is this possible?
6. Why are monetary systems often described as being monetary standards? What is the distinction between commodity monetary standards and fiat standards?
7. In the older gold monetary systems, how credible were the claims that all money was safe? that each country had easy access to foreign markets?
8. What were claimed to be the advantages of having gold monetary systems operate automatically? What did a country have to do to get its domestic monetary system to operate automatically?
9. Distinguish between the stability of a country's price level and the "parity" of its price level with the price levels of other countries.

---

[1]The plural indicates our acceptance also of a second agreement formulated at Bretton Woods for the establishment and operation of the International Bank for Reconstruction and Development.

Which of these was supposed to be a resulting advantage of the automatic operation of gold standards?

10. How did gold-coin and gold-bullion standards differ from each other? How did each of these variants of the gold standard differ from the gold-exchange variant?

11. Explain the meaning of these terms as applying to gold standards: credit money, free coinage, gratuitous coinage, seigniorage. Do governments still earn seigniorage in the manufacture of coins? Explain.

12. Why is it said that safety in the sense of redeemability was especially emphasized in bimetallic monetary systems? Why were such systems plagued by the operation of Gresham's law?

13. Briefly describe the principal weaknesses of the gold standard as seen by advocates of the fiat standard. What were the principal positive arguments of these people in favor of the fiat standard?

14. What is the nature of the "fusion" that is said to be the pattern of present-day monetary systems?

CHAPTER 4

MONETARY SYSTEM OF THE
UNITED STATES: DOMESTIC FEATURES

GOLD

Gold as the standard of value

As authorized by the Gold Reserve Act adopted on January 30, 1934, President Franklin Roosevelt on the following day proclaimed the standard of value of the United States to be the dollar equal to $15\frac{5}{21}$ grains of gold nine-tenths fine. The nine-tenths fine designation was a carry-over from gold coinage days when, indeed, nine-tenths of the weight of gold coins was gold and the remaining one-tenth was alloy added for hardening. But we became accustomed to saying that the gold dollar as the standard of value was equal to $\frac{9}{10}$ of $15\frac{5}{21}$ grains or 13.7142857+ grains of fine or pure gold—and, for short, simply 13.714 grains of fine gold—and that gold had an official value of $35 per fine ounce (480 grains ÷ 13.7142857+). However, on the basis of a further authorization adopted by Congress early in 1972, the fine gold weight of the dollar was reduced to 12.6315789+ grains, so that $38 became our official price for an ounce of gold (480 ÷ 12.6315789+). When, therefore, we say that this or that is worth so many dollars, we presumably mean gold dollars of, let us say, 12.632 grains.

Equality of purchasing power?

In a gold standard, the purchasing power of all moneys in circulation per unit is supposed to be equal to that of the standard of value, but whether this is so in the United States at the present time is a debatable question. We should expect it to be debatable in a system in which gold-standard and fiat-standard principles and rules are fused. It is clear that, in buying goods in foreign countries, Americans are able to get as much for their paper money, coins, and demand deposit dollars per unit as they would get for 12.632 grains of fine gold, and that foreigners' spending for American goods in whatever kinds of dollars they acquire can get as much per dollar as they would get for 12.632 grains of fine gold. But most dollars are spent by Americans in our own markets, so that the question is whether these dollars have as much purchasing power as gold coins of equal denominations would have. The debate becomes all the fuzzier when we consider the proposition that the dollar sustains the value of gold at $38 an ounce and that 12.632 grains of fine gold do not sustain the purchasing power of the dollar. This proposition unquestionably has much merit. If the United States were to demonetize gold, that is, to offer all its gold reserves for sale in the market, the market price would surely fall far below $38. And if we were to raise the official price of gold to, say $70, or lower it to, say $25—actions that would be called, respectively, a devaluation and a revaluation of the dollar—it would be likely that the market price of gold would quickly move toward the new official price. Accordingly, it appears that the market price of gold per ounce usually stays close to $38 for no reason other than that it is our official price.

Uncertainty about the parity of purchasing power of 12.632 grains of fine gold and units of our domestic moneys in American markets is made all the greater because the U.S. Treasury does not buy and sell gold in open markets either at home or abroad at its official price or at any other price. In March 1968, the monetary officials of ten leading industrial countries of the so-called free world (the "group of ten") agreed to discontinue buying and selling gold in the open market and to confine their gold dealings, therefore, to transactions among themselves, with other members of the International Monetary Fund, and with the IMF itself. Even though the market price of gold in London, Frankfort, and other foreign markets has at times risen considerable distances above $38 an ounce, the policy of March 1968 has remained continuously in effect, and reasons for its suspension or abrogation are not apparent at the present time.

Gold regulations

A further source of uncertainty about the parity of purchasing power between gold and domestic moneys is the array of regulations concerning the ownership of gold and transactions in it to which the American people are subject. Individuals and enterprises are permitted to buy at home and abroad as much gold jewelry and other fabricated gold articles as they can afford and want, and they may sell this material freely at home and abroad. Coin collectors and coin dealers may buy and sell at home and abroad and hold as many gold coins minted in the United States before April 5, 1933, and foreign gold coins minted before 1934 as they can obtain and the same rule applies to gold certificates issued by the U.S. Treasury before January 30, 1934, of the type that previously passed from hand to hand as paper money. (These yellow-backed pieces of paper money of various denominations were backed 100 percent by gold reserves, so that they were often described as "warehouse receipts" for gold coin.) Moreover, people may invest in gold-bearing ores if they want to, and dentists, sculptors, and other persons engaged in gold-using industries, professions, and arts can freely get limited amounts of gold for their work without a lot of red tape. And most importantly, domestic mining companies can freely sell gold "recovered from natural deposits" to foreign buyers *other than* foreign central banks and other monetary authorities of foreign governments.

Individuals and enterprises that handle substantial amounts of gold in their businesses, industries, professions, and arts must generally obtain licenses from the U.S. Treasury in order to buy gold from domestic mining companies, refiners, and dealers, as well as to import it from foreign countries. Thus domestic mining companies, though free to sell gold to foreign buyers (except central banks and monetary authorities), are generally limited at home to selling to licensees. The licensees include refiners, dealers in gold bullion, manufacturing jewelers, and dental supply houses. Such licensees are required to keep records and make reports to the Treasury strictly accounting for gold acquired, sold or used, and scrap recovered. Licenses are also required for importing foreign gold coins made after 1933, and the applicant must convince the Treasury that the coins to be imported have "recognized special value to collectors of rare and unusual coins," and that they were "originally issued for circulation within the country of issue." For the exportation of such coins, separate export licenses are required.

For the average American, the most important feature of our gold regulations is likely to be that they do not permit him to hold gold bullion and post-1933 foreign gold coins as an investment or speculation. Although he could buy gold in these forms in Paris, Zurich, and other foreign markets, *our* regulations do not permit him to hold such gold either at home or abroad. Nor may he invest in the securities of any foreign enterprise that holds a substantial part of its assets in gold "as a store of value or as, or in lieu of, money." We should notice, therefore, that the American gold market is much different from the principal continental markets in Europe that are generally free of licensing requirements and other restrictions—markets in which gold hoarders are free to buy and sell.

Gold reserves

The gold bullion that the U.S. Treasury holds is money. Although this gold does not get into domestic circulation as a medium of exchange and although there is doubt about the service of the gold dollar as the domestic standard of value, gold bullion is used as an international medium of exchange and the gold dollar is unquestionably the means by which we measure the values of foreign goods, services, investment securities, and other assets. Because of gold's weak domestic role and its important international role, indeed, most of what needs to be said further about gold as money can best be deferred to Chapter 5, in which the international features of our monetary system are described.

At this point, however, a few facts about the U.S. Treasury's gold bullion should be stated. (1) Most of this gold has a lien on it equal at any time to the amount of gold certificates held by the Federal Reserve banks. At the end of June 1970, for example, the Treasury's gold holdings at $35 an ounce amounted to $11,889 million, while the gold-certificate holdings of the Federal Reserve banks amounted to $11,045 million,[1] so that only the balance of $844 million was "free gold" as a net asset of the Treasury. The gold certificates held by the Federal Reserve banks are redeemable at face value in gold bullion when the gold is needed to settle international obligations.[2] Such redemption is subject to the consent of the U.S. Secretary of the Treasury, but such consent is surely governed by the wishes of the President. (Actually, the gold certificates, though they are listed as such among the assets of the Federal Reserve banks, have no physcial existence. They are credits on the books of the Treasury payable to the Reserve banks in the form of gold certificates. But so-called transactions in gold certificates, including redemption, are handled by book entries without need of counting and transferring a multitude of pieces of paper.) (2) None of the gold bars owned by the Treasury and none of the so-called gold certificates owned by the Federal Reserve banks are held for the redemption of currency and demand deposits held by the American people, nor are they held to satisfy reserve requirements pertaining to these moneys, since no legal reserve requirements for gold reserves for these moneys now obtain. (3) The Treasury does not augment its stock of gold bullion by buying from domestic mining companies, from any other domestic source, such as dealers in gold reclaimed from jewelry, or in foreign gold markets. Nor does it sell from its stock of gold bullion to either domestic or foreign industrial, professional, or artistic processors of gold. In a word, in accordance with the decision of March 1968, the U.S. Treasury does not engage in market transactions in gold at home or abroad.

SUBSIDIARY COINS

For use as mediums of exchange in small transactions, our coinage laws provide for the issuance of dollars, half dollars, quarters, dimes, 5-cent pieces, and cents. The dollars, half dollars, quarters, dimes, and 5-cent pieces are composed of combinations of copper and nickel; and the cent is 95 percent copper and 5 percent zinc. All these coins are classified as subsidiary coins, which means that they are deliberately given face values in excess of the market values of the metals they contain. Even in gold-standard days, it was recognized that such coins are accepted for convenience and not because of the market value of their metallic content—a recognition that was newly demonstrated, as it were, by the ready public acceptance of silverless quarters and dimes, and half dollars with 40 percent silver, as pro-

---

[1]*Federal Reserve Bulletin*, July 1970, pp. A12, A75.
[2]For a description of such transactions, see Chapter 7.

vided for by the Coinage Act of 1965, in place of coins of the same denominations that were formerly issued with 90 percent silver, and later the acceptance of silverless dollars and half dollars as provided for by the coinage legislation of December 31, 1970. Although the 5-cent piece and the cent are subsidiary coins in the sense of the relationship between their face and market values, they are sometimes classified separately as "minor coins," and nobody is likely to argue about their minor purchasing power.

Elasticity

Our issues of subsidiary coins have been provided with the moderate degrees of elasticity they need to serve well as means of payment in small transactions. When people want more of these coins in exchange for paper money and demand deposits and near-moneys, such as savings deposits, they have no difficulty in getting them, and when they want fewer, they find that banks and other financial institutions readily accept excess supplies in exchange for paper money and deposit balances. It is recognized that long-run expansibility of coin issues is especially important as the number of small transactions increases with population growth and business expansion and as more coins are specially needed, as for parking meters and vending machines. But there is also provision for seasonal expansion and contraction, as during and after the Christmas shopping season. To illustrate with figures, coins in circulation outside the U.S. Treasury and the Federal Reserve banks were reported at $5691 million at the end of 1968 and at $6021 million at the end of 1969, indicating long-run expansion; but the following January figures for the two years were, respectively, $5673 million and $5986 million,[3] indicating in both instances some seasonal contraction.

It should be added that, although such figures are adequate to demonstrate elasticity in our coin supplies, they are far from accurate in measuring the quantities of coins actually being used as money. Large quantities are in the hands of coin collectors and dealers and even larger quantities of the pre-1965 half dollars, quarters, and dimes of 90 percent silver content have undoubtedly been melted down. And, of course, some have been lost and some hidden away and forgotten. Much the same can be said for virtually all of the silver dollars that continue to be reported as being "in circulation" month after month at $482 million. As for the melting of silver coins, it is not illegal. A ban on the melting and exportation of silver coins was imposed in May 1967 but was removed in May 1969.

Circulation mechanics

The machinery to provide the flow of coins into and out of circulation is well-greased. The Federal Reserve banks hold abundant supplies ready for shipment to commercial banks from which they are expected to flow directly to the public through withdrawals from deposit accounts, or indi-

---

[3]*Federal Reserve Bulletin,* various issues.

rectly through other financial institutions that, in turn, withdraw from their commercial bank deposit accounts. The coin supplies of the Federal Reserve banks are accumulated by return flows from the public through the commercial banks but chiefly from deposits by the U.S. Treasury of newly minted coins. All newly minted coins are distributed among the twelve Federal Reserve banks as Treasury deposits in proportion to expected needs of additional coins in the districts they respectively serve. Assume, for example, that at a given time the Treasury deposits $500,000 of new coins at all the Reserve banks. The deposits would affect Federal Reserve assets and liabilities as follows (with assets, as in a balance sheet, shown on the left-hand, or debit, side and with liabilities entered on the right-hand, or credit, side):

FEDERAL RESERVE BANKS

| Cash | +500,000 | Deposits: | |
| | | U.S. Treasurer | +500,000 |

Then, should commercial banks get shipments of coins of, say, $450,000, their asset accounts and the Federal Reserve asset and liability accounts would be affected as follows:

FEDERAL RESERVE BANKS

| Cash | −450,000 | Deposits: | |
| | | Member bank reserves | −450,000 |

COMMERCIAL BANKS

| Vault cash | +450,000 | | |
| Reserve with FR | −450,000 | | |

Finally, should other institutions and individuals (called, collectively, the "nonbank public") make coin withdrawals of $300,000 from demand deposits and $80,000 from time deposits at the commercial banks, their assets and the commercial banks' assets and liabilities would be affected in this way:

COMMERCIAL BANKS

| Vault cash | −380,000 | Demand deposits | −300,000 |
| | | Time deposits | − 80,000 |

NONBANK PUBLIC

Coins	+380,000		
Demand deposits	−300,000		
Time deposits	− 80,000		

When the nonbank public deposits excess supplies of coins in demand and time accounts at the commercial banks and the commercial banks pass them on to the Federal Reserve banks, the pluses and minuses of the third and second transactions, respectively, are reversed.

PAPER MONEY

Federal reserve notes

From the standpoint of quantities outstanding at all times, Federal Reserve notes are the most important kind of hand-to-hand money or currency in our monetary system. They hold this position by a wide margin. At the end of May 1970, for example, their outstanding volume amounted to $46,985 million while the volume of all other kinds of currency reported to be in circulation outside the U.S. Treasury and the Federal Reserve banks, including silver dollars and other coins, amounted to only $6680 million.[4]

Federal Reserve notes are issued in denominations of $1, $5, $10, $20, $50, and $100. The Federal Reserve Act also authorizes denominations of $2, $500, $1000, $5000, and $10,000, but $2 notes have never been issued, and a decision was made in July 1969 by the Treasury and the Federal Reserve authorities to discontinue the issuance of notes in the four denominations above $100, as well as to permanently withdraw from circulation notes in these denominations when they appear at the Federal Reserve banks as in shipments of currency from commercial banks.

Outstanding Federal Reserve notes are carried on the books and balance sheets of the Federal Reserve banks as liabilities, and they are guaranteed by the federal government. The liability classification harks back to the pre-1933 situation when they were redeemable in gold coin; in effect, they were promises to pay in gold coin. Now, however, the Federal Reserve banks have no obligation to redeem or convert the notes. Since they are legal tender, we could say that, as liabilities, they are payable only in themselves. For this reason, indeed, the guaranty of the notes by the federal government appears to be meaningless.

Despite the nonredeemability of the notes, the Federal Reserve banks are required to hold collateral of face value at least equal to the face amount of outstanding notes as "security." The Board of Governors of the Federal Reserve System can require the Reserve banks to hold more collateral than this, but it has never done so. The collateral may consist of gold certificates, SDR certificates,[5] Treasury obligations, and commercial paper in whatever proportions the individual Reserve bank chooses. (Commercial paper consists of such things as bankers' acceptances bought by the Reserve banks in the open market and promissory notes on which commercial banks borrow from the Reserve banks.) Actually, the Reserve banks pledge as "secu-

---

[4]*Federal Reserve Bulletin,* July 1970, p. A16.
[5]See Chapter 7.

rity" very little, if any, of their holdings of commercial paper, so that the collateral consists entirely or almost entirely of gold certificates and Treasury obligations, the latter predominating by a wide margin. The pledged collateral is put under the control of the chairman of the Reserve bank's board of directors who serves as "Federal Reserve agent" in supervising its note-issue operations. In view of irredeemability, however, all this fuss about pledging collateral and controlling it is also largely meaningless.

Elasticity   The capacity of the Federal Reserve banks to expand and contract their note issues quickly and by large amounts is the principal source of elasticity in our currency system. This is indicated by the very fact that the volume of Federal Reserve notes in circulation at all times far exceeds the combined volume of all other kinds of hand-to-hand money. Some elasticity in coin issues is necessary, as noted previously, but people want paper money rather than coins when they decide to make large withdrawals from demand and time deposits in hand-to-hand money, and they chiefly want to deposit paper money when they decide that their holdings of hand-to-hand money are excessive. When we consider all the demand deposits, all the near-moneys, and all the obligations of governments, business firms, and consumers that are payable in legal tender should depositors and creditors want it, we must conclude that some kind of legal-tender paper money must have a very great degree of elasticity. In our system, the issues of Federal Reserve notes meet this need in an excellent way.

Our dependence on Federal Reserve note issues for elasticity is three dimensional: long-run, seasonal, and emergency. Expansion in note issues is needed year after year to keep pace, as it were, with the growth of business activity and the accompanying increased volume of transactions that people decide to effect with hand-to-hand money. And within each year, according to a pattern that repeats itself from year to year, more hand-to-hand money is wanted for transactions on some days, weeks, and months than at other times, as during and after the Christmas shopping season and before and after national holidays. Additionally, there are possibilities of panics occurring, with people losing confidence in banks and other financial institutions and trying to make huge withdrawals of hand-to-hand money from them. These are remote possibilities, it is true, but they must be prepared for and be cooled quickly, should they become realities, by quick outflows of notes in order to meet the withdrawal demands. In a panic situation, proving to depositors that they can get hand-to-hand money if they want it will doubtless convince them that they really do *not* want it—that they simple wanted it to be sure that their deposits were "safe." All this also implies that we depend on Federal Reserve notes for contraction in the volume of outstanding hand-to-hand money when needs decrease—for their disappearance from circulation in return flows to the Reserve banks happens when recessions occur in the long-run movement of business activity, the Christmas shopping season is over, and panics are cooled.

Further Circulation Mechanics The machinery for the issuance and retirement of Federal Reserve notes is splendidly geared to serve the requirements of three-dimensional elasticity. Each Federal Reserve bank holds large quantities of unissued notes for which it has already set aside gold certificates and Treasury obligations to meet the collateral requirements; and these are available for immediate shipment to commercial banks as requested. Likewise, each Reserve bank holds large amounts of unpledged gold certificates and Treasury obligations that it can quickly pledge as collateral for additional unissued notes already on hand. And the U.S. Bureau of Engraving and Printing in Washington, D.C., always stands ready to send large quantities of notes from its inventories to the individual Reserve bank on orders from the Board of Governors, as requested by the bank's board chairman in his role as Federal Reserve agent. Alternatively, the Federal Reserve banks always stand ready to accept from commercial banks whatever quantities of notes they want to send for credit in their reserve accounts. As thus received, the notes are "out of circulation" and they are no longer carried as a liability in the Reserve banks' balance sheets. They may be held under the control of the individual Reserve banks for reissue, or they may be surrendered to the control of the Federal Reserve agents who then release the collateral previously pledged for them. In either case, the notes are, as it were, only "scraps of paper"—they will become money again only when reissued!

The workings of the Federal Reserve note-issue machinery may be illustrated in terms of what happens to the liabilities of the Reserve banks and the assets of commercial banks as a result of shipments of notes. Assuming that a commercial bank gets a shipment of $400,000 of Federal Reserve notes to be charged, as a withdrawal, against its account, the results would be as follows:

FEDERAL RESERVE BANK

Federal Reserve notes	+400,000
Deposits	
Member bank reserves	−400,000

COMMERCIAL BANK

Vault cash	+400,000
Reserve with FR	−400,000

And of course, the same liabilities and assets would be affected, with the pluses and minuses in opposite directions, if the shipment were made by the commercial bank to the Reserve bank for credit in its reserve account.

Other paper money

The "left-overs" of the greenback issues of the Civil War period are the only kind of paper money in addition to Federal Reserve notes that remain available for regular circulation in the United States. Some of these "United States notes," as they are officially called, were retired after the Civil War but legislation adopted in 1878 provided that notes received by the Treasury, as in tax payments, were to be "reissued and paid out again and kept in circulation." At the time, the outstanding volume of the notes amounted to approximately $347 million, but in November 1964 the Treasury decreased this figure to $323 million in a decision that by then $24 million of the notes had been "destroyed or irretrievably lost"—a kind of write-down that had been authorized by the Old Series Currency Adjustment Act adopted in 1961.

All other classes of paper money still reported to be "in circulation"—reported to total $301 million at the end of May 1970—are in the process of retirement. Retirement means that, as they appear at the Federal Reserve banks in shipments of currency from commercial banks, they are charged against the Treasury's deposit accounts and are then destroyed. The principal class of paper money "in process of retirement" are silver certificates that had been outstanding in amounts approaching $2.5 billion as late as 1965. They had been redeemable, unit for unit, in silver dollars (or in equivalent amounts of silver bullion, as ordered in May 1967) but legislation adopted on June 24, 1967, provided for suspension of redemption in silver one year later. The only other kind of paper money now in the process of retirement that was once of great importance in our monetary system —especially between 1863 and 1913—is the national-bank note. By satisfying certain requirements, any national bank could issues notes of this class but the note-issue privilege of national banks was, in effect, suspended in 1935.

In monetary transactions, we rarely encounter greenbacks, silver certificates, national-bank notes, and other minor kinds of paper money that are now in the process of retirement. Many of these notes have rarity values and are held in paper-money collections, and probably more have been "destroyed or irretrievably lost" than the Treasury has estimated.

DEMAND DEPOSITS

Importance of demand deposits

From the standpoint of volume, demand deposits are our most important kind of money. In May 1970, for example, the average daily amount outstanding was reported at $152.6 billion, while the volume of Federal Reserve notes in circulation at the end of that month was reported at only $47 billion. Even comparative figures such as these understate the importance of demand deposits as means of payment, as it is estimated that at least 90 percent of transactions, as measured by total monetary value, are settled by transfers among demand deposits. Not 90 percent of the *number* of transactions, but that percentage of monetary value. Obviously, most small transactions are settled by the use of paper money and coins, but when we study the sizable payments, it is equally obvious that they are settled in most instances by checks drawn on demand deposit accounts. So important is the use of demand deposits in the quantitative monetary functions, so peculiar are the procedures for their expansion and contraction, and so important is the control of this expansion and contraction for the prevention of inflation and deflation and for the attainment of other goals, such as full employment, that Chapters 6 and 7 are devoted to them. At this point, the analysis must be brief.

Payments in legal tender and transfers

Demand deposits are obligations chiefly of commercial banks to pay on demand as ordered by their depositors by means of written instruments, that is, checks. Like other obligations to pay in domestic money, the bank's obligations to pay can be satisfied without question by payment in legal tender, but most people who get rights to payment by way of checks do not want this kind of payment. They are quite satisfied to have the amounts of the checks transferred from the drawers' demand deposits to their own, and the banks maintain a marvelous array of internal bookkeeping and interbank arrangements for making such transfers with very little use of paper money and coins. Because, indeed, demand deposits are commonly used and generally accepted as mediums of exchange, without need of their conversion anywhere along the line into paper money and coins, we always classify them as a distinct kind of money.

Reports of demand deposits

Although the demand-deposit concept is reasonably clear, there are some differences of opinion about what should be included as demand deposits as a component of the total monetary stock. Accordingly, we should know that the most widely respected data for demand deposits, including the figure of $152.6 billion for May 1970 mentioned above, are estimates of the Board of Governors of the Federal Reserve System compiled on the basis of its own definitions. For one thing, the Federal Reserve classifies as demand deposits not only deposits that are truly payable on demand as checks are presented for payment, but also deposits that are payable in less than 30 days and deposits payable on notice of less than 30 days. For another thing, the Federal Reserve deducts from its compilations of demand deposits on banks' books "cash items in process of collection" and "Federal Reserve float"[6]—and nobody quarrels about this. Assume that John Doe receives a check for $1000 drawn by Richard Roe on bank A, and that Doe deposits this check in his demand deposit account at bank B. Bank B sends

---

[6]See Chapter 7.

the check to bank A for payment, but until bank A receives it and pays, Doe and Roe both have demand deposit balances of $1000. However, bank B carries the check temporarily as an asset on its books in the account "cash items in process of collection." Accordingly, the Federal Reserve would come up with the right total for outstanding demand deposits by deducting bank B's cash items of $1000 from the $2000 sum of Doe's and Roe's balances.

Still further, the Federal Reserve includes in its reported demand deposit totals foreign deposits at both the Federal Reserve and commercial banks but excludes all domestic interbank deposits, that is, commercial bank reserve accounts and so-called clearing balances at the Federal Reserve banks and all the demand deposit balances that domestic banks keep with one another. Again, there is general agreement with these definitional decisions, since the foreign deposits are available for spending and are likely to be spent while the interbank balances, though available for spending, are kept more or less intact as cash reserves rather than for spending.

But there is a considerable disagreement about the exclusion from reported demand deposit totals of Treasury deposits at both the Federal Reserve banks and the commercial banks that usually amount to several billions of dollars. The Federal Reserve says that these deposits "have little influence on the expenditures of the Federal Government." But because of the exclusion, the quantity of demand deposits in circulation can seem to be decreasing in some months simply because a considerable amount of tax payments are flowing from taxpayers' accounts to the Treasury accounts, or increasing in other months because the Treasury is spending more than it is currently receiving in tax and other payments from the public. The Federal Reserve tries to "correct" for such flows between the public and the Treasury by making certain "seasonal adjustments" to its figures. Thus the May 1970 figure given above was unadjusted, while the seasonally adjusted figure for the same months was $156.2 billion. However, many economists think that the adjustment procedure is certain to be inaccurate, so that it would probably be better to include Treasury deposits at both the Federal Reserve and commercial banks in total demand deposits as a component of the total money stock.

LEGAL TENDER

Although our legal-tender laws have at times been peculiar and even unclear, the most recent statement, in an act approved on July 23, 1965, is quite straightforward:

> All coins and currencies of the United States (including Federal Reserve notes and circulating notes of Federal Reserve banks and national banking associations), regardless of when coined or issued, shall be legal tender for all debts, public and private, public charges, taxes, duties, and dues.

Of all the kinds of money currently in circulation, therefore, only demand deposits are not legal tender. If you would prefer paper money or coins, you need not accept a check for a payment due you.

FOR REVIEW

1. Describe the role of gold in the present domestic monetary system of the United States.
2. Why is it questionable whether our domestic moneys have purchasing power per dollar equal to that of 12.632 grains of fine gold?
3. Describe the regulations that apply at the present time to the ownership of gold by American individuals.
4. What is the nature of "gold certificates" held by the Federal Reserve banks? For what purposes can they be used?
5. Why are all of our coins of current mintage said to be subsidiary coins? Does this description call into question their safety or acceptability? Discuss.
6. How do Federal Reserve notes get into circulation? How are excess quantities withdrawn from circulation?
7. What kinds of assets do the Federal Reserve banks set aside as collateral for Federal Reserve notes? Does such collateral make Federal Reserve notes more acceptable than they would otherwise be? Discuss.
8. Is it of any importance to the proper functioning of our monetary system that Federal Reserve notes are legal tender? Explain.
9. What is the relative importance of demand deposits as mediums of exchange by comparison with paper money and coin?
10. Do you think that Treasury deposits at the Federal Reserve and commercial banks should be included in the country's reported money supply? Why or why not?
11. Of our three most popular kinds of money, which are legal tender and which are not?

PROBLEM

Indicate how the assets and liabilities of the Federal Reserve banks, the commercial banks, and the nonbank public would be affected, if at all, by each of the following transactions:

1. The Treasury deposits $750,000 of newly minted coins at the Federal Reserve banks.
2. Commercial banks get shipments of $220,000 in coins and $650,000 in Federal Reserve notes from their Federal Reserve banks, with the withdrawals charged against their reserve accounts.
3. Customers of commercial banks make withdrawals of paper money and coins of $600,000 from demand deposit accounts and of $180,000 from time deposit accounts.

CHAPTER 5

MONETARY SYSTEM OF THE UNITED STATES: INTERNATIONAL FEATURES

MEMBERSHIP IN THE INTERNATIONAL MONETARY FUND

The features of our monetary system as described in Chapter 4 can be said to be features of the system as it operates domestically on the basis of fiat-standard rules. Even so, the domestic system has obvious connections internationally. Foreigners obtain our coins, Federal Reserve notes, and dollar demand deposit balances—chiefly deposit balances—when they sell goods to us, and we do not restrict them in spending these dollars in our markets or in markets of third countries.

Since we give such spending assurances because of our membership in the International Monetary Fund (IMF), its articles of agreement that we accepted by the adoption of the Bretton Woods Agreements Act in 1945 must be said to be an integral part of our monetary system. Actually, the assurances are given to other countries that are members of the IMF rather than to their people individually, but the result is much the same as if they were given directly to these peoples. Our strong support of the IMF is fitting because we were the prime mover in its establishment, because we continue to believe in the desirability of what it does and is trying to do, and because, indeed, our dollar has occupied a key role in its operations. We give this support even though the fund's rules with their gold-standard flavor appear to be contradictory, at least in some aspects, to our domestic fiat-standard rules. Despite apparent contradictions, we are willing to join our domestic system to the fund's international system as an embodiment of the fusion that is characteristic of the modern monetary systems of leading countries.

Objectives of the IMF

Statement of Objectives We believe in the desirability of what the IMF does and is trying to do because we accept its objectives, as we should since we had the leading role in their formulation. These objectives are stated as follows:

(i)   To promote international monetary cooperation through a permanent institution which provides the machinery for consultation and collaboration on international monetary problems.

(ii) To facilitate the expansion and balanced growth of international trade, and to contribute thereby to the promotion and maintenance of high levels of employment and real income and to the development of the productive resources of all members as primary objectives of economic policy.

(iii) To promote exchange stability, to maintain orderly exchange arrangements among members, and to avoid competitive exchange depreciation.

(iv) To assist in the establishment of a multilateral system of payments in respect of current transactions between members and in the elimination of foreign exchange restrictions which hamper the growth of world trade.

(v)   To give confidence to members by making the Fund's resources temporarily available to them under adequate safeguards, thus providing them with opportunity to correct maladjustments in their balance of payments without resorting to measures destructive of national or international prosperity.

(vi) In accordance with the above, to shorten the duration and lessen the degree of disequilibrium in the international balances of payments of members.

Interpretation   This statement of objectives means that the IMF has been assigned the task of helping member countries to cope with temporary shortages of means of international payment needed to meet obligations that originate in transactions on current account with other countries. The fund's help is expected to enable members to overcome such shortages in reasonable periods of time by moderate shifts of policy rather than by drastic actions, such as the imposition of controls on their foreign exchange markets. The fund is not expected to use its resources in more or less hopeless efforts to help any member to overcome chronic current account deficits that indicate a "fundamental disequilibrium" in the member's international economic position. Payments required for current account transactions are defined as including the following:

1.   All payments due in connection with foreign trade, other current business, including services, and normal short-term banking and credit facilities.

2.   Payments due as interest on loans and as net income from other investments.

3. Payments of moderate amount for amortization of loans or for depreciation of direct investment.
4. Moderate remittances for family living expenses.

As so described, current account payments are contrasted with "capital transfers," such as payments for land and buildings located in foreign countries and for securities issued by these countries or by enterprises located there. Accordingly, the fund is not expected to use its resources to help members make investments of these kinds or to clear up balance-of-payments deficits that result from such investments.

The facilities of the IMF were designed to supplement its members' ordinary banking facilities that normally arrange all kinds of international payments. The commercial banks continue as the principal dealers in foreign currencies, and most international payments are arranged through them. They continue to build up demand deposit balances with correspondent banks in foreign countries, and continue to supply drafts drawn on these balances to importers and other people who have payments to make abroad. If, however, the commercial banks exhaust their foreign balances in current account transactions without having means to replenish them in other ways, they can depend on the fund for additional balances. The central bank of the member country can buy the needed foreign currencies from the fund and then sell them to its commercial banks.

Par values, exchange rates, and redeemability

Par Values Each member of the IMF is expected, as quickly as its monetary reserves permit, to establish a par value for its monetary unit in terms of gold or United States dollars, and to obligate itself not to change the initial par value without consulting the fund, and not to change it, in any case, above 10 percent upward or downward without the fund's specific consent. The articles of agreement provide that a member "shall not" propose changes in the par value of its currency except to correct fundamental disequilibriums in its balance of payments. Nevertheless, the fund has no power to prevent changes within the 10 percent limit even when it is convinced that no fundamental disequilibriums exist to justify the changes. On the other hand, the articles direct the fund to approve changes beyond the 10 percent limit when it is satisfied that they are needed to correct fundamental disequilibriums, and they make the interesting point that, if the fund is so satisfied, it is not to object to proposed changes "because of the domestic social or political policies" of the members that propose the changes. If a member makes changes beyond the 10 percent limit without the fund's consent, it may withhold the use of its facilities from the member, and eventually, if the quarrel is not patched up, require it to withdraw from membership.

As a member, the United States originally set the par value of the dollar at $15\frac{5}{21}$ grains of gold nine-tenths fine—the level proclaimed under the

Gold Reserve Act of 1934—while all other member countries adopted the practice of stating the par values of their monetary units as equal to so many United States dollars or cents. Nevertheless, setting dollars-or-cents values for monetary units has obviously been only an indirect way of giving them gold values. Accordingly, a member other than the United States that wants to change the par value of its monetary unit can do so in terms of dollars or cents or in terms of gold, as it may choose.

Exchange-Rate Parities   As soon as a member country establishes a par value for its monetary unit, it thereby sets pars of exchange between its unit and the units for all other currencies with established par values. As of late 1971, for example, the British pound had a declared value of $2.6057 and the Belgian franc, a declared value of 2.2316 cents. At that time, therefore, the par of exchange in New York on London and in London on New York (since both markets quote the pound-dollar relationship in dollars) was $2.6057; in New York on Brussels, it was 2.2316 cents, and in Brussels on New York, 44.81 francs; and in London on Brussels, it was .022316/ 2.6057 of a pound (about 0.856 penny), and in Brussels on London, 116.76 francs. Until late December 1971 each member country made a commitment to keep spot rates of exchange in its market for the currencies of other member countries from fluctuating beyond a range of 1 percent above and below such pars of exchange. At that time, however, the IMF authorized its member countries to extend this range to $2\frac{1}{4}$ percent above and below the pars. Although this authorization was described as "temporary," expectations were that a wider range such as $2\frac{1}{4}$ percent would eventually be authorized on a permanent basis. (As the term is used in this context, spot rates are rates charged for foreign currencies where the buyer gets them immediately or immediately gets instruments payable in them on demand.)

Redemption and Conversion Obligations   The steps that an IMF member will take to keep its exchange rates within the permitted range are directly related to the status the member has assumed under Articles VIII and XIV of the Bretton Woods Agreement. If the member has not accepted responsibility for the redemption or conversion of other members' holdings of its currency under Article VIII, it will doubtless have reserved rights to exercise direct controls over exchange rates and transactions in its market as is permitted by Article XIV. But if it has accepted the obligations of Article VIII—as have all the leading industrial member countries as well as a goodly number of "less-developed" members—it forgoes rights to impose direct exchange controls on current account transactions[1] and assumes specific responsibilities for redemption or conversion of other members'

---

[1] It may impose controls on current account transactions with nonmember countries and their peoples unless the fund decides that such control would be contrary to its objectives.

holdings of its currency. It has two options: (1) it can make a commitment to redeem such holdings in gold, or (2) it can make a commitment to convert them into the currencies of the members that want to get rid of these holdings. If it chooses the second option, it still reserves the right to redeem in gold should it want to do so, but it is never directly obligated to redeem in gold. A member that chooses the first option needs only to stand ready at all times to buy and sell gold at a fixed price in terms of its currency (with the price adjusted for "handling charges" not exceeding a specified limit). Such a readiness to buy and sell gold fulfills the member's responsibility with regard to exchange-rate stability, and it has no obligation to take any other kind of action, such as dealings in foreign exchange markets, to keep rates within the permitted range. A member that chooses the second option obliges itself to buy back balances of its currency held by any other member and to pay in the other member's currency (or in gold, if it so decides). However, a proviso here is that the "other member" must say that the balances to be bought back were recently acquired in current account transactions or that its own currency is needed for current account transactions. While "buy backs" are effected at the par of exchange between the two currencies involved, they are not likely to have much influence otherwise in keeping exchange rates stable. Hence members that choose the second option must generally engage in rather extensive transactions in foreign exchange markets to keep rates within the permitted range.

Redemption   From the beginning of IMF operations until August 15, 1971, the United States was the only member country with a standing commitment to buy and sell gold at what is called a "fixed price." All through this period we stood ready to buy gold from all other members of the fund at $34.9125 an ounce ($35 minus a handling charge of 0.25 percent) and to sell gold to all other members at $35.0875 an ounce ($35 plus the handling charge of 0.25 percent). Our commitment to sell gold at a fixed price in dollars was really, of course, a promise to redeem in gold all dollars held by other IMF members that they might choose to use to buy gold from the Treasury.

However, on August 15, 1971, President Nixon announced that "temporarily" the United States would not redeem in gold or other reserve assets dollars held by foreign governments and central banks. After lengthy discussions and conferences among our representatives, the representatives of nine other leading industrial member countries (constituting with us the so-called "group of ten"), and officials of the IMF, announcements were made on December 18 and 19, 1971 that we had agreed to a devaluation of the dollar of approximately 7.89 percent, that the ten countries had agreed to realignments of pars of exchange among their currencies, and that the IMF had agreed to a "temporary regime" of permitting exchange rates to fluctuate within a range of $2\frac{1}{4}$ percent above and below these realigned pars. But the announcements reported no promise or demand for the restoration of the redeemability in gold of foreign-held dollars. A "proper degree of convertibility" in the IMF system was simply recognized to be a matter deserving discussion that should be "promptly undertaken."

(In addition to the United States, the "group of ten" includes Belgium— also representing Luxembourg—Canada, France, West Germany, Italy, Japan, the Netherlands, Sweden, and the United Kingdom.)

Conversion   The buy-back and rate-stabilization operations of second-option members can probably best be explained by means of illustrations. For a buy-back transaction, assume that the National Bank of Belgium (Belgium's central bank) asks the Bank of England to buy back £50,000 that it claims it recently acquired in current account transactions. To meet its buy-back obligation, the Bank of England would have to pay 5.84 million Belgian francs as determined by the pound-franc par of exchange. It might deliver some Belgian francs already owned, buy them in one or more foreign exchange markets (provided that its transactions would not cause rates to go beyond the permitted range), or buy them from the IMF by using its "drawing rights" there. For an illustration of a rate-stabilization operation, let us refer to the very important spot rate between our dollar and the British pound. The par for this rate in both New York and London is $2.6057, and England has a commitment to keep this rate within the range $2.5471–$2.6643. Assume, then, that a big demand for dollars in London occurs at a time when the British banks hold only limited supplies of dollars (as demand deposits at American commercial banks). The pressure of demand prompts the British commercial banks to raise the rate at which they are willing to sell spot dollars, and the rate soon threatens to go higher than $2.54 by approaching $2.5471 (these being expensive prices for dollars). At this point, the Bank of England begins to look for dollars. It wants to acquire dollars to sell to the British commercial banks so that they will have no reason to further increase the spot selling rate for dollars. It would hardly try to buy dollars in Paris, Frankfort, or other foreign markets, since buying there, because of the close interrelationships among markets, would tend to cause the London rate for dollars to go up rather than to hold it down. Accordingly, it might take either of two other courses in its quest for dollars: it could exercise its "drawing rights" at the IMF—in effect, buying dollars for pounds—or it could sell gold to the IMF for dollars. And, of course, it could continue to maintain and intensify its downward pressure on the dollar exchange rate in London as long as it had "drawing rights" and gold for use in obtaining dollars.[2] An interesting aspect of the gold transaction is that England would, in effect, be redeeming pounds in gold, although having no standing commitment to do that.

---

[2]However, its options would not be limited solely to the two mentioned. For a further discussion of these matters, see Chapter 25.

Drawing rights

IMF as Merchant in Currencies The foregoing references to drawing rights at the IMF calls attention to a very important area of its operations that requires a rather lengthy description. The fund is not simply a set of rules concerning par values of currencies, pars of exchange among them, and limitations on exchange-rate fluctuations. It is a merchant in the currencies of all its members, and its merchandising of currencies is directed to supplying members with means of payment to meet obligations to other members that originate in current account transactions as previously described. It operates in the expectation, as it were, that at most times the members will be able to meet their current account obligations to other members out of the proceeds of export sales, with each member's exporters selling their receipts in foreign currencies to their own banks, and its importers buying foreign currencies needed for payments from these commercial banks. But there is also the expectation that, from time to time, some member countries will run into serious difficulties in trying to meet net current account obligations to foreigners. The proceeds of their export sales will fall substantially short of the payment they must make for imports, and their reserves of gold and foreign currencies will be inadequate to supply the difference. A country might be inclined to try to overcome such difficulties by adopting such measures as paying subsidies to exporters, raising tariff duties to restrict imports, freeing its exchange rates from parity rules, and imposing operating restrictions in its foreign exchange market. But such measures would tend to defeat the very purposes for which countries band together to set up international monetary facilities, such as the IMF. Accordingly, the IMF concept is that the country should use its drawing rights in order to get the foreign currencies needed to meet its net current account obligations and thus avoid measures that would be inimical to the smooth flow of international trade.

Quotas and Subscriptions The drawing rights of each member of the IMF depend on the size of its "quota" and on the amount of its currency that the IMF holds from time to time. The quota is the amount of its subscription to the resources of the fund. Quotas for the forty-five nations that were represented at Bretton Woods were agreed upon at the conference itself (except for Denmark for which the setting of a quota was postponed), and the quotas of other countries that have since become members have been initially set by the fund itself. Since 1945, there have been three increases in quotas for almost all of the members at uniform percentage rates—one of 50 percent in 1959, one of 25 percent in 1966, and one of about 35 percent in 1970. In addition, there have been numerous increases in the quotas of individual members, almost all of them as requested by these members themselves. Throughout the career of the fund, the United States has had by far the largest quota, and this has meant not only that its subscription has been largest, but also that its block of votes in the fund's management has been largest. Our present quota is $6700 million and the next largest (in pre-1972 dollar equivalents) are those of the United Kingdom, $2800 million; West Germany, $1600 million; France, $1500 million; Japan, $1200 million; Canada, $1100 million; and Italy, $1000 million. At the end of 1970, the total quotas of all 117 members of the fund amounted (in dollar equivalents) to $28,433 million.[3]

As equal to quotas, subscriptions to the resources of the IMF, both original subscriptions and increases, have been generally payable at 25 percent in gold and 75 percent in the currency of the subscribing member.[4] Thus the United States has paid into the fund $1675 million worth of gold (at $35 an ounce, of course) and $5025 million in dollars. However, for countries having limited reserves of gold and dollars, the IMF has exercised its authority to permit gold payments of less than 25 percent, with the deficiencies compensated by additional currency payments. Moreover, the fund has generally accepted members' noninterest-bearing notes or other obligations in lieu of their currencies to the extent that the currencies have not been needed for the fund's buying and selling operations. Thus the United States dollars owned by the fund consist of a demand deposit balance at the Federal Reserve Bank of New York and U.S. Treasury notes of a special series, with the notes being available at face value for additions to the demand deposit balance whenever the fund wants to make this conversion. This means that the assets of the fund consist almost exclusively of gold and members' currencies (in the form of demand deposits at members' central banks and notes of their treasuries), and that its "liabilities" consist almost exclusively of the members' equity accounts that represent their subscriptions.

Purchases and Sales   A member's drawing rights in the IMF at any time are its capacity to acquire the currencies of other members in exchange for

---

[3]International Monetary Fund, *International Financial Statistics*, February 1971, pp. 8–9.
[4]If a member reduces the par value of its monetary unit, it is required to pay into the fund an additional amount of its currency to compensate for the reduction in the "gold value" of the fund's existing holdings of that currency; and if a member increases the par value, the fund is required to return to it an amount of its currency equal to the increase in the "gold value" of its holdings. By a large majority vote of the members, the fund itself may make uniform changes in the par values of the monetary units of all members that do not specifically object, but uniform changes do not require in- and out-payments of currency unless these are also voted. Likewise, they do not reduce members' rights, without the fund's consent, to change (initial) par values in the 10 percent range. Such a uniform change would actually amount to an increase or decrease in the official United States gold price. That no uniform change has yet been effected is indicated, therefore, by the holding of our gold price at $35 an ounce throughout the fund's career until early 1972 when it was changed to $38 for a different reason.

its own currency.[5] Its acquisitions of other currencies are said to be "purchases," so that one may say that it sells its own currency to the fund in buying the currencies of other members, or probably better, that it uses its own currency to buy other currencies. It may also pay gold for other currencies, but such transactions are exceptional, so that, in the typical transaction, the fund's holdings of the buying member's currency goes up while its holdings of the currencies sold go down. These ups and downs in the fund's currency holdings are effected at the pars of exchange. Assume, for example, that the United States wants to buy 50 million Belgian francs. Since the parity of the Belgian franc in terms of the dollar is 2.2316 cents, we would pay $1,115,800, and the fund's demand deposit account at the Federal Reserve Bank of New York would go up by that amount while its account at the National Bank of Belgium would go down by 50 million francs as it made delivery. On the fund's own books, the transaction would affect two of its asset accounts as follows:[6]

UNITED STATES DOLLARS

+ 1,115,800

BELGIAN FRANCS

− 50,000,000

Gold-Tranche and Credit-Tranche Drawings As was said previously, a member's drawing rights depend on its quota and the fund's holdings of its currency. The rules are rather complex, so that it should be helpful to use figures for illustration as we go along. Let us assume that country X's quota is $800 million and that the IMF holds $600 million of X's currency at a time when X wants to buy currencies of other members. It could immediately buy $200 million worth of the other currencies with no questions asked; its drawing rights are said to be "virtually automatic" until payments into the fund of its own currency cause the fund's holdings of that currency to reach 100 percent of its quota. Country X would be said to be using its "gold-tranche position" to buy or to be making "gold-tranche" purchases. The French word *tranche* means "slice," and this is a "gold slice" equal to 25 percent of X's quota because it stands for drawing rights given to X because of the 25 percent of its subscription to the fund's resources that it paid in gold. At any time, then, a member's gold-tranche drawing rights

---

[5]The discussion here and in the following paragraphs concerns members' drawing rights in the operations of the fund's "general account." Since the beginning of 1970, members that are participants in its "special drawing account" have been allocated "special drawing rights" (SDRs) that are described later in this chapter.
[6]Ignoring a service charge of $5579 that we would also have to pay if the transaction were a credit-tranche purchase, as described later.

are equal to its quota minus the fund's holdings of its currency at that time, if this subtraction gives a positive result. (If the positive result is more than 25 percent of the member's quota, the excess is often referred to as the member's "super gold-tranche" position or drawing rights.)

Suppose, however, that country X wants to buy $700 million worth of other currencies. It would then be using up all its gold-tranche drawing rights, all its drawing rights in its "first credit tranche" and in its "second credit tranche," and one half of the drawing rights in its "third credit tranche"—each credit "slice" also being equal to 25 percent of its quota. Unlike gold-tranche drawing rights, drawings in the credit tranches require the fund's consent. Country X would have to convince the fund that it needed the credit-tranche drawings in order to meet extraordinary obligations on current account that originated because of temporary balance-of-payments difficulties rather than because of a fundamental disequilibrium in its international position. And the fund would probably insist that country X take appropriate steps at home, as by monetary control and fiscal policy actions, to remove the causes of the difficulties. Even with the fund's consent, moreover, its willingness to sell currencies to country X would not ordinarily go so far as to permit X to exhaust its drawing rights in two and a half credit tranches in a single transaction, since the general rule is that, once the fund's holdings of a member's currency reaches 100 percent of the member's quota, drawings in any one year must not cause such holdings to rise by more than 25 percent of the quota. Still further, the credit tranches do not go on forever in number. Except for less-developed member countries for which the fund can make special concessions, the credit tranches are limited to four by the rule that says, in effect, that a member has no further drawing rights when the fund's holdings of its currency reach 200 percent of its quota.

The fund's currency transactions have significant similarities to the transactions of the typical foreign department of a large commercial bank—similarities in the characteristics of transactions, although not in their size and variety. The fund's currency holdings are very much larger than the holdings of the typical bank, the average size of its transactions is also much larger, and it buys and sells many currencies in which the typical bank rarely deals. The similarities have four sources: (1) its service charge on its credit-tranche currency sales, (2) its payment of interest to some members, (3) its charging of interest to other members, and (4) its right to require members to "repay" their drawings.

Charges and Interest Payments The fund's service charge for credit-tranche sales of currencies resembles the profit commercial banks seek by way of spreads between their buying and selling rates for foreign currencies. This charge is 0.5 percent of the amount that the buying member pays in its currency for the foreign currencies that it buys. In the illustrative purchase of 50 million Belgian francs by the United States given above, the charge would be $5579 on the assumption that the purchase was a credit-tranche transaction. (In July 1969 a service charge at the same rate on gold-tranche purchases was discontinued.)

The fund pays interest at a uniform rate on the average amount by which its holdings of each member's currency in given periods falls short of 75 percent of the member's quota. Although the rate paid is a modest one, it resembles interest payments by banks on time deposit accounts.

Much more significant, however, are the fund's interest charges on its average holdings of each member's currency in excess of the member's quota, because interest charges give these excess holdings the complexion of loans, with the whole procedure resembling the charging of interest on bank loans. The interest charges are progressive, so to say, in two dimensions: they go higher the larger the amount of excess holdings, and they go higher the longer the duration of such holdings. At the present scale, the lowest rate, 2 percent a year, begins to apply after 3 months of excess holdings, and it remains in effect for 15 months of holdings in the first two credit tranches and for 9 months of holdings in the third and fourth credit tranches. After these initial periods, the rates in all credit tranches rise every 6 months by one half of a percentage point per annum. When the rate reaches 4 percent on any portion of the fund's excess holdings of a member's currency, the fund and the member are required to discuss how the fund's holdings can be reduced, if they have not already made an agreement about this. If the member agrees, or if it has agreed, to "repay" all the excess holdings within 5 years from the dates of the drawings that caused the excess holdings, the interest charges do not go above 5 percent a year; but if there is no agreement, or if the member fails to fulfill an agreement, the interest charges can continue to rise to whatever level the fund decides.

Repayment Obligations Even more important than interest charges in giving the drawings of IMF members in the credit tranches the complexion of bank loans are the members' obligations to "repay" those drawings. The usual procedure is for members to make specific agreements with the fund to repay over a period of 3 to 5 years from the dates of the drawings. The repayment obligations of the member can be fulfilled in two ways: (1) by its using, in agreed proportions, gold, convertible currencies, and "special drawing rights" in the fund itself (to be described later) to repurchase the fund's credit-tranche holdings of its currency; and (2) by purchases of its currency from the fund by other members. The first way hardly requires explanation, because the member simply uses some of its monetary reserves to buy back some of its own currency. But the second way, too, should not be difficult to understand. The fund's credit-tranche holdings of a member's currency go down if the member repurchases, but they also go down if the fund sells some of this currency to other members. The effects of the two transactions on the fund's holdings of the member's currency are identical, so that it regards its sales of that currency to other members as repayments by the member itself. Accordingly, it is quite possible for a member's *apparent* repurchase obligations to be whittled down and even to vanish as a result of other members' purchases of its currency from the fund; and indeed it is possible for the member additionally to get gold-tranche drawing rights as a result of purchases by other members. For illustration, assume that country X's quota is $800 million, that the fund holds $1000 million of X's currency at the beginning of a certain period, and that X makes no further drawings during the period. During the period, however, other countries buy $100 million of X's currency, and this is regarded as a repayment by X of half of its drawings in its first credit tranche. Were other countries to buy $300 million of X's currency, the result would be the full repayment of its credit-tranche drawings and the establishment for it of gold-tranche drawing rights of $100 million.

Other Repurchases   Apart from repurchases of their currencies that members must make on the basis of agreements with the fund, they sometimes must make repurchases or additional repurchases as determined by formulas in the articles of agreement. By application of the formulas, the amounts of these required repurchases, if any, are mathematically related to the size of members' monetary reserves at the end of the fund's financial year (April 30), net changes in the amounts of these reserves during the year, and net changes in the fund's holdings of the members' currencies during the year. It is noteworthy that required repurchases in this category may extend to fund holdings of members' currencies in their gold-tranche positions; in other words, they may be required to the point where the fund's holdings of members' currencies would be reduced to 75 percent of their quotas. However, total formula repurchases from year to year usually amount to much less than repayments on the basis of agreements.

Finally, each member may voluntarily repurchase fund holdings of its currency for gold or for "special drawing rights" if the fund is willing to accept them in lieu of gold. In this category, the fund is required to sell back to the member holdings of its currency in excess of its quota, but it need not consent to sales beyond this—sales that would give the member a gold-tranche position. Such a consent would mean, of course, that the transaction would be voluntary on both sides.

Provisions about capital transfers

Although members' drawings from the IMF are generally restricted to currencies needed to meet temporary current account deficits, its articles of agreement permit drawings for capital transfers "of reasonable amount required for the expansion of exports or in the ordinary course of trade, banking, or other business." Moreover, each members is free to use gold-tranche currency purchases for foreign investment, and there is no restriction on its use of its own "resources of gold and foreign exchange" for foreign investment so long as this investment is in accord with the fund's objectives.

On the other hand, members that have accepted the obligations of Article VIII, although they thereby have agreed not to impose controls on current account transactions in their foreign exchange markets, remain free to control capital transfers in whatever ways they choose. When, indeed, a member would have to use credit-tranche drawings to meet "a large or sustained outflow of capital," the fund may request the member to exercise controls in order to prevent such a use, and declare it to be ineligible to use the fund's resources should it fail to comply.

Stand-by arrangements

Most of the currency drawings of members in their credit tranches are made according to the terms of "stand-by arrangements" previously agreed to between them and the fund. This means that, typically, the member anticipates that within the next few months or the next year it is likely to need credit-tranche drawings of given amounts of foreign currencies and immediately gets a fund commitment to provide these amounts when actually needed. As a condition for making such a commitment, the fund may require the member to take certain actions designed to remove the causes of its balance-of-payments difficulties. Most of the fund's stand-by arrangements are 1-year commitments, but regardless of duration, they are subject to a service charge of 0.25 percent of the amounts arranged. However, the charge is credited against the ordinary charge of 0.50 percent for drawings to the extent that the stand-bys are actually drawn upon.

Arrangements to borrow

In recognition of the probability that its holdings of the currencies of leading members would be insufficient to meet drawing requests in periods of severe international monetary disturbances, the fund has agreements with ten of these members (Belgium, Canada, France, West Germany, Italy, Japan, the Netherlands, Sweden, the United Kingdom, and the United States) to borrow specified amounts of their currencies in such emergencies. Should there be a flight from, say, the French franc to the West German mark, the fund might not have enough marks to meet the drawing requests of the Bank of France—hence the provision of having a pre-arranged commitment from West Germany to supply the needed marks. The fund's "arrangements to borrow" are expected to remain in effect indefinitely. Under these arrangements, the total commitments of the ten countries to lend (in dollars or dollar equivalents) amounted to $5901 million at the end of December 1970, and gross borrowings up to that time had amounted to $2155 million. The commitment of the United States to lend is $2 billion.[7]

---

[7]*Ibid.*, p. 16.

If a member has a gold-tranche position at the time it lends to the fund, as it is likely to have, this position is not reduced in any way because of the increased fund holdings of its currency that result from the loan. If, indeed, it subsequently needs foreign currencies to meet balance-of-payments deficits of its own, it has additional drawing rights of the gold-tranche character up to the amount of the loan.

Special drawing rights

All the details about quotas in the fund, subscriptions to its resources, and its purchases and sales of currencies given in the preceding pages have been descriptive of the setup and operations of its "general account." But an extraordinary new facility was added on January 1, 1970, with the establishment of its "special drawing account."

Need of Continual Growth of Monetary Reserves   For many years before 1970, there had been great anxiety among monetary statesmen and economists about shortages of the kinds of assets that countries want to hold as monetary reserves—assets that they regard as "safe" in the sense of being fully acceptable at face value by other countries for the settlement of obligations due them. It was expected that the shortages would grow progressively worse, because all countries would want continual increases in their monetary reserves to keep pace, as it were, with continual increases in the volumes of their international transactions. Such increases in reserves could hardly be expected to come from gold production, since the net flow of gold into monetary reserves was obviously quite scanty from year to year and, indeed, negative in the three years 1966–1968. The increases could come from the creation of more dollars by the United States and more pounds by the United Kingdom, because these two moneys were being widely held as "reserve currencies"; but many holders were becoming quite reluctant to accept and hold greater quantities of dollars and pounds, seeing themselves as giving away goods, land, buildings, securities, and so on for demand deposit balances that the United States and the United Kingdom could create unlimitedly. General-account drawing rights in the fund could be expanded by means of increased quotas and subscriptions, as in 1959 and 1966, but such increases would not result in genuine increases in world monetary reserves, because gold-tranche drawing rights obtained by gold payments to the fund are obviously matched by reductions in subscribing members' gold reserves, and increased credit-tranche drawing rights are usable only with the fund's consent. Hence came the extraordinary decision that the fund itself should *create* a new kind of international money—a "reserve asset" that would augment the monetary reserves of its members and be available as a means of settling international obligations without giving rise to equal obligations to repay or repurchase.

Allocations of SDRs   The new "reserve asset" was and is called "special drawing rights" (SDRs) to distinguish it from the general-account drawing rights of IMF members. The unit value of SDRs was made equal to that of the United States dollar—at a metric-system weight of 0.888671 gram of fine gold. (In January 1972, the SDR unit value was raised to $1.0857 because of our impending dollar devaluation.) To inaugurate the new system, it was decided that 3.5 billion SDR units would be created on January 1, 1970, an additional 3 billion units at the beginning of 1971, and a further 3 billion units at the beginning of 1972. And a further decision was to allocate these units to members that chose to participate in the new system in proportion to their fund quotas on the days immediately preceding the allocation dates. Accordingly, at the top end of the scale in the first two allocations of 1970 and 1971, the United States received, respectively, 866.9 and 716.9 million units; the United Kingdom, 409.9 and 299.6 million; West Germany, 201.6 and 171.2 million; and France, 165.5 and 160.5 million; while at the bottom end, Botswana and Lesotho each received 500,000 and 535,000 units and Gambia, 800,000 and 856,000 units. In the first two allocations, only 3414 million units and 2949 million units respectively were actually allocated, because Nationalist China (Taiwan) did not take its allocations although it agreed to be a "participant" in the special drawing account, and several of the smaller members—ten in the first allocation, and eight in the second—decided not to become participants for the time being.[8] Countries that are not members of the fund are not eligible to be participants in its special drawing account.

Use of SDRs with IMF as Intermediary   As a reserve asset designed to be comparable with gold as a means of settling international obligations, SDRs are used chiefly in transactions among participating fund members, rather than between participants and the fund itself as in the case of general-account transactions. In most instances, however, the fund acts as an intermediary in arranging SDR transactions among members. When a participant needs convertible currencies to meet balance-of-payments obligations, it notifies the fund of its needs and offers an equivalent amount of its SDRs in payment, and the fund then *designates* the participant that is to receive these SDRs. The participant so designated is *obligated* to accept the SDRs and to deliver convertible currencies of equivalent amount. However, no participant can be required to accept SDRs if acceptance would cause its SDR holdings to exceed three times the amount of its cumulative allocations, although it may voluntarily go beyond this limit. In the typical transaction, it is the designated participant's own currency that is wanted and is delivered. If, for example, the fund designates that France shall deliver to the

---

[8]International Monetary Fund, *International Financial Statistics,* May 1970, p. 7, and *International Financial News Survey,* January 13, 1971, pp. 1–2.

United Kingdom the many millions of francs equivalent to 10 million SDR units, France makes the francs available in the Bank of England's demand deposit account at the Bank of France, and the fund, in its SDR records, transfers 10 million units from the United Kingdom's account to that of France. And France is presumably willing to accept the SDRs in exchange for francs, much as it would be willing to accept gold, in the expectation that sooner or later it will use them, in turn, to meet balance-of-payments obligations of its own. But France would probably be unwilling to accept unlimited amounts of SDRs in exchange for its goods, just as it would be unwilling to accept an unlimited amount of dollars—hence the limitation on acceptance obligations at the level at which acceptance would cause its SDR holdings to exceed three times its allocations. (Another way by which a participant can avoid getting overloaded with SDRs that it does not want is to refuse to accept its share in new SDR allocations, as it has the privilege to do. As a result of such a refusal, it need not accept SDRs beyond the amounts that would bring its holdings to three times the allocations it had previously accepted.)

Choice of Participants to Receive SDRs   In designating participants to receive SDRs offered by other participants, the fund usually chooses participants that have strong reserve and balance-of-payments positions—participants that can afford to be generous, one may say. But it may also designate participants with the aim of helping or forcing them to "reconstitute" their monetary reserves. In the discussions that led up to the establishment of the fund's special drawing account, fear was repeatedly expressed that some participants, because of uncertainties about the quality and long-run acceptability of SDRs, would quickly use their allocations to acquire more desirable reserve assets, especially gold, and is was thought that the gold reserves of the United States might suffer severe drains. Accordingly, the amendments to the fund's articles of agreement by which the SDR facility was set up have several provisions aimed at persuading participants to use their gold reserves, gold-tranche drawing rights, and their reserves of convertible foreign currencies proportionally with SDRs in meeting balance-of-payments obligations.

Although, therefore, participants are encouraged to look upon SDRs as being as freely useful as gold as a component of monetary reserves, there is an "expectation" that they will not use SDRs "for the sole purpose of changing the composition" of their reserves "as between special drawing rights and the total of gold, foreign exchange, and reserve position in the fund." If, then, a participant uses a lot of its SDR allocations to meet balance-of-payments obligations—a use substantially out of proportion to its use of other monetary reserves—it is "expected" to try to reacquire SDRs to "reconstitute" its reserves, that is, to restore the proper proportions. The fund can assist by designating it as the participant to receive SDRs offered by other participants. Indeed, the fund's power of designation is the principal weapon that it has to force participants to reconstitute their reserves. If a participant displays no enthusiasm toward reconstitution, the fund can still designate it as the recipient of SDRs offered by other participants, and as mentioned previously, it has an obligation to accept. Another provision aimed at reconstitution of reserves is the rule that each participant must hold SDRs, on a daily average basis over each of successive 5-year periods, equal to 30 percent of its total allotments. While, therefore, a participant can "spend" at once its annual allotments, it must, at some time in a 5-year period, reacquire and hold SDRs in amounts much in excess of 30 percent of its allotments in order to satisfy the requirement for average daily holdings.

Direct Transactions in SDRs If a participant wants to use SDRs to buy back balances of its currency owned by other participants, it can bypass the fund and go directly to these other participants with its proposals. But a participant so approached is not obligated to make such an exchange; its consent to the transaction is necessary. If it does consent, its holdings of SDRs as recorded on the fund's books are increased, and the holdings of the participant that is buying back its currency are reduced.

When the buy-back arrangement was provided for, it was expected to be especially useful to the United States as a means of conserving its gold reserves. It was thought that foreign countries with unwanted dollar accumulations might be persuaded to accept SDRs from us in exchange for excess dollars rather than to use them to buy gold from the U.S. Treasury.

Fund Transactions in SDRs The fund itself may acquire and use SDRs in several kinds of transactions with participating member countries. It is required to accept them in collecting assessments that it is authorized to make from time to time against participants in order to cover the operating expenses of the special drawing account, and it voluntarily accepts them in collecting the annual charge that participants must pay on their total cumulative allocations of SDRs. The fund is required to accept SDRs for obligatory repurchases of credit-tranche drawings in the prescribed proportion of the repaying countries' monetary reserves, and it may accept them, in lieu of gold, when participants want to buy back fund holdings of their currencies in excess of amounts they are required to buy back.

One use to which the fund puts the SDRs acquired in these ways is to make annual interest payments to participants on their holdings of SDRs. The annual interest rate on participants' *holdings* of SDRs must be the same as the annual charge rate on their cumulative *allocations*. The rate is now $1\frac{1}{2}$ percent, and the arrangement means that, on a net basis, participants pay interest on amounts by which their holdings fall short of their allocations, and they receive interest on amounts by which their holdings exceed

their allocations. Presumably this should be an inducement to some participants, however slight, to hold their allotments and to others to accept and
hold SDRs in excess of their allotments.

Other uses to which the fund may put its acquisitions of SDRs are three:
(1) delivery in exchange for gold or acceptable currencies in order to help
participants to reconstitute their monetary reserves; (2) delivery to participants in exchange for their currencies when the fund's holdings of these
currencies have become "scarce"; and (3) delivery by agreement with participants in other kinds of general-account transactions. For the second type
of transaction, as listed here, the participant is obligated to turn over to the
fund supplies of its "scarce" currency for SDRs, provided that, as usual,
its acquisition of these SDRs does not cause its holdings to exceed three
times its cumulative allotments.

The fund's acquisitions of SDRs in its own name are carried as an asset
in its general account, and this asset is reduced, of course, as it makes payments and deliveries of the kinds described.

"Paper Gold"?   The monetary statesmen and economists who have been
the most ardent advocates of the creation of SDRs as a new reserve asset
and the most ardent supporters of their free and wide use as a means of
international payment generally anticipate that eventually SDRs will completely replace gold—that gold as money will be finally recognized as a
"barbarous relic" of the past and will be demonetized, that is, dumped on
the market for industrial uses and private hoarding should people still want
to hoard it. One may say that popular allusions to SDRs as "paper gold"
are expressions of this anticipation. But many people who are wise about
monetary affairs are much less enthusiastic. In their view, SDRs are only
promises to pay whose acceptability to the individual participant will continue to depend on his confidence that other participants always will be
willing to give merchandise, services, securities, and other things in exchange
for SDRs. And they contrast such acceptability, clouded with uncertainties,
with the cloudless acceptability of gold that is not a promise to pay and
that still seems to be wanted for its own sake.

The experience of the fund and the participants in the use of SDRs has
been much too short for a realistic judgment about this. It does seem reasonable to say that, so far, the SDR facility has been working well—perhaps
even better than was expected for its early years even by its most ardent
advocates and supporters. But for that realistic judgment, we can only
wait and see.

FOR REVIEW

1. What kind of commitment, if any, does the United States make to
    foreign individuals who acquire or hold Federal Reserve notes or dollar
    demand deposits?

2. Is it not a gross exaggeration to say that the articles of agreement of the IMF are really an integral part of the monetary system of the United States? Discuss.

3. What is the United States trying to accomplish by its membership in and support of the IMF?

4. What is meant by the par value of the currency of a member country of the IMF? How is the par value of the United States dollar expressed? the par values of the monetary units of other member countries?

5. What is the nature of the "par of exchange" between the currencies of two member countries of the IMF? What is the basic IMF rule about limiting exchange rate fluctuations in relation to pars of exchange?

6. Under what circumstances may a member country of the IMF change the par value of its currency? Are there prescribed limits to such changes? Explain.

7. To what extent do member countries of the IMF have an obligation to redeem in gold quantities of their currencies acquired by other members?

8. If the IMF is a merchant in currencies, where did or does it get the currencies that it buys and sells?

9. In what form does the IMF hold the dollars provided by the United States in relation to our "quota"? Does it stand ready to sell these dollars to individuals? to commercial banks? Explain.

10. Distinguish between the gold-tranche and the credit-tranche drawing rights of a member of the IMF.

11. What kinds of restrictions, if any, typically apply to the use of a country's gold-tranche drawing rights at the IMF? its credit-tranche drawing rights?

12. Why are credit-tranche drawings at the IMF said to be quite similar to borrowings from it?

13. How can a country's "repayment obligation" to the IMF because of credit-tranche drawings be satisfied?

14. In IMF operations, what is a stand-by arrangement? the general arrangement to borrow?

15. What was so special about the IMF's establishing facilities for "special drawing rights" in 1970?

16. If the United States wanted to buy some Italian lire with SDRs, how could it go about doing this?

17. What obligations do participating countries have to accept SDRs? to hold SDRs in relation to the IMF's total allocations to it?

PROBLEMS

1. As of March 31, 1971, the IMF's holdings of United States dollars, Brit-

ish pounds, and Mexican pesos (Mex$) were as shown in the following IMF asset accounts. Also shown are the quotas of the three countries and the par values of their monetary units at that time.

QUOTA: $6,700,000,000 UNITED STATES DOLLARS	$1 = 13.714 GRAINS OF GOLD
Mar. 31	$5,020,000,000
QUOTA: £1,166,666,667 UNITED KINGDOM POUNDS	£1 = $2.40 UNITED STATES
Mar. 31	£1,641,875,000
QUOTA: MEX$4,625,000,000 MEXICAN PESOS	Mex$1 = 8 UNITED STATES CENTS
Mar. 31	Mex$3,091,250,000

A. On March 31, 1971:
  (1) In terms of its own currency, what was the gold-tranche position of each of the three countries, if any?
  (2) In what amounts in terms of its own currency, if at all, did each country have existing repurchase obligations because of credit-tranche drawings?
  (3) According to the IMF's customary rules, and assuming its consent for credit-tranche drawings, what capacity in terms of its own currency did each country have to buy other currencies in a 12-month period?

B. Assuming that on April 1, 1971, Mexico bought £5,000,000 from the IMF for Mex$150,000,000, what would have been the effects of this transaction on:
  (1) the IMF's currency assets?
  (2) the gold-tranche positions of Mexico and the United Kingdom?
  (3) the credit-tranche repurchase obligations of these two countries?

C. Assuming that on April 2, 1971—as a transaction additional to that of April 1—the United Kingdom bought US$48,000,000 from the IMF for £20,000,000, what would have been the effects of this transaction (disregarding the IMF's service charge) on:
  (1) the gold-tranche position of the United States?
  (2) the credit-tranche drawing rights of the United Kingdom and its credit-tranche repurchase obligations?

D. Assuming that on April 3, 1971—as a transaction additional to those of April 1 and 2—the United States bought Mex$500,000,000 from the IMF for US$40,000,000, what would have been the effects on:
  (1) the gold-tranche positions of Mexico and the United States?
  (2) their credit-tranche drawing rights and their credit-tranche repurchase obligations?

E. After the completion of the transactions of April 1–3, 1971, what
    would have been:
    (1) the IMF's holdings of the three currencies?
    (2) the gold-tranche position of each of the three countries, if
         any?
    (3) the credit-tranche repurchase obligations of each country, if
         any?
    (4) the capacity of each country, in terms of its own currency to
         purchase other currencies in a 12-month period, assuming the
         IMF's consent to credit-tranche purchases according to its
         customary rules?

2. As of the end of March 1971, the total allocations of SDRs that had
    been made to the United States, the United Kingdom, and Mexico, and
    their holdings on that day were as follows in millions of units:

	ALLOCATIONS	HOLDINGS
United States	1583.8	1442.6
United Kingdom	709.5	481.8
Mexico	85.0	87.4

A. As of March 31, 1971:
    (1) In terms of SDRs, what capacity did each of these countries
         have to buy the currencies of other participants?
    (2) What was the total number of SDR units that each of these
         countries was obligated to accept from other participants in
         exchange for its own currency or other convertible currencies?
B. With the par value of the British pound at US$2.40 and that of the
    Mexican peso at 8 United States cents, what effects on the SDR
    holdings of the three countries would result from purchases in ex-
    change for SDRs:
    (1) of £10,000,000 from the United Kingdom by Mexico?
    (2) of Mex$500,000,000 from Mexico by the United States?
C. What effects, if any, would the two transactions under B have on
    the SDR holdings and the currency holdings of the IMF itself?

CHAPTER 6

DEMAND DEPOSITS AS MONEY

By a very wide margin, demand deposits are our most important kind of money from the standpoint both of the quantity outstanding and of the total dollar volume of transactions that are settled by their use. By a very wide margin, also, demand deposits are obligations of commercial banks to pay at once legal tender as directed by orders, that is, by checks, written by the depositors. Indeed, commercial banks are distinguished from all other classes of financial institutions for the very reason that they hold the demand deposit accounts of the general public. We saw in Chapter 4 that Federal Reserve reports of outstanding demand deposits include also commercial bank deposits payable in less than 30 days or on notice of less than 30 days and some deposits at the Federal Reserve banks, such as deposits of foreign governments and international institutions, and exclude deposits that commercial banks keep as reserves at the Federal Reserve banks and with one another. However, such inclusions and exclusions hardly require continual attention, so that our discussion of the sources, uses, and qualities of demand deposits and the expansion and contraction of their volume in this chapter and in Chapter 7 can best concentrate on the demand deposits of the public at the commercial banks that are truly payable on demand.

THE SOURCES OF DEMAND DEPOSITS

The sources of demand deposits are peculiar. The volume outstanding does not increase by the printing of pieces of paper at the U.S. Bureau of Engraving and Printing and the distribution of these pieces of paper, as in the case of Federal Reserve notes, or by the manufacturing operations of the mints and the distribution of their product, as in the case of coins.

Sources in general

Instead, demand deposits are increased by *increases* in every kind of asset held by the commercial banking system not offset by decreases in other assets or by increases in the system's liabilities and stockholders' equity accounts other than demand deposits themselves; and they are also increased by *decreases* in every kind of liability and equity account of the commercial banking system, other than demand deposits themselves, not offset by changes in other assets and liabilities and equity accounts. But the sources of demand deposits can have negative movements, as they often do, so that *decreases* in assets of the commercial banking system that are not offset and *increases* in the system's liabilities and equity accounts that are not offset cause decreases in the volume of demand deposits.

Take, for example, the making of a deposit of, say, $10,000 in paper money and coins in a demand deposit account. The effects on the assets and liabilities of the commercial banking system are as follows (with assets as usual on the left-hand, or debit, side and liabilities on the right-hand, or credit, side):

COMMERCIAL BANKING SYSTEM

Vault cash	+ 10,000	Demand deposits	+ 10,000

Thus the increase in the asset "vault cash" causes an increase in demand deposits of the same amount, since the asset increase is not offset in any way. In the opposite direction, a withdrawal of $10,000 in paper money and coin by a demand depositor would raise vault cash and this would cause an equal decrease in demand deposits.

Next, assume that bank customers transfer $50,000 of balances in savings accounts to their checking accounts. The results are as follows:

COMMERCIAL BANKING SYSTEM

		Demand deposits	+ 50,000
		Time deposits	− 50,000

Here the decrease in the time deposit liability causes an increase in demand deposits, since there are no offsetting changes in other assets and liabilities or in equity accounts. A transfer of $50,000 of balances from demand deposits to time deposits, on the other hand, would obviously decrease demand deposits by that amount—a decrease that could be said to be caused by the increase in the time deposit liability.

Suppose, however, that the savings depositors withdraw $12,000 in paper money and coin. The result is this:

COMMERCIAL BANKING SYSTEM

Vault cash	− 12,000	Time deposits	− 12,000

Here the decrease in the time deposit liability has no effect on demand deposits because it is exactly offset by the decrease in the vault cash asset.

Again, assume that customers of bank A deposit in their demand deposit accounts $75,000 of checks drawn on bank B, that A sends the checks to B for payment, and that B pays and A accepts payment by way of their reserve accounts at the Federal Reserve banks. The results for the two banks are as follows.

BANK A

Reserve at FR	+75,000	Demand deposits	+75,000

BANK B

Reserve at FR	−75,000	Demand deposits	−75,000

For bank A, the increase in its reserve account at the Federal Reserve bank, as an asset, causes its demand deposits to increase by an equal amount, but for bank B, the result is the opposite: the decrease in its reserve account causes a decrease in its demand deposits of the same amount. However, for the commercial banking *system* in which A and B are combined with all other commercial banks, there is no net change in anything, because the two asset changes cancel out as do the two changes in demand deposits.

For a further illustration, assume that customers draw checks for $15,000 payable to commercial banks themselves for services supplied. The banks would temporarily take up the $15,000 in an income account, and then combine it with all other income for a given period and deduct all expenses for the period and carry the resulting net figure for profit to the stockholders' equity accounts that they call "undivided profits"—equity accounts comparable to the "earned surplus" accounts of other classes of business corporations. For the purposes of the illustration, however, let us assume that the banks have no additional income and no expenses. With this assumption, the effects would be as follows:

COMMERCIAL RANKING SYSTEM

Demand deposits	−15,000
Undivided profits	+15,000

Accordingly, the increase in the equity account, since it is not offset in any way, causes an equal decrease in demand deposits.

For a final illustration in this group, assume that commercial banks buy chairs and desks at a cost of $25,000 and issue cashiers' checks in payment. The checks are so called because they are drawn on the banks by their own cashiers (or treasurers) and they, in themselves, are classified as demand deposits because they are obligations of the banks to pay legal tender on presentation for payment. Hence the effects are as follows:

COMMERCIAL RANKING SYSTEM

Furniture and fixtures	+25,000	Demand deposits	+25,000

Once again, therefore, an increase in an asset results in an equal increase in demand deposits since it is not offset in any way by changes in other assets, liabilities, or equity accounts. From year to year, the asset account for furniture and fixtures would be gradually reduced by charges for depreciation, an item of expense. But such reductions would have no effects on demand deposits since they would be offset (disregarding all other expenses and all income) by reductions in the undivided profits account.

Loans and investments as sources

Nevertheless, the principal ways by which the volume of demand deposits is expanded are the granting of loans by the commercial banks and their buying of investment securities; and the principal ways by which the demand deposit volume is reduced is the repayment of loans to the commercial banks and their sales of securities from their holdings to buyers outside the commercial banking system. This means that increases in outstanding demand deposits in billions of dollars from year to year are chiefly caused by increases in outstanding loans of the commercial banks and in their holdings of securities, and that decreases—generally occurring in short periods and in much smaller amounts—are chiefly caused by curtailment in commercial bank loans and investments.

Because of the role of commercial bank loans and holdings of securities, as just stated, the commercial banks are often said to "create" money in the form of demand deposits through their lending and investing operations—that, indeed, they are the most important "creators" of money in our economy, because demand deposits are our most important kind of money in volume and use. As we will see in Chapter 7, there is good reason to speak of "creation" in this context, although we will also see that the commercial banks' acts of creation are complex rather than simple and direct like the creation of Federal Reserve notes and coins and that they involve an intriguing paradox.

Lending and Discounting For the moment, however, let us confine our attention to the simpler relationships between demand deposits and commercial bank lending and investment, that is, relationships in terms of assets, liabilities, and equity accounts of the character illustrated in the foregoing pages. When a commercial bank grants a loan, it acquires a claim on the borrower for repayment, and this claim is an asset. The asset is intangible but it is almost always evidenced by a promissory note signed by the borrower. Almost always, too, the borrower wants the amount of the loan—the "proceeds"—to be simply added to his demand deposit balance. For a loan of, say, $80,000, the result would be as follows:

COMMERCIAL BANKING SYSTEM

| Loans and discounts | +80,000 | Demand deposits | +80,000 |

Thus, according to the pattern repeatedly illustrated earlier, the asset increase would cause an equal increase in demand deposits, since there would be no offsetting changes in other assets or in liabilities or equity accounts. Suppose, however, that somebody borrows $20,000 and takes the proceeds in paper money. The effect would be this:

COMMERCIAL BANKING SYSTEM

Vault cash	− 20,000
Loans and discounts	+ 20,000

No increase in demand deposits would result because the increase in one asset would be fully offset by the decrease in the other.

Actually, most borrowings, from commercial banks take the form of "discounts" rather than "loans."[1] In borrowing on a discount basis, the borrower gets less than the face amount of his note as proceeds and has the obligation to pay the face amount at maturity,[2] the difference being his interest obligation. If, for example, a borrower signs a note for $40,000 payable in 1 year and if the bank discounts the note at the rate of 6 percent per annum, the borrower gets as proceeds $37,600 and has the obligation to pay $40,000 at the note's maturity. The borrower would not be paying interest "in advance," as is sometimes said about transactions of this kind, since interest always accrues with the passing of time; he simply pays interest of $2400 at maturity on an advance of $37,600. But we should notice that the *effective rate* of interest he pays is not really 6 percent but 6.383

---

[1]Although there is a conceptual distinction between loans and discounts, as described here, it is customary to use the single term *loans* to refer to both kinds of bank advances when the context does not require making the distinction.

[2]If, however, the note is interest-bearing, the borrower may get more than the face amount as proceeds, and the obligation to pay at maturity will surely be more than the face amount. Although the discounting of interest-bearing notes is much less common than the discounting of noninterest-bearing notes, it is helpful to have an illustration. Assume that a businessman receives from one of his customers a promissory note for $40,000 maturing in 1 year and bearing interest at 8 percent. On the day he gets it, he endorses it and takes it to his bank which is willing to grant an advance on it, that is, to discount it. The bank's discount rate is 6 percent. The maturity value of the note is $40,000 plus $3200 for interest at 8 percent, or $43,200 in total. It is this maturity value that the bank discounts, and the "discount" at 6 percent is $2592. Accordingly, the businessman as borrower gets $40,608 as proceeds and has the obligation as endorser to pay $43,200 at the note's maturity if his customer, the maker of the note, does not pay at that time. On its books, the bank enters the transaction as a "discount" by adding $43,200 to its loans-and-discounts asset account while adding $40,608 to the businessman's demand deposit account and $2592 to its own unearned-discount liability account. (Observation: the quotation marks are designed to call attention to the weird use of the term *discount* as a noun to mean both the transaction and the amount deducted in the transaction for interest—a use that becomes all the more confusing when the term is also used as a verb and as an adjective, as it has been in this footnote. Though the footnote is the author's, he disclaims guilt for using the term *discount* so lavishly. That is the way it is used in financial circles, and the student may as well prepare himself to try to understand what it means in different contexts.)

percent ($2400 ÷ $37,600)—which indicates why the astute people who manage commercial banks prefer the discount procedure!

If the borrower in the transaction just described wanted to take the proceeds of his discounted note as an added balance in his demand deposit, the effects on commercial bank assets and liabilities would be as follows:

COMMERCIAL BANKING SYSTEM

Loans and discounts	+ 40,000	Demand deposits	+ 37,600
		Unearned discount	+ 2,400

Thus the asset increase would be partially offset by the increased liability for unearned discount, so that demand deposits would go up by the net difference.

Repayment of Loans In most instances, demand deposits simply vanish as loans are repaid, since the usual procedure is for borrowers to make repayment by drawing checks on their demand deposit accounts payable to the lending banks. In borrowing and while spending loan proceeds, the borrowers expect to be able to replenish their demand deposits sufficiently in order to meet their obligations at maturity, and of course, the banks would not lend in the first place were they to lack confidence in borrowers' capacity to do this. Assume, then, that the loan of $80,000 and the discount of $40,000 of the foregoing illustrations are to be paid off by checks drawn by the borrowers on their demand deposit accounts at the lending banks. For the loan, let us additionally assume that it was for 1 year at 6 percent interest, so that the borrower's repayment check amounts to $84,800. The effects would be as follows:

COMMERCIAL BANKING SYSTEM

Loans and discounts	− 80,000	Demand deposits	− 84,800
		Undivided profits	+ 4,800

Thus demand deposits are extinguished because of the asset reduction *plus* the increase in the undivided profits account. (Undivided profits increase, of course, because the interest received is income, and because, as in earlier illustrations, all other items of income and expenses are disregarded.)

For the repayment of the discount of $40,000, the borrower's check would be exactly that amount since it already included his interest obligation. But as the bank would now have earned the interest, there would no longer be a reason for it to show a liability for unearned discount, so that the effects of the repayment would be as follows:

COMMERCIAL BANKING SYSTEM

Loans and discounts	− 40,000	Demand deposits	− 40,000
		Unearned discount	− 2,400
		Undivided profits	+ 2,400

With the potential effects on demand deposits of the changes in unearned discount and undivided profits canceling out,[3] the actual decline in demand deposits would be the amount of asset reduction.

Investment in Securities　The effects on the volume of demand deposits of the acquisition and disposal of investment securities by the commercial banking system closely parallel the effects of loan grants and repayments. We would expect to see such a parallelism, since, in obedience to restrictive government regulations, commercial banks confine their acqustions of securities almost exclusively to debt instruments like U.S. Treasury bills and notes and government and corporation bonds. And of course, the issuance of such instruments is an act of borrowing no less than the issuance of promissory notes to commercial banks as evidences of borrowing there. But the parallelism also obtains when the commercial banks invest in and dispose of common and preferred stocks to the limited extent that is permissible.

The parallelism can be seen most clearly when commercial banks buy debt instruments directly from issuers located in their own communities. Assume, for example, that a commercial bank buys at par $50,000 of bonds being used by the government of the city where it is located. The city treasurer would probably want the proceeds of this sale to be credited to the city's demand deposit account, so that the effects would be as follows:

COMMERCIAL BANKING SYSTEM

Municipal securities	+ 50,000	Demand deposits	+ 50,000

According to the usual pattern, therefore, the increase in bank assets causes an equal increase in demand deposits, because it is not offset in any way by changes in other assets or liabilities or in equity accounts. Nevertheless, the result would be the same for the commercial banking system were the bank of the foregoing illustration to make an out-of-town purchase of corporation bonds at a par value of, say, $50,000. Were it to pay by drawing a check on its reserve account at the Federal Reserve bank, its assets would be affected as follows:

BUYING BANK

Reserve at FR	− 50,000
Corporation bonds	+ 50,000

No increase in demand deposits occurs, but the seller of the corporation bonds would surely deposit the check at his bank, and that bank would send the check to the Federal Reserve bank for credit in its reserve account, with the following effects:

---

[3]In actual practice, the bank would make periodic transfers from the unearned discount account to undivided profits as portions of the discount were earned with the passing of time.

DEPOSITORY BANK			
Reserve with FR	+ 50,000	Demand deposits	+ 50,000

For the commercial banking *system,* therefore, the two changes in reserve accounts would cancel out, with the increase in security holdings of the one bank then being exactly matched by an increase in demand deposits on the books of the other.

Disposal of Securities   The two principal ways by which the security holdings of the commercial banking system are reduced are redemptions at maturity and sales outside the system. If the city treasurer of the foregoing illustration drew a check for $50,000 to redeem the city's bonds held by the bank that invested in them, the effects would obviously be the reverse of the effects of the original investment: the bank's investment asset would go down by $50,000 causing demand deposits of equal amount to vanish. In the case of a resale of the corporation bonds by the bank that invested in them—a resale to a nonbank buyer—the effects would be largely the reverse of the effects of the original investment, but not necessarily exactly so. That would depend on the selling price. Suppose, for example, that the bank is able to sell the bonds at $51,000. The nonbank buyer would draw a check for that amount on his bank, the selling bank would present the check to this bank for payment, and payment would be completed (let us assume) through the two banks' reserve accounts at the Federal Reserve banks. Disregarding all other items of income and expense of the selling bank, the profit on sale of $1000 would add to its undivided profits, so that the over-all effects would be:

SELLING BANK			
Reserve with FR	+ 51,000	Undivided profits	+ 1,000
Corporation bonds	− 50,000		

DEPOSITORY BANK			
Reserve with FR	− 51,000	Demand deposits	− 51,000

For the commercial banking system, therefore, the two changes in reserve accounts would cancel out, and the reduction in assets of $50,000 plus the increase in the equity account of $1000 would cause the decrease of $51,000 in demand deposits.

USE OF DEMAND DEPOSITS

Demand deposits can retain and, indeed, continually improve their status as our principal kind of money in volume and use for many reasons, among which the following are surely most important:

1. They can be readily used as a medium of exchange through the use of checks.
2. The usefulness of checks as a means of transferring demand deposit balances is, in turn, greatly enhanced by (a) their endowment by law with the quality of negotiability, and (b) the extensive network of facilities that are maintained by the commercial and Federal Reserve banks for the speedy presentation of checks for payment to the banks on which they are drawn.
3. Demand deposits generally have purchasing power and acceptability for payments equal, dollar for dollar, with the purchasing power and acceptability of paper money and coins.
4. Demand deposits are generally regarded as having a high degree of safety.

THE NATURE OF CHECKS

Demand deposits would hardly be a convenient medium of exchange were it necessary for the depositor to visit his bank and there make arrangements with a teller to transfer portions of his deposit balance to the people to whom he wants to make payments. But such time-consuming actions are quite unnecessary. To use his deposit to make payments, he need not visit the bank at all, and he can even add to his deposit by mail. All he has to do is to write checks as orders to pay, and in the course of a single day, he can write as many of these orders as he chooses, even hundreds or thousands. And the bank is contractually obligated to obey these orders provided that the depositor has a sufficient *collected* balance[4] to cover them.

Definition

Because checks are negotiable instruments, a good definition of a check must incorporate all the features that are required for negotiability by the Uniform Commercial Code that has been adopted in all states. Such a definition is this: a *check* is a written unconditional order of a depositor on a bank to pay to the order of a designated party or to the bearer a specified sum of money on demand. Checks are "bills of exchange" but they are distinctive in that, as orders to pay, they are drawn only on banks, while other types of bills of exchange may be drawn on anybody who has obligations to pay. The writer of a check is the *drawer*, the bank on which the check is drawn is the *drawee*, and the person or institution designated to receive payment is the *payee*.

Kinds of Checks   Checks vary greatly in color, size, and other features, although all must satisfy the terms included in the foregoing definition.

---

[4]For the meaning of this term, see p. 113.

There are also variations according to the status of the drawers and drawees, and these are of some significance. One special class is the "certified check" which is so called because payment to the payee or a subsequent "holder in due course" is specially guaranteed by the drawee bank. A certified check is made out in the regular way and is then presented to the drawee bank, which stamps or writes "accepted," "certified," or "guaranteed" on its face, with the date and its signature. Banks are under no obligation to certify checks, their obligation being, rather, to pay checks properly presented during regular banking hours, but they usually certify simply as a matter of routine service for their customers. (A bank is said to "pay" checks drawn on itself; if it gives paper money or coins for checks drawn on other banks, it is said to "cash" these checks. It has no obligation to cash checks—even those drawn on the U.S. Treasury.)

Among banks themselves, another kind of check, called a "bank draft," is used. Banks find it convenient to keep accounts with one another to facilitate their operations, and they may draw on these accounts in the same manner as ordinary depositors. A bank draft, therefore, differs from the check of an individual only in that it is drawn by one bank on another. In many kinds of transactions, banks drafts are more acceptable than personal checks drawn by individual depositors, and most banks accordingly "sell" drafts to their customers, usually charging a small fee for the service. Thus a person who must make a payment in "New York funds" may obtain from his bank a draft upon its "correspondent bank" in New York City with which it maintains a deposit balance. Bank drafts are also used in buying and selling foreign currencies, as when an American bank sells a draft payable in sterling drawn on its account held with a bank in London. Such drafts on foreign banks are often called "bankers' sight drafts," or "bankers' demand drafts," to distinguish them from domestic bank drafts.[5]

A check drawn on a bank by one of its own officers, who has been duly authorized, is known as a "cashier's check," or "treasurer's check." Cashiers' checks are commonly used by banks in meeting their payrolls and other operating expenses. Like bank drafts, some are sold to holders of demand deposit accounts for transactions in which their personal checks would not be acceptable. And holders of savings and other time deposit accounts, who have no right to draw checks against these accounts, often buy cashiers' checks when they have large payments to make. Moreover, bank-issued travelers' checks are really a kind of cashiers' checks.

For time depositors and others who would like to make certain payments by drawing their own checks, although having no demand deposit accounts, many banks provide "bank money orders." The customer applies to the bank for the right to draw each check or "money order" of this kind, draws the instrument on the bank itself and signs it, and makes payment for the

---

[5] For an explanation of the use of bank drafts for making international payments, see Chapter 24.

amount of the check and the bank's service charge in hand-to-hand money or by having his time deposit balance reduced. In effect, then, the bank simply gives him a temporary demand deposit account for the exact amount of the check.

Negotiability of checks

Negotiability and Assignability   The widespread use of checks would be virtually impossible were it not for the special quality of *negotiability* that has been given them by law in all states. This quality makes it possible on occasion for the receiver of a check to have rights to payment superior to the rights possessed by the person who transferred it to him. The privileged quality of negotiability has been given only to checks, other bills of exchange, promissory notes, stock certificates, and a few other commercial instruments. All other kinds of property are merely *assignable,* which means that a transferee can obtain rights in the property no better than the rights of the transferor.

The distinction between assignability and negotiability may be illustrated. Suppose that a person has mortgaged his home for $8000—that he has given his creditor a binding claim, or *lien,* against the property for that amount. This person now decides to sell the property and sets his selling price at $20,000. He does not tell the buyer that there is a mortgage of $8000 against the property, and the buyer, neglecting to have the title searched, does not discover the existence of the mortgage. The buyer pays $20,000 and later receives notice from the mortgagee that the claim of $8000 must be paid. Because the mortgage as a lien on the property itself cannot be eliminated by a mere transfer of title, the buyer cannot escape the obligation although he has been misled. Here, then, is an instance of assignability, for the buyer got rights in the property no better than the seller had.

Now consider an illustration of negotiability. A businessman makes out a check payable to "cash" or to "bearer" for $250, signs it, and gives it to one of his employees with instructions to pay certain bills. The employee, however, takes the check to an appliance store, buys a television set for himself, and gives the check in payment. The employee, it is clear, has no rights in the check except to use it as his employer directed, but the appliance merchant has no warning of this defect in the title of the employee. The check is in proper form, it is properly signed, and the merchant would probably think that it had been made out to the employee for wages. When the employer finds that the employee has embezzled his money, he is unable to force the merchant to return an equal sum or any other amount, for according to the law, the merchant is a "holder in due course" and has independent rights in the check—rights that, in this instance, are superior to the rights of the employee who transferred it.

Advantage of Negotiability   The foregoing illustrations show why the transfer of negotiable instruments is a much simpler matter than the transfer of many other kinds of property. If checks did not possess the quality of negotiability, their use in transferring demand deposit balances would be severely limited. Not only would banks have to be vigilant to detect fraudulent and forged checks—a necessary safeguard even when checks are negotiable—they would have to be concerned with the goodness of customers' titles to every check presented for payment, cashing, or deposit.

Requisites for the Negotiability of Checks An instrument is not made negotiable simply by calling it a check, a bill of exchange of another type, or a promissory note. It must satisfy the requirements of negotiability as stated in the Uniform Commercial Code. For checks, these requirements are as follows:[6]

1. The instrument must be in writing and signed by the drawer.

2. It must contain an unconditional order to pay a specific sum of money, and in general, it must contain "no other promise, order, obligation, or power." Orders to pay in commodities or services, while they may be valid contracts after acceptance and may then be assignable, can never be negotiable. The order to pay must be unconditional: if the money is to be paid only if the payee does this or that, the instrument is not negotiable.

3. The instrument must be payable on demand, that is, when it is presented to the drawee bank during regular banking hours.

4. It must be payable to the order of a designated party or to bearer. A written order on a bank to pay "to John Jones" is not negotiable, but such an order, if properly drawn in other respects, is negotiable if payable "to the order of John Jones." The word *order* indicates that the bank is to pay John Jones or anybody else to whom Jones directs payment to be made. This is important because a major objective of state legislatures in providing for the negotiability of some kinds of instruments is to ease their passing from hand to hand. Even more, therefore, does the drawer of a check promote ease in passing when he makes it payable "to bearer," since he thereby directs the bank to pay whoever presents it for payment.

5. Finally, the instrument must name the bank that is being ordered to pay or otherwise identify it "with reasonable certainty." In writing checks, most people use the forms supplied by the banks themselves with their names as drawees printed thereon, so that there is no problem here. Sometimes, however, one needs to transform a blank piece of paper into a check by writing all the required details on it, or to use a check form designed for general use, with the drawee bank's identification as well as other details to be filled in—in which instances, it is pleasant and convenient for him to remember the name of his bank. Should he forget it, he could satisfy the

---

[6]Uniform Commercial Code, Art. 3, secs. 102, 104. As negotiability is a matter of great complexity, the student should know that the discussion in these paragraphs only touches the highlights, as it were.

identification requirement "with reasonable certainty" by designating, say, "the bank at the northwest corner of Main Street and Jefferson Boulevard in South Bend, Indiana."

Holders in Due Course   Everyone who accepts a check is not necessarily a "holder in due course," that is, he does not necessarily get rights independent of, and possibly superior to, the rights of the transferor. To qualify as a holder in due course, he must satisfy certain conditions:[7]

1. He simply cannot qualify at all if "the instrument is so incomplete, bears such visible evidence of forgery or alteration, or is otherwise so irregular as to call into question its validity, or terms of ownership, or to create an ambiguity as to the party to pay."

2. He must not know that the drawee bank has already refused to pay the check (if it has so refused).

3. He must take the check in good faith and for value. Thus a person who receives a check as a gift does not qualify as a holder in due course because he gives nothing of value in exchange for it.

4. Finally, he must not know "of any defense" against the check or "claim to it on the part of any person." Had the appliance merchant of the illustration known that the employee had the duty to use the check of $250 to pay his employer's bills, he would not have been a holder in due course.

When the holder of a check is unable to satisfy all the foregoing requirements, he may nevertheless have a good title to it, and he may be able to obtain payment or to enforce his claim to payment. However, his right to payment can be defeated by certain "defenses" that drawers and drawee banks would not have were he a holder in due course. For example, the person who receives a check as a gift has no grounds to take legal action to force payment if the donor tells his bank not to pay the check, but a transferee of a check who qualifies as a holder in due course is in a strong position to force the drawee bank to pay even though the drawer has told it not to pay.

Endorsements   Checks that are made payable to the bearer can be passed from hand to hand without any formalities, since their drawers have ordered the drawee banks to pay whoever presents them. Recognized by law as bearer instruments are checks made payable to "cash" and to specified parties *or* bearer, as "Pay to John Doe or bearer" and "Pay to the order of John Doe or bearer."

When a check is payable to the order of a designated party, it cannot be passed from hand to hand unless he authorizes such transfers. If he wants to do so, he *endorses* the check by writing his name across the bank. But endorsement is something more than a mechanical procedure incidental to the passing of checks to other parties. Each endorser makes certain war-

---

[7]*Ibid.*, Art. 3, secs. 302, 304.

ranties:[8] that he has good title to the check or that he is authorized to obtain payment on behalf of somebody who has good title, and that the transfer is otherwise rightful; that all signatures are genuine or authorized; that the check has not been materially altered; and that he has no knowledge of any insolvency proceeding instituted against the drawer (or against the drawee bank in the case of a certified check). In addition, a qualified endorser—one who uses words such as "without recourse" in his endorsement—warrants that he has no knowledge of a "defense" that is good against him; while an unqualified endorser—one who does not use words such as "without recourse"—warrants definitely that no party has a "defense" that is good against him, and obligates himself to pay the amount of the check to the party to whom he transfers it or to any subsequent holder should the drawee bank refuse to pay.[9] Because the obligation of the unqualified endorser to pay is contingent on nonpayment by the drawee bank, he is said to be secondarily liable for payment. But such secondary liability doubtless enhances the usefulness of checks because it is an additional safety factor. For banks, it provides protection when they increase depositors' balances for deposited checks drawn on other banks, because they have the right to revoke such increases when the drawee banks refuse to pay.

THE CLEARING OF CHECKS

Greatly contributing to the usefulness of checks as means of transferring demand deposit balances is the extensive and intricate network of facilities that the commercial and Federal Reserve banks maintain for their "clearing"—for presenting them to the drawee banks for payment as quickly as possible. In a well-managed bank, the rule is that a depositor has no right to make withdrawals from a deposit balance that originates from deposits of checks drawn on other banks until the depository bank has had enough time to collect payment on these checks. Until payment has been collected, such a balance is an "uncollected balance," and the bank reserves the right to refuse payment on checks drawn against it and to mark them with a notation, such as "drawn against uncollected funds." Therefore, if it took banks a long time to collect payment on checks on other banks deposited by their customers, these customers would surely complain about poor service, and were the delays in collection frequent and prolonged, the customers would doubtless insist that their debtors pay in paper money rather than by means of checks. No wonder, then, why the commercial and Federal Reserve banks are constantly seeking new ways to speed their clearing procedures.

---

[8] *Ibid.,* Art. 3, secs. 414, 417.

[9] The warranties of a person who transfers "for value" a bearer negotiable instrument without his endorsement are the same as the warranties of an unqualified endorser; however, they run only in favor of his immediate transeferee.

Classification for clearing

In the matter of clearing, every commercial bank worthy of the name cashes, pays, and receives for deposit three classes of checks: (1) checks drawn on itself, commonly called "us checks"; (2) checks drawn on other banks in its home city or community; and (3) checks drawn on banks elsewhere—on "out-of-town banks." It does not have to worry about clearing checks drawn on itself—there is no place to send them to, since they have already been presented for payment to itself as drawee. It takes care of them in its own bookkeeping department, subtracting from the deposit balances of the drawers, and adding to the balances of depositors whatever amounts have not already been paid in paper money and coins. (Since the amounts of certified checks are deducted from the drawers' accounts at the time of certification, they are deducted from the liability account *certified checks outstanding* when paid. Likewise, the bank's own cashiers' checks, when paid, are deducted from the liability account *cashiers' checks outstanding.*)

Clearing channels

In small cities or communities where there are only two or three banks, each bank typically employs messengers to deliver to the others checks drawn on them and to demand payment, and of course, messengers from the others deliver checks to it with demands for payment. In larger cities and communities, however, the common practice is for the banks to exchange checks among one another at clearinghouses which they themselves maintain. Typically, all the large banks of a community are members of the clearinghouse, and smaller banks either use messengers for direct presentation of checks to drawee banks or get the large banks to take their checks to the clearinghouse. For the clearing of checks drawn on out-of-town banks, most banks send them to the Federal Reserve banks of their respective districts or to metropolitan commercial banks known as "correspondent banks," depending on the Reserve and correspondent banks to present the checks to the drawee banks for payment. Subject to an exception for "nonpar banks" to be mentioned later, any bank can simultaneously use the clearing services of both the Federal Reserve bank of its district and of one or more correspondent banks. Especially deserving mention is the fact that the correspondent banks extensively use Federal Reserve clearing services in passing to drawee banks those checks received from out-of-town banks as well as those received from local customers.

It is noteworthy that, in the clearing of checks, payment by drawee banks is rarely made in paper money and coins—an important fact that supports the claim that demand deposits are truly money in that they are commonly used and generally accepted as mediums of exchange without any need for their conversion into something else. In local clearings by messengers and through clearinghouses, payment is usually made by drafts (checks) drawn on the Federal Reserve or correspondent banks or by telegraphic or telephonic transfers on the books of these institutions. And collections of payments on checks sent by out-of-town banks are generally simply added to the deposit accounts of the sending banks on the books of the Federal Reserve and correspondent banks, while the deposit balances of the paying banks are reduced.

Clearinghouses

A clearinghouse need be nothing more than a simple room or office where messengers from the banks of a community can meet to transfer the checks that each bank presents to the others for payment. Actually, many clearinghouses have quite elaborate facilities maintained by associations of which the banks of the community are members. And the clearinghouse associations themselves often do much more than simply provide clearing facilities, adding such activities as the regulation of banking hours and practices, the promotion of good public relations, and the operation of facilities for the exchange of credit information—in a word, serving as trade associations for the banks of the cities in which they operate.

Clearing Procedure   Assume that in a certain city there are six banks associated in a clearinghouse. Of the checks it has received from its depositors and other customers, each bank daily sorts those drawn on the other five banks and puts them into individual packages, at the same time preparing a statement of the total payment due from each. At a set hour, messengers of the banks are ready at the clearinghouse to deliver the packages. Bank A's messengers have five packages, each representing its claim on one of the other banks, and the total obviously representing the amount due bank A from the others, collectively. The messengers of each of the other five banks in turn have a package of checks drawn on bank A, and the total of the five packages is the amount that bank A owes the others, collectively. If the latter total is greater than the former, bank A must pay the difference; if the former is greater, bank A has the right to receive payment equal to the difference. The manner in which the clearing is made may be illustrated with figures as follows:

| | CHECKS DRAWN ON | | | | | | |
	BANK A	BANK B	BANK C	BANK D	BANK E	BANK F	TOTALS
Bank A brings		$ 6,000	$ 3,000	$ 2,000	$ 4,000	$ 5,000	$ 20,000
Bank B brings	$ 4,000		7,000	5,000	3,000	2,000	21,000
Bank C brings	2,000	5,000		2,000	1,000	5,000	15,000
Bank D brings	4,000	3,000	6,000		4,000	3,000	20,000
Bank E brings	5,000	6,000	4,000	6,000		3,000	24,000
Bank F brings	2,000	4,000	3,000	5,000	3,000		17,000
Totals	$17,000	$24,000	$23,000	$20,000	$15,000	$18,000	$117,000

The table may be summarized as follows:

BANK	CHECKS RECEIVED (DEBITS)	CHECKS BROUGHT (CREDITS)	DEBIT BALANCE	CREDIT BALANCE
Bank A	$ 17,000	$ 20,000		$ 3,000
Bank B	24,000	21,000	$ 3,000	
Bank C	23,000	15,000	8,000	
Bank D	20,000	20,000		
Bank E	15,000	24,000		9,000
Bank F	18,000	17,000	1,000	
Totals	$117,000	$117,000	$12,000	$12,000

Settlement of Balances   Banks B, C, and F must pay their respective debit balances, or a total of $12,000, and banks A and E are entitled to receive $12,000 in the proportions indicated by their credit balances. Bank D neither pays nor receives payment since its claim against the other banks is exactly equal to its obligation to them. (Such an exact balancing of claims against obligations would rarely, if ever, occur in actual clearinghouse operations, but the possibility is included in the illustration in order to emphasize the fact that clearing is essentially the offsetting of claims and counterclaims.) Thus $117,000 of checks are cleared by the payment of only $12,000. The clearing of great volumes of checks with relatively small balances to be paid and received is a commonplace in clearinghouse operations. Moreover, as mentioned previously, the payment of the balances is usually a matter of bookkeeping entries in the deposit accounts of paying and receiving banks at the Federal Reserve and correspondent banks.

Federal reserve clearing facilities

The Federal Reserve Act, as adopted on December 23, 1913, gave the Board of Governors of the Federal Reserve System the authority to act as a clearing agent for the twelve Federal Reserve banks and to require the Reserve banks in turn to act as clearing agents for the member banks in their districts. In first exercising the latter authority, the board ordered the Reserve banks to be prepared by June 1915 to serve as clearing agencies for their member banks. The Reserve banks then announced their willingness to accept for collection checks drawn on all member banks that had agreed to *remit at par.* To remit at par means that a bank will pay the full face amount of checks drawn on it—that it will make no deduction from the face amount for any real or imaginary expenses incurred in making payment.

The original arrangement was known as the "voluntary" system in that each member bank could choose whether it would remit at par. The voluntary system was not successful, as most of the member banks wanted to retain full discretion concerning remittance charges. Most of the member banks continued to clear out-of-town checks through correspondent banks located in the large cities, as they had done before the establishment of the Federal Reserve facilities.

Present System   The voluntary system was therefore supplanted by a "compulsory" one in July 1918. The new system, which continues in operation at the present time, is compulsory only in the sense that each member bank is required to make payment at par on checks drawn on it that are presented for payment by the Reserve banks. On the other hand, the member bank may deduct remittance charges in making payment on checks drawn on it presented for payment by other organizations or individuals, but no member bank does so. Member banks have no obligation whatever to cash at face value or to receive for deposit at face value checks drawn on other banks, whether or not they are member banks. It may refuse to cash these checks or to accept them for credit to deposit accounts. Thus the student should not be surprised if a member bank deducts a "service charge" when cashing his check drawn on another bank; although he may be offended, he should know that the member bank violates no Federal Reserve rule in making such a deduction. Finally, the member bank is free to decide how extensively, if at all, it will use the Federal Reserve clearing facilities to collect payment on checks drawn on other banks.

All member banks are privileged to use the Federal Reserve clearing facilities free of charge; and nonmember banks can also obtain free clearing services by agreeing to remit at par and to keep with the Federal Reserve banks of their respective districts deposit balances sufficient to cover any charges that may be made against them for items that are uncollectible. A clearing bank can send to its Reserve bank checks drawn on banks located in any part of the United States provided that the drawee banks are committed to remit at par to the Reserve banks. The volume of checks handled in recent years by the Reserve banks is shown in Table 6-1. Think of it— billions of items with face values totaling trillions of dollars!

Checks sent to a Federal Reserve bank by a clearing bank are sorted according to the locations of the drawee banks. For those that can be presented to drawee banks quickly, as through the clearinghouse of the city where the Reserve bank is located, the clearing bank receives immediate credit on its books; for others, credit is given according to "time schedules" by which it can be deferred as long as 2 business days. In all cases, each drawee bank to which checks are presented is required to make immediate payment at par. It can pay by simply authorizing the Reserve bank to charge its deposit account on the Reserve bank's books; it can send hand-to-hand money, with the Reserve bank bearing the expenses of shipment (unlikely in most instances); or with permission, it can draw a draft on its account at a correspondent bank payable to the Reserve bank.

Clearing within a Single Reserve District   For an illustration of the use of Federal Reserve facilities for clearing checks among banks located in a

Table 6-1   **Check Clearings of the Federal Reserve Banks, 1959–1970**[a]

YEAR	NUMBER OF ITEMS (IN MILLIONS)	AMOUNT (IN BILLIONS)
1959	3258	$1130
1960	3419	1154
1961	3631	1198
1962	3873	1283
1963	4069	1364
1964	4319	1475
1965	4607	1634
1966	5021	1894
1967	5420	2044
1968	5905	2351
1969	6503	2774
1970	7158	3332

[a] Excluding United States government checks, postal money orders, and checks drawn on the Reserve banks themselves.
Source: Board of Governors of the Federal Reserve System, *Annual Reports.*

single Federal Reserve district, assume that John Jones, who lives in South Bend, Indiana, receives a check for $2000 from Richard Roe, who lives in Joliet, Illinois. Jones deposits the check in his demand deposit account at bank A in South Bend, and bank A forwards it with others to the Federal Reserve Bank of Chicago. The Federal Reserve Bank of Chicago then sends the check to bank B in Joliet on which it is drawn, and bank B, after making appropriate entries on its books, cancels it and turns it over to Roe with the monthly statement of his account. The canceled check is evidence to Roe that his obligation to Jones has been paid. As for the three banks, their assets and liabilities are affected as follows:

BANK A OF SOUTH BEND

Reserve with FR	+ 2,000	Demand deposits:	
		John Jones	+ 2,000

BANK B OF JOLIET

Reserve with FR	− 2,000	Demand deposits:	
		Richard Roe	− 2,000

FEDERAL RESERVE BANK OF CHICAGO

	Member bank reserves:	
	Bank A	+ 2,000
	Bank B	− 2,000

Interdistrict Clearing   When a Federal Reserve bank receives for clearing checks drawn on banks outside its own district, it sends them to the other

Reserve banks (or their branches) for presentation to the drawee banks.[10] But a Reserve bank that collects payments from drawee banks does not settle directly with the Reserve bank that sends its checks for collection. Instead, payments among the Reserve banks themselves are completed through the Interdistrict Settlement Fund (ISF) at the U.S. Treasury in Washington, D.C. The ISF is simply a set of accounts supervised by the Board of Governors of the Federal Reserve System in which a large portion of the Reserve banks' "gold certificates due from the Treasury" are held as deposit balances. Each Federal Reserve bank wires the Board of Governors a daily statement of the total amount of checks it has received from the other Reserve banks and their branches. This total is charged against the Reserve bank sending the report, and the other Reserve banks are credited with the amounts they have sent it. When reports have been received from all the Reserve banks, a clearing schedule similar to that given above for a clearinghouse is prepared, and transfers among the accounts of the twelve banks in the ISF are then made for the net debits and credits.

For an illustration in terms of a single check, assume that John Jones, who still lives in South Bend, receives a check for $5000 from Richard Roe, who now lives in Augusta, Maine. The check is deposited in bank A of South Bend, which forwards it to the Federal Reserve Bank of Chicago. The latter sends the check to the Federal Reserve Bank of Boston, which passes it on for payment to bank B of Augusta, the drawee. At the same time, the Federal Reserve Bank of Boston notifies the Board of Governors of the transaction (combined with all others of a similar character), and when all is done, the assets and liabilities of the four banks and the ISF are affected as follows:

BANK A OF SOUTH BEND

Reserve with FR	+5,000	Demand deposits: John Jones	+5,000

FEDERAL RESERVE BANK OF CHICAGO

Gold certificates	+5,000	Member bank reserves: Bank A	+5,000

FEDERAL RESERVE BANK OF BOSTON

Gold certificates	−5,000	Member bank reserves: Bank B	−5,000

[10]By arrangement with its district Reserve bank, a clearing bank may send checks directly to other Federal Reserve banks and their branches and, in some instances, directly to the drawee banks. It notifies the district Reserve bank of such sendings and receives credit on the latter's books in the usual way on the basis of the time schedules. When the volume of clearings warrants, moreover, a Federal Reserve bank can require clearing banks to send directly to the other Reserve banks and their branches.

BANK B OF AUGUSTA

| Reserve with FR | − 5,000 | Demand deposits: | |
| | | Richard Roe | − 5,000 |

INTERDISTRICT SETTLEMENT FUND

	Gold certificates due:	
	Reserve Bank of Chicago	+ 5,000
	Reserve Bank of Boston	− 5,000

Correspondent bank clearing facilities

Many of the large metropolitan banks strenuously compete with the Federal Reserve banks in providing clearing services as correspondents of other commercial banks. As clearing operations are expensive, the large banks do not want the clearing business for its own sake, but they strive to excel in clearing services as a means of attracting deposits from out-of-town banks. In many large banks, the deposits of out-of-town banks are as much as 30 or 40 percent of total deposits, so that they are a very important source of funds for loans and investments. Moreover, the out-of-town banks that use the clearing services of metropolitan banks are likely to go to them also for other kinds of services for which fees and commissions are charged.

In trying to gain a competitive advantage, many of the city correspondent banks have clearing rules and arrangements more liberal than those of the Federal Reserve banks. They are much less insistent on the sorting of clearing items by destination than the Reserve banks, and usually grant immediate credit for all items sent in without regard to the time required to present them to the drawee banks. Despite this competitive attitude, however, the correspondent banks themselves freely use the facilities of the Federal Reserve banks, so that great quantities of checks sent by out-of-town banks to correspondent banks eventually go through Federal Reserve channels.

THE PURCHASING POWER OF DEMAND DEPOSITS

The foregoing references to remittances at par and remittance charges indicate why it is appropriate to raise the question of whether demand deposits have purchasing power, dollar for dollar, equal to that of paper money and coins. Today the answer is generally "yes," although it has not always been so, and it is still not so in some localities—localities especially concentrated in certain Northcentral and Southeastern states.

Charges related to demand deposits

If you present a check for $100 for payment to the bank on which it is drawn, and it pays you $99.50 in paper money and coins, it is not "remitting at par." The 50-cent deduction is a "remittance charge," and it will destroy the "parity" of purchasing power between demand deposits and paper money and coins. If it is your bank that levies remittance charges or if you receive many checks drawn on banks that levy such charges, you will surely conclude that having $100 in demand deposits is not quite so good as having $100 in paper money and coins.

But you may ask: "What about the service charges I must pay my bank for having and using my checking account there, and what about the so-called collection charges that I have paid at several banks for cashing checks drawn on other banks? Do not these kinds of charges also destroy the parity of demand deposits?" As for the service charges, perhaps you have a "special" checking account in which you may keep whatever balance you wish but which you can use only by buying a pad of blank checks at 10 cents a check. Or perhaps you have a "regular" checking account of moderate size for which you must pay a dollar a month if the average or minimum balance falls below $200 or $300, and in the use of which you must pay 10 cents for each of your checks the banks pays in the course of a month over and above the "free" ones it allows you, this number being proportional to the deposit balance you maintain. Or perhaps you have a regular checking account of substantial size which the bank "analyzes" each month to determine whether or not you should be required to pay a service charge—the analysis giving you credit for the portion of your average balance on which the bank is in a position to earn interest, and charging you for the number of deposits made, the number of checks and other "cash items" in these deposits, the number of your checks paid, and the quantities of coins handled.

Nevertheless, the common opinion and the opinion of the Federal Reserve authorities is that parity is destroyed only when drawee banks fail to honor checks drawn on them at face value—when they deduct remittance charges. Service charges on checking accounts are, indeed, expenses of using them as mediums of exchange, but such charges are comparable with the expenses you would incur while driving your car here and there in order to pay bills with paper money and coins. And collection charges are essentially justifiable interest charges, because a bank that pays out paper money and coins immediately when cashing a check drawn on another bank is likely to wait 2 or more days before obtaining payment from that other bank.

Federal reserve promotion of par remittance

When the clearing facilities of the Federal Reserve System were established, thousands of banks were making deductions for remittance charges. The early clearing rules of the Federal Reserve banks stipulated that they would accept for collection only checks that were drawn on banks willing to make payment at par on presentation, and that the sending of checks by mail was to be regarded as equivalent to presentation at the counters of the drawee banks. The Reserve banks, furthermore, would not undertake to collect checks for any banks that did not agree themselves to remit at par.

Since the usefulness of the Federal Reserve clearing facilities was destined to remain limited as long as many banks refused to remit at par, drastic actions were taken by the Reserve banks to force remittance at par universally. Bundles of checks were assembled and presented by agents at the counters of obstinate banks, with demands for immediate payment in paper money and coins. Such a practice, instead of persuading banks to yield, aroused a great deal of resentment, for many bankers were quite reluctant to give up remittance charges that had been a substantial source of income. In some districts, lawsuits were brought against the Reserve banks to enjoin them from using forceful tactics, and several state legislatures passed laws that specifically authorized their chartered banks to levy remittance charges.[11] Some of the court decisions favored the Reserve banks and others went to the remittance-charging banks; at any rate, the litigation prompted the Reserve banks to adopt a policy of conciliation.

Present situation

At the present time, therefore, the Reserve banks do not attempt to compel banks to remit at par, but they perform no clearing services for nonpar banks, nor do they accept for collection checks drawn on such banks. Hence banks on the par list must find some means outside the Federal Reserve to collect payment on checks drawn on nonpar banks.

The great majority of banks, and virtually all institutions of significant size, now remit at par. At the end of 1970, however, there were still 501 banks that had not agreed to discontinue remittance charges on checks presented by the Federal Reserve banks. Most of the nonpar banks are relatively isolated institutions located in communities of less than 2500 population. As Table 6-2 shows, the nonpar banks are largely clustered in the Southeastern states and in the Dakotas.

Table 6-2   **Banks Not on Federal Reserve Par List, December 31, 1970**

LOCATION	NUMBER OF BANKS	LOCATION	NUMBER OF BANKS
Louisiana	94	Tennessee	41
North Dakota	91	North Carolina	22
South Dakota	87	Texas	20
Arkansas	68	South Carolina	17
Alabama	61	Total	501

Source: *Federal Reserve Bulletin,* February 1971, p. A97.

[11]For a summary of these actions, see *Digest of Rulings of the Board of Governors of the Federal Reserve System* (to October 1, 1937), pp. 72–76.

THE SAFETY OF DEMAND DEPOSITS

As our most important kind of money in volume and use, demand deposits have a high degree of safety, although not quite so high as that of paper money and coins. It is still possible for commercial banks to fail, and bank failures can result in the nonpayment of depositors' claims in whole or in part—virtually always, in actual experience, in partial nonpayment. Apart from the competence and integrity of bank managements, the possibilities of failure and of losses to depositors depend chiefly on four things: (1) the cash assets that banks hold, (2) their holdings of other assets, (3) whatever measures of special protection are given to some depositors, and (4) whether or not the banks have their deposits insured by the Federal Deposit Insurance Corporation. However, we should keep in mind that these sources of protection for demand depositors are shared, in most instances, with savings depositors and the holders of other classes of time deposits, and that nondeposit claims against banks, as for unpaid bills for fuel, light, and supplies, usually have claims against assets pro rata with the claims of depositors.

Cash assets or primary reserves

Most readily available to meet the claims of depositors (and nondeposit creditors) are banks' cash assets—their "primary reserves," as these assets are usually called. These cash assets or reserves consist of paper money and coins held by the banks in their own vaults and deposit balances held by them with the Federal Reserve banks and correspondent banks—balances convertible on demand into paper money and coins. Accordingly, a bank that has deposits of $1 million on its books and $150,000 of primary reserves is in a position to meet immediately the withdrawal of 15 percent of its deposits.

The federal government and all the state governments except Illinois prescribe minimum cash reserve requirements for the commercial banks in their respective jurisdictions, and they stipulate in what forms the reserves may be held. Under state law, varying proportions of the required reserves may be kept as paper money and coins and as demand balances with other banking institutions, including the Federal Reserve banks; and under federal law, applying to the member banks of the Federal Reserve System, vault cash in any amount can be counted in meeting reserve requirements, but all the rest of the required reserves must be held as demand balances with the district Reserve banks. Banks often hold more than the legal minimums—indeed, this is almost always so with most of the member banks, because they find it greatly convenient to hold balances with city correspondent banks.

Claims on other assets

Like the creditors of other kinds of business enterprises, the holders of deposits in a commercial bank are protected by all its assets—not only by its primary reserves, but also by its outstanding loans, its receivables of other kinds, its holdings of investment securities, its building and equipment, and other sundry assets. Should the bank fail, all these assets would be liquidated and distribution made to the depositors and other creditors of equal rank on a pro rata basis. Only if the proceeds of liquidation were more than enough to pay off the depositors and all nondeposit creditors in full would there be something left for the stockholders.

Safety for deposits by way of banks' noncash assets is promoted by government loan and investment regulations and by examinations conducted by the supervisory authorities. The supervisory authorities and their examiners give much attention to the quality of bank assets, holding that every dollar of deposits must be matched by more than a dollar of assets of unquestionable soundness.

Special protective provisions

Some deposits in commercial banks are given preferential treatment, so that they have a higher degree of safety than deposits not so treated. Special protection is usually provided by pledging designated assets, especially government obligations from the banks' investment portfolios, or by giving prior liens on all assets to the deposits eligible for preferential status.

In their respective spheres, federal and state laws generally authorize banks to give special protection to "public funds," that is, deposits of government bodies themselves, funds under court jurisdiction placed in deposit accounts, and deposits made by the banks' own trust departments in their banking departments. At the same time, the laws generally prescribe that government officials having custody of public funds, judges, and trust officers must not make deposits in any banks or banking departments that refuse to provide the authorized protection.

The larger the amount of a bank's deposits that are protected by specific asset pledges and first liens on all assets, the greater is the weakening of the claims of all other depositors and nondeposit creditors. Accordingly, federal and state laws generally forbid banks to provide special protection for deposits other than the classes mentioned in the preceding paragraph. But another way by which asset protection is often weakened is by the pledging of assets by banks as collateral on loans they obtain from the Federal Reserve and correspondent banks. In the event of bank failure, the Federal Reserve and correspondent banks would have first claim on the pledged collateral for the payment of the principal and interest on their loans. On the other hand, many banks borrow long-term money by selling "subordinated debentures," the contracts for which provide that, in the event of bank failure, the depositors must be paid off in full before the debenture holders get anything on their claims. In effect, the buyers of such debentures contribute to bank assets but voluntarily take positions inferior to depositors as claimants.

Deposit insurance

In the thinking of a very great majority of all bank depositors the principal source of safety for their deposits is surely deposit insurance as sponsored by the federal government and provided by its agency, the Federal Deposit Insurance Corporation (FDIC). This confidence in deposit insurance is indicated by the refusal of most people to place deposits in non-insured banks and to limit their deposits in any insured bank to no more than $20,000, the amount of the insurance coverage per depositor per insured bank. At the end of 1970, for example, deposits in 13,511 insured commercial banks amounted to $482.5 billion, while deposits in 147 non-insured commercial banks amounted to only $2.9 billion. As of June 30, 1970, the FDIC estimated that 99.0 percent of accounts in insured banks had balances not exceeding $20,000 and that the total of insured balances amounted to 63.6 percent of total deposits held by insured banks (both percentages including deposits in insured mutual savings banks).[12]

Insurance Coverage   The FDIC's insurance program provides protection not exceeding $20,000 for all deposits that any person or organization maintains "in the same right and capacity" in any insured bank.[13] A person who has a checking account of $12,000 in his own name and for his own benefit is fully insured, while one who, under the same circumstances, has a checking account of $27,000 is insured only for the amount of $20,000. Likewise, a person who has in his own name and for his own benefit a checking account of $11,000 and a savings account of $13,000, both at the same insured bank, gets insurance protection of only $20,000.

But persons and organizations can have two or more accounts in a single insured bank and have insurance coverage of $20,000 for each, provided that each is held according to a differing "right and capacity." For example, a husband and wife can have three separate accounts insured, one in the name of the husband, one in the name of the wife, and a joint account in both names. Another example is a partnership account and the separate personal accounts of the members of the partnership. Again, separate coverage is provided for an individual's personal account and for such accounts that he has in his own name but as a trustee for others; should he open ten accounts as trustee for ten different persons, each account would have full insurance coverage of $20,000. This rule applies to deposits made by the trust department of a bank in its banking department, each trust account having insurance coverage of $20,000 for its share in the total deposits

---

[12]Federal Deposit Insurance Corporation, *Annual Report*, 1970, pp. xii, xiii, 198, 199. For further reference to insured mutual savings banks, see Chapter 10.

[13]This coverage was originally $2500 when the insurance system was launched on January 1, 1934. It was raised to $5000 in mid-1934, to $10,000 in 1950, to $15,000 in 1966, and to $20,000 in December 1969.

made. Governmental bodies, too, can get insurance protection of $20,000 in each of several accounts in a single insured bank, as when officials, employees, or agents having custody of government funds in different official capacities open separate accounts.

Worth mentioning, too, is that insurance coverage is based on the deposits maintained by any person or organization in a given "right and capacity" in a single insured bank, and not on his deposits among insured banks in general. Hence a person who wants full protection for a cash balance of $80,000 that he wants to hold entirely in his own name and for his own benefit can get it by simply depositing $20,000 in each of four insured banks.

Assessment on Insured Banks   The insured banks emphasize that because they pay assessments for deposit insurance, it must not be regarded as a government handout. The assessments are payable semiannually at the rate of $\frac{1}{24}$ of 1 percent on the average of total deposits held at the beginning and end of each period of 6 months (with some prescribed adjustments). Out of its annual assessment revenue, the FDIC meets its operating expenses and makes provisions for losses, and then allocates $33\frac{1}{3}$ percent of the remaining "net assessment income" for investment in U.S. Treasury obligations to be held in its "deposit insurance fund," and $66\frac{2}{3}$ percent as a credit to the insured banks. The credit is prorated to each insured bank according to the amount of its assessment liability for the year in which the "net assessment income" was derived by the FDIC. In any year, therefore, an insured bank is assessed at the semiannual rate of $\frac{1}{24}$ of 1 percent, but its assessment is reduced by the credit apportioned to it from the preceding year. Since 1951, when credits were first allowed, they have amounted annually to more than half the total assessment liabilities of the insured banks (about 57 percent in the year 1970). Accordingly, it is appropriate to say that the cost of insurance amounts to less than half the quoted semiannual rate.

The basis of the assessment, it should be observed, is the average of total deposits on the books of the insured banks, and not merely the average total of the insured portions of accounts. Such a basis has the effect of placing a disproportionate burden on the larger banks, because accounts with balances far above $20,000 tend to concentrate with them; it has the effect of breaking down any close correlation between the assessment paid and the incidence of risk. A bank that holds a $1 million account of a business corporation pays the assessment on the full account even though only $20,000 of it is insured; while a bank whose total deposits amount to $1 million, none of them being in excess of $20,000, pays exactly the same assessment for the $1 million but has insurance coverage of the entire amount. Nevertheless, the big banks refrain from complaining about this, because they do not want to offend the smaller banks from which they hope to attract deposit balances and fee-paying service assignments as correspondents.

Confidence in Deposit Insurance   Confidence in the deposit insurance system is surely well-placed. The FDIC has met all its operating expenses and all its losses as insurer out of the income on the Treasury obligations in which its "deposit insurance fund" is chiefly invested, so that all the net assessments paid by the insured banks and the left-over interest on Treasury obligations have been added annually to the fund. At the same time, losses to depositors in "terminated cases" among 489 insured banks that failed in the whole period of the FDIC's operations from January 1, 1934, to the end of 1970 amounted to only $2,307,000.[14]

Although the deposit insurance fund—at $4380 million by the end of 1970—might seem small in relation to the huge amount of deposits in insured banks at that time, it is most unlikely that the banks holding most of these deposits will fail. The very confidence that people have in the insurance system should preclude panic withdrawals from banks even in times of rather severe economic distress. Even if the deposit insurance fund should be exhausted as a result of more bank failures than we are inclined to anticipate, the FDIC could borrow as much as $3 billion from the Treasury, an amount that the Treasury is *directed* by Congress to lend if needed "for insurance purposes." And always in the background is the thought that Congress could hardly permit the FDIC itself to fail, because its failure would be a blow of unprecedented proportions to the people's confidence in the whole financial system.

Moreover, the FDIC has many rights and powers to try to decrease its losses as an insurer: the right to serve as receiver for failed national banks as well as for failed state-chartered banks when so appointed (and many state laws specify that it is to be appointed in this capacity); the right of subrogation with respect to the claims of depositors it pays off; powers to examine insured banks and to require them to submit reports as means of judging their managers' competence, to require them to carry burglary and indemnity insurance, and to expel them for continued illegal practices or "unsafe and unsound" practices (but with depositors' balances held at the time of expulsion remaining protected for two years); and to rush to the assistance of shaky banks—"hazardous" banks, the FDIC calls them—by making deposits in them, granting loans to them, buying assets from them, or arranging their absorption by stronger banks in mergers.

Subrogation and Losses   The FDIC's right of subrogation means that it gets claims against the assets of failed banks equal to the amount of insured deposits that it pays off, and this is obviously a means by which its losses are sharply limited. To illustrate, assume that the financial position of an insured bank as indicated by its book accounts at the time of its failure was as follows:

---

[14]*Ibid.,* p. 6.

| Assets | $900,000 | Deposits | $820,000 |
| | | Stockholders' equity | 80,000 |

Assume further that all deposits of $20,000 or less, plus $20,000 for each account greater than that, totaled $750,000, so that this is the amount that the FDIC paid out as insurer. It thereby got a claim of $750,000 against the bank, and depositors had remaining claims of $70,000 on the uninsured portions of their accounts. The stockholders also had a claim of $80,000, but a claim payable only after full payment to the FDIC and the depositors. Now, assume that the books prove to be wrong, and that only $656,000 is realized on the sale of the assets. The loss on sale wipes out the stockholders' inferior claim, and leaves only enough to pay 80 cents on the dollar of depositors' claims, including that of the FDIC as subrogated creditor. Accordingly, the FDIC recovers $600,000 while taking a loss of $150,000, and the depositors recover $56,000 on the uninsured portions of their accounts, taking a loss of $14,000. John Doe who had a balance of $30,000 in his deposit account at the time of the bank's failure gets $20,000 from the FDIC and a further $8000 from the liquidation of the bank's assets, thus suffering a loss of $2000.

FOR REVIEW

1. Explain how changes in the assets, liabilities, and equity accounts of commercial banks affect the volume of demand deposits.
2. What are the principal ways by which commercial banks expand and contract the volume of demand deposits?
3. Do the customers of commercial banks have any influence on the volume of demand deposits on the books of these banks? Discuss.
4. What is a check? a cashier's check? a certified check? a bank draft?
5. Explain how the negotiability of checks enhances their convenience as means of transferring balances in demand deposit accounts.
6. To be legally negotiable, what requirement must a check satisfy?
7. Why would a merchant, in receiving checks from customers, want to to be in a position as "holder in due course"? How could he qualify to be such a holder?
8. What is meant by the clearing of checks? Why do good clearing facilities enhance the convenience of demand deposits as mediums of exchange?
9. What are the principal channels through which checks are cleared in the United States?
10. In relation to the use of demand deposits and checks, what are the distinctions between service charges, collection charges, and remittance charges?

11. What are the principal sources of safety for demand deposits? Are demand deposits as safe as Federal Reserve notes? Discuss.
12. Describe the scope of the insurance program of the Federal Deposit Insurance Corporation.
13. Do depositors in insured banks that fail lose all the balances in their accounts in excess of $20,000? Explain.

PROBLEMS

1. Show in T accounts how the assets and liabilities of the Merchants National Bank would be affected by each of the following transactions. For all expense and income items, use an undivided-profits account, even though in actual practice other accounts would be used temporarily for these items.

   A. Holders of demand deposit accounts deposit $12,000 in paper money and coins.
   B. Holders of demand deposit accounts deposit $400,000 of checks drawn on out-of-town banks on which Merchants collects payment through the Federal Reserve bank in its district by a credit to its reserve account there.
   C. A demand depositor opens a savings account by drawing a check of $8000 payable to Merchants itself.
   D. Merchants issues a cashier's check for $15,000 in payment for office equipment.
   E. Merchants discounts a customer's $25,000 1-year promissory note at 6 percent, crediting his demand deposit account for the proceeds.
   F. A customer offers for discount a promissory note for $40,000 due in 1 year and bearing interest at 6 percent received from one of his own debtors. Merchants discounts the note at 8 percent and credits the customer's demand deposit account for the proceeds.
   G. The borrower in transaction E pays off his obligation at its maturity by drawing a check for $25,000 on his demand deposit account payable to Merchants.
   H. Merchants buys Treasury obligations at their par value of $120,000, paying by drawing a check on its reserve account at the Federal Reserve bank in its district.
   I. Of the securities bought in transaction H, Merchants later sells $70,000 face amount at $70,500 to one of its demand depositors. The buyer pays by drawing a check payable to Merchants.

2. Indicate in T accounts how the assets and liabilities of the commercial banks, the Federal Reserve banks, and the Interdistrict Settle-

ment Fund would be affected, if at all, by each of the following transactions. Assume that payments due to and from commercial banks are made and received through reserve accounts at the Federal Reserve banks.

A.   For bank A located in its district, the Federal Reserve Bank of Atlanta collects payment on $500,000 of checks drawn on bank B, which is also located in the Atlanta district.

B.   For bank C located in its district, the Federal Reserve Bank of Kansas City collects payment through the Federal Reserve Bank of Minneapolis on $700,000 of checks drawn on bank D, located in the Minneapolis district.

3–5.   At the time of its suspension for insolvency, each of the three insured banks named below had asset, deposit, and capital accounts on their books as indicated in the column under its name. Also entered in this column is the total amount of deposits the FDIC paid off as insurer, as well as the total amount of cash it realized in liquidating the bank's assets in its role as receiver.

	(3) PEOPLES NATIONAL BANK	(4) MECHANICS STATE BANK	(5) NATIONAL BANK OF BANNON
Assets	$900,000	$5,200,000	$8,000,000
Deposits	820,000	4,800,000	7,400,000
Capital accounts	80,000	400,000	600,000
Deposit payoff by FDIC	700,000	4,200,000	6,300,000
Cash realized in liquidation	738,000	3,600,000	4,440,000

In each instance, state how much of the cash realized in liquidation would go to the depositors of the bank on the uninsured portions of their balances, the bank's stockholders, and the FDIC. Also state in each instance how much in total would be recovered by a depositor who had $30,000 on deposit at the time of the bank's suspension.

CHAPTER 7

THE EXPANSION AND CONTRACTION
OF DEMAND DEPOSITS

It was explained in the preceding chapter that demand deposits are "created" by the commercial banks through their granting of loans and buying investment securities. Nevertheless, the capacity of the commercial banks to create demand deposits through lending and investing is always closely limited in relationship to the amount of their cash assets, that is, their "primary reserves," the portions of these cash assets they are required by law to hold as percentages of their demand and time deposits, and whatever additional portions they decide that they must hold to meet withdrawal demands or for other reasons of safety or convenience. The cash assets or primary reserves consist of paper money and coins on hand, demand deposit balances or "reserve accounts" at the Federal Reserve banks, and demand deposit balances at domestic correspondent banks.

For the individual commercial bank, lending and investing capacity at any time is generally limited to the amount of its *excess reserves*, that is, the amount of its cash assets over and above those that it needs to meet the legal reserve requirements and those that it decides it must hold additionally for safety or convenience. This is a fact because the bank must expect to lose cash assets as it pays for securities and as borrowers withdraw the proceeds of loans by writing checks. But if a commercial bank can lend or invest only the amount of its excess cash reserves, it would not seem to be creating anything, just as a student would not seem to be creating anything if he lends an extra 10-dollar bill to a classmate.

Nevertheless, we have a paradox: *the system of commercial banks can do what the individual commercial bank cannot do*. It can "blow up" a dollar of excess reserves into several dollars of new demand deposits. The cash assets that the individual bank loses by lending and investing will generally be acquired by other commercial banks, which then acquire new lending and investing capacity; and when these latter banks also lose cash assets by expanding their loans and investments, still other banks are likely to acquire them. And so on, theoretically, to infinity. If, to satisfy legal reserve requirements and for additional safety and convenience, commercial banks generally hold reserves equal to 10 percent of their demand deposits, the *system* can expand demand deposits by an amount equal to ten times excess reserves; if 12½ percent, eight times; if 20 percent, five times; if 25 percent, four times, and so on, with the multiplier always equal to the reciprocal of the percentage chosen. It is because of the "blow-up" processes of the *system*, therefore, that commercial banks are said to be creators of money in the form of demand deposits.

THE PROCESS OF EXPANSION

To illustrate how it is possible for the commercial banking system to expand demand deposits through lending by a multiple of excess reserves, partial balance sheets of four banks are presented below and are subsequently adjusted to show the results of a series of assumed transactions. Cash in vault, demand balances at correspondent banks, and reserve balances at the Federal Reserve banks are entered collectively as primary reserves, and the loans and discounts and demand deposits of the four banks start at identical levels simply for convenience and clarity in exposition.

BANK A

Primary reserves	250,000	Demand deposits	800,000
Loans and discounts	500,000		

BANK B

Primary reserves	160,000	Demand deposits	800,000
Loans and discounts	500,000		

BANK C

Primary reserves	160,000	Demand deposits	800,000
Loans and discounts	500,000		

BANK D

Primary reserves	160,000	Demand deposits	800,000
Loans and discounts	500,000		

Let us assume that, as a matter of fixed policy, each of these banks maintains a 20 percent reserve against demand deposits. It is apparent, then, that banks B, C, and D have no excess reserves, for the primary reserves of each are exactly equal to 20 percent of its demand deposits. Bank A, however, has excess reserves of $90,000 as it needs only $160,000 of reserves against its deposits of $800,000.

Assume, then, that bank A, having no reason to keep the excess reserves idle, decides to lend $90,000 to some of its customers who have applied for loans. The loans are made by adding $90,000 to the customers' deposit accounts, and the pertinent accounts then appear as follows:

BANK A

| Primary reserves | 250,000 | Demand deposits | 890,000 |
| Loans and discounts | 590,000 | | |

But as the borrowers do not negotiate the loans to let the additional balances lie unused in their deposit accounts, it can be assumed that they draw $90,000 of checks to meet business expenditures. It may be further assumed, for the sake of simplicity, that all the checks drawn are received by customers of bank B, who deposit them in their accounts. Bank B sends the checks for payment to A and the latter pays out of its primary reserves. The balance sheets of the two banks are affected as follows:

BANK A

| Primary reserves | 160,000 | Demand deposits | 800,000 |
| Loans and discounts | 590,000 | | |

BANK B

| Primary reserves | 250,000 | Demand deposits | 890,000 |
| Loans and discounts | 500,000 | | |

Despite the withdrawal of $90,000, bank A remains in a safe position because its primary reserves are exactly equal to 20 percent of its demand deposits. Bank B, however, now has excess reserves: it needs reserves of $178,000 against demand deposits of $890,000; hence the excess amounts to $72,000. Bank B, let us say, lends $72,000 to customers by increasing their deposit accounts. The pertinent accounts then appear in its balance sheet as follows:

BANK B

| Primary reserves | 250,000 | Demand deposits | 962,000 |
| Loans and discounts | 572,000 | | |

Again it is logical to assume that the customers want to make immediate use of the money borrowed, so that they draw checks against their accounts for $72,000. The payees deposit the checks at bank C, it collects payment from B, and the balance sheets of the two banks become

BANK B

| Primary reserves | 178,000 | Demand deposits | 890,000 |
| Loans and discounts | 572,000 | | |

BANK C

| Primary reserves | 232,000 | Demand deposits | 872,000 |
| Loans and discounts | 500,000 | | |

Bank B's primary reserve position is satisfactory as the 20 percent requirement is fulfilled; but bank C now has excess reserves of $57,600 (actual reserves of $232,000 less required reserves of $174,400). Bank C, therefore, grants loans of $57,600, and its balance sheet then appears as follows:

BANK C

| Primary reserves | 232,000 | Demand deposits | 929,600 |
| Loans and discounts | 557,600 | | |

The proceeds of the loans are drawn upon in full and the checks on bank C are deposited at bank D, and D collects payment from C, so that the balance sheets of these two banks appear as follows:

BANK C

| Primary reserves | 174,400 | Demand deposits | 872,000 |
| Loans and discounts | 557,600 | | |

BANK D

| Primary reserves | 217,600 | Demand deposits | 857,600 |
| Loans and discounts | 500,000 | | |

Bank C's reserves are now equal to 20 percent of its demand deposits, and it can make no further loans on the basis of its present resources; but as D's required reserves amount to $171,520, and its actual reserves are $217,600, it is in a position to lend the difference, which amounts to $46,080. If the loans are granted and the checks are deposited in bank E, the deposits and primary reserves of that bank will be increased by $46,080.

Infinite series of new deposits

Let us see what has happened thus far. On the basis of the excess primary reserves of $90,000 originally held by bank A, the demand deposits of bank B were expanded by $90,000, those of C by $72,000, those of D by $57,600, and those of E by $46,080. Thus by the independent action of the first four of these banks, demand deposits were expanded in the amount of $265,680 on the basis of only $90,000 of excess reserves as originally held by A. Further steps in the expansion, as well as the over-all process of expansion, are shown in the table on the following page.

Such an unlimited succession of figures for new deposits, in which each amount is equal to a fixed percentage of the preceding amount, is what mathematicians call an infinite geometrical progression or series. The total

	RECEIVES DEPOSITS OF	SETS ASIDE RESERVES OF	LENDS
Bank A			$ 90,000
Bank B	$ 90,000	$18,000	72,000
Bank C	72,000	14,400	57,600
Bank D	57,600	11,520	46,080
Bank E	46,080	9,216	36,864
Bank F	36,864	7,373	29,491
Bank G	29,491	5,898	23,593
Other banks (in turn)	117,965	23,593	94,372
Totals	450,000	90,000	450,000

of the progression in our illustrative case,[1] it will be noted, comes to $450,-000, which is five times the first figure of the progression, $90,000. As long, indeed, as each figure is equal to 80 percent of the preceding figure, the sum of any such progression will always be equal to five times the first figure. Thus we are able to say, as before, that any excess reserves in the commercial banking system can be the basis of a fivefold creation of demand deposits if a reserve ratio of 20 percent is maintained.

Criticism

Because the illustration has been simplified for reasons of clarity, certain objections may be offered. In the first place, we know that the demand for loans at each bank would not always be exactly equal to that bank's excess reserves. This objection is not valid, however, as we are merely investigating the banks' capacity to expand demand deposits, but not necessarily the probabilities of expansion.

A second objection is that all the checks drawn against bank A are not likely to be deposited in B. Granted. But wherever the checks are deposited, they will provide, not one bank, but many banks with increased primary reserves totalling $90,000. Some of the checks, in fact, may be redeposited at A itself, but in that event A would discover that its primary reserves had not been drawn to the extent anticipated. It would therefore be in a position to make new loans in the amount of the excess reserves remaining.

A third objection, stated in terms of the illustration, is that the recipients of the $90,000 of checks drawn upon bank A are likely to be just as reluctant to let their deposits lie idle at B as were the drawers of the checks, that is, the borrowers from A. In consequence, B must be prepared to pay out the entire $90,000—which it could not do without having its reserves sadly de-

---

[1]The sum of an infinite geometrical progression is found by the formula $s = a/(1 - r)$, where a is the first term of the series and r is the ratio (less than 1) of each term to the preceding one. Substituting figures from the illustration, we get: $s = \$90,000/(1 - 0.80) = \$450,000$.

pleted if it persists in lending $72,000. This appears to be a potent objection, but it arises because the illustration was simplified. If the $90,000 had been used to buy merchandise from many firms and had been deposited in small amounts in many banks in various parts of the country, as would probably be the case, the new deposits would immediately assume a stable character —a character in keeping with the normal growth of deposits in a period of expanding bank lending. It is true that the many firms with deposits in many banks would draw checks against the $90,000 of new deposits, but the same firms and others would be making deposits of checks received from people borrowing at other institutions throughout the banking system. In this way, checks drawn against individual banks would generally be offset by other checks deposited with them, so that no single bank need fear a large adverse clearing balance.

Expansion beyond the amount of excess reserves

If all the banks of the system are expanding their loans in an amount beyond their excess reserves, any individual bank will not place itself in a dangerous position by adopting the same policy. If all banks lend to the extent of 125 percent of their excess reserves, it is probable that none will be dangerously affected because checks drawn on the various banks against the new deposits will tend to balance each other in the clearing process. Checks for larger amounts will be drawn against each bank, but in turn, checks for larger amounts will be reaching the depositors of each bank.

The fact remains, however, that the banking system as a whole continues to be restricted by the amount of primary reserves available and the desired reserve ratio; in other words, loans may be made at a more rapid pace, but new demand deposits may not be created to a greater extent than five times the excess reserves if the banks want to maintain a reserve ratio of 20 percent, ten times if 10 percent, and so on. Moreover, the individual bank ordinarily does not know at what rate other banks are expanding their loans.

By way of summary, it is worth repeating that, in general, a bank cannot lend more than the amount of its excess reserves because it must expect checks to be drawn against the full amount of its loans. A bank may expect that some of the checks will come back to it for deposit, but it has no assurance that that will happen. If, in the illustration, bank A had loaned $120,000 instead of $90,000, and if the full amount of the loans had been drawn out, the bank would have been left with only $130,000 of primary reserves— considerably less than the required 20 percent.

Expansion by means of bank investments

Although the foregoing illustration was presented entirely in terms of the lending activities of banks A, B, C, and so on, it is important to emphasize that the purchase of investment securities by the commercial banks has identical effects upon demand deposit expansion. Expansion by way of investment deserves emphasis because the total investment holdings of the commercial banks have recently been averaging about 30 percent of their total loans and investments. If bank A were to buy $90,000 worth of securities from its customers, giving them credit in deposit accounts, if the customers drew checks to the full amount of the new deposits, and if the payees of the checks deposited them at bank B, B would have $90,000 of new deposits and excess reserves of $72,000, which it also could use for the purchase of securities. If it did so use them, bank C would gain new excess reserves, which would be available for investment, and so on.

The process of expansion, moreover, does not vary in any essential aspect when banks buy securities in the open market rather than directly from their own customers. Were bank A to purchase $90,000 worth of securities in the open market, it would be likely to make payment by means of a bank draft drawn on its correspondent bank or on its Federal Reserve bank. But the payee of the draft—the seller of the securities—would deposit it in his bank somewhere in the country; and when the depository bank had sent the draft through for payment, A would lose $90,000 of primary reserves and the depository bank would gain an equal amount—of which $72,000 would be excess or free reserves available for lending or investment.

THE PROCESS OF CONTRACTION

A net loss of primary reserves from the commercial banking system, occurring at a time when it has no excess reserves and no access to new reserves, necessarily leads to a multiple contraction of demand deposits if the customary reserve ratio is to be maintained. Likewise, a multiple contraction of demand deposits must take place if the commercial banks want to build up their reserve ratios—as in times of banking panic—and if, at the same time, they can obtain no outside assistance, as from the Federal Reserve banks.

Suppose that a group of commercial banks—A, B, C, and so on—have individually $160,000 of primary reserves, $500,000 of investments, and $800,000 of demand deposits, and suppose that depositors at bank A withdraw $90,000 of hand-to-hand money. The pertinent accounts in bank A's balance sheet then appear as follows:

BANK A

Primary reserves	70,000	Demand deposits	710,000
Investments	500,000		

Let us assume, as before, that each of the banks wants to maintain a reserve ratio of 20 percent. Thus A needs reserves of $142,000 and as it has only $70,000 remaining, it is deficient in the amount of $72,000. It therefore sells $72,000 of investment securities and these are purchased by a depositor at bank B who draws a check against that bank in payment. Bank A presents the check to B and the latter pays out of its primary reserves. The affected accounts in the statements of the two banks then become

BANK A

| Primary reserves | 142,000 | Demand deposits | 710,000 |
| Investments | 428,000 | | |

BANK B

| Primary reserves | 88,000 | Demand deposits | 728,000 |
| Investments | 500,000 | | |

By the sale of some of its investment securities, A has thus been able to restore itself to a satisfactory position, but B is now deficient in reserves. It should have reserves of $145,600, but its actual reserves amount to only $88,000. To make up the difference, it sells $57,600 of investment securities and these are bought by a depositor at bank C who draws a check in payment. Bank B presents the check to C and receives payment, following which the pertinent accounts of the two banks appear as follows:

BANK B

| Primary reserves | 145,600 | Demand deposits | 728,000 |
| Investments | 442,400 | | |

BANK C

| Primary reserves | 102,400 | Demand deposits | 742,400 |
| Investments | 500,000 | | |

Bank B's reserve position is now satisfactory, but C finds itself with a deficiency of $46,080, since it needs reserves of $148,480 and has only $102,400. It therefore sells $46,080 of investment securities.

And so it goes. It is hardly necessary to carry the illustration further, for it should already be apparent that the process of contraction follows exactly the same course—in reverse—and involves exactly the same figures as the process of expansion, which was analyzed at greater length. It should be apparent, too, that the over-all result must be the same in both expansion and contraction: that, in terms of the illustration, the availability of $90,000 of excess primary reserves makes possible an expansion of $450,000 of demand deposits, while the loss of $90,000 of needed reserves requires the elimination of $450,000 of demand deposits.

THE SOURCES OF COMMERCIAL BANK
PRIMARY RESERVES

In observing thus far the process by which demand deposits may be expanded throughout the commercial banking system in an amount several times the available excess reserves, we merely assumed that $90,000 of excess reserves were originally held by bank A. It now becomes necessary to inquire into the forces or factors that determine the volume of primary reserves the commercial banking system will have at any given time, and that, by expanding and contracting, will cause changes in this volume of reserves. The importance of such an inquiry can be realized when we reflect that any event that introduces new primary reserves into the banking system is capable of starting the whole process of demand deposit expansion; and that, conversely, any event that extinguishes needed primary reserves tends to cause a multiple contraction of demand deposits.

Commercial bank holdings of primary reserves at given times and changes therein over periods of time are determined by the dollar values of what are called "factors supplying reserve funds" and "factors absorbing reserve funds," the magnitudes of which are published by the Board of Governors of the Federal Reserve System on four bases: weekly averages of daily figures ending with Wednesday, the Wednesday figures themselves, monthly averages of daily figures for each calendar month, and end-of-the-month figures.[2] The supplying factors are so named because an expansion in any of them results in *an increase of equal amount* in commercial bank primary reserves; and the absorbing factors, because an expansion in any of them results in *a decrease of equal amount* in commercial bank primary reserves. But all the factors of both classes can also decrease and thereby cause results opposite the results of increases. Decreases in supplying factors cause equal decreases in commercial bank primary reserves, and decreases in absorbing factors cause equal increases in these primary reserves.[3] Nevertheless, because there are thirteen factors in all, as listed below, the effects of changes in any one factor or in a group of factors may be offset in whole or in part by changes in other single factors or groups.

The factors supplying reserve funds are the following:

1. United States government securities held by the Federal Reserve banks.[4]
2. Discounts and advances of the Federal Reserve banks.

---

[2]The importance that the Federal Reserve authorities themselves ascribe to the factors supplying and absorbing reserve funds is indicated by their presentation of the factor reports as the lead-off tables in the huge array of tabular data published in each monthly issue of the *Federal Reserve Bulletin*.

[3]The effect on primary reserves of changes in the factors can be best understood perhaps if we keep in mind the algebraic law of signs. The factors supplying reserve funds are plus items (+), and the factors absorbing reserve funds, minus items (−). Thus an increase in a supplying factor (+ +) or a decrease in an absorbing factor (− −) has the effect of expanding reserves; and a decrease in a supplying factor (− +) or an increase in an absorbing factor (+ −) has the effect of reducing reserves.

[4]Including securities of federal agencies other than the U.S. Treasury. Although the Federal Reserve banks have authority to invest in the debt issues of various federal agencies, such as the federal home loan banks, they generally confine their investment entirely or almost entirely to "direct" Treasury obligations.

3. Float.
4. Other Federal Reserve bank assets.
5. Gold stock.
6. SDR certificate account.
7. Treasury currency outstanding.

The factors absorbing reserve funds are the following:

1. Currency in circulation.
2. Treasury cash holdings.
3. Treasury deposits at the Federal Reserve banks.
4. Foreign deposits at the Federal Reserve banks.
5. Other deposits at the Federal Reserve banks.
6. Other Federal Reserve bank liabilities and capital.

Federal reserve reports on the factors

The factor reports of the Federal Reserve are designed to show how the magnitude of the factors supplying and absorbing reserve funds in combination determine the amount of the *reserve balances of member banks on deposit at the Federal Reserve banks.* These reserve balances of member banks, in turn, are one of the two principal determinants of the capacity of the whole commercial banking system to create new money in the form of demand deposits (with reserve requirements and needs as the second). This is so because the member banks of the Federal Reserve System—all commercial banks having federal charters, that is, national banks and almost all of the larger state-chartered banks[5]—consistently hold more than 80 percent of the assets and deposits of the whole system. It is so also because these reserve balances of the member banks determine their capacity to get and hold paper money and coins as primary reserves of a different form, as well as to supply paper money and coins (as reserves) to nonmember banks for which they are correspondents.

Only to the extent that commercial banks count as primary reserves the demand balances they keep with other commercial banks does the direct influence of the factors supplying and absorbing reserve funds on the money-creation capacities of the commercial banking system break down. If bank A sends a quantity of paper money and coins to bank B for deposit, it recognizes no change in the amount of its primary reserves, while B regards this money as an addition to its own reserves; yet there is no accompanying change in any of the supplying and absorbing factors. Also deserving mention is the fact that the shifting of deposits and reserves from bank to bank in the commercial banking system, and the shifting of balances between demand and time accounts, cause changes more or less continuously in the amount of excess reserves without affecting the total volume of reserves.

---

[5]For additional details about the member banks, see Chapters 9 and 16.

If checks drawn on banks subject to a 17 percent reserve requirement are deposited in and cleared by banks subject to a 12 percent requirement, with a resulting shift of reserves, the amount of excess reserves is obviously increased. Similarly, excess reserves are increased if customers who have balances in demand deposit accounts subject to a 17 percent reserve requirement transfer them to time accounts subject to a 6 percent requirement.

Illustrations of factor effects

In order to show how the factors supplying and absorbing reserve funds combine to determine the volume of member bank reserve balances at the Reserve banks, Table 7-1 presents end-of-the-month statistics of the factors

Table 7-1   **Factors and Reserves, January 31, March 31, and August 31, 1970 (in millions of dollars)**

	JANUARY 31	MARCH 31	AUGUST 31
Factors supplying reserve funds:			
United States government securities held by Federal Reserve banks	55,739	55,785	59,978
Discounts and advances of Federal Reserve banks	1,565	684	538
Float	2,544	2,827	1,510
Other Federal Reserve bank assets	2,012	2,191	1,187
Gold stock	11,367	11,367	11,367
SDR certificate account	200	400	400
Treasury currency outstanding	6,853	6,911	7,045
Total	80,280	80,165	82,025
Factors absorbing reserve funds:			
Currency in circulation	51,869	52,701	54,669
Treasury cash holdings	640	566	468
Treasury deposits at Federal Reserve banks	1,127	1,192	1,056
Foreign deposits at Federal Reserve banks	152	200	173
Other deposits at Federal Reserve banks	692	839	750
Other Federal Reserve liabilities and capital	2,163	2,172	2,352
Total	56,643	57,670	59,468
Member bank reserves at Federal Reserve banks	23,637	22,495	22,557

Source: *Federal Reserve Bulletin,* April, June, and October 1970, pp. A4–A5.

and reserves for the three months January, March, and August 1970. It will be noted that in each column the total of the factors supplying reserve funds minus the total of the absorbing factors equals the amount of member bank reserve balances at the Reserve banks. Between January 31 and August 31, member bank reserve balances decreased from $23,637 million to $22,557 million, for a net decrease of $1080 million. How can we explain this decrease? We can do so by an analysis as presented in Table 7-2.

Table 7-2   **Changes in Factors and Reserves, January 31 to August 31, 1970 (in millions of dollars)**

	NET CHANGE[a]	CHANGES SUPPLYING RESERVES	CHANGES ABSORBING RESERVES
Factors supplying reserve funds:			
United States government securities held by Federal Reserve banks	4239	4239	
Discounts and advances of Federal Reserve banks	− 1027		1027
Float	− 1034		1034
Other Federal Reserve bank assets	− 825		825
Gold stock	0		
SDR certificate account	200	200	
Treasury currency outstanding	192	192	
Factors absorbing reserve funds:			
Currency in circulation	2800		2800
Treasury cash holdings	− 172	172	
Treasury deposits at Federal Reserve banks	− 71	71	
Foreign deposits at Federal Reserve banks	21		21
Other deposits at Federal Reserve banks	58		58
Other Federal Reserve liabilities and capital	189		189
Total		4874	5954
Net decrease in member bank reserves		1080	

a Differences between amounts in first and third columns of Table 7-1.

Factors supplying reserve funds

United States Government Securities Held by Federal Reserve Banks   Federal Reserve bank holdings of United States government securities may well be described as the most important of the thirteen factors that affect commercial bank primary reserves, because increases and decreases in these holdings are the principal means by which the Federal Reserve controls the volume of reserves and therefore the volume of money in circulation.[6] Because of this importance, Federal Reserve transactions in Treasury obli-

---

[6]It is important to emphasize that the transactions referred to here involve the *ownership* of Treasury obligations by the Federal Reserve banks. The Reserve banks also buy and sell government securities as fiscal agents of the Treasury (see Chapter 20), but securities so handled never appear as assets on the Federal Reserve books.

gations are closely coordinated. They are effected by the Federal Reserve Bank of New York for what is called the "system open market account" (SOMA) under the direction of the Federal Open Market Committee (FOMC), which is composed of the seven members of the Board of Governors of the Federal Reserve System and five presidents of Reserve banks.[7] Thus the Reserve banks neither decide on nor carry through transactions in Treasury obligations individually.

In buying and selling Treasury obligations for the portfolios of the twelve reserve banks, SOMA confines its dealings to a small group of large nonbank dealers that "make markets" in these obligations and to a small group of large metropolitan banks known as "dealer banks"—about twenty dealers and dealer banks in all. But the nonbank dealers and dealer banks, in turn, buy and sell Treasury obligations in transactions with banks and other investors in all parts of the country, so that reserves created by SOMA purchases may be acquired by banks in many parts of the country, and SOMA sales may cause reserve losses to banks in many areas.

The creation and extinguishment of commercial bank reserves through SOMA transactions is direct and immediate. When SOMA buys from dealer banks, it simply credits the reserve accounts of these banks for the cost of the securities. But when it buys from nonbank dealers, the credits also go to the reserve accounts of member banks, with the dealers, in turn, getting credits of equal amount in their demand deposit accounts on the books of these banks. (Each dealer has an arrangement with a member bank for the handling of his SOMA transactions through the bank's reserve account.) To illustrate, assume that SOMA buys Treasury obligations at a cost of $250,000.[8] Whether it buys from a dealer bank or a nonbank dealer, the effect on the books of the Federal Reserve banks collectively is as follows:[9]

FEDERAL RESERVE BANKS

United States		Deposits:	
government securities	+ 250,000	Member bank reserves	+ 250,000

If it is a dealer bank that is selling the securities to SOMA, the effect on the books of the commercial banking system is this:

---

[7]For further details on the composition and functions of the Federal Open Market Committee, see Chapter 16, and on the operations of the system open market account, Chapter 20.

[8]Although changes in the factors as they affect the books of the Federal Reserve banks usually involve millions of dollars, and often billions, it will be convenient to use rather modest figures in the illustrations.

[9]The student will find it advantageous to examine immediately the complete statement of the twelve Federal Reserve banks combined as presented in Chapter 17. He should also refer to it from time to time in the course of the discussion in the remainder of this chapter, noting the tie-ins between the factors and Federal Reserve assets and liabilities.

COMMERCIAL BANKING SYSTEM

Reserve at FR	+250,000	
United States government securities	−250,000	

And if it is a nonbank dealer who sells to SOMA, the effect is this:

COMMERCIAL BANKING SYSTEM

Reserve at FR	+250,000	Demand deposits	+250,000

If, on the other hand, SOMA sells Treasury obligations from the portfolios of the Federal Reserve banks at a price of $250,000 the effect on their books is the reverse of that given above; and the effect on the books of the commercial banking system is the reverse of one or the other of the effects of its purchase, as shown above, depending on whether the buyer is a dealer bank or a nonbank dealer.

Discounts and Advances of the Federal Reserve Banks   The relationship between changes in the volume of discounts and advances of the Federal Reserve banks and changes in commercial bank reserve balances is also direct. This is necessarily so because almost all discounts and advances are loans granted by the Reserve banks to member banks. As the borrowing banks usually ask to have the amounts of the loans credited to their reserve accounts, expansions in "discounts and advances" of the Reserve banks and in the reserve accounts usually take place in identical amounts simultaneously. The borrowing banks are not even required to sign promissory notes, since they have standing commitments to the Reserve banks to repay all loans taken plus interest at the "discount rate" the Reserve banks have in effect. Assume, for example, that the Reserve banks grant loans to member banks of $100,000 with the member banks asking for credits to their reserve accounts. The asset and liability accounts of the Reserve banks (collectively) and the commercial banking system would be affected as follows:

FEDERAL RESERVE BANKS

Discounts and advances	+100,000	Deposits: Member bank reserves	+100,000

COMMERCIAL BANKING SYSTEM

Reserve at FR	+100,000	Liabilities for borrowed money	+100,000

In repaying loans due the Federal Reserve banks, the member banks customarily have the payments, including interest, charged against their reserve balances. Continuing the illustration and assuming that the payments, including interest of, say, $600, are so charged, the effects of repayment on the books of the Federal Reserve banks and the commercial banking system would be as follows:

FEDERAL RESERVE BANKS

Discounts and advances	− 100,000	Deposits:	
		Member bank reserves	− 100,600
		Surplus	+ 600

COMMERCIAL BANKING SYSTEM

Reserve at FR	− 100,600	Liabilities for borrowed money	− 100,000
		Undivided profits	− 600

We observe that the commercial banking system suffers a net loss of $600 of reserves as a result of the two transactions of borrowing and repayment, a loss attributable obviously to the interest charged. In terms of the factors supplying and absorbing funds, however, this reduction in reserves *is caused by* the increase in the absorbing factor "other Federal Reserve liabilities and capital." Surplus is a capital account on the Federal Reserve books, and as such, it is a component of "other Federal Reserve liabilities and capital"; its increase by $600, therefore, causes reserves to fall by the same amount. (Actually, of course, the credit to surplus on the Federal Reserve books and the debit to undivided profits on the books of the commercial banking system would come from their respective "profit and loss" accounts after combination with all other income and expense items for the pertinent accounting periods.)

Float   The Federal Reserve banks create and extinguish commercial bank reserves in connection with their services in clearing checks for both member and nonmember banks as described in Chapter 6. They create reserves when they credit the accounts of banks that send in checks for collection— "sending banks," let us call them—before they themselves have collected payment on these checks from the banks on which they are drawn—"drawee banks." And they extinguish reserves when, in any period, their collections from drawee banks exceed the credits they are currently giving to sending banks. At all times, however, the Reserve banks are late in their collection of payment from drawee banks in relation to their "time schedules" for credits to sending banks,[10] so that there is always outstanding a net amount of reserves created in the clearing operations. This net amount is known as the "float." On a daily basis in recent years, the float has usually been well over $1 billion and on quite a few days it has gone over $3 billion.

An illustration should clarify the process of reserve creation in clearing operations. Assume that member banks send in $80,000 of checks that, ac-

---

[10]See Chapter 6.

cording to the time schedules, are subject to deferred credit of 2 business days. An entry is made on the books of the Federal Reserve banks as follows:

FEDERAL RESERVE BANKS

Cash items in process		Deferred availability	
of collection	+80,000	cash items	+80,000

Now assume that at the expiration of 2 business days only $50,000 of the checks have been presented to the drawee banks, and that, for that amount, they have authorized the Reserve banks to reduce their reserve balances to effect payment. The following changes thus take place on the Federal Reserve books and on the books of the sending and drawee banks:

FEDERAL RESERVE BANKS

Cash items in process		Deposits:	
of collection	−50,000	Member bank reserves	+30,000
		Deferred availability	
		cash items	−80,000

SENDING BANKS

Reserve at FR	+80,000		
Cash items in process			
of collection	−80,000		

DRAWEE BANKS

Reserve at FR	−50,000	Demand deposits	−50,000

Thus the sending banks gain $80,000 of reserves while the drawee banks lose only $50,000, so that the commercial banking system has a net gain of $30,000. The Federal Reserve banks will quickly catch up on this transaction, perhaps in another day or two, but they will be falling behind simultaneously on other such transactions. Hence the float, though having a wide range of variations, is a continuous source of commercial bank primary reserves. The amount at any time, one will have observed, is the net difference between the Federal Reserve asset account *cash items in process of collection* and the liability account *deferred availability cash items*. In the illustration, the first of these accounts was reduced to $30,000 while the latter was reduced to zero.

Other Federal Reserve Bank Assets As a factor supplying reserve funds, *other Federal Reserve bank assets* include foreign currencies at their dollar values, the banking premises of the Reserve banks (land, buildings, and equipment), and bankers' acceptances, as well as many miscellaneous asset items of no particular importance to our study in this chapter, such as accrued interest receivable and prepaid expenses.[11]

When the Federal Reserve Bank of New York buys bankers' acceptances from dealers, it pays for them by issuing officers' checks (similar to the cashiers' checks issued by commercial banks), which the dealers deposit in their accounts at commercial banks. The commercial banks, in turn, send the checks to the Reserve bank for credit to their reserve accounts. When acceptances mature, the Federal Reserve Bank of New York presents them to the accepting banks for payment, and the latter typically direct that payment be taken by charges against their reserve accounts. Thus the effects of transactions in bankers' acceptances on reserves parallel the effects of transactions in Treasury obligations. In a similar way, commercial bank reserves are created when any Federal Reserve bank buys, say, office machines and pays by issuing an officers' check, and when the seller deposits the check at a commercial bank and the commercial bank sends it to a Reserve bank for credit in its reserve account.

Much more important among the "other assets" of the Reserve banks in recent years have been foreign currencies. Carried at their dollar values on the books of the Reserve banks, these currencies are chiefly acquired in "swaps" with foreign central banks, as described in Chapter 25. A swap may be initiated by the Federal Reserve when a supply of a given country's currency is needed to buy back excess supplies of dollars being acquired by its central bank, or it may be intiated by a foreign central bank because it needs dollars to sell to its commercial banks for payments to be made to American exporters and other claimants. For the purposes of this discussion, let us take a transaction of the second type by assuming that a foreign central bank initiates a swap valued at $600,000. In effect, it sells $600,000 worth of its currency for an increase in its deposit account of $600,000 at the Federal Reserve banks, so that their asset and liability accounts are affected as follows:

FEDERAL RESERVE BANKS

Foreign currencies[12]	+ 600,000	Deposits:	
		Foreign	+ 600,000

In the first instance, therefore, the increase in other Federal Reserve bank assets is exactly offset by the increase in the absorbing factor "foreign de-

---

[11]In its reports of the factors, the Board of Governors does not include holdings of bankers' acceptances among "other Federal Reserve bank assets" but simply adds them into the total of "Reserve bank credit outstanding" with a footnote so saying. But there is no good reason why holdings of bankers' acceptances should be orphaned in this way. For a description of bankers' acceptances as financing instruments and their market, see Chapter 11.

[12]In Federal Reserve parlance, "other assets denominated in foreign currencies."

posits at the Federal Reserve banks," so that no change in commercial bank reserves results. But the central bank of the foreign country will surely sell the newly acquired dollars to commercial banks located there by means of checks drawn on the Reserve banks. The commercial banks of the foreign country will then deposit these checks at commercial banks in the United States, and the latter will send them to the Reserve banks for credit to their reserve accounts, with the following results:

FEDERAL RESERVE BANKS

	Deposits:	
	Member bank reserves	+600,000
	Foreign	−600,000

COMMERCIAL BANKING SYSTEM

Reserve with FR	+600,000	Demand deposits:	
		Foreign	+600,000

Accordingly, the increase in reserves is directly attributable to the decrease in foreign deposits at the Federal Reserve banks, although it is not improper to say that it is indirectly attributable to the increase in other Federal Reserve bank assets.

Gold Stock   Following the decision of the United States and other leading countries in March 1968 to confine their gold transactions to central banks and the IMF and to abstain from transactions in the open market, as buying from mining companies,[13] the buying and selling of gold by the Treasury have had no direct effect on commercial bank reserves. In a purchase transaction, for example, the results are the same as in a swap initiated by a foreign central bank, as just described. In the one instance, the foreign central bank, in effect, buys dollars in exchange for some of its own currency; in the other, it buys dollars with gold; and in both instances, it gets payment by credit to its dollar deposit accounts at the Federal Reserve banks. But following the gold transaction, as following the swap transaction, American commercial banks are likely to get new reserves as the foreign central bank sells to its commercial banks dollar checks drawn on the Reserve banks, and as these checks are deposited at American commercial banks and sent to the Reserve banks for payment—all as previously described.

For illustration, assume that the Treasury buys $700,000 worth of gold from a foreign central bank and pays by directing the Federal Reserve Bank of New York to transfer this amount from its deposit account to that

---

[13]See Chapter 4.

of the foreign bank.[14] The effect on the Treasury's books and on the books of the Federal Reserve banks would be as follows:

U.S. TREASURY

Gold	+700,000
Deposits at FR	−700,000

FEDERAL RESERVE BANKS

Deposits:		
U.S. Treasurer		−700,000
Foreign		+700,000

Thus we have opposite changes of equal amount in two factors absorbing reserve funds, foreign deposits and Treasury deposits at the Federal Reserve banks, and commercial bank reserves are not affected.

But is not *gold stock* a factor in supplying reserve funds? Since it has obviously increased, should not the result be an immediate increase in commercial bank reserves of $700,000? There is, indeed, no doubt concerning the increase in the gold stock, but its potential influence on commercial bank reserves is nullified by an increase in still a fourth factor—the absorbing factor "Treasury cash holdings." Gold is one of the cash assets of the Treasury, and again, there is no doubt that the Treasury now has $700,000 more in gold than it had before. In sum, four factors are affected by the gold purchase, but they cross cancel in such a manner that commercial bank reserves are not affected.

However, the Treasury is not likely to be satisfied to have its deposit accounts at the Reserve banks remain depleted because of the gold purchase. It should not have its spending capacity reduced as a result of *buying money* in the form of gold. Accordingly, it is likely to replenish its deposit accounts at the Reserve banks by "depositing" gold certificates of $700,000 with them (in reality, of course, giving them "gold credits" on its own books[15]). The results would be as follows:

U.S. TREASURY

Deposits at FR	+700,000	Gold certificates due FR	+700,000

FEDERAL RESERVE BANKS

Gold certificates	+700,000	Deposits:	
		U.S. Treasurer	+700,000

[14]This illustration and the subsequent description of a gold sale ignore the Treasury's "handling charge" of 0.25 percent of the value of the gold bought and sold, because including it would not alter the described effects of the gold transactions in any significant way.

[15]See Chapter 4.

But, again, commercial bank reserves are not affected, because there are opposing changes in two factors absorbing reserve funds: Treasury cash holdings would be reduced, because it would now have a gold liability of $700,000 against its gold asset of the same amount, and Treasury deposits at the Reserve banks would be increased by an equal amount.

In a similar way, gold sales by the Treasury to foreign central banks affect the four factors referred to in the preceding paragraphs, but in a cross-canceling way so that commercial bank reserves are not affected. In order to free gold for sale, the Treasury cancels gold certificates due the Reserve banks and the Reserve banks charge this *withdrawal* against the Treasury's deposit accounts. Thus opposing changes in two absorbing factors occur: the Treasury's cash holdings increase and its deposits at the Reserve banks decrease. Then the Treasury delivers the gold to the foreign central bank and receives payment through a transfer from the deposit balance of the foreign bank at the Federal Reserve banks to its own deposit accounts there. In this way, gold stock and foreign deposits at the Reserve banks both decrease, canceling out potential effects on commercial bank reserves, while Treasury deposits at the Reserve banks increase and Treasury cash holdings decrease, also with canceling-out results.

However, the commercial banks are likely to have lost reserves *preceding* the gold purchase by the foreign central bank. The commercial banks of the foreign country probably decided that their dollar deposits at American commercial banks were excessive and sold the excess to their central bank by drawing checks on their American balances payable to the central bank. The central bank probably deposited these checks at the Reserve banks, with the Reserve banks charging the reserve accounts of the drawee banks in collecting payment on the checks. At this point, then, the foreign central bank probably decided that it, too, had an excessive amount of dollars and chose to use some of them to buy gold from the Treasury.

SDR Certificate Account   When the Treasury gives dollars in exchange for SDRs tendered by other countries that are participants in the special drawing account of the International Monetary Fund,[16] it pays the dollars out of its deposit accounts at the Federal Reserve banks into the deposit accounts there of the foreign central banks that deliver the SDRs. Accordingly, there are equal offsetting changes in two absorbing factors—Treasury deposits and foreign deposits—with no effect on commercial bank reserves. But in acquiring SDRs, as in acquiring gold, the Treasury buys international money, and its spending power at home should not be reduced as a result of the transaction. For this reason, it gets its deposit accounts at the Reserve banks replenished in the amount of dollars paid out for the SDRs by giving the Reserve banks credits on its books in its SDR certificate account (just as it gives them gold certificate credits when it buys gold). Here the in-

---

[16]See Chapter 5.

crease in the SDR certificate account, a supplying factor, is offset by the equal increase in Treasury deposits, an absorbing factor, so that, again, the reserves of the commercial banks are not affected. With the SDR acquisition transaction designated by the letter a and the replenishment transaction by the letter $b,$ and assuming that the number of SDR units acquired had a dollar value of $950,000, the results on the books of the Treasury and the Federal Reserve banks would be as follows:

U.S. TREASURY

SDRs	$+950,000a$	SDR certificates	$+950,000b$
Deposits at FR	$\begin{cases} -950,000a \\ +950,000b \end{cases}$		

FEDERAL RESERVE BANKS

SDR certificate account	$+950,000b$	Deposits:	
		U.S. Treasurer	$\begin{cases} -950,000a \\ +950,000b \end{cases}$
		Foreign	$+950,000a$

As with gold acquisitions by the Treasury, its acquisitions of SDRs have effects on commercial bank reserves only when the foreign central banks sell the dollars paid for them to their commercial banks by means of checks drawn on the Reserve banks, and when these commercial banks deposit the checks at American commercial banks that send them to the Reserve banks for credit in their reserve accounts. In terms of the factors, however, this increase in commercial bank reserves results directly from the reduction in foreign deposits at the Reserve banks and only indirectly from the SDR transaction.

Treasury Currency Outstanding The supplying factor *Treasury currency outstanding* consists primarily of all the coins, from dollars to cents, that the Treasury has issued over the years, regardless of who now holds them. In much smaller amounts, it also includes the remaining greenbacks of the Civil War period, silver certificates that have not yet been retired, and other paper moneys "in process of retirement," such as national-bank notes, for which the Treasury has accepted liability.

As thus described, it is readily apparent that changes in "Treasury currency outstanding" are chiefly additions to the issues of coins as manufactured by the mints. We saw in Chapter 4 that the output of the mints is deposited at the Federal Reserve banks to the credit of the Treasury in its deposit accounts there; and now we can add that, with respect to factor influences, increases in Treasury currency outstanding from this source are exactly offset by equal increases in Treasury deposits as an absorbing factor. Accordingly, it is only when the Treasury spends the proceeds of its coin deposits (including the seigniorage it earns on coinage) that commercial bank reserves are increased. But such an increase in commercial bank reserves is attributable directly to the decrease in Treasury deposits and only indirectly to the increase in Treasury currency outstanding.

Factors absorbing reserve funds

Currency in Circulation Because the factor reports of the Federal Reserve are designed to show the sources of member bank reserves on deposit at the Reserve banks and the causes of changes therein, the absorbing factor *currency in circulation* is reported as the amount of paper money and coins "outside the Treasury and the Federal Reserve banks." If a member bank makes a withdrawal of paper money and coins from its Reserve bank chargeable against its reserve account, this account is obviously reduced; and if it ships paper money and coins to its Reserve bank for credit in its reserve account, this account is obviously increased.

Because, however, vault cash is a component of commercial bank primary reserves, shipments to the Reserve banks out of vault cash and additions to it by means of shipments of paper money and coins from the Reserve banks do not change the level of total reserves. More significant, therefore, is the amount of paper money and coins outside the Treasury, the Federal Reserve banks, and the commercial banks—all three—since the commercial banks lose primary reserves when their customers withdraw hand-to-hand money, and they regain reserves when their customers deposit such money. Thus the commercial banking system lost approximately $19 billion of primary reserves in the 5 years of World War II, 1941–1945, in which hand-to-hand money outside the Treasury and the Federal Reserve and commercial banks increased by that amount. A fabulous figure! But it is interesting to observe that this reserve drain was more than offset by purchases of Treasury obligations by SOMA—a deliberate use of a factor supplying reserves to offset an absorbing factor's enormous change.

It is true, nevertheless, that sizable increases in the volume of paper money and coins outside the commercial banks soon require a flow of such money from the Reserve banks. On experiencing a drain of vault cash, the commercial banks call on the Reserve banks for shipments of hand-to-hand money to replace that which they have lost.[17] As soon as the shipments are made, currency in circulation "outside the Treasury and the Federal Reserve banks" is increased. To illustrate, let us say that the Reserve banks, in making up packages for shipment as requested by commercial banks, enclose $20,000 in coins and $180,000 in Federal Reserve notes, and that they are authorized to charge the shipments against the reserve accounts of the banks requesting them. The accounts of the Reserve and commercial banks are affected as follows:

---

[17]Some banks ask their correspondents for hand-to-hand money, but the correspondents, in turn, are most likely to meet these requests by making withdrawals from the Reserve banks.

FEDERAL RESERVE BANKS

Cash	−20,000	Federal Reserve notes	+180,000
		Deposits:	
		Member bank reserves	−200,000

COMMERCIAL BANKING SYSTEM

| Vault cash | +200,000 |
| Reserve with FR | −200,000 |

Accordingly, the transaction causes no change in commercial bank reserves, the reserve loss presumably having already taken place because of withdrawals from the banks' vault cash.

Treasury Cash Holdings   As a factor absorbing reserve funds, *Treasury cash holdings* comprise its *free* gold—the value of gold bullion held in excess of the face amount of gold certificate holdings of the Federal Reserve banks—temporary accumulations of Federal Reserve notes, greenbacks, and coins received from taxpayers and others, and a few minor items. Although totals of all these items can change substantially from week to week, such changes are usually offset exactly or approximately by opposing changes in Treasury deposits at the Federal Reserve banks, as we noted in the gold transaction previously described. As a factor acting independently, therefore, Treasury cash holdings usually affect commercial bank reserves only in a small way.

At rare intervals, however, Treasury cash holdings have been affected by extraordinary transactions of large dollar amounts, as in their increase by more than $2.8 billion as a result of the devaluation of the dollar in 1934, the use of portions of this "profit" in 1946 and 1959 for subscription payments to the IMF, and the use of another portion of $500 million in the fall of 1953 to augment federal spending power at a time when it was cramped by tight borrowing restrictions.

Treasury Deposits at the Federal Reserve Banks   But if Treasury cash holdings ordinarily have little independent influence on reserves, its companion factor absorbing reserve funds *Treasury deposits at the Federal Reserve banks* is one of the most spectacular performers in the whole history of finance. Into these deposit accounts are poured the tens of billions of dollars of federal tax revenues and proceeds of the sales of its debt instruments, and out of it, also in tens of billions of dollars, come the disbursements to meet the military and civilian payrolls, interest on the national debt, and the principal of maturing obligations, and to pay for all kinds of military and civilian equipment, supplies, and services. At most times, nevertheless, the Treasury's deposit balances at the Reserve banks will not be of fantastic size; on the contrary, the total rarely goes much above $1 billion, and usually it falls well below that figure. One reason for this is that the Treasury chooses to keep most of its day-to-day deposit balances as demand deposits with thousands of commercial banks in all parts of the country—deposits that are called "tax and loan accounts" and from which transfers to the Reserve banks are ordered when its balances there become depleted. A second reason for rather modest Treasury deposit balances in relationship to federal spending is that both its deposit accounts at the Reserve banks and its tax and loan accounts at the commercial banks are constantly being replenished by tax collections and sales of new issues of its debt instruments.

How changes in Treasury deposits at the Federal Reserve banks affect the primary reserves of the commercial banking system is not at all difficult to understand. Taxpayers and the buyers of new issues of Treasury obligations customarily make payment by drawing checks on their accounts at the commercial banks. The checks are deposited by the U.S. Internal Revenue Service and other offices of the Treasury at the Federal Reserve banks,[18] the Reserve banks return them to the commercial banks for payment, and the commercial banks normally pay by having their reserve accounts reduced. If, for example, taxpayers' checks amount to $400,000, the books of the Federal Reserve and commercial banks would show the following changes:

FEDERAL RESERVE BANKS

	Deposits:	
	Member bank reserves	−400,000
	U.S. Treasurer	+400,000

COMMERCIAL BANKING SYSTEM

Reserve with FR	−400,000	Demand deposits	−400,000

When the federal government spends money, the foregoing process is simply reversed. The disbursing officers of the government draw checks on the Treasury, the payees of the checks deposit them or have them cashed at the commercial banks, the commercial banks send them to the Federal Reserve banks for payment, and payment is effected as the Reserve banks increase the reserve accounts of the commercial banks and reduce the deposit accounts of the Treasury.

Foreign and Other Deposits at the Federal Reserve Banks   The two absorbing factors *foreign deposits* and *other deposits at the Federal Reserve banks* may be treated jointly because changes in them affect commercial

---

[18]Many payments to the Treasury are actually deposited in tax and loan accounts at the commercial banks. But when the Treasury orders transfers from these accounts to the Federal Reserve banks, it is as if the taxpayers' and security buyers' checks were being directly deposited at the Reserve banks. Though the timing varies, the result is the same.

bank reserves in exactly the same way. Indeed, we have already had three illustrative references to foreign deposits at the Reserve banks where we saw why decreases in them cause equal increases in commercial bank reserves—decreases resulting from sales by central banks of dollars obtained by gold sales to the Treasury, in exchange for SDRs, and in swap arrangements with the Reserve banks themselves. For an illustration of an opposite effect, assume that the commercial banks of a foreign country draw checks on their demand deposits at American commercial banks in selling dollars to the central bank of that country. If the foreign central bank deposits these checks at the Federal Reserve banks, the checks are presented to the drawee banks for payment, and these banks pay by having their reserve accounts at the Reserve banks reduced.

The "other deposits" at the Reserve banks include their own outstanding officers' checks, the so-called clearing balances of nonmember commercial banks that choose to use the Federal Reserve clearing facilities, the deposits of federal corporations and agencies other than the Treasury, and deposits of certain international organizations, such as the IMF. A single illustration should suffice to show why increases and decreases in these deposits cause opposing changes of equal amounts in commercial bank reserves. Assume that member banks are paying their semiannual assessments to the Federal Deposit Insurance Corporation by drawing checks on the Federal Reserve banks themselves. The FDIC deposits these checks at the Reserve banks, and the latter reduce the reserve accounts of the drawers and increase the deposit balance of the FDIC. On the other hand, when the FDIC issues checks in meeting its payroll, they are deposited at the commercial banks, the commercial banks send them to the Reserve banks, and balances there are switched in the opposite direction.

Other Federal Reserve Liabilities and Capital The absorbing factor *other Federal Reserve liabilities and capital* comprises the outstanding capital stock of the Reserve banks, their surplus and other capital accounts, and all their liabilities other than Federal Reserve notes, deposit liabilities, and deferred availability cash items. These liabilities include unearned discount on Treasury obligations purchased, accrued wages, and other accrued operating expenses.

We have already used an illustration showing why increases in "other Federal Reserve liabilities and capital" cause decreases of equal amounts in commercial bank reserves. In the second illustration of the workings of the factors, the Federal Reserve banks granted loans to member banks of $100,000 on which they charged interest of $600. Accordingly, while the loans caused an increase in reserves of $100,000, the repayment of the loans with interest caused a reserve reduction of $100,600, with the net reduction of $600 attributable to the increase of that amount in the surplus accounts of the Reserve banks.

For a further illustration, assume that certain member banks have expanded their capital stock and surplus, so that, in accordance with the requirements of membership,[19] they must subscribe to additional stock in the Federal Reserve banks in their respective districts. They would most likely pay for the stock by directing the Reserve banks to charge its cost against their reserve accounts. In this way, the increase in Federal Reserve "capital" would be the cause, as it were, of an equal decrease in commmercial bank reserves.

FEDERAL RESERVE CONTROL

The forgoing description of the nature and behavior of the thirteen factors absorbing and supplying reserves has indicated that the volume of primary reserves held by the commercial banking system can be affected by actions of the Federal Reserve, the Treasury, government corporations and agencies, and foreign and international institutions that have deposits at the Federal Reserve banks, and finally, the people generally by withdrawing and depositing paper money and coins. But the actions of the Federal Reserve must dominate all the others if it is to fulfill its responsibility as the central bank—its duty to control the volume of bank reserves and therefore the volume of money in circulation as a means of trying to achieve goals of full employment, price-level stability, and a good rate of economic growth.

Are the powers of the Federal Reserve strong enough to give it this control—this position of dominance? The answer is "unquestionably yes." In fact, its virtually unlimited capacity to buy and sell U.S. Treasury obligations in the open market is alone sufficient to give it very great control of reserve and money volumes, and this is why Federal Reserve holdings of Treasury obligations were described earlier in this chapter as the most important of the thirteen factors. The Federal Reserve can give the commercial banks new reserves by granting them loans at the "discount window" and then take away an equal amount by selling Treasury obligations in the open market. It may observe that the commercial banks are losing reserves through a reduction in the float or by reason of large withdrawals of paper money and coins by the public, but it can take quick action to replace these losses by buying Treasury obligations in the market. It can supply dollars to a foreign central bank in a swap arrangement, but as the foreign bank dispenses these dollars in such a way that they get into the hands of American commercial banks, the Federal Reserve can offset the reserve effects by selling Treasury obligations. If the Treasury overestimates its short-run expenditure needs and makes too large withdrawals from its tax and loan accounts at the commercial banks, the Federal Reserve can make good their reserve losses by open-market purchases of Treasury obligations. All this means that the Federal Reserve can employ

---

[19]See Chapter 16.

open-market buying and selling to offset undesirable reserve changes being caused by factors over which it has no direct control, while engaging in additional open-market transactions to move positively toward a quantitative monetary target, such as "easier money" or "tighter money."

But if the commercial banks are individually limited in their capacity to create demand deposits through lending and investing, because of the likelihood that they will lose primary reserves in amounts equal to the proceeds of their loans and investments, are not the Federal Reserve banks limited similarly in their capacity to create reserves through purchases of Treasury obligations? As they continue year after year to create more reserves in order to keep pace with expanding business activity—and often, indeed, to *promote* expansion—will they not be drained of their own reserves as the commercial banks call for more hand-to-hand money to meet the withdrawal demands of their depositors? The answer to these questions is, of course, that the Reserve banks *create* most of the hand-to-hand money needed to meet the calls of the commercial banks: they simply issue more Federal Reserve notes! They are able to replace one kind of liability, their deposit accounts, with another kind, their notes—and this is a prerogative that no commercial bank enjoys.

In sum, the Federal Reserve banks, unlike the commercial banks, have no need to worry about their own solvency, since they can meet their obligations of all kinds by issuing their own legal tender paper money, that is, Federal Reserve notes.

FOR REVIEW

1. What are the primary reserves of a commercial bank? Why is it said that the bank's lending and investing capacity depends on the amount of these reserves? Does this capacity depend on anything else? Explain.
2. If a commercial bank has excess reserves of $70,000, and if it customarily keeps reserves equal to 15 percent of its demand deposits, how much can it safely add to its loans and investments? Explain.
3. If the commercial banking system has excess reserves of $70,000, and if it customarily keeps reserves equal to 15 percent of its demand deposits, how much can it safely add to its loans and investments? Explain.
4. Why are the factors supplying and absorbing reserve funds so called? What are the seven supplying factors? the six absorbing factors?
5. What is the relationship, at any time, between the total of the supplying factors, the total of the absorbing factors, and the reserve balances of member banks at the Federal Reserve banks? between the factor totals and vault cash of member banks? between the factor totals and the primary reserves of the whole commercial banking system?
6. What changes in which factors could offset an increase in United

States government security holdings of the Reserve banks? an increase in currency in circulation?

7. From the standpoint of monetary control, which of the factors supplying and absorbing reserves is the most important? Why is it so described?

8. Explain how Federal Reserve transactions in United States government securities cause changes of equal amounts in commercial bank primary reserves.

9. Explain why an increase in "discounts and advances" of the Federal Reserve banks causes an equal increase in commercial bank primary reserves, while repayments of these loans with interest cause decreases in reserves exceeding the loan amounts.

10. When the Treasury buys gold from a foreign central bank, which of the factors supplying and absorbing reserves are affected? What is the usual effect on commercial bank primary reserves?

11. What is "float" as a factor supplying reserves? Under what circumstances does "float" decrease and thereby absorb reserves?

12. What is the distinction between "Treasury currency outstanding" and "currency in circulation" as factors affecting commercial bank reserves?

13. How are commercial bank reserves affected by Treasury decisions about how much of its deposit balances it will keep in tax and loan accounts?

14. Why is it said that foreign central banks and the American people can affect the size of commercial bank reserves?

15. Does the Federal Reserve have sufficient control over the factors supplying and absorbing reserves to do an effective job in regulating the money supply?

16. Why is it said that the Federal Reserve banks have no need to worry about their solvency?

PROBLEMS

1. The factors supplying and absorbing reserve funds were of the following amounts, in millions of dollars, on the dates entered as column heads:

	NOVEMBER 30, 1970	JANUARY 31, 1971
Treasury deposits at FR banks	587	976
Foreign deposits at FR banks	136	129
Other deposits at FR banks	692	769
Discounts and advances of FR banks	300	308
SDR certificate account	400	400
Treasury cash holdings	458	467
Treasury currency outstanding	7,108	7,172

Currency in circulation	56,357	55,348
United States government securities		
held by FR banks	61,294	61,783
Float	2,028	2,750
Gold stock	11,117	10,732
Other FR bank assets	1,015	1,326
Other FR liabilities and capital	2,302	2,217

A. Construct a table similar to Table 7-1, and determine what must have been the respective amounts of reserves of member banks on deposit at the Federal Reserve banks on the two days.

B. Construct a table similar to Table 7-2 to indicate what factor changes caused the change in member bank reserves on deposit at the Federal Reserve banks between November 30, 1970, and January 31, 1971.

2. Indicate what effects, if any, each of the following transactions would have on specific asset and liability accounts of the Federal Reserve banks and the commercial banks. Indicate also (a) which of the factors supplying and absorbing reserve funds would be affected, (b) the dollar amounts of these effects, and (c) the resulting dollar effects, if any, on member bank reserves on deposit at the Reserve banks. (Assume in all instances that payments between the Federal Reserve banks and member banks are made through the member banks' reserve accounts on the books of the Reserve banks.)

A. The Treasury deposits $500,000 of newly minted coins at the Federal Reserve banks.

B. Employees of the federal government deposit payroll checks of $800,000 at a member bank that sends them to the Federal Reserve bank where it receives payment on them.

C. A member bank gets a shipment of $20,000 in coins and $280,000 in Federal Reserve notes from a Reserve bank.

D. A member bank sends to a Federal Reserve bank $750,000 of checks drawn on other member banks. At the end of 2 business days, the sending bank is credited in full, but the Reserve bank has received payment from drawee banks on only $550,000 of the checks.

E. A foreign central bank buys United States government securities in the American market at a cost of $600,000, making payment by drawing a check on its deposit balance at the Federal Reserve Bank of New York. The check is deposited by the seller at a member bank that receives payment on it by sending it to its Reserve bank.

F. At its "cash window" in Washington, the Treasury sells $100,000 face amount of savings bonds for $75,000, receiving payment in paper money and coins.

G. A newly established national bank, having set up a reserve account at the Federal Reserve bank in its district, buys and pays for $250,000 of stock in that Reserve bank.

H. A member bank borrows $365,000 from the Federal Reserve bank in its district. Five days later it repays the loan plus interest of $250.

I. The Federal Reserve's system open market account buys $425,000 par value of Treasury obligations from a member bank.

J. A Federal Reserve bank collects payment from a member bank on a check for $700,000 drawn on the member bank by a foreign central bank in buying gold from the Treasury. The Treasury delivers the gold and withdraws $700,000 from its gold certificate account "due" the Reserve banks.

K. A foreign central bank deposits at the Federal Reserve Bank of New York a check for $950,000 received from the Treasury for SDR units of that value. The Treasury credits the Federal Reserve banks for $950,000 "due" on its SDR certificate account with them.

CHAPTER 8

MONETARY AND BANKING HISTORY
OF THE UNITED STATES

EARLY CONDITIONS AND DEVELOPMENTS

Dearth of metallic money

The American colonists brought very little gold and silver with them, and only insignificant gold deposits and none of silver were found in the colonies. In return for their exports, they preferred to import tools and other manufactured goods rather than gold and silver for monetary purposes. Accordingly, a general shortage of metallic money prevailed throughout the colonial period, and many nonmetallic commodities, such as wampum, beaverskins, tobacco, and rice, as well as a variety of paper issues, were widely used in the monetary capacities. The coins that did circulate came chiefly from the West Indies and were mostly of Spanish and Portuguese origin, with the Spanish dollar, or "piece of eight," leading in popularity. All these kinds of money—foreign coins, nonmetallic commodities, and paper issues—were from time to time made legal tender for the payment of public and private obligations in the several colonies.

Accounts were commonly kept in terms of the British system of pounds, shillings, and pence, and the colonial governments attempted to fix by legislation ratios between the Spanish dollar and the British shilling. Because they did not adopt a uniform ratio, however, great confusion in valuation among the colonies resulted.

Colonial paper money

Because of the perennial shortage of coins, the colonies experimented with several kinds of paper money. Beginning with Massachusetts in 1690, most of the colonies at one time or another issued "bills of credit" to meet extraordinary expenditures that could not be financed out of current revenues. These bills circulated from hand to hand like modern Federal Reserve notes. They were supposed to be redeemed in short periods of time and were customarily made receivable for tax payments. At other times, some of the colonial governments issued "loan bills" simply to provide mediums of exchange. Like the bills of credit, the loan bills were government promises to pay; but instead of being payable out of tax revenues, they depended for redemption on the people who first borrowed and spent them. Individuals could obtain supplies of the loan bills by mortgaging property as security while promising to make installment repayments in the bills themselves, in silver, or in some other acceptable medium, and agreeing to pay interest on the amounts taken. Similar loan bills were issued by "loan banks" sponsored by groups of merchants. The procedure of putting the bills of loan banks into circulation and of retiring them was much the same as for government loan bills.

In many instances, these varieties of paper money were issued to great excess, so that they tended to depreciate rapidly. The exchange value of many issues fell as low as 10 percent of their face value. On the other hand, some issues, such as those of the Pennsylvania "public banks" of 1723 and 1739, were wisely managed and were of great benefit in spurring business activity by providing much-needed mediums of exchange. Because of excessive issues, however, the British government in 1751 forbade the issuance of legal tender paper money in New England, and in 1764 it extended the prohibition to the other colonies. Nevertheless, a goodly volume of paper money was still outstanding at the outbreak of the American Revolution.

Paper money of the Continental Congress

The confused state of the money supply in the colonial period was paralleled by the situation in the period of the Revolution. Coins were quite rare, and those in circulation were a motley array of Spanish, British, Portuguese, Dutch, and French issues.

One of the first acts of the Continental Congress was to authorize the printing of $2 million of paper money. For this issue, the dollar sign is appropriately introduced, since the money was declared to be redeemable in Spanish dollars or the gold or silver equivalent. This promise of redemption, though never fulfilled, presaged the adoption of the dollar rather than the British pound as the monetary unit of the United States, and government accounts thereafter were kept in terms of dollars. The Continental Congress thought that the states would take care of the redemption of the paper money, and rough attempts were made to apportion the liability to them on the basis of population. But the states displayed little enthusiasm toward accepting such a liability.

From 1775 to 1779, forty issues of this kind of paper money, totaling approximately $242 million, were authorized by the Continental Congress. Because, however, some of the earlier issues were partially replaced by new issues, the entire amount was not outstanding at any one time. In addition, some of the states issued paper money totaling $210 million, the greater portion coming from Virginia and the Carolinas. Very early in the course of the war, the quantity of paper money in circulation far exceeded all reasonable medium-of-exchange needs, and as a result the money quickly depreciated. By May 1781, the paper had ceased to circulate as money, its depreciation having reached a level where a hundred paper dollars had purchasing power equal to about one dollar in silver. Later the depreciation became even greater.

Money in the period of the Confederation

As they became effective in 1781, the Articles of Confederation gave few monetary powers to the central government, but the Congress of the Confederation had one notable achievement when in 1786 it selected the dollar with decimal fractions as our monetary unit. The Mint Ordinance of 1786 also provided for the minting of gold, silver, and copper coins, but as it turned out, only copper coins were produced.

Another notable development of the Confederation period was the emergence of banks in the modern sense, that is, as institutions quite different from the "loan banks" of the colonial period. This was an important development because, in several subsequent decades in which there were many difficulties with the coinage, the early banks supplemented it with their issues of circulating bank notes that were generally of good quality and well-managed, and with the beginnings, as it were, of demand deposits as means of payment.

The first and most important of the early banks was the Bank of North America that opened for business in Philadelphia in January 1782 under a charter granted by the Congress of the Confederation. Because it was possible to get only about $70,000 from individual subscriptions to the bank's capital, Congress itself bought stock in the amount of $200,000, paying for it in specie. Although the Confederation government was the principal stockholder, it left the management in private hands. Because of misgivings about the power of the Congress of the Confederation to charter a banking institution, the bank obtained a charter from the state of Pennsylvania in 1782. The Bank of North America performed good services on behalf of the Confederation as well as the general public. Large loans were granted to the Confederation government at a time when, because of its lack of independent taxing power, it was handicapped by having to appeal to the states for funds. Loans of the bank also enabled private individuals to expand their business activities.

Other banks of this period were the Bank of Massachusetts, chartered in 1784, and the Bank of New York, which was established in the same year although it operated without a charter until 1791.

THE PERIOD OF BIMETALLISM, 1792–1862

Bimetallism at 15 to 1

Coinage Act of 1792   Under the Constitution, the federal government has the power to coin money and to regulate its value as well as the value of foreign coins circulating in the United States,[1] and the states are forbidden to coin money and to "emit bills of credit."[2] Congress exercised its exclusive powers for the first time in the adoption of the Coinage Act of April 2, 1792, which established a bimetallic standard. There was nothing peculiar about this, as monetary systems in other countries were generally bimetallic at that time. The gold dollar, not to be coined, was given a fine gold weight of 24.75 grains; and the silver dollar, a weight of 371.25 grains of fine silver. The ratio was thus 15 to 1. The legislation provided for the opening of a mint in Philadelphia and for the coinage of gold eagles, half eagles, and quarter eagles, worth $10, $5, and $2.50, respectively, and silver dollars, half dollars, quarter dollars, dimes, and half dimes, as well as copper cents and half cents. The free coinage of gold and silver in the denominations mentioned was authorized.

The coinage of copper cents and half cents began in 1793, silver in 1794, and gold in 1795. Because of the early shortage of domestic coins, Congress provided for the temporary acceptance of certain foreign coins in the payment of import duties and taxes, and in 1793 such coins were made legal tender for a 3-year period for all purposes at stipulated ratios to the dollar. As the mint was unable to supply an adequate coinage, the designation of certain classes of foreign coins as legal tender was extended from time to time to 1857.

Difficulties with the Coinage   When the mint ratio of 15 to 1 was selected in 1792, it was quite close to the market ratio of the values of gold and silver, but toward the close of the century the market value of silver began to fall. This meant that the American mint ratio overvalued silver and undervalued gold, so that it was not advantageous to import gold into the United States. France adopted a mint ratio of 15.5 to 1 in 1803; thus gold was obviously more valuable there than in the United States. As a matter of fact, only moderate amounts of gold were coined in the United States until the mint ratio was changed in 1834.

Perplexing difficulties also beset the silver dollar, for American traders were able to exchange our silver dollars in the West Indies for the somewhat heavier Spanish silver dollars. It was profitable to export our silver dollars, exchange them for Spanish dollars, and import the latter and have them melted down and recoined at the mint. In consequence, domestic silver dollars tended to disappear from circulation, and throughout this period the chief American coin in circulation was the silver half dollar. The situation was so vexatious that President Thomas Jefferson in 1806 suspended the coinage of the silver dollar, and this decision remained in effect for 20 years.

---

[1] Art. I, sec. 8, par. 5.
[2] Art. I, sec. 10, par. 1.

Banking developments

Banks, Notes, and Deposits   But the banks were having a better time of it. In fact, Congress established the Bank of the United States under federal charter in 1791 even before it set up a monetary system for the country in the Coinage Act of the following year. And the number of banks under state charters grew steadily—to twenty-eight in 1800, to eighty-eight in 1811, and to 329 in 1830. Thus the coinage was progressively supplemented as more and more banks came into operation and granted loans by issuing their own paper money in the form of bank notes that were typically made payable "in specie to the bearer on demand." Likewise, demand deposits on the books of these banks continued to grow in amounts and in the frequency of their use as a means of payment.

However, the Bank of the United States and its successor of the same name established in 1816 deserve special consideration as the first incursions of the federal government into the banking field. Each of these banks had some features of a central bank long before the establishment of the Federal Reserve System, and judging from what happened in other countries to early banks of its kind, it would very probably have developed into a full-fledged central bank had it been permitted to continue in operation.

Charter of the First Bank   The charter of the first Bank of the United States authorized a capitalization of $10 million, of which one fifth was to be subscribed by the federal government. The government's subscription was made possible by a loan granted by the bank itself—a loan to be repaid in ten annual installments. The remainder of the stock was to be sold to private individuals whose subscriptions were to be paid in four semiannual installments consisting in total of one fourth specie and three fourths in 6 percent bonds of the federal government. The par value of the shares was put at $400, and individual subscriptions were limited to a maximum of 1000 shares. Despite these provisions of the charter calling for payments of $2 million in specie by the private subscribers, it is probable that only about one fourth of that amount was so paid.

The management of the bank was vested in a board of twenty-five directors elected by the stockholders, but no stockholder was permitted to cast more than thirty votes, and foreign stockholders had to be present in person to vote. The charter required the directors to be stockholders of the bank and citizens of the United States, and not more than three fourths of them were eligible for reelection from year to year. The directors, who received no compensation, were empowered to choose a salaried president.

The bank was authorized to issue $10 million of notes, which were not legal tender but were receivable for all obligations due the federal government as long as the bank continued to redeem them at par in specie. The bank was authorized to receive deposits, as well as to make loans both to the general public and to the federal and state governments. Its loans were to bear interest at not more than 6 percent. The total granted at any time to the federal government, except by special permission of Congress, was to be limited to $100,000, and that to each state, to $50,000. It could sell its holdings of government bonds but could not buy additional bonds in the market.

Branches of the parent bank were established in Boston, New York, Baltimore, Washington, Norfolk, Charleston, Savannah, and New Orleans. The head office was located in Philadelphia.

Operations of the First Bank   The charter of the bank, unless renewed, was to expire in 20 years. During that period, the bank's operations were highly successful, and its services to the federal government were especially noteworthy. Besides making the initial loan for the government's stock subscription of $2 million, the bank from time to time made other large advances to the U.S. Treasury. In 1796, for example, the total indebtedness of the federal government to the bank reached $6.2 million. As the bank insisted on the payment of the debt, the government sold some of its holdings of bank stock in 1796 and 1797, and the remainder in 1802. The government realized a profit of $671,860 on the sale and in the meantime had received dividends totaling $1,101,720. The bank's services as fiscal agent were also of benefit to the Treasury, for it moved government funds about the country by means of its branches at a time when most of the revenue was collected as customs duties in the seaboard cities.

As for its services to the general public, the bank supplied good circulating notes during a period in which gold and silver were scarce and in which trade would have otherwise been impeded for lack of adequate mediums of exchange. Its policy of sending the notes of state-chartered banks to the issuing banks for redemption and of refusing to receive such notes unless redeemable in specie, tended to keep these issues within reasonable bounds. Also, the bank acted as a depositary for private accounts and made loans to merchants and others for business transactions.

Closing of the First Bank   When we consider the good work of the first Bank of the United States, we have difficulty in understanding why its charter was not renewed. But opposition to it had continued throughout its career. The state banks, as they grew in number and size, naturally opposed the rechartering because they were anxious to be rid of a strong competitor. Misgivings about the constitutionality of the bank's federal charter were often voiced by its critics. The claim that the bank was an "undemocratic monopoly" was also a strong argument against it; and an even stronger one was that 18,000 out of the 25,000 shares of the bank's outstanding stock were owned by foreigners, chiefly by British investors. It was argued that the foreign owners of this stock might exercise a dangerous influence not only on the affairs of the bank but also on the economic development of the country.

The opponents of the bank were successful in their campaign, and the rechartering bill was defeated in the Senate on February 20, 1811, by the tie-splitting vote of the presiding Vice President. The bank, accordingly, proceeded to wind up its affairs and to suspend operations as a federal institution. In liquidation, it paid $434 on each $400 share outstanding.

Need of a New Bank The absence of the first Bank of the United States was sorely felt during the period of the second war with England beginning in 1812. The number of state banks increased from 88 to 246 in the period from 1811 to 1816, and because the restraining influence of the national bank was removed, they issued notes in excessive quantities. At the same time, less specie was available for the redemption of notes, for approximately $7 million had been sent abroad to pay off the stockholders of the first Bank of the United States. As a result of the excessive note issues, the exportation of specie, and the abnormal war conditions, all the state banks of the country except those of New England suspended specie payments in 1814. The federal government itself suffered losses estimated at $5 million in accepting depreciated and worthless state bank notes in the period from 1814 to 1817.

As early as 1814, Alexander Dallas, the Secretary of the Treasury in the administration of President James Madison, advocated the establishment of a new national bank. He contended that the bank could grant loans to the Treasury at a time when the government's credit was insecure, that a well-designed national note currency would be created, and that the new institution could gradually lead the state banks to a resumption of specie redemption. A bill to establish a bank was passed in January 1815, but it was not acceptable to Secretary Dallas, and President Madison accordingly vetoed it. A more acceptable bill received the President's signature on April 10, 1816, and the bank opened for business in January 1817.

Charter of the Second Bank The second Bank of the United States was authorized to sell $35 million of capital stock of $100 par value, of which 20 percent was subscribed by the federal government and paid for in its own bonds. Private subscriptions, limited individually to 3000 shares, were made payable in three installments, consisting in total of one fourth specie and three fourths government bonds. As with the first bank, this provision of the charter was violated; of the $7 million required, only about $2 million was paid in specie. The regulations respecting the bank's management were almost identical with those of its predecessor, except that the President of the United States was to choose five of its twenty-five directors. The bank was authorized to issue notes in an amount equal to its capital stock in denominations of not less than $5. The notes were made receivable by the federal government for all public dues, and the bank was made subject to a penalty of 12 percent a year on the face value of its outstanding notes should it suspend specie payment.

In return for the exclusive privilege of operating under a federal charter, the bank obligated itself to pay the government a charter fee of $1.5 million, payable in three equal annual installments, and to serve as fiscal agent without compensation. The federal government, on its part, agreed to keep its own money as deposits with the bank unless the Secretary of the Treasury should decide otherwise, in which event he was to submit to Congress a written explanation of the reasons for his decision.

Career of the Second Bank   The second national bank got off to a bad start. Many subscribers were allowed to obtain stock by merely turning their personal promissory notes over to the bank. The bank made loans to the stockholders on terms that permitted them to use the stock—sometimes unpaid for—as collateral. Many people, including some of the bank's officers, speculated in its stock. Several of the bank's branches located in the South and West issued notes in excessive quantities, and as they were redeemable at any branch, the effect was to drain specie from the more conservatively managed branches in the East. In 1818, as a result of reckless management, the Baltimore branch failed with a net loss of $3 million. So unsatisfactory was the bank's behavior that a bill was introduced in Congress in January 1819 to set aside its charter. This action led to the resignation of William Jones, the bank's first president, and it was permitted to continue in operation under a new president, Langdon Cheves.

Cheves succeeded in putting the bank into sound condition by restricting its note issues, curtailing loans, and adopting other conservative policies. Although he did restore the bank to a position of strength, his strict policies robbed it of much of its usefulness.

In 1823, Nicholas Biddle, who succeeded Cheves as president, expanded the bank's operations, enlarged the quantity of its outstanding notes, and adopted a more liberal policy toward the granting of loans. Under Biddle the bank moved forward in the pattern of the first national bank. It served the federal government adequately as fiscal agent, helped to finance the growth of private business, and curbed the issue of state bank notes by sending them to the issuing banks for redemption. In all likelihood, the bank would have operated during the remainder of its 20-year charter period as a well-managed institution and would have obtained an extension of its charter without difficulty had not the question of rechartering become a burning political issue.

The Rechartering Controversy   The story of the rechartering controversy has been told many times, and it is necessary here to give only the minimum details. Questions about the power of Congress to charter a bank were still constantly raised, although the Supreme Court had established a constitutional foundation for the bank's charter in two celebrated cases, *McCulloch v. Maryland* and *Osborn v. United States Bank.*[3] President Andrew Jackson, in his first message to Congress in December 1829, raised the question of

---

[3] 4 Wheaton 316 (1819) and 9 Wheaton 738 (1824).

constitutionality despite the decisions in these cases; and it was possible for him as a good Democrat to do so, for the decision had been handed down by a Supreme Court headed by the Federalist John Marshall. As the decisions denied the right of state governments to tax the branches and notes of the national bank, the Democrats had reason to oppose the continuance of the bank. State banking interests were also, as a matter of course, opposed to the recharting. And it may be added that the very atmosphere of "Jacksonian democracy" was not healthful for a "monopoly" such as the bank was said to be.

Despite all these elements of danger for the bank, Jackson might have been persuaded to agree to an extension of its charter had not the question of extension become a leading issue in the presidential campaign of 1832. Henry Clay, the candidate of the Whigs, made the extension of the bank's charter a major campaign goal, and he intimated that the bank would be forced to close if Jackson were reelected. Jackson's victory, therefore, virtually spelled the doom of the bank, and indeed even before the election, in July 1832, Jackson had vetoed one bill for extending the charter.

As a result of a misunderstanding, Jackson apparently came to believe that the bank was insolvent. In 1832 he asked the bank, as the government's fiscal agent, to accumulate a reserve of specie to be used to pay off some outstanding government bonds. Biddle suggested that the financing be deferred, and Jackson took this advice to mean that the bank was unable to carry out his instructions. Jackson then ordered the Secretary of the Treasury to deposit all future revenues in state banks beginning September 26, 1834, and to exhaust the deposits at the Bank of the United States by drawing on them to meet current expenditures. The officers of the bank, despairing of obtaining a renewal of the charter under such circumstances, proceeded to curtail loans and to limit other business. The bank ceased operations as a national institution on March 3, 1836. However, it obtained a charter from the state of Pennsylvania, but it was so badly managed that it had to suspend operations in 1841.

Bimetallism at 16 to 1

While the second Bank of the United States was pursuing its checkered career, Congress gave some thought to the unsatisfactory state of the coinage. But the thought was neither hurried nor strenuous, since it was not until 1834 that legislation aimed at improvement was adopted. Suggestions were made from time to time that the exportation of domestic coins be prohibited, that a silver standard be adopted, and that the gold-silver ratio be changed to make it conform more closely with the foreign market ratio. From time to time, too, committees of both the Senate and the House engaged in studies of the coinage question and produced some interesting reports.

Coinage Acts of 1834 and 1837   Finally came the decision of 1834 to retain bimetallism but to change the mint ratio, a decision that was incorporated in the Coinage Act of that year. The gold content of the gold dollar was reduced from 24.75 grains to 23.2 grains, but the silver content of the silver dollar was left unchanged at 371.25 grains, so that a new mint ratio of 16.002 to 1 resulted. As the market ratio of the two metals in Europe was still around 15½ to 1, Congress should have known that the new mint ratio would overvalue gold, but it is not clear from the historical record whether this overvaluation of gold was intended or was a misunderstanding. At any rate, the stage was set for the operation of Gresham's law resulting in a coinage flow opposite to that which had been in force for many years—toward the retention of gold in circulation and the expulsion of silver.

(In the Coinage Act of 1837, a further slight change was made in the gold content of the gold dollar, raising it to 23.22 grains, and making the mint ratio 15.988 to 1. The change was made for technical reasons for the convenience of the mint, and of course, the slight variation in the ratio left it quite close to 16 to 1.)

Because the fractional silver coins had a metallic composition in exact proportion to the silver dollar, they also had a foreign market value in excess of their monetary value at home. For a variety of reasons, nevertheless, they were slow in disappearing from circulation, and it was not until the middle 1840s that the process of their expulsion accelerated. On the other hand, it was now easy to keep gold coins in circulation. Although the United States continued to have an unfavorable balance of trade, large investments made here by foreign capitalists caused gold to flow into the country.

Provision for Subsidiary Coinage   The flow of gold from California following the discovery there in 1848 caused its value to fall in relationship to silver and resulted in an even greater undervaluation of silver at the mint. As a consequence, silver coins largely disappeared from circulation. In 1849, the coinage of a gold dollar was authorized for the first time, and in 1853, a 3-cent piece composed of silver and copper was issued. These actions relieved somewhat the acute shortage of coins of small denominations, but it was not until the adoption of the Coinage Act of 1853 that adequate relief was obtained. This legislation reduced the silver weight of the half dollar and the other fractional silver coins, suspended their free coinage, and made them legal tender only to the amount of $5. The reduction in the silver weight, which amounted to approximately 6.9 percent, was barely sufficient to make the face value of the coins greater than the foreign market value of the silver of which they were composed.

Because silver dollars were rare while gold coins circulated freely, the legislation of 1853, by reducing the fractional silver coins to the status of subsidiary coins, had the effect of putting the United States on a *de facto* gold coin standard. Officially, however, our monetary system was still bimetallic because the 1792 provision for the free coinage of the silver dollar remained in effect.

State banking before the Civil War

The expiration of the charter of the second Bank of the United States in 1836 left the field of commercial banking entirely open to the exploitation of state banks, and as Table 8-1 shows, they grew rapidly in number and in volume of operations. Many banks were well-managed during this period and served their customers safely and efficiently, especially those located in the Northeast, but many others engaged in "exploitation" in the evil sense of the word. For many areas of the country and for lengthy periods, this was the era of "wildcat banking."

Table 8-1   **Growth of State-Chartered Banks, 1837–1862 (dollar amounts in thousands)**

YEAR	NUMBER OF BANKS	CAPITAL	NOTES	DEPOSITS	LOANS
1837	788	$290,772	$149,186	$189,818	$525,116
1840	901	358,443	106,969	119,856	462,897
1845	707	206,046	89,609	114,358	288,617
1850	824	217,317	131,367	146,304	364,204
1855	1307	332,177	186,952	235,557	576,145
1860	1562	421,880	207,102	309,735	691,946
1862	1492	418,140	183,792	357,466	646,678

Source: U.S. Bureau of the Census, *Historical Statistics of the United States, 1789–1945* (Washington, D.C., 1949), p. 263.

The only asset that many banks derived from their issues of "capital stock" was an assemblage of the promissory notes of the subscribers to this stock—a very doubtful asset, and one providing nothing for the redemption of the notes that the banks themselves issued in granting loans to customers. The banks' own notes were supposed to be redeemable in gold or silver coins on demand, but reserves in gold and silver coins were often scanty or non-existent. In fact, some banks were set up in out-of-the-way places to make it difficult for the holders of their notes to present them with demands for payment. Even the notes of well-managed banks were not uniform in denominations, size, color, and paper quality, so that counterfeiting flourished. Thus, a "counterfeit detector" published in 1839 described 1395 varieties of counterfeit or altered notes thought to be in circulation.

Independent treasury system

When President Jackson decided to bypass the second Bank of the United States as depository and disbursing agent for federal revenues, various state banks were selected to serve in this capacity. These "pet banks," as they came to be called, were carefully chosen for the competence of their managements, and, in addition, they had to abide by an array of federal regulations in order to continue to qualify. Nevertheless, several of them ran into financial difficulties of such severity that the federal government suffered losses on some of its deposits with them. This experience led it to decide to act as its own banker, and it set up a framework for so acting in the establishment of an "independent treasury system" in 1846. In the U.S. Treasury in Washington, D.C., and in "subtreasuries" located in principal cities throughout the country, the government collected all its tax revenues and from them it made all its disbursements—all in "hard money," as it refused to accept the notes of state banks and checks drawn on them.

The drawing of gold and silver coins into the federal government's treasuries through tax collections and their subsequent disbursement necessarily had significant effects on the quantity of money available for private transactions, so that the Treasury's fiscal operations tended to be a source of disturbance to private business activity. Before the Civil War, the disturbances were not great because of the limited scope of the government's operations, but after the war they became more pronounced, so much so that the Treasury came to rely more and more on national banks as depositories, as was permitted by the National Bank Act adopted in 1863.

Even then, however, the arrangement was not entirely satisfactory, for the Secretary of the Treasury had full power to select depository banks as well as to decide upon the division of funds among the banks and the treasuries. The quantity of money available for private transactions, therefore, could be materially affected by decisions of the Secretary, and his decisions, in turn, could obviously be influenced by political considerations. Finally, in 1913, the Federal Reserve banks were authorized to act as depositories and fiscal agents of the federal government, and they proceeded to fulfill these duties so efficiently that the independent treasury system was discontinued by legislation adopted in 1920.

THE PERIOD OF THE FIAT STANDARD, 1862–1879

Eight months after the beginning of the Civil War, with the firing on Fort Sumter in April 1861, the New York banks announced that they could no longer redeem their notes in gold, and banks throughout the country followed with similar announcements. Even before this, under authority of legislation passed in July 1861, the U.S. Treasury had been issuing noninterest-bearing notes which were really a kind of paper money. A total of $50 million was authorized, and the notes were made receivable for all public dues. Although the notes were declared to be redeemable in gold on demand, the Treasury quickly followed the banks in suspending redemption— an action that meant a *de facto* shift from the bimetallic standard to a fiat standard.

The greenbacks

Issuance Legislation adopted on February 25, 1862 authorized the Treasury to issue $150 million of noninterest-bearing notes of which one third were to be used to redeem the demand notes authorized in the preceding year and the balance to meet current expenditures. The new notes—which soon came to be known as "greenbacks"—were to be issued in denominations of not less than $5, and they were made legal tender for all private and most public purposes. They were not made directly redeemable in gold, but they could be exchanged for 6 percent bonds that were declared to be redeemable in gold in 20 years or callable for redemption at any time after 5 years.

A second issue of $150 million of greenbacks was authorized in July 1852; of this issue, as much as $35 million could be given denominations from $1 to $5. A final round of $150 million was authorized by legislation adopted in January and March 1863, and in this instance the entire amount could be in denominations of $1 or more. Moreover, the 1863 legislation did not permit the conversion of the notes into "gold bonds," and it suspended as of July 1, 1863, the right of conversion of the earlier issues. Thus total issues of $450 million were in circulation during the war period. In addition, approximately $163 million of short-term interest-bearing Treasury notes were turned out, and as they were also legal tender they are includable with the paper money issues of the period.

Depreciation   Because the greenbacks were not redeemable in gold, they quickly became less acceptable than gold coins in the market: prices were higher when payment was made in greenbacks than when made in gold. For the most part, in keeping with the theory of Gresham's law, gold coins disappeared from circulation, as the people, having more confidence in the coins than in the greenbacks, preferred to hoard them and to use the greenbacks for current transactions. Thus we say that the greenbacks depreciated in relationship to gold, or alternatively, that gold "went to a premium." The extent of the depreciation varied from time to time during the war according to the changing fortunes of the armies, the credit position of the Treasury, and the prospects of ultimate redemption. The greatest depreciation was reached in the summer of 1864 when, on the average during July and August, it stood at 61 percent; that is to say, that people could buy with $39 in gold as much as they could buy with $100 in greenbacks.

The great depreciation of the greenbacks also made the fractional silver coins worth more as metal than as money, so that they were rapidly withdrawn from circulation. As in the period before 1953, an acute shortage of small coins ensued. To remedy this, the Treasury issued large quantities of legal tender paper money in fractional denominations and also authorized the use of postage stamps—manufactured without glue—as legal tender in small transactions; and city governments and merchants, without legal sanction, printed a variety of paper tokens, often called "shinplasters."

Charters for national banks

When Salmon P. Chase was chosen in 1861 as Secretary of the Treasury in the Cabinet of President Abraham Lincoln, he began almost immediately to promote the establishment of a new system of national banks—not a system of exclusive character as typified by the two Banks of the United States and their branches, but a system of numerous independent banks operating under federal rather than state charters. He believed that such new institutions would be able to supply a paper money of uniform quality that would be acceptable throughout the country and that would bring about a gradual elimination of the notes of the state-chartered banks. Chase first made his proposal to Congress in 1861 but it was not acted upon, and a bill introduced in the following year was defeated in the House. Although President Lincoln recommended the adoption of Chase's plan in his message to Congress in December 1862, the proposal was again defeated in the House in January 1863. The administration then turned to the Senate for support, and that body was able to pass the bill by a narrow margin; the House then concurred, and the legislation was signed by the President on February 25, 1863.

So few national banks were established, so few state banks converted to national charters, and so defective was the legislation of 1863 in general that it was replaced in entirety by a new act that became law on June 3, 1864. Hence the act of 1864—with many amendments over the years—is the legislative foundation of our present system of national banks.

As originally adopted, the 1864 legislation provided that national banks could be established with capital stock of $50,000 to $200,000, the specific amount depending on location; that an amount equal to one third of each bank's capital stock, or $30,000 if greater, must be invested in Treasury bonds; that on the basis of such bonds, the bank could issue an equal amount of notes designed for general circulation as money; and that all national banks would be subject to the general supervision of the Comptroller of the Currency, an officer of the Treasury Department.

In view of the requirement that each bank chartered under the National Bank Act invest a large portion of its original funds in government bonds, many historians believe that the creation of a market for these bonds at a time when the Treasury's credit position was weak was a prime objective of the legislation. If so, the objective was not realized, for the chartering of new national banks proceeded quite slowly until almost the end of the Civil War. Indeed, the national bank system would probably have remained of secondary importance in our financial structure had not Congress placed an annual tax of 10 percent on the face value of outstanding notes of state banks, a tax that became effective on July 1, 1866. The tax was obviously prohibitive, for the state banks would have had to lend their notes at rates of interest in excess of 10 percent to earn any net income whatever.

As it was quite commonly thought at that time that note issuance was a primary function of commercial banks, and that such banks could not profitably operate without that function, most of the state banks either suspended operations or surrendered their state charters and got national ones. Though there were 1562 state banks in operation in 1860, only 247 remained in 1868, and while only sixty-six national banks were in operation in the fall of 1863, the number had increased to 1640 in 1868.[4] In the closing years of the 1860s, therefore, the United States achieved a degee of unification in commercial banking never equaled before or since.

Resumption of gold redemption

The Resumption Act of 1875 directed the Treasury to redeem in "coin" any greenbacks that might be presented for redemption on or after January 1, 1879. "Coin" could mean either gold or silver, but the Treasury interpreted it to mean gold, and because its gold holdings were scanty in relationship to the volume of greenbacks outstanding, it sold bonds for gold over a period of several months in 1877 and 1878—mostly in foreign markets—to augment its reserves. As the date for resumption approached, the premium on gold gradually declined and finally disappeared in December 1878. When gold was at last available, it is interesting to remark, very few of the greenbacks were presented for redemption. The notes that did come in were used by the Treasury in meeting its ordinary expenditures, in accordance with the direction of legislation passed in 1878 that notes received were to be "reissued and paid out again and kept in circulation."

"Crime of '73"

Another important monetary event of the early post-Civil War period was the dropping by Congress in the Coinage Act of February 12, 1873 of the silver dollar from the list of coins that the mints were authorized to turn out. But the event was hardly world-shaking at the time it happened. Because of the undervaluation of silver by the 1834 and 1837 mint ratios of approximately 16 to 1, it had been profitable for decades to dispose of silver in foreign markets, and only moderate quantities of silver dollars had been coined after 1834. Within a short time, however, the devotees of silver money were bitterly denouncing the legislation of 1873 and were calling it the "Crime of '73."

The bitterness of the silver people grew as an extraordinary fall in the market value of silver occurred—a fall caused by a rapid expansion in the output of silver and a world-wide decline in its monetary demand. Discoveries of rich deposits, such as those of Nevada in the period 1859–1866, opened up important new sources of supply, while many developments abroad pointed toward the downgrading of silver as a monetary metal, including the weakening of the bimetallic system of the Latin Monetary Union through the defeat of France in the Franco-Prussian War, the establishment of the gold standard in the monetary laws of the new German Empire unified by Bismarck, and the decline in the hoarding demand of Oriental peoples. The average market ratio of silver to gold, which had been 15.57 to 1 in 1870, declined to 16.16 to 1 in 1874, to 16.64 to 1 in 1875, to 17.75 to

---

[4]U.S. Bureau of the Census, *Historical Statistics of the United States, 1789–1945* (Washington, D.C., 1949), pp. 264–265.

1 in 1876, and to 18.05 to 1 in 1880.[5] Beginning soon after 1873, therefore, owners of silver would have found it highly advantageous to sell it to the mints in the United States and to obtain and export gold; and had the free coinage of both metals prevailed at that time, the United States would have moved rapidly toward a *de facto* silver standard.

THE PERIOD OF THE GOLD COIN STANDARD, 1879–1933

But a "limping" standard at the start

When the Resumption Act went into effect on January 1, 1879, the United States was for the first time officially on a gold coin standard. For many years, nevertheless, finding an appropriate place in our monetary system for silver continued to be a vexatious and disturbing problem.

Bland-Allison Act   To redress the grievance felt by the inflationist elements of the country because of the "Crime of '73," Congress in 1878 passed the Bland-Allison Act, which ordered the Secretary of the Treasury to buy silver in the market for an indefinite period. Monthly purchases at current market prices were not to exceed $4 million or to fall below $2 million. The silver was to be coined as dollars of the former weight and fineness, that is, containing 371.25 grains of fine silver, and silver certificates in denominations of $10 or more could be issued against silver dollars held in the Treasury. The new silver dollars were made full legal tender, and as nothing was said about their redemption in gold, the state of the monetary system was confused. The presence of legal-tender credit money whose redemption in gold was not explicitly assured justified the description of the monetary system as a "limping" standard in contradistinction to a full-fledged gold coin standard.

As 291,200,000 ounces of silver were purchased under the Bland-Allison Act over a period of 12 years, the continued production of new silver dollars tended to exceed the monetary needs of the country or, at least, the need of a coin that was unpopular because of its size and weight. In consequence, the silver dollars quickly returned to the U.S. Treasury in the payment of taxes and other obligations. As far as circulation went, anyway, the situation was improved in 1886 when Congress authorized the issuance of silver certificates of $1, $2, and $5 denominations, for it was much easier to keep the paper money in circulation.

Redemption of Fractional Coins   The Resumption Act had ordered the Treasury to turn out fractional silver coins to redeem the outstanding frac-

---

[5]*Annual Report of the Director of the Mint,* 1952, p. 67.

tional paper money issued during the course of the Civil War. But so many of the coins were issued that they frequently passed only at a discount. To correct this situation, legislation passed in 1879 provided that subsidiary coins could be redeemed at the Treasury "for lawful money" if presented in amounts of $20 or multiples thereof. But "lawful money" included the silver dollars and the silver certificates authorized by the Bland-Allison Act; hence the "limping" character of the monetary standard was accentuated.

Sherman Silver Purchase Act   When the Bland-Allison Act was repealed in 1890, the country was not given relief from the shower of silver; instead, the Sherman Silver Purchase Act, calling for even heavier purchases, was enacted. The silver bloc was not satisfied with the Bland-Allison Act because a rising market value of silver resulted in smaller purchases by the Treasury, since the buying was done in terms of dollars. The Sherman Act, accordingly, directed the Treasury to buy as much as 4½ million ounces a month if available in the market, and to pay any price up to coinage value, that is, $1 for 371.25 grains. The silver was to be paid for by the issuance of new silver certificates (known as the "Treasury notes of 1890") that were made redeemable, quite strangely, in either gold or silver at the option of the Secretary of the Treasury—something that sounded like a return of bimetallism. The certificates were made legal tender except for payments contracted for in other kinds of money. Certificates amounting to $155,931,000 were issued in payment for 168,675,000 ounces of fine silver before the repeal of the Sherman Act in 1893.

Drain of Gold Reserves   The steady flow of silver certificates into the monetary stream, together with other disturbing occurrences, made it difficult to maintain gold redemption in the decade of the 1890s. Although it was permissible for the Treasury to redeem both the Bland-Allison certificates and the notes of 1890 in silver, gold redemption was freely provided. When, therefore, economic conditions became disturbed and people began to fear for the safety of the monetary system, they exchanged much of their paper money for gold. Financial difficulties in Europe caused foreign bankers to convert their investments in the United States into gold, and to export it in order to build up their reserves at home. At the same time, the revenues of the federal government were falling off, although concurrently, pensions for Civil War veterans increased. As the excessive circulation of money caused interest rates to fall, this occasioned further exports of gold for investment at higher rates abroad.

These conditions reached their culmination in the panic of 1893, and during the ensuing depression, the demand for gold very nearly caused the United States to suspend gold redemption. Time after time, the gold reserves were drawn down to low levels through the redemption of silver certificates. Although President Grover Cleveland, in the autumn of 1893, was able to persuade Congress to repeal the Sherman Silver Purchase Act, it was necessary for the government in the years 1894 to 1896 to sell $262 million of bonds to obtain gold to meet redemption demands. The determination of the government to maintain gold redemption, and the improvement in economic conditions generally, finally led to an easing of the gold drain, and the standard seemed to be safe.

Currency Act of 1900

It was generally thought that the defeat of William Jennings Bryan, who campaigned for "free silver" in the presidential elections of 1896 and 1900, would permanently settle the silver issue; but, as we shall see, it took another 70 years to do that. Bryan wanted the free and unlimited coinage of silver at the old ratio of 15.988 to 1; since the market ratio in 1896 was 30 to 1, his position was clearly untenable. Had he won either election and had he succeeded in having his proposal enacted, the United States would have found itself with a silver standard, for it would have been enormously profitable to export gold for sale abroad, and to import silver and have it coined.

But Bryan did not win in 1896, and before he had the chance to run again, Congress enacted legislation on March 14, 1900—well before the election of that year—declaring the gold dollar to be our "standard unit of value." This legislation was officially called the "Currency Act," although it is more commonly referred to as the "Gold Standard Act." It directed the Secretary of the Treasury to keep all other forms of money at par with gold, and this apparently meant that all kinds of hand-to-hand money, including the silver certificates, the notes of 1890, and the fractional coins, were to be redeemable in gold on demand. A gold fund of $150 million was to be maintained for the redemption of the greenbacks and the Treasury notes of 1890.

Revival of state-chartered banking

Even before the Civil War, especially in the larger cities, rapid progress had been made in the use of checks drawn on bank demand deposits as a means of payment, and the development greatly accelerated in the 1870s. Many bankers and would-be organizers of new banks thus came to realize that, after all, banks could operate profitably though lacking the right to issue their own paper money, that is, circulating notes. Such a realization led to a revival of interest in state-chartered banking. Applications for state charters were approved in increasing numbers, especially after 1880, and by 1899 the number of state banks, at 4451, exceeded that of national banks, at 3583. Charters for both classes of banks were granted liberally in the early years of the present century but at a more rapid pace for state banks. A total of 17,542 state banks were in operation in the year 1914, and substantially fewer than half as many national banks, 7525.[6]

---

[6]U.S. Bureau of the Census, *op. cit.*, pp. 264, 266.

Gold and silver, 1900–1933

After the adoption of the Currency Act of 1900, respect for and devotion to the gold coin standard grew steadily, and its general acceptance as the best possible monetary standard for the foreseeable future entrenched it in a strong position. At the same time, the power and influence of the bimetallists, the silver-purchase advocates, and other proponents of abundant money supplies largely went into eclipse, although without actually expiring, as will be seen later.

In the whole period from 1900 to the early 1930's, then, the preeminent position of the gold coin standard was not seriously threatened at any time. During World War I, there were restrictions on the exportation of gold and on its use in domestic industry, and people were urged, as a matter of patriotism, to turn in their gold coins to banks so that they could be accumulated as a national reserve, and such restrictions and urgings could be said to amount to a suspension of the gold standard. But if so, the suspension was short-lived, as the restrictions were removed in June 1919, and supplications concerning the disposition of gold coins were heard no more.

During the period of World War I, also, there was some further tampering with silver, but not of a kind to threaten the position of gold. By the terms of the Pittman Act of April 23, 1918, the United States melted down about 259 million silver dollars and sold the bullion to Great Britain, which needed it for monetary purposes in India—as a means of quieting the natives who had a special fondness for hard money. But the Pittman Act also directed the Treasury to replace this silver by purchases in the market—which was a kind of victory for the "silver interests," but not nearly of the proportions of the silver-purchase legislation of 1878 and 1890 and, later on, of the 1930s and 1940s.

Considering the relative insignificance of these developments concerning gold and silver, one readily concludes that the most important monetary event of the entire period from 1900 to the crisis of the early 1930s was the adoption of the Federal Reserve Act on December 23, 1913, with its provisions for a new kind of money—Federal Reserve notes—that was destined to serve us most admirably and for central banking facilities, albeit facilities of a rather peculiar kind.

All of which means that the gold coin standard seemed to be strong and safe while the banking system was in a state of almost constant disorder, confusion, and inefficiency, and it was this kind of shambles that the Federal Reserve Act was designed to clear up.

Defects in the banking system

The multiplication in the number of commercial banks in the 1880s and 1890s and in the early years of the present century, previously referred to, was hardly a movement in the direction of a stronger, more efficient commercial bank structure. Many of the newly chartered banks were undercapitalized and poorly managed—they were simply additional weak units in a system in which there were already too many weak units. And the system in a collective sense had many defects and weaknesses of its own, among the most important of which were the following:

1. Inelasticity and perverse elasticity in the issuance and retirement of national bank notes. Because these notes were issued on the basis of pledged Treasury bonds having the "circulation privilege," their expansion and contraction depended more on the state of the revenues and expenditures of the federal government, and therefore on its need of borrowing, than on the tempo of business activity and the need of paper money in circulation.

2. The machinery for the clearing and collection of out-of-town checks was slow, roundabout, and burdened with remittance charges.

3. The reserve regulations that applied to the commercial banks were poorly designed for preventing crises and panics. Though requirements seemed to be high, there was a considerable element of fiction in the way reserves were counted; and to the extent that reserves were not scattered in the vaults of individual banks, they tended to be concentrated as deposits at New York banks. As profit-seeking institutions, the New York banks had no strong reason to be concerned about the well-being or even the survival of their out-of-town bank customers that made these deposits.

4. Relationships between the Treasury and the commercial banks were defective because of the operations of the independent treasury system. Although the Treasury employed some of the national banks as depositories and fiscal agents, its allocation of funds between its own offices and these national banks was often haphazard. As a result, business disturbances occurred at times because of poor planning of federal fiscal operations and deposit decisions.

5. Obviously lacking was any single agency with power and responsibility to force upon the thousands of banks tighter managerial policies, safer modes of operation, and more efficient procedures. The Comptroller of the Currency and the state bank officials were largely occupied with routine matters of chartering and supervision, and it hardly occurred to them to try to coordinate their policies. Too often, indeed, these officials thought of themselves as being in competition with one another. And of course, there was no single agency to promote interbank relationships aimed at collective capacities to weather periods of stress and crisis.

6. The foreign exchange facilities of the country were primitive in scope and quality, so that business firms had to depend largely on British banks for their foreign trade financing. An important reason for this was that national banks were not permitted to accept time drafts drawn under letters of credit and were thus excluded from using the principal

international deferred-payment financing device. Although some state banks had the power to accept time drafts, there was no well-developed discount market in which accepted drafts could be sold.

7. Channels for interregional flows of loan funds were quite inadequate, so that banks in a given area might have excess loan funds with little demand for loans, while banks in other areas had little lending capacity with big loan demands. As evidence of this, the levels of interest rates often tended to vary markedly from region to region.

Federal Reserve Act

Although several chapters elsewhere in this text are devoted to the background, structure, and operations of the Federal Reserve System as our central bank, and although there are numerous references to it in other chapters, it should be instructive to have a brief outline here of the principal innovations of the Federal Reserve Act, as follows:

1. A degree of unification and coordination in banking was to be achieved by the establishment of twelve regional "central banks" and the creation in Washington of a board vested with supervisory powers. The twelve banks were expected to promote the unification of banking in their respective districts in that state banks were invited to voluntarily share the "membership" in the system required of national banks.[7] The Federal Reserve Board and the officials of the regional banks were given powers thought to be adequate for coping with future emergencies. It was expected that the Federal Reserve banks would accumulate in time most of the gold reserves of the country, so that the metallic foundation of the nation's monetary and banking systems would be marshaled under a unified management.

2. The inelasticity and perverse elasticity in the supply of paper money was to be overcome by the issuance of Federal Reserve notes, with reserves and collateral consisting of gold and commercial paper rather than government bonds; and according to the original design, the national bank notes were to be retired or at least replaced by "Federal Reserve bank notes," as a second kind of Federal Reserve paper money.

3. The weaknesses in the administration of bank reserves were to be corrected by the requirement that member banks keep a large portion of their reserves (and by an amendment of 1916, all their reserves) as deposits with the Federal Reserve banks. These provisions made possible a reduction in the size of required reserves.

4. National banks were authorized to distinguish between time and demand deposits and to greatly reduce reserves held against the time accounts. For the first time, therefore, they were enabled to compete on

---

[7]Although the number twelve is used here, the Federal Reserve Act provided for the establishment of not fewer than eight or more than twelve regional banks.

relatively equal terms with state banks in seeking savings and other
time balances.

5. To improve the mechanics for the clearing and collection of checks, the
    Federal Reserve Act authorized the Federal Reserve Board to function
    as a clearing agency for the twelve Reserve banks, and the Reserve banks
    in turn were required to perform clearing services for the member insti-
    tutions within their respective districts as ordered by the board.

6. As a means of promoting foreign trade financing by American banks,
    the national banks were authorized within certain limits to issue letters
    of credit and to accept time drafts drawn under them, and other pro-
    visions of the legislation were designed to encourage foreign branching
    by American banks.

7. In the matter of relationships between the U.S. Treasury and the bank-
    ing system, the legislation authorized the Reserve banks to act for the
    federal government as fiscal agents and depositories. (As was mentioned
    earlier in this chapter, these tasks were undertaken so efficiently by the
    Reserve banks that the independent treasury system was discontinued
    by legislation adopted in 1920.)

8. Finally, national banks were authorized, with the permission of the
    Federal Reserve, to engage in the trust business—another innovation
    aimed at equalizing competition between national and state institutions.

Toward a banking crisis

Many of the provisions of the Federal Reserve Act were highly successful in eradicating some of the monetary and banking difficulties and sources
of malfunction that had plagued the country for years and decades, as well
as in softening others. And many of the good results began to be realized
with surprising speed, as in the superior performance of Federal Reserve
notes by comparison with national bank notes, improvements in check
clearing facilities and procedures, the strengthened competitive position of
national banks, and the excellence of the working relationships between
the Federal Reserve banks and the Treasury.

But some other provisions of the Federal Reserve Act were not well-
designed. The idea of having "regional central banks," instead of one for
the whole country, was an absurdity, as became increasingly evident in the
1920s when, for example, the Reserve banks got in one another's way in
their open-market operations, and especially when the locus of power
seemed to many to be at the Federal Reserve Bank of New York rather than
at the headquarters of the Federal Reserve Board in Washington.

Nevertheless, the principal defects of the Federal Reserve Act were its
omissions—its lack of significant provisions for the strengthening of the
commercial banks individually and for the promotion of public confidence
in them, as, for example, a system of deposit insurance which the Senate
had wanted but which the House had rejected. The country continued to
be served or disserved by thousands of small, weak banks, many of them

undercapitalized, poorly managed, and without significant access to stronger institutions for help in time of need. Even the access of these banks to the Federal Reserve banks was quite limited, because of the non-membership of most of the state-chartered banks, and because, even for the member banks, the lending capacity of the Reserve banks was hedged about with many restrictions.

Thus the Federal Reserve Act did little to alter the stage setting for a banking crisis. Its coming was delayed by the boom of World War I and the highly prosperous conditions of most of the 1920s, but even in the 1920s there were many hundreds of bank failures. These occurred chiefly in farming areas, for the economic state of agriculture in the 1920s was one of depression and not of prosperity. The number of chartered commercial banks reached its highest year-end level at the end of 1921 with 21,327 state banks in operation and 8154 national banks for a total of 29,481, but already a wave of bank suspensions was gathering momentum.[8] In the years 1921–1929, the total number of suspensions—particularly concentrated in farming areas, as said previously—was 5413 including 4647 state-chartered banks and 766 national banks, and there were additional suspensions of 301 unincorporated "private" banks. Then, with the coming of the Great Depression in and after 1929, the wave of suspensions engulfed the urban areas of the country, with 4081 state-chartered banks, 846 national banks, and 175 private banks joining the failure rolls in the 3 years 1930–1932.[9]

Merging of crises

Meanwhile, a crisis was developing in Europe, beginning with the failure of the Kredit Anstalt, a large Austrian commercial bank, in May 1961, and spreading quickly to Germany and then to England. So ill-prepared was England to withstand the resulting "flight from the pound" that it suspended its gold standard on September 21, 1931, that is, it stopped redeeming the pound in gold bullion. Following this action by Britain, rumors began to spread that the gold standard of the United States would soon fall also, and we, in turn, experienced a "flight from the dollar." In a period of only 6 weeks following Britain's suspension, foreigners with dollar assets withdrew about $725 million in gold—close to one sixth of our total gold reserves at that time. Because of our willingness to pay gold, this first panic abated, but a new wave of gold withdrawals amounting to $450 million occurred in May and June 1932. Although this second flight from the dollar also subsided, the domestic situation had by then become so distressed that a major financial collapse seemed to be unavoidable.

The huge swellings in the ranks of the unemployed, the complete shutdowns of many factories, multiplications of the number of breadlines and the persons on them, and for the banks in particular, the continual parade

[8]*Ibid.*, pp. 264, 266.
[9]*Ibid.*, p. 273.

of closings caused a general loss of confidence in those that still remained open. People turned to hoarding—gold coin if they could get it, but if not, any other kind of paper money or coins would do. In state after state, the banks found that they could not meet withdrawal demands, and state governments came to their temporary rescue by declaring "bank holidays" ostensibly to celebrate some obscure persons or events in their histories never before thought worthy of much notice. As early as October 1932, a holiday of 12 days was proclaimed in Nevada, but most of the holidays of other states were proclaimed in February and the first few days of March 1933. New York, the stronghold of American banking, gave way on March 4, the day of President Franklin Roosevelt's first inauguration, and banks almost everywhere were in a state of suspension on that day.

THE PERIOD OF A FUSED FIAT-GOLD STANDARD, 1933–

In the field of money and banking, the Roosevelt administration faced two major problems: (1) to decide what to do about gold and with the gold coin standard, and (2) to get the commercial banks back into operation in a condition of such strength that the people's confidence in them would be restored.

Fall of the gold coin standard

In the matter of the gold coin standard, the early actions of the Roosevelt administration presaged its disestablishment, although it is most unlikely that this was immediately decided. In view of the acuteness of the crisis, the administration apparently had to make quick day-to-day decisions without pondering over their final results.

Nationalization of Gold Whatever its viewpoint, one of the first actions of the Roosevelt administration was the issuance on March 6 of a presidential proclamation that forbade banks to pay out gold and silver coins and bullion, to export these metals, and to "earmark" them in their vaults for foreign accounts. Then, under authority of the Emergency Banking Act adopted 3 days later, the President issued a series of executive orders further forbidding the exportation of gold coins, bullion, and certificates except by permission of the Secretary of the Treasury, and requiring everybody to deliver whatever gold coins, bullion, and certificates he might have to the Federal Reserve banks or to member banks of the Federal Reserve System in exchange, dollar for dollar, for other kinds of money.

Abrogation of the Gold Clause This nationalization of gold left none legally available for meeting outstanding obligations that had been declared to be payable in gold coins "of the weight and fineness" or "of the standard of value" existent at the time the obligations were incurred.

Obligations with such a "gold clause" were outstanding in enormous amounts, including large volumes of "gold bonds" of business corporations and the federal government's own "Liberty bonds" issued during World War I. Accordingly, a joint resolution of Congress signed by the President on June 6 abrogated the gold clause in all such contracts and outstanding debts, providing that all gold-clause obligations could be settled, dollar for dollar, in any legal tender, and forbidding the insertion of gold clauses in new contracts. One notable aspect of this action by Congress was its repudiation of an important contractual commitment of the federal government itself.[10]

A Gold-Buying Experiment   A little before this, a peculiar piece of legislation had been adopted—a rider to the Agricultural Adjustment Act of May 12, 1933, that came widely to be known as the "Inflation Amendment." This amendment authorized the President to reduce the gold weight of the gold dollar by as much as 50 percent, to restablish a bimetallic standard

---

[10]When the dollar was officially devalued in January 1934, the gold weight of the new dollar was fixed at 59.06 + percent of the former weight. Many creditors who had contracts payable in gold dollars of the old weight felt that they should receive more of the "59-cent dollars" than the contracts nominally called for. Lawsuits were therefore brought in the federal courts in which plaintiffs asked for payment of exactly or approximately $1.69 + (1 ÷ 0.5906) in legal tender money for each dollar in gold that had been promised; four such cases reached the Supreme Court. Two of the cases involved the payment of principal and interest on "gold bonds" issued by railroad companies (*Norman v. Baltimore and Ohio R.R.*, and *United States v. Bankers Trust Company*, 294 U.S. 240); one involved legal tender gold certificates (*Nortz v. United States*, 294 U.S. 317); and the fourth was concerned with the payment of principal upon the Liberty bonds of the federal government (*Perry v. United States*, 294 U.S. 330).

In its decisions, announced on February 18, 1935, the court held in the first place that Congress possessed the right to abrogate the gold clause as it existed in private contracts and in the contracts of state and local governments—this in accordance with its constitutional power to regulate the value of money. Second, the court held untenable the claim of the plaintiff who sought to recover from the federal government a sum in legal tender money far in excess of the face value of the gold certificates that he had been compelled to surrender. At best, he might have had the right to receive an equal face amount in gold coins, but he would not have been able to export them or to hold them within the country without a license; on the contrary, he would have been obligated to surrender the gold coins to the Treasury at face value for other kinds of money. Finally, the Supreme Court held that Congress did not have the authority to abrogate the gold clause as it applied to the contracts of the federal government itself, as in the Liberty bonds. Nevertheless, the owner of the Liberty bonds upon which suit was brought could not recover, the court decided, because he had not shown that he had been damaged by the action of Congress. Had the general price level changed in inverse proportion to the devaluation, recovery would presumably have been possible.

To forestall renewed efforts of the government's creditors to recover more than the face value of outstanding Treasury bonds and other obligations, Congress, by a joint resolution effective January 1, 1936, closed the Court of Claims to further suits. The federal government as a sovereign power can be sued only by its own consent; in this instance, the consent was permanently withdrawn.

at a gold-silver ration of his own choice, and to order the issuance of $3 billion of greenbacks of the Civil War variety to be used to pay off the principal of outstanding Treasury bonds.

The President ignored the provisions about bimetallism and greenbacks, but he picked for decisive action the provision that authorized him to devaluate the gold dollar. At his direction, the Reconstruction Finance Corporation—whose principal job was succoring tottering railroads, banks, and other financial institutions—began in August 1933 to offer to buy newly mined domestic gold at prices well above the former official price of $20.67 an ounce. The objective was to force prices in general to rise to the 1926 level, or at least wholesale prices, since 1926 was then the base year of the BLS index of wholesale prices. The "great deflation" that had been accompanying the Great Depression was to be reversed. Higher prices, by expanding profit margins, or more likely, by reducing loss margins, would encourage business firms to expand productive operations, and thus general business recovery would come about.

The theory was undoubtedly that of a professor of agricultural economics at Cornell University, George F. Warren, who was a close adviser to the President. His thought was that the great deflation had been caused by a world-wide shortage of gold, and that the appropriate remedy was to increase the gold supply—something that could be done at a stroke by increasing its price in terms of dollars. But as a test of the validity of his theory, the gold-buying experiment was undertaken under just about the worst possible circumstances. Since gold had already been nationalized, the only business that was likely to be stimulated by higher prices for gold was the gold mining industry!

Gold Reserve Act

By the end of January 1934, President Roosevelt was ready to set a definitive weight for the "new" gold dollar. Although he already had power to do this under the Inflation Amendment, he evidently wanted a further explicit authorization from Congress. Moreover, he wanted the Treasury to take title to all gold coins, bullion, and certificates held by the Federal Reserve banks,[11] and the seizure required specific action by Congress. Accordingly, on January 30, 1934, the Gold Reserve Act was adopted—an enactment that, with the Bretton Woods Agreements Act of 1945, gives us the fused fiat-gold monetary system that we now have. Because, therefore, the Gold Reserve Act is unquestionably to be classified as *basic* monetary legislation in effect at the present time, it surely deserves description in some detail.

---

[11]The gold coins, bullion, and certificates originally surrendered by the public to the member banks of the Federal Reserve System had, in turn, been surrendered by them to the Federal Reserve banks.

Principal Provisions The Gold Reserve Act vested in the federal government title to all gold coins, bullion, and certificates held by the Federal Reserve banks, and authorized the Treasury to give the Reserve banks credit on its books, dollar for dollar at the old rate, in compensation for these assets. The Treasury credits set up for the Federal Reserve banks were made payable in gold certificates of a new kind; and the Federal Reserve Act was amended in numerous places to substitute "gold certificates" for "gold," as in the reserve requirements applying to Federal Reserve notes and the deposit liabilities of the Reserve banks.

The devaluation power given to the President by the Inflation Amendment was modified by a provision stating "nor shall the weight of the gold dollar be fixed in any event at more than 60 per centum of its present weight." The Gold Reserve Act also provided that any profit realized through the devaluation of the dollar was to be turned into the Treasury as a "miscellaneous receipt" and that any loss that might occur through a subsequent revaluation upward would also be absorbed by the Treasury. Of the profit from devaluation, $2 billion was appropriated to an Exchange Stabilization Fund for the purpose of controlling the value of the dollar in international (foreign exchange) transactions. The fund was placed under the control of the Secretary of the Treasury subject to the supervision of the President.

The Gold Reserve Act provided that gold should no longer be coined for circulation in the United States, that "no currency of the United States shall be redeemable in gold" except as permitted by the Secretary of the Treasury with the approval of the President, and that existing gold be reduced to bars of a weight and fineness determined by the Secretary.

The Secretary of the Treasury was given numerous powers, all subject to the approval of the President. He was authorized to prescribe regulations for the use of gold in industry, the professions, and the arts; its acquisition by the Federal Reserve banks for the settlement of international obligations; and its use for other minor purposes. At his discretion, the gold certificates owned by the Reserve banks could be redeemed in gold when necessary to maintain the "equal purchasing power of every kind of currency of the United States." He was empowered to buy and sell gold at home and abroad in any amounts "at such rates and upon such terms and conditions as he may deem advantageous to the public interest." He also received authority to deal in gold, foreign currencies, credit instruments, and securities for the account of the Exchange Stabilization Fund.

Finally, in awkward phraseology, the Gold Reserve Act declared the gold dollar to be our "standard unit of value."

Devaluation of the Dollar By a proclamation issued on January 31, 1934, President Roosevelt officially reduced the weight of the gold dollar, nine-tenths fine, from 25.8 grains to $15\frac{5}{21}$ grains. This action effected a devaluation of approximately 40.94 percent, making the new price of gold $35 a fine ounce.[12] The total gold holdings of the government before the act of devaluation amounted to approximately $4043 million, and the President's proclamation immediately increased their dollar value to $6849 million. Two billion dollars of the increment were set aside in the newly created Exchange Stabilization Fund, and the remainder became a part of the general cash balance of the Treasury.

Loose Ends   Even for the domestic monetary system, the Gold Reserve Act and the President's proclamation were not well-rounded, complete jobs. The President continued to have the power to make further changes in the official value of gold as long as he stayed within the range between 50 and 60 percent of its pre-1934 official value; and the Secretary of the Treasury had the peculiar authority to buy and sell gold "at such rates and upon such terms" as he might choose. But there was no harm in this. The President's power to change the official value of gold was permitted to expire as of June 30, 1943, and the power of the Secretary of the Treasury to vary prices and terms for buying and selling is quite generally understood to have been abrogated by provisions of the Bretton Woods Agreements Act that are obviously at odds with the exercise of such a power.

More important, therefore, was the failure of the Gold Reserve Act to eliminate gold reserve requirements—changed to gold certificate requirements—applicable to Federal Reserve notes and the deposit liabilities of the Federal Reserve banks. If paper money, silver coins, and demand deposits were no longer to be redeemable for domestic purposes in gold, there was not much sense in having a gold certificate "backing" for this money or to have its expansibility restricted by certificate "requirements." Eventually, indeed, the gold certificate requirements were removed, but under circumstances of stress and concern that could have been avoided. These requirements were reduced in June 1945 because of wartime gold drains and huge increases in Federal Reserve notes and demand deposits in circulation, and then eliminated for Federal Reserve deposit liabilities by the act of March 3, 1965, and for Federal Reserve notes by the act of March 18, 1968, with these later actions taken because of misgivings of foreign holders of dollars about the availability of our gold reserves to redeem these dollars.

Bretton Woods Agreements Act

As Basic Legislation   As adopted on July 31, 1945, the Bretton Woods Agreements Act completed, as it were, the legislative foundation for our present fused fiat-gold monetary standard, the primary part of which had

---

[12]The gold value of the new dollar was equal to 59.0623815 percent of that of the old dollar; hence an ounce of gold that was formerly worth $20.67183462 was now worth $20.67+ ÷ 59.06+, or $35.

been laid by the Gold Reserve Act of 1934. The 1945 legislation had the effect of incorporating in our own basic monetary laws our duties, responsibilities, and rights as a member of the International Monetary Fund as provided for in its "articles of agreement."

The 1945 legislation authorized the President to accept membership for the United States in the IMF and directed the Secretary of the Treasury to pay over to it the gold and dollars we subscribed to its resources—the amount of our "quota." In becoming a member, we declared the par value of the dollar to be $15\frac{5}{21}$ grains of gold nine-tenths fine—the same value, of course, that the President had proclaimed in January 1934 under the Gold Reserve Act—and we undertook to redeem dollars held by other members of the fund at $35 an ounce plus our usual handling charge of 0.25 percent, and to accept gold from other members and the fund itself in exchange for dollars at $35 an ounce, less the handling charge. At the same time, the legislation forbids the President and our representatives in the fund's administration to agree to any change in the par value of the dollar without the specific consent of Congress.

Details about the structure of the IMF, how it operates, and the duties, responsibilities, and rights of member countries were presented at length in Chapter 5, and further details about some of these features may be found in Chapter 25 and about the major problems it faces at the present time, in Chapter 26.

Further Actions   In 1959, 1966, and 1970, our "quota" in the IMF was increased, bringing it at the end of 1970 to $6,700 million—meaning that from the beginning we had paid in 25 percent of this amount in gold and the balance in dollars and noninterest-bearing Treasury obligations convertible by the IMF into dollars on demand.

In addition, by the act of June 19, 1968, the United States accepted a role as a "participant" in the fund's new facility for special drawing rights (SDRs) that became operative at the beginning of 1970—agreeing, in effect, to recognize SDRs as an international reserve asset and to accept them, within prescribed limits, as a new kind of international money. But details about SDRs are also presented in Chapter 5.

A move that further affected our position in the IMF and our monetary relationships with its member countries was the action we took early in 1972 to further devaluate the dollar. The devaluation amounted to approximately 7.89 percent, and it gave the dollar a new fine gold weight of approximately 12.632 grains and placed our new official value of gold at $38 an ounce.

Rescue and reform for the banks

Returning to 1933, we find the Roosevelt administration facing its second major problem in the field of money and banking: that of getting the commercial banks back into operation in a manner that would restore the

people's confidence in them. As it turned out, however, it decided to go
well beyond this in the direction of reform in both commercial banking and
central banking—always, of course, with the consent and support of Congress and, in some instances, with its modifying, adding to, and deleting
proposals coming from the White House.

Rescue and Restoration   President Roosevelt's proclamation of March 6,
1933, previously referred to in the matter of gold, declared a nation-wide
"bank holiday" for all commercial banks. The holiday was to continue for
4 days, but on March 9 it was extended for an indefinite period. Then,
under authority of the Emergency Banking Act of March 9, the President
issued an executive order aimed at getting "sound" banks back into operation quickly. He empowered the Secretary of the Treasury to license
national banks and state member banks to reopen and proceed with customary operations, with the licensing actually to be done by the Federal
Reserve banks acting as the Secretary's agents. At the same time, the executive order authorized state supervisory authorities to permit the reopening
of their chartered banks that were not members of the Federal Reserve
System.

Most of the commercial banks that were judged to be "sound" were permitted to reopen during the first 4 business days of the week of March 12,
and by March 29, about 12,800 of the approximately 18,000 banks that had
been in operation before the crisis were functioning on an "unrestricted"
basis.[13] Many additional banks were subsequently permitted to reopen,
but the delay itself indicated varying degrees of "unsoundness" in their
condition as judged in March. On the other hand, between March 6 and
the end of the year, 2340 banks had been placed in receivership (including
179 licensed banks), and this number was in addition to 408 banks that had
been suspended between January 1 and March 4. At the end of the year,
at any rate, the President, by a proclamation of December 30, turned back
to the state authorities the jurisdiction over nonmember state banks that
he had assumed by the holiday proclamation of March 6.

Banking Act of 1933   In the Banking Act of June 16, 1933, Congress and
the administration turned to the task of reform, concentrating at this stage
on trying to clear up the weaknesses in the commercial banking system that
had been overlooked at the time of the adoption of the Federal Reserve Act
in 1913, as well as weaknesses that had developed since then. Its principal
provisions along this line were the following:

1.   Establishment of the system of deposit insurance, to start on January 1,
     1934, at the modest level of $2500 per depositor per insured bank (but
     raised to $5000 effective July 1, 1934, by a later amendment).

---

[13]*Federal Reserve Bulletin,* April 1933, p. 209.

2. Prohibition on the payment of interest on demand deposits by member banks of the Federal Reserve System, with provisions for restrictions on their payment of interest on time deposits.
3. Increased capital requirement for new national banks located in smaller communities—really a doubling of this requirement from $25,000 to $50,000.
4. Several new kinds of restrictions on investment by member banks, and very tight restrictions on their underwriting of and dealing in securities.
5. Prohibition on lending by member banks to their own executive officers, and close restrictions on their lending to "affiliates," such as holding companies and other subsidiaries of these holding companies.
6. Delegation of power to the Federal Reserve Board to remove directors and officers of member banks found guilty of violations of law or of "unsafe and unsound" banking practices.

Banking Act of 1935 By contrast, the principal objective of the Banking Act of August 23, 1935, was to reform our central bank structure. In essence, it discarded the idea of "regional central banks" of the Federal Reserve Act by concentrating power in the Washington supervisory agency hitherto called the Federal Reserve Board but now to be reconstituted and renamed as the Board of Governors of the Federal Reserve System. And not only a concentration of power, but new powers for the new board: to set and change reserve requirements applicable to the demand and time deposits of member banks, to dictate the classification of these deposits, to "review and determine" the discount rates charged by the Federal Reserve banks, and especially to constitute a majority of the membership of the Federal Open Market Committee. The FOMC had been set up by the Banking Act of 1933 to determine the open-market operations of the Federal Reserve banks—the most powerful instrument of monetary control, as described in Chapter 7—but the then Federal Reserve Board had been entirely excluded from its membership.

But the Banking Act of 1935 also had some further reform measures for the commercial banking system, most importantly a greatly expanded capacity of the Federal Reserve banks to lend to their member banks and therefore to come to their aid in time of difficulty. Other such measures were the requirement that national banks accumulate surplus accounts equal to their capital stock accounts, a prohibition on the payment of interest on demand deposits by insured nonmember banks, and the delegation of authority to the Federal Deposit Insurance Corporation to limit the payment of interest by insured nonmember banks on time deposits.

Hail and farewell to silver

Renewed Enthusiasm for Silver Buying Although the Roosevelt administration ignored the provisions of the Inflation Amendment of 1933 that authorized the reestablishment of a bimetallic monetary standard, it yielded readily to revived pressures for new and extraordinarily generous programs of silver buying. It started on this course with a presidential proclamation issued in December 1933 to ratify an agreement prepared at a "World Economic Conference" held during the preceding summer in London—an agreement by which the principal silver-producing and -using countries hoped to promote stability in the world silver market. As the United States accepted major responsibility for withholding silver from the world market, the President directed the Treasury to buy at 64.64 cents a fine ounce all domestic silver produced from the date of his proclamation and offered to it.

Then came the Silver Purchase Act of June 19, 1934, which envisaged "doing something for silver" more generous than anything else that had been done for it since bimetallism. The Treasury was authorized to buy silver until its market price—which had averaged about 35 cents an ounce in 1933—reached its "official" United States value of $1.29+ per fine ounce,[14] or until the country's silver reserves (including silver in circulating coins) reached 25 percent of our combined gold and silver reserves. Although the Treasury was authorized to pay up to $1.29+ a fine ounce, it continued to pay 64.64 cents except for silver already held in private stocks on May 1, 1934, for which the offering price, as prescribed in the law itself, was 50 cents an ounce. But even better things were to come. Whereas the Treasury had had some discretion about buying, the act of July 6, 1939, ordered it to buy all newly mined domestic silver offered at a new higher price of 71.11 cents a fine ounce, and the act of July 31, 1946, further hiked the prescribed price to 90.5 cents. However, the 1946 legislation authorized the Treasury to sell silver at any price not less than 90.5 cents, thereby rejecting, as it were, the reserve and price goals of the 1934 legislation.

Transformation in the Silver Market   But in the 1950s and early 1960s extraordinary developments were taking place in the silver market—in a direction opposite the developments of the 1870s and 1880s when silver experienced its first great plunge in value. Current production of silver outside the Iron Curtain was progressively falling short of demands for coinage and industrial uses, the deficiency in output rising from about 60 million ounces in the early 1950s to about 140 million ounces in 1961. Coinage demands increased because of the resumption of silver coinage in many foreign countries, the normal growth in coin requirements with expanding populations and transactions, and extraordinary additional needs for use in vending machines, coin telephones, and parking meters, for the payment of tolls and sales taxes, and for meeting the wants of an ever-

---

[14]The fraction in this value is the run-on fraction 0.2929 . . . , and the value itself originated with the Coinage Act of 1792 with its provision for a silver dollar of 371.25 grains of fine silver. Thus an ounce of silver (480 grains) was given a value of 480 ÷ 371.25, or $1.2929 . . . .

growing army of coin collectors and speculators. Expanded industrial demand resulted from new or enlarged uses of silver in photography and office copying machines, in electrical contacts, switching equipment, and batteries, and as solder and alloys in the manufacture of jet aircraft and missiles, as well as in the production of silverware. As a result of these developments, the price of silver in the New York market rose slightly above the Treasury's selling price of 91 cents an ounce in early 1959, and it became advantageous for silver users to buy from the Treasury.

Bowing Out of Silver   In the light of these market developments, we began a retreat from silver money. But the retreat was a rather leisurely one, considering the rapidly growing prospects that the market price of silver would go well above the "melting point" of fractional silver coins as soon as the Treasury stopped offering silver at prices below that level, and considering the increase in the hoarding of these coins in anticipation that they would soon be worth more as metal than as money.

There were four major steps in the retreat. First came the repeal of the silver-purchase legislation by the act of June 4, 1963, with a provision for the issuance, for the first time, of Federal Reserve notes in the $1 denomination to take the place of $1 silver certificates. Then came the Coinage Act of July 23, 1965, which substituted a combination of copper and nickel (cupronickel) for the silver in the quarter and dime, and which reduced the silver component of the half dollar from 90 percent by weight to 40 percent. The third step was the suspension of the redeemability of silver certificates in silver bullion as provided for by the act of June 24, 1967, the suspension to be effective one year later. (By order of the Secretary of the Treasury, as authorized by the act of June 4, 1963, redeemability in silver dollars had been changed in March 1964 to redeemability in bullion.) And finally came the legislation of December 31, 1970, which provided for cupronickel dollars and half dollars, but also, as a last gasp for silver money, 150 million "Eisenhower dollars" to contain by weight 40 percent silver. Twenty million of the Eisenhower dollars were to be highly polished "proof coins" to be offered for sale at $10 each, and the remainder, at $3 each. Meanwhile, the Treasury had turned over its remaining reserves of silver bullion to the military stockpile, so that it was necessary to make a reverse transfer for the minting of the silver-containing Eisenhower dollars.

FOR REVIEW

1. What kinds of money were used as mediums of exchange and as the standard of value during our colonial period? What difficulties with money were experienced in that period?
2. What actions about money did the Continental Congress take during the period of the American Revolution? What actions were taken under the Articles of Confederation?

3. What were the principal provisions of the Coinage Act of 1792? What was the nature of the subsequent difficulties with the gold coinage and the silver dollar?

4. What were the principal arguments for and against the establishment of the first Bank of the United States? Why was its charter not renewed?

5. Why were the Coinage Acts of 1834 and 1953 adopted? Did they fulfill their objectives? Explain.

6. In what ways was the second Bank of the United States mismanaged? Why did the question of its rechartering become an important political issue?

7. To what extent did commercial banking under state charters develop in the period before the Civil War? What were "wildcat banks"? "pet banks"?

8. Why did the federal government set up the "independent treasury system" in the 1840s? How well did it function? Why was it discontinued?

9. What happened to bimetallism in the United States and elsewhere in the 1870s?

10. Why did banking under state charters almost vanish in the late 1860s and then have a great resurgence later in the century?

11. Why is the Federal Reserve Act described as the most important monetary event in the United States between 1900 and 1933?

12. Under what circumstances was the gold coin standard suspended in 1933? Was the suspension justified? Discuss.

13. What is meant by the "abrogation of the gold clause" as occurring in 1933? What did the Supreme Court decide about the constitutionality of this action?

14. Why are the Gold Reserve Act of 1934 and the Bretton Woods Agreements Act of 1945 described as the basic monetary legislation of our present system?

15. Why and how was the dollar devaluated in 1934? How was it possible for a "profit" to result from the devaluation? Who got it?

16. What was the basic objective of the Banking Act of 1933? of the Banking Act of 1935?

17. What were the principal developments in the period 1965–1970 pertaining to the position of silver in our monetary system?

II

FINANCIAL INSTITUTIONS AND MARKETS

CHAPTER 9

FINANCIAL INSTITUTIONS: CENTRAL AND COMMERCIAL BANKS

Many times in the preceding chapters, references were made to the Federal Reserve System as our central bank because of its responsibility and powers to control the money stock, and to the commercial banks because of their role as the principal creators of money. But the student should know these institutions more intimately. Moreover, he should be acquainted with several other classes of institutions that are important in directing money flows in the economy and with the markets in which they operate.

In the present chapter, accordingly, a start will be made with an analysis of the characteristics that financial institutions have in common, to be followed with an examination of the major structural features of the Federal Reserve System and the commercial banking system and some of their interrelationships. Then, in Chapter 10, the structure and functions of other major classes of financial institutions will be studied, and finally, in this part of the textbook, the shape and scope of the markets in which financial institutions operate will be analyzed in Chapter 11.

GENERAL CHARACTERISTICS

Financial institutions are distinguished from all other kinds of business enterprises in that their principal operations are directed to accumulating the temporarily idle money of the public and passing it on for spending to borrowers and to sellers of securities. They are financial intermediaries. Some classes of financial institutions accumulate money by "accepting" demand deposits, savings deposits, other time deposits, or a combination of these; some sell shares to people who become their "members"; some sell their own issues of stocks, bonds, investment certificates, and promissory notes; some sell insurance policies and annuity contracts; some employ still other techniques for getting money accumulations; and some use two or more of these procedures. Much of the money accumulated by financial institutions is passed on as loans directly arranged with borrowers; but much, too, is passed on, as it were, impersonally, as by buying in the open market stocks and debt instruments issued by governments, business corporations, and other seekers of funds.

Some of the subclasses of financial institutions are called "banks," "banking firms," or "banking houses," while others are rarely, if ever, so labeled. Because, indeed, it is not at all clear why a distinction is made, we must immediately recognize that the term *bank* has no clear-cut meaning. Thus a savings and loan *association* does much the same thing as a mutual savings *bank* in its procedures of acquiring money and lending it out; and consumer loans of some finance *companies* are comparable with those of credit *unions* and commercial *banks*. We simply must accept the popular usage.

Sources of money accumulations

Saving   Saving is the principal source of the money that financial institutions accumulate. *Saving* is current money income left after the payment of taxes that income receivers decide not to spend for consumer goods, at least temporarily. The income receivers may defer their spending for consumer goods for short or long periods, or they may never spend their saved money income for such goods. Meanwhile, however, the saved money income is available to them. What do they do with it?

They may hoard it in safe-deposit boxes or under mattresses, but decisions in this direction are usually insignificant in relationship to the total volume of saving. They may invest the saved money income in new means of production, such as factory machinery and equipment, store and office buildings, houses and other residential properties, trucks and other rolling stock, and inventories. This is obviously the decision of individuals who spend saved money income for new homes, and it is outstandingly the decision of nonfinancial business enterprises that have no intention of spending their savings at any time for consumer goods but for the expansion of their productive facilities. Again, savers may decide to turn their savings over to other persons and nonfinancial enterprises for new productive facilities or to governments in order to cover their deficits. This is done chiefly, of course, by buying in the market securities issued by the nonfinancial enterprises and governments. Finally, among the principal choices that savers have, they may entrust their saved money income to financial institutions. The financial institutions strongly urge them to do this by offering rewards in the form of interest or dividends (and sometimes prospects of "capital gains," that is, profits from sales of portfolio securities), by promising to provide many kinds of services, and with some exceptions, by giving the greatest assurances that savings entrusted to them will be safe. Indeed, financial institutions in their respective classes, and among classes, compete strenuously with one another to capture the affections of savers, and many of them hope to corral savings temporarily held by savers for later purchases of capital facilities and securities, in addition to savings held by savers who have no such spending intentions.

We should add that, in effect, many income receivers have contractual obligations to financial institutions to save. If they have previously obtained loans from these institutions to enable them temporarily to spend beyond their incomes, they must save out of subsequent income flows in order to meet their repayment obligations. Always keep in mind therefore that money made available to financial institutions for loans and security buying includes both "new" deposits and the like and repayments on loans previously granted and retirements of security holdings by their issuers.

Other Sources A second important source of money accumulations of financial institutions is newly created money—a source that, in the first instance, is tapped almost exclusively by the commercial banks. As we know by now, the individual commercial bank participates in a process of money creation when it credits demand deposit accounts for the proceeds of loans and security purchases, and it can be said to be an accumulator of this newly created money until the borrowers and security sellers make withdrawals. Moreover, as we also know, withdrawals generally appear as demand deposits in other commercial banks, so that the *system,* as it were, holds on to the newly created money as accumulations of the de-positors' temporarily idle holdings.

A further source of money accumulation by financial institutions is the importation of money from foreign countries. Foreigners may sell some of their currencies to commercial banks for demand deposit balances payable in dollars, and such balances, though drawn on by the foreigners, tend to stay with the commercial banking system until a transaction in reverse of the original one occurs. In a similar way, foreigners may obtain deposit balances at commercial banks when the central banks of their countries sell them dollars obtained by drawings from the IMF or by sales of gold or SDRs to the U.S. Treasury.

Finally, some money flows to financial institutions may come from dishoarding. But if hoarding is likely to be small in relationship to the volume of saving, as said previously, dishoarding in any period is not likely to be an important means of accumulation to the institutions.

Disposal of money accumulations

In order to continue to attract money flows from savers and other holders of idle balances, financial institutions must quickly pass on the money they accumulate—or most of it—to individuals, enterprises, and governments for spending. They must put the money to work in order to earn income to pay the interest or dividends they have promised, to meet the costs of the services they provide (to the extent that fees and commissions do not cover these costs), and, indeed, to strengthen their assurances of safety.

Because they are financial intermediaries, they spend very little of the money they accumulate for physical facilities, inventories, and the like, as manufacturing companies do, but put most of it to work by giving it to borrowers and security sellers for spending for such things.

Some classes of financial institutions, including savings and loan associations, consumer finance companies, and credit unions, are highly specialized in their choice of loan outlets and the kind of securities they buy. Others, especially the commercial banks, are wide-ranging in their search for numerous outlets for their money accumulations. And still others, including life insurance companies and business finance companies, take positions between close specialization and generalization. Much depends on the basis from which the institutions get their charters or licenses, since charters and licenses generally authorize the carrying on of activities of specified kinds, and since the laws impose rules and regulations on the charter holders and licensees. But much depends, too, on the ingenuity of institutional managers in devising new operating procedures that do not appear to violate the traditional rules and regulations. In recent years, at any rate, there has been a strong drive toward generalization. Restrictions have become increasingly irksome to the managers of many financial institutions, and they have sought new powers of lending and security buying by amendments to laws and regulations or by reinterpretation of existing laws and regulations.

A peculiar aspect of the "passing-on" operations of financial institutions is that there is always a considerable interchange of money among them, so that, for substantial amounts accumulated, the collecting institutions are not the ultimate suppliers to spenders. Commercial banks keep deposits with other commercial banks, and almost all institutions of other classes keep most of their cash balances as checking accounts at the commercial banks. In reverse directions, the commercial banks are lenders to one another and to many institutions of the other classes. Trust institutions and mutual savings banks invest in the common stocks of commercial banks. Life insurance companies buy bond issues of finance companies. Some investment companies invest in the stocks of several other kinds of financial institutions. Some pension funds have savings accounts at savings and loan associations. Most of the residential mortgage loans originated by mortgage bankers are transferred to life insurance companies and mutual savings banks. Many other such interchanges could be cited, but those mentioned should be sufficiently illustrative.

Contribution to economic welfare

The work that financial institutions do (with exceptions for the few that are deliberately fraudulent) is quite beneficial to economic society—they are not parasitic as some people suspect. The principal benefits to savers individually by way of income returns, services, and safety have already been mentioned, and the principal benefits to the individuals, enterprises, and governments to which the financial institutions lend and whose securities they buy are almost as obvious. For the typical home buyer, for example, getting a mortgage loan from a financial institution is surely more convenient, less time consuming, and probably less embarrassing than trying to collect the needed money from relatives and friends; and much the same can be said for the typical business enterprise that seeks loans from financial institutions rather than directly soliciting savers.

In an over-all sense, moreover, financial institutions collectively make very important contributions to economic stability and growth. Indeed, it is reasonable to say that their collective function of accumulating savings and passing them on for expenditure is essential for economic stability and growth. For economic stability to prevail in any period of time of significant length, it is necessary that spending for capital goods—new productive facilities, including housing and inventories—plus government deficit spending be equal to planned saving, that is, the saving that people want to do and expect to be able to do out of their money income of the period. Accordingly, the financial institutions, by their unceasing efforts to attract savings and by their policies of quickly passing these savings on for the financing (chiefly) of spending for capital goods and government deficits greatly help to bring about such an equality or equilibrium. For economic growth, it is necessary that spending for capital goods plus government deficit spending exceed planned saving. Although such an excess could come from the dishoarding of money previously hoarded, it is made possible chiefly by financial institutions, perhaps in a limited way by the importation of money from foreign countries, but predominantly, again, by the creation of new money in the form of demand deposits by the commercial banks on the basis of additional primary reserves supplied by the Federal Reserve.

Merchants of credit

Credit and Debt   The operations of financial institutions are so thoroughly involved with promises to pay that they are often called "merchants of credit." *Credit* may be defined as *the right to receive payment or the obligation to make payment on demand or at some future time on account of an immediate transfer of goods.* As the origin of the term implies (*credere*, to trust), credit is based on the faith or confidence that the creditor reposes in the ability and willingness of the debtor to fulfill his promise to pay. In a credit transaction, the right to receive payment and the obligation to make payment necessarily originate at the same time and for the same amount; indeed, the two phrases simply describe the transaction from the respective points of view of the creditor and the debtor. Although the term *debt* is often used in specific reference to the debtor's obligation to pay, debt and credit actually mean the same thing, allowing for the difference in viewpoint. Thus it could be much more pleasant to refer to the national "credit" in the vicinity of $400 billion rather than the national "debt" of that amount—looking at it from the standpoint of the owners of Treasury securities.

The goods acquired in the present in a credit transaction may consist of physical assets, such as commodities and real property, money, or intangible rights. When money is obtained on credit, the intent of most borrowers is to use the money immediately to obtain physical assets, so that, ultimately the transaction is one whereby physical assets are obtained by means of credit. In many instances, however, the debtor obtains money on the basis of a promise to repay, not with the intention of using it himself to acquire physical assets, but with the intention of advancing it to others for such a purpose. And this, of course, describes the procedure of most financial institutions in acquiring money from savers and others against promises to repay.

Role of Rights to Payment　Intangible rights have a prominent place in the extension, use, and extinguishment of credit. Indeed, a credit itself is such a right—the creditor's right to receive a stipulated payment from the debtor at a specified time or on demand. But the "goods" received by the debtor in the present may also consist of rights, as when he gets a promise to pay from the creditor in exchange for his own promise to pay. Exchanges of rights of this description are especially common in the operations of financial institutions. Such an exchange is typified in the procedure of commercial banks in granting loans to customers. The customer signs a promissory note that sets forth the time and amount of his obligation to repay, and the bank credits his demand deposit account for the amount of the loan, thereby obligating itself to pay this amount as ordered by a check or checks to be drawn by the customer. Likewise, investment bankers, in underwriting a bond issue, sign an agreement with the issuer promising to pay for the entire issue at a designated price and time, but in return, they receive the bonds which are themselves the issuer's promises to pay interest and principal.

Rights and Obligations of Financial Institutions　Consider the abbreviated statement of the assets, liabilities, and capital of all insured commercial banks at the end of 1969, as presented in Table 9-1, as an indicator of how financial institutions are surrounded, as it were, with promises to pay. Except for paper money and coins on hand, bank premises, and a few minor items such as supplies inventories (not shown separately), all the assets are rights to receive payment: from other banks for "cash items" drawn on them and sent to them for payment and on deposit balances held with them, from government and business corporations for interest and principal on holdings of their securities, and from borrowers for interest and principal on loans granted. And all the liabilities, by the very reason that they are so called, must be obligations to pay: to demand and time depositors, to other banks for borrowed money, to employees for accrued wages, to governments for accrued taxes, and so on. Even among the capital accounts, "capital notes and debentures" are obligations to pay their holders interest and principal, leaving only the stock and surplus accounts outside the realm of promises to pay. Allowing for the exceptions mentioned, then, all these are the promises that financial institutions live by—and men and women, too, either individually or through their enterprises or governments that are both the creditors and the debtors of the financial institutions.

SPECIAL POSITION OF THE COMMERCIAL AND CENTRAL BANKS

In any description of financial institutions as accumulators and dispensers of savings and other temporarily idle money, a special position must be reserved for the commercial and central banks. The commercial banks deserve special recognition because of their capacity to create money in the form of demand deposits. Like other financial institutions, they accumulate money against promises to pay, but their promises or obligations to pay on demand are themselves commonly used and generally accepted as mediums of exchange. *What is basically a promise to pay money is treated by the public as money itself.*

In turn, the central bank deserves special recognition because of its unique responsibility to control the quantity of money in circulation in order to promote the general welfare—to try to achieve full employment, price-level stability, and so on. In most developed countries, the central bank directly controls the quantity of paper money in circulation because it is the exclusive issuer of this kind of money, its issues taking the form of bank notes; and it controls the quantity of demand deposits because of its capacity to alter the volume of the commercial banks' cash reserves that determine their capacity to create demand deposits.

So extraordinary is the position of the central bank that there is doubt whether it should be called a "financial institution" in any ordinary sense. In order to create reserves for the commercial banks, as by granting loans to them or by buying Treasury obligations in the open market, the Federal Reserve banks need no accumulation of anybody's temporarily idle money. They do, indeed, hold deposits of member banks, the Treasury, government agencies, and foreign governments and central banks, but their lending and investing capacity does not derive from these deposits. All these deposits could be withdrawn without diminishing the capacity of the Reserve banks to go on creating reserves by their own lending and investing operations. The withdrawals could easily be met by the issuance of new Federal Reserve notes, and the proceeds of further Reserve bank lending and investing could also be paid out in still more Federal Reserve notes. Essentially, therefore, the power of the Federal Reserve to vary the amount of commercial bank reserves derives from its capacity to issue paper money unlimitedly, and not from any accumulation of money already existing.

Table 9-1   Assets, Liabilities, and Capital of All Insured Commercial Banks, December 31, 1969 (in millions of dollars)

ASSETS

Currency and coin		7,347
Deposits with Federal Reserve and other banks		41,394
Cash items in process of collection		40,594
U.S. Treasury obligations	54,530	
Federal agency securities	9,772	
Obligations of state and local governments	58,944	
Other securities	2,140	
Loans and discounts	286,752	
	412,138	
Less reserves for losses	6,179	405,959
Bank premises, furniture, and fixtures		8,070
Other real estate owned		361
Customers' liability on acceptances outstanding		3,309
Other assets		17,503
Total assets		524,536[a]

LIABILITIES

Demand deposits	240,131
Time deposits	196,859
Liabilities for borrowed money	18,654
Acceptances outstanding	3,387
Other liabilities[b]	25,929
Total liabilities	484,960

CAPITAL

Capital notes and debentures	1,998
Preferred stock	103
Common stock	10,529
Surplus	17,461
Undivided profits	8,427
Surplus reserves	1,058
Total capital	39,576
Total liabilities and capital	524,536

[a] Items do not add exactly to this total because of rounding.
[b] Including minority interests in consolidated subsidiaries of $3.3 million.
Source: Derived from Federal Deposit Insurance Corporation, *Annual Report,* 1969, pp. 258–261.

CHARTING MONEY FLOWS

In Figure 9-1, we attempt to picture many of the propositions concerning money flows and the roles of financial institutions discussed in the preceding pages of this chapter—with, indeed, a few propositions added.

All the financial institutions except the Federal Reserve System are shown appropriately in the position of "intermediaries" between savers (standing also for dishoarders and foreign suppliers of funds) on the one side, and investment spenders—spenders for capital facilities—and governments that want money to cover their deficits, on the other side. But financial institutions are not intermediaries for all money flows from one side to the other, as is shown by the bifurcated arrow going from savers to the money and capital markets and to investment spenders. This arrow indicates that (1) savers may themselves spend for new productive facilities, as when individuals buy new homes and business proprietors, partners, and corporations use retained earnings to acquire productive facilities, such as machinery and inventories; and that (2) savers may buy securities in the money and capital markets and thus make their savings available to the sellers of these securities whether domestic spenders for capital facilities, spenders on foreign projects, or governments. (For brief definitions at this point, the money market is the market in which money is loaned for periods not exceeding 1 year, and the capital market is one in which money is loaned for periods of more than 1 year and in which corporate stocks are bought and sold.) The remaining savings are shown as flowing to financial institutions by way of deposits and "security buying" —the purchase of various kinds of instruments that institutions issue.

Within the financial institutions' quadrangle, the commercial banks are marked off because of their special powers to create money in the form of demand deposits, but their separation by a dotted line indicates that they remain in the general class of financial institutions as accumulators of savings. The consumer credit institutions also get special notice by a dotted line and by an arrow going, as it were, against the savings flow, in recognition of their peculiar role of accumulating savings to pass on to borrowers who want to spend for consumer goods beyond their current incomes, that is, to dissave. The U-shaped arrow drawn between the financial institutions and the money and capital markets calls attention to the interchange of money accumulations among financial institutions, as described earlier, an interchange in which the commercial banks and consumer credit institutions participate (despite the dotted-line segregation). And the arrow from the financial institutions to the money and capital markets and the arrows from these markets to investment spenders and governments are designed to represent the main flows of money accumulations from the financial institutions, many of these flows on the basis of loans directly negotiated and the remainder by way of purchases in the markets of new issues of securities of investment spenders and governments.

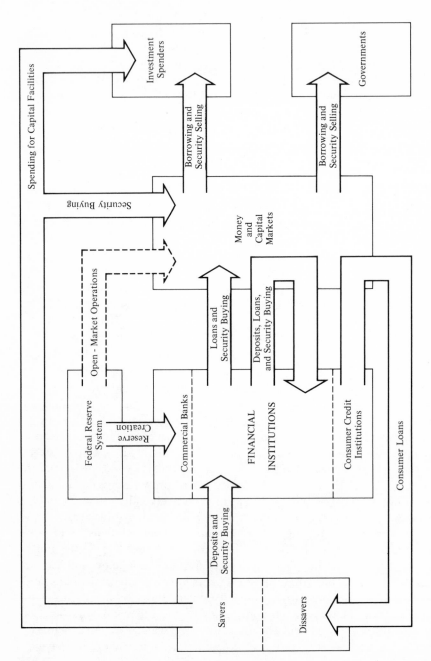

Figure 9-1. Savings Flows and Financial Institutions as Intermediaries

Finally, the Federal Reserve System, as our central bank, has a position outside of and above the quadrangle for financial institutions, because of doubts about whether it is a financial institution in the ordinary sense, but especially because it is supposed to control money creation in such manner that everything else in the picture will function in ways conducive to the general welfare. Since, however, its control is exercised chiefly by regulating demand deposit creation by the commercial banks, its solid outflow arrow is shown as going directly to these banks. At the same time, a second arrow indicates that the Federal Reserve engages in market transactions, especially in Treasury obligations, but the arrow is dotted rather than solid to indicate that these transactions are designed to affect commercial bank reserves rather than to supply money elsewhere, as to the Treasury to cover its deficits.

(In a chart like Figure 9–1, some scholars would interpose the money and capital markets between savers and the financial institutions on the left-hand side as well as on the right-hand side. Their reasoning is that the financial institutions sell to savers various kinds of short-term and long-term "financial assets"—demand deposits, time deposits, promissory notes, insurance policies, bonds, stocks, and so on—and that such sales can appropriately be called money and capital market transactions. While such a point of view and its terminology are quite acceptable, the interposition is omitted from Figure 9-1 in order to avoid complexity.)

THE FEDERAL RESERVE SYSTEM AS OUR CENTRAL BANK

Structure

As it is well known that there are twelve Federal Reserve banks in operation in the United States, the frequent references that have been made to the Federal Reserve System as our central bank in the singular may seem to be inaccurate. Truly, however, the System is unitary in character. Despite the separate operation of the twelve Reserve banks (plus, indeed, their twenty-four branches), all their activities that have to do with money creation and control are closely coordinated *and directed* by the Board of Governors of the Federal Reserve System whose headquarters are located in Washington, D.C., and by the Federal Open Market Committee that meets there every 3 or 4 weeks.

The Board of Governors is composed of seven persons who are chosen by the President with the advice and consent of the Senate for 14-year terms. The terms are staggered with the term of one member expiring at the end of January in each even-numbered year. All the important powers of monetary control that national governments usually allocate to their central banks are concentrated by the federal government in the Board of Governors, except for the power of determining the open-market operations of the Federal Reserve banks, which is the most important money-control power of all. This power the Board shares with five presidents of Reserve banks who join it in composing the Federal Open Market Committee (FOMC). The FOMC always includes the president of the Federal Reserve Bank of New York, with the other four presidential places rotated from year to year among the presidents of the other eleven Reserve banks. If it did not have to share the open-market power with the five Reserve bank presidents, the Board of Governors could well be called our "central bank," with the Reserve banks and their branches regarded as operating facilities of this central institution. In recognition of the sharing of power, therefore, the logical conclusion would seem to be that our central bank is the Board of Governors and the FOMC jointly, with the Reserve banks and their branches as operating facilities.

Functions

The primary responsibility of the Federal Reserve is to control the quantity of money in circulation in such manner as to promote the general welfare. Responsibility requires power, and the Board of Governors has the power to control the issuance of Federal Reserve notes, as we noted in Chapter 4, and joined with the five Reserve bank presidents in the FOMC, to control the quantity of commercial bank primary reserves and presumably, therefore, their creation of demand deposits, as we noted in Chapter 7. These powers are supplemented in various ways, most notably by the board's authority to set reserve requirements applicable to the deposit liabilities of the commercial banks that are members of the Federal Reserve System (as described later in this chapter), to set maximum rates of interest that member banks may pay on time deposits, and to establish margin requirements for certain kinds of loans for the purchase of stocks and bonds.

In its control of the quantity of money in circulation, a central bank is expected to prevent financial crises and panics. In attempting to curb inflation, in particular, it must not be so restrictive as to bring about a "liquidity crisis"—a situation in which business enterprises that are normally rated as "strong" cannot get enough money to meet current operating expenses and maturing debts. If it has inadvertently been too restrictive, it should "backtrack" quickly and take action to provide for very large conversions of noncash assets into money. This is what is generally meant by references to the central bank as the "lender of last resort." Business enterprises cannot get money because other lenders have no money to give them, but the central bank, as lender of last resort, should have ample means to supply these money requirements, in order to prevent or curb panic. Because the money and reserve creating capacities of the Federal Reserve itself are not subject to reserve requirements, it is always in a very strong position to act as lender of last resort. The only question we might ask is whether it will recognize a developing crisis quickly enough and be sufficiently generous in meeting it.

Finally, the Federal Reserve, like the central banks of other countries, is expected to be the principal adviser of the national government in all matters of finance, and especially in regard to the government's own finances and fiscal policy. The point is that, for maximum effectiveness, the money-control policies of the Federal Reserve must be coordinated with the debt-management and fiscal policies of the Treasury, so that there should always be a close "working relationship" between the two agencies. It is probable that the Federal Reserve is, indeed, the principal financial adviser to the Treasury, although we cannot be certain because of the intangibles involved in advisory capacities and working relationships and because advice may be sought but not followed.

THE COMMERCIAL BANKING SYSTEM

Wide range of operations

The commercial banks are distinguished from all other classes of financial institutions because they create and hold the demand deposits of the general public. They have other notable features and accomplishments that tend to set them apart from other classes of financial institutions, but not entirely, because there is at least some sharing with other classes. They are the most important accumulators of savings in time deposits. In total assets, they collectively lead by a very wide margin.

They engage in so many fields of financing that they are often called "department stores of banking." They are the principal short-term lenders to business enterprises, but they are also responsible for a large volume of intermediate-term loans to business firms. In competition with other mortgage lending institutions, they grant large numbers of loans for the construction and purchase of residential property; in competition with other consumer credit institutions, they hold the leading position in granting consumer loans; and in competition with other farm credit institutions, they account for a large volume of loans for many purposes to farmers. They are the principal lenders to brokers and dealers in securities who borrow to finance their customers' purchases "on margin," and they account for an additional large volume of loans to one another as well as to financial institutions of other classes.

The commercial banks invest in securities of many classes of issuers. Some of the larger ones buy and sell government securities in capacities as dealers, and almost all are willing to act as agents for their customers in executing orders to buy and sell securities of all kinds. The larger commercial banks, too, maintain the great bulk of foreign exchange facilities, and many smaller ones have correspondent relationships with these banks to enable them also to buy and sell foreign currencies.

Finally—and this list is not exhaustive—the commercial banks supply a very large proportion of institutional trust services by which they manage specific arrays of segregated assets as executors and administrators of decedents' estates, as guardians of the property of minors and mental incompetents, and as trustees and agents.

Structure

We are said to have a *dual* commercial banking system, because both the federal government and the state governments charter commercial banks. Those chartered by the federal government are always recognizable by having the word *national* in their names, even if it is added at the end, as in the case of the Chase Manhattan Bank National Association (often abbreviated to N.A.). National banks receive their charters from the Comptroller of the Currency, an officer of the Treasury Department, and they are subject throughout their careers to his regulatory supervision. They are required to be members of the Federal Reserve System and to have their deposit accounts insured by the Federal Deposit Insurance Corporation. Significant among the features of membership in the Federal Reserve System are requirements that member banks hold cash reserves as percentages of their deposits at levels fixed by the Board of Governors and keep their interest payments on time deposits within the maximum rate limits set by the board. Other important features are the ownership by the member banks of all the stock of the Federal Reserve banks, their subjection to numerous rules and regulations of the Federal Reserve Act and the Board of Governors in addition to rules about reserves and interest payments, and their ready access to many services provided by the Federal Reserve banks —provided, for the most part, without charges.

State banks or state-chartered banks get their charters from state officials who are variously known as secretaries, commissioners, and superintendents of banking (and sometimes by other names), and like national banks, they continue to be subject to the regulatory supervision of the chartering official. Many "state banks" are really "trust companies" that have been primarily authorized, as it were, to provide trust services to the public, but have been additionally authorized to engage in the commercial banking business. On the other hand, many institutions chartered as commercial banks, both national and state, have been additionally authorized to engage in the trust business, so that, at the present state of development, the distinction is of little significance. State-chartered banks are eligible for membership in the Federal Reserve System, that is, they may become members if they apply and are accepted. If they are accepted, they must have their deposit accounts insured by the FDIC. Almost all of the large state-chartered commercial banks are members, but a great majority of the smaller ones are not. But nonmember state banks may still get their deposit accounts insured by the FDIC by application and acceptance, and all but about 200 have applied and been accepted.

Cross-classification

Using a cross-section view based simultaneously on charter sources, membership in the Federal Reserve System, and deposit insurance, we have four classes of commercial banks: (1) national banks that are members and insured, (2) state member banks that are insured, (3) state nonmember banks that are insured, and (4) state nonmember noninsured banks. The number and assets of the banks of these four classes individually and in certain pertinent combinations as of June 30, 1970, are presented in Table 9-2.

Table 9-2   **Status, Number, and Assets of Commercial Banks, June 30, 1970**
(assets in billions of dollars)

STATUS	NUMBER	ASSETS
National banks	4,637	312.5
State member banks	1,166	117.2
Total member banks	5,803	429.7
State nonmember insured banks	7,675	96.8
Total insured banks	13,478	526.5
State nonmember noninsured banks	193	4.1
Total commercial banks	13,671	530.6
Total nonmember banks	9,034	218.1
Total state-chartered banks	7,868	100.9

Source: *Federal Reserve Bulletin,* May 1971, pp. A22–A23.

FOR REVIEW

1. What is the common function that distinguishes all financial institutions collectively from other classes of business enterprises? Why are the financial institutions described as intermediaries?
2. What are the principal sources of the money accumulations of financial institutions? In general terms, what are the principal outlets for these money accumulations?
3. What justification is there for saying that financial institutions make important contributions to economic welfare?
4. What is credit? What is the relationship between credit and debt? Why are financial institutions said to be merchants of credit?
5. Why are commercial banks recognized as having a special position among financial institutions? What is peculiar about their obligations to pay on demand as a kind of credit?
6. Why is the central bank accorded a special position in the discussion in this chapter? Why is there uncertainty about the classification of the central bank as a financial institution?
7. What is peculiar about the disposal of the money accumulations of consumer credit institutions? What effects does this disposal have on saving? On investment spending?
8. Why is it said that the United States has only one central bank despite the obvious fact that we have twelve Federal Reserve banks?

9. What are the principal functions of a central bank?
10. How are commercial banks distinguished from all other classes of financial institutions? What are some of the reasons for their description as department stores of banking?
11. For what reason is our commercial banking system described as a dual system?
12. What is indicated by descriptions of some of our commercial banks as national banks? as member banks? as insured banks?

CHAPTER 10

OTHER FINANCIAL INSTITUTIONS

SAVINGS AND LOAN ASSOCIATIONS

Functions

Savings and loan associations are said to have two principal functions: to encourage thrift and to grant loans to customers for the acquisition of homes.[1] They try to encourage thrift by paying what they hope will be attractive rates of interest on savers' balances left with them in what may be collectively called "savings accounts,"[2] and they devote a very large proportion of the savings thus accumulated in granting long-term mortgage loans to customers individually for the acquisition of single-family homes. Much smaller amounts of their funds are held as cash and invested in U.S. Treasury obligations for liquidity purposes, and are loaned for the purchase and construction of homes for two to four families and multi-family properties; with still smaller amounts going into loans for the repair, modernization, and equipping of residential property, for the acquisition of business property, and for college and university education.

Although many savings and loan associations also have limited powers to invest directly in real property and in municipal securities, their highly specialized character as residential mortgage lenders is indicated by the fact that 72.8 percent of their collective assets at the end of 1969 consisted of mortgage loans on homes for one to four families and that another 7.2 percent consisted of mortgage loans on other residential property.[3]

---

[1]Although the single designation *savings and loan associations* is used in this description, such institutions are also known in various localities as savings associations, building and loan associations, homestead aid associations, cooperative banks, and building societies.

[2]Although a large number of associations call these accounts "share accounts" and call the return paid on them "dividends," preference for the designations *savings accounts* and *interest* has grown rapidly in recent years.

[3]Derived from United States Savings and Loan League, *Savings and Loan Fact Book,* 1970, pp. 36, 93.

Mutual and stock associations

Most of the savings and loan associations are *mutual* institutions, which means that individually they are run primarily for the benefit of the holders of savings accounts and borrowers, and not specifically for profits as are the usual business corporations. It also means that the holders of savings accounts typically have certain ownership rights, similar to those of stockholders in ordinary business corporations but not entirely so. All the income of a mutual association, after the payment of expenses including taxes and allocations to a "reserve for losses" and other surplus reserves, is available for the payment of interest to the holders of savings accounts, provided that the rates do not exceed the maximums permitted by supervisory authorities.

In a few states, however, there are large numbers of *stock* savings and loan associations whose operating goal, as in other profit-seeking corporations, is to have substantial amounts of income left for the stockholders after the payment of expenses including interest to holders of savings accounts. Stock associations are especially prominent in California, Illinois, Ohio, and Texas. Of a total of 5898 associations with total assets of $162.2 billion in operation at the end of 1969, 736 were stock associations with assets of $33.4 billion.[4]

Federal and state charters

As in commercial banking, we have a dual system for the chartering and supervision of savings and loan associations. Associations chartered by the federal government always have the word *federal* in their names. They are chartered and supervised by the Federal Home Loan Bank Board, an agency composed of three persons chosen by the President with the advice and consent of the Senate and having its headquarters in Washington, D.C. However, the board delegates much of the work of decision making about charters and supervision to the twelve federal home loan banks that are scattered throughout the country and that individually serve geographical areas comparable to the areas served by individual Federal Reserve banks. All federal associations are mutual institutions, so that the stock associations are necessarily state-chartered. In many states, the officials who charter and supervise commercial banks also charter savings and loan associations and supervise their operations; while, in others, the chartering and supervision of associations are responsibilities of other officials.

Membership in the Federal Home Loan Bank System

All federal savings and loan associations are required to be members of the Federal Home Loan Bank System, and state-chartered associations are eligible for membership by application and acceptance, as are mutual savings banks and life insurance companies. In each of the twelve geo-

---

[4]*Ibid.*, pp. 56, 58.

graphical areas of the system, the member institutions own all the stock of the federal home loan bank, often keep with it demand or time deposits or both, and have rather liberal borrowing privileges; at the same time, they are subject to its supervisory powers as delegated by the Federal Home Loan Bank Board.

For savings and loan associations, membership has been very popular because the home loan banks have been especially generous in granting loans to supply members with money to meet extraordinary withdrawals from savings accounts. To hold their popularity with savers, associations need at all times to be able to meet withdrawal requests at once, but their own capacities in this direction are limited because of the large proportions of their assets that are tied up in long-term mortgage loans. Hence the ready availability of loans from the home loan banks is quite attractive to them. Indeed, membership in the Federal Home Loan Bank System is often said to be *essential* for any association that does a significant volume of business —a proposition supported by the fact that the 2071 federal and the 2676 state-chartered associations that were members at the end of 1969 held 98 percent of the assets of all associations then in operation.[5]

Because of long traditions against borrowing, mutual savings banks and life insurance companies have been much less enthusiastic about membership. For life insurance companies, indeed, enthusiasm has been virtually nil, as only one such company has been a member in recent years. But among mutual savings banks, the tradition against borrowing has recently been breaking down, as evidence by an increase in their membership from twenty at the end of 1961 to forty-four at the end of 1969.[6]

Loans of the Home Loan Banks   In addition to lending generously in order to enable member institutions to meet withdrawals from savings accounts, the federal home loan banks have been liberal in lending to them in order to help them cope with seasonal fluctuations in loan demands of their own customers. For the members, net inflows from holders of savings accounts and from loans repayments typically have seasonal patterns substantially different from the seasonal patterns of loan outflows, so that it is helpful to them to be able to borrow from the home loan banks in months when net inflows of savings and loan repayments are small or negative and loan demands are high, and then to repay in the months when these flows are reversed. Loans of the home loan banks for meeting members' seasonal cash needs are generally for short terms, but they also have the power to grant loans with maturities up to 10 years—a power used to supply loan funds to members located in areas where there are chronic shortages of "mortgage money." Over the years, however, the home loan banks have not displayed

---

[5]*Ibid.*, p. 113.
[6]*Fact Book*, 1962, p. 106; 1970, p. 113.

much enthusiasm for lending for the longer periods, although they have recently made some moves toward greater liberality in this area.

Loan Funds for the Home Loan Banks For the federal home loan banks, the principal source of funds for lending in recent years has been the sale of debt instruments designated "notes" and "bonds" in the open market. The notes have maturities up to 1 year, and the bonds have generally had maturities from 1 to 2 years or slightly longer, although there have recently been several bond issues with 5-year maturities—indicative of the banks' moves in the direction of longer-term lending to the member institutions. Although these notes and bonds are not guaranteed by the federal government, they rank high in investment quality as do all securities issued by "federal agencies." Other sources of loan funds for the home loan banks are the equity investment of the member institutions—both their stock holdings and the banks' retained earnings—and demand and time deposits kept by member institutions with the banks.

Insurance for savings accounts

All federal savings and loan associations are required to have their savings accounts insured by the Federal Savings and Loan Insurance Corporation (FSLIC), and state-chartered associations also have access to this insurance program by way of application and acceptance. Because the states of Maryland, Massachusetts, and Ohio have their own insurance systems for the associations they charter, the number of FSLIC-insured associations is smaller than the membership of associations in the Federal Home Loan Bank System. Although mutual savings banks and life insurance companies are eligible for membership in the Federal Home Loan Bank System, they are not eligible for FSLIC insurance. Mutual savings banks are eligible for deposit insurance with the Federal Deposit Insurance Corporation, and for the policyholders of life insurance companies, the federal government sponsors no protective program.

The features of the insurance program of the FSLIC are almost exactly the same as those of the FDIC program except in the matters of assessments and management. The insurance coverage for each saver in a given "right and capacity" in each insured institution is $20,000, and the FSLIC has powers to require certain kinds of rules and regulations be observed by the insured associations, to examine them, to require them to report their condition from time to time, to expel associations for illegal and "unsafe and unsound" practices, to aid "hazardous" associations with financial assistance, and to serve as receiver for insured associations that are suspended. As for assessments on insured associations, the FSLIC system differs from the FDIC system chiefly in two provisions. One is that, for most of the associations, regular assessment payments in cash are suspended when the FSLIC's insurance "reserves" (that ubiquitous word meaning in this instance all its assets minus a small amount needed to pay or offset a few miscellaneous liabilities) stay at a level equal to or above 2 percent of the savings accounts of all insured associations. The other differing provision is that when the FSLIC's insurance reserves fall below 2 percent by a substantial margin, most associations are required to pay from year to year both their regular assessments and "prepayments" against assessments to be due in subsequent years. As for management, the Federal Home Loan Bank Board is also the board of trustees of the FSLIC, so that the FSLIC does not have an aspect of independence comparable to that of the FDIC in the commercial banking field.

MUTUAL SAVINGS BANKS

In organization, sources of funds, and loan and investment policies, mutual savings banks closely resemble savings and loan associations. There are no federal facilities for the chartering of mutual savings banks, so that all currently in operation have their charters from the state governments. Only eighteen states have provisions for such chartering, and, indeed, a very large proportion of the mutual savings banks are concentrated in the Northeastern section of the country. At the end of 1969, 468 of a total of 496 were located in the New England and Middle Atlantic states. And even in the Northeast, there is a big concentration in three states only: Massachusetts, New York, and Connecticut, with these states having 173, 122, and 69 mutuals, respectively, at the end of 1969.[7]

As the designation *mutual* indicates, mutual savings banks have no stockholders, so that they are presumably operated for the primary benefit of their depositors. Unlike holders of savings accounts in mutual savings and loan associations, however, the depositors have no ownership rights, as in choosing directors. They are recognized as being creditors, and management is in the hands of self-perpetuating boards of trustees or boards of "corporators" who choose the trustees from among their own members. *Self-perpetuation* means that the remaining members of a board choose successors for members who die or resign or who are removed by legal proceedings.

Sources of funds

By a wide margin, the principal source of funds for mutual savings banks are the savings of customers deposited with them in savings accounts, mostly "regular" passbook accounts. Although the mutuals reserve contractual rights to require advance notice for withdrawals from the passbook accounts, they never enforce these rights, so that the full balances of the accounts are actually payable on demand, although not by means of checks. Other sources of funds are accumulated earnings as indicated in surplus accounts and surplus reserves and occasional borrowings by some from commercial banks and the federal home loan banks.

---

[7]Federal Deposit Insurance Corporation, *Annual Report*, 1970, pp. 242–248.

Loans and investments

Like savings and loan associations, mutual savings banks are primarily interested in granting long-term mortgage loans for the acquisition of residential property. However, they have wider investment powers than associations, and the use of these wider powers results in a more diversified array of assets for the mutuals collectively, as indicated in Table 10–1. Especially noteworthy are their significant volume of mortgage loans for purposes other than residential and their substantial holdings of corporate securities including a moderate amount of corporate stocks.

Deposit insurance and memberships

Massachusetts requires all of its mutual savings banks to insure their deposit accounts with its own insuring organization, the Mutual Savings Central Fund. Eight Massachusetts mutuals are also insured by the Federal Deposit Insurance Corporation, as are the mutuals of all other states except for one located in Maine. FDIC insurance for the deposits of mutual savings banks is exactly the same as for deposits in insured commercial banks, that is, the maximum coverage in each is $20,000 for each depositor for accounts held in a given "right and capacity." In addition to having eligibility for membership in the Federal Home Loan Bank System, as mentioned previously, mutual savings banks are eligible for membership in the Federal Reserve System. However, the mutuals have never found Federal Reserve membership to be attractive. Never have more than three belonged at one time, and none have belonged since 1962.

LIFE INSURANCE COMPANIES

In total asset holdings, the life insurance companies rank third in importance among our financial institutions, following commercial banks and the trust institutions. Here we refer to the legal-reserve life insurance companies with which the general public is most familiar—companies whose regulation and modes of operation differ from those of certain fraternal organizations that sell policies only to their own members; mutual savings banks that, in three states, participate in life insurance programs of a special character; and governmental bodies that provide policies for special groups, as for servicemen and veterans.

The legal-reserve companies are so called because individually they are required to hold "admitted" assets at all times at least equal in total value to the amount of their liabilities—liabilities that are chiefly estimates of accumulated obligations to policyholders and holders of annuity contracts and their beneficiaries, and that are carried as such in accounts called "policy reserves." Assets are "admitted" if they satisfy the standards that the states have established in considerable detail in order to govern lending and investing by the life companies subject to their respective jurisdictions. On the other hand, policy reserves, as estimates, are a very peculiar kind of liability, differing in their uncertainty from the liabilities of almost all other kinds of business enterprises. The state laws set certain rules for determining how large the policy reserves should be, but their size and growth depend very importantly on the individual company's "actuarial assumptions," that is, its assumptions about mortality and about the amount of income from premiums and its investments it will add to the reserves from year to year. These assumptions are also, of course, principal determinants of the periodic premiums that individual companies decide to charge policyholders for the various kinds of policies they sell.

Table 10-1   Assets of All Mutual Savings Banks, December 31, 1969[a] (dollar amounts in millions)

	AMOUNT	PERCENT OF TOTAL
Cash and due from banks	891	1.2
United States government obligations	3,243	4.3
Obligations of states and subdivisions	198	0.3
Corporation and other bonds	8,655	11.6
Corporation stocks	2,213	3.0
Residential real-estate loans	48,683	65.3
Other real-estate loans	7,455	10.0
Other loans	1,940	2.6
Other assets	1,284	1.7
Total	74,562	100.0

[a] Before deduction of valuation reserves.
Source: Federal Deposit Insurance Corporation, *Annual Report,* 1969, pp. 262–263. (Percentages supplied by the author.)

Stock and mutual companies

A large majority of life insurance companies are stock companies with profit motives comparable to those of business corporations in other fields of enterprise, while the remainder are mutuals that are ostensibly operated for the primary benefit of the policyholders. As of June 30, 1969, 1656 stock companies were reported to be in operation and only 156 mutuals.[8] But the mutuals have been in operation much longer, on the average, than the stock companies, and accordingly, have had much more time to sell policies and accumulate assets, so that, in terms of assets and "insurance in force," they dominate the industry. Thus the assets of the mutuals amounted to $134.5 billion at the end of 1969 while the asset holdings of the stock companies at that time totaled $62.7 billion.[9]

---

[8]Institute of Life Insurance, *Life Insurance Fact Book,* 1970, p. 108.
[9]*Ibid.,* p. 68.

Premiums and other receipts

Were life insurance companies to limit their activities to the sale of term insurance, their functions as financial institutions would not be important. Term insurance is designated to provide protection only. A company with only 1-year term policies outstanding, and with premium rates based on current mortality experience, would find its yearly outlays to beneficiaries and for expenses about equal to its premium receipts, so that it would have little to lend or invest. Actually, rates for term policies are higher than expenses and mortality experience require, so that such a company would accumulate a moderate amount of savings.

But most policies sold by insurance companies are not of the term variety. Term insurance is not attractive to many people because, though it may be renewable from time to time without repeated medical examinations, the premiums rise with each renewal. As the policyholder gets older, he must pay more and more because of the increasing risk of death. Most people prefer level-premium policies, such as "whole life" or "limited-payment life" policies, by which they contract to pay from year to year exactly the same premium as that with which they start. But the risk of death still rises with advancing age, so that policyholders must pay substantially more in the earlier years of their contracts than they would for term insurance to balance off, as it were, the relatively low payments of later years. It is here, of course, that the important savings element enters, since the excess payments of the earlier years are just as truly savings as balances in accounts at commercial banks, savings and loan associations, or mutual savings banks. Moreover, these savings or most of them are readily available to the policyholder as the "cash surrender value" of his policy if he decides to have it canceled.

The policyholder accumulates savings at a much faster pace if he buys an endowment policy, for he must pay much higher premiums than would be paid on a level-premium life policy of the same face amount. Such a policy provides for the payment of the face amount on the death of the insured during the contract period, but it also calls for the payment of the face amount to the insured or his beneficiary at the end of the contract period if he is still living. Most insurance companies also sell annuity contracts on which they collect periodic payments or lump sums and incur the obligation to pay the annuitant a specified sum of money periodically (usually monthly), beginning at a designated time and extending for a designated period of years or for the remainder of the annuitant's life. Obviously, the savings-accumulation function largely overshadows the protective function in the annuity sector of an insurance company's activities.

Premiums received by life insurance companies, to the extent that they are not needed to meet current expenses and contractual payments to insureds, beneficiaries, and annuitants, are generally available for loans and investments. Accordingly, interest and dividends on loan and invest-ment portfolios, less related operating expenses, constitute an additional savings flow to the life companies for which they seek new loan and in-vestment outlets. In the year 1969, the legal-reserve companies had interest and other income of $9.4 billion to supplement their premium receipts of $34 billion.[10]

Table 10-2 **Assets of Life Insurance Companies, December 31, 1969** (dollar amounts in millions)

	AMOUNT	PERCENT OF TOTAL
United States government obligations	4,124	2.1
Bonds of state and local governments	3,221	1.6
Bonds of foreign governments[a]	2,889	1.5
Corporation bonds:		
Railroad	3,608	1.8
Public utility	17,963	9.1
Industrial and miscellaneous[b]	49,968	25.4
Corporation stocks	13,707	7.0
Mortgage loans	72,027	36.5
Real estate	5,912	3.0
Policy loans	13,825	7.0
Other assets	9,964	5.0
Total	197,208	100.0

[a] Issues of foreign governments and their subdivisions (very largely Canadian).
[b] Including about $3 billion of bonds of foreign enterprises, chiefly Canadian; $233 million of bonds of international agencies such as the International Bank for Reconstruc-tion and Development; and $265 million of nonguaranteed bonds of federal agencies.
Source: Institute of Life Insurance, *Life Insurance Fact Book,* 1970, pp. 70–71, 79, 82.

Loans and investments

As Table 10–2 indicates, most of the investment money of life insurance companies goes into securities of business enterprises, especially bonds of public utility and industrial corporations, and real-estate mortgage loans. The huge post-World War II expansion of business capital facilities and the equally great residential housing boom gave the insurance companies an unprecedented opportunity to increase their holdings in these areas, and they have continued to concentrate on corporation bonds and mortgage loans. The regulatory laws still strictly limit investment in the stocks of business corporations, although a moderate but progressive relaxing of these restrictions has been occurring in recent years. Moreover, many states have recently amended their laws to permit life insurance com-panies to invest pension fund monies largely or wholly in segregated port-

[10]*Ibid.,* p. 57.

folios of common stocks should this kind of investment be directed by the creators of the pension funds. As for mortgage loans, a strong concentration on urban properties, both commercial and residential, prevails. At the end of 1969, 92 percent of the total dollar amount of these loans were on urban real estate and only 8 percent on farms.[11]

Finally, a word about policy loans that rose from $7.7 billion or 4.8 percent of total assets at the end of 1965 to $13.8 billion or 7 percent of assets at the end of 1969.[12] Policyholders generally have the contractual right not only to withdraw the cash surrender values of their policies by canceling them but also to borrow these amounts while keeping their policies in force by continued payments of premiums. As interest rates on policy loans, as set in the policies themselves, do not generally exceed 6 percent per annum, the extraordinarily high interest rates prevailing on loans elsewhere in the period 1965–1969 account for the big surge in policy loans. Such a surge, however, is not very pleasant for the insurance companies; it tends to confuse their cash-flow forecasting and compels them to forgo some opportunities for lending and investing elsewhere at much higher rates of interest.

TRUST INSTITUTIONS

Although most of the trust services that are supplied by financial institutions in the United States are services of trust departments of commercial banks and trust departments of trust companies that also engage in commercial banking, trust services and commercial banking services are markedly different in scope and in institution-customer relationships. The performance of the two kinds of services by single institutions under one roof, so to say, has resulted from a series of historical accidents rather than because of a logical functional union. When you make a deposit with a commercial bank or in the commercial banking department of a trust company, you have no right to direct how your money is to be used; instead, your right is simply to get the same amount of money back when you want it or at a specified time, as with certificates of deposit, and almost always with an addition for interest in the case of savings and other time deposits. When, however, you turn cash or other assets over to a trust department, it is strictly obligated to do with these assets what you direct if you choose to give directions, and to strictly account for what it has done and is doing with them and with the income earned on them. By legal requirements, the asset holdings of trust departments must be carefully segregated from the assets of banking departments, although an exception generally permits temporary deposits in banking departments of cash accumulated in various accounts in the trust departments of the same institutions.

---

[11]Computed from *ibid.*, p. 88.
[12]*Ibid.*, pp. 70–71.

Scope of trust services

The principal services of trust institutions are services as executors and administrators of decedents' estates; guardians of the property of minors and mental incompetents; trustees under deeds of trust, trust agreements, and wills; and agents in a wide array of capacities. In acting as executor or administrator, the trust institution "collects" the assets of a decedent's estate, pays its debts and taxes, meets the expenses of administration, and distributes the balance to the heirs—all under the direction of the probate court to which it must make an accounting. As guardian of a minor or mental incompetent, the trust institution holds and manages his property until he is legally recognized as being capable of managing his own affairs —as when a minor reaches the age of 21—meanwhile using income from the property and portions of the principal, if necessary, to meet his living expenses. As trustees, trust institutions take title to, hold, and manage property as allocated to them by decedents in their wills (testamentary trusts), as conveyed to them by individuals during their lifetimes (living, or *inter vivos,* trusts), and as conveyed to them by business corporations, nonprofit institutions, and governmental bodies. Also for business corporations, trust institutions act as trustees under indentures or agreements on the basis of which bonds and equipment-trust certificates are issued—act for the protection of the buyers of these securities. As agents, trust institutions provide safekeeping and custodial services, hold property under escrow, act as registrars and transfer agents for corporate securities, distribute interest and dividends on these securities, and manage property in few or many ways, according to the instructions of the owners.

Because all these kinds of services are performed by trust institutions, they are often collectively called "trust services"; but we should observe that many do not involve trusteeships. Trusts and trusteeships exist only when legal titles to given properties are held by the trust institution (or by one or more individual trustees) and the equitable titles or "beneficial interests" are held by others. In any event, most of the work of trust institutions is concerned with the management of properties or arrays of properties for the benefit of heirs of decedents' estates, wards of guardianships, trust beneficiaries, and the principals of agency contracts, and not for the benefit of the trust institutions themselves or their stockholders as in the case of banking operations. (Benefits to the trust institutions are derived from fees and commissions for their services, as provided for by agreement, court decrees, or law, whether or not they are covered by income from the property managed.)

Accumulation of savings

Because trust institutions are classified as financial institutions, they must be accumulators of savings that they pass on to spenders. In many instances, the assets they receive for management represent savings already passed on for expenditure, as when they are directed to continue to hold stocks and bonds included in decedents' estates or turned over to them by creators of living trusts. But they also receive cash that they are directed to invest, some of it accumulated over long periods and some derived out of current income. Savings flows out of current income are typified by periodic additions of cash to trust accounts that men and women establish for their children and periodic contributions by business corporations and nonprofit institutions to pension trusts established for their employees.

Investment discretion

In many instances, trust institutions have little or no discretion in deciding what to do with savings they accumulate. The people and organizations that turn assets of various kinds over to them for management (including probate courts in exercising jurisdiction over decedents' estates and guardianships) direct that these assets be held. Or if they turn cash over, they give specific instructions on how it is to be invested. In such instances, it is the duty of the trust institution to obey.

But in many instances, also, trust institutions are given full discretion in choosing investments. Money is turned over to them with instructions to invest it in ways that, in their judgment, will best serve the purposes for which it is turned over; or noncash assets are turned over with authority for their sale and reinvestment should the trust institutions decide that changes would be advantageous. But instructions and authorizations of these kinds do not give trust institutions a wild degree of freedom in choosing investments. Their investment judgment is supposed to be that which "men of prudence, discretion and intelligence exercise in the management of their own affairs," and they can be surcharged for losses if judges and juries decide that their judgment was imprudent.

A third possibility is for trust institutions to receive property for management without any instructions at all, a circumstance that is most likely to occur when testators name trust institutions as trustees in their wills without consulting them in advance about investment policy. But a lack of instructions does not mean unlimited investment discretion for the trust institution. In a few states, it can invest only in the securities, mortgage loans, and other kinds of assets that are specifically authorized in "legal lists" promulgated by state authorities. In many states, the prudent-man rule applies. And in still other states, of a steadily diminishing number, a portion of each trust account must be invested in legal-list assets while the balance is left to the judgment of the trust institution on the basis of the prudent-man rule.

Common trust funds

Although trust institutions are subject to a basic legal rule that requires them to keep the assets acquired in and for each decedent's estate, guardianship, and trust segregated from all other assets, they often take advantage of an exception to the segregation rule that permits them to take cash from many such accounts for "collective" investment. However, this may be done only if it is not precluded in one way or another by investment instructions contained in wills, decrees of probate courts, and trust agreements.

Assets held collectively constitute a *common trust fund,* and units or shares in it are allocated to the participating accounts in proportion to their contributions to it. Thus the assets of estate A may include 100 units in the common trust fund, the assets of trust account B may include 500 units, and so on. The income of the common trust fund is distributed to the participating accounts in proportion to the units each holds, and withdrawals of contributions are made at the unit value of total fund assets at current market prices. Some trust institutions maintain several common trust funds concurrently, as one for legal-list investments, one for investment in common stocks, and one for "balanced" investment in stocks and bonds.

Investment preferences

The most recent comprehensive data we have about the asset holdings of trust institutions are those of 1969 collected by the bank supervisory agencies of the federal government from the trust departments of insured commercial banks. They reported total assets of $280 billion in 1,028,406 accounts classified as personal trusts, estates, guardianships, personal agencies, employee-benefit trusts, and employee-benefit agencies. At market values of late 1969, for the most part, the assets included $181 billion of common stocks, $33 billion of government obligations, federal, state, and local, and $38 billion of corporate and other bonds.[13]

INVESTMENT COMPANIES

Investment companies sell their own issues of securities to the public, chiefly common stock, in order to acquire savings for investment in the securities of other enterprises—chiefly the securities of manufacturing and other "operating" companies, and again, predominantly their common stock. For the typical investment company, therefore, common stock is simultaneously the principal means by which the public's savings are accumulated and the principal outlet for these accumulations. Collectively, the investment companies weight their investment portfolios heavily in favor of common stocks, because their dividend rates are often higher than interest rates on bonds, but especially because of the much greater possibilities of capital gains. For this reason, they make a strong appeal to

---

[13]Federal Deposit Insurance Corporation, *Trust Assets of Insured Commercial Banks, 1969* (Washington, D.C., 1970), table 1.

many people of moderate means who regard their stockholdings in investment companies as having potential rates of return substantially greater than interest rates currently being paid on time deposits by commercial banks, mutual savings banks, and savings and loan associations. But a disadvantage is also widely recognized: unlike deposit-receiving institutions in meeting withdrawals, the investment companies do not undertake to redeem their stock at the prices investors paid for it.

Classification of investment companies

Among the various ways in which investment companies are classified, the classification that distinguishes between open-end and close-end companies is especially significant.

Mutual Funds   In number and assets, the open-end companies predominate by a wide margin. For reasons that are not clear or particularly logical, they are known as *mutual funds,* and they are distinguished by their continuous offerings of shares of their common stock to all who may be willing to buy, and by their commitment to redeem shares at "current asset value." The current asset value of each share of a company's outstanding stock is determined daily or twice a day by the following formula:

$$\frac{\substack{\text{Investment portfolio} \\ \text{at market value}} + \substack{\text{other assets} \\ \text{including cash}} - \text{liabilities}}{\text{Number of shares outstanding}}$$

Most mutual funds sell shares of their common stock from day to day at the price determined by this formula plus a sales charge or "load" that generally ranges from 9 to 2 percent depending upon the size of individual sales, as for example, 9 percent on sales up to $25,000, 7 percent on sales between $25,000 and $50,000, and so on until the 2 percent rate is reached on sales in excess of $500,000. However, a goodly number of no-load funds organized and managed by investment advisory firms are in operation.

The formula values of shares, as they vary from day to day, are also important in relationship to the commitments of mutual funds to redeem their shares. For most funds, the formula value is exactly the redemption price; however, a few deduct a moderate redemption charge.

Closed-End Companies   Closed-end investment companies do not make continuous offerings of additional shares of their stock, nor do they undertake to redeem outstanding shares when their holders wish to convert them into cash. If a closed-end company wishes to issue additional stock, it typically gets investment bankers to underwrite and sell a sizable issue at one sale, so that the additional financing is completed quickly. Many closed-end companies never add to their stock issues, and many others do so only rarely. As for conversion into cash, the holder of shares must find buyers in the market, as for stocks held in manufacturing and other nonfinancial corporations, probably with the assistance of security dealers or brokers.

Some closed-end investment companies have become such without really aiming in that direction, as when manufacturing companies have sold their operating facilities and have invested the sales proceeds in arrays of the securities of other corporations, in place of winding up their affairs and going out of business.

Investment policies

When investment companies file registration statements with the federal Securities and Exchange Commission (SEC) as required by the Investment Company Act if they operate in interstate commerce or intend to do so, they must declare what their respective investment policies are or will be. Such a declaration must also be made in the companies' prospectuses that they are required to tender to all persons and organizations to which they offer their securities for sale. The purpose of registration statements and prospectuses is to prevent fraud and to ensure that prospective buyers of these securities will have all "material facts" needed for wise investment decisions. If the SEC is satisfied that no fraud is involved and that all material facts about an investment company's affairs have been revealed, it has no power to prevent the sale of its securities even when it judges the company's declared investment policy to be highly speculative or even absurd.

On the basis of their declared investment policies, investment companies get classification labels, such as "diversified common stock companies," indicating that they invest exclusively or almost exclusively in a wide list of common stocks; "balanced companies," designating a spread of holdings among bonds, preferred stock, and common stock; "bond companies," "preferred stock companies," "bond and preferred stock companies," and "foreign securities companies," designations that are self-explanatory; and "specialty companies," a designation indicating a peculiar kind of investment concentration, as in speculative common stocks, low-priced common stocks or bonds, or the securities of a single industry. In relationship to income and capital-gains goals of their investment policies, investment companies are often additionally classified as "income," "growth," and "mixed" companies. For example, a company that has income as its main objective will probably concentrate its investments in the common stocks of corporations that are liberal in distributing current earnings as dividends, while one that has growth as its principal goal will be likely to concentrate on common stocks that are expected to rise substantially in market value although current dividend payments may be small or nil.

PENSION FUNDS

Aside from the assets of the social security, railroad retirement, and civil service retirement programs of the federal government, most of the assets of pension funds—those of state and local governments, business corporations and other business enterprises, and private nonprofit institutions—are held by trust institutions and life insurance companies. Accordingly, classifying pension funds as a distinct type of financial institution might appear to be straining for an identification that has little meaning. But it is the pension funds that accumulate savings and decide what to do with them, so that, in these actions, they clearly resemble financial institutions of other classes. They do, indeed, turn most of these accumulations over to trust institutions and life insurance companies, but this is simply an interchange among institutions of the kind referred to in the preceding chapter.

Structure of pension funds

Moreover, pension funds have organizational structures quite distinct from the structures of trust institutions and life insurance companies. In establishing pension programs, state legislatures, city councils, corporate boards of directors, the boards of nonprofit institutions, and in a few instances, labor unions find it essential to name officials who are to administer the programs, and these officials then fulfill roles comparable to those of officers of other financial institutions. It is they who work with trust institutions and life insurance companies in the management of the assets of the funds, and indeed, in some instances, they have the power to decide what kinds of assets are to be acquired and how much of each kind. The officials of pension funds, moreover, have many administrative duties that trust institutions and life insurance companies do not want or will not accept—duties of deciding who among employees are eligible to participate in the program, who are vested with pension rights, who may begin to receive pension payments early because of physical and mental disabilities, who are eligible to retire early for other reasons, and so on.

Still further in the matter of structure, the employees covered in pension programs may be likened to savers who have deposits with other classes of financial institutions. This is clearly the position that employees have with regard to their own contributions, since, almost without exception, pension programs provide that such contributions are returnable to the employee, usually with interest, if he resigns or is fired. But employees may also be likened to those savers in respect to employers' contributions—a matter of much greater importance, because most programs do not require employee contributions and many others provide for them only if employees wish to contribute, and especially because employers' contributions collectively greatly exceed employee contributions. Because employer contributions to pension funds are a kind of compensation for labor service and, therefore, an income flow to employees, and because they cannot be immediately spent for consumer goods, they clearly take the complexion of employee savings. However, we must recognize that the savings are collective rather than individual until the time the employee becomes vested with pension rights. *Vesting* means that, if the employee resigns or is fired after the date on which it occurs, he still is entitled to receive pension payments beginning at normal retirement age equal to the payments earned until the time of resignation or dismissal.

Trusteed and insured pension funds

Trusteed Pension Funds In trusteed pension programs, the assets of the pension funds are generally held by trust institutions, usually on an individually segregated basis, but also, in many instances, with the assets collectively held in common trust funds with units or shares of participation allocated to the individual pension accounts. Incomplete statistics indicate that, in a substantial majority of trusteed programs, the trust institutions are given full discretion to decide how pension fund contributions are to be invested, although the trust institutions, in making investment decisions, often consult with the administrative officials of the funds. In other trusteed programs, the trust institutions share investment judgments with one or several individual co-trustees; in others, they hold fund assets as trustees but with investment decisions entirely the responsibility of individual co-trustees; and in still others, fund assets are held by the trust institutions in agency capacities with investment decisions made by "outside" trustees. In all the arrangements in which the trust institutions have no investment responsibility or share it, the "outside" trustees or co-trustees are generally the administrative officials of the pension funds.

Insured Pension Funds In insured pension programs, pension fund contributions are customarily used to buy annuity or life insurance contracts for each covered employee by a variety of arrangements, three of which may be briefly described. As measured by the number of employees covered, the most popular arrangement has been "deposit administration." In this arrangement, a separate account for each pension program is accumulated from contributions and from investment income credited on accumulations and is charged with a "load" for expenses. Then, as each covered employee retires, the lump-sum cost of an annuity contract under which payments are to begin immediately and are to continue monthly for the remainder of his life is charged against the account.

Another popular arrangement is for the employer to buy annually a deferred annuity contract for each covered employee, so that, on retirement, he gets a monthly pension equal to the sum of the payments promised in the series of deferred annuity contracts bought for him during his working years.

Many smaller employers wish to combine their pension commitments with life insurance protection for their employees, and a popular way of doing so is to acquire for each covered employee a retirement income insurance policy. If the employee dies before reaching retirement age, his beneficiaries get the face amount of the policy (or possibly its cash surrender value, if greater); and if he lives to retirement age, the cash surrender value is used to acquire an annuity contract for the payment of the promised monthly pension.

Investment policies

The assets of the pension funds of the federal government, including the Social Security Trust Fund, consist exclusively of cash, Treasury obligations, and obligations of federal agencies. Similarly, a large number of the pension funds of state and local governments are invested greatly and sometimes exclusively in government obligations, federal, state, and local; while others have substantial investments in corporate stocks and bonds, especially bonds. Most of the assets of nongovernmental insured pension funds are scattered in an undifferentiated way among all the assets of the life insurance companies as presented in Table 10-2 for 1969. However, the Institute of Life Insurance reported that, at the end of that same year, the legal-reserve companies held $3.5 billion in segregated portfolios for pension funds—presumably entirely or almost entirely common stocks— while total reserves for the insured funds amounted to $37.9 billion.[14] The Securities and Exchange Commission reports periodically on the assets of noninsured "private" pension funds—predominantly the trusteed funds of individual business corporations, but including also trusteed multi-employer funds and funds of nonprofit institutions. Its asset data for December 31, 1970, are presented in Table 10-3.

Table 10-3   **Assets of Private Noninsured Pension Funds, December 31, 1970** (in millions of dollars)

	BOOK VALUE[a]	ESTIMATED MARKET VALUE[a]
Cash and deposits	1,780	1,800
United States government securities	3,030	3,000
Corporate and other bonds	29,210	24,500
Preferred stock	1,860	1,700
Common stock	51,080	64,600
Mortgages	4,240	3,600
Other	4,660	4,200
Totals	95,850	103,500

[a] Items do not add exactly to totals because of rounding.
Source: Securities and Exchange Commission, *Statistical Bulletin,* May 1971, p. 23.

[14]*Fact Book,* pp. 37, 38.

SECURITY DEALERS AND BROKERS

Firms of security dealers and brokers are financial institutions that have two primary functions: (1) to assist business corporations and governments to acquire funds through sales of new issues of stocks, bonds, and other debt instruments; and (2) to help individual and institutional investors to recover funds previously invested in stocks and bonds. A few firms largely confine their activities to the first of these functions; a much larger number spread their activities across both functional areas in varying proportions; and a still larger number rather closely restrict their operations to the second function.

In channeling savings flows to ultimate spenders, security dealers and brokers follow procedures that are essentially different from the procedures of life insurance companies, pension funds, and other financial institutions that favor investment in long-term securities. In place of accumulating savings and then seeking issues of stocks and bonds in which to invest these savings, they make arrangements with corporations and governments that want to sell new issues of stocks and bonds and with holders of previously issued stocks and bonds who want to sell their holdings, and then, as it were, seek savers willing to buy securities coming from these two sources. They are dealers and brokers in securities who aim to earn income by way of profits and commissions on security transactions, rather than by way of dividends and interest through the holding of securities. It is true that, as *dealers*, they buy securities in their own names with their own or borrowed funds; nevertheless, they ordinarily buy only when they have expectations of being able to resell quickly at higher prices. And in the many transactions in which they act as *brokers* or agents, they simly attempt to find buyers for the securities that their customers wish to sell and to find sellers of securities that their customers wish to buy, charging commissions when they succeed in arranging sales.

Investment banking

The function of assisting business corporations and governments to acquire long-term funds through sales of new issues of stocks and bonds is called "investment banking." Such assistance is best given, one may say, when security firms are willing to "underwrite" new issues. To underwrite a security issue is to guarantee that the issuing corporation or government will receive on a designated day a specified amount of money as proceeds of the issue. When, for example, security firms in the role of investment bankers underwrite "at 98" a corporation's bond issue of $10 million, they guarantee that on the designated day the corporation will receive $9.8 million less an amount for selling expenses previously agreed on. However, their profit depends upon the price at which they are able to sell the bonds to investors. In the usual procedure, the bankers make good on their guaranty by buying the whole security issue outright, and they then promptly make a "public offering" at an announced price. In terms of the illustration, this price might be, say, 99½. If they succeed in selling at that price, they earn a gross profit of $1.50 per $100 of bonds; if they cannot find enough buyers at that price, they "pull the peg" and sell at whatever prices they can get, thereby accepting profit margins less than $1.50 and taking losses on sales at prices less than 98.

Another procedure of underwriting is to guarantee sales of security issues on a stand-by basis. This procedure is most frequently used when corporations make offerings of additional shares of their common stock to their existing common stockholders. Such a corporation wishes to sell at the offering price all the shares that it offers, and it can get assurances of full sale if it is able to find investment bankers who are willing to make a commitment to "stand by" to buy whatever shares it fails to sell directly. For such a guaranty, the bankers receive a commission on the entire issue, and they expect to be able to earn an additional profit on the shares they take and offer for resale.

In most underwritings, the investment bankers are able to sell entire security issues (and shares of stock taken in stand-bys) before the dates on which they are obligated to make payment to the issuers, so that they need to draw on their own funds only to meet regular operating expenses. When sales lag, however, they must make up deficiencies in sales proceeds out of their own funds or with borrowed money. Even here, however, they expect to be able to replenish these funds or to repay borrowings largely through further sales of the underwritten securities, even when these sales result in losses because of lowered offering prices.

In many instances, investment bankers are unwilling to underwrite new security issues but are willing to attempt to sell them as agents. These are said to be "best-efforts" commitments, because the bankers agree only to do the best they can to sell, and accept obligations to pay the issuers only to the extent that sales are actually made. Best-efforts commitments are chiefly made for new issues of common stocks of corporations of small and medium sizes that are not well-known to the investing public, and they are chiefly entered into by smaller, less-well-known security firms, since the larger, more reputable firms of investment bankers will generally avoid asking their customers to buy anything that they themselves are unwilling to underwrite.

Transactions in outstanding securities

Many individuals and organizations would not invest in stocks and bonds were they not to have reasonable assurance that they could find buyers for these securities rather quickly should they wish to resell. Good facilities for the resale of outstanding securities may thus be said to be quite important for the promotion of savings flows to corporations and governments by way of their sales of new issues. It is important to corporations, for example, that people are willing to turn their savings over for new shares of stock even when some of these people will hold the stock for only short periods of time. They get the investors' savings through the original sales of the stock, and subsequent market transactions do not diminish the amount of savings thus accumulated. These market transactions simply mean that buyers of outstanding stocks are substituted for the sellers as contributors of savings to the corporations. Moreover, resales of securities in the market are often the means by which sellers get money to invest in new issues—the means by which, in effect, they transfer savings from the corporations or governments to which they had previously contributed to the issuers of the new securities.

The services of security dealers and brokers in helping individual and institutional investors to recover funds previously invested in stocks and bonds are generally reasonably fast because of the extensive array of market facilities they maintain and are reasonably fair because of the integrity of most firms, but with fairness also depending on a large body of government regulations. The market facilities are the stock exchanges and the over-the-counter securities market, this being an all-inclusive classification, because the *over-the-counter market* is defined as the broad market in which security transactions are effected if they are not handled through the facilities of the stock exchanges. Both on the stock exchanges and in the over-the-counter market, some security firms "make markets" in given outstanding security issues. This means that they are willing at all times (but occasionally subject to delays) to quote prices at which they will buy or sell stocks and bonds of these issues in their own names as dealers. This is the role taken by "specialists" on the stock exchanges and by security firms that are said to maintain "dealer positions" in specified securities in the over-the-counter market. But regardless of special interests of this kind in given issues, most security firms will undertake as brokers to attempt to find buyers and sellers for all kinds and issues of securities outstanding. Their transactions as brokers are effected through the stock exchanges if they are members and the securities are traded there; in the over-the-counter market, if the securities are not traded on exchanges of which they are members; or in the over-the-counter market, whether or not the securities are traded on exchanges, if they are not members of these exchanges.

FINANCE COMPANIES

On the basis of the classes of borrowers to which they direct most of their loans, finance companies have a threefold classification: business finance companies, sales finance companies, and consumer finance companies. In all three classes, the companies are variously proprietorships, partnerships, and corporations, but with few exceptions, the larger ones are corporations, with these corporations having large proportions of total loans outstanding.

A distinguishing feature of finance companies generally is that they depend upon borrowing to obtain most of their loan funds, rather than by taking deposits or selling stock or "shares" of some kind. When possible, the typical finance company obtains a substantial share of its loan funds by long-term borrowing in addition to the equity investment of its proprietors or stockholders and the remainder by short-term borrowing that is especially depended upon to take care of fluctuations in the loan demands of its own customers. For much of their short-term borrowing, finance companies rely on the commercial banks as lenders. But the larger companies also borrow extensively in the open market by selling short-term promissory notes[15] to all individuals and institutions that are willing to buy, and they shift substantial amounts of their borrowings back and forth between commercial banks and the open market in consideration of the availability of money and the terms on which they may borrow from the two sources.

Business finance companies

Two subclasses of business finance companies are recognized: factoring companies (or, simply, *factors*) and commercial finance companies. Both subclasses concentrate on the short-term financing of business enterprises on the basis of the "accounts receivable" of these enterprises, that is, their claims against customers who buy on deferred-payment terms.

Factors   Factors buy outright the accounts receivable of their customers or "clients," obligating themselves to pay for these receivables on a computed "average due date" less a commission generally ranging between 1 and 2 percent. They take full responsibility for the quality of the receivables they buy, making credit investigations, approving sales, making collections, searching for delinquent account debtors, and accepting losses on approved accounts that turn out to be uncollectible. It is for these services that the commission is charged. However, factors are also willing to make advances to clients on receivables before their average due dates. It is this additional service that chiefly justifies the classification of factors as financial institutions, because advances are, in effect, loans on which repayment is obtained by collecting from the client's account debtors and because the factors charge interest (in addition to the commission) for the period from the date of each advance to the average due date of the receivables involved.

Commercial Finance Companies   The ordinary procedure of commercial finance companies differs from that of factors in that they simply grant loans on the security of clients' accounts receivable pledged with them. The loans generally range from between 70 and 90 percent of the face value

---

[15]See Chapter 11.

of the pledged accounts. Although commercial finance companies often advise clients on credit matters, they take no responsibility for the quality of the pledged accounts. In other words, they "have recourse" against clients for pledged accounts that turn out to be uncollectible; the client must substitute good accounts or pay off in cash the amount loaned on the uncollectible ones. Many commercial finance companies also grant short-term inventory loans to dealers in producers' durable equipment, including farm machinery, and buy from these dealers the installment payment contracts of ultimate buyers of this equipment—in effect, therefore, granting intermediate-term loans to these buyers.

Sales finance companies

Although sales finance companies are generally classed as a principal type of consumer credit institution, they also have an important role as short-term lenders to business enterprises. Their principal objective is to acquire installment payment contracts that consumers sign when buying cars, television sets, home heating equipment, and other consumer durable goods. But they know that the dealers in these goods must have a varied stock on hand to display and deliver to buyers, and that most dealers do not have sufficient cash of their own to carry adequate inventories. So the typical sales finance company grants short-term "wholesale" or "floorplan" loans to dealers for inventory acquisition on the basis of commitments that they will sell all or most of their consumer installment contracts to it. Though it charges interest on its loans to dealers, it does not expect to earn much, if anything, from this source; it expects to get its profits chiefly from the high-yield consumer contracts.

In retail sales of consumer durable goods in which a sales finance company provides the financing, the buyers ordinarily do not enter into direct negotiations with it. It supplies the dealer with contract forms, gives him instructions on how they are to be completed, and states the terms and conditions on the basis of which it will buy sales contracts from him: chiefly requirements about down payments (cash or trade-ins), frequency of installment payments, maximum maturity, insurance coverages that buyers must obtain and pay for (especially important in automobile sales), and the "finance charge" to be added to the buyers' obligations. As sales are made, the dealer completes the details of each contract, has the buyer sign it, and subsequently sells the contract to the finance company. The sales finance company then notifies the buyer of the assignment of the contract, and directs him to make his installment payments to it rather than to the dealer. In most states, the "contract" itself is a conditional sales instrument by which the dealer (and then the finance company after the assignment to it) retains a "security interest" in the goods until all installment payments have been made, and in which the buyer gives his specific promise to make these installment payments.

Consumer finance companies

Consumer finance companies concentrate on granting loans to consumers and devote very little, if any, of their resources to lending to business firms or elsewhere. They lend to consumers for almost anything that consumers wish to buy, although they appear to emphasize in their advertising the advantages of getting a loan from them in order to pay off all your outstanding bills so that you will then have payments to make to only one creditor. They are the people who tell you that, if you call friendly so-and-so and tell him of your needs, they will have the money waiting for you when you get to their office. Perhaps it is not quite so easy, but we still may say that consumer finance companies grant many consumer loans to people who are not qualified to borrow elsewhere.

In their lending operations, consumer finance companies are probably the most closely regulated of all financial institutions. Under the "small-loan laws" as adopted by the various state legislatures, such a company must have each of its offices separately licensed, keep prescribed records, use prescribed forms, make reports to state officials, and subject itself to examination by these officials. Its outstanding loans to any borrower must at no time exceed a stipulated maximum, such as $300 in Alabama, $500 in Maryland, $800 in Illinois, $1000 in Michigan, and $1400 in New York. It must not charge interest in excess of stipulated rates; as in Arizona, 3 percent a month on unpaid principal balances not exceeding $300, 2 percent a month on balances between $300 and $600, and 1 percent a month on balances between $600 and $1000; or as in Minnesota, $2\frac{3}{4}$ percent a month on balances up to $300, $1\frac{1}{2}$ percent on balances between $300 and $600, and $1\frac{1}{4}$ percent a month on balances between $600 and $900. It is strictly limited in the kinds and amounts of additional charges it may levy and in the kinds of things it may accept as collateral for its loans. It must limit the maturities of its loans to designated periods, and it must generally allow borrowers to pay off their loans ahead of due dates with no further interest charges or with interest rebates, depending upon how interest is charged and how and when prepayments are made.

Although the general rule under the small-loan laws has been that a consumer finance company may carry on no other business in its loan office or offices, a recent development in many states has been to permit such companies to obtain additional licenses under such statutes as "industrial loan acts" and "installment loan acts." The additional licenses permit loans to individual borrowers much in excess of the maximums of the small-loan laws but at rates of interest substantially below the permitted rates of these laws. ("Industrial" loan acts and comparable "industrial" bank acts are so called because they were originally passed to promote the establishment of institutions to lend primarily to wage earners in manufacturing and other industries—not for lending to the industries themselves. A large number of "industrial banks" and "industrial loan companies" remain in operation without also having small-loan licenses, so that they are recognized as distinct types of consumer credit institutions.)

Overlapping and conglomeration

For many large finance companies especially, the foregoing separate descriptions of classes and subclasses tends to be functional rather than organizational. That is to say, many have divisions or subsidiaries that are separately engaged in factoring, lending on accounts receivable, buying consumer installment contracts, granting loans as licensees under small-loan laws, and so on. In divisions and subsidiaries, a few cover the entire field, while others are not so broad in the scope of their operations although not confining themselves to single functions.

CREDIT UNIONS

A *credit union* is a cooperative corporation in which all members, who have some bond of mutual interests, contribute savings to a pool to be used for loans to members, principally consumer loans. As for commercial banks and savings and loan associations, we have a dual system of chartering of credit unions, so that in all states—except Alaska, Delaware, Hawaii, Nevada, South Dakota, and Wyoming, which have no credit union laws—"federal" credit unions and state-chartered ones operate, as it were, side by side.

According to a report of the Credit Union National Association, 23,761 credit unions were in operation in the United States at the end of 1969, with estimated membership of approximately 21.6 million persons and assets of $15.9 billion, including outstanding loans of $12.9 billion. The members' total savings, in what are variously called "savings accounts" and "share accounts," were estimated at $13.7 billion. The typical credit union is a small institution, about 54 percent of them having assets at the end of 1969 of not more than $200,000 individually. At that time, nevertheless, 14.6 percent of the unions had assets individually of more than $1 million and 2.5 percent of more than $5 million.[16]

Organization

Credit unions may be operated successfully, as a general rule, only when the "bonds of mutual interests" among the members are reasonably strong; at any rate, some "bonds" of this kind are required by both the federal and state governments in granting charters. The employees of a small manufacturing company or of a "shop" in a larger one, the members of an office force, church parish, or chapter of a fraternal society, the constituents of a

---

[16]*International Credit Union Yearbook*, 1970, pp. 1, 15.

labor union "local"—groups of these kinds should be sufficiently cohesive to operate a credit union successfully.

A general rule is that each member of a credit union must be the owner of at least one share of stock, typically of $5 or $10 par value. Many members of credit unions buy many additional shares or, in some, put much or all of their savings into deposit accounts, thus making the unions a principal or even an exclusive depositary for their savings. Regardless of the number of shares each member owns, however, he only has one vote in the election of directors and the personnel of a "credit committee" and on policy questions submitted for members' decisions. Other funds for loans are derived from small entrance fees for new members, "fines" for delinquency in loan repayments, occasional loans obtained from commercial banks, and accumulated earnings not paid out as dividends.

In the typical setup, the board of directors chooses a president, one or more vice-presidents, a treasurer, and a secretary from among its own membership. Typically, too, the treasurer is the most active officer in the additional role as general manager. He has custody of the union's funds, receives loan applications, and working with the credit committee, grants the loans and supervises them while outstanding.

Loans to members

Except for loans to other credit unions, each credit union is permitted to grant loans only to its own members. In the case of federal credit unions, except for very small ones, outstanding loans to each member may not exceed $2500 or $2\frac{1}{2}$ percent of the union's capital and surplus, if less, if the loans are unsecured, or 10 percent of capital and surplus if secured.

No law, federal or state, permits credit unions to charge more than 1 percent interest a month on the declining unpaid balances of loans. Many credit unions charge less than the maximum permitted rate, some reducing the interest charge by granting "rebates" on the basis of earnings. The interest received on loans and income from other sources are used to cover operating expenses, to set up reserves in order to absorb losses, and to pay dividends to the members on their savings balances.

Insurance for savings in credit unions

Late in 1970 Congress passed legislation creating a new federal agency to manage an insurance program for the protection of savers' balances in credit unions. Closely modeled on the FDIC and FSLIC systems, the program for credit unions requires all federal credit unions to be insured and makes insurance available to state-chartered unions on the usual basis of application and acceptance. Members' savings balances are individually insured up to $20,000, and the insured union must pay semiannual assessments of $\frac{1}{24}$ of 1 percent of total savings balances as "premiums" for their coverage.

THE COOPERATIVE FARM CREDIT SYSTEM

For most farmers in most localities, the principal sources of loans are commercial banks, life insurance companies, and finance companies. The commercial banks are especially important as lenders to farmers not only because of their big lead in the volume of their outstanding farm loans, but also because of the many purposes for which they lend and the wide range of the maturities of their loans. On the other hand, loans of life insurance companies are almost exclusively mortgage loans for the acquisition of farm land and buildings and their improvement, while the loans of finance companies are chiefly advances for the acquisition of farm machinery that are granted, as it were, by their purchase of farmers' installment payment contracts from dealers.

Nevertheless, these sources of farm loans are extensively supplemented by the facilities of a "cooperative farm credit system" sponsored by the federal government. For many farmers, indeed, the lending institutions sponsored by the federal government are more important as sources of funds than the "ordinary" institutions, depending on financing needs as they vary from farmer to farmer, ease of access to the different kinds of institutions, their credit standards as applied to loan applications, and their interest rates, maturities, provisions for installment repayment, and other customary loan terms.

Structure

The cooperative farm credit system consists of twelve federal land banks, over six hundred federal land bank associations, twelve federal intermediate credit banks, about five hundred production credit associations, and thirteen banks for cooperatives, all subject to the regulatory jurisdiction of an independent federal agency called the Farm Credit Administration (FCA). As the supervisory head of the cooperative system, the FCA is composed of the Federal Farm Credit Board, the Governor of the FCA, and four deputy governors. The board has thirteen members of whom twelve are chosen by the President with the advice and consent of the Senate and the thirteenth is chosen by the Secretary of Agriculture. The board, in turn, appoints the Governor and the deputy governors. Because the board is a part-time policy-making body, much of the work of administration, including decision making, falls to the Governor of the FCA as assisted by his deputies.

As in the geographical structures of the Federal Reserve and Home Loan Bank Systems, the country has been divided into twelve districts with a federal land bank, a federal intermediate credit bank, and a bank for cooperatives located in a principal city in each of the districts. The three banks of each district have a single board of directors known as a "farm credit board" but separate presidents as chief administrative officers chosen by the board. Although each of the three banks has distinct lending and supervisory responsibilities and separate arrays of assets and liabilities, there is considerable overlapping among them in the use of facilities and personnel. The thirteenth bank for cooperatives—strange departure in our financial structure from the magic number twelve!—is called the "Central Bank for Cooperatives" and is located in Washington, D.C.

Loan facilities and flows

The cooperative idea works this way: When owners and prospective owners of farms in a given area wish to obtain mortgage loans from the land bank of the district, they apply to the FCA for a corporate charter for a federal land bank association or join an association already in operation. They apply to the association for their loans, and if the association is willing to accept responsibility for these loans (on a corporate limited-liability basis), it sends the applications to the land bank. The land bank grants the loans to the association and the association then grants the loans to the applicants.

In a similar way, when farmers of a given area wish to use the cooperative facilities to obtain short- and intermediate-term loans for such purposes as the planting, harvesting, and marketing of crops, the purchase, feeding, and marketing of livestock, the repair and improvement of farm buildings, and the acquisition of machinery and equipment, they apply to the FCA for a corporate charter for a production credit association or join one already in operation in their vicinity. They then apply to the association for their loans, and if the association is willing to grant them, it obtains the necessary funds by borrowing in turn from the federal intermediate credit bank of the district.

Again, if the farmers of a given area belong to purchasing, marketing, and business-service cooperatives, and if the cooperatives need money to stock seed, feed, and fertilizer for resale to their members, to buy up members' crops for sorting, grading, packing, and selling, to erect buildings, such as receiving and sorting stations and storage facilities, and to finance other similar needs, they may apply to the bank for cooperatives of the district for loans—short-term or intermediate-term depending upon the purpose of the loan. Finally, the Central Bank for Cooperatives grants loans to the district banks and participates with them in granting loans to cooperatives when these loans exceed the district banks' lending limits. (The purchasing, marketing, and business-service cooperatives mentioned here are *not* chartered by the FCA; they are generally corporations or voluntary associations formed under state law by groups of farmers who decide that collective buying or marketing or both would be advantageous. Probably the best known of such cooperatives is the California Fruit Growers' Association, which markets the citrus crops of many members under its "Sunkist" label.)

Ownership arrangements and security issues

In connection with all the lending mentioned in the preceding paragraphs, stock subscriptions equal to stipulated proportions of loans (generally 5 percent) are required. In borrowing from a federal land bank association or a production credit association, a farmer buys stock in it, and these associations buy stock in the district federal land bank and federal intermediate credit bank in relationship to their borrowings from them. Likewise, the purchasing, marketing and business-service cooperatives buy stock in the banks for cooperatives in connection with the loans obtained from them, and these banks buy stock in the Central Bank. The objective has been to have all the FCA institutions fully owned directly or indirectly by farmers—an objective that now obtains although the Treasury held majority ownership interests in many of these institutions for long periods and minority interests for additional long periods.

Very large proportions of the loan funds of the land banks, the intermediate credit banks, and the banks for cooperatives are obtained by sales of their debt instruments in the open market, with the land banks favoring long-term bonds because they are long-term lenders, and the intermediate credit banks and banks for cooperatives generally getting their money by issues of short-term "debentures." Although these bonds and debentures have no principal or interest guaranties of the Treasury, they are highly regarded in investment circles for safety.

FOR REVIEW

1. What are the principal sources and uses of funds of savings and loan associations? Why are some of these associations called federal associations? mutual associations? insured associations?

2. Why do most of the savings and loan associations find it advantageous to be members of the Federal Home Loan Bank System?

3. What is peculiar about the geography, ownership, and management of mutual savings banks?

4. On the basis of what kinds of contracts have our life insurance companies accumulated huge amounts of savings? What are their principal outlets for these savings accumulations?

5. What kinds of activities are described as trust services? By what kinds of institutions are such services performed? In what varying capacities do the institutions perform these services?

6. In performing trust services, what freedom of choice, if any, do trust institutions have in selecting investments? Explain.

7. Why is it said that common stock is extraordinarily important in the operations of investment companies?

8. How does one go about investing his money in a mutual fund? What are the procedures and terms of making withdrawals?

9. Explain the distinction between trusteed and insured pension funds. What is the major source of money accumulations for both these classes of pension funds?

10. What is the distinction, if any, between a security dealer and an investment banking firm?

11. What is meant by the underwriting of a new security issue? What is stand-by underwriting? a best-efforts commitment?

12. What kinds of financial services are provided by factors and commercial finance companies?

13. What is the distinction between wholesale and retail financing as engaged in by sales finance companies?

14. How are consumer finance companies distinguished from other sub-classes of finance companies?

15. What is a credit union? What are the principal sources of funds for credit unions? What do they use these funds for?

16. Why are the federal land banks and other federally sponsored institutions in the farm credit field described as constituting a cooperative farm credit system?

CHAPTER 11

FINANCIAL MARKETS

MONEY AND CAPITAL MARKETS

Financial markets comprise all the facilities by means of which people arrange to lend and borrow money and to use it to buy and sell corporate stocks. According to generally accepted terminology, each economically developed country has only two financial markets: a money market and a capital market. A money market comprises all the facilities by means of which people arrange to borrow and lend money for periods not exceeding 1 year;[1] and a capital market, the facilities by means of which they arrange to borrow and lend money for periods exceeding 1 year and to buy and sell corporate stocks. Accordingly, a country's money market is often referred to as its "market for short-term funds," and its capital market, the "market for long-term funds."

Market subdivisions

In the United States, both the money and capital markets have many subdivisions for each of which the term *market* is often separately used. Thus it would appear that we have a great number of financial markets, rather than only two, but the liberal usage of the term *market* is so widespread that we can hardly avoid accepting this usage. Among subdivisions, the distinction between *primary* and *secondary* markets is especially important. In primary markets, individuals, business enterprises, and governments try to obtain money in exchange for their debt instruments, and corporations additionally try to obtain it by offering new issues of their stock; in secondary markets, individuals and institutions try to sell to other investors bonds and stocks that they own and loans that they have previously granted. Also important in the matter of market subdivisions is the distinction between

---

[1] A money market may also be said to include facilities for the purchase and sale of money itself, which means, in most instances, the purchase and sale of foreign currencies in exchange for domestic money.

markets in which deals are *negotiated* directly between borrowers and lenders and buyers and sellers and *open* markets. In a market in which negotiated deals are effected, seekers of money go directly to lenders and buyers of stocks and bonds and try to make arrangements for getting the money; while in an open market, debt instruments and stocks are exchanged for money without any significant contacts between the sellers of these instruments and the buyers. When a businessman applies to a commercial bank for a short-term loan to acquire inventory, discusses the details with a loan officer, has his credit worthiness investigated, and comes to an agreement on the amount and terms of the loan, this is a negotiated transaction in a primary market; but when a finance company finds buyers for an issue of its 90-day promissory notes that it offers broadside to the investing public, this is a transaction in an open primary market. In a similar way, when a man sells fifty shares of General Electric common stock from his holdings to his next-door neighbor, this is a negotiated deal in a secondary market, while the sale would be a transaction in an open secondary market were it made through the agency of a member firm of the New York Stock Exchange.

Again, there are many subdivisions in the money and capital markets according to the kinds of loans that are granted and the classes of securities that are bought and sold. Examples are the markets for short-term loans to business enterprises, mortgage loans on business properties, mortgage loans on residential properties, consumer loans for automobile buying, the bonds and stocks of domestic corporations, the bonds and stocks of foreign corporations, U.S. Treasury obligations, and the obligations of state and local governments. Finally, many geographical subdivisions of the money and capital markets obtain, as the market for short-term business loans in Detroit, the residential mortgage market in New Orleans, the market on the Pacific Coast for the promissory notes of finance companies, the national market in the stocks of prominent corporations, and the national and international markets in Treasury bills.

Market volume and activity

As measured by the volume of loans and debt instruments of different classes and corporate stocks outstanding at given times, the relative importance of some of the major subdivisions of the money and capital markets is indicated in Federal Reserve flow-of-funds reports. Data from the report for December 31, 1970, are presented in Table 11–1. But such data are far from accurate as indicators of *activity* in the various markets, in the sense of loans granted and repaid and securities issued, retired, bought, and sold in the course of, say, a year. As a rule, markets for short-term loans and securities are much more active than bond and mortgage loan markets, principally for two reasons: (1) because short-term lending and repayment and short-term security issuance and redemption are transactions that, by definition, are likely to be repeated frequently in the course of a year; and (2) because many of the short-term securities have the qualities of liquid assets,[2] so that, even during the short periods that individual issues are outstanding, they are often bought and sold repeatedly as a temporary means of investing idle money. Again, repeated transactions in the secondary market in the common stocks of prominent corporations are commonplace —some of them having, indeed, huge "turnovers"—while secondary market transactions in the bonds of the same corporations are so few by comparison that their markets are often described as being "thin."

Scope of this chapter

In the subsequent discussion of the money and capital markets in this chapter, we can hardly cover every kind of market facility available. Some market facilities were referred to in significant ways in Chapter 10, and others in earlier chapters, at least by implication. Other facilities can best be treated in later chapters, as in Chapters 13–15 for most of the lending and investing operations of the commercial banks, and in Chapters 23–25 for transactions in foreign moneys. For the present chapter, therefore, we must choose from the standpoints of importance and convenience of placement, at the same time giving most emphasis to open-market facilities. For convenience, too, it is appropriate to begin with a general treatment of government securities markets rather than to break this treatment into separate discussions under money market and capital market headings.

Table 11-1 **Debt Instruments and Corporate Stocks Outstanding, December 31, 1970 (in billions of dollars)**

United States government securities	299.7
Obligations of federal agencies	38.3
Obligations of state and local governments	143.4
Corporation and foreign bonds	206.5
Home mortgage loans	280.1
Other mortgage loans	170.4
Consumer credit	126.8
Commercial bank loans[a]	155.5
Other loans	140.7
Corporate stocks[b]	911.6
Total	2473.0

[a] Loans not included in other categories as listed.
[b] At market value.
Source: Federal Reserve Bulletin, March 1971, p. A71.10.

GOVERNMENT SECURITIES MARKETS

U.S. Treasury direct obligations

Measured by total dollar volumes of transactions, the market in direct obligations of the U.S. Treasury is the most important financial market that

---

[2]See Chapter 1.

we have—far more important than the New York Stock Exchange and, indeed, all our stock exchanges combined. For March 1970, for example, principal dealers in direct Treasury obligations reported that their average *daily* purchases and sales amounted to $2861 million, while average daily sales of stocks on all stock exchanges amounted to approximately $507 million.[3]

The Treasury's *direct* obligations are debt instruments that evidence its own borrowings and that state its commitment to repay at designated maturities. They differ from *securities of federal agencies*, on some of which the Treasury guarantees payment of principal and interest but on most of which it has no payment obligation at all. Although the Treasury occasionally borrows from the Federal Reserve banks in what could be called "negotiated transactions," most of its borrowed funds are obtained by open-market sales of new issues of its bills, notes, and "marketable" bonds.

Treasury Bills Treasury bills are money market instruments throughout their lives, since they never have maturities beyond 1 year. Every week the Treasury puts out two issues of bills, one to mature in 91 days and the other in 182 days; and each month it puts out a bill issue to mature in 9 months and another to mature in 1 year.[4] In late 1970, the weekly issues were averaging about $1.9 billion for the 91-day bills, $1.4 billion for the 182-day bills, $500 million for the 9-month bills, and $1.2 billion for the 1-year issues. Occasionally, too, the Treasury sells issues of "tax anticipation bills." These are so called because their maturity dates are set close to important tax-payment dates, and are designed, as it were, to bring in, well before the due dates of tax payments, funds accumulated by corporations and other taxpayers to meet tax obligations. Such issues run for various periods—but always less than 1 year—depending upon the date of issue and the tax-payment dates at which they are aimed. The proceeds of the regular weekly and monthly issues are ordinarily used to redeem the maturing issues put out 91 days, 182 days, 9 months, and 1 year earlier. However, the Treasury sometimes gets "new money" by stepping up the volume of its weekly and monthly offerings, and sometimes it reduces the net volume of outstanding bills by making new offerings smaller than maturing issues. On the other hand, maturing tax anticipation bills are accepted in payment of federal taxes or, if not offered for tax payments by the holders, are redeemed out of these revenues.

A peculiar aspect of Treasury bills is that the Treasury does not designate the rates of interest they shall earn. Instead, it offers the bills on an auction basis, alloting the issues to the highest bidders, that is, the bidders who are satisfied with the lowest rates of interest (discount). For example,

---

[3]*Federal Reserve Bulletin,* June 1970, p. A44, and Securities and Exchange Commission, *Statistical Bulletin,* July 1970, p. 10.
[4]The maturities sometimes vary 1 day or 2 because of holidays.

an investor might successfully bid for some 91-day bills at a price of 98.400, a bid indicating that he would be satisfied to earn approximately 6.5 percent per annum on his allotment. Another investor bidding, say 98.390, and thus indicating a hope for a slightly higher rate of return, might have his bid rejected because the entire offering could be allotted at bids higher than 98.390. On the other hand, to encourage smaller investors to get into the bill market, the Treasury is willing to make individual allotments up to $200,000 of each offering of bills to such investors on a noncompetitive basis. However, many "smaller" investors are necessarily excluded from buying even on a noncompetitive basis, since $10,000 is the minimum denomination for bills. For each offering, then, the total of the noncompetitive allotments is subtracted from the total offering and the balance is allocated to the competitive bidders, with the noncompetitive buyers paying at the average price of the accepted competitive bids.

All Treasury bills are issued payable to the bearer: they cannot be registered in the names of the owners at the Treasury or the Federal Reserve banks. Accordingly, owners must be on guard against dangers of fire, theft, and other causes of disappearance.

Treasury Notes and Bonds Notes are the Treasury's intermediate-term debt instrument and bonds are its long-term instrument. Note issues have maturities ranging from slightly more than 1 year to 7 years, while bonds issued in the past couple of decades have had maturities ranging from 5 to 40 years.

In offering new issues of notes and bonds, the Treasury stipulates the rates of interest they will bear, although it can hardly be said to have a free hand in setting these rates. It must be guided by conditions of tightness or ease in the financial markets, giving particular attention to rates currently being paid on other kinds of intermediate- and long-term indebtedness. Because the Treasury always wishes to have its new flotations of debt instruments oversubscribed, it has customarily erred somewhat in the direction of liberality in setting the interest rates it will pay. However, the error can be avoided if it offers notes and bonds on an auction basis— a procedure that was inaugurated in the fall of 1970 with respect to notes. Prospective buyers of an issue may be expected to bid prices above par value if the Treasury sets too high an interest rate, and below par value if it sets too low an interest rate, so that the premiums and discounts will compensate, as it were, for any error in the set rate.

In the period 1965–1971, on the other hand, the Treasury had no free hand in offering marketable bonds, because federal law set a ceiling of 4¼ percent for their coupon interest rate. Bonds bearing that rate would have been salable only at prices far below par because of the high market rates then prevailing. In March 1971, however, Congress authorized the issuance of $10 billion of marketable bonds without regard to the 4¼ percent ceiling.

Interest on notes and bonds is payable semiannually on par value at the rates designated at the time of issuance. Both kinds of instruments may be obtained in bearer form with coupons for interest attached or in registered form. If registered, the names of the owners are recorded on the books of the Federal Reserve banks, and transfers must also be recorded. However, holders of bonds and notes of one form may readily exchange them for the other form if they so choose.

Original Sale of Treasury Marketable Obligations   In selling its bills, notes, and marketable bonds, the Treasury does not directly use the services of security dealers, brokers, or other middlemen; however, it does rely greatly on the service facilities of the Federal Reserve banks in their capacity as "fiscal agents of the United States."[5] Having decided to put out a new issue of securities, it makes a general announcement of the type, the date of issue, the price and rate of interest (except, of course, for bills), the maturity, and the details on making payment. Details on payment may provide, for example, that the new issue is being offered only in exchange—always voluntary—for a maturing issue, or that either cash or maturing instruments will be accepted in payment for units of the new issue. For commercial banks, an important consideration is whether or not they may pay by simply crediting the Treasury's tax and loan accounts on their own books.

In effect, the Treasury's announcement invites everybody to enter subscriptions for the securities to be marketed. As thus invited, any person or organization may enter a subscription at the Federal Reserve bank in the district, and when payment has been made in the prescribed manner, the Reserve bank makes delivery of the securities. Usually, however, subscribers do not get as much as they ask, because total subscriptions exceed the total volume of securities offered. The subscriber can feel, however, that he is not being unfairly treated, because subscriptions are scaled down on a pro rata basis; indeed, because he, too, expects an oversubscription, he probably subscribes for more of the issue than he wants anyway! The only preference ordinarily shown by the Treasury is one in favor of those "smaller" investors once again—a provision that subscriptions up to $200,000 will be allotted in full even when it is necessary to scale down all those beyond that level.

Dealers and the Market   Although the Treasury does not ask security dealers to assist with the original sale of its debt instruments, they fulfill an indispensable function in helping to maintain a strong and active market for the Treasury obligations. This is an important function because many institutions and individuals would not invest in these obligations in the first place were they to lack assurances that they could readily resell at prices not subject to wide fluctuations, at least in short periods. There are two

---

[5]For a description of Federal Reserve fiscal agency services, see Chapter 16.

classes of dealers: nonbank security firms and large metropolitan commercial banks known as "dealer-banks." Some of the nonbank security firms specialize in buying and selling government securities—usually issues of federal agencies and of state and local governments as well as direct Treasury obligations—while others engage in many additional transactions of the securities business.

The very fact that a security firm or large commercial bank declares itself to be a dealer in government securities of particular classes means that it will carry inventories of these securities and will "make markets" in them by standing ready at all times (except, possibly, in brief periods of extreme disorder in financial markets) to quote prices at which it will be willing to buy large amounts and other prices at which it will sell large amounts. The offering prices will, of course, be greater than the bid prices, since the dealers derive their income from profits on price spreads rather than from commissions. Nevertheless, the spreads are usually quite narrow, because the dealers depend on voluminous transactions for their profits rather than on substantial margins on individual transactions.

Money Market Facilities for Nonbank Dealers Because nonbank dealers in government securities carry their inventories chiefly by means of borrowed funds and because all their borrowing is short term, the market facilities by which they get these funds are generally recognized as constituting a distinct subdivision of the money market. Even in relatively short periods, the sources of borrowed funds often shift substantially, depending upon the availability of money for lending among these sources. At virtually all times, the commercial banks are an important source, and they grant both "call loans" and time loans typically running for only a few days. The call loans are so named because the dealer can repay on notice of 1 day and the lending bank can demand repayment on notice of 1 day. Other important sources of borrowed money—sometimes more important collectively than the commercial banks—are life insurance companies, other financial institutions, and nonfinancial business corporations.

Borrowings by dealers often take the form of repurchase agreements by which the dealer sells securities from his inventory with a contractual obligation to buy back exactly the same securities in a few days at a slightly higher price, with the price differential representing interest on what amounts to a secured loan. In the matter of repurchase agreements, the Federal Reserve Bank of New York, on behalf of all the Reserve banks, occasionally assists the dealers by providing them with funds by way of such contracts—when, as it were, their usual sources of funds for carrying Treasury obligations are greatly diminished. This help is not altruistic, because the Federal Reserve wishes no wide or frequent price fluctuations to develop in the market when the dealers have insufficient money to perform their customary buying and selling functions.

Securities of federal agencies

The market for the debt instruments of federal agencies can be described as an adjunct to the market for direct Treasury obligations, because carrying inventories of these instruments and dealing in them are generally additional functions of the security firms and banks that deal in the direct obligations. The market for agency securities has grown greatly in significance in recent years because of the rapid growth in the volume of such securities issued and outstanding. Between the end of 1964 and the end of 1969, the volume of outstanding agency securities increased from about $14 billion to $44 billion, or by approximately $30 billion, while the volume of Treasury marketable issues increased from about $213 billion to $236 billion, or by only approximately $23 billion.[6]

The principal contributors to the big growth in outstanding agency securities in the 1964–1969 period were the federal home loan banks, the Federal National Mortgage Association (FNMA, or "Fanny Mae"), the federal land banks, the federal intermediate credit banks, and the banks for cooperatives—all of these, except the FNMA, to get funds chiefly for relending to stockholding "member" institutions as described in the preceding chapter. However, the borrowings of the FNMA have been and are aimed in the same direction as those of the home loan banks—in order to expand the capacity of home-mortgage lending institutions to grant new mortgage loans on residential property by buying from them residential mortgages already on their books.

The securities issued by federal agencies are variously called "notes," "debentures," "bonds," and "participation certificates." Among agencies, the terminology is by no means uniform. While instruments called "notes" almost always have maturities of not more than 1 year, instruments called "debentures" and "bonds" often have maturities as short as 2 or 3 years. Participation certificates are so called because they represent interests, so to say, in an array of assets pledged for their safety and held by the issuing agency as trustee, such as residential mortgage loans held by the Government National Mortgage Association as security for its certificates, and loans to promote exports held by the Export-Import Bank. Collectively, at any rate, a large proportion of agency issues are short-term, and a large proportion of the remainder have maturities at the time of issuance of not more than 5 years.

Securities of state and local governments

The debt instruments that state and local governments issue as means of borrowing are known collectively as "municipal" securities, or simply as "municipals." They are also often referred to as "tax exempts," because of the extraordinary provision of the Internal Revenue Code that exempts the

---

[6]Board of Governors of the Federal Reserve System, *Flow of Funds Accounts, 1945–1968* (Washington, D.C., 1970), p. 57, and *Federal Reserve Bulletin*, various issues.

interest paid on them from the levies of the federal corporation and individual income taxes.

Maturities   At the time of their original sale, most issues of municipal securities are long-term, since the principal purpose of their sale is to finance the construction of schools, highways, and other public facilities that are expected to have long lives, as well as to pay off maturing securities previously issued for construction. However, a major percentage of so-called long-term issues have serial maturities, which means that portions of each issue come due each year even when the maturity of the final portion may be 20 to 30 years. In a typical serial issue, therefore, some of the securities are really short-term, others intermediate term, and the remainder long-term. Only a small proportion of municipals are short-term entirely at the time of issuance; these are usually "notes" or "warrants" to meet ordinary expenditures and to be paid out of tax receipts or to meet construction costs and to be paid out of the proceeds of later bond issues.

Investment Qualities   Because of wide differences in the revenue sources of the great number of state and local governments that engage in debt financing—and, therefore, in their apparent capacities to meet interest and principal obligations—municipal securities have a wide range of ratings from the standpoint of safety. Differences in ratings also result from variations in the revenue sources that issuing governments are willing to allocate to meet interest and principal obligations—variations that, among other things, account for a basic distinction between their "general obligations" and their "revenue bonds." On its general obligations, a government is said to pledge its full faith and credit—to pledge, in effect, that it will use all its taxing powers to the limit in order to pay interest and principal; while on its revenue bonds, its pledge is to use revenues from a given source in order to meet these obligations, as fees received from water users for waterworks bonds, and tolls received from highway users for toll-road bonds.

Original Sale   For the original sale of security issues, a state or local government customarily publishes details about each proposed issue (and details about its financial position and records) with a general invitation for bids for the entire issue aimed at security dealers that specialize in government securities, other investment banking firms, and commercial banks that deal in municipals. The government accepts the bid that will result in the lowest net interest cost to it, or if it judges all the bids to be unsatisfactory, it rejects all as it reserves the right to do.

As in dealing in securities generally, the successful bidder buys in the expectation of being able to resell quickly at a higher price. For small issues, the security firm or dealer-bank may try to find buyers entirely on its own; but for larger issues, it will surely invite other security dealers and dealer-banks to join it in an underwriting syndicate in which all will participate in the resale effort and all will share the risk of not being able to resell at or above the price guaranteed to the issuing government. Nevertheless, a significant minority of issues, especially issues of revenue bonds, are exempted from competitive-bidding rules, so that many are sold in negotiated deals with single investment banking firms or dealer-banks, with the single firm or bank deciding whether or not it wants to assemble a syndicate.

Secondary Market   The principal market facilities for the buying and selling of municipal securities already outstanding are supplied by security firms and commercial banks that specialize in trading in government issues, as well as by some generalized security firms that have departments that specialize in the same area. As with Treasury obligations, these security firms and dealer-banks carry inventories of the municipals for which they are willing to "make markets," and they continually quote prices at which they will sell out of these inventories and at which they will buy to add to them. The security firms and dealer-banks are especially concerned with providing good secondary markets for the municipal issues that they have previously participated in underwriting, but many include numerous additional issues in their market making. On the other hand, secondary markets for a large number of issues of governments whose credit standings are inferior or are not well-known to investors are sometimes hard to find, although most security firms and banks will try to find buyers or sellers on an agency basis, that is, as brokers, if not as dealers.

Even for large outstanding issues of high-rated state and local governments, the secondary market is not so "broad, deep, and resilient" as that for Treasury obligations. This means that the dealers sometimes vary their price quotations by substantial amounts from transaction to transaction—especially when important classes of investors, such as the commercial banks, are buying and selling in huge amounts, or when the dealers themselves are anxious to add to their inventories in anticipation of falling market rates of interest or to reduce these inventories in anticipation of rising market rates.

OTHER SUBDIVISIONS OF THE MONEY MARKET[7]

The acceptance market

Nature and Use of Bankers' Acceptances   A *banker's acceptance* is a written order (draft) drawn on a bank by an individual or firm directing payment of a specified sum of money to the order of a designated party or to bearer at a specified future date, with the bank, by its "acceptance" of the

---

[7]Deferred to later chapters are descriptions of two important subdivisions of the money market: the federal funds market and the foreign exchange market. For the federal funds market, see Chapter 13, and the foreign exchange market, Chapters 23 and 25.

order written on it, committing itself to make the payment as directed. Essentially, therefore, bankers' acceptances are much the same as certified checks; in both, the drawee banks, by their written acceptance or certification, agree to make payment as ordered. But a certified check orders payment on demand, while payment on an acceptance is to be made on the designated future date. The maturities of acceptances generally range from 30 to 180 days.

Bankers' acceptances are used chiefly in financing the movement of goods in international trade, although some also are used for the domestic shipment and storage of goods. Of the $5973 million of acceptances reported to be outstanding in the United States at the end of July 1970, $2294 million had originated in import transactions, $1198 million in export transactions, and most of the balance in shipments between foreign countries, in the storage of goods in foreign countries, and in the storage of goods within the United States. The use of acceptances has greatly expanded in recent years, with the outstanding volume rising from $1229 million at the end of January 1960 to $5973 million at the end of July 1970, as just indicated.[8]

Origin of the Draft To illustrate how a banker's acceptance originates, let us say that an American firm is buying a shipment of textiles from a British firm, that payment is to be made in dollars, and that the British exporter requires the American importer to get a commercial letter of credit from an American bank. The British exporter could require the American importer to pay cash before the goods were shipped, but such terms might not be acceptable to the importer. Again, the exporter could draw a draft directly on the American importer, but his acceptance and promise to pay would not be likely to be valued so highly as the acceptance of a reputable American bank.

The American importer goes to his bank—in New York City, let us say —and asks that the letter of credit be issued in favor of the British exporter. The letter of credit is an authorization to the exporter to draw the draft. When the importer obtains the letter of credit, he signs a contract in which he agrees to pay the bank the amount of the acceptance (plus a commission) in time for the bank to pay it off at maturity. When the British exporter receives the letter of credit, he delivers the textiles to the steamship company and gets in return a bill of lading that gives the holder the right to obtain the goods when they are delivered in the United States. He then draws the draft and takes it, with the bill of lading and the letter of credit, to his bank in England. He may merely ask the bank to collect payment for him, but more likely he will ask it to discount the draft, that is, to give him its present value in sterling, so that he may have money with which to go on with his regular operations.

---

[8]*Federal Reserve Bulletin,* November 1960, p. 1258; September 1970, p. A37.

Draft Becomes an Acceptance   After the British bank discounts the draft, it sends it, with the bill of lading and the letter of credit, to its correspondent bank in the United States. This bank presents all documents to the American bank that issued the letter of credit. If all terms of the transaction have been properly met, the American issuing bank writes its acceptance across the face of the draft, with the date and its signature; by this action, the bank agrees to pay the face amount of the draft at maturity. At that moment, the draft becomes a banker's acceptance.

The accepting bank keeps the bill of lading and files away the letter of credit that has now served its purpose. Usually the bill of lading is given to the importer in exchange for a document by which the bank retains a "security interest" in the imported goods. The importer can then claim his goods by presenting the bill of lading to the steamship company.

Disposal of the Acceptance   Suppose that the acceptance is due 60 days "after sight," that is, 60 days after the American issuing bank accepted it. What happens to it in the meantime? The American correspondent bank would be holding it, but it would belong to the British bank. The British bank might direct the correspondent to hold the acceptance until maturity, in which case it would be financing the trade transaction. In effect, it would be making a loan to the American importer, since it had paid off the British exporter and had not itself received payment. Or the British bank, wanting to have its dollar balance on the correspondent's books increased immediately, might direct it to sell the acceptance in our money market. If that were its choice, a bank located anywhere in the United States might buy the acceptance as a short-term investment. The buying bank would be making a loan to the American importer, although it might know little or nothing about him, his credit position, and the nature of the transaction that gave rise to the acceptance. Clearly, its loan would be an impersonal open-market one rather than a negotiated deal.[9]

Accepting Institutions and Investors in Acceptances   The principal accepting institutions in the United States are the large commercial banks of New York City and San Francisco, their international banking subsidiaries, and American branches and agencies of foreign banks.

Unless a bank buys its own acceptances, it neither lends nor borrows money in creating acceptances. It merely, as it were, *lends its good name* to the individual or firm that obtains a letter of credit from it, and this individual or firm is the borrower *of money*. The money, in turn, is loaned by whoever holds the acceptance as an investment instrument from the time of its acceptance until its maturity. Actually, many accepting banks do buy their own acceptances, thus making themselves lenders of money as well as

---

[9]Letters of credit and bankers' acceptances may be used in many ways, but the text illustration should suffice at this time. The use of acceptance will be examined further in a later discussion of foreign exchange instruments. See Chapter 24.

of their good names. Other important classes of buyers are other commercial banks, the Federal Reserve banks, mutual savings banks, nonfinancial business corporations, and foreign central and commercial banks.

Federal Reserve Banks as Buyers For many years, the Federal Reserve banks held a peculiar position in the acceptance market by standing ready at all times to buy at posted discount rates any quantity of acceptances of "prime" quality offered by member banks and recognized dealers. By thus giving the member banks and dealers an assured market for excess supplies of acceptances, the Federal Reserve intended to promote a wider use of this type of instrument. However, in March 1955, the policy of buying at the option of member banks and dealers was discontinued. This move did not signify a loss of interest in promoting the use of acceptances, but the introduction of Federal Reserve discretion in buying.

At the present time, therefore, member banks and dealers may offer acceptances to the Federal Reserve Bank of New York (which does the buying and selling for all the Reserve banks) as well as offer to buy acceptances held by it, but the New York institution may accept or reject the offers as it chooses. Moreover, it need not await offers but may buy and sell on its own initiative in the open market.

Continuing as a means of supporting the acceptance market—but still at the discretion of the Federal Reserve authorities—is the practice of the Federal Reserve Bank of New York in buying acceptances from nonbank dealers under "repurchase agreements." By this arrangement, a dealer sells with the obligation to buy back the acceptances within a specified short period of time. Selling on the basis of repurchase agreements is the equivalent of obtaining short-term loans for the carrying of acceptances; hence dealers are likely to ask for this accommodation when they have insufficient funds to buy and carry all the acceptances offered them.

Middlemen in the Acceptance Market Serving as middlemen in the acceptance market are the dealers to whom reference has already been made. There are only seven dealer firms in operation, and a majority of these are primarily dealers in government securities. The dealers buy and sell in their own names, that is, they act as principals rather than as brokers or agents. Like Treasury bills, acceptances are bought and sold on a discount basis, the dealer taking as his profit the spread between the discount rate at which he buys and that at which he sells—a spread that has been ranging between $\frac{1}{8}$ and $\frac{1}{4}$ of 1 percent per annum. Although the bulk of acceptances are both created and held for investment in New York City, the dealers also reach buyers elsewhere through correspondent institutions and by telephone, telegraph, and mail.

The commercial paper market

Nature of Commercial Paper and Its Issuers A second market in which business enterprises obtain short-term loans without direct negotiation with the ultimate lenders is the market for commercial paper. Open-market commercial paper consists of unsecured promissory notes of several classes of issuers, with round face amounts ranging from $5000 to as high as $1 million, generally made payable to the bearer, and with maturities ranging from 3 to 270 days.

Among the issuers, finance companies dominate the market. The larger finance companies offer their notes directly and continuously to all classes of investors who may be interested in buying. They announce the rates of interest they are offering, with the scale graduated upward for the longer maturities, and they give their notes face amounts and maturities as wanted by investors who come to them and their selling agents with money to lend. Within a few minutes, a company may issue to an individual investor a 7-day note for $10,000 bearing interest at its lowest announced rate and to a corporate treasurer who has excess cash for temporary investment, a 90-day note for $1 million bearing interest at the higher announced rate for this longer maturity. But most finance companies do not have the national reputations and sales facilities for the "direct placement" of their notes among investors. Yet many have sufficient reputations to qualify for open-market borrowing, and they gain access to the market by finding dealers who are willing to buy their paper for resale. In such a transaction, the dealer buys an assortment of promissory notes of the face amounts and maturities that he designates, since he must keep in mind what his investing customers will want. Such "dealer-placed" paper is usually noninterest-bearing, and the usual procedure is for the dealer to offer to buy the issue at rates of discount that vary according to maturities and, from time to time, according to the changing supply and demand situation in the money market. He makes his offer in the hope of being able to resell the notes to his customers at slightly lower rates of discount, although he chiefly depends for his profit on a commission charged the issuer ranging from $\frac{1}{8}$ to $\frac{1}{4}$ of 1 percent on a per annum basis.

For many decades until the late 1960s, well-known high-rated manufacturing and mercantile corporations were the principal issuers of commercial paper apart from the finance companies. But the late 1960s brought many bank holdings companies and some of their nonbank subsidiaries and many public utility and transportation companies into the market as borrowers, as well as additional industrial corporations, especially firms in the oil and steel industries. A growth in outstanding commercial paper from about $9 billion at the end of 1965 to almost $40 billion at the end of May 1970[10] indicates the great surge in the popularity of the market. Most of the "bank-related" issuers of commercial paper offer their notes directly to investors, as do a few of the large nonbank enterprises, but most of the nonbank corporate issuers depend upon the dealers to find buyers for their notes.

---

[10]*Federal Reserve Bulletin,* September 1970, p. A37.

Attractions of the Open Market Because the finance, manufacturing, mercantile, public utility, and transportation companies[11] that borrow by the sale of their notes in the open market must have strong credit reputations, they could, as a rule, borrow equal amounts of money directly from commercial banks. In fact, many of these companies use both of these sources of short-term funds simultaneously, with many of the large finance companies, for example, having lines of credit with scores of commercial banks. Nevertheless, they are inclined to prefer the open market for several reasons. One is that the rates of interest (or discount) they pay on their commercial paper are less than the commercial banks charge on direct loans. Closely related to this advantage is another concerning the cost of funds: they have the full use of the money borrowed in the open market, whereas the commercial banks, in granting direct loans, often enforce "minimum-balance rules." By such a rule, a commercial bank stipulates that the borrower must not let his demand balance fall below 10, 15, or 20 percent of his outstanding loans, and this, of course, immobilizes a portion of the funds borrowed. Another advantage of open-market borrowing is that it enhances the borrower's power to bargain with the commercial banks for better terms on direct loans. Finally, a borrower's success in finding many buyers for its notes in the open market strengthens its credit reputation generally; as a result, its search for funds in other directions may be greatly eased, as in finding buyers for its long-term obligations.

The Role of Dealers Because commercial paper consists predominantly of the notes of finance companies and bank holding companies, and because the larger finance companies and most of the bank holding companies offer their notes directly to investors, the role of dealers in the market might appear to be a minor one. At the end of May 1970, for example, outstanding finance company and bank-related paper sold directly was reported at $25,637 million, while paper sold through dealers was reported at only about half as much at $13,952 million. Nevertheless, the latter figure for dealer-placed paper was obviously anything but a minor one. Indeed, the dealers had shared handsomely in the market boom of the late 1960s, with their outstandings rising from a level of only $1903 million at the end of 1965.[12]

Although borrowing in the open market is often described as an "impersonal" transaction, the relationships between dealers and the business firms that sell issues of promissory notes to them are by no means impersonal. Such a firm must make application for the dealer's services and submit to a thorough credit investigation. The dealer wishes to have every assurance that the firm will be able to pay its notes at their maturities. While buyers of commercial paper are free to make their own investigations of the credit

---

[11]The reason for the incursion of bank holding companies and their nonbank subsidiaries as open-market borrowers is separately discussed in Chapter 13.
[12]*Ibid.*

positions of the issuers, they are inclined to rely on the dealer's recommendations, so that a default would seriously injure his reputation. Because, moreover, the dealer usually buys outright from the issuer, he will surely have frozen in his hands an issue that proves to be unattractive to investors.

Once a dealer has bought an issue of promissory notes, he seeks to resell them to investors as quickly as possible. Because his commission rate is small, he depends upon quick turnover for a reasonable rate of profit. Dealers try to include in their lists of offerings notes of varying maturities, issuers, denominations, and prices, so that each investor may make a selection to meet his individual requirements. Investors are frequently permitted to buy the notes on an option basis; by this arrangement, they are allowed 10 days or 2 weeks to make an independent credit investigation, and they are then privileged to return the notes to the dealer if dissatisfied with their quality.

Investors in Commercial Paper   While many of the large metropolitan banks have, in effect, become borrowers on open-market commercial paper by way of the issues of their holding companies and other affiliates, these banks have never shown much interest in investment in the paper of other classes of issuers. But many smaller banks throughout the country have long been important among buyers of commercial paper. For these banks, buying commercial paper is a means of expanding loan portfolios without the burdens of extensive credit investigation and follow-up, as in direct lending, and especially attractive in periods when loan demands in their immediate localities are relatively weak.

However, nonfinancial business corporations are the principal investors in the directly offered notes of the large finance and holding companies. Such investment has been especially convenient for corporate treasurers because of the willingness of the issuers to tailor the face amounts and maturities of their notes exactly as wanted—even maturities of a few days, as "over the weekend." Moreover, the notes generally pay interest at higher rates than can be earned on short-term Treasury obligations of equal maturities, and the corporate treasurers are glad to get the additional margin of income, convinced that the additional margin of risk is slight.

Other important classes of investors in commercial paper are trust institutions, college endowment funds, life insurance companies, investment companies, and individuals.

Market for certificates of deposit

A new open-market instrument originated early in 1961 when a large commercial bank in New York City announced that it would issue negotiable time certificates of deposits (CDs) and that a dealer in government securities had agreed to provide market facilities for them. Since then the market has boomed, with many additional banks in New York and other principal cities issuing their own CDs, and with many additional dealers in government securities providing secondary market facilities for them. Outstanding CDs in denominations of $100,000 or more reached a peak of over $24 billion in November and December 1968—a level substantially exceeding the amount of commercial paper at that time.

While large-denomination negotiable CDs grew enormously in popularity in the 1960s, there were sharp setbacks in amounts outstanding in the latter months of 1966 and in March and April 1968, followed by a decline of more than $13 billion from early December 1968 to the end of 1969. In 1970, however, the popularity of CDs was progressively restored, so that the volume outstanding at the end of that year exceeded that of the 1968 peak. The reason for gyrations of the periods mentioned is that the success of large commercial banks in selling (issuing) new CDs and in renewing maturing ones depends upon the maximum rates of interest that the Federal Reserve permits them to pay. Because a CD is a time deposit, and because almost all the issuers of the large-denomination CDs are member banks of the Federal Reserve System, they cannot go beyond the Federal Reserve rate maximums. And when interest rates on other open-market instruments go beyond these maximums as in the 1966, 1968, and 1969 episodes, the banks can hardly escape difficulties in trying to sell new CDs and to get holders of maturing ones to renew them.

Nature of CDs and the Market   As issued by a commercial bank, a time certificate of deposit, or CD, is a receipt for money deposited. A marketable CD, as signed by the bank, states that the amount deposited plus interest at a designated rate is payable on a stipulated date to the order of the depositor or to the bearer—however the depositor himself wishes it. Marketable CDs always have maturities of at least 30 days, since deposits payable in less than 30 days are classified by the Federal Reserve as demand deposits on which no interest may be paid. Because the CD is payable to order or to bearer, it is negotiable; accordingly, the depositor, if he wants cash before the stipulated maturity date, may sell it to somebody else who has money for temporary investment or, more probably, to a dealer. Whoever holds the CD at maturity—legitimately, of course—is entitled to payment of the face amount plus interest by simply presenting it to the bank that issued it.

Before 1961, many smaller commercial banks issued certificates of deposit to business corporations and other customers who felt that their demand deposit balances were too large, and who wanted, therefore, to earn a return on portions of these balances by transfers to time deposits. But the large metropolitan banks did not generally provide time deposit facilities for their corporate customers, although many had savings deposit facilities for individuals and nonprofit institutions. These banks thought that their large corporate customers would simply make transfers from demand to time accounts, thereby increasing their expenses for interest payments, but without adding to the total volume of their deposits. But corporate treasurers grew increasingly reluctant to let excessive balances lie idle in their demand deposit accounts, so that they drew more and more on these accounts to buy Treasury bills and other open-market instruments. Faced with strong and expanding loan demands, the metropolitan banks concluded that they could not afford to lose these deposits. Thus came their quick embrace of CDs as something to offer the corporate treasurers as an attractive alternative to investment in Treasury obligations, commercial paper, and the like.

Although many smaller banks continue to issue CDs, their instruments are rarely bought and sold in the open market. Buyers of short-term open-market instruments want strong assurances that the issuer will surely pay at maturity, and in general, it is only the large metropolitan banks that can give such assurances. Although a small bank's CDs with face amounts not exceeding $20,000 per depositor have the protection of the FDIC's deposit insurance, the dealers are not interested in them because the expense of handling numerous instruments of small face amounts would exceed their gross profit margins. Moreover, large corporations with millions of dollars to invest for short periods in the money market naturally go to the big banks with which they already have their major demand deposit balances.

For these reasons, CDs as open-market instruments are predominantly the issues of big banks to big nonfinancial business corporations, as is indicated by the fact that most are issued with face amounts of $1 million. Accordingly, most of the market transactions in outstanding CDs in which the dealers participate involve certificates of this denomination, although there are some transactions in CDs as "small" as $500,000, and even, on occasion, as low as $100,000.

Market Transactions   Many of the large CDs originate by direct arrangements between the issuing banks and their corporate customers as well as customers of other classes, including state and local governments, foreign governments and central banks, and wealthy individuals. A customer simply uses excess balances in its demand deposit account with a given bank by "buying" that bank's own CDs with the maturities it wishes, provided, of course, that it is satisfied with the rate of interest that the bank offers. For the bank, the only immediate effect is a decrease in its demand deposits and an increase in its time deposits of equal amounts. However, many banks also acquire time deposits via the CD route by issuing bearer instruments, with interest rates and maturities thought to be attractive, and offering them through the dealers to prospective buyers.

But the dealers have much more to do than simply find buyers for newly issued CDs that banks wish to offer to investors generally. Many holders of CDs dispose of them before their maturities. They offer these CDs to the dealers who are willing to quote buying prices in the expectation that they will be able to resell rather quickly at slightly higher prices. A reason for sales to dealers is that original buyers of CDs sometimes overestimate the time that the cash invested will not be needed for operations or other necessary uses. For most sales to dealers, however, a more common reason is that original buyers, to get the advantage of higher interest rates on longer maturities, take CDs with maturities longer than they would otherwise want. Assume, for example, that a corporate treasurer has several million dollars of excess cash that he wishes to invest for 60 days. His bank tells him that it will pay interest at $5\frac{1}{2}$ percent per annum on 60-day CDs, but $6\frac{1}{2}$ percent on 6-month CDs. He would be very likely to take the 6-month instruments, expecting to be able to sell them to a dealer 60 days later at face value plus interest for the 60 days at $5\frac{1}{2}$ percent, and hoping for an additional premium! (If the market yield on instruments coming due in 4 months were, say, 6 percent at the time of sale to the dealer, the dealer should be willing to pay a premium on a $6\frac{1}{2}$ percent CD coming due in 4 months.) Another corporate treasurer, having money to invest for 4 months, might be quite willing to buy these CDs from the dealer, paying not only the premium mentioned but also an additional one as compensation to the dealer. Although the amounts of these premiums would moderately reduce the rate of yield on the CDs, this reduced yield would surely still be at least as good as that obtainable on any other 4-month instrument of comparable quality. The second treasurer, unlike the first, might anticipate rising market rates of interest, so that he would wish to avoid maturities longer than 4 months.

The Eurodollar market

Eurodollars and Eurobanks Eurodollars are deposits of United States dollars in banks outside the United States. Anybody who receives payments in dollar instruments or who holds dollar assets, such as Treasury obligations or commercial paper, may contribute to the supply of Eurodollars. For example, a British exporter who receives a dollar draft on an American bank in payment for goods exported may decide to deposit this draft as a dollar time deposit with a London bank rather than to sell it for sterling. Perhaps he will so decide because he wants to have dollars available in a month or two for dollar payments he must make, or because the London bank is willing to pay interest at a higher rate on the dollar deposit than on a sterling deposit of equivalent amount. The London bank may be willing to pay a higher rate on the dollar deposit, in turn, because it knows that Eurodollar borrowers are willing to pay higher rates of interest on such borrowings than on sterling loans.

Backing the Eurodollar deposit at the London bank would be an equal demand deposit balance in an American bank, because the London bank would send the dollar draft received from the British exporter to its American correspondent bank for credit in its demand deposit there. In lending Eurodollars, therefore, the British bank would simply draw a draft on its American correspondent payable to the borrower. If the British borrower turned over the draft in payment for some imports from West Germany, the German exporter might deposit it in a dollar account at a bank in, say, Frankfort, and the Frankfort bank, on sending the draft to its American correspondent for deposit, would then have the Eurodollar deposit of the German exporter backed by its own dollar demand deposit in the United States. Assuming that the British bank's loan equaled the full amount of the dollar time deposit of the British exporter, there would then be dollar deposits on the books of "Eurobanks" equal to twice the amount of the Frankfurt bank's demand deposit balance at its American correspondent bank. ("Eurobank" is the designation given to a bank anywhere in the world that accepts deposits denominated in foreign currencies and repayable in these currencies.) Thus a multiple expansion of Eurodollars on the basis of a given demand deposit balance in the United States is conceivable, comparable to demand deposit expansion within the United States on the basis of given amounts of cash assets as described in Chapter 7.

Scope of the Eurodollar Market   The Eurodollar market is actually a segment of a broad international market in many "Eurocurrencies" in which deposit and loan transactions are effected in many currencies outside the countries whose currencies are involved—not only dollar deposits at and dollar loans granted by banks outside the United States, but also sterling deposits at and sterling loans granted by continental European banks, deposits at and loans by British banks of German marks and French francs, and so on. And despite the prefix *Euro*, Eurocurrencies include the United States dollar, as already indicated, but also other non-European currencies, such as the Canadian dollar and the Japanese yen; and banks located in many areas outside Europe also participate in the market, especially American and Canadian banks, and banks located in the Near and Far East and in Latin America.

Nevertheless, the international Eurocurrency market is dominated by transactions in the United States dollar, with the volume of Eurodollar deposits estimated at about $40 to $45 billion at the end of 1969.[13] The Eurodollar market is described as a "wholesale" market in that individual transactions, especially among Eurobanks, usually range from $500,000 to $5 million. There are many transactions among Eurobanks, because these banks often redeposit Eurodollars with one another to take advantage of slight differentials in interest rates offered from country to country. The Eurodollar deposits themselves, including such redeposits, are preponderantly time deposits, ranging from "overnight money" and deposits payable on notice of 2 days or 7 days to deposits payable in 180 or 360 days.[14] Because of this, Eurodollar deposit expansion is not of the same character

---

[13]Federal Reserve Bank of Cleveland, *Money Market Instruments* (Cleveland, Ohio, 3d ed., 1970), p. 104.
[14]*Ibid.*, p. 72.

as demand deposit expansion in the United States as referred to in the second preceding paragraph, because time deposits are not readily available means of payment like demand deposits. And even when Eurodollar deposits are demand deposits, multiple expansion is probably quite limited, since "leakages" from the market tend to be large. If the German exporter of the illustration were to use his dollar draft to invest in the American money or capital market, his dollars would be "repatriated." The Frankfort bank would have no addition to its Eurodollar deposits, and demand deposit balances of Eurobanks at American banks, on which the creation of Eurodollars depends, would be reduced.

Participation of Americans in the Eurodollar Market Since the description of the Eurodollar market is placed in these pages as if it were a subdivision of the *American* money market, we must emphasize that it is most appropriately classified so only to the extent that Americans supply funds to it and obtain funds from it. In the period of its most rapid growth beginning about 1966, Americans have been chiefly demanders of funds rather than suppliers. Although Americans own many billions of dollars that could easily be deposited with Eurobanks, they have been discouraged from doing so by restrictive policies of the federal government designed to reduce our balance-of-payments deficits. Since early 1965, American financial institutions have been limited by "guidelines" in their lending abroad and in their keeping of balances with foreign banks—guidelines that appear to be closely observed because the financial institutions know that they could be made compulsory at any time. Since early 1965, too, American business corporations that have important branch or subsidiary facilities in foreign countries or that otherwise engage extensively in international business have also been subject to guideline limitations on their cash balances held abroad, their returning of earnings of foreign branches and subsidiaries for reinvestment abroad, and their borrowing in American financial markets for spending abroad—guidelines that were, as a matter of fact, made compulsory at the beginning of 1968.

For the financing of their foreign operations, therefore, many American nonfinancial business corporations have had good reasons to go to Eurobanks to borrow dollars. Although they would generally qualify to borrow sterling from British banks, francs from French banks, and so on, they often find it much more convenient to have dollars available for much of the spending they wish to do. In many countries, too, restrictions imposed on Eurodollar loans are typically far fewer than those imposed on loans in domestic currencies for intercountry investment spending. Large American commercial banks also have been very important among borrowers of Eurodollars as means of expanding their lending and investing capacities at home, especially during periods of restrictive monetary policy imposed by the Federal Reserve. Beginning in 1966, an extraordinary expansion in the number of foreign branches of large American commercial banks developed, with the branches, new and old, getting assignments to accumulate Eurodollars to be "loaned" to the parent banks in the United States.[15]

OTHER SUBDIVISIONS OF THE CAPITAL MARKET

Apart from transactions in government securities having maturities of more than 1 year, transactions in the capital market are chiefly the buying and selling of new issues of corporate stocks and bonds, their subsequent resale among investors, and the granting of real-estate mortgage loans and, in some instances, their subsequent transfer among lenders. Accordingly, the capital market can be said to have subdivisions for corporate stocks, for corporate bonds, and for mortgage loans, plus a special one, as it were, for "Eurobonds," in addition to the subdivisions concerned with long-term government securities. And in keeping with the usual patterns of financial markets, each of these subdivisions may be said to have primary and secondary market facilities, with some of these facilities further classified as open-market facilities and others as facilities for negotiated deals.

Because most consumer loans are granted for intermediate terms, a separate sector of the capital market must also be recognized as existing for them. However, most consumer loans originate by direct negotiation between borrowers and lenders and are retained by the lenders until maturity, so that open-market and secondary market facilities for them are of slight importance.

Market for corporate stocks

In the establishment of corporations of small and medium sizes, stock sales to the incorporators are usually the principal source of cash and other assets, and for many of the corporations that continue to be closely held, stock continues to be the principal source of assets for many years. For larger corporations whose stock is widely held, new issues of stock from year to year are much less important as means of financing than new issues of bonds. In the first 8 months of 1970, for example, bond issues of more than $100,000 individually offered for cash sale in the United States by business corporations other than investment companies amounted to $18,122 million, while common and preferred stock issues exceeding $100,000 offered for cash sale by these corporations amounted, respectively, to $4511 million and $737 million.[16] However, the dollar volume of market transactions in stocks is many times greater than the dollar volume of market transactions in bonds—a circumstance that indicates that changes in the ownership of stocks, considered collectively, occur much more

---

[15]For some details concerning the establishment of foreign branches and foreign banking subsidiaries by American banks, see Chapter 12.

[16]Securities and Exchange Commission, *Statistical Bulletin,* November 1970, p. 14.

frequently than changes in the ownership of bonds. In terms of dollar amounts, therefore, secondary market facilities for stock transactions are much more important than primary market facilities. Moreover, the secondary market facilities are important *for the sale of new issues*, because many people would not invest in new issues if they were not given reasonable assurances that they could resell without too much difficulty, and many people get the money to invest in new issues by selling stocks already held.

Primary or New-Issues Market   A principal procedure by which corporations acquire cash for new issues of their stock is by making offerings to their existing stockholders. Each stockholder is given "rights" to subscribe in the ratio of his present holdings to the total amount of the corporation's stock already outstanding. If he subscribes, he surrenders the subscription warrant that evidences his subscription rights, and pays in cash at the offering price. If he sells his "rights," the buyer of the warrant surrenders it and pays in cash. Other procedures by which a corporation issues new stock to limited groups rather than to the public at large include its sale to bondholders who exercise rights to buy provided by stock-purchase warrants attached to their bonds, its exchange for outstanding convertible bonds, its exchange for the stocks (or directly for the assets) of other enterprises in mergers, its sale to corporations' own executives who have previously been given options to buy and to their employees generally by way of employee-purchase and -savings plans, and finally, its occasional sale in bulk to institutional investors, especially mutual funds.

When, on the other hand, corporations wish to offer new issues of their stocks broadside to the public, they usually hope to get investment banking firms to take over full responsibility for the offer. They ask the investment banking firms to underwrite their issues,[17] and firms so approached make careful investigations much like those of other financial institutions in deciding whether or not to grant long-term loans to applicants. If they decide to underwrite, they work closely with the corporations in getting the issues ready for the market, particularly in seeing that the requirements of federal and state laws for security sales are met. Most underwritings of corporate stock issues are negotiated deals individually handled by the issuing corporation and a single investment banking firm that is said to serve as "originator" of the issue. However, some corporations, especially railroad corporations and public utilities, offer their new stock issues by the competitive-bidding route when required to do so by federal or state regulations. At any rate, the originator or successful bidder typically assembles other investment banking firms in an underwriting syndicate in order to share the risk of failure to sell at the public offering price, and then joins the syndicate members—including itself, of course—with

---

[17]As pointed out in the preceding chapter, corporations often also get investment bankers to underwrite their "rights offerings" to their existing stockholders. See Chapter 10.

other security firms that accept invitations to participate in a "selling group," so that numerous potential investors can be reached quickly.

Sometimes, however, investment bankers agree to help with broadside offers of new corporate stock issues only on an agency or "best-efforts" basis. This is a rather common arrangement for offerings of stock issues of moderate size of corporations that are not well-known to investors. Because the bankers take no direct risk of financial loss in undertaking to try to sell on this basis, they may spend little time in investigating the issuers and helping them to prepare their issues for the market.

Stock Exchanges   The stock exchanges are the most obvious facilities that we have for the buying and selling of stocks already outstanding—for transfers in ownership among investors. Fourteen stock exchanges operate in the United States, but the New York Stock Exchange and the American Stock Exchange, both located in New York City, dominate by wide margins. Of total sales of stocks on all stock exchanges in 1969 at $175,311 million, the New York Stock Exchange had sales of $129,603 million, or approximately 74 percent of the total, and the American had sales of $30,074 million, or about 17 percent. Sales on the leading "regional" exchanges were those of the Midwest Stock Exchange of $5988 million, the Pacific Coast Stock Exchange of $5422 million, and the Philadelphia-Baltimore-Washington Stock Exchange of $2529 million.[18]

On the New York and American exchanges, buying and selling are restricted to the stocks of corporations that have applied to have their stocks "listed," disclosed a large amount of financial information about themselves, agreed to continue to disclose such information and to abide by other rules, and have had their applications approved by the exchange and by the Securities and Exchange Commission. On other exchanges, transactions take place in stocks that have been listed in a similar way, but also in various groupings of stocks that have been admitted to "unlisted trading"—stocks formally listed on other exchanges. A single stock may be listed formally on two or more exchanges.

Only the individuals and security firms that are members of an exchange have access to the various posts on its "floor" at which various assortments of stocks are bought and sold, so that, on the exchange itself, transactions are effected exclusively among members. But many of the members of each exchange undertake to buy and sell for nonmembers as commission brokers, that is, in agency capacities. It is this service that makes the exchanges important secondary markets for stock, because it gives the public indirect access to them. Buy and sell orders flow to the commission brokers from all parts of the country and from foreign countries—or from given geo-

---

[18]Securities and Exchange Commission, *Statistical Bulletin*, March 1970, p. 11. (Percentages supplied by the author.)

graphical areas in the case of the regional exchanges outside New York City—and the brokers meet at the various posts to complete these orders as directed.

Over-the-Counter Market From the standpoint of the number of issues that are bought and sold, the over-the-counter secondary market in corporate stocks is much more important than all the stock exchanges collectively. This is so because there are thousands of issues of stock outstanding not listed on stock exchanges that people want to buy and sell. Some of these are quite "active" in the sense that there are voluminous transactions in them—a large number being more active that many listed issues—while a great number account for only occasional transactions individually. Moreover, many transactions in listed stocks take place in the over-the-counter market. If you wish to sell 100 shares of a listed stock that you own, you do not have to sell it through a member of the stock exchange on which it is listed. You can sell it wherever and to whomever you choose. If you offer it to a security firm that is not a member of the same stock exchange, it, in turn, can pass it on to whomever it chooses, whether or not a member of that exchange.

Apart from ultimate investors as buyers and sellers, the principal operators in the over-the-counter market for stocks are security firms that are called "broker-dealers." They are so called because, from transaction to transaction, they are generally privileged to choose whether to buy or sell in their own names as dealers on a profit-seeking basis or simply to try to find matching buyers and sellers as brokers (agents) on a commission basis. Many broker-dealer firms are diversified in various ways, some being simultaneously members of one or more stock exchanges, some serving importantly as underwriters of new security issues, some acting as brokers or dealers in one or more of the general classes of government securities, some operating as broker-dealers in corporation bonds, and some including in the scope of their operations two or more or all of these additional functions. But there are many that largely confine their activities to brokerage and dealing in stocks.

As specifically operating in the over-the-counter secondary market for corporate stocks, at any rate, many security firms individually "make markets" in given stocks in the usual sense of carrying inventories of these stocks and standing ready to quote prices at which they will buy and sell them in their own names as dealers. They are especially inclined to make markets in stocks whose original sale they participated in underwriting, although, for the individual firm, making markets is not necessarily limited to such issues. On the other hand, thousands of outstanding stock issues have no markets made for them by broker-dealer firms, because of rarity of transactions, smallness of issues individually, or the relative obscurity of the corporations that issued them. However, for almost any stock, no matter the thinness of its market, it is almost always possible to find over-the-counter firms that are willing to act as brokers in trying to find buyers or sellers, as the case may be.

Third Market   Individual sales outside the stock exchanges of large blocks of listed stocks are often said to be transactions in the "third market." Although such sales are, by definition, over-the-counter transactions, the third-market designation calls attention to their extraordinary size, who the buyers and sellers are, and why the stock exchanges are bypassed. The large size of the transactions typically indicates that both the buyer and seller are large financial institutions, such as mutual funds and trust institutions, and lower commission charges explain why the stock exchanges are bypassed. The buying institution concludes that the price arranged in the over-the-counter market plus the broker's commission is less than the total cost would be by buying through a member of the stock exchange, and the selling institution concludes that this price minus the broker's commission is better than the proceeds would be by way of a sale on the stock exchange.

Market for corporation bonds

New-Issues Distribution   Many new bond issues are sold to existing security holders, chiefly to common stockholders who are, in some instances, stockholders of the bond-issuing corporations and, in others, stockholders of other corporations. Bonds sold to corporations' own common stockholders are chiefly issues that are convertible into common stocks or that have stock-purchase warrants attached to them. Bonds "sold" to the common stockholders of other corporations are also principally convertible bonds that are offered in exchange for the common stocks of corporations that the issuing corporations want to acquire in merger transactions. The use of bonds in this manner can be reasonably called "sales" because they are the source of much of the purchasing power by which absorbing corporations acquire, in effect, the assets of absorbed corporations. Such offerings of convertible bonds in exchange for the common stocks of other corporations were especially prominent in the feverish merger movement of the 1960s.

An even more important channel for the sale of new bond issues is "private placement" with institutional investors, especially life insurance companies and trust institutions. The financial officers of a corporation go to, say, a large life insurance company, describe their needs for long-term funds, and ask it to supply these funds. After an investigation that turns out favorably, the life company makes a commitment to buy the bonds, or perhaps it agrees to buy 50 percent of the issue while saying that it will find other insurance companies to take the balance. Or perhaps the corporation's financial officers go to an investment banking firm with their plea for long-term bond financing, and the investment bankers, after favorable consideration, decide that the best market for the bond issue would be institutional investors rather than the investing public. Accordingly, in an agency capacity, they contact institutional investors, and if they find buyers, they are paid a "finder's fee" by the issuing corporation. An advantage of private placements to bond-issuing corporations is that they are often able to arrange with the institutional investors to spread the "take-downs" of their bonds over rather lengthy periods of time, so that the proceeds come to them only when needed for their spending projects.

A third important procedure for financing by means of new bond issues is to have them underwritten by investment banking firms, with the underwriting firm taking full responsibility for subsequent resales to the investing public or sharing this responsibility with other firms assembled by it in an underwriting syndicate. As is customary in underwriting procedures, the bankers guarantee that they will pay a stipulated dollar amount for the bonds on a designated date, with their profit depending upon their success in reselling at higher prices—and preferably, of course, at the "public offering price." Under federal and state laws, some business corporations, such as railroads and electric power companies, are required to offer their new bond issues, or most of them, for competitive bids; but manufacturing, mercantile, and other corporations that are not subject to such legal requirements almost invariably take their propositions for public sale of bond issues to single investment banking firms, so that, if agreement is reached, the results are "negotiated deals."

Very few bond issues are sold by investment bankers on a best-efforts basis, and certainly not by reputable banking firms because they are most reluctant to ask their customers to buy something that they themselves are unwilling to underwrite.

Secondary Markets In buying new corporate bond issues in bulk, institutional investors, such as life insurance companies, expect to hold them until maturity or until other retirement dates if there is provision for periodic retirement. The investment policy of life companies, for example, is to concentrate on bonds and long-term mortgages, and they like the assurances of long-run income at the rates of interest stipulated in these instruments. Should they need to resell corporate bonds from their portfolios, their market would be largely limited to "private placements" with other institutional investors. Because privately placed bonds are not ordinarily registered with the SEC at the time of original sale to the institutional investors, registration would be required for a resale offering to the public.

For the resale of corporate bonds held by the typical investor, the principal facilities are those of the over-the-counter market. The outstanding bond issues of many business corporations are listed on the stock exchanges, but as with listed stocks, and indeed, to a greater extent, many transactions in these issues are effected in the over-the-counter market.

And of course, only the over-the-counter facilities are available for nonlisted bonds. As in handling other classes of securities, security firms that operate in the over-the-counter market can generally choose whether to act as dealer or broker from one transaction to the next. Some make markets as dealers in given issues, especially in issues that they have participated in underwriting; and virtually all are willing to act as brokers in trying to find buyers and sellers for much longer lists of bonds in which they may have no dealer interests.

The Eurobond market

Eurobonds are bonds that are payable in a currency other than the currencies of the countries in which the bonds are originally sold. Bonds whose interest and principal are payable in United States dollars by American corporations as issuers are Eurobonds if originally sold in capital markets other than our own; and likewise for bond issues of foreign corporations having interest and principal payable in home-country currency but originally sold outside the home country.

Participation by American Corporations   Like the Eurodollar market discussed earlier in this chapter, the Eurobond market is an international, or "global," one, so that the prefix *Euro* does not imply that either the issuers or the buyers are confined to European countries. As we would expect from the participation of Americans in most international markets, they also participate in the Eurobond market. But our participation is very largely confined to issuing dollar bonds for sale abroad rather than to buying bonds offered by issuers located in foreign countries. Investment by Americans in sterling bonds offered for sale outside the United Kingdom by British corporations, franc bonds offered outside France by French corporations, and so on, is largely precluded by our "interest equalization tax" that is specifically designed to restrict capital outflows from the United States which would add to our balance-of-payments deficits.

On the other hand, the guideline restrictions on American corporations' investment abroad of dollars acquired in the United States have made the Eurobond market especially attractive to these corporations. Wanting to expand their foreign operations while being limited in the amount of domestic dollars they are permitted to spend abroad, many of these corporations have sold dollar bonds in many foreign markets. Actually, the bonds have been chiefly issues of "financing subsidiaries" of the American corporations with principal and interest guaranteed by the parent corporations. The "financing subsidiaries" have generally been foreign-chartered corporations, with Luxembourg and the Bahama Islands especially favored as charter sources because of their light taxes on such enterprises.

Choice of Eurobond Issues   If an American corporation has a branch factory in, say, Belgium, why would not it or its financing subsidiary issue bonds payable in Belgian francs and offer them for sale exclusively in Belgium? One reason is that the capital market in Belgium, as in most foreign countries, is not nearly so well-developed as ours, so that there might be great difficulty in raising the amount of Belgian francs needed. Another is that Belgium, such as most foreign countries—and as the United States itself in recent years with its guidelines and interest equalization tax—has restrictions on borrowing by foreigners in its capital market, but restrictions that are applied much less rigorously to the use of Eurodollars in bond buying. And a third reason, closely related to the other two as stated, is that American corporations and their financing subsidiaries have been able, in most instances, to get large numbers of financial institutions scattered in many countries to underwrite each of their Eurobond issues, so that it has been possible, in effect, to reach long-term investors in many countries and localities simultaneously.

The real-estate mortgage loan market

Loans granted for the purchase and construction of real property, that is, land and buildings, are called "mortgage loans" because, in almost all instances, the borrower is required to pledge the property to the lender as security for the loan. The document by which the pledge is made is the mortgage. It is recorded in the same government office in which deeds are recorded as a notice to the public, as it were, that the lender has a lien on the property that will generally take precedence over claims against it subsequently originating. The borrower also signs a mortgage note in which he specifically promises to repay the loan—probably in periodic installments—with interest at a designated rate. He also binds himself to other "covenants," such as to keep the property in a good state of repair, to pay taxes levied on it, and to provide adequate fire insurance coverage. If he defaults on his interest or principal obligations or the additional covenants, the lender is privileged to take legal action to get clear title to the pledged property and to sell it to recover the unpaid principal of its loan and accumulated unpaid interest. If, on the other hand, the borrower meets all his obligations, the lender gives him a written document called a "satisfaction of mortgage," and this is also publicly recorded as notification to all who may be interested that the lender's lien no longer obtains.

Total mortgage loans outstanding in the United States at the end of 1970 were reported at approximately $450.5 billion, broken down as follows: on one-to-four-family homes (chiefly single-family homes), $280.1 billion; on multi-family properties (residential properties for five or more families), $57.8 billion; on "commercial" properties (including factory buildings and other real property often separately classified as "industrial"), $81.4 billion; and on farms, $31.2 billion.[19] The figures, however, do not include out-

---

[19]*Federal Reserve Bulletin,* March 1971, p. 71.12.

standing bond issues secured by real-property mortgages that are especially prominent in the financial structures of railroads and public utilities. As for the mortgage lenders, the data in Table 11-2 indicate that savings and loan associations, life insurance companies, commercial banks, and mutual savings banks, in that order, have the top positions, although we note the lead of life insurance companies and commercial banks in mortgage lending on properties other than one-to-four-family homes. Worthy of note, too, are the substantial holdings of federally sponsored credit agencies, a classification which includes, of course, the federal land banks, the Government National Mortgage Association, and the Federal National Mortgage Association, as well as the large holdings of "households" (chiefly individual investors in Federal Reserve terminology).

Table 11-2   **Outstanding Mortgage Loans and Their Holders, December 31, 1970 (in billions of dollars)**

HOLDERS	HOME MORTGAGES[a]	OTHER MORTGAGES	TOTAL
Savings and loan associations	125.5	25.1	150.6
Life insurance companies	26.7	47.6	74.3
Commercial banks	41.8	30.2	72.0
Mutual savings banks	37.6	20.5	58.1
Households	13.7	29.4	43.1
Federally sponsored credit agencies	15.3	7.5	22.8
Federal government	6.0	3.4	9.4
State and local retirement funds		6.2	6.2
Finance companies	5.9		5.9
Private pension funds	4.2		4.2
State and local governments	2.2		2.2
Other	1.3	0.5	1.8
Total	280.1[b]	170.4	450.5[b]

[a] On one-to-four-family homes.
[b] Items do not add exactly to these totals because of rounding.
Source: Federal Reserve Bulletin, March 1971, pp. A71.10–A71.11.

Primary Market   A very large proportion of all mortgage loans are arranged by direct negotiation between borrowers and lending institutions. An individual who wants to buy or build a house for his own occupancy applies personally for a loan at a savings and loan association, a mutual savings bank, or a commercial bank; a farmer who wants to buy additional land or put up farm buildings submits his application to a commercial bank, a federal land bank association, or a branch lending office of a life insurance company; and a "builder" or "developer" who wants to put up a store or office building or construct a shopping center goes directly to a life insurance company or possibly to a commercial bank with his application. Each of these applicants may, of course, go from one lending institution to others with his application, either because he is turned down by the first ones to which he applies or because he wants to shop around in order to find out where he can obtain the best deal.

In addition to direct negotiation as an outstanding feature of mortgage lending procedure, a second important feature, so to speak, is the intention of the lending institutions to hold until maturity the mortgage loans they grant. The principal classes of lending institutions grant mortgage loans because they want long-term investments on which they may depend for a steady stream of income that is largely predictable on the basis of interest rates originally set in the loan contracts. In ordinary circumstances, indeed, they are likely to be displeased if borrowers seek to prepay their principal obligations, that is, to pay off principal ahead of due dates—an attitude that is indicated by prepayment penalties that are commonly written into mortgage loan contracts. In ordinary circumstances, too, the mortgage lending institutions do not worry greatly about the apparent illiquidity of mortgage portfolios. They look to other assets and continued inflows of new savings from depositors and other customers to supply cash needs. Since, moreover, most mortgage loan contracts provide for principal repayments in installments, lending institutions expect a continual flow of repayments as an important additional source of liquidity.

Mortgage Bankers One important group of mortgage lenders are exceptional in not wanting to hold for their own long-term investment any sizable proportion of the mortgage loans they arrange. These are mortgage banking firms that have two principal functions: (1) to originate mortgage loans to be passed on to the long-term investing institutions, and (2) to service these mortgage loans on behalf of the transferee institutions as long as they are outstanding. As originators of mortgage loans, they engage in the direct negotiations with loan applicants, investigate their credit worthiness, run checks on titles to properties to be mortgaged, have the mortgage documents prepared (and later recorded), and handle all the other details necessary for the proper "closing" of the loans. As servicers of outstanding mortgage loans, the mortgage bankers collect installment payments of interest and principal (to be passed on, of course, to the institutions to which the mortgage loans have been transferred), seek delinquent mortgagors, assure that mortgage covenants about repairs, taxes, and insurance are fulfilled, and take foreclosure proceedings against mortgaged properties when, after defaults, they are judged to be necessary. The mortgage bankers receive separate fees from the transferee institutions for origination and for servicing, but their income is chiefly earned from servicing fees since they continue as long as loans are outstanding while, for the individual loan, the origination fee is paid only once.

Most of the origination and servicing work of mortgage bankers is performed on behalf of life insurance companies. A life company that wants to spread its mortgage loans over a wide geographical area selects mortgage banking firms in many locations as its "correspondents" and gives them quotas of the amounts of mortgages of different kinds that it will accept from them in given periods of time, provided always that prescribed quality standards are met. In some instances, the mortgage bankers get approval for proposed loans and the money for them from the insurance companies before the loans are closed; but more often, they grant the loans out of their own money and get reimbursed on selling the loans to the insurance companies—this is what makes them bankers rather than brokers. Moreover, many grant additional loans without regard to quotas, because they want to have mortgage loans "on the shelf" ready for sale to institutions, such as mutual savings banks and commercial banks, that rarely set quotas because of uncertainties concerning the amount of money they are going to have available for investment in mortgage loans. For carrying mortgage loans in their own names pending later sale, the mortgage bankers often obtain short-term loans from commercial banks with the mortgages put as collateral security. This financing procedure is known as "mortgage warehousing."

Secondary Market Facilities   Although mortgage bankers can be said to serve as middlemen in the mortgage market, their facilities are hardly to be classified as constituting a secondary market. Theirs is a one-way street, as they rarely buy mortgages from lending institutions that want to liquidate some of their holdings.

The fact is that secondary market facilities for mortgage loans are rather poorly developed except for loans insured by the Federal Housing Administration (FHA) and loans guaranteed by the Veterans Administration (VA). The difficulty in developing good secondary markets for "conventional" mortgage loans—those not insured or guaranteed—is that these loans lack uniformity in quality. Every mortgage loan is different from all others in that a specific parcel of property in a given location is pledged for its safety, and its quality depends on the value of this property in relationship to the unpaid balance of the loan, the competence of the original grantor of the loan, the thoroughness of its investigation of the credit worthiness of the borrower and of his title to the mortgaged property, the borrower's behavior in maintaining the property, the laws of the state pertaining to titles, the rights of mortgagees, foreclosure procedures, and so on, and many other factors. Unless you make a careful investigation, you do not know what you are getting if you buy an outstanding mortgage loan on a house located in Arizona or a store building located in Vermont —and investigations as well as continual supervision after you have bought the loan can be expensive.

If, however, some bystanding highly reputable institution is willing to protect you against losses on the mortgage loans you buy, its protective role will give these loans a uniformity in quality that they would otherwise lack. This is why secondary market facilities have been much better for

FHA-insured and VA-guaranteed loans than for conventional loans. Even so, these facilities have been chiefly provided by agencies owned or directly sponsored by the federal government rather than by private financial institutions—by the Government National Mortgage Association established in 1968 and owned and operated by the federal government, and for a much longer period, by the Federal National Mortgage Association (FNMA) which for much of its life was operated and largely capitalized by the federal government but which has been transferred to private ownership and management though remaining subject to government regulations and supervision.

At least, however, the government sponsored agencies have been making significant moves toward providing secondary market facilities for conventional mortgage loans—most notably the FNMA's move in the spring of 1971 to take on the buying and selling of conventional loans, and the similar move in the same period by the Federal Home Loan Mortgage Corporation that was established in 1970 to provide secondary market facilities for the member institutions of the Federal Home Loan Bank System. Nevertheless, secondary market institutions in any field are usually expected to be sellers as well as buyers, so that a continuing source of dissatisfaction among mortgage lenders is that secondary institutions, although buying large amounts of mortgage loans from year to year, have been unable to sell any substantial amounts from their portfolios—even FHA-insured and VA-guaranteed mortgage loans.

FOR REVIEW

1. What is a financial market? Why is each developed country said to have only two financial markets? What are they? How are they distinguished?
2. What is the distinction between primary and secondary financial markets? between open markets and markets for negotiated deals?
3. Why is the market for Treasury obligations, especially for short-term ones, much more active than other financial markets?
4. What are Treasury bills? What maturities do Treasury bills have? What is peculiar about the procedure of their original sale?
5. In what characteristics do Treasury notes and marketable bonds differ from Treasury bills?
6. In the primary and secondary marketing of Treasury marketable obligations, what roles are played by the Federal Reserve banks and security dealers?
7. What kinds of securities are classified as "federal agency securities"? Describe the market facilities for these issues.
8. Why is a distinction made between the general obligations of state and local governments and their revenue issues? Why are both of these classes of securities called "tax exempts"?

9. What are bankers' acceptances? What are they principally used for? Describe how an acceptance originates.

10. In money market transactions, what are repurchase agreements? In what subdivisions of the market are they used? What is the procedure in their use?

11. What kinds of enterprises are principal issuers of commercial paper? Why do these enterprises prefer issuance of commercial paper to direct borrowing from commercial banks?

12. What are certificates of deposit (CDs)? How can one account for the huge increase in large-denomination CDs outstanding in recent years?

13. What are the functions of dealers in the market for bankers' acceptances? the market for commercial paper? the market for CDs?

14. What are Eurodollars? Eurocurrencies in general? Explain how it is possible for the outstanding amount of Eurodollars to exceed their dollar backing in deposit accounts in the United States.

15. What is the scope of the primary market for corporate stocks? the secondary market? the third market?

16. Describe the procedures by which new issues of bonds are used for financing by business corporations.

17. Why have many American corporations found it advantageous to borrow in the Eurobond market?

18. What classes of our financial institutions are principal grantors of real-estate mortgage loans? What are the functions of mortgage bankers in the mortgage loan market?

COMMERCIAL BANKING

CHAPTER 12

COMMERCIAL BANKING STRUCTURE

THE ESTABLISHMENT OF NEW BANKS

Background

Legislative Charters. Until almost the middle of the nineteenth century, state legislatures jealously guarded their right to grant charters for new commercial banks, and every charter had to be specially authorized by legislative enactment. This prerogative was often used unfairly for political preferment. A legislature controlled by one political party or faction would grant no charters to groups aligned with other parties or factions. In many instances, moreover, certain state officials had authority to control the stock subscriptions of new banks and to decide who might and who might not buy stock; they, too, often acted from unfair political motives.

The system was one that invited graft and corruption. To enjoy the benefits of restricted competition, groups that were successful in obtaining charters opposed the granting of additional ones to others. Such groups not infrequently offered bribes to convert legislators to their point of view. Hence those who wanted to get charters had a reason to offer even larger bribes to support their charter applications. In consequence, there was no assurance that persons having the best qualifications for managing banks would be able to obtain charters.

Origin of "Free Banking" The favoring of the few and the exclusion of the many in the granting of bank charters came in the course of time to be looked on as most undemocratic. Those who obtained charters were regarded as monopolists, the recipients of special privilege, and quite out of place in a country where everybody except the slave was supposed to be free and equal.

Opposition to banking monopolies and the demand for equal treatment for all culminated in the adoption of state "free-banking laws," beginning with Michigan in 1837. Under these laws, anybody or any group with sufficient money for stock subscriptions and having other qualifications to fulfill the minimum requirements as stipulated in the legislation could obtain a charter as a matter of right. A state official was given the power to issue new charters according to a prescribed method of procedure. The official ordinarily was given little discretion, so that a charter could not be refused if the applicants were able to satisfy the requirements of the law.

"Free Banking" at present

The chartering of commercial banks under state jurisdiction has remained "free" to the present time, and the National Bank Act, first adopted in 1863 and completely revised in 1864, also provided for free commercial banking under federal charters. In our day, therefore, any group of persons able to satisfy the stipulations of the banking code of the state or federal government *theoretically* has the right to establish a new commercial bank.

As a practical matter, however, it is by no means easy at the present time to obtain commercial bank charters from the federal government and from most of the state governments. The thousands of bank failures that occurred in the 1920s and early 1930s convinced legislatures and bank supervisory authorities that the establishment of innumerable weak, competing banks would be advantageous neither for their incorporators nor for the communities in which they proposed to operate.

Criteria for a New Bank To secure a commercial bank charter at the present time, the promoters must be able to show that a new bank is needed in the community where it is to be located, and that the proposed institution has reasonable prospects for success. The Comptroller of the Currency, who is the head of the national banking system, and the state superintendents and secretaries of banking make comprehensive investigations to determine whether new charters should be granted. A survey is made of the community in which the proposed bank is to operate. How many banks are already in operation there? Are they efficiently managed? How do the rates of interest they charge on loans compare with rates charged by banks in other cities and towns? Are their services adequate? Is there a need of additional banking services? Would competition be beneficial or harmful? The government authorities consider the prospects of business expansion in the community, and the probable long-range need of additional banking services.

Consideration is also given to the probable character of the proposed institution for which a charter is requested. What are the qualifications of the organizers and the prospective officers of the new bank? Have they had experience in banking? What is the financial position of the people who will subscribe to its stock and that of the proposed directors? Do they have excellent business connections, so that they will be able to bring profitable accounts to the new institution? Will the new bank, by taking business away from the banks already in operation, seriously weaken them?

Not only do the bank supervisors take into account the arguments in support of the proposed institution advanced by the promoters, they willingly hear all opposing arguments set forth by the officers of existing banks as well as by other "interested" persons. It should be apparent, therefore, that receiving a bank charter is a relatively rare privilege; in many instances, the applicants cannot satisfy the criteria suggested by the foregoing groups of questions.

Application for a Charter As there are fifty state banking systems in the United States, in addition to the national system, it would be confusing and probably tiresome to try to make an over-all survey of organizational procedures and requirements. In the subsequent discussion, therefore, attention will be confined largely to the procedure of obtaining a federal charter and to the provisions of the National Bank Act concerning capital stock, surplus, boards of directors, and so on.[1]

The promoters of a new national bank must first apply to the Comptroller of the Currency for permission to organize the bank. The application is made by filing a standard form supplied by the Comptroller, and it must be signed by at least five of the prospective shareholders, preferably by several of the proposed officers or directors. The signers must supply information about their residence, business interests, personal wealth, and banking experience, and state how many shares of stock they will buy. The application also states whether a bank building will be erected or bought, and at what cost, or if a building is to be leased, the rental to be paid. The name of the proposed bank is given, and the Comptroller is asked to "reserve" it. Finally, the applicants must testify that no fees or commissions have been paid or will be paid in the sale of the proposed bank's stock.

After the application to organize has been received by the Comptroller, he delegates a national bank examiner to investigate the proposal. It is the examiner's duty to file a report recommending the acceptance or the rejection of the application. To gather information to support his recommendation, he may interview the promoters and the would-be officers of the proposed bank, the officers of existing banks, prominent businessmen, public officials, and others whose opinions should be pertinent, and he may even call meetings to give the general public opportunities to voice opinions for and against. The Comptroller does not ordinarily rely solely on the report of the examiner in making his decision; he usually calls for further information and advice from the Federal Reserve bank of the district, the Federal Deposit Insurance Corporation, and personnel on his own Washington staff. If he is satisfied that a new bank is needed and that the proposed institution will have good prospects for successful operation, he authorizes the promoters to proceed with the organization of the bank and the acceptance of subscriptions to its stock.

---

[1]Most of the laws applicable to national banks are found in Title 12 of the *United States Code.*

Articles of Association   After the stock of the bank has been subscribed, the organizers prepare articles of association, which must be signed by at least five natural persons,[2] and a copy of which must be filed with the Comptroller. The articles of association are similar in all important particulars to the articles of incorporation of a nonbank business corporation. According to the law, they "shall specify in general terms the object for which the association is formed, and may contain any other provisions, not inconsistent with law, which the association may see fit to adopt for the regulation of its business and the conduct of its affairs."[3] A second document called the "organization certificate" must also be filed with the Comptroller; it states the name and location of the bank, the dollar amount of its capital stock and the number of shares, and the names and addresses of the stockholders with the number of shares held by each.

Election of Directors   When these preliminaries have been followed, it is appropriate for the stockholders to proceed with the election of directors. Each director is required to take an oath affirming (1) that he is the owner of the requisite number of shares; (2) that in fulfilling his duties, he will "diligently and honestly administer the affairs" of the bank; and (3) that he will not knowingly violate, or permit to be violated, the federal banking laws. To show that this requirement of the law has been met, a *certificate of oaths of directors* must be filed with the Comptroller.

Other Preliminaries   Next, the newly chosen directors usually prepare and adopt *bylaws*. The bylaws may be described as an internal code that supplements the articles of association in setting rules and regulations for the bank's operations. They include provisions about the annual meeting of the stockholders, the sending of notices of meetings, and the keeping of minutes of actions taken at meetings; regulations about the time and place of directors' meetings, the number of directors required for a quorum, and the composition and duties of committees named by the board; provisions about the selection of officers, their bonding, and the designation of their duties; rules about the issuance of stock certificates, the sale of new stock, and the transfer of stock; a statement of the hours during which the bank will be open for business; the designation of an official seal; and the procedure for amending the bylaws.

The directors then choose the officers of the bank, among whom there must be at least a president, a vice-president, and a cashier. Since a national bank must be a member of the Federal Reserve System, an application is made to the Federal Reserve bank in the district to buy the amount of stock required for membership.[4] The stock must be paid for before the

---

[2]That is, human beings, as distinct from artificial legal "persons," such as corporations.
[3]*United States Code*, Title 12, sec. 21.
[4]See Chapter 16.

bank is permitted to open for business. Then, as an additional preliminary, the directors must notify the Comptroller of the Currency on standard forms that the down payments required on the bank's own stock subscriptions have been received.

Finally, when the Comptroller is satisfied that all the requirements of the law have been fulfilled, he issues a *certificate of authority to commence business* that must be published in a local newspaper daily or weekly over a period of 60 days. In the meantime, however, the bank may open its doors and launch its operations.

Capital Stock and Surplus The minimum amounts of capital stock that newly organized national banks are required to have vary according to the size of the cities and towns in which the banks are to operate. Banks established in communities of 6000 population or less must have capital stock of at least $50,000; in cities having more than 6000 but not more than 50,000 inhabitants, at least $100,000; and in cities of more than 50,000 inhabitants, at least $200,000. In outlying areas of cities of more than 50,000 population, the Comptroller may permit the establishment of banks with only $100,000 of capital stock provided that state-chartered banks in the same localities are authorized to operate with capital stock of that amount or less.

The stock of national banks must be issued in shares having par values not exceeding $100. No-par stock is not permitted. For the stock of a new bank, 50 percent of the purchase price must be paid before the bank opens for business, and the remainder must be paid by monthly installments within 6 months from the date on which the Comptroller issues the certificate of authority to commence business. All subscription payments must be in cash. In addition, the law requires national banks to begin business with paid-in surplus equal to 20 percent of the amount of their capital stock to cover organization expenses and the losses that may occur during the first year or two. This requirement can be met, of course, by the sale of the stock at a price at least 20 percent above its par value.

STOCKHOLDERS AND DIRECTORS

Stockholders

As a rule, the banking laws place no limitations on individual holdings of bank stock,[5] although it is not normally possible for a single individual or organization to own all the outstanding stock of a bank. The laws stipulate the minimum size of banks' boards of directors, as well as the minimum amount of stock that must be owned by each director, so that

---

[5]Except for the ownership of bank stock by other banks and by holding companies, as discussed later in this chapter.

at least such minimum amounts—"directors' qualifying shares"—must be distributed among those who are to serve as directors.

The stockholders of a bank have rights and privileges similar to those enjoyed by the stockholders of other classes of business corporations. They have the right to receive stock certificates stating the number of shares standing in their names; to sell or otherwise dispose of their stock; to inspect the bank's books and records—but this right is very limited— to participate in earnings when dividends are declared by the board of directors; to take action in court to prevent the bank from committing illegal acts as well as *ultra vires* acts, that is, acts outside the scope of the authorized powers of the bank; to subscribe to new stock issues in proportion to their current holdings; and to share in the assets in the event of dissolution. As owners, moreover, holders of a bank's stock have the right to participate in its management by way of the usual corporate procedure of electing the board of directors. As in nonbank business corporations, the board is presumably amenable to the will of the stockholders, but the stockholders are usually quite content to have the board formulate all operating policies. Nevertheless, they reserve authority to vote on certain kinds of proposed actions, such as changes in the volume and features of stock issues, amendment of the articles of association, and the merger of the bank with other institutions. The stockholders of a bank usually have an annual meeting at which a report of the bank's activities is made, the directors for the ensuing year are elected, and general questions of policy are discussed. On questions of policy, stockholders usually have one vote for each share of stock they own, but in the election of directors of national banks, each stockholder has, for each share, as many votes as there are directors to be elected. Thus a stockholder who owns 100 shares, in voting in an election of ten directors, would have 1000 votes, and these could be cast in total for one director, or split up in any way desired. This device, known as cumulative voting, is designed to enable the minority stockholders to obtain representation on the board of directors.

Board of Directors

Legal Stipulations The board of directors of a national bank must have not less than five nor more than twenty-five members; they must be citizens of the United States; and at least three fourths of them must have resided in the state, territory, or district in which the bank is situated, or within 50 miles of the bank's head office, for at least 1 year preceding their election. The residence requirement remains in force during the directors' terms of office. Any stockholder who owns $1000 par value of stock in his own right is eligibile for election, but those who hold stock in trust for others, such as trustees under wills, may not be chosen.

Duties and Responsibilities The directors of a commercial bank are expected to exercise "reasonable prudence and diligence" in its management. They become subject to criminal penalties for certain violations of the law and to lawsuits for damages if their negligence or infractions of the law result in losses to depositors and stockholders. Absence from the meetings of the board does not ordinarily excuse a director from responsibility for actions taken by it, for one who accepts a position of this kind is under obligation to fulfill it and not to resign from it by default.

Specifically, it is the duty of the directors to formulate the general operating policies of the bank, to select the officers and supervise their work, to examine the books or have them examined periodically, and to decide on the distribution of earnings. The directors need not burden themselves with responsibility for making all kinds of routine decisions, for they may rightfully delegate many of the powers of administration to the officers. Nevertheless, they are not justified in giving the officers a free hand; that is to say, they should establish specific standards that the officers are required to observe. Many boards, for example, permit the officers to grant individual loans to stipulated maximum amounts, such as $25,000 or $50,000, but reserve the right to pass upon applications for loans of larger amounts. Similarly, decisions about buying large amounts of investment securities are ordinarily reserved to the board. The directors do not guarantee the good faith and honesty of the officers whom they select, but if misdeeds of officers are called to their attention—perhaps in the course of audits or examinations—they must promptly make corrections; otherwise they themselves may be charged with negligence.

The entire board of directors need not give detailed consideration to every matter that comes within its jurisdiction, for it is possible to establish directorial committees, such as loan, investment, personnel, and auditing committees, whose resolutions will be adopted as a matter of course by the full board. For example, the officers may be able to get quick judgments on proposed loans from a loan committee without having to await a regular meeting of the board.

Directors have another duty not mentioned in banking laws and court decisions, but still of outstanding importance: the duty of bringing profitable business to the bank. Unless possessing special competence as administrators, most directors would not remain long in their jobs if their "connections" were not a source of profitable accounts. The existence of this duty explains why most bank directors are business and professional men and women of outstanding prominence in their respective communities.

Criminal and Civil Penalties Designated as crimes in both federal and state laws are certain kinds of actions that bank directors may be tempted to take or approve. These actions include granting loans and giving gifts to bank examiners who, as employees of the bank supervisory authorities, actually examine or have power to examine the given bank; contributing bank funds to political parties and candidates for public office; accepting commissions personally for granting loans; wilfully entering false information in books, statements, or reports; certifying checks for amounts exceeding the drawers' deposit balances; publishing false advertisements about deposit insurance; and, of course, fraud and embezzlement. Besides making themselves subject to fines, imprisonment, or both for such actions, directors are financially responsible to stockholders and depositors for resulting losses.

Other actions, while not criminal in character, can give rise to financial liability. These include the granting of loans beyond the limits permitted by law; the payment of dividends that result in "impairments" of the capital stock, that is, causing the fair value of the stockholders' remaining investment to be less than the par value of the stock; and all the shades and degrees of negligence generally referred to simply as "mismanagement."

UNIT BANKING AND MULTIPLE BANKING

Most of the commercial banks of the United States have individually only one office or "shop" in which all their business operations are centered. They are thus said to be "unit banks," and we are said to have, in rather broad areas of the country, a unit banking system. But our banking structure is far from being unitary in its over-all complexion, for we have had major developments in branch banking and group banking, and a smaller development in chain banking—three phases of what is sometimes called "multiple banking."[6] Branch banking occurs when a single bank carries on its business in two or more offices at separate locations; group banking when a holding company controls the operations of two or more banks; and chain banking, when an individual, the members of a family, or other closely associated persons control the operations of two or more banks.

Survival of unit banking

The prevalence of unit banking in the United States is a most remarkable phenomenon. It is remarkable because it has continued through an era that has seen the spread of great branch organizations in virtually every other field of business enterprise—branch factories established by manufacturing companies, branch assembly plants, chain department stores, theaters, food stores, drugstores, and gasoline stations, branch warehouses for distribution, and so on. It is remarkable also because it departs radically from the pattern of commercial banking in most foreign countries where such banking is concentrated in a handful of large institutions, each with numerous branches.

---

[6]The terms *unit banking* and *multiple banking* have no direct relationship with the term *dual banking,* which simply describes the fact that in the United States both the federal and state governments charter commercial banks.

The chief explanation for the survival of unit banking in the United States appears to be that legislation aimed at curbing the growth of "bigness" and "concentration" in banking has been much more effective than similar legislation supposedly applying to other business fields. By the adoption of antitrust laws and related measures, we have from time to time announced intentions to check all tendencies toward the concentration of economic power wherever they might appear, but we have usually been only half-hearted toward carrying this intention into effect. In the field of banking, however, intentions and their implementation have generally gone hand in hand. The fear of a concentration of "money power" in the hands of a few bankers has been more compelling than fear of concentration of economic power in the hands of a few corporations in, say, the automobile, oil, and steel industries, so that restrictive legislation related to bank organization has been enforced with considerable vigor.

Another reason for the continuance of unit banking in the United States originates in limitations in the powers of state governments. Although each state charters commercial banks, it cannot give these banks the right to open branches in other states or to "do business" in them as distinguished from "doing business" in interstate commerce. Moreover, each state has been strongly inclined to limit the activities of the banks of other states within its own borders. A bank may grant loans to residents of other states and transact other business with them as long as these operations qualify as transactions in interstate commerce; but intrastate transactions are subject to the restrictions and prohibitions of the states in which they take place. The federal government, in turn, has acquiesced in such arrangements. Since the adoption of the National Bank Act in 1863, it has not permitted national banks to establish interstate branches.

Misgivings about unit banking

Although unit banks dominate in numbers, we are not sure that they give us the best banking system. Perhaps our restrictions on the development of branch banking have been too severe. It may be that we have condemned many communities to poor banking services by forbidding their inefficiently managed banks to sell out to highly efficient metropolitan institutions for conversion into branches. Perhaps we have done the same thing by preventing the efficient institutions from going into these communities to establish new branches to provide kinds and qualities of services the existing unit banks fail to provide. Perhaps, indeed, we have carved out little areas of monopoly in many communities for single banks, whether or not efficiently managed, by refusing admittance to the branches of other banks, as well as by refusing to charter new competitive unit banks. It may be that we have made a sacred cow of state boundary lines, deliberately refusing to acknowledge the interstate character of many metropolitan areas and industrial regions.

BRANCH BANKING

Features of a branch banking system

In a country where the commercial banking structure is largely unitary, most banking offices are individually independent of all others in matters of ownership and control, being owned and operated by a separately chartered banking corporation that is distinguishable from all others. In a country where branch banking predominates, by contrast, each bank typically has a "head office" in a principal city and, scattered over the country or in given regions, many subordinate offices—the branches, of course—in all of which, so to say, its business operations are spread. And of course, it is possible to have a combination of these two kinds of structures, as in the United States—where, however, the branch organizations are limited to individual states.

A branch banking enterprise, such as Barclay's Bank in England or the Bank of Montreal in Canada, is a single corporation having a single board of directors, only one group of stockholders, and a single aggregate of assets and liabilities. Branches or offices are opened in many communities, each under the supervision of a manager who is an employee of the national institution and who is subject in all respects to the rules and regulations set down by the national board of directors and officers. Whether or not each branch has available full banking services depends chiefly upon its location. In important cities, the branches of a national institution provide most if not all of the services available at the head office itself, although the granting of large loans may require approval at the head office, and much detailed work, such as some phases of credit analysis, may be handled at the head office rather than locally. In small communities and in the outlying districts of large cities, on the other hand, the branches are often little more than tellers' windows engaged simply in accepting and paying deposits and in receiving applications for loans. Similarly, if commercial banking were to be restructured in the United States on a nation-wide branch basis, each bank would have a head office in a major city, and the local "banks" in other cities and towns would be merely subordinate offices. We might have not more than thirty or forty great national organizations, each with scores or hundreds of branches in all or many parts of the country. Anyway, the "problem" of branch banking in the United States is primarily a question of whether or not nation-wide or, at least, regional branch banking should be permitted.

Pros and cons of branch banking

As just indicated, the pros and cons of branch banking, as they pertain to the present situation in the United States, may best be thought of as arguments for and against nation-wide or regional branch banking, rather than arguments for and against branch banking confined to state or county lines as is now the situation in many states. In the following examination of the arguments, therefore, the term *branch banking* should be understood to stand for branch banking on a much broader geographical scale than we now have, and the term *unit banking* to include limited-area branch banking, such as now obtains in many states.

Proponents of branch banking argue that it makes possible such a diversification of loans that somewhat greater risks can be taken with some of them—to the benefit of new ventures and borrowers of weaker credit standings—than can be accepted by unit banks. At the same time, it is argued that over-all safety of loan portfolios—and therefore safety for depositors—is assured because the larger loans will be subject to approval at the head office without regard to the string-pulling pressures to which officers of unit banks are likely to be subjected. Economies of operation, they believe, are all in favor of branch organizations, including the concentration of much routine work at the head office so that duplicate departments can be eliminated, and the carrying on of business in unpretentious offices rather than in "Greek temples," such as unit banks seem to think are necessary. Superior managerial personnel is available to branch organizations, it is claimed, because they are able to attract the most competent people by paying handsome salaries—an argument that is emphasized because poor management has been generally claimed to be the most important cause of weakness in unit banks. Proponents of branch banking further argue that better services can be had in branch systems than from the usual type of unit banks. Although branches located in the smaller communities may have only limited facilities at hand, they can arrange through the head office for services of all kinds. Finally, it is held that the rarity of failures among foreign branch banking organizations, as contrasted with the thousands of suspensions of unit banks in the United States, clearly proves the greater safety of branch systems.

The people who oppose the extension of branch banking in the United States hold that branch organizations tend to ignore the peculiar needs of individuals and communities, for the whole banking structure becomes impersonal. Although branch managers may want to cooperate with the businessmen and other prospective borrowers of their localities, they are handicapped ·because they must strictly observe regulations adopted and decisions made by directors and officers at the head office, who may know very little about peculiarities in the conditions of these localities. A further claim is that branch organizations drain funds from the smaller communities to the big cities because the national officers are likely to be more interested in lending huge sums to great national corporations than in granting thousands of small loans to small businessmen in numerous hamlets and villages. In regard to safety, the opponents of branch banking claim that we have now achieved a large measure of safety in unit banking through the development of nation-wide deposit insurance, the weeding out of unsound banks, and the closer integration of the thousands of banks that remain. Finally, and most importantly, the critics of branch banking claim that its extension would result in a dangerous concentration of economic power in the hands of a few national officers of the branch organizations—a concentration similar to that which obtains in so many of our industries because of their relative freedom to transcend state boundary lines, to absorb competitors, to acquire and establish subsidiaries, and in other ways to progress toward monopoly.

Development of branch banking in the United States

Early Development   The extension of branch banking was not an important question in the United States until after the year 1909, when California departed from precedent by permitting state-wide branch banking. Before the Civil War, a considerable development of branch banking took place, but political and economic conditions generally militated against the success of branch organizations. The two Banks of the United States had branches, but their charters were not renewed; and though several state branch organizations were established, particularly in the South and the West, most of them failed before or during the Civil War. The National Bank Acts of 1863 and 1864 made no provision for branch banking, although an amendment of 1865 authorized the Comptroller of the Currency to grant national charters to state banks already having branches. The regulations, however, were so restrictive that most of the state banks that reconstituted themselves as national institutions preferred to obtain separate charters for each branch. In the year 1900, only eighty-seven commercial banks in the United States were operating branches, and they averaged only slightly more than one branch each, having a total of 119.[7]

California's action in relaxing restrictions on branch banking was soon matched by other states, and by 1915 state commercial banks had 759 branches in operation. But there was no immediate change in federal regulations, so that national banks had only twenty-six branches in operation in 1915.[8] The Federal Reserve Act, as adopted in 1913, permitted the establishment of foreign branches by American banks but failed to provide for any extension of domestic branching by national banks. The first concession of the federal government in the direction of domestic branch banking came in an amendment to the banking laws adopted in 1918. This amendment permitted state banks to obtain national charters while retaining any branches already in operation, but such banks could not thereafter establish new branches. Likewise, in absorbing state banks by merger, national banks could continue in operation any branches already founded by the state institutions.

A further breach in the restrictions of federal law was made in 1922 by a

---

[7]Board of Governors of the Federal Reserve System, *Banking and Monetary Statistics,* Washington, D.C., 1943, p. 297.
[8]*Ibid.*

ruling of the Comptroller of the Currency that had no specific legislative sanction. It permitted national banks to open additional offices—"tellers' windows"—in their home cities, provided that such action was not explicitly forbidden by state law. Additional offices were merely to receive and pay deposits and to accept applications for loans.

McFadden Act of 1927 Doubts and disputes about the legality of the Comptroller's ruling of 1922 led to further consideration of the whole question of branch operation by national banks and state member banks of the Federal Reserve System, and Congress finally took a stand by adopting the so-called McFadden Act of February 25, 1927. Although this legislation was hailed in some quarters as a liberalization of federal law, it was really quite restrictive. It did permit national banks to engage in city-wide branch banking, but city-wide banking is scarcely branch banking in the sense discussed in this chapter. In cities of 25,000 to 50,000 population, each national bank could have one branch; in cities of 50,000 to 100,000 population, two branches; and in cities of more than 100,000 population, any number approved by the Comptroller of the Currency. Even so, city branches could be opened by national banks only in states in which state chartered banks had the same privilege.

The McFadden Act also permitted state banks, when converting into national banks, and national banks when merging with one another, to retain all branches in operation as of the date of the approval of the act. State banks could join the Federal Reserve System and retain all branches in operation on February 25, 1927, but all branches established after that date outside home office cities would have to be relinquished by state banks desiring to join, and state banks that were already members were to forfeit their membership should they establish new branches outside their home cities. The McFadden Act thus attempted to restrict branching by state banks as well as by national banks, although state law might be more generous in the matter. Finally, the legislation permitted national banks to retain branches already in "lawful operation," as well as single branches operated with or without official sanction for 25 years or more.

Present Federal Regulations Although many of the states continued after 1927 to relax their laws relating to branch banking, nothing further was done to amend the federal laws until after the banking crisis of the early 1930s. The collapse of thousands of unit banks suggested once again comparison of the safety records of unit and branch banking systems, and Congress, in the Banking Act of 1933, finally created the framework for a more extensive development of branch banking. As the provisions of the legislation of 1933, with amendments of the Banking Act of 1935, the Act of July 15, 1952, and the Act of September 28, 1962, at present govern the establishment of branches by national and state member banks, they deserve examination in some detail.

1. In the first place, Congress shifted major responsibility to the states by permitting them to decide whether or not branch banking should be encouraged. If a state allows its chartered banks to establish branches throughout its juridiction, then a national bank operating in that state may establish branches on a state-wide basis; if a state permits only city-wide branch banking, then national banks are similarly restricted; and if a state limits branch banking to some other geographical unit, as the county, then national banks are similarly limited.

2. In establishing out-of-town branches, national banks and state member banks must satisfy certain capital stock and surplus requirements. The federal law stipulates that any such bank must have total capital stock equal to that which would be required if the head office and its out-of-town branches, located in different cities, towns, and villages, were separate national banks, and in any case, not less than the capital stock and surplus required of state banks by state law. For example, a national bank or a state member bank located in a city of more than 50,000 population and having a branch in another city of more than 50,000 population and one in a city of 5000 population would be required to have $450,000 of capital stock, unless the state law prescribed a higher capital stock and surplus requirement, in which circumstance the latter requirement would prevail.

3. Regardless of the authorization of state law and its capacity to satisfy the capital stock requirements, a national bank must have the permission of the Comptroller of the Currency to open branches or to change their location. Likewise, the approval of the Board of Governors of the Federal Reserve System must be had for the establishment of new branches by state member banks and for the retention by newly admitted state member banks of branches established outside their home cities after February 25, 1927. State nonmember banks that are insured by the Federal Deposit Insurance Corporation must obtain its consent to change the location of branches and to open new ones.

4. Finally, national banks are permitted to open seasonal agencies in resort communities for the receipt and payment of deposits without regard to the capital requirements that otherwise apply to branch operations. The privilege may be exercised, however, only if the branches are located in the head-office counties of the national banks concerned, if the respective state governments specifically permit county-wide branch banking, if the resort communities are not served by other banks, and if the Comptroller of the Currency approves.

Despite the liberalization of the federal regulations, in no instance does American law permit nation-wide branch banking of the pattern and scope found in Canada, England, France, and many other countries. Because state governments decide the extent to which branch banking may be expanded, branch organizations are necessarily limited by state boundary lines.[9]

State Regulation of Branch Banking   Nineteen states, as listed in Table 12-1, permit state-wide branching by commercial banks, and district-wide branching has been authorized by Congress for the District of Columbia.

Table 12-1   **State Branch Banking Laws in Effect in June 1969**

	PERMITTING STATE-WIDE BRANCHING	
Alaska	Idaho	South Carolina
Arizona	Maine	South Dakota
California	Maryland	Utah
Connecticut	Nevada	Vermont
Delaware	North Carolina	Virginia[a]
District of Columbia	Oregon	Washington
Hawaii	Rhode Island	
	PERMITTING LIMITED-AREA BRANCHING[b]	
Alabama	Michigan	Ohio
Georgia	Mississippi	Pennsylvania
Indiana	New Hampshire	Tennessee
Kentucky	New Jersey	Wisconsin
Louisiana	New Mexico	
Massachusetts	New York	
	PROHIBITING BRANCHING	
Arkansas	Kansas	North Dakota
Colorado	Minnesota	Oklahoma
Florida	Missouri	Texas
Illinois	Montana	West Virginia
Iowa	Nebraska	Wyoming

[a] Through conversion into branches of banks absorbed in mergers.
[b] As in head-office counties, in head-office and contiguous counties, or in specially designated banking districts (as in New York and New Jersey).
Source: Federal Reserve Bulletin, March 1970, pp. 201–202, 210.

Sixteen states permit branching in home-office counties, home-office and contiguous counties, or other areas less than state-wide, as within the home-office "banking district" as demarcated in New York and New Jersey. And the remaining fifteen states generally prohibit all branching, although

---

[9]But there are a few exceptions that somehow got by, as, for examples, a Pennsylvania branch operated by a New Jersey bank and two branches in the state of Washington and one in Oregon operated by a California bank. See Federal Deposit Insurance Corporation, *Annual Report,* 1969, p. 250.

Table 12-2   Growth of Branch Banking, 1945–1970[a]

	END OF YEAR			
	1945	1955	1965	1970
Number of commercial banks	14,011	13,716	13,804	13,688
Number of banks with branches	1122	1659	3140	3994
Number of branches	3947	6710	15,486	21,424
Number of branches in leading branch banking states:				
California	891	1174	2377	2994
New York	671	1025	1920	2429
Pennsylvania	118	466	1229	1723
Ohio	175	366	946	1298
Michigan	179	376	889	1205
North Carolina	150	324	733	1121
New Jersey	131	257	665	1007
Virginia	89	160	538	806
Massachusetts	137	260	565	735
Indiana	79	163	468	632
Washington	112	202	405	556
LOCATION OF BRANCHES, DECEMBER 31, 1970:[b]				
In head-office cities			7991	
Outside head-office cities:				
In same counties			7031	
In contiguous counties			3713	
In noncontiguous counties			3773	

[a] A branch is defined as "any branch bank, branch office, branch agency, additional office, or any branch place of business . . . at which deposits are received, or checks paid, or money [is] lent." Data do not include "facilities" other than branches maintained by commercial banks at military and other government establishments. "Facilities" numbering 219 were being maintained by 152 banks at the end of 1970.

[b] Including 1084 branches of mutual savings banks.

Source: Federal Reserve Bulletin, June 1946, pp. 672–673; April 1956, pp. 398–399; April 1966, pp. 600–601; and April 1971, pp. A94–A95.

a few have minor exceptions, as for additional "offices" to receive and pay deposits as distinct from branches with wider operating scopes.

In many states, the laws stipulate that branches may be established only in communities not already served by banks; and several states require the closing of branches in the event that independent banks are opened in the communities where the branches have been in operation. Other regulations commonly found in state laws pertain to the capital stock that banks must have in order to establish branches, the additional amounts of stock required for each branch, the maximum number of branches that may be established by any one bank, and the population of the communities in which branches may be opened.

Spread of branch banking since 1945

As the data of Table 12-2 reveal, the growth of commercial banking since 1945, in terms of offices for handling business, has been entirely a growth in branches and not in the number of banks. While the number of banks fell moderately from the end of 1945 to the end of 1970, the number of banks that have branches increased by 2872 and the number of branches, by 12,477. However, the data for leading branch banking states (listed in the order of their leadership in 1970) indicate that throughout the period, branching has been quite heavily concentrated in a few states— as it was in 1970 when the top six states had slightly more than half of the total number of branches. Moreover, the figures on the location of branches within states presented in the lower portion of the table (with the inclusion of data for mutual savings banks) indicate that as late as the end of 1970 approximately two thirds of all branches were located in the head-office cities and counties of the parent banks.

Foreign branches and foreign banking subsidiaries

Foreign Branches   Under federal law, national banks and state member banks are permitted to establish foreign branches, defined as branches in foreign countries and in "dependencies and insular possessions" of the United States, if they have at least $1 million of capital stock and surplus, and if they get the approval of the Federal Reserve Board of Governors for each branch that they wish to set up. The books of each branch must be kept separately from those of all others as well as from the books of the parent bank, and the branches are subject to examination by the board.

Until the 1960s, American banks were slow in establishing foreign branches, as they were generally satisfied to handle their international business by means of correspondent relationships with foreign banks located in the principal money centers. At the end of 1959, only seven American banks had foreign branches for a total of 132 located in thirty countries including "dependencies and insular possessions." However, foreign branching accelerated in the 1960s, especially in 1968 and 1969, as many additional banks established branches and banks already having branches added to their lists. At the end of 1967, fifteen banks had 295 branches located in 54 countries, but by the end of 1969, 53 banks had 460 branches in 59 countries.[10] The huge expansion of 1968–1969 was especially prompted by the banks' drive to expand their domestic lending and investing capacity, despite the Federal Reserve's restrictive monetary policy, by attracting Eurodollars as referred to in Chapter 11.

The 1969 array of branches included 235 in Latin America, including

---

[10]Board of Governors of the Federal Reserve System, *Annual Report*, 1959, p. 90; 1967, p. 323; and 1969, p. 312.

38 in Argentina, 32 in the Bahama Islands, 26 in Panama, 23 in Colombia, and 18 in Chile; 103 in Europe, including 37 in the United Kingdom, 17 in Germany, 11 in France, and 10 in Belgium; 77 in the Far East, including 13 each in Hong Kong and Japan and 11 in India; 6 in the Near East and 1 in Africa; and 38 in overseas areas and trust territories of the United States, including 18 in Puerto Rico and 13 in the Virgin Islands.[11] Collectively, all these branches had assets of $26,783 million at the end of 1969, indicating an increase of $9912 million in that year[12] (omitting from both figures "due from head offices and United States branches" representing very largely if not entirely Eurodollars assembled by the branches and "loaned" to head offices and branches at home).

Foreign Banking Subsidiaries   In addition to its authorization for foreign branching, federal law provides national banks with three avenues for participation in international banking by way of investment in the stocks of corporations so engaged. Such investment is also open to state banks to the extent that state laws permit. Within prescribed limits, national banks may invest directly or indirectly in the stocks of foreign banks, the stocks of domestic corporations that are chartered to engage in international banking but that limit their operations according to restrictions agreed to between them and the Federal Reserve Board of Governors (*agreement corporations*), and the stock of corporations chartered by the Board of Governors itself to engage in international banking *and financing* (*Edge Act corporations*). The agreement and Edge Act corporations may invest, in turn, in the stocks of foreign banks, and the Edge Act corporations may additionally invest in foreign corporations outside the commercial banking field. The Edge Act corporations are not permitted to establish domestic branches, but with the approval of the Board of Governors, they may establish branches in foreign countries, while the agreement corporations may have both domestic and foreign branches if so permitted by the Board of Governors and, for domestic branches, by state law.

Typically, American banks establish international banking corporations as wholly owned subsidiaries except for directors' qualifying shares. According to a Federal Reserve report, there were five agreement corporations and sixty-three Edge Act corporations in operation at the end of the year 1969.[13]

GROUP AND CHAIN BANKING

In many states, the gathering together of numerous banking offices under the control of single interests has not always awaited the enactment of permissive laws. Although it might be impossible to establish branches with-

---

[11]*Ibid.*, 1969, p. 313.
[12]Derived from *Federal Reserve Bulletin*, September 1970, p. 740.
[13]Board of Governors of the Federal Reserve System, *Annual Report*, 1969, p. 314.

out the sanction of law, most of the advantages of branch banking could be achieved by the formation of groups and chains. From the point of view of the controlling interests, control by means of group and chain arrangements can, indeed, be superior to branch setups. Through the operations of a holding company, for example, control can be exercised over banks located in different states, whereas branching, as we have seen, is limited by state boundary lines. Again, a holding company can integrate in a single system national banks, state banks that are members of the Federal Reserve System, and state nonmember banks. It is also possible for the holding company to control corporations in fields of finance other than commercial banking, although since 1934, the inclusion of investment banking subsidiaries in group systems has been prohibited by federal law.

Extent of group and chain banking

Although a few groups and chains were in operation before 1901, the development of such organizations has been almost exclusively a phenomenon of the twentieth century. Group banking had its most rapid early growth in the decade of the 1920s, with most of the outstanding present-day groups getting their starts at that time. At the end of 1931, ninety-seven groups comprising 978 banks and 1219 branches were in operation,[14] but by the end of 1969, the number of groups had shrunk to eighty-six, comprising 723 banks and 2674 branches. Nevertheless, group banking remains very much alive, as indicated by an increase in the total deposits of group banks and their branches from $22,526 million to $62,574 million in the 6-year period ending December 31, 1969.[15]

As for chain banking, there has always been uncertainty about its prevalence. A holding company may be known, but it is often quite difficult to trace the ownership of stocks by individuals in two or more banks and especially to discover how closely different owners may be associated in their control interests and ideas. The Board of Governors of the Federal Reserve System used to publish estimates of the scope of chain banking—admittedly incomplete—but it gave up this task after reporting its estimate for the end of 1945. For that date, it estimated that there were 115 chain systems comprising 522 banks and seventy-four branches.[16] Moreover, the generally accepted definition of chain banking given earlier in this chapter is probably much too narrow. Much stock in commercial banks is owned by mutual savings banks, life insurance companies, and investment companies, and by commercial banks themselves in their trust departments. In some instances, indeed, individual commercial banks, in their role as

---

[14]C. E. Cagle, *Banking Studies*, Washington, D.C.: Board of Governors of the Federal Reserve System, 1941, pp. 134, 136.
[15]*Federal Reserve Bulletin*, June issues, 1964, p. 783; and 1970, p. A95.
[16]Joint Economic Committee, *Monetary Policy and Management of the Public Debt*, Washington, D.C.: Government Printing Office, 1952, p. 552.

trustees, own substantial amounts of their own outstanding stock. In many instances, too, commercial banks grant loans on the security of pledged bank stocks, and it is possible that, by such lending, they gain some degree of influence over the banks whose stock is pledged. From the standpoint of concentration of power, therefore, the communities of interest that may exist among financial institutions in voting their stock holdings in given commercial banks, as well as the total influence of some of these institutions singly, may be much more important than the ownership of individuals or of groups of individuals in two or more banks.[17]

Regulation of group banking

The establishment of holding companies to control simultaneously two or more separately chartered banks offered opportunities for manipulative practices, and abuses were not slow in appearing. Groups were sometimes organized to make profits for the promoters, rather than to further an integration of banking that could be said to serve the public interest. Holding companies could deliberately strengthen one bank at the expense of other banks in its group. For example, a holding company might strengthen the asset position and increase the income of a subsidiary bank in which it had virtually a 100 percent stock ownership by shifting the better assets from a subsidiary in which it controlled, say, only 51 percent of the stock. In instances where the holding companies owned controlling interests in investment banking affiliates, subsidiary commercial banks could be ordered to buy securities offered for sale by the investment banking subsidiaries even when they might be of poor quality.

As these and other abuses of group banking become too frequent, Congress and some of the state legislatures took steps to curb them.

State Regulation In many states, the commercial banks are not permitted to invest in the stocks of other commercial banks, and in many others, such investment is closely restricted. In general, however, restrictions on ownership by holding companies are not so tight. According to a Federal Reserve report, the status of state regulation in 1969 was as follows:

> 30 States do not have specific legislation regulating registered bank holding companies. Of the remaining States, five require state approval of the acquisition of banks by holdings companies; four restrict such acquisitions, generally by specifying the maximum percentage of a bank's stock or of the total deposits in the State that the holding company may control; and 12 prohibit registered bank holding companies.[18]

---

[17]For the details of an extensive investigation of institutional and individual communities of interest in the largest member banks of the Federal Reserve System, see House Committee on Banking and Currency, *Chain Banking: Stockholder and Loan Links of 200 Largest Member Banks*, Washington, D.C.: Government Printing Office, 1963.
[18]*Federal Reserve Bulletin*, March 1970, p. 202.

Federal Regulation To the extent that holding companies control banks located in several states or control national as well as state banks, the problem of regulation is clearly one with which only the federal government can adequately cope. In the Banking Acts of 1933 and 1935, Congress provided for limited supervision over holding companies that controlled member bank subsidiaries by denying them the right to vote the stock of these subsidiaries should they not get voting permits issued by the Federal Reserve Board of Governors. But a holding company could avoid federal regulation by choosing not to apply for a voting permit, although it would thereby be deprived of voting power. Moreover, the legislation did not reach holding companies that had only nonmember subsidiaries. Even greater weaknesses in the legislation were its lack of curbs on the expansion of group systems and its failure to require holding companies to avoid activities unrelated to banking, whether undertaken directly or through nonbank subsidiaries. So argued the Board of Governors in many of its annual reports to Congress, as well as in its testimony before Congressional committees.

Although Congress finally granted the board some of the powers it had long sought by passing the Bank Holding Company Act of 1956, this legislation was so loaded with exemptions and exclusions that it became subject to widespread criticism. So Congress tried again in 1966, adding amendments designed to plug most of the loopholes, but making one gesture toward liberality by repealing the voting-permit provisions of the legislation of the 1930s. Hardly, however, had the 1966 amendments been adopted when concern began to mount about bank holding companies of a different kind. Almost "revolutionary" in the speed and scope of its development was the establishment of holding companies individually controlling *only one bank*, but with some having additional subsidiaries in other lines of business, with these and others making moves toward acquiring other such nonbank subsidiaries, and with all generally free to go into whatever business areas they might choose. At the end of 1970, accordingly, Congress added another group of amendments to the basic holding company legislation of 1956, this time making its regulations applicable uniformly to both group holding companies and one-bank holding companies.

However, something should be said about the one-bank holding companies themselves before we proceed with a survey of the federal regulations as they now apply.

ONE-BANK HOLDING COMPANIES

Development

Although one-bank holding companies had had a long history, their growth before the late 1960s was generally considered to be unimportant because most of them controlled small banks and many others were "conglomerate" business corporations that had bought controlling interests in single banks as profit-seeking ventures more or less incidentally to their acquisitions of controlling interests in manufacturing, mercantile, and transportation enterprises and in other nonfinancial corporations. As late as the end of 1965, the 548 banks that were controlled by one-bank holding companies had only $13.9 billion of deposits (as of June 30, 1964) equal to only 4.5 percent of total deposits of all commercial banks.[19]

But the disquieting development that began to accelerate sharply in 1967 was the acquisition by one-bank holding companies of a large number of the biggest banks of the country, with the acquisitions engineered by the directors of the banks themselves. By April 1, 1970, the number of banks controlled by one-bank holding companies had risen to 1116, and these banks held (as of June 30, 1969) $138.8 billion of deposits equal to 32.6 percent of total deposits of all commercial banks.[20]

Objective

Before the adoption of the federal regulations of 1970, the principal reason for decisions of the directors of individual banks to set up holding companies had been to enable single families of corporations—the bank, the holding company, and the holding company's other (nonbank) subsidiaries—to continue the bank's normal activities while adding many other kinds of activities outside the scope of operations permitted by law to the bank itself. Accordingly, a usual procedure of the holding companies had been to establish nonbank subsidiaries, as insurance and travel agencies, investment companies, mortgage banking firms, commercial finance companies, sellers of computer services, equipment lessors, and so on. Another common procedure had been for the holding companies to buy controlling interests in independent firms already engaged in such areas and then to continue them in operation as subsidiaries. As long as a holding company confined its operations and those of its nonbank subsidiaries to areas of the kinds just listed—areas claimed to be "reasonably" related to commercial banking—it was said to be a "congeneric" (meaning "of the same kind"), but if it went beyond such areas, as into manufacturing and merchandising, it was said to be a "conglomerate."

Ease in establishment

In the 1967–1970 period of rapid growth of one-bank holding companies, the simplicity of the procedure by which they could be set up was especially appealing to bank directors. All that a bank's directors had to do was to get an ordinary corporate charter for the holding company under the state's general incorporation statute and then to persuade the bank's stock-

---

[19]Federal Reserve Bank of Chicago, *Business Conditions*, July 1970, p. 6.
[20]*Ibid.*

holders to exchange their shares of bank stock for shares in the holding company. And persuasion was usually a pushover, since stockholders had every reason to anticipate that earnings per share on the holding company's stock, to be derived from a broadened range of activities, would be substantially higher than earnings per share to be expected were they to hold the bank's own stock.

Federal regulation

As it now applies to both group holding companies and one-bank holding companies, the federal law defines a *bank holding company* as a corporation, partnership, or other entity (but not including an individual human being) that directly or indirectly owns, controls, or has the power to vote 25 percent or more of any class of "voting securities" of a commercial bank; or that controls the election of a majority of the directors of a commercial bank; or that is found by the Board of Governors, after it has provided an opportunity for a hearing, to exercise "a controlling influence over the management and policies" of a commercial bank. Entities that would become bank holding companies as a result of buying bank stock or taking other actions to gain control of one or more banks must have advance permission of the Board of Governors to take such actions. And all entities that fall within the scope of the definition—let us continue to call them "holding companies"—must register with the board, subject themselves and their subsidiaries to examination by it, and obey the provisions of the law as well as the regulations that the law authorizes the board to adopt and enforce.

Restrictions on Control of Commercial Banks As a general rule, a registered bank holding company must get permission of the Board of Governors for additional acquisitions of bank stocks having voting power. However, it needs no such permission to buy additional stocks in banks in which it already holds a majority of the voting shares or to buy stock in other banks as long as its holdings of voting shares in each do not exceed 5 percent of the total voting shares outstanding. On the other hand, the legislation stipulates that, if a holding company wants to buy stock in banks located in states other than the state in which its banking subsidiaries were principally concentrated (as measured by deposits) on May 9, 1956, or whenever it became a holding company, if later, the Board of Governors must deny permission unless the states in which the banks are located *have specific provisions in their laws* allowing such purchases.

Under the 1966 amendments, the board is directed to give the Comptroller of the Currency an opportunity to object to proposed holding company acquisitions of national banks, and likewise for state supervisory authorities with respect to acquisitions involving state banks. Despite objections, however, it may still approve of an acquisition after a hearing. The board is also directed to withhold approval of every proposed acquisition unless it is convinced that "the anticompetitive effects . . . are clearly outweighed in the public interest by the probable effect of the transaction in meeting the convenience and needs of the community to be served." Even further, it must notify the U.S. Attorney General of its approvals of proposed acquisitions and give him 30 days to take action in court, if he so chooses, to prevent their completion on grounds of antitrust law violation.

Restrictions on Engaging in Other Lines of Business   Since bypassing the restrictions of banking laws on banks' ranges of activities was the principal reason for the establishment of one-bank holding companies in the late 1960s, the 1970 amendments were especially designed to preserve these restrictions or at least some of them. Nevertheless, Congress gave to the Board of Governors principal responsibility for deciding what kinds of activities are "so closely related to banking" as to be permissible and what kinds are so unrelated as to be forbidden. In making such decisions, the board is directed by Congress to take into consideration whether engaging in given kinds of activity by holding companies and their nonbank subsidiaries would have benefits to the public outweighing "possible adverse effects, such as undue concentration of resources, decreased or unfair competition, conflicts of interest, or unsound banking practices."

On the basis of applications of individual holding companies, the board is empowered to grant permission for their direct or indirect engagement in designated kinds of activities, and by general rule, it may authorize all registered holding companies to engage in specified kinds of activities. When, however, it decides in individual cases or by general rule that specified kinds of activities must be avoided, holding companies already so engaged must either discontinue these activities or give up their role as bank holding companies, that is, they must divest themselves of bank control. But the holding companies are given several years to make their decisions and to effect the prescribed changes in their status. Moreover, the board may exempt certain one-bank holding companies from the divestment provisions of the law and its own general rules, especially those that before July 1, 1968, were individually controlling only a "small bank."

BANK MERGERS

The combination of two or more existing banks into one, by merger or consolidation,[21] is a further means of reducing the number of unit banks

---

[21]Although the federal and state banking laws are by no means uniform in their use of terms, a *bank merger* may be said to occur when one bank absorbs another and continues in operation under its own charter, that is, it survives; while a bank consolidation may be said to occur when a new bank is chartered and it absorbs two or more existing banks, with the latter surrendering their charters. In the text discussion, however, the single term *merger* stands for both the merger and the consolidation.

and concentrating bank assets and powers in the hands of fewer people. Because the bank merger movement has been especially strong in the post-World War II period, it has given rise to new fears of the stifling of competition, an elimination of loan facilities for small businessmen, and other dangers. In the period 1950–1969, as Table 12-3 shows, 2965 commercial

Table 12-3   **Mergers of Commercial Banks, 1950–1969[a]   (assets in millions of dollars)**

	BANKS ABSORBED			BANKS ABSORBED	
YEAR	NUMBER	ASSETS	YEAR	NUMBER	ASSETS
1950	91	1,129	1960	136	2,795
1951	84	1,778	1961	133	5,995
1952	99	820	1962	193	2,207
1953	115	1,200	1963	151	3,519
1954	216	4,064	1964	139	2,238
1955	225	9,615	1965	167	2,096
1956	186	2,964	1966	136	1,645
1957	165	2,302	1967	122	2,889
1958	151	2,559	1968	130	2,185
1959	171	3,688	1969	155	3,986
			Totals	2965	59,674

[a] Including, in a few instances, absorptions of institutions like savings and loan associations and safe deposit companies.

Sources: Derived from House Committee on Banking and Currency, *Hearings before Subcommittee No. 2 on Regulation of Bank Mergers,* Washington, D.C.: Government Printing Office, 1960, p. 19, and annual reports of the Comptroller of the Currency and the Federal Deposit Insurance Corporation.

banks with total assets of $59,674 million were absorbed by other institutions. In the same period, about 2600 new banks were chartered, but new banks generally start on a modest scale while banks absorbed in mergers are often of substantial sizes. Sometimes, indeed, they are very large, as, for example, the Bank of Manhattan Company that, with $1629 million of assets, was absorbed in 1955 by what is now the Chase Manhattan Bank; the Corn Exchange Bank and Trust Company, with assets of $821 million, absorbed in 1955 by the Chemical Bank and Trust Company, and the New York Trust Company, with assets of $859 million, absorbed in 1959 by the combined Chemical Corn Exchange Bank; and J. P. Morgan & Company, Inc., with assets of $983 million, absorbed in 1959 by what is now the Morgan Guaranty Trust Company.[22] The adoption of federal bank merger legislation in 1960 seemed to stop mergers among giants—except for the

[22]House Committee on Banking and Currency, *Hearings before Subcommittee No. 2 on Regulation of Bank Mergers,* Washingotn, D.C.: Government Printing Office, 1960, pp. 16, 23, 136.

1961 merger in New York City of the Manufacturers Trust Company with assets of $3845 million and the Hanover Bank with assets of $2156 million —but since its adoption, there have been many absorptions of small and medium-sized banks by very large instititions, as well as numerous combinations among the smaller banks themselves.

Reasons for mergers

An important reason for the strong merger movement that has continued to the present time is the anxiety of absorbing banks to get ready-made branches. Where branch banking laws permit, absorbed banks may be converted into branches, and if these banks themselves have had branches in operation, this is all the better for the absorbing bank. A comparable reason is the desire of absorbing banks to get departments and facilities already developed and groups of loyal customers already gained by the institutions to be absorbed. In this regard, big banks in large cities have found their correspondent business with out-of-town banks to be growing at a rate much below the rates of growth of other phases of banking, especially "retail banking"—the granting of consumer and home-purchase loans, the building up of savings deposits, and the like. Wanting to get into retail banking quickly, they often decide on mergers with institutions already having extensive operations in this area as the best way to proceed. Other objectives of bank mergers are the reduction of the burden of overhead expenses by spreading them over larger volumes of operations, improvement in management by obtaining desirable personnel of absorbed banks, acquiring the capacity to grant larger loans to individual borrowers, and, it is surely fair to add, reduction in competition and enjoyment of the satisfaction of growth in power and prestige.

In a goodly number of mergers, the impetus comes not from the absorbing banks but from banks that want to sell out. Elderly managements that want to retire without having developed bright young people to take over are very likely to shop around for institutions that will buy them out at fair prices. Banks that are operating in the red or that are in danger of insolvency for other reasons may be quite happy to save something for the stockholders by selling out; indeed, the supervisory authorities, especially the Federal Deposit Insurance Corporation, will surely encourage them to do so by giving direct assistance in arranging mergers.

Federal bank merger legislation

Before the adoption of the federal bank merger legislation in 1960, the Comptroller of the Currency and the FDIC appeared to have no responsibility to disallow mergers on grounds of their probable monopolistic or other anticompetitive effects, and the power and responsibility of the Federal Reserve Board of Governors in this area were patently weak and uncertain. At the same time, there was uncertainty about the role that the

U.S. Department of Justice should play in contesting on antitrust grounds mergers approved by the bank supervisory agencies. Although the 1960 legislation seemed to be aimed at resolving the questions of jurisdiction and responsibility largely in favor of the supervisory agencies, the Attorney General decided that it did not diminish his duty to attack bank mergers which he thought to be violative of the antitrust laws. He stepped up actions in the courts to prevent the completion of mergers already approved by the supervisory agencies, and in the case of the merger of the Manufacturers Trust Company and the Hanover Bank that had already been completed, he asked the court to order its undoing. The situation was so confused that Congress could hardly avoid returning to the fray to try to clear up the difficulties, as it did in 1966 by adopting amendments to the 1960 legislation to clarify allocations of authority and to set guidelines and rules of procedure.

As the federal legislation now reads, the rule is that no mergers among insured banks may take place without the written consent of the Comptroller of the Currency if the surviving institution is to be a national bank; the Board of Governors, if a state member bank; or the FDIC, if a nonmember insured bank. In passing on merger proposals, each of the supervisory agencies is to take into consideration "the financial and managerial resources and future prospects of the existing and proposed institutions, and the convenience and needs of the community to be served." Each agency must request reports from the other two supervisory agencies and the Attorney General on the competitive factors involved, and these reports must be presented within 30 days—or 10 days if the agency asking for them declares that an "emergency" requires quick action. Indeed, these reports may be dispensed with if the agency decides that a merger must be effected at once to prevent the failure of one of the banks to be merged. As in the case of acquisitions by holding companies, the supervisory agency is directed not to approve proposed mergers unless it finds that the anticompetitive effects "are clearly outweighed in the public interest" by probable advantages to the community to be served. After approval, the merger may not be effected for 30 days in order to give the Attorney General the opportunity to take action in court to prevent it on antitrust grounds. But if he does not take such action within 30 days, the only ground left to him for attacking the merger as effected are the antimonopoly provisions of the Sherman Antitrust Act. However, the holdup is for only 10 days for "emergency" mergers as previously declared by the supervisory agency, and not at all for mergers to prevent bank failures.

FOR REVIEW

1. What is meant by free banking? Are people free at the present time to establish new commercial banks?

2. On the basis of what criteria does the Comptroller of the Currency

approve or reject applications for the establishment of new national banks?

3. Describe the procedure that must be followed by the organizers of a new national bank.

4. What rules apply at the present time to the capital stock and surplus of national banks?

5. What are the rights of the owners of bank stock? To what extent do owners of bank stock have decision-making powers concerning the bank's management? Explain.

6. What are the functions of the directors of a commercial bank? For what kinds of action are they subject to criminal and civil penalties?

7. Why does the commercial banking system of the United States continue to be predominantly one of unit banks and of branch banking confined to individual states?

8. Can you add any arguments to those presented in this chapter in favor of, or in opposition to, regional or nation-wide expansion of branch banking?

9. What conditions must a national bank satisfy to establish branches?

10. In general terms, how liberal are the state governments in permitting commercial banks to establish branches?

11. Distinguish between group and chain banking. Why is there some uncertainty at the present time about the nature of chain banking?

12. How can one account for the great growth in the number of one-bank holding companies in the period 1967–1970?

13. What are the principal restrictions of present federal law on expansion in the control of banks by holding companies? in their control of other kinds of business enterprises?

14. Why have there been a great number of bank mergers in recent years? For banks that are subject to federal supervision, who has the final word on the legality of their mergers? Explain.

CHAPTER 13

PRIMARY AND SECONDARY RESERVES

PRIMARY RESERVES

In any well-managed commercial bank, a senior officer or perhaps a committee is charged with the responsibility of watching the "money position" of the bank from hour to hour to determine what lending and investing capacity is available or, on the other hand, what deficiencies in the bank's cash assets are developing. Watching a bank's "money position" implies not only a continual consideration of the amount of its cash assets in relationship to the amounts of its demand and time deposits and the reserve needs that apply to them; it implies the forecasting of changes in cash assets and deposit liabilities to be expected in the ordinary course of business during the day and in the next few days; and it implies the making of many decisions about the use of excess cash (not expected to be needed immediately for ordinary operations) in quick, specially selected loan and investment operations, and about prompt actions to cancel deficiencies already obtaining. The forecasting has to do with effects on cash assets and deposits to be anticipated through clearing operations at the local clearinghouse and with the Federal Reserve banks, deposits and withdrawals of out-of-town correspondent banks, transfers from and to U.S. Treasury tax and loan accounts, large withdrawals from the deposit accounts of major customers soon to be made as courteously reported in advance by their treasurers, and so on. The whole idea is that the watchers of the bank's "money position" want to be sure that it will have enough cash assets for needs but also to quickly put to interest-earning work whatever cash is available over and above needed amounts.

Any bank's *reserve needs* may be said to be the cash "reserve requirements" set by law or government regulation plus any additional amounts of cash assets that the bank decides it should have as a matter of continuing policy. For many large banks, needs and legal requirements are thought to be identical; but for other large banks and most of the smaller ones, needs are typically regarded as exceeding legal requirements, and in many instances by wide margins.

Nature, functions, and distribution of primary reserves

Cash Assets as Primary Reserves   The cash assets of commercial banks constitute their *primary reserves.* They consist of paper money and coins on hand or "vault cash," reserve balances on deposit at the Federal Reserve banks (for member banks), clearing balances at the Reserve banks (for nonmember banks that use the Federal Reserve clearing facilities), and demand deposit balances at other domestic commercial banks.

We may think that a commercial bank should also count as primary reserves the "cash items" that it has sent out to other banks for payment—checks drawn on them, Treasury note and bond coupons sent to the Federal Reserve banks for payment, and the like. But the individual bank must expect these outgoing cash items to be well-balanced—or perhaps over-balanced—by incoming items drawn on it and dispatched to it for payment by other banks. However, probable excesses in either direction are surely to be considered in the forecasting referred to in the first paragraph of the chapter, and actual excesses as they develop surely require decisions related to "money position."

Functions of Primary Reserves   It would appear that the principal reason banks have for holding primary reserves is to protect their solvency—to enable them at all times to meet the withdrawal demands of their depositors as well as to make other necessary cash outlays. This is surely so for banks' holdings of vault cash, since it would be quite demoralizing to them—and even more so to their depositors—should they be unable to meet the depositors' requests for paper money and coins. And solvency appears to be the objective of reserve requirements imposed by state governments on their chartered banks. But solvency does not appear to be an important objective of reserve requirements imposed on member banks of the Federal Reserve System, since the amount of reserves they are required to hold is obviously much greater than needed to meet cash-payment obligations that are likely to materialize from day to day, and since the reserves they do hold to satisfy the requirements seem not to be freely available to meet cash-payment obligations because of the penalties for deficiencies to which they are subject. We must, therefore, agree with the bankers that the reserve requirements set for member banks are designed principally to make effective the money-control objectives of the Federal Reserve rather than for the protection of solvency.

This aspect of the reserve requirements that apply to member banks is important for the whole commercial banking system and for the welfare of the whole economy, because the member banks dominate the system, consistently having over 80 percent of the total assets and the total deposits of all commercial banks. Because of this dominance, any treatment of primary reserve management must concentrate almost of necessity on management by the member banks, as is done in this chapter. But management by nonmember banks need not be entirely excluded, and it is not.

Distribution of Primary Reserves   In the first place, virtually all commercial banks, both member and nonmember, want to keep their vault cash at the lowest possible level commensurate with their capacity at all times to make payments that must be made in paper money and coins. Although vault cash may be counted in meeting reserve requirements imposed by all federal and state laws and regulations, it clutters the place, takes valuable storage space in the vaults, has to be counted from time to time to be sure that it is really there, is subject to embezzlement and burglary, and costs premiums for burglary and indemnity insurance.

Secondly, virtually all commercial banks, except the major banks of New York City, find it advantageous to hold substantial demand deposit balances at correspondent commercial banks located in principal cities. Not in all principal cities for the individual bank, of course, but typically for it a balance with a New York City bank and one with a bank located in a principal city in the geographical area in which it operates, and possibly balances with one or two banks located in other principal cities of the area or elsewhere. Keeping deposit balances with correspondent banks in principal cities is advantageous to nonmember banks for two reasons: (1) such balances generally satisfy reserve requirements imposed by state laws and regulations; and (2) they are the basis on which the correspondent banks provide many "free" services to the depositing banks. Because of the role of these balances in meeting legal reserve requirements, nonmember banks have no reason to try to hold them down to levels that will only suffice to compensate the correspondents for the "free" services provided. On the other hand, demand balances with correspondent banks do not count in meeting the legal reserve requirements that apply to member banks, so that these banks have good reason to trim balances with correspondents to levels just high enough to ensure the continued flow of the services they seek.

Finally, member banks collectively keep most of their cash assets as reserve balances at the Federal Reserve banks, since only these balances and their vault cash satisfy the reserve requirements to which they are subject. And the larger member banks, especially, try to keep these reserve balances at levels that, with vault cash, will be only enough to satisfy the requirements. They deplore holding "idle cash"—especially at times when loan and investment opportunities abound. What is more, their dislike for idle cash is typically a day-to-day attitude. If primary reserves are in excess supply today, why not lend the excess for 1 day, and if the excess continues tomorrow, why not relend for another day? If a deficiency develops tomorrow, perhaps the repayment of the 1-day loan will cover it, or if not, why not obtain a 1-day loan to supply it? Good money position management would seem to require affirmative answers to these questions, provided that opportunities for 1-day lending and borrowing are readily available —as they generally are, especially in the "federal funds" market to be described a little later.

Member bank reserve requirements

Classification of Deposits and Member Banks   The member banks of the Federal Reserve System are required to hold primary reserves equal to certain percentages of their demand and time deposits as prescribed from time to time by the Board of Governors of the system within the limits set by the Federal Reserve Act. As indicated earlier, the required reserves must be kept as vault cash or as deposit balances with the Federal Reserve banks, and it should be added here that it is up to the individual member bank to decide how much of the required reserves it wants to keep in one form or the other. The Board of Governors may limit the counting of vault cash for satisfying the requirements, but we can think of no reason why it is likely to do so. The Federal Reserve Act distinguishes between demand and time deposits and classifies the member banks as being either "reserve city banks" or "country banks" (or for the latter, banks "not in a reserve city," as the law itself says). It gives the board the authority to decide what kinds of deposits are demand deposits and what kinds are time deposits, as well as to add to and make deletions from the list of cities that are classified as reserve cities.

The board defines as *demand deposits* all deposits of individuals, partnerships, corporations, and governmental bodies payable on demand, in less than 30 days, or on notice of less than 30 days; similar deposits of other domestic banking institutions and of foreign banks; certified checks and cashiers' checks outstanding; and letters of credit and travelers' checks sold for cash. However, to find the net amount of demand deposits to which the reserve requirement applies, the member bank is permitted to deduct the following from the "gross" amount of the foregoing items: deposits with other incorporated domestic banks, other than the Federal Reserve banks, subject to withdrawal on demand; cash items in the process of collection; and cash items on hand that will be presented for payment or forwarded for collection within 1 day. *Time deposits* are defined as deposits that are payable in not less than 30 days or that are subject to notice of withdrawal of 30 days or more, and the classification includes savings deposits of individuals and nonprofit institutions, so-called open-account time deposits of business corporations, and both negotiable and nonnegotiable certificates of deposit.

The reserve city banks are chiefly the large banks of about fifty of our principal cities that hold substantial deposit balances of out-of-town banks ("interbank balances"), while the country banks are all member banks located outside these cities, as well as many smaller banks in them that have been given special dispensations by the Board of Governors from the reserve-city classification.

Ranges of Reserve Requirements The ranges within which the Board of Governors is authorized to fix reserve requirements for the member banks are as follows (in percentages of deposits):

	APPLYING TO	
RESERVES FOR	RESERVE CITY BANKS	COUNTRY BANKS
Demand deposits	10–22	7–14
Time deposits	3–10	3–10

(It was not until 1935 that the board first got a continuing power to change reserve requirements applicable to member bank deposits. It was authorized to vary the requirements between the percentages then in effect and levels of double those percentages. For the demand deposits of New York and Chicago banks then classified as "central reserve city" banks, the permitted range was 13–26 percent; of reserve city banks, 10–20 percent; and of country banks, 7–14 percent; and for the time deposits of all three classes, 3–6 percent. By the terms of legislation adopted in 1959, New York and Chicago were shifted to the reserve city classification, and the maximum rate for the demand deposits of reserve city banks was raised to 22 percent. Finally, legislation adopted on a temporary basis in 1966 and made permanent in 1968 empowered the board to go as high as 10 percent in the time deposit requirement for both reserve city and country banks.)

To illustrate how the board uses its authority to set requirements, those in effect in December 1970 may be cited as follows (again as percentages of deposits):[1]

	APPLYING TO	
RESERVES FOR	RESERVE CITY BANKS	COUNTRY BANKS
Demand deposits:		
Up to $5 million	17	12½
Over $5 million	17½	13
Savings deposits	3	3
Other time deposits:		
Up to $5 million	3	3
Over $5 million	5	5

---

[1]Also in effect in December 1970 were several special reserve requirements that had been added by the board over a period of several years to strengthen the effectiveness of its policy of restrictive monetary control. In the main, and subject to some exceptions, these special provisions classified as "deposits" subject to reserve requirements: (1) borrowings by member banks by sales of their promissory notes (as by issuing open-market commercial paper); (2) borrowings by "affiliates" of member banks—holding companies having controlling interests in the member banks and other controlled subsidiaries of the holding companies or of the member banks themselves—to the extent that the proceeds of these borrowings are used to expand the member banks' lending and investing capacity; (3) borrowings by member banks from their foreign branches (which chiefly take the form of Eurodollars, as mentioned in Chapter 11); and (4)

Determination of Required Reserves   In determining whether each member bank holds reserves as required, computations are made on an average daily basis for weeks ending at the close of business on Wednesdays. Suppose, for example, that a member bank is checking its reserve position for the week—the "reserve computation period"—ending Wednesday, December 16. It takes the average of the demand and time deposits on its books at the close of business on each day of the *second preceding week,* that is, the week ending Wednesday, December 2. It then applies to these averages of demand and time deposits the respective reserve percentages prescribed by the Board of Governors to find the amount of reserves needed to meet the board's requirement. It then substracts from this "amount of reserves needed" its average holdings of vault cash at the close of business daily in the week ending December 2, and the remainder is the reserve balance it should have at the district Federal Reserve bank on an average daily close-of-business basis in the week ending December 16. (To put it in other words, reserves that satisfy the requirements are average daily balances at the Reserve bank in the reserve-computation week plus average daily holdings of vault cash in the second preceding week.)

To illustrate, assume that a country bank had average daily demand deposits of $40 million, average daily savings deposits of $35 million, average daily time deposits of other kinds of $25 million, and average daily vault cash of $1,800,000 in the week ending December 2; and that the reserve requirements in effect were those that obtain in December 1970, as given above. The computation just described would be as follows:

Required for demand deposits:	
On $5 million at 12½ percent	$ 625,000
On $35 million at 13 percent	4,550,000
Required for savings deposits:	
On $35 million at 3 percent	1,050,000
Required for other time deposits:	
On $5 million at 3 percent	150,000
On $20 million at 5 percent	1,000,000
Total required reserves	7,375,000
Less average daily holdings of vault cash	1,800,000
Average daily reserves required at Federal Reserve bank during week ending December 16	$5,575,000

If the member bank had only $5,400,000 in its reserve account at the Federal Reserve bank at the close of business on the first 6 days of the week

---

the deposits of foreign branches to the extent that, in excess of certain "base-period" amounts, they are "used" to buy assets from the parent member banks and to grant loans to residents of the United States.

ending December 16, it could still satisfy the requirement exactly by build-ing up its reserve on the seventh day to $6,625,000. Its average daily re-serve account would then be

$$\frac{(6 \times \$5,400,000) + \$6,625,000}{7}$$ or $5,575,000.

Reports, Carryovers, and Penalties   As events actually occur (continuing the illustration), our member bank would make its regular weekly report to its Federal Reserve bank on Thursday, December 3, giving its daily fig-ures for demand and time deposits and holdings of vault cash[2] for the week ending December 2. The Federal Reserve bank kindly undertakes to do all the necessary computations. Two weeks later, it would report to the mem-ber bank what its requirements were for the week ended December 16, how much it had in its reserves to satisfy the requirements, how much these reserves were in excess of the requirements or deficient, and the amount of its "carry-over" if any.

As for this carry-over, the rule is that any excess reserves in any reserve-computation week may be applied to meeting the requirements of the next week, and that any deficiency in a reserve-computation week may be made up or offset, without penalty, by an excess position in the following week. But carry-overs of excesses and deficiencies are restricted to amounts not exceeding 2 percent of the requirements in the week from which the carry-over is taken. Moreover, carry-overs that are not used up or made up in the following week may not be carried to succeeding weeks. For illustra-tion, assume that a member bank has reserve requirements of $100,000 in 2 successive weeks with no carry-overs from the week preceding the first of these 2 weeks. If its average daily reserves as applicable to the first week actually amounted to $98,000, it could make up the deficiency by carrying average daily reserves of $102,000 applicable to the second week. Or if its average daily reserves applicable to the first week were $102,000, it could get by with average daily reserves of $98,000 applicable to the second week. If, on the other hand, it had average reserves of only $95,000 applica-ble to the first week, it would be immediately subject to a penalty on the deficiency of $3000 not subject to the carry-over privilege, or if the bank had average daily reserves of $98,000 applicable to the first week and only $100,000 applicable to the second week, it would be subject to a penalty on the deficiency of $2000 of the first week which, after being carried over, had not been offset in the second week.

Penalties for deficiencies of the kinds just illustrated are levied on their amounts at a per-annum rate equal to 2 percentage points above the dis-count rate for regular lending by the Federal Reserve banks to member banks. With the regular discount rate at, say, 5 percent, the penalty for a week's average daily deficiency of, say, $200,000 would be $200,000 × 0.07 × $\frac{7}{365}$, or approximately $269. But there is not much sense in incur-

---

[2]And for its transactions in the federal funds market, as discussed later in this chapter.

ring penalties for deficiencies, since member banks may borrow from the Reserve banks at the lower discount rate if unable to clear up deficiencies by other means.[3]

Requirements and Management   All the computations involved in the determination of required reserves, excesses, deficiencies, and carry-overs on the basis of some figures from 1 week and others from 2 weeks earlier might seem to be unduly complicated. Actually, however, the opposite is true: reserve management for the member bank is made much easier than it had been with former arrangements. The managers of its money position know well ahead of time, so to say, how much reserves they are going to need as balances at the Federal Reserve bank on an average daily basis during a given reserve-computation week. They do not wait for the Federal Reserve report to find what their reserve position was for the past week; instead, they make their own computations of requirements, and then, during the reserve-computation week, take actions to adjust their reserve balances to keep them in line with what they must be.

Actions to eliminate deficiencies in reserve accounts

The principal kinds of action that member banks are likely to take to increase their reserve balances at the Federal Reserve banks, should they be running deficiencies, may be outlined as follows:

1. To transfer balances from correspondent banks to the Federal Reserve banks, if these balances are thought to be more than enough to compensate the correspondents for their services. For larger banks, however, this is an unlikely kind of action, as they will customarily avoid keeping excessive balances with correspondents.
2. To "buy" from other member banks excess reserves that they have on deposit at the Federal Reserve banks, that is, to buy "federal funds." *Buying* in this context means borrowing, and *federal funds* are, by definition, deposits at the Federal Reserve banks. (We should especially note that they have nothing to do with the finances of the federal government or the Treasury.) Deficient member banks may buy federal funds from correspondent banks, by direct negotiation with other banks in their local communities or elsewhere, or in the open market. The federal funds market is a very important subdivision of the money market; as such, it will be examined in some detail shortly.
3. To demand repayment of outstanding "call loans" to security dealers. As a rule, the security dealers expect that such repayment demands will be made from time to time and do not resent them. In order to

---

[3]For an analysis of Federal Reserve lending policies and practices, see Chapters 17 and 20.

repay, the security dealers are ordinarily able to borrow from other banks, so that the net effect is for the calling bank to gain reserves and for the banks that grant new loans to the dealers to lose reserves —much as in a federal funds transaction. While member banks typically have other call or demand loans on their books, especially "margin loans" to individual customers for the speculative purchasing and carrying of stocks, they would be unlikely to call these as a means of adjusting their reserve positions. These customers would surely resent repayment calls for such a purpose, and many would probably be inclined to shift their banking business elsewhere.

4. To borrow from the Federal Reserve banks. As a rule, the member banks are reluctant to borrow from the Reserve banks, and they much prefer to adjust their reserve positions by buying federal funds from other member banks, as long as interest rates on federal funds do not significantly exceed the Federal Reserve discount rate. If, however, federal funds are not available or if the interest-rate differential is judged to be excessive, member banks overcome their reluctance and turn to the Reserve banks for loans.

5. To sell assets held as "secondary reserves." This is the most probable action when a bank's money managers decide that a reserve deficiency that has developed is likely to be "chronic"—that it is likely to continue without interruption for several weeks or months. Though it would probably be possible to make up the deficiency by purchases of federal funds from day to day, it is also probable that the interest cost on federal funds would exceed the earnings rate on the secondary reserves to be sold. Accordingly, profit goals would suggest sales from the secondary reserves as the better course.

Federal funds market

As already defined, federal funds are deposit balances at the Federal Reserve banks. They consist very largely of the reserve accounts of member banks; but as being or becoming available to the commercial banks, other financial institutions, and nonfinancial business corporations and individuals, they include also the clearing balances of nonmember banks at the Reserve banks, outstanding checks drawn on the Treasury and drawn by foreign governments and central banks on their deposit balances at the Reserve banks, and outstanding officers' checks (cashiers' checks) issued by the Reserve banks themselves.

Market Sectors and Participants As already indicated also, the market for federal funds is important as a major subdivision of the money market chiefly because it comprises the facilities by which member banks sell excess reserves to other member banks that have deficiencies. The market has many geographical sectors, ranging from sectors limited to given cities to the nation-wide facilities, with the latter including, as it were, facilities for negotiated transactions and open-market facilities. Member banks in given cities, communities, and regions frequently buy and sell excess reserves among one another by direct negotiation. At the same time, many of these banks participate in the national market, especially by way of transactions with their correspondent banks located in the principal cities. A metropolitan correspondent bank will typically sell federal funds to out-of-town banks that keep deposit balances with it even when it itself has reserve deficiencies. It does so in the expectation of being able to obtain federal funds elsewhere in order to offset these sales as well as to clear its existing deficiencies. Typically, too, it will buy excess reserves from the out-of-town banks even when it already has excess reserves of its own, expecting to be able to sell the excesses from both sources to other banks.

From the standpoint of volumes of transactions, the large metropolitan banks are, indeed, the principal buyers and sellers of federal funds by reason of large transactions among one another as well as transactions with the out-of-town banks for which they serve as correspondents. Transactions among the metropolitan banks themselves include purchases and sales directly negotiated and transactions in the open market. For open-market transactions, banks simply notify the security dealers who act as federal funds brokers how much they have to sell and what rates of interest they are asking, and banks that wish to buy, on calling the brokers, are told what banks are selling, how much they are offering, and the rates of interest asked. In offering federal funds in the open market, a bank makes its offering, in effect, to all banks that want to buy and that are willing to pay the interest rate designated. As the open market functions, however, the offerings tend to be limited to large banks since individual sales usually amount to at least $1 million.

Net Buyers and Sellers   While some of the smaller member banks engage in federal funds transactions only occasionally, the large ones typically buy and sell large amounts from day to day, and often, in fact, they both buy and sell on the same day. Collectively, however, they are almost always net buyers as their positions stand at the close of business from day to day. Thus the large banks that voluntarily make weekly reports of their assets and liabilities to the Federal Reserve—approximately 340 in number—reported that their holdings of federal funds purchased totaled $17,013 million at the close of business on September 16, 1970, while their outstanding sales were $8192 million.[4] For the week ended that day, the forty-six largest member banks reported average daily purchases of $9240 million and average daily sales of $2456 million, with their average net purchases of $6784 million[5] amounting to approximately 54 percent of

---

[4]*Federal Reserve Bulletin*, November 1970, pp. A26, A30.
[5]*Ibid.*, p. A8.

their average daily required reserves for the week! Such figures indicate, of course, that the smaller banks are collectively net sellers of federal funds in large amounts—something to be expected, since these banks are much more likely than the larger ones to carry excess reserves more or less continuously as a matter of policy.

Procedure   Most transactions in federal funds are 1-day deals, and the mechanics of completing them are quite simple. The most common procedure is to give a Federal Reserve bank an order by telephone call or telegram to credit the reserve account of the buying bank for the dollar amount of a sale and to debit the reserve account of the selling bank for the same amount, with an additional instruction to reverse these entries on the following day. In a separate action, the buying bank then pays the selling bank interest at the agreed-upon rate on the 1-day "loan."

SECONDARY RESERVES

A principal reason why the managers of member banks think that reserve requirements imposed on them by the Federal Reserve are excessive for protection-of-solvency objectives is their conviction that solvency can be protected just as well by holdings of readily marketable short-term securities of high quality that can be quickly converted into cash if and when it is needed to meet cash drains—securities that they classify collectively as "secondary reserves." Since securities held as secondary reserves yield interest income, their preference for these assets over nonearning primary reserves as a means of protecting solvency is not difficult to understand.

Functions of secondary reserves

Replenishment of Primary Reserves   Even with primary reserve requirements that they regard as excessive, bank managers generally conclude that they still must hold substantial amounts of secondary reserves— especially if they try to manage their primary reserves in a manner to keep them no greater, or not much greater, than is legally required. Because deficiencies are subject to penalties, they want to have on hand noncash assets that can be quickly turned into cash without significant losses when deficiencies are likely to be so prolonged that buying federal funds on a day-to-day basis or borrowing from the Federal Reserve banks would hardly be an appropriate remedy.

Meeting Loan Demands and Other Commitments   But banks want to be prepared to do more than to replenish cash that has been drained in ordinary day-to-day withdrawals of depositors that exceed their new deposits. The typical commercial bank has outstanding at all times many "lines of credit" by which it has made commitments to grant loans of specified amounts within specified periods to business corporations, other business enterprises, and other customers. As the bank must ordinarily expect the proceeds from loans to be withdrawn rather quickly,[6] it will want to hold secondary reserves sufficient, through quick conversion into cash, to cover extraordinary withdrawals expected to result from line-of-credit loans. And if the bank has reason to expect extraordinary cash drains at other times for other reasons, as withdrawals of paper money and coins during the Christmas shopping season or to meet commitments to local governments to buy issues of their short-term warrants pending tax receipts, it will want to hold secondary reserves in proportions related to these expectations. It would obviously make little sense to hold primary reserves for weeks or months in anticipation of drains for reasons such as these, when the wherewithal could be held temporarily in interest-bearing secondary reserves.

All this does not mean, of course, that a bank would decide that at any given time it must hold enough secondary reserves to meet *all* extraordinary cash drains expected to occur within, say, a year. Loans are repaid, municipalities collect taxes and redeem their warrants, and paper money and coins flow back after the Christmas shopping season. Hence the management of secondary reserves must take account of replenishment to be expected from such sources as well as expected drains.

Qualities of secondary reserves

High Credit Quality and Ready Marketability   What kinds of interest-paying securities qualify for inclusion among banks' secondary reserves? The answer has already been largely given in the mention of readily marketable short-term high-quality securities. That securities held as secondary reserves should be of high quality from the standpoint of the credit standing of their issuers hardly requires argument. Since secondary reserves are held in the expectation that there will be a need to convert them into cash to meet cash-payment obligations, one wants to be sure that their issuers will surely pay them off at maturity—that possibilities of default are nonexistent or, at worst, extremely slight.

But a bank may need cash before the maturity dates of the securities it holds as secondary reserves; hence the requirement for ready marketability. Thus small outstanding security issues of obscure business corporations or obscure local governments, even when of high quality, are not likely to qualify because of probable difficulties in finding buyers for them at fair prices should it be necessary to sell before their maturities. Ready marketability implies, therefore, broad markets in which there are many potential demanders who will surely come into the market to buy,

---

[6]See Chapter 7.

if not at the offering price at the moment, at offering prices *in ordinary circumstances* only slightly lower.

Emphasis on Short Maturities   The reference to market prices indicates why emphasis is given to *short-term* securities for secondary reserves. There is a risk of loss on the sale of any interest-bearing security because of increases in market rates of interest—a risk that attaches to Treasury obligations, which, of course, are of impeachable credit standing, as well as to securities of other issuers of eminent credit reputations. If a high-quality security is bought at a price that will yield 5 percent per annum if held to maturity, and if a month later market yields on securities of the same class with equal remaining periods to maturity have risen to 6 percent, the market price of the security bought earlier will surely fall below the price paid for it. But because of the short maturity, the drop in its market price will be quite moderate. The drop would be much greater if the maturity were 5, 10, or 20 years. In fact, we can say that the longer the maturity, the greater the drop in market price would be.

In emphasizing short maturities for the securities acquired as secondary reserves, therefore, banks have in mind the absurdity of investing in something whose loss on sale, should sale be necessary, may equal or exceed the interest earned during the holding period. It would be just as well or better to hold primary reserves instead.

Inclusion of Intermediate-Term Securities   While "short term" generally means maturities of not more than 1 year, and while banks' secondary reserves are usually concentrated in short-term securities as thus defined, many bank managers regard their secondary reserves as also including readily marketable high-quality securities with maturities of 2 or 3 years, and sometimes even 4 or 5 years. In their cash-flow forecasting, they distinguish between net cash outflows that are very likely to take place within a year and those that, in the same period, are possible but hardly to be confidently expected. For the highly probable net cash outflows, they want securities for their secondary reserves that are truly short-term (as customarily defined), but for the possible additional outflows they are often willing to take some greater risks of market-price drops in inter-mediate-term securities, provided that interest yields on them are significantly higher than on the short-term securities. There is always the consoling thought that intermediate-term securities become short-term ones with the passing of time and another that substantial capital gains may be realized on the sale of intermediate-term securities if there is a significant fall in market rates of interest.

Types of investments for secondary reserves

As suggested by the earlier discussion in this chapter of primary reserve management, excess cash that is expected to be available for only a few days or weeks can probably be most conveniently sold from day to day in the federal funds market, granted as call loans to security dealers, or granted as time loans to the dealers for the number of days or weeks of expected availability. Should, however, a demand for federal funds and dealer loans be lacking (or inconvenient to arrange, as for smaller banks), the typical bank that wants to promptly put idle cash to work would probably invest in Treasury bills having approximately the same number of days or weeks until maturity.

For the investment of excess cash expected to be available for longer periods if not invested but expected to be needed for cash drains within 1 year, commercial banks collectively appear to concentrate their choice rather heavily on Treasury bills and other Treasury obligations maturing within a year. A plentitude of such Treasury issues is available, and banks can generally get as much as they want without a bloody scramble in the market, and the secondary market is "broad, deep, and resilient" so that opportunities for quick resale at relatively stable prices can usually be anticipated with confidence. At the end of 1969, commercial bank holdings of Treasury obligations maturing within 1 year were estimated at approximately $16.8 billion—an amount equal to about one third of their primary reserves.[7] At that time, the commercial banks' holdings of securities of state and local governments exceeded their holdings of Treasury obligations of all maturities, and although maturity breakdowns are not available, it is probable that the commercial banks were classifying substantial proportions of these municipal securities as secondary reserves for reasons of high quality, short maturities, and ready marketability. Given these qualifications, indeed, commercial banks generally have reason to prefer such securities to Treasury obligations because of their tax-exemption feature. Likewise for security issues of federal agencies: although commercial banks' holdings of these issues are much less than their portfolios of direct Treasury obligations and municipals, they have reason to prefer them for short-term secondary reserves over direct Treasury obligations because of their higher interest yields, provided, as always, that they are among those that are readily marketable. Finally, larger banks often have holdings of bankers' acceptances that they regard as excellent for their secondary reserves, and similarly for holdings of open-market commercial paper of smaller banks.

For secondary reserves to meet cash drains that are thought to be possible within 1 year but not probable the commercial banks very largely confine their security selection to Treasury and municipal securities having intermediate-term maturities. In fact, their holdings of intermediate-term Treasury obligations usually substantially exceed their holdings of Treasury

---

[7]Derived from the Treasury survey of the ownership of its securities as reported in the *Federal Reserve Bulletin,* November 1970, p. A43, and from Federal Deposit Insurance Corporation, *Annual Report,* 1969, p. 258.

issues having maturities within 1 year, as at the end of 1969 when their investment in issues having maturities from 1 to 5 years was estimated at $27.4 billion.[8]

FOR REVIEW

1. What is meant by a bank's money position? Why it its management said to include forecasting?
2. What kinds of assets are included in banks' primary reserves? What kinds satisfy the reserve requirements that apply to member banks?
3. What classes of banks are likely to have primary reserve needs over and above the legal reserve requirements? For what reasons are they likely to have additional needs?
4. What purposes are served by legal reserve requirements?
5. Why do banks try to limit as closely as possible the portion of reserves they hold as vault cash?
6. What is the general attitude of member banks toward keeping demand balances with correspondent banks? the attitude of nonmember banks?
7. How does the Federal Reserve classify demand deposits and time deposits for the application of its reserve requirements?
8. Within what percentage ranges does the Federal Reserve have the power to set reserve requirements applicable to the deposits of member banks?
9. What can commercial banks do to eliminate deficiencies in their reserves as legally required?
10. What are federal funds? What accounts for the huge volume of daily transactions in the federal funds market?
11. By what procedures are loans in the federal funds market customarily granted and repaid?
12. For what reasons do commercial banks hold certain kinds of assets that they call "secondary reserves"?
13. Why is shortness of maturity of secondary reserves emphasized? ready marketability?
14. Do Treasury bills typically qualify for banks' secondary reserve? Treasury notes? bankers' acceptances?

PROBLEM

In the week ending Wednesday, June 2, the average daily demand deposits of the First National Bank amounted to $12 million, its savings

---

[8]Derived from the Treasury ownership survey as reported in the *Federal Reserve Bulletin*, November 1970, p. A43.

deposits, to $9 million, and its other time deposits, to $5 million. Its average daily holdings of vault cash in that week amounted to $400,000.

A. For the "reserve computation week" ending June 16, what average daily reserve balance at the Federal Reserve bank would the First National Bank need to satisfy the reserve requirements applying to it as a member bank, assuming these requirements to be 12 percent for demand deposits, 3 percent for savings deposits, and 4 percent for other time deposits?

B. Assuming that the First National Bank had an allowable carry-over of $150,000 of excess reserves from the reserve computation period ending June 9, what would it need as an average daily reserve balance at the Federal Reserve bank for the week ending June 16?

C. Assuming that the average daily reserve balance of the First National bank at the Federal Reserve bank amounted to $1,437,000 in the week ending June 16, that it had no carry-over from the preceding week, and that it did not have excess reserves in the following week, what would be the penalty for the deficiency in the week ending June 16, with the Federal Reserve discount rate at 5 percent?

CHAPTER 14

LOANS AND DISCOUNTS

LOANS AND INVESTMENTS OF COMMERCIAL BANKS

Although commercial banks are privately owned business enterprises, they have been given the extraordinary power to create money in the form of demand deposits, as well as to extinguish money so created. How wisely do they use this power? How well do they serve the public interest in using it? We know that the power is chiefly used in the expansion and contraction of their loans and investments, so that the question of public interest can be restated as three others: For whom do the commercial banks create money? For what purposes? Do these purposes serve the public interest? In this chapter and in Chapter 15 we will be looking for answers to these three questions, although answers to the third will generally be left for the student to express. In the present chapter, we shall be concerned with the creation of money by way of the lending operations of commercial banks—with the outlets, purposes, and administration of loans—and in Chapter 15 with the more impersonal process of money creation through open-market purchases of investment securities. With regard to the latter, we have already considered in Chapter 13 commercial bank investment in secondary reserves; and with regard to both avenues of money creation, we have had references at numerous places in other earlier chapters.

In the course of our present inquiry, we shall see that the commercial banks create money in order to enable business enterprises to meet current operating expenses, such as are incurred in buying raw materials and finished goods and in employing labor, to acquire machinery and equipment, and even, in some instances, to acquire plant sites and buildings; to enable farmers to obtain seed, feed, and fertilizer, to pay hired hands, to drain and fence land, and to erect various kinds of farm buildings; to enable governmental bodies—federal, state, and local—to meet all kinds of expenditures of both the current and capital kinds; to help consumers to buy automobiles, household furniture, electrical appliances, and other consumer goods and services; to assist individuals and families to buy residential property and to modernize their homes; to provide funds to speculators to buy and hold stocks and bonds, commodities and real property; and to support and encourage many other kinds of activities.

Three viewpoints

The study of the lending and investment operations of commercial banks should not be looked upon simply as the analysis of certain kinds of managerial policies and techniques. If it were only this, the devotion of two chapters and part of a third in this textbook would be quite unwarranted. It is true that the student who plans a career in commercial banking may be most interested in policies and techniques, as he will expect to apply them when he becomes a loan or investment officer; but the purpose of this lengthy treatment of loans and investments extends far beyond the interest of the prospective banker, worthy though those interests may be.

Anyone who ever expects to borrow from the commercial banks—whether by obtaining direct loans or, as an officer of a business corporation or a governmental body, by selling securities to them—should be much concerned with bank loan and investment policies and techniques. Under what circumstances is it possible to obtain a loan from a bank or to sell investment securities to it? What terms do banks prescribe? What do they want in the way of collateral security? What kinds of loans do they favor? How much can they lend to individual borrowers? Are there certain kinds of loans that they are not permitted to grant? How is the credit position of the prospective borrower evaluated? What is the significance of endorsements and guaranties? What documents are used? Questions such as these indicate that the capacity of bank customers to manage their own financial affairs must be immeasurably enhanced if they know what course banks take in their lending and investing activities.

Finally, the study of bank lending and investing policies and techniques is important for an understanding of the business culture of our times. The student who is little interested in finance as such must realize, nevertheless, that the commercial banks, by granting loans and buying securities, exert a profound influence on the course of economic development. To the extent that newly created demand deposits are spent in hiring idle factors of production to increase output, the commercial banks would appear to act wisely in creating them; but to the extent that they are used merely to bid up the prices of factors already employed, the banks would appear to act against the public interest. While the banks themselves can argue, with good reason, that ultimate responsibility for the volume of demand deposits rests with the Federal Reserve, they can hardly deny that, by picking and choosing among loan applicants and security issuers, they retain considerable power of influence over output, employment, and price developments. And even less, indeed, can they deny that their power is very great, through picking and choosing, to determine which business enterprises, farmers, households, public bodies, and so on will be encouraged and promoted through their loans and investments and which will be allowed to go begging. They are truly important as arbiters of economic destiny.

Preference for lending

Reasons for Preferring Loans　Collectively, commercial banks much prefer lending to investment in securities. After acquiring securities for their secondary reserves in amounts thought to be sufficient, they typically choose to devote all or most of their remaining lending and investing capacity to loans, provided that loan demands of credit-worthy applicants are great enough to use up this capacity, and provided that they are not fearful of sharp adverse criticism by bank examiners. They are chiefly geared for lending. Most of their personnel of officer ranks are lending officers, and by comparison, their investment officers are few. They can usually earn higher rates of interest on loans than on investment securities, after allowing for the much higher costs incurred in loan administration than in the management of investment portfolios. But, more than this, they know that their prestige and popularity in the communities they serve would suffer severe damage were they to reject many loan demands of credit-worthy applicants while expanding their holdings of securities not needed for secondary reserves. And Congress and the state legislatures might raise questions of why they should have money-creating powers.

Experience in the 1960s　The preference of commercial banks for loans was rather well-illustrated by the generally divergent changes from year to year in the volumes of the outstanding loans and security holdings of all insured commercial banks in the 1960s, details of which are presented in Table 14-1. In the analysis of these data, we should keep in mind that we had a recession beginning in 1960 and extending into early 1961; that recovery was slow at first and loan demand moderate; that the loan demand began to accelerate in 1962 and reached proportions of extraordinary intensity in the years 1965–1969, except for some weakening in 1967; that the Federal Reserve was liberal in supplying the commercial banks with reserves into 1966, when its monetary policy became extremely tight; and that the Federal Reserve's monetary policy was expansive in 1967, moderately restrictive in 1968, and extremely tight again in 1969.

In 1961, therefore, the insured banks were able both to take care of the moderate expansion in the loan demand and to add an even larger amount to their holdings of securities. Thereafter, however, taking care of the loan demand clearly took strong precedence over adding to investment portfolios, and this was so even in 1967, when additions to security holdings slightly

Table 14-1   Changes in Outstanding Loans and Security Holdings of Insured Commercial Banks, 1961–1969[a] (in millions of dollars)

YEAR	LOANS	U.S. TREASURY	STATE AND LOCAL	OTHER	TOTAL SECURITIES
		SECURITY HOLDINGS			
1961	7,285	5569	2,767	305	8,642
1962	15,216	− 125	4,479	896	5,250
1963	15,910	−3154	5,028	686	2,560
1964	19,163	− 224	3,733	− 21	3,488
1965	26,018	3378	5,136	933[b]	2,691
1966	17,342	−3306	2,352	1589[b]	635
1967	18,254	6325	8,989	3663[b]	18,978
1968	29,272	1942	8,571	1466	11,978
1969	24,487	−9641	552	− 768	− 9,857
Totals	172,947	−5992	41,607	8749	44,365

[a] Decreases indicated by minus sign; all other figures are increases. In some instances, items do not add exactly to horizontal totals because of rounding.

[b] Excluding changes in stock holdings of national banks except stock of the Federal Reserve banks.

Source: Federal Deposit Insurance Corporation, *Annual Reports.*

exceeded the loan expansion. The loan demand weakened somewhat in that year because of a "mini-recession" that occurred in its early months. Especially valiant were the substantial expansion in loans in the tight-money year 1966 accompanied by a slight growth in security holdings, and, much more so, the substantial loan expansion of 1969 largely made possible by the sharp cutback in security holdings.

CLASSIFICATION OF LOANS

The loans of commercial banks can best be classified on the basis of what borrowers intend to do with the money they obtain. On this basis, there are six major classes: business loans, farm loans, loans for the purchasing and carrying of securities, consumer loans, home mortgage loans, and a miscellaneous class including interbank loans, direct loans to governmental bodies, and loans granted by banks to their own officers and employees. This is essentially the classification used by the Federal Deposit Insurance Corporation in its compilations of loan statistics of insured banks, of which a sample is presented in Table 14-2. Although all kinds of real-estate loans are combined in a single class in the FDIC reports, they can easily be redistributed to the other classes on the basis of the subdivisions listed, with real-estate loans "secured by other properties" being allocated to business loans. "Loans to other financial institutions" are chiefly loans to sales finance and consumer finance companies. Since the finance companies are primarily lenders to consumers, much of their borrowings from the commercial banks eventually get into the hands of consumers; but from

Table 14-2   **Loans and Discounts of All Insured Commercial Banks, December 31, 1969ᵃ (dollar amounts in millions)**

DESCRIPTION	AMOUNT	PERCENT OF TOTAL
Commercial and industrial (including open-market paper)	108,394	37.8
Loans to farmers (excluding loans on real estate)	10,324	3.6
Loans to brokers and dealers in securities	5,647	2.0
Other loans for purchasing or carrying securities	3,995	1.4
Real-estate loans:		
Secured by farmland	3,993	1.4
Secured by residential properties:		
Insured by the Federal Housing Administration	7,825	2.7
Guaranteed by the Veterans Administration	2,596	0.9
Not insured or guaranteed by FHA or VA	33,859	11.8
Secured by other properties	22,053	7.7
Subtotal	70,326	24.5
Other loans to individuals:		
Passenger-automobile installment loans	22,706	7.9
Credit cards and related plans	3,722	1.3
Other retail consumer installment loans	6,270	2.2
Residential repair and modernization installment loans	3,655	1.3
Other installment loans for personal expenditure	9,936	3.5
Single-payment loans for personal expenditure	17,066	5.9
Subtotal	63,356	22.1
Loans to domestic commercial and foreign banks	2,425	0.8
Loans to other financial institutions	14,939	5.2
All other loans (including overdrafts)	7,347	2.6
Total	286,752	100.0

ᵃ Before deduction of reserves for losses and excluding sales of federal funds.
Source: Federal Deposit Insurance Corporation, *Annual Report*, 1969, p. 259. (Percentages supplied by the author.)

the standpoint of the commercial banks themselves, loans granted to the finance companies are simply a subclass of business loans.

Business loans

The general order of business loans are usually subclassified as short-term loans and term loans. A year is the generally recognized dividing line between the two subclasses—any business loan having an original maturity of 1 year or less is a short-term loan, and any having an original maturity of more than 1 year is a term loan. As a rule, the short-term loans are for working capital purposes, while term loans provide money for the acquisition of machinery and other equipment, so that the subclassification, although it appears to be based upon the time element, actually tends to distinguish among purposes.

Short-term Loans   Commercial banks hold in high favor short-term loans to business enterprises for productive purposes. No matter how widely they extend their lending operations in new fields, they seem to accept a unique responsibility for the supplying of working capital to business firms —almost as if working capital loans are thought to justify their possession of the money-creating power. Their attitude is that every business enterprise must have money to buy stocks of goods, whether raw materials, semifinished manufactures, or finished goods, to carry an appropriate volume of its customers' obligations (accounts receivable), to pay payrolls, and to meet other current operating expenses; that it should have enough money of its own to take care of a moderate volume of activity without outside help; and that it is fully justified in going to the banks to borrow when activity expands beyond the "moderate" level. If an enterprise operates for 4 months at 60 percent of capacity and for the remaining 8 months of the year at full capacity, it should be able to operate through the less active period with its own resources, but it has good reason to call on the banks for assistance in stepping up operations in the more active period. The insistence of many bankers on the "annual cleanup" of working capital loans—that is, that the borrower should have no outstanding working capital loans for some period of the year—is an expression of this attitude.

Short-term loans for working capital are often described as "self-liquidating." The idea is that the money provided by the banks is spent on productive operations that, in a short period of time and in the normal course of affairs, should produce a return flow of money with which the loans can be repaid. If a merchant borrows to acquire a stock of goods for resale, and if he sells for cash, a month or 2 may be sufficient for the self-liquidation of the loan; if he sells on account, allowing his customers, say, 60 days for payment, the loan may require a maturity of 3 or 4 months, but it should be no less self-liquidating—to be repaid out of the merchant's collections from his customers.

Lines of Credit   In connection with their short-term lending for business purposes, commercial banks often establish *lines of credit* for customers who borrow frequently and who are faithful in fulfilling the terms of their obligations. A line of credit is a commitment of a bank to a customer to lend him, within a stated period of time, any amount that he cares to take up to a specified maximum. As lines of credit can be opened for a month, a quarter, a production season, a year, or other convenient period, they enable bank customers to plan their business operations with confidence that the necessary money will be forthcoming as it is needed. Customers who have lines of credit avoid prolonged negotiations every time they want to increase their borrowings. Instead, the negotiations take place when the lines of credit are applied for. A manufacturer who has a line of credit of $50,000 may actually borrow only $25,000 or $30,000 if that is all he needs, but he knows that his request for additional money will be honored whenever he presents it.

A bank's obligations to meet the terms of its outstanding lines of credit are usually described as a "moral responsibility," but sometimes banks provide "firm commitments" whereby they bind themselves contractually to grant such loans as the customers request up to specified maximums. For both kinds of lines, it is customary for banks to charge the full rate of interest only on amounts actually borrowed; and for firm commitments, they usually charge a nominal rate, possible 0.5 percent or thereabout, on the unused portions of the lines.

Although lines of credit are quite advantageous to bank customers for business planning, they have restrictive effects upon the banks' own freedom of action. Even in periods of economic crisis, they will make every effort to honor requests for loans coming from customers with established lines of credit, whether or not these lines are firm commitments. Thus at times when the banks may be anxious to convert earning assets into money, they will surely feel obligated to grant new loans in accordance with the terms of their established lines.

Term Loans   The proportion of total business loans granted by commercial banks having original maturities of more than 1 year—and therefore classified as "term loans"—is surprisingly large. There is no regular reporting of term lending by commercial banks generally, but the Federal Reserve publishes monthly reports of outstanding term loans of about 160 large commercial banks, as well as quarterly changes in them. At the end of September 1970, for example, the term loans of these banks amounted to $32,622 million equal to 40 percent of total "commercial and industrial" loans of $81,168. The proportions of term loans to total loans of this class were especially large in advances to the mining industry (including crude petroleum and natural gas) at 83 percent; to petroleum refiners, at 76 percent; transportation companies, 75 percent; manufacturers in primary metals, 72 percent; and unclassified foreign business firms, 73 percent. Other large proportions of term loans were outstanding to firms in the chemical and rubber industries at 64 percent; manufacturers of transportation equipment, 55 percent; machinery manufacturers, 49 percent; and firms in the service industries, 44 percent.[1]

Term loans are granted by commercial banks to finance the acquisition

---

[1]*Federal Reserve Bulletin,* November 1970, p. A31. (Percentages supplied by the author.)

of facilities, such as machinery and equipment by manufacturers; counters, shelves, showcases, and delivery trucks by retail merchants; the furnishings and equipment of hotels, restaurants, theaters, beauty salons, and repair shops; office facilities of professional people; and busses, trucks, and trailers of transportation companies. And despite the rule of "annual cleanup," some of them are granted for working capital. Banks account for their large volumes of term lending on several grounds: that many of the borrowers could not conveniently and economically raise longer-term money by the sale of stocks and bonds; that the term loans simply substitute for intermediate- and long-term corporation bonds that they would be inclined to buy anyway; that portions of most term loans are really short-term advances, because of contractual provisions requiring installment repayment; and that term lending is more realistic than the older practice of granting short-term loans with "understandings" that the loans would be renewed from time to time.

Farm loans

In a broad sense, farm loans are business loans, for farming is a kind of business activity. Like the manufacturer or merchant, the farmer needs short-term money to buy raw materials—seed, feed, fertilizer, and other supplies—to meet payrolls, and to pay other current operating expenses; and like the manufacturer or merchant, he needs intermediate- and long-term funds to buy land, to prepare it for productive use, to erect buildings, and to buy machinery and equipment. Commercial banks located in farming areas may have few outlets for productive loans other than those that develop from farmers' needs; for them, indeed, "business loans" must be largely farm loans.

Nevertheless, it is customary to differentiate between business loans and farm loans because lending to farmers poses several kinds of problems not ordinarily encountered in other areas of lending. For one thing, it is difficult to draw the line between the farm as a business enterprise and the farm as a household. For another, many farmers are more dependent on commercial banks and other financial institutions for loans than the average businessman in other fields. Again, the fate of farm loans is closely bound with natural forces—temperatures, rainfall, winds, and so on. Most important of all, the long-continued problem of general maladjustment in our agricultural economy—evidenced by recurring surpluses of some crops, soil exhaustion in one-crop areas, subsistence farming, and the like —make the administration of farm loans a specialized type of activity.

Loans for purchasing and carrying securities

To provide customers with funds to buy and hold investment securities, commercial banks grant loans of three subclasses: (1) loans to investment banking firms for the flotation of new bond and stock issues; (2) call and time loans to brokers and dealers who operate in the securities markets; and (3) loans to individuals who want to buy securities "on margin."

In undertaking to float issues of securities for corporations and governments, investment banking firms generally agree to pay the issuers for all the securities at stipulated prices within short periods. Their usual expectation is that quick sales of the securities to investors will give them the money for these payments. Sometimes, however, sales fail to keep pace with expectations, and payment dates find the investment bankers short of funds. In such circumstances, commercial banks are asked for loans to make up the deficiencies. These loans are usually safeguarded by pledges of the unsold securities, although other collateral is sometimes required.

Most of the funds borrowed by individuals for the "purchasing and carrying of securities" are supplied by commercial banks, either by direct loans to these people (item 3 in the foregoing list), or by loans to brokers and dealers (item 2) who in turn lend to their customers individually. Neither of these two classes of loans is self-liquidating, since the securities involved in the transactions are generally long-term issues—or perpetual in complexion, as in the case of common stocks. Nevertheless, they are generally short-term loans, and indeed, many are call or demand loans since the ultimate borrowers are speculators who expect to close out their "positions" in given securities within short periods, either to "take profits" or to limit losses; and the close outs give them the money to repay the banks, or to repay the dealers and brokers who can then repay the banks.

The bulk of the loans granted by commercial banks for speculative transactions in common stocks and bonds convertible into stocks are subject to restrictions imposed by the Federal Reserve Board of Governors by its Regulation U (by authority of the federal Securities Exchange Act), and brokers and dealers are subject to comparable restrictions by the board's Regulation T in lending to their customers. Both of these regulations set "margin requirements" that limit individual loans to specified percentages of the value of the securities acquired, and their objective is to prevent excessive use of borrowed funds, as judged by the board, for speculation in stocks and convertible bonds.[2]

Consumer loans

Consumer loans are granted to individuals for buying for their own use automobiles, television sets, other electrical equipment for the home, and household furniture, for meeting the costs of home modernization and repair, for "consolidating" personal debts already outstanding elsewhere, and so on. As the use to which a consumer loan is put brings no direct financial

---

[2]For further details about these regulations and their objectives, see Chapter 20.

returns, the borrower must have some unrelated means to pay—typically, of course, a "good" job. In judging consumer loan applications, therefore, banks must place great weight on the integrity of the applicants and the adequacy and stability of their income-earning capacities.

Until about 1930, commercial banks generally regarded consumer loans with strong disfavor. They granted loans to sales finance companies and other institutions that themselves were lending to consumers, but they could classify these as business loans, as they still do. However, the big decline in the 1930s in applications for business loans of all kinds prompted many commercial banks to venture further and further into direct lending to consumers. In the post-World War II period, this kind of lending has been promoted with great enthusiasm, so much so that the commercial banks are now the leading lenders to consumers by a wide margin. At the end of September 1970, the outstanding consumer loans of commercial banks were reported at $50,113 million, equal to about 52 percent of total consumer loans of all lending institutions and equal to about 40 percent of all consumer credit estimated to be outstanding.[3]

Home mortgage loans

Loans granted to individuals for the purchase and construction of homes for their own use have an important place in the loan portfolios of commercial banks, as the data on Table 14-2 indicate. Rapid growth of lending in this area, as in consumer loans, dates from the 1930s; it was especially stimulated by the establishment of the mortgage insurance programs of the Federal Housing Administration set up in 1934. As in consumer loans, too, nothing is ordinarily added to a person's sources of income through the borrowing of money to buy a home, so that integrity and income-earning capacity already established are important criteria in judging risks. Nevertheless, banks get an added element of safety in granting home mortgage loans, even if not insured, since a reasonable resale value for real property can usually be counted on—a prospect often not applying to personal property acquired by way of consumer loans.

Classified as business loans, rather than as home mortgage loans, are advances by commercial banks to individuals and firms for the construction of apartment buildings and other residential property for rental, as are those granted to "developers" for the building of houses for resale. Loans to developers, however, are usually succeeded by home mortgage loans as the completed properties are sold to individuals; thus many commercial banks favor loans to developers, not for their own sake, but to get a goodly share of the home buyers' mortgage loans expected to follow.

---

[3]Derived from *Federal Reserve Bulletin,* November 1970, pp. A54, A55.

LOAN INSTRUMENTS

Promissory notes

Borrowers' Notes Promissory notes signed by the borrowers are the principal formal instruments used by commercial banks in their lending activities. By signing a promissory note, the borrower, of course, promises to pay the face amount of the note (on a *discount*) or the face amount plus interest at a stated rate (on a *loan*[4]) on demand or at a specified future time. For many term loans to business enterprises, repayment in quarterly, semi-annual, or annual installments is promised; and the promise of payment in installments is all the more frequent in consumer and home mortgage loans, in connection with which monthly installments are usually required. Demand notes are most commonly used in granting loans for the purchasing and carrying of securities, but they are by no means uncommon in loans for business purposes. The lending bank can call at any time for the payment of a demand note, and on the other hand, the borrower has the right to pay it off at any time he chooses; nevertheless, the loan may be outstanding for a lengthy period—as long, one may say, as the bank and the borrower continue to be satisfied with the arrangement existing between them.

Some of the note forms used by commercial banks are quite complex documents—much more so than the simple note forms in which there is a bare recital of the promise to pay a stated sum of money on demand or at a specified time "to the order of" the bank. The fine print in the complex note forms sets up a wide range of safeguards for the bank, such as its right to take action for payment "without demand, notice, or protest," its right to offset its own obligation to the borrower on deposit accounts against the amount of the note "whether due or not due," and its right to apply any of the borrower's property in its possession to the payment of the note "at, before, or after" maturity. But while it is always advisable that we read the fine print carefully, we may take solace in knowing that the typical bank is much more interested in managing its loans in a routine, businesslike way than in taking drastic action "at, before, or after" maturity.

A note having only the signature of the maker (borrower) and no endorsements is known as a "single-name instrument" because the borrower alone is responsible for its payment.

Discount of Other Notes Promissory notes signed by parties other than the borrowers are sometimes used as loan instruments. In a few areas of business, it is customary for buyers of goods to give promissory notes to the sellers instead of having the transactions merely recorded in open ledger accounts, as is, of course, the usual procedure in most fields of business

---

[4]For the technical distinction between a loan and a discount, see Chapter 6.

enterprise. The holders of customers' notes originating in this way may endorse them and have a bank discount them, that is, advance their present value. In such a transaction, the original maker of each note is primarily liable, and the borrower as endorser is secondarily liable; hence the note is described as a "double-name instrument."

Drafts and acceptances

Other double-name instruments are the *trade acceptance* and the *commercial draft*. These are alike in most respects. Such an instrument is drawn by a creditor against a debtor directing him to pay to the order of a designated party or to the bearer a specified sum of money on demand or at a designated future time. The creditor himself may be the designated party (the payee), or a bank that acts as collection agent or that discounts the instrument may be named as the payee. A commercial draft may be used for any type of transaction, as when a debtor has failed to pay a book account within the time allowed. A trade acceptance, on the other hand, bears a statement on its face that it originated in a genuine merchandise transaction; it is supposed to be drawn, therefore, by a seller of goods on the buyer. Trade acceptances are usually classified as "self-liquidating instruments," because the sale of the merchandise should provide the funds with which they can be paid off at maturity.

A commercial draft may order the debtor (the drawee) to pay on demand, in which event to accept the draft is to pay it. Again, a commercial draft or a trade acceptance may be drawn for payment at some future time, and the drawee indicates his willingness to fulfill the terms of the instrument by writing the word *accepted*, the date, and his signature across the face. Holders of accepted drafts and trade acceptances may ask commercial banks to discount them, and the banks, if they do so, rely on the credit of the drawees who are primarily liable as acceptors and on the credit of the drawers who are secondarily liable.

CREDIT ANALYSIS

Character, capacity, and capital

Safety is the watchword in commercial bank lending. Bankers want to be reasonably sure that the principal of their loans will be repaid even when, because of their selection of the better risks, they may have to accept lower rates of interest than other lenders charge. Even a well-managed bank will have some of its loans become uncollectible in whole or in part; if it did not have some such losses, the conclusion would be that "good" management was being carried to a point of extreme conservatism. Nevertheless, keeping losses to very small proportions of total loans is always a goal, for the relatively weak capital-asset ratios of commercial banks mean that "impairments of capital" can result all too easily from losses.

Judgment on the safety of loan outlets is generally said to be based upon the threefold criteria of character, capacity, and capital. Character refers to the personal integrity of prospective borrowers—their intention (even, we may say, their anxiety) to meet their obligations without default of any kind. Capacity measures the managerial ability of prospective borrowers —their ability to use wisely and efficiently whatever funds a bank may advance. Capital is the measure of the borrowers' own resources to which, as it were, the loans of the banks will be added—the plant and equipment already owned, its location, its layout, the nature and extent of the markets in which the borrowers sell, and so on. Character is an indispensable criterion in all kinds of lending—banks do not want to deal with people who lack integrity. The other two criteria, however, are of more or less importance depending upon the nature of the loan.

If a prospective borrower is unable fully to satisfy the credit department of a bank on the basis of capacity and capital, his application is not necessarily rejected. Instead, a fourth criterion is considered: collateral. The applicant may have some valuable property that he is willing to pledge to improve the quality of the loan. With a pledge of property, the bank expects to be able to obtain payment by its sale should the borrower be otherwise unable to repay. But collateral does not rule out the three basic criteria, for banks are not dealers in commodities, real estate, and corporate stocks and bonds. They much prefer the payment of loans to the sale of pledged collateral as a means of collection.

As a general rule, therefore, bank customers who can make good scores on the tests of character, capacity, and capital can borrow on an unsecured basis; while those who have some significant shortcomings in capacity or capital must provide "security" either by pledging property or by obtaining the cosignatures or endorsements of other responsible parties. However, the acceptability of cosigners and endorsers is, in turn, based on evaluations of their character, capacity, and capital.

Sources of credit information

In arriving at judgments about the character, capacity, and capital of loan applicants, the credit departments of banks draw information from several sources. In consumer lending, the cost of extensive credit investigations would be prohibitive because of the small size of the average loan; hence the applicants themselves must be relied upon to supply most of the information, although it is usually desirable to verify their disclosures with some outside checkings. For most of the other kinds of loans that commercial banks grant, however, a well-stocked credit file for each borrower is generally regarded as indispensable, and banks spend liberally in accumulating data for such files.

Internal Records   In building up a credit file, the credit department of a bank can often find information of major significance in the records of the bank's own operating departments. If the customer has borrowed from the bank in the past, the records will show what amounts were borrowed, what rates of interest were paid, what guaranties or kinds of collateral were provided, whether payments were made promptly, whether renewals of loans were asked for, whether there were any disputes about terms after the loans had been granted, and so on. The records of the commercial department will disclose the average balance maintained in the customer's checking account, maximum and minimum balances over a given period of time, the number and amount of overdrafts, and the profitability of the account in the sense of the bank's earnings of interest or of its levying of service charges. The records of other departments should indicate the extent to which the customer uses the various services made available by the bank and the income it derives from such patronage.

Information from the Customer   The applicant for a loan should know more about his own affairs than anybody else hence he should be the best source of information. By means of personal interviews, direct investigations by bank personnel, the analysis of financial statements, and correspondence by mail, most of the significant facts about the applicant's business may be obtainable. If it is not clear what the applicant did with a large sum of money on hand a year ago, the best way to find out is to ask him. If some of the ratios computed from his financial statements are out of line with those of other comparable business enterprises, he may be able to explain why they are out of line. Rather than having the credit analysts theorize about why certain bookkeeping adjustments were made in the applicant's surplus accounts, the better method is to ask him why the adjustments were made and to have him justify them.

But if there is some suspicion about the applicant's character, his defects of character, if they really do exist, may tempt him to "doctor" the information he gives to a bank's credit department. Nevertheless, this need not be an excuse for unsafe loans. If the applicant states that his plant and equipment are of the finest kinds, a bank officer can visit the plant to find out for himself. If the applicant says that there is no outstanding mortgage on his plant and equipment, a search of public records at the county recorder's office will disclose whether or not he is telling the truth. And if there are misgivings about the accuracy of his financial statements, the bank can insist that they be certified by a reputable firm of public accountants.

Bank and Trade Checkings   Commercial banks are liberal in supplying credit information to one another. They give generously in the expectation of being generously treated when they, in turn, seek credit information from other institutions. Credit exchange bureaus are maintained by many clearinghouse associations, and many metropolitan banks that specialize in correspondent banking take pride in the extensive body of credit information they have available for the use of the banks that do business with them. Thus a bank need not have past dealings with a loan applicant to find how he has managed his banking affairs before coming to it. As soon as he discloses to the loan officer that he has borrowed from time to time at this or that bank, the credit department proceeds with its "checking" with it.

Businessmen, too, are usually liberal in supplying the commercial banks with credit information about their customers. If a customer has been prompt in meeting his obligations, the businessman is likely to be pleased to put in a good word for him; and if the customer has been slothful, the businessman will probably not hesitate to let the banks know about it. The loan applicant, therefore, will ordinarily be asked to give the names of several business firms from which he buys materials and supplies on account, and letters will go to these firms to inquire how he has behaved in his relations with them.

Although most well-run banks prefer to undertake their own bank and trade checkings, they often, in addition, subscribe to the services of credit-rating agencies that specialize in compiling data related to the creditworthiness of business enterprises. Doubtless the best known of these is Dun & Bradstreet, whose service extends over the whole range of business; but there are also several agencies that confine their work to particular industries, such as the Jewelers Board of Trade in the jewelry industry and the Lumberman's Credit Association, Inc., in the furniture and woodworking industries.[5]

Other Sources Other sources of information, while generally less important than the sources already mentioned, often turn up data that might otherwise be overlooked. The clipping from local newspapers of significant items about borrowing customers is a common procedure of credit departments, as is the examination of public records for information about pending lawsuits, bankruptcy proceedings, and the like. As it is important to know developments and trends in the industries in which customers are engaged, bank lending officers generally read extensively in trade journals and government reports.

SECURITY FOR BANK LOANS

Security is provided for bank loans by means of guaranties and pledges of property. The guaranties are of the nature of cosignatures and endorsements whereby parties other than the borrowers assume responsibility for the payment of obligations on the default of the borrowers. Guaranties

---

[5]For a description of the work of these and other such agencies, see Herbert V. Prochnow and Roy A. Foulke, *Practical Bank Credit*, 2d rev. ed., New York: Harper & Row, 1963, pp. 62–134.

may be placed on the borrowers' notes or they may be evidenced by separate documents, and pledges may also be incorporated in note forms or made in separate instruments.

Guaranties

Private Parties　Guaranties of private parties are often used to annul, as it were, the limited liabilities of stockholders in business corporations. If the stock of an applicant corporation is closely held by one or a few stockholders, the banker is likely to decide that they should assume full responsibility for the repayment of the loan applied for—that they should not "hide behind" the legal entity status of the corporation when they, in effect, get the full benefits of the loan. Another use of guaranties occurs when strong parent corporations guarantee the repayment of loans granted to subsidiaries with weaker credit standings; here again, of course, the veil of the legal entity doctrine is drawn aside.

Relatives and friends of prospective borrowers are often prevailed upon to cosign or endorse the borrowers' notes, and if the character, capacity, and capital of these people are stronger than the similar qualities of the borrowers, the bankers are pleased to have their guaranties. In some business lending, guaranties of this kind may not be difficult to obtain, as when fathers guarantee the notes of their sons to help them get their business careers off to good starts and when silent partners guarantee the notes of the enterprises in which they have substantial financial interests.

Government Agencies　One of the most significant developments in the field of finance since the early 1930s has been the creation and extension of facilities of the federal government for the guaranty of many kinds of loans granted by commercial banks and other financial institutions. As planned, such guaranties have generally had the effect of encouraging lending institutions to pour loan funds into channels that would otherwise be unattractive or to stipulate terms that would otherwise be unacceptable.

The protective arrangements of the federal agencies include loan insurance, loan guaranties, participations in granting loans, commitments to participate, and commitments to take loans that lending institutions want to transfer. In the field of business lending, certain arrangements of these kinds may be worked out by commercial banks with the Small Business Administration and the Veterans Administration; and for the financing of military contracts, the Army, Navy, Air Force, and other procurement agencies of the federal government may enter into similar arrangements under the terms of the Defense Production Act of 1950. For commercial banks that engage in international lending, protective arrangements are available from the Export-Import Bank. In the area of housing loans, protective commitments of several kinds are provided by the Federal Housing Administration, the Veterans Administration, and the Farmers

Home Administration. In farm lending, price-support loans granted by commercial banks are eligible for protection by the Commodity Credit Corporation; certain kinds of farm ownership and improvement loans, by the Farmers Home Administration; and various classes of loans to qualified war veterans, by the Veterans Administration. And finally—but far from exhausting the list—the student himself is likely to be fully aware of the guaranties of the Department of Health, Education, and Welfare for loans to meet costs of college and university education.

Pledges of property

Stocks and Bonds   On loans for the purchasing and carrying of securities, the security itself is almost always provided by the "good delivery" to the lending bank of the stocks and bonds for the acquisition of which the loans are granted. But stocks and bonds are frequently pledged as security for other classes of loans. A businessman who borrows to buy merchandise may pledge government bonds that he holds as a nonbusiness investment; a corporation that is borrowing to buy equipment may pledge stocks held in a subsidiary; and in borrowing for consumption, an individual may pledge his holdings of the common stock of an industrial corporation. Stocks and bonds are conveniently passed from hand to hand as pledges, and the banks, if selective in accepting such collateral, have assurances of a market for reimbursing themselves should loans be defaulted.

Inventories   Inventories of raw materials, goods in process, and finished goods are pledged by many borrowers as security for bank loans. In some lines of business, such pledges are provided as a matter of course, as, for example, the pledging of automobiles by dealers when they obtain loans to acquire their "floor stocks."

The safety of a bank's inventory loans appears to be enhanced when the pledged goods are in the possession of reliable but "disinterested" third parties rather than in the possession of the borrowers themselves. When goods are delivered to a transportation company for shipment, the bill of lading can be made out to the order of the bank, and the bank, in turn, can hold it as a document of title until the loan has been paid off or satisfactory arrangements for its payment have been made. Again, the goods can be stored in a public warehouse owned and operated by a licensed warehousing company—a "bona fide bailee for hire"—with instructions to issue the warehouse receipt (likely to be made nonnegotiable) to the bank. The bank can then authorize release of the goods in whole or in part only when the loan repayment has been made or satisfactorily arranged. More conveniently for the borrower, the goods can be stored in his own premises under the control of a licensed warehousing company: this is known as "field warehousing."

Nevertheless, commercial banks grant many loans on the security of inventories that remain in the possession and under the control of the borrowers. Under the Uniform Commercial Code, a bank (or other lender) may retain a "security interest" in such an inventory provided that a "financing statement" of the proper form is filed in the designated government office as notice to the public of its prior claim. However, a risk remains—that growing out of the legal rule that if goods are sold in the ordinary course of business to buyers who are unaware of the bank's security interest, the buyers get good title. Nevertheless, such arrangements are still acceptable when the bank has confidence in the borrower's character although obviously having some reservations about his capacity or capital.

Receivables   Although the volume of interbusiness accounts receivable outstanding at any time amounts to tens of billions of dollars,[6] the proportion pledged on bank loans is relatively small. Such receivables are chiefly book or ledger accounts—simply, we may say, the claims that sellers have against business customers who have bought on a deferred payment basis. The outstanding volume is very large, because it is standard practice for most manufacturing companies to sell on account to wholesalers and for most wholesalers to sell on account to retailers and service establishments.

There are several reasons why interbusiness receivables are pledged to only a limited extent in bank lending. Many holders of such receivables do not need to borrow, many have assets of other kinds that can be pledged more conveniently, and others have superior credit ratings that enable them to borrow on an unsecured basis. Another reason it that there are many complexities in arranging for and supervising loans secured by receivables, so that many banks decide that they cannot afford to employ specially trained personnel for this work. Still another reason is that many firms that need to "cash" their receivables prefer the services of factors and commercial finance companies that are specialists in "accounts-receivable financing."[7]

Equipment and Real Property   Large numbers of bank loans are secured by pledges of machinery and equipment—loans granted for the acquisition of factory machinery by manufacturers, store fixtures by merchants, "rolling stock" by transportation companies, office equipment by business firms in general, machinery and other facilities by farmers, and automobiles, mobile homes, boats, television sets, and other durable goods by consumers. In many instances, moreover, loans granted for purposes other than the acquisition of equipment are secured by pledges of equipment already owned by the borrowers.

---

[6]The Securities and Exchange Commission estimated the volume of receivables on the books of nonfinancial business corporations at the end of June 1970 at $271.4 billion, including amounts due from the federal government totaling $4.4 billion. (*Statistical Bulletin,* October 1970, p. 26.)

[7]See Chapter 10.

Additional large numbers of bank loans are secured by mortgages on real property—land and buildings. Almost all loans granted for the purchase and construction of such property are secured by the property itself, including urban lots, farm land, factory, store, and office buildings, warehouses, and single, double, and multi-family dwellings. In addition, real property is often pledged when its purchase or construction is not involved; in borrowing for quite different purposes, the borrowers may agree to pledge real property already owned outright.

REGULATION OF BANK LENDING

In granting loans, commercial banks are subject to numerous legal restrictions—some enacted by Congress and the state legislatures, and others promulgated by the federal and state supervisory officials in keeping with the discretionary authority vested in them by the legislative bodies. Beyond the letter of the law and official regulations, there are more restrictions imposed, as it were, in the course of bank examinations. As a matter of fact, criticisms of bank examiners are often more important in shaping loan policies than are the laws and specific regulations. In any event, all three kinds of restrictions emphasize safety—the safety of depositors. The regulatory authorities and examiners are not especially interested in the contribution given loans may make to the public welfare as by promoting economic stability and growth—their interest centers on the probability of repayment at maturity so that depositors will not be endangered by losses. The loan to the Smith Corporation may be judged to be "good" because it has put up adequate collateral, although it is using the money to put out a useless patent medicine, while that granted to Jack Brown may be relegated to the "substandard," or "doubtful," classification because he is not a very good risk, although he is using the money to pay his son's college tuition.

The judgments of bank examiners are most difficult, if not impossible, to describe, but a sampling of the specific laws and regulations applicable to bank lending can be presented. The margin regulations that apply to loans for purchasing and carrying securities have already been mentioned; for the rest, let us review the more important regulations that apply to national banks (and that, in some instances, are extended to state banks that are members of the Federal Reserve System).

10 Percent rule

The most important restriction pertinent to the lending operations of a national bank is the rule that it must not have outstanding at any time loans to any person, partnership, association, or corporation that exceed 10 percent of the bank's capital stock and surplus. In the application of this rule, loans made to the several members of a partnership are regarded as loans to the partnership; and loans made to corporate subsidiaries where the parent company owns or controls majority interests are regarded as loans to the parent company itself. The liability of borrowers as endorsers or guarantors of negotiable instruments, except for accommodation endorsements,[8] is included in the 10 percent limitation.

There are many exceptions to the 10 percent rule, including loans secured by goods in process of shipment, warehouse receipts covering readily marketable staples, or Treasury obligations, and discounts of business paper on which parties other than the borrowers are the principal obligors. In some cases, the exceptions are such that no limits remain; in others, loans equal to certain percentages of capital stock and surplus in addition to the basic 10 percent are permitted. So numerous are the exceptions, indeed, that we might conclude that the rule itself is meaningless. But this is not so, for it does apply to unsecured loans, to loans secured by stocks and bonds (other than federal obligations), and to loans secured by real estate and equipment. As the average size of loans of these three classes, especially of the first class, tend to be substantially larger than those of the classes for which exceptions are made, the rule is quite effective in limiting the size of loans—in limiting the capacity of banks to risk excessive proportions of their resources on the success or failure of a few favored borrowers.

Other loan regulations

Loans to Affiliates   National banks and state member banks are limited in the amounts that they may lend to their "affiliates." These include corporations that hold a controlling stock ownership in the lending bank, corporations that the lending bank controls through stock ownership, and corporations that are simultaneously controlled with the lending bank by a parent company. The member bank is not permitted to have outstanding at any time loans to any one affiliate in excess of 10 percent of the bank's capital stock and surplus or loans in excess of 20 percent to all its affiliates collectively. The loans, moreover, must be secured by collateral. If obligations of the federal government, the securities of certain federal agencies, or certain classes of instruments that are eligible for discounting at the Federal Reserve banks are put up as collateral, their market value at the time loans are granted must be at least equal to the amount of the loans; if securities of state and local governments, their market value must exceed by at least 10 percent the amount of the loans; and if other types of securities, their market value must exceed by at least 20 percent the amount of the loans. Furthermore, a loan to an officer, director, employee, or

---

[8]Where a party endorses a negotiable instrument without "consideration," that is, without compensation or benefit to himself, as a means of helping another party to the instrument to borrow or otherwise obtain credit—such as the relatives and friends mentioned earlier.

representative of an affiliate is regarded as a loan to the affiliate itself to the extent that the proceeds are used for its benefit.

The foregoing limitations do not apply, however, to banks' affiliates that are engaged principally in international banking, those whose sole functions are to own and manage the banks' premises, affiliates engaged in the safe-deposit business, those engaged solely in holding Treasury obligations or obligations of certain federal agencies, and a few others.

Loans Related to the Public Interest   As a means of safeguarding the public welfare, national banks are not permitted to grant loans on the security of their own outstanding stock placed as collateral. This regulation is designed to prevent insidious impairments of bank capital, such as occurred frequently in the early decades of the nineteenth century when subscribers "paid" for their stock by borrowing from the bank itself and leaving the stock as collateral.

Also as a matter of public welfare, every national bank and state member bank is forbidden to grant loans to its executive officers unless each loan is approved by the board of directors, and the total outstanding at any time to any officer does not exceed $30,000 for the acquisition of a house for his own occupancy, $10,000 for the education of his children, and $5000 for all other purposes. All such loans must be made due and payable on demand of the bank if the officer borrows at other banks in amounts exceeding these limits, and he must make a written report to his board of directors on his borrowings at other banks should they exceed the limits. The objective of these rules is to prevent the "milking" of banks by insiders.

Other regulations to safeguard the public interest forbid banks to lend trust funds to their officers, directors, and employees and to grant loans (or give gifts) to bank examiners who have authority to examine them, and forbid bank officers, directors, and employees to accept payments from customers for arranging loans.

Real Estate Loans   Before the adoption of the Federal Reserve Act, national banks were not permitted to grant loans on the security of real estate, but that legislation and subsequent amendments to the national banking laws opened the way for such loans, subject to certain restrictions. A general restriction is that a national bank may not lend on real estate mortgages in the aggregate an amount exceeding its total capital stock and surplus, or 70 percent of its savings and other time deposits, whichever amount is greater.

In arranging individual real estate loans, national banks are generally limited to first mortgages on improved property. Loans may be granted for amounts up to 90 percent of the appraised value of pledged real estate for periods not exceeding 30 years, provided that installment repayment is required at a rate sufficient to retire the entire principal within the period for which each loan is granted; up to 66⅔ percent of appraised value for periods not exceeding 20 years if installment repayment provisions are such that the entire principal will be retired within 20 years; and up to 66⅔ percent of appraised value with maturities not longer than 10 years where provisions for installment repayment require repayment in a period not exceeding 10 years.

As a rule, real estate loans insured by the Federal Housing Administration, guaranteed by the Veterans Administration, insured by state governments and state agencies, or having participations of the Small Business Administration are exempt from the foregoing limitations applicable to individual loans (although remaining subject to the terms and conditions prescribed by the insuring, guaranteeing, and participating agencies). Also exempt are loans advanced for the construction of residential property, farm buildings, and industrial and commercial property maturing within 60 months. For the exemption to apply to a loan for the construction of industrial or commercial property, however, another lender, such as a life insurance company, must have made a commitment to take over the financing and to provide funds for the full repayment of the bank upon the completion of construction. Excluded from the classification of real estate loans are advances granted to manufacturing and other industrial enterprises on the basis of their general credit standing but secured by pledges of real estate simply as a matter of "precaution against contingencies."

Interest regulations

Federal banking laws also limit the rates of interest that national banks may charge on their loans. The general rule is that a national bank may charge whatever rates are permitted by the state in which it is located, or a rate one point higher than the Federal Reserve discount rate on 90-day commercial paper, whichever of these is greater. If the state government has not stipulated maximum rates for bank loans, then a rate of 7 percent is substituted in the foregoing general rule. A national bank does not violate the law if, in addition to charging the maximum rate of interest permitted, it makes reasonable service charges for credit investigations, collection of installment payments, examination of titles, and similar operations.

If a national bank charges interest at a rate in excess of that permitted, the full interest receivable is forfeited; in the event that the interest has already been paid, the borrower has the right to recover twice its amount.

FOR REVIEW

1. In your judgment, is any class of the loans granted by commercial banks likely to be injurious to the public welfare? Discuss.
2. How did the performance of commercial banks in the late 1960s indicate their preference for lending over investing?

3. As granted by commercial banks, what are working capital loans? term loans?
4. To what classes of borrowers, in addition to business firms, do commercial banks chiefly lend?
5. In the lending operations of commercial banks, what are lines of credit? firm commitments?
6. Why are bank loans for purchasing and carrying long-term securities typically short-term loans and even, in some instances, demand loans?
7. How do commercial banks rank with other institutions as grantors of consumer loans?
8. How are promissory notes used in connection with the lending operations of commercial banks?
9. Explain the meaning of character, capacity, and capital as criteria for credit judgments.
10. From the standpoint of commercial banks, is the security of their loans really enhanced by endorsements of parties other than the borrowers? Discuss.
11. What kinds of assets are most commonly pledged as security for bank loans?
12. Explain how the 10 percent rule is applied in lending by national banks.
13. What kinds of enterprises are classified as affiliates of member banks? To what extent, if at all, are member banks restricted in lending to such affiliates?
14. What are the principal rules that apply to real-estate mortgage lending by national banks?
15. Are national banks limited in any way on the rates of interest they charge on loans? Explain.

CHAPTER 15

INVESTMENTS

INVESTMENT STANDARDS AND CHOICES

Investment capacities

Given their strong preference for lending over investment in securities, commercial banks collectively have little "left-over capacity," if any, to add to investments beyond secondary reserve needs in periods of strong loan demands and restrictive Federal Reserve monetary policy, as in the years 1966 and 1969. It is true that the management of some banks, especially smaller ones, try to uphold the traditions that their total loans, for reasons of safety, should not exceed 50, 55, or 60 percent of their total deposits, and that they become more and more reluctant to add to their loan portfolios when loans outstanding approach and reach such levels. That the larger banks do not bind themselves to such traditions was indicated by the growth in the 1960s of ratios of loans to deposits of reserve city member banks, as shown in Table 15-1. We note that, although the country member banks and the insured nonmember banks also had substantial increases in loan to deposit ratios, the increases did not go nearly so high as for the larger banks. However, we must keep in mind the possibility that expansion in loan demands at the smaller banks was not so great as at the larger banks.

Whatever the reasons, smaller banks typically have capacity at all times to invest in securities in amounts beyond secondary reserve needs, and the larger banks have the capacity in times of moderate loan demands, whether this moderation is a continuing phenomenon, as in lengthy periods of less-than-buoyant business activity, or a result of falls in business activity from buoyant levels that may or may not become prolonged. Regardless of the ways by which investment capacities beyond secondary reserve needs may originate, at any rate, the principal questions for consideration in this chapter concern the standards that guide commercial banks in selecting securities for their "bond accounts" and the choices they actually

Table 15-1   **Ratios of Loans of Commercial Banks to Deposits at End of Years 1960–1969 (in percentages)**

| YEAR | MEMBER BANKS | | | COUNTRY BANKS | NONMEMBER INSURED BANKS |
| | RESERVE CITY BANKS | | | | |
	NEW YORK	CHICAGO	OTHER		
1960	53	50	52	49	48
1961	53	50	52	49	48
1962	58	54	55	51	51
1963	62	60	59	54	53
1964	60	60	59	55	54
1965	67	66	63	57	55
1966	69	69	64	58	57
1967	65	66	61	57	56
1968	67	71	63	58	57
1969	77	81	72	62	62

Source: Computed from *Federal Reserve Bulletin,* various issues.

make presumably in keeping with these standards. A bank's "bond account" is well-named for holdings of investment securities that are thought not to be of secondary reserve quality—judged to be lacking in one or two of the qualities that secondary reserves should have—because federal and state laws generally prohibit investment by commercial banks (except, of course, by their trust departments) in common and preferred stocks, with exceptions made only for stockholdings in the Federal Reserve banks, certain classes of affiliates, and in a few other kinds of ventures to be described later.

Standards

Standards of Supervisory Agencies   Federal and state laws declare some rules to govern investment by commercial banks, and bank supervisory agencies generally have powers to impose further regulations—powers specifically delegated to them by the laws or implied from the broad responsibility that they have to keep depositors protected. In consideration of such an apparent responsibility, the supervisory agencies have traditionally concentrated on standards designed to ensure that investment securities acquired by the commercial banks subject to their respective jurisdictions will be safe in the ordinary sense of the strong credit standing of their issuers and therefore of insignificant possibilities of default. (Actually, such standards have applied and continue to apply to secondary reserves as well as to bond-account securities, since the regulations rarely make distinctions of this kind.) Standards aimed at safety leave little room for defense by bank investment officers that securities of poorer grades are acquired and held because of their higher interest yields, or because of good possibilities of capital gains as the financial positions of their issuers improve. In their judgments about what banks should invest in, the supervisory agencies accept no responsibility toward trying to help them maximize their profits, and they are especially critical of security holdings judged to be "distinctly and predominantly speculative."

Traditionally, too, both federal and state supervisory agencies, in their emphasis on safety, have placed great reliance on the ratings of securities by organizations, such as Standard and Poor's Corporation and Moody's Investors Services, Inc., generally holding that banks should confine their investments to the top four grades including, in the case of Moody's ratings, securities rated Aaa, Aa, A, and Baa—or in the parlance of finance men, "triple a," "double a," "a," and "b double a." However, the supervisory agencies have long said, as they continue to say, that bank investment officers should not accept such ratings as a matter of course—that they themselves should give some time to security analysis for judgments about the safety of high-rated securities and, therefore, about the reliability of the ratings themselves. And this is good advice—to the extent, at least, that it encourages forecasting of what may happen later—since Standard and Moody's not infrequently lower the ratings of outstanding securities when they observe that the affairs of the issuers are deteriorating. The supervisory authorities also say that bank investment officers, in selecting securities, should not conclude that they are limited to rated issues—that they should feel free to invest in unrated ones, provided that they apply analytical tests more or less comparable to the tests applied by the rating services.

Presumably with secondary reserves chiefly in mind, the supervisory agencies have also emphasized rather strongly over the years "marketability" as a desirable quality for investment securities acquired by commercial banks. Their concept of marketability has generally been quick salability at prices not far from the prices paid for the securities, or in other words, the constant availability of buyers who are willing to pay prices not subject to wide fluctuations. Accordingly, bank examiners, as representatives of the supervisors, tend to be critical of banks that, in their judgment, "go too far out" in the maturities of the securities they buy—especially so, of course, if substantial proportions of investment portfolios have long maturities.

Standards as Applied   It appears that commercial banks collectively observe stricter standards in selecting securities for their bond accounts—and surely for their secondary reserves—than the standards "recommended," shall we say, by the supervisory agencies. Many confine their bond-account holdings very largely to securities rated in the two top grades, as well as to unrated securities that investment officers decide would deserve ratings in these two grades; and many others avoid going below the third grade, whether so classified by the rating services or by themselves on the basis of their own analyses. No doubt they have in mind the possibilities of deteriorating financial positions of issuers, and they do not want to be told by bank examiners that they should sell this or that security—at a loss—because it has fallen in investment quality.

For smaller banks especially, bond-account holdings are often limited to rated securities in the two or three top grades and include very few if any unrated ones. While the investment officers of these banks may think that they are quite capable of reaching sound judgments about the investment qualities of unrated securities, they are often fearful that bank examiners will not agree with these judgments. They anticipate no criticism from examiners on holding of *rated* securities in the two or three top grades.

Choices

Qualities for the Bond Account If only securities of high quality from the standpoint of safety are selected for banks' bond accounts, we may ask what is the difference between holdings in these accounts and secondary reserves. The word *bond* largely indicates where the difference is, but not entirely so. Secondary reserves are *short-term*, high-quality, *readily marketable* securities, while the general attitude toward bond-account securities is that, in ordinary circumstances, they should have longer maturities than secondary reserves, and that their marketability—despite supervisors' suggestions—need not be greatly emphasized.

They should have longer maturities because, except in periods when Federal Reserve monetary policy is severely restrictive, interest yields on bonds and other debt instruments of longer maturities are appreciably higher than short-term yields. The idea is that banks (and other investors) have two choices in striving for higher yields on the interest-paying securities they buy: either to buy securities of lower grades or to "go out" to longer maturities. With their emphasis on high quality, the banks choose the second of these courses.

As for marketability, the expectation is that they will be held to maturity or at least until the passing of time will have made them short-term instruments. After such time lapses, considering the high quality of the securities and the fact that instruments of short maturities of any high-rated issuer usually have better secondary markets than its longer-term instruments, they would presumably deserve to be reclassified as "secondary reserves." If bank investment officers were greatly concerned about the marketability of securities selected for their bond accounts, the concern in itself would be an indication that no such selection should be made—that, instead, securities immediately qualifying as secondary reserves should be selected.

Concentration in Government Securities As long as they obey legal limitations and observe the quality standards of the supervisory agencies, commercial banks are generally free to choose for their bond accounts whatever kinds of debt instruments they prefer—notes, mortgage, debenture, or collateral trust bonds, equipment trust certificates, participation certificates, and so on. Likewise, they have great freedom in choosing among issuers—manufacturing and mercantile corporations, mining companies, railroads and public utilities, domestic governments at all levels and their "agencies," foreign governments and enterprises, and so on.

But the remarkable fact concerning their investment policy is that, to an extraordinary degree, they confine their holdings to securities issued by domestic governments, federal, state, and local, and their agencies. As indicated in Table 15-2, the security holdings of all commercial banks at the

Table 15-2   Security Holdings of Commercial Banks, Selected Years, 1945–1970 (in billions of dollars)

END OF YEAR	U.S. TREASURY[a]	FEDERAL AGENCIES[b]	STATE AND LOCAL GOVERNMENTS	CORPORATION BONDS	TOTAL
1945	90.4	1.1	4.0	2.2	97.7
1948	62.4	2.0	5.7	1.9	72.0
1951	61.3	1.6	9.2	2.2	74.3
1954	68.9	3.7	12.6	1.9	87.1
1957	59.2	2.4	13.9	1.4	76.9
1959	60.2	1.9	17.0	1.2	80.3
1961	67.2	3.0	20.3	0.9	91.4
1963	64.1	4.7	30.0	0.8	99.6
1965	60.8	6.1	38.6	0.8	106.3
1966	57.3	5.9	41.0	0.9	105.1
1967	63.5	9.1	50.0	1.6	124.2
1968	65.8	10.3	58.6	1.9	136.6
1969	56.5	10.1	59.2	1.9	127.7
1970	61.7	13.1	70.4	2.4	147.6

[a] Direct and guaranteed issues.

[b] Including loan participation certificates.

Source: Board of Governors of the Federal Reserve System, Flow of Funds Accounts 1945–1968, Washington, D.C., 1970, pp. 58–59, and Federal Reserve Bulletin, March 1971, pp. A71.13, A71.18.

end of 1970 (including secondary reserves that are not distinguished from bond-account holdings in published reports) comprised Treasury direct and guaranteed obligations of $61.7 billion, nonguaranteed issues of federal agencies of $13.1 billion, obligations of state and local governments of $70.4 billion, and only $2.4 billion of corporation bonds (including bonds of foreign enterprises and possibly governments). Thus securities of domestic governments amounted to 98.4 percent of total investment portfolios![1]

Investment in Treasury Obligations   As we saw in Chapter 13, Treasury

[1]Ignoring stockholdings of member banks in the Federal Reserve banks and some other holdings of stock, all of relatively insignificant amounts.

direct and guaranteed obligations are held by commercial banks chiefly as secondary reserves. In the Treasury survey of the ownership of its direct obligations for March 31, 1971 (estimated to reach about 90 percent of commercial bank ownership), holdings of commercial banks were reported at $15,966 million in issues with maturities to 1 year, $26,684 million in issues with maturities from 1 to 5 years, $6553 million in issues having maturities from 5 to 10 years, and only $633 million in issues with maturities over 10 years.[2] As these figures are representative of the maturity distributions of recent years, they indicate that, even beyond their investment in Treasury issues for secondary reserves, commercial banks confine themselves chiefly to intermediate-term issues and largely avoid the long-term ones.

Investment in Municipals   The enthusiasm of commercial banks for investment in the security issues of state and local governments has grown steadily throughout the post-World War II period, with increases in holdings occurring from year to year without interruption and with an extraordinary spurt coming in the 1960s and in 1970 with holdings increasing from $17.0 billion at the end of 1959 to $70.4 billion at the end of 1970. In many of the post-war years, as Table 15-2 shows, the commercial banks added to their holdings of municipals while cutting back—in some years, quite sharply—their holdings of Treasury obligations. The enthusiasm of the commercial banks for municipals has had three principal sources: (1) their tax-exemption feature, (2) steady improvements in secondary market facilities for them, and (3) the banks' strenuous competition in the 1960s for time deposits on which they had to pay (and were permitted to pay) much higher interest rates than had prevailed earlier.

The attraction of the tax-exemption feature is obvious. With most banks of significant size being subject to a federal corporation income tax rate of about 50 percent (on income in excess of $25,000), they find it pleasant to have a kind of income that fully escapes this taxation. In April 1971, for example, average market yields on Treasury bonds maturing or callable in 10 years or more, on state and local bonds rated "triple a," and on corporation bonds rated "triple a" (both ratings by Moody's) were, respectively, 5.75 percent, 5.22 percent, and 7.25 percent.[3] In which of these would you invest if you had to pay federal income tax at about 50 percent on the interest to be earned on the Treasury and corporation bonds but nothing at all on the income to be earned on the municipal issues?[4]

---

[2]Federal Reserve Bulletin, May 1971, p. A43.

[3]*Ibid.*, p. A34.

[4]Although, for the commercial banks, the choice would surely go to the municipals, that choice would not necessarily be best for individuals, even if the person is in the 50 percent bracket of the individual income tax. In the case of the Treasury bonds, a market yield of 5.75 percent meant that they had to be selling far below par value because of their low coupon rates of interest. Accordingly, much of the yield *to matu-*

Improvements in secondary markets for municipal securities have meant that substantial proportions of these securities, as they get close to their maturities, can be regarded as excellent secondary reserves—in substitution, we may say, for equal amounts of Treasury short-term obligations that the banks would otherwise want to hold.

Finally, strenuous competition for time deposits, as a reason for enthusiasm for municipals, is closely related to their tax-exemption feature. It might appear strange for a bank to be paying 7 percent interest on certificates of deposit (CDs) while holding large amounts of municipal securities paying only, say, 6 percent. But with the interest payment on the CDs a deductible expense for income tax computation and with the corporate tax rate at about 50 percent, the "after-tax cost" of the interest payment would be only about 3½ percent. Thus with the interest earned on the municipals being tax free, the gross income differential would be about 2½ percent.

Investment in Federal Agency Securities   Also growing steadily in the esteem of commercial banks in recent years have been the nonguaranteed security issues of many federal agencies. As with municipal security holdings of commercial banks, we get no regular reports of maturity distributions of their holdings of agency issues. Nevertheless, it seems safe to say that many of the latter are held as secondary reserves because of short maturities and greatly improved secondary markets for them, and the remainder, for banks' bond accounts—replacing, as it were, Treasury direct obligations of comparable amounts in both these categories because of their higher interest yields.

Spacing the maturities

If interest rates paid by issuers of longer-term securities are higher than rates paid on their short-term issues, as they generally are, and if commercial banks select only high-quality securities for their bond accounts, they can earn the higher rates both on their bond accounts and on much of their secondary reserves. With the passing of time, the longer-term securities become short-term ones, and since they are of high quality—and presumably readily marketable then for reasons of both quality and maturity—they deserve to be classified as "secondary reserves." But the issuers of the securities that are now secondary reserves continue to pay interest on them at the original rates.

Hence comes the idea of "spacing the maturities" of bond-account investments. With maturities of these investments spread rather evenly for

---

ity (which is the meaning of a market yield) would be realized as a capital gain subject to the lower tax rate that applies to such gains. Moreover, Treasury bonds owned by decedents at the time of death can be used *at face value* plus accrued interest in paying federal estate taxes, regardless of the (low) price at which a decedent may have bought them or how shortly before death he may have bought them.

the length of whatever maturity scale is adopted, some of them will move into the secondary reserve classification from month to month or perhaps from quarter to quarter. Then, as secondary reserves mature and are paid, the money, if not needed for primary reserves or meeting loan demands, can be largely reinvested at the end, so to say, of the maturity scale. Over a period of years, then, there can be a continual movement of securities from the bond account into the secondary reserves, a continual movement of secondary reserves into cash as maturities occur, and a constant reinvestment of some of this cash, if not all, in relatively high-yielding, long-term issues.

INVESTMENT REGULATIONS

In addition to establishing standards for commercial bank investment or giving supervisory agencies authority to set standards, federal and state banking laws spell out certain kinds of specific prohibitions and restrictions, as well as some specific investment authorizations. Such prohibitions, restrictions, and authorizations are especially important as found in federal law, since they apply not only to national banks but also generally to state member banks, and indeed, a few apply to all commercial banks. As they directly apply to national banks, most are contained in paragraph 7 of section 5136 of the Revised Statutes, but section 9 of the Federal Reserve Act provides:

> State member banks shall be subject to the limitations and conditions with respect to purchasing, selling, underwriting, and holding of investment securities and stock as are applicable in the case of national banks under paragraph "seventh" of section 5136 of the Revised Statutes, as amended.

In the matter of authorization, however, state member banks must have approval under state law in addition to the grants of power in federal law. At any rate, considering the broad application of the federal legislation, we may well confine our attention to it to get the flavor and to understand the scope of the kinds of rules referred to.

By way of introduction, it is pertinent to say that federal law is quite restrictive on investment in stocks by member banks, national and state, and for all commercial banks, on their *dealing* in securities as distinguished from buying and selling for their own secondary reserves and bond accounts, as previously described. As for investment in bonds and other debt instruments, federal law sets down few rules, leaving it to the Comptroller of the Currency to establish standards and, by implication, to set rules. After stating what forms of debt instruments are being referred to, paragraph 7 of section 5136 of the Revised Statutes restricts investment in them "under such further definition of the term 'investment securities' as may by regulation be prescribed by the Comptroller of the Currency." And as indicated above, "definitions" of the Comptroller are made to apply also to the investment choices of state member banks.

Investment in stocks

Stock of Federal Reserve Banks and Subsidiaries   All member banks are *required* to buy stock in the Federal Reserve banks in their respective districts as a condition of membership.[5] Beyond this, however, their permanent stockholdings are limited to the stocks of subsidiary and service corporations established for certain specified functions. A subsidiary may be established for the sole purpose of owning and maintaining the building or buildings in which the bank carries on its operations, but the total amount invested in its stock and granted in loans to it may not exceed the amount of the bank's own capital stock, unless the Comptroller of the Currency grants permission to national banks for larger amounts of financing, or the Board of Governors, to state member banks. Likewise, a member bank may establish a subsidiary to engage in the safe-deposit business, but without special permission, it must not invest in the subsidiary's stock any amount in excess of 15 percent of its own capital stock and surplus. Again, member banks are authorized to invest amounts not exceeding 10 percent of their capital stock and surplus in "bank service corporations" owned by two or more banks. The role of such corporations is to provide data-processing or other clerical, bookkeeping, or statistical services to the stockholding banks.

Finally in the area of subsidiaries, member banks are authorized to invest in the stocks of one or more foreign banks and in the stocks of one or more domestic corporations organized to engage in international banking or in international banking and financing (agreement corporations and Edge Act corporations, respectively, as briefly described in Chapter 12.) For any national bank, however, total stock investments in foreign banks and international banking and financing corporations are limited to 25 percent of its own capital stock and surplus.[6]

Additional Authorizations   The federal housing legislation authorizes member banks to invest in the common stock of the Federal National Mortgage Association, now a "federally sponsored" private agency that provides secondary market facilities for residential mortgage loans. Financial institutions that sell mortgage loans to the FNMA are required to subscribe to its common stock in amounts related to the unpaid principal of the loans sold; hence the stock-purchase authorization to member banks enables

---

[5]See Chapter 16.
[6]This investment limitation is imposed by the Federal Reserve Board of Governors, which has special jurisdiction in this area, rather than by the Comptroller of the Currency.

them to use the FNMA's services. Also by way of federal housing legislation, member banks are permitted to invest in the stock of corporations that are organized to provide housing for families and individuals of low and moderate income, as well as in partnerships and joint ventures in which these corporations may participate.

Finally, member banks (and nonmember insured banks, when permitted by state law) are authorized to invest in the stock of "small business investment companies." This authorization permits a radical departure from the traditions of commercial bank domestic investment, for the functions of small business investment companies is to advance equity funds, as long-term loans, to small business enterprises. Under federal law, therefore, commercial banks are empowered and even officially encouraged to acquire *ownership* interests in domestic private business enterprises other than affiliates. But the departure is not very radical as measured by the size of investments that may be made in the stocks of small business investment companies. A member bank's investment in any such company may not exceed 50 percent of the company's "equity securities" having actual or potential voting rights, nor may its investment in all small business investment companies exceed 5 percent of its own capital stock and surplus.

Other Stock Transactions   Member banks make many loans on the security of pledged stocks, and in the event of default, they may take title to such stock. The regulations provide that stock so acquired must be sold within a "reasonable" period of time—a period presumably determinable from market conditions.

A member bank is not permitted to grant loans on the security of its own stock or to buy shares of its own stock in the market, but such shares may come into its possession as a result of actions to force payment on loans and the like. Although the bank is permitted to take title in such circumstances, it is required to sell the stock within 6 months.

Investment in bonds

Another 10 Percent Rule   As for loans of national banks, federal law itself establishes a general rule aimed at investment diversification. Applying to all member banks, this rule limits each member bank's holdings of the debt instruments of "any one obligor or maker" to amounts not exceeding 10 percent of the bank's own capital stock and surplus. However, the 10 percent rule does not apply to Treasury obligations, the obligations of most of the federal agencies whether or not guaranteed by the Treasury, and the general obligations of state and local governments.[7]

---

[7]For the distinction between general obligations of state and local governments and their "revenue bonds," see Chapter 11.

Other Rules   When member banks buy bonds or other debt instruments at prices in excess of their par or face values, they are required to charge the premiums to expense accounts immediately or to amortize these premiums, that is, to charge portions of them periodically so that the book value will have been reduced to the par value at or before maturity. If a member bank buys debt instruments that are convertible into the obligor's stock at the bank's option or that have stock-purchase warrants attached, it must immediately write off any part of the purchase price that represents a payment for the conversion feature or the warrants, that is, any amount exceeding the "investment value" of the security *as a debt instrument*. This rule is in line with the idea, of course, that member banks should not speculate in stocks or on developments in the stock markets. Finally, member banks are forbidden to invest in debt instruments that are convertible into stock at the option of their issuers.

Dealing in securities

Background   Before 1933, many commercial banks not only bought investment securities for their own portfolios but engaged in underwriting security issues, that is, guaranteeing to the issuers the sale of the securities at stipulated prices. Then as now, underwriting guaranties were most commonly fulfilled by the outright purchase of entire issues of securities that the banks undertook to resell to their customers. The banks thus acted as security merchants in buying at wholesale and selling in smaller lots at retail. Although this kind of activity normally came within the specialized province of investment banking firms—as it still does—many commercial banks enthusiastically invaded the field, especially in the late 1920s. They opened specialized bond or trading departments or organized separate corporations known as "security affiliates."

The combination of investment banking and commercial banking functions within single institutions, or within groups of affiliated institutions, gave rise to many "conflicts of interest" between commercial banks and their customers. Hearings held in 1932 and 1933 by the U.S. Senate Banking and Currency Committee disclosed many practices that, at the least, were of doubtful morality and that, at the most, approached the fraudulent. Many people, as a matter of course, turned to the commercial banks for advice about buying securities, but all too often, the banks recommended securities that they or their affiliates were bringing out as underwriters. As advisers they were presumably acting in the interests of their customers, but as merchants in securities they often appeared to lose sight of those interests.

Divorcement   In view of the revelations of the Senate committee, Congress decided that, from the standpoint of public welfare, commercial banking and investment banking functions are incompatible, and in the Banking

Act of 1933 it took action to separate them. This law, with later amendments, forbids any person, firm, or other organization "engaged in the business of issuing, underwriting, selling, or distributing" investment securities to "engage at the same time to any extent whatever in the business of receiving deposits." Moreover, the officers, directors, partners, and employees of firms that are primarily engaged in security underwriting are declared to be ineligible to serve as directors, officers, or employees of member banks of the Federal Reserve System; however, the Board of Governors is empowered to make some exceptions.

As a general rule, then, commercial banks are not permitted to participate directly or indirectly as underwriters in the flotation of new security issues, or to act as dealers in issues already outstanding, that is, as merchants in securities, buying and selling in their own names for profit.

But There Are Exceptions In adopting legislation, Congress often makes exceptions to its own rules, and in legislation pertaining to securities, it almost always does so for issues that it itself authorizes. Accordingly, it empowers member banks, without limit, to deal in Treasury direct obligations and to underwrite[8] and deal in the obligations of most of the federal agencies. But the exceptions go beyond these. Member banks may also underwrite and deal in general obligations of state and local governments without limit. Then there are exceptions for underwriting and dealing in certain classes of securities provided that the Comptroller of the Currency decides that national banks (and, therefore, also state member banks) may invest in these securities for their secondary reserves and bond accounts. The Comptroller has so decided for security issues of the International Bank for Reconstruction and Development, the Inter-American Development Bank, and the Asian Development Bank, and his attitude has generally been favorable toward the revenue issues of state and local governments, as distinguished from their general obligations.

There was a big hassle in the 1960s between the Comptroller and the Federal Reserve Board of Governors about underwriting and dealing in such revenue issues, with the Comptroller holding that national banks could underwrite and deal in some of them, and the Board holding that state member banks must not underwrite and deal in any. By legislation adopted in 1968, however, Congress resolved the dispute in favor of the Comptroller by giving him the authority to decide which revenue issues member banks may invest in and which, therefore, they may also underwrite and deal in. But all underwriting and dealing that are subject to decisions of the Comptroller fall within the limits of the 10 percent rule. This means that the holdings of any member bank in the securities of any issuer in the

---

[8]As was pointed out in Chapter 11, the Treasury depends upon no financial institutions to underwrite its direct obligations.

decisional classes as underwriter, dealer, and investor must not exceed 10 percent of its capital stock and surplus.

Data on Trading Accounts According to an FDIC report on the security portfolios of all commercial banks at the end of 1969, holdings in their "trading accounts," that is, holdings in their capacities as underwriters and dealers, amounted to $3255 million, broken down as follows (in millions of dollars):[9]

U.S. Treasury securities	1012
Federal agency securities	468
Obligations of states and subdivisions	1756
Other securities	20

Commercial Banks as Brokers Finally in the matter of security transactions, member banks (and nonmember banks, as well) are permitted to buy and sell all kinds of securities as brokers for their customers. In so serving, they ordinarily transfer the customers' buy and sell orders to member firms of the stock exchanges and to dealers in the over-the-counter market.

FOR REVIEW

1. Why are small banks more likely to be interested in bond-account investment than are large banks?
2. How do commercial banks' bond-account investments typically differ from their secondary reserves?
3. What quality standards do bank supervisory authorities generally insist upon for banks' bond-account investments?
4. Why do commercial banks strongly favor Treasury obligations for their investment portfolios? obligations of federal agencies? obligations of state and local governments?
5. What have been the apparent effects on the investment policy of commercial banks of their strenuous competition in recent years for time deposits?
6. What is meant by "spacing the maturities" as an investment policy for commercial banks? What advantages are claimed for this policy?
7. To what extent is investment by state member banks regulated by the federal government? their dealing in securities?
8. What limitations apply to national banks and state member banks with respect to their investment in stocks?
9. What is the scope of the 10 percent rule that applies to investment by

---

[9]These amounts were included in the figures for total security holdings at the end of 1969, as presented earlier in this chapter.

national banks? What kinds of investments are exempted from this rule?

10. What is the distinction between investment in securities and dealing in them? What kinds of securities are banks generally permitted to deal in?

11. How does a bank's trading account differ from its bond account and from its secondary reserves?

THE FEDERAL RESERVE AS CENTRAL BANK

CHAPTER 16

ORIGIN AND STRUCTURE OF THE FEDERAL RESERVE SYSTEM

ORIGINS OF THE FEDERAL RESERVE SYSTEM

Background developments that led to the adoption of the Federal Reserve Act in 1913 are often said to have begun in the year 1893. It was the panic of that year and the ensuing depression that brought to bankers, businessmen, and statesmen a realization of the weaknesses of the American banking system. In a very real sense, the people of this country began to look at foreign banking systems with humility to discover the reasons for their greater strength and stability. The complacency that had marked attitudes toward banking in the United States was severely shaken.

Early proposals for reform

At first, the reformers devoted their attention almost exclusively to the problem of improving the bank note issues, apparently believing that most of our monetary and banking difficulties would be solved if the national bank notes could be endowed with the quality of elasticity. Thus the American Bankers Association, in its Baltimore convention of 1893, advocated the adoption of a bank note system similar to that of Canada—a system in which all the banks that issued notes would be jointly obligated for their safety. But Canada with only a few banks and the United States with thousands were hardly comparable; and the proposal was received coldly, especially by the larger, stronger banks.

Although the presidential campaign of 1896 had problems of money and banking, including Bryan's proposal for "free silver," as its chief issues, the victorious Republicans were unwilling to sponsor a broad program of reform. Realizing this, certain private interests representing bankers and businessmen called a "currency convention" in Indianapolis in 1897. The convention appointed a commission to study banking problems and to prepare proposals for submission to Congress and the President. The commission included in its recommendations a note issue jointly guaranteed by all issuing banks, and based on commercial paper rather than on U.S. Treasury bonds; limitations on the operations of the independent treasury system;[1] the allocation of a gold reserve by the Treasury specifically for the greenbacks issued during the Civil War; and the adoption of legislation to permit an extension of branch banking. But these proposals were not well-received in Congress, for the leaders there remained unenthusiastic about comprehensive reform legislation in the monetary and banking fields. However, they did yield to the extent of passing the Currency Act of March 14, 1900, an enactment usually cited as the "Gold Standard Act."

"Gold Standard Act"

Despite the imposing alternative title usually attributed to it, the Currency Act was not important as reform legislation; indeed, it was a makeshift bill hurried through Congress to enable the Republican leaders to claim, in the presidential campaign of 1900, that they had fulfilled their campaign promises of 1896. The new legislation merely declared our unit of value to be the gold dollar; it accepted the recommendation of the monetary commission of 1897 by creating a gold redemption fund of $150 million for the greenbacks and the Treasury notes (silver certificates) of 1890; and it provided for the refunding of outstanding Treasury bonds by issues of "consols" bearing 2 percent interest. It was thought that setting a low interest rate on these bonds would make them unattractive for purposes other than as collateral for the note issues of the national banks. Nothing was done about branch banking; instead, a provision was included to permit the establishment of new national banks with capital stock of only $25,000 in communities of less than 3000 population.

Far from improving the banking structure, the Currency Act was in a certain sense harmful. As a result of the provision permitting the establishment of new national banks with capital stock of only $25,000, the number of small, weak banks rapidly increased. So rapid, indeed, was this expansion that the Comptroller of the Currency found the job of supervision virtually impossible, and he had to be satisfied to keep in check only the worst abuses. Moreover, the failure of Congress to include in the Currency Acts thoroughgoing measures to provide elasticity in the monetary system permitted—in the subsequent period of rapid growth in economic activity—repeated stringency in the quantity of paper money, a stringency often acute in the autumn crop-marketing season.

Panic of 1907 and the Aldrich-Vreeland Act

The panic of 1907 was a crowning argument in support of the position of the reformers. The nation-wide suspension of banking operations, the failure of hundreds of banks, the suspension of gold payments, and the

---

[1]See Chapter 8.

recourse to clearinghouse certificates and scrip as mediums of exchange convinced the congressional leaders that reform must be forthcoming, if for no other reason than to save their own position of power.

Even in these circumstances, Congress dallied and passed no monetary legislation until May 30, 1908, and its efforts then were not at all comprehensive. The Aldrich-Vreeland Act, as the legislation is designated, provided for emergency issues of notes by "national currency associations"—groups of ten or more national banks with combined capital stock and surplus of at least $5 million—and by individual banks, when permitted by the Secretary of the Treasury. For the first time, commercial paper, the bonds of the state and city governments, and certain other classes of securities could be accepted by the Comptroller of the Currency as collateral for bank note issues. More important were the provisions for the appointment of a "national monetary commission" to analyze the whole question of reorganizing the financial structure.

The National Monetary Commission, which consisted of nine senators and nine representatives, was organized almost immediately, and it continued its work until March 1912 when it was dissolved. College and university professors and other expert students of money and banking were called to Washington to do the detailed work of research, and twenty-three volumes of their findings were published. While the commission was still carrying on its investigation, a bill for banking reform was drawn and presented to Congress. This bill—called the "Aldrich bill"—provided for the establishment of a central bank in Washington to be named the "National Reserve Association." The proposed institution was to have branches in each of fifteen districts into which the country was to be divided. All banks of the country were to be eligible for membership in the National Reserve Association provided that they were able to satisfy certain requirements. An important stipulation was that the national banks were to be supplanted by the association in the issue of bank notes. The association was to have other powers resembling those of central banks abroad.

At the time that the Aldrich bill was introduced, control of Congress had passed to the Democrats; and its cool reception was to be expected, since it had been sponsored, however halfheartedly, by the Republicans. But aside from the matter of party politics, the Aldrich bill was an inadequate proposal in many respects. Critics claimed that it had been designed to preserve in full measure the interests and powers of the banking fraternity while showing small concern for the interests of the general public. At any rate, little attention was given in it to some of the basic defects of the banking system, such as the concentration of reserves in New York City and the cumbersome facilities for the clearing and collection of checks.

Federal Reserve Act

When the Democrats took control of the House Banking and Currency Committee, they immediately set to work upon a substitute measure, building in some particulars upon the Aldrich bill, but introducing many independent ideas of their own. The plan of a single central bank with branches was discarded, for the Democrats—then the party of "states' rights"—were fearful of the concentration of the "money power" in the East. In its place, a plan calling for the establishment of a group of relatively independent regional banks was introduced. The first draft of the new legislation, to be known when adopted as the Federal Reserve Act, was completed in October 1912. The election of President Wilson in the following month, and the assurance that he would have adequate control of both houses of Congress, presaged the adoption of the Democratic proposals. Much work, however, remained to be done. Many alternative plans were considered, the objections of special interests had to be met, and numerous compromises were necessary. In consequence, the Federal Reserve Act did not become law until December 23, 1913, and the first Federal Reserve Board did not take office until August 10, 1914.

The Federal Reserve Act provided that the Secretary of the Treasury, the Secretary of Agriculture, and the Comptroller of the Currency should serve as the "Reserve Bank Organization Committee." It was the duty of the committee to divide the country into from eight to twelve districts, in each of which one of the proposed regional banks would be opened. After holding hearings in cities throughout the country, receiving the pleas of bankers, businessmen, and others who favored one location or another, and studying the financial organization of the various regions, the committee finally decided that twelve reserve districts should be demarcated.

As the original Federal Reserve Act has been amended on numerous occasions, it would be confusing to trace all the changes introduced from 1913 to the present time. In the subsequent description of the structure and functions of the Federal Reserve System, therefore, the present situation will be of chief interest. But it should be kept in mind that the amendments that have been adopted from time to time—particularly those of the Banking Act of 1935—have had the effect of making the present Federal Reserve structure quite different from that envisaged by the founders. We have rejected, as it were, the idea of regional central banking as embodied in the original Federal Reserve Act and have, in effect, made the Board of Governors in Washington *the* central bank and converted the twelve Federal Reserve banks to the status of operating arms of the Washington institution.

STRUCTURE OF THE FEDERAL RESERVE SYSTEM

The functions of the Federal Reserve System as our central bank are shared by four agencies, or groups of agencies, as follows:[2]

---

[2]Two other relatively unimportant agencies in the Federal Reserve System may be mentioned. The *Conference of Presidents* (originally *Governors*) *of the Federal Reserve*

1. The Board of Governors.
2. The Federal Open Market Committee.
3. The Federal Advisory Council.
4. The Federal Reserve banks and their branches.

Board of Governors

Of outstanding importance for the functioning of the Federal Reserve System are the comprehensive powers of the Board of Governors situated at the apex. All the major powers of the system are predominantly, if not exclusively vested in it, and all significant actions are either initiated by it or carried out with its approval and supervision. There is little of importance that the Federal Reserve banks may do without the board's sanction. Although its powers are declared in detail in the Federal Reserve Act as amended to the present time—just as they are described in some detail in subsequent portions of this chapter and in Chapter 20—we should keep in mind at the outset that they constitute a virtually complete control of the Federal Reserve System as our central bank.

Composition of the Board The Board of Governors on February 1, 1936, replaced a similar but less-powerful supervisory agency, known at the "Federal Reserve Board" which had been provided for in the original legislation of 1913. The board is composed of seven members who are appointed by the President with the advice and consent of the Senate. The term of office is 14 years, although members are appointed for "staggered" terms so that every 2 years the term of office of one member expires. Thus continuity in policy is expected to be preserved although rotation in office is provided for. A member who serves a full term of 14 years is not eligible for reappointment. The President designates one member as chairman, and one as vice-chairman; these offices are held for 4-year terms, with the possibility of reappointment.

Not more than one member may be appointed from any Federal Reserve district, and the President, in making appoints, "shall have due regard for a fair representation" of the financial, agricultural, industrial, and commercial interests of the country as well as of its geographical divisions. During his term of office (and for 2 years thereafter if he leaves office before the end

---

Banks has had an interesting history, for, early in the career of the system, it gained such power and prestige as seriously to threaten the authority of what was then the Federal Reserve Board; but it now occupies a subordinate position, and its function, like that of the Federal Advisory Council, is to consult with and advise the Board of Governors. It holds two or more meetings each year.

The Conference of Chairmen of the Federal Reserve Banks is also insignificant at the present time from the viewpoint of administrative authority. The influence of the chairmen (also known as the "Federal Reserve agents") has been submerged as a result of the provision of the Banking Act of 1935 making the president of each Reserve bank its chief executive officer. The Conference of Chairmen ordinarily meets once a year with the Board of Governors.

of his appointed term), a member of the Board of Governors is not permitted to hold "any office, position, or employment" in any member bank, nor may he be, during his term of office, a stockholder, director, or officer of any banking institution, whether or not it is a member bank. The President may remove members from office for cause.

The Board as a Government Agency   The charge has sometimes been made that the Federal Reserve System is a private banking organization, and that Congress has delegated its power "to coin money" for the private profit of a favored group. Hence the fact must be stressed that the Board of Governors is purely a government agency. Neither the banking fraternity nor any other group is specially represented on the board, and it is responsible to no nongovernmental clique. The stockholders of the Reserve banks—that is, the member banks—have no power whatsoever to control the decisions of the board.

To allude to the Federal Reserve System as a "private" organization proves to be a gross distortion of fact when the far-reaching powers of the Board of Governors are examined. As indicated above, they are comprehensive—in detail, reaching into almost all phases of the operations of the Reserve and member banks.

Powers Relating to the Structure of the System   In relation to the structure of the Federal Reserve System, the Board of Governors has, first of all, the power to adujst the boundaries of the twelve Federal Reserve districts. Until 1959, this power had been little used, as only a few minor adjustments of district boundaries had been made. But the admission of Alaska and Hawaii to statehood in that year required a more comprehensive action. The board enlarged the twelfth Federal Reserve district, the headquarters city of which is San Francisco, to include both of the new states. A similar power is the board's authority to classify cities and other communities as reserve cities and "country districts." This authority is of some importance, since reserve requirements applicable to the demand deposits of member banks always differ according to these classifications, and since the capacity of member banks to attract deposit balances of other banks depends upon the classification of the communities in which they are located.

The board is also authorized by law to establish facilities for the clearing and collections of checks among the twelve Reserve banks and their branches. This authority is exercised in the functioning of the Interdistrict Settlement Fund as described in Chapter 6.

Finally, in this group is the power of the board to assess the twelve Federal Reserve banks semiannually for funds to meet its administrative expenses. Though a government agency, the Board of Governors receives no appropriations from Congress for salaries and other expenses. Its expenses are met by the assessments levied on the Reserve banks in proportion to their capital stock and surplus accounts. In the year 1969, these assessments amounted to approximately $15 million.[3]

Federal Open Market Committee

The Federal Open Market Committee is an agency of great importance in the structure of the Federal Reserve System, since it has the authority to determine when and in what volume the Reserve banks will buy and sell Treasury obligations, bankers' acceptances, foreign currencies, and certain additional kinds of securities and "paper." The power to decide about transactions of the Reserve banks in Treasury obligations is, by far, the *most important power of monetary control* possessed by the Federal Reserve.

Early Promotion of Coordinated Open-Market Policy   The need of coordinated action in the purchase and sale of Treasury obligations and other securities by the twelve Reserve banks was early recognized, for it was easily possible for one Reserve bank to defeat the monetary objectives of another. Thus if the Federal Reserve Bank of New York decided to restrict the volume of its loans to member banks, its action could be nullified by the purchase of securities in the New York market by another Reserve bank.

As early as 1922, efforts were made to unify open-market operations. In that year, the Reserve banks upon their own initiative set up a committee composed of the governors (presidents) of the Reserve banks of Boston, New York, Philadelphia, and Chicago to supervise open-market operations; in the following year, the governor of the Cleveland bank was added, and the committee, designated the Open Market Investment Committee, was taken under the wing of the Board of Governors.[4] As the governor of the Federal Reserve Bank of New York dominated the Open Market Investment Committee, and as the Reserve banks not represented on the committee were jealous of the power of the New York bank, the committee was reorganized in 1930 as the Open Market Policy Conference, composed of the governors of all the Reserve banks.

Provisions of the Banking Acts of 1933 and 1935   The foregoing open-market agencies were extralegal in character, as no provision for them was included in the Federal Reserve Act and its amendments; accordingly, no Reserve bank was compelled to cooperate with them or to follow their advice in the purchases and sale of securities. In the Banking Act of 1933, however, Congress officially recognized the usefulness of an open-market agency

---

[3]*Annual Report of the Board of Governors,* 1969, p. 323.

[4]Although the Washington agency of the Federal Reserve System was known as the "Federal Reserve Board" before February 1, 1936, the present designation "Board of Governors" may conveniently be used even when reference is made to conditions and events antedating 1936.

by establishing the Federal Open Market Committee composed of one representative of each of the Reserve banks.

The Board of Governors objected, however, that though it was given the right to lay down rules and regulations for the guidance of the committee, it was not represented on it nor could it participate in policy decisions. In consequence, the Banking Act of 1935 reconstituted the committee and gave it plenary powers to dictate to the Reserve banks the character and extent of their open-market operations. "No Federal Reserve bank," reads a provision of the legislation, "shall engage or decline to engage in open-market operations . . . except in accordance with the direction of and regulations adopted by the committee."[5]

The Federal Open Market Committee is now composed of the seven members of the Board of Governors and five representatives of the Reserve banks. One representative is chosen annually by the Federal Reserve Bank of New York and one by each of the following groups of Reserve banks: Boston, Philadelphia, and Richmond; Cleveland and Chicago; Atlanta, Dallas, and St. Louis; and Minneapolis, Kansas City, and San Francisco. The board of directors of each Reserve bank has one vote in choosing the representative of its group, and only Reserve bank presidents and first vice-presidents are qualified for election. Another president or first vice-president is chosen by each group as an alternate.

Any member of the Federal Open Market Committee may be elected as its chairman or vice-chairman; these officials are chosen by the members at the first meeting in January to serve for the current year. For many years now, however, the chairman of the Board of Governors has invariably been chosen as the chairman of the committee.

Federal Advisory Council

The Federal Advisory Council is composed of twelve members, one chosen annually by the board of directors of each of the Federal Reserve banks. The members are usually distinguished commercial bankers who are chosen because of their prominence in the respective districts. The Reserve banks may vote them a stipulated compensation, with the approval of the Board of Governors, but the office is primarily an honorary one.

The council has no authority to direct any of the activities of the Federal Reserve System. It meets at least four times a year to consult with and advise the Board of Governors on matters relating to business conditions, the operations of the Reserve banks, and questions of policy. The recommendations of the council, which the board is free to accept or reject, are occasionally given wide publicity in daily newspapers and financial journals.

Federal Reserve bank and branches

The principal operating units of the Federal Reserve are the twelve Reserve banks and their branches. A Reserve bank is located in an important

---

[5]Section 205, amending section 12A of the Federal Reserve Act.

ctiy in each of the districts as originally mapped by the Organization Committee, and twenty-four other cities are directly served by branches established to facilitate the operations of the parent Reserve banks. Each Reserve bank was originally given a 20-year charter by the federal goverenment, but the charters were made of indefinite or perpetual duration by legislation adopted in 1927.

The boundaries of the Federal Reserve districts (allowing for the inclusion of Alaska and Hawaii in the twelfth district, as mentioned earlier[6]) and the location of the Reserve banks and their branches are shown in the map in Figure 16-1.

Capital Stock of the Reserve Banks The Federal Reserve Act required each Reserve bank, at the time of its organization, to have minimum subscribed capital stock of $4 million, divided into shares of $100 par value. The stock is subscribed by the member banks in amounts equal to 6 percent of their own capital stock and surplus, although only one half of each subscription must be paid in, the balance remaining subject to call. In view of the money-creating powers of the Reserve banks, which are in no way dependent upon the amount of their outstanding stock, it is most unlikely that the unpaid balances will ever be called. The original legislation authorized the sale of stock to the general public and to the Treasury should such sales be necessary to supply each bank with the minimum capital required, but the subscriptions of the member banks were adequate and this expedient did not need to be employed.

The combined paid-in capital stock of the Reserve banks at the end of November 1970 amounted to more than twenty-nine times the total originally stipulated. Individually, the capital stock accounts of the Reserve banks varied at that time from the $16 million of the Federal Reserve Bank of Minneapolis to that of the Federal Reserve Bank of New York which approximated $184 million.[7] Because the member banks must subscribe for additional stock when they increase their own capital stock or surplus, and must surrender a portion of it when their capital stock or surplus is reduced, the outstanding capital stock of the Reserve banks necessarily varies according to the total capital stock and surplus of all the member banks.

Distribution of Earnings The Federal Reserve Act authorizes the Reserve banks to pay cumulative dividends of 6 percent each year on the paid-in stock held by the member banks. Under no circumstances can the stock-holding member banks enjoy a return exceeding that rate.

The regulations governing the distribution of net earnings in excess of dividend requirements have been changed several times. The original legislation of 1913 provided for the allocation of one half of excess earnings to

---

[6]Alaska is included within the area served by the Seattle branch of the Federal Reserve Bank of San Francisco, while Hawaii is placed within the area served by the San Francisco head office.

[7]*Federal Reserve Bulletin,* December 1970, p. A13.

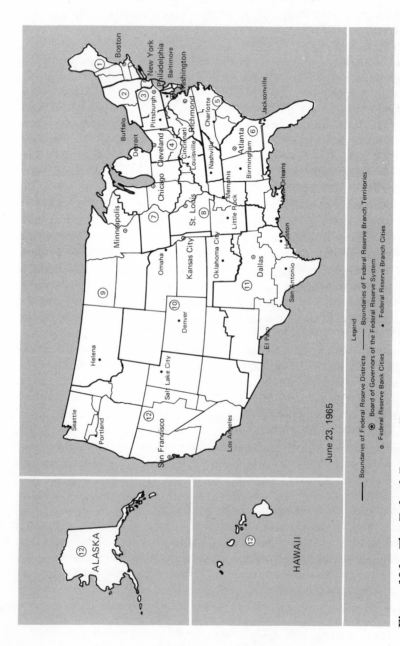

June 23, 1965

Legend

—— Boundaries of Federal Reserve Districts ——— Boundaries of Federal Reserve Branch Territories
⊛ Board of Governors of the Federal Reserve System
⊙ Federal Reserve Bank Cities • Federal Reserve Branch Cities

Figure 16.1 The Federal Reserve System—Boundaries of Federal Reserve Districts and Their Branch Territories

each Reserve bank's surplus account until it should be equal to 40 percent of the capital stock account. The remaining half was payable to the federal government as a franchise tax. An amendment adopted in 1919 stipulated that all excess earnings were to be turned into the surplus account until it should equal 200 percent of the paid-in capital; thereafter, 10 percent of excess earnings were to go to surplus, and the remainder to the Treasury as a franchise tax. The Banking Act of 1933 altered the distribution of earnings once again. The Reserve banks were required to subscribe to the stock of the Federal Deposit Insurance Corporation in an amount equal to one half of their surplus as of January 1, 1933. The surplus account of each bank was therefore divided, and the total amount of the subscription, approximately $139 million, was written off the books. At the same time, however, the provisions for the payment of a franchise tax were repealed.

Beginning in 1947 and continuing through 1958, the Federal Reserve banks by direction of the Board of Governors paid into the Treasury approximately 90 percent of their annual earnings after expenses and dividends. In 1959, the board decided that in subsequent years the surplus account of each Reserve bank would be limited to 200 percent of its paid-in capital stock. Each Reserve bank was therefore directed to pay to the Treasury an amount equal to its "excess surplus" at the end of 1959, that is, the amount of surplus exceeding the 200 percent limit, and to continue to make payments to the Treasury each year of all current net earnings not needed for dividends and to maintain the surplus account at the 200 percent level. Early in 1965, the board made a further decision in the same direction, this time bringing the surplus limit down to 100 percent of the paid-in capital stock, and again requiring the Reserve banks to make extraordinary payments to the Treasury—the amounts by which their surplus accounts at the end of 1964 exceeded the new 100 percent limit—as well as to continue regular payments of all net current earnings not required for dividends and for credits to surplus accounts to keep them at the 100 percent level. All these payments since 1947 have been technically designated as interest on outstanding Federal Reserve notes; as such, they have been voluntary, although it is obvious that Congress could at any time have made them compulsory by simply requiring payments of equal amounts in a restoration of the franchise tax.

From November 1914, when the Federal Reserve banks were opened for business, until the end of 1969, their total net earnings amounted to approximately $21,326 million, out of which only $767 million had been distributed to the member banks as dividends. Payments to the Treasury included $149 million on account of the franchise tax, about $139 million as the subscription to the stock of the FDIC (this eventually going to the Treasury when the FDIC's stock was retired), $19,610 million as interest on Federal Reserve notes, and a miscellaneous item of about $2 million. After an internal adjustment of about $11 million, all these allocations left total surplus of approximately $669 million at the end of 1969.[8]

Board of Directors Each Reserve bank is managed by a board of nine directors who are chosen in part by the Board of Governors and in part by the member banks. Three of the board members, known as "class A directors," are desginated as the representatives of the banking interests of a Reserve district; and three, the "class B directors," represent the commercial, industrial, and agricultural interests of the district. Directors of these two classes are elected by the member banks. The class B directors must not be officers, directors, or employees of any other banking institutions. The "class C directors," also three in number, are appointed by the Board of Governors to represent the public interest. They must have been residents of their respective districts for at least 2 years preceding their appointment. One of them, who must be a person of tested banking experience, is designated by the Board of Governors as chairman of the Reserve bank's board of directors; a second class C director is named deputy chairman. Class C directors, during their term of office, must have no other banking connections, either as director, officer, employee, or stockholder.

The term of office of all directors is 3 years. Each year a class C director is appointed by the Board of Governors, and a class A director and a class B director are elected by the member banks. The member banks are grouped in each district in three classes—large banks, banks of intermediate size, and small banks—and each group takes its turn every third year in choosing the class A and class B directors of that year. This classification is based on the idea that the interests of the three groups may not necessarily coincide, so that each should have fair participation in choosing board members. In general, however, little interest is shown by the member banks in the election of directors.

Executive Officers The chief executive officer of a Federal Reserve bank is the president; he is chosen for a term of 5 years by the bank's board of directors, subject to the approval of the Board of Governors. One or more vice-presidents may also be selected, the appointment of the first vice-president also being subject to the approval of the Board of Governors. Actually, each Reserve bank has several vice-presidents, as well as many other officers of lower ranks.

The Federal Reserve Act as adopted in 1913 was somewhat vague in its provisions concerning executive officers, although apparently the chairman of each bank's board of directors—who is also known as its "Federal Reserve agent"—was intended to assume the lead in handling administrative

---

[8]Derived from *Annual Report of the Board of Governors*, 1969, p. 339.

affairs. The Reserve banks, nevertheless, took upon themselves the responsibility of naming their own chief executive officers—called "governors"—and in the early years there were spirited contests between chairmen and governors for administrative supremacy. In the course of time, however, the governors won a clear decision—a decision affirmed by the Banking Act of 1935, for it explicitly provided that the governor of each Reserve Bank, but redesignated as "president," should be its chief administrative officer.

As principal executive, therefore, each Reserve bank president is now responsible for the execution of the policies formulated by the board of directors or by the Board of Governors in Washington, as the case may be. All other officers and employees are directly subject to his authority in the performance of their duties.

In accordance with the intent of the Banking Act of 1935, the Board of Governors deprived the board chairmen of many of the powers that they had formerly enjoyed, putting their jobs on a part-time basis. Each chairman, however, still retains several statutory powers, including the right to preside and vote at board meetings, the duty of maintaining an office for the Board of Governors on the premises of the Reserve bank, the duty of making reports to the Board of Governors, and the authority to supervise the note issues of the Reserve bank to which he is attached.

The compensation paid to each chairman is determined by the Board of Governors but is furnished by the Reserve bank; the compensation of the president, vice-presidents, and other officers and employees is determined by the board of directors, subject to the approval of the Board of Governors.

Branches of the Reserve Banks   Twenty-four branches of the Federal Reserve banks are now in operation. In several instances, branches were established apparently to assuage the injury felt by some major cities because they were not selected for the location of head offices; and in others, their establishment was more clearly designed to provide better facilities to serve the member banks. However, the growth of population and the volume of transactions between member banks and the branches have long since wiped out distinctions so based. For a long time, better service facilities for the member banks have been emphasized, and all developments have been in the direction of greatly expanding branch activities, so that in scope of operations all branches have come to resemble closely their parent Reserve banks themselves.

Although the branches are not separately capitalized, each has its own board of directors of not less than three or more than seven members. A majority of one is chosen by the board of directors of the parent bank and the remainder by the Board of Governors. The work of each branch is supervised by a manager who, in almost all instances, is ranked as a vice-president of the parent bank.

With the permission of the Board of Governors, any Reserve bank may establish foreign branches and agencies and name foreign correspondents, but most of the foreign business of the system is done through the Federal Reserve Bank of New York and its correspondents abroad.

Powers of the Board of Governors   The Board of Governors has broad authority to supervise the operations of the Reserve banks and their branches. Some of these powers have already been mentioned: the appointment of three class C directors for each bank and a minority of the directors for each branch, the approval of the nomination of presidents and first vice-presidents, and the approval of the compensation paid by the Reserve banks to all their officers and employees.

The Reserve banks are required to submit weekly statements of their financial condition to the board, and it may require them to write off their books any assets it deems to be worthless. Moreover, the Reserve banks are examined periodically by a corps of examiners under the direction of the Board of Governors.

Were a Reserve bank to indulge in operations in violation of the law, the board could suspend its operations, take possession of it, operate it during the period of suspension, reorganize it, and even liquidate it. Of a similar nature is the power of the board to suspend or remove any director, officer, or employee of a Reserve bank for cause. However, there has been no occasion for the use of this group of powers.

The board has authority to pass on the establishment of branches, agencies, and correspondents by the Reserve banks. It may compel a Reserve bank to establish a branch or agency within its district or to close a branch or agency already in operation. If a Reserve bank undertakes to establish a branch or agency in a foreign country or in an insular possession of the United States or to appoint correspondents there, it must obtain the approval of the Board of Governors. In addition, the board has the power to supervise, regulate, and limit transactions between the Reserve banks and foreign banks and bankers.

The Board of Governors supervises the issuance of Federal Reserve notes. It authorizes the Comptroller of the Currency to deliver new batches of notes to the Reserve banks, and establishes regulations for the safeguarding of the gold certificates, Treasury obligations, and commercial paper held by the Federal Reserve agents as collateral for notes outstanding.[9]

In the exercise of a final power in this area, the board supervises the check-clearing and collection facilities of the Reserve banks and regulates the charges they may levy for collecting payment on items other than checks, such as notes, drafts, acceptances, and bond coupons.

The question of independence

In recent years, the Federal Reserve has been subjected to a continual barrage of criticism. Whatever may be the scope of specific attacks, many

---

[9]Very little safeguarding is needed for gold certificates, since, as mentioned in Chapter 4, they are almost entirely "gold credits" on the books of the Treasury.

tend ultimately to condemn its "independence"—its high degree of immunity from responsibility to and control by the President, Congress, and the voting public.

Attacks on Independence   Many economists, members of Congress, and other students of monetary affairs have aimed their attacks at the Board of Governors and the Federal Open Market Committee for what they regard as errors in money-control policies. In the 1950s, the two agencies were accused of going overboard in their fears of inflation and of often adopting restrictive policies that choked off business expansion even when the rate of unemployment was unconscionably high and many capital facilities were idle; and the recessions of 1953–1954, 1957–1958, and 1960–1961, occurring as they did at such short intervals, were cited as evidencing unduly restrictive monetary policies. In the early 1960s, the Federal Reserve authorities were accused of again going overboard in concern about our international balance-of-payments developments; and in the later 1960s, of shifting much too abruptly and intensely to positions of tightness, as in 1966 and 1969, and then reversing these positions too liberally.

Nevertheless, the critics hardly expect any money-control agency to be free of error in policy decisions. They are not disturbed so much by the alleged errors themselves as by the circumstances that make possible, in their opinion, a perpetuation of errors. Their grievance is that the Board of Governors and the Federal Open Market Committee are not accountable to anybody for their errors, and that a policy widely regarded as ill-conceived cannot be reversed by vote of the public or by direction of the elected representatives of the public, the President and the members of Congress. It is argued, therefore, that the Federal Reserve authorities constitute a "fourth branch of the government," comparable in many ways to the Supreme Court in remoteness from control by the electorate. As a consequence, the critics say, the President and his advisers cannot formulate a national economic program to cope with unemployment and to promote growth with any assurance that the Federal Reserve authorities will exercise their money-control powers to support and advance it. Indeed, they add, restrictive Federal Reserve policies may nullify the expansionary effects of tax reduction, spending, debt management, and other fiscal and economic policies decided on by the President and Congress. They further argue that the voting public holds the President responsible for what happens to business activity during his term of office, even when his direct powers of monetary control are severely limited, and even when monetary control enormously influences business developments. It is strange, they say, that the President, who is the representative of all the people, must sometimes engage in behind-the-scenes "begging" to try to get the Federal Reserve authorities to support his economic policies.

Legal Provisions for Independence   The "independence" of the Federal Reserve authorities, about which the critics complain, has not come about by accident. It is in the law. The student must surely have seen this in the description of the structure of the Federal Reserve System. For the Board of Governors, independence originates in the 14-year term of office, equal to three and a half Presidential terms; in the "staggered" terms and their dating (one to expire on January 31 in each even-numbered year, so that a newly elected President gets the opportunity to choose a member of the board only after he has been in office for more than a year, and the opportunity to choose only one additional member during his 4-year term unless there are deaths or resignations); in its freedom from any appropriations go-around with Congress, since it gets its "spending money" from the assessments on the Reserve banks; and its lack of accountability for its expenditures, since they are not subject to audit and criticism by the General Accounting Office, the government's "watchdog" agency.

The independence of the Federal Open Market Committee is largely that of the board itself, since it constitutes a majority of the committee, but there is an additional degree of independence in that the five Reserve bank presidents are, in a sense, even more remote from the authority of the President, Congress, and the voting public. For each Federal Reserve bank, independence originates in the election of six of its nine directors by the member banks, and the appointment of the other three by the "independent" Board of Governors; in the choice of its president and first vice-president by these directors with the approval of the Board of Governors; and in its accountability only to the Board of Governors for its operating expenditures. Even the Federal Advisory Council—despite its apparent lack of significant influence on Federal Reserve policy decisions—is criticized for its remoteness from the public, a remoteness that results from choosing its members by the boards of directors of the Reserve banks and the invariable limiting of these choices to commercial bankers.

Defense of Independence   The principal argument in defense of the "independence" of the Federal Reserve appears to be that it must be free to protect the public from unwise fiscal policies of Congress and the President. This has surely been the traditional viewpoint of the defenders of its independence, even when, in recent years, they may have avoided stating this viewpoint so bluntly. The substance of the argument is that Congress and the President are subject to innumerable public pressures to increase the government's spending programs; that, to retain their popularity and to gain reelection, they are strongly inclined to yield to these pressures; that, for the same reasons, they are disinclined to provide additional tax sources to meet the costs of new spending programs; that, therefore, they are willing to accept chronic budgetary deficits as the best way to proceed; and that, if the Federal Reserve authorities expand the quantity of money to finance these deficits, the result can only be severe and prolonged inflation. If, on the other hand, the Federal Reserve authorities are free to restrict expansion in the quantity of money, and if they do restrict it, then the Treasury must borrow the people's savings to meet the deficits—and this is not inflationary. It is argued that the need of independent monetary control as a means of curbing unwise fiscal policies has been acknowledged by various Congresses and Presidents by their adoption and approval of the provisions for "independence" contained in the Federal Reserve Act and its amendments.

Closely related to the argument just presented is one to the effect that insulation "against private or public pressures" is essential for proper monetary control. The Board of Governors itself expressed this argument some years ago as follows:

> Because money so vitally affects all people in all walks of life as well as the financing of the government, the task of credit and monetary management has unique characteristics. Policy decisions of an agency performing this task are often the subject of controversy and frequently of a restrictive nature; consequently, they are often unpopular, at least temporarily, with some groups. The general public in a democracy, however, is more apt to accept or tolerate restrictive monetary and credit policies if they are decided by public officials who, like the members of the judiciary, are removed from immediate pressures.[10]

Still another argument in defense of the existing Federal Reserve setup is that acknowledged errors in policy have not resulted from defects in this setup but from lack of adequate data on current economic developments, deficiencies in forecasting tools, weaknesses in the money-control instruments themselves, and indeed, lack of knowledge and understanding of relationships between changes in the quantity of money and other economic phenomena. It is argued that direct monetary control by the President or by Congress would be equally subject to error on account of such deficiencies in information, instruments, and understanding.

Finally, defenders of the Federal Reserve's "independence" argue that, despite admitted errors, its over-all record in monetary control has been good, so that it would be foolhardy to make sweeping changes.

Proposals for Change   Despite the final argument just stated, many proposals for changes in the structure of the Federal Reserve System have been made in recent years—some of them, indeed, quite "sweeping" in scope. Probably most attention has been given to the proposals of the Commission on Money and Credit, whose report was published in the summer of 1961.[11]

---

[10]Joint Committee on the Economic Report, *Monetary Policy and the Management of the Public Debt,* Part 1, Washington, D.C.: Government Printing Office, 1952, p. 242.

[11]The Commission on Money and Credit was organized in 1958 to study "policy questions of critical importance" pertaining to the structure and functions of our financial

It recommended that the membership of the Board of Governors be reduced to five members having overlapping 10-year terms. One term would expire in every other odd-numbered year, so that the President would be enabled to choose one member shortly after taking office. Occupational and geographical qualifications for members of the board would be eliminated, and members could be reappointed although they had served full 10-year terms. The chairman and vice-chairman of the board would be chosen by the President "from among the board's membership" for 4-year terms coterminous with his own term. Thus the first appointee of the President could also be appointed chairman. The commission further recommended that the Federal Open Market Committee be abolished and that the power to direct the open-market operations of the Federal Reserve banks be vested exclusively in the Board of Governors. Rather strangely, however, it also recommended that the board be *required* to consult with the twelve presidents of the Reserve banks in establishing its open-market policy and in setting discount rates and reserve requirements. Finally, in the structural area, the commission recommended that the Federal Advisory Council be reconstituted to be "broadly representative of all aspects of the American economy." The board of directors of each Reserve bank would make at least two nominations, and the Board of Governors would make a selection among the nominees, one from each district, for a twelve-member council having terms of 3 years. The council would meet with the board at least twice a year.[12]

MEMBER BANKS OF THE FEDERAL RESERVE SYSTEM

The commercial banks that are members of the Federal Reserve System are really *outside* the system defined as our central bank. Although the member banks choose six of the nine directors of each of the Federal Reserve banks and although the Reserve banks contribute five of the twelve members of the Federal Open Market Committee, the influence of the individual member bank on Federal Reserve decisions by way of these

---

institutions, and to recommend "changes in laws, government regulations, or the administrative practices of government or private institutions." It had 25 members, chiefly bankers, other businessmen, and members of leading law firms, but with representatives also from labor and farm organizations and the academic profession. The commission was sponsored by the Committee for Economic Development, a distinguished private research organization that had long been active in making recommendations on public policy. The commission's studies and findings were published in many volumes, and its principal recommendations with supporting statements were published in the single volume *Money and Credit: Their Influence on Jobs, Prices, and Growth* (Englewood Cliffs, N.J.: Prentice-Hall, Inc., 1961).

[12]Commission on Money and Credit, *Money and Credit: Their Influence on Jobs, Prices, and Growth,* Englewood Cliffs, N.J.: Prentice-Hall, Inc., 1961, pp. 85–90.

connections is so remote as to be inconsequential. Nevertheless, having as members those commercial banks that own most of the assets and that have most of the deposits of all commercial banks is helpful to effect monetary control, so that a consideration of the member bank situation is appropriate for this chapter. At the end of June 1970, for example, the member banks held 79.9 percent of total commercial bank deposits although they comprised only 46.4 percent of the total number of commercial banks.[13] Such percentages indicate, of course, that the average member bank is much larger than the average nonmember bank. Indeed, almost all of the larger banks of the country are members.

Help for monetary control comes chiefly by way of the reserve requirements set by the Board of Governors to which all member banks are subject. The Federal Reserve could still exercise effective control over the quantity of money if there were no member banks, provided that most of the commercial banks were subject to cash reserve requirements of substantial size under state laws; but control is greatly eased when a very large proportion of the deposits of the commercial banking system is directly subject to the reserve requirements set by the board itself.

Qualifications of member banks

All national banks are required to be members of the Federal Reserve System. The action of the Comptroller of the Currency in granting national charters to newly organized banks and to converted state nonmember banks immediately admits them to membership, without need of further approval of the Federal Reserve authorities. The withdrawal or expulsion of national banks from the Federal Reserve System, on the other hand, requires the immediate surrender of their national charters.

Incorporated state banks, including commercial banks, mutual savings banks, trust companies, and industrial banks, may voluntarily join the Federal Reserve System if they are able to satisfy the requirements of membership. Other state-chartered and state-licensed financial institutions, such as savings and loan associations, sales finance companies, consumer finance companies, and credit unions, are not eligible for membership.

For eligible state institutions, the principal qualifications for membership are as follows: (1) the passing of an entrance examination, (2) sufficient capital, (3) subscription to stock in the Federal Reserve bank in the district, (4) observance of reserve requirements, (5) payment at par on checks presented for payment by the Federal Reserve banks, (6) submission to regular examination by Federal Reserve examiners and to requirements for reports of condition, and (7) observance of most of the federal banking laws applicable to the operations of national banks.

In passing upon the application of a state bank for membership, the

---

[13]Computed from *Federal Reserve Bulletin,* December 1970, p. A19.

Board of Governors considers its financial history, the nature of its business operations, the character of its service to the community in which it is located, the qualifications of its directors and officers, the strength of its capital structure, and the scope of its corporate powers. The books of the applicant are subjected to a thorough examination, and various adjustments, such as the writing off of doubtful assets, may be required as a condition for admission.

The general rule on capital is that a state bank seeking admission to the Federal Reserve System must have capital stock and surplus that the Board of Governors finds to be adequate in relation to "the character and condition of its assets and to its existing and prospective deposit liabilities and other corporate responsibilities." If its capital stock and surplus are less than would be required of a new national bank in the same locality,[14] it must be insured by the FDIC at the time of its admission. After admission, the state bank may not reduce the amount of its capital stock without the permission of the board. Because mutual savings banks do not issue capital stock, the rule that applies to them requires surplus and "undivided profits," that is, retained profits not carried to the surplus account, equal to the capital stock that national banks situated in the same communities would be required to have. Actually, no mutual savings bank has belonged to the system since 1962.

Details concerning the other principal qualifications of membership, as listed above, are presented elsewhere in this textbook; hence it should not be necessary to discuss them at this time.

Expulsion and withdrawal of member banks

The Board of Governors is empowered to expel member banks from the Federal Reserve System if it finds them guilty of violations of the applicable federal banking laws or of its own regulations, or if it finds that they have ceased to exercise banking functions without the appointment of a receiver or liquidating agent. On the other hand, state member banks, whatever their reasons may be, may voluntarily withdraw from the Federal Reserve System by filing with the board a 6-months notice of their intention to withdraw. The board can waive the notice requirement.

Upon expulsion or withdrawal, a member bank must surrender its stock in the Federal Reserve bank, and at the same time, of course, it must forfeit all the rights and privileges of membership formerly enjoyed. The stock is redeemable at par, and in addition, the withdrawing bank is allowed accrued dividends at the rate of 0.5 percent per month.

Supervision of member banks

In addition to passing upon the admission of state banks as members of the Federal Reserve System, the Board of Governors has the authority to

---

[14]For the capital requirements of national banks, see Chapter 12.

subject the state members to examination and to require them from time to time to submit reports on their assets, liabilities, and capital accounts with supporting details. The routine work of examination is normally performed, not by the board's own examiners, but by examiners employed by the district Reserve banks. At whatever times it may choose, however, the board may order special examinations of any member banks, whether national banks or state-chartered members.

The board approves or rejects applications for the establishment of branches of state member banks and for their absorption of other banks in mergers; passes upon proposed reductions in the amounts of their capital stock; has authority to permit a director, officer, or employee of any member bank (or a private banker) to be a director, officer, or employee of not more than one additional member bank; and decides on the removal of officers and directors of member banks for continued violations of the law or for unsafe and unsound banking practices.

With regard to the operations of member banks, the board determines within certain limits the reserves they must hold in proportion to their deposits; sets the maximum rates of interest they may pay on savings and other time deposits; and interprets and enforces the federal laws pertaining to their loans and investments.

Advantages of membership

Many of the advantages of membership will be indicated or implied in the discussion of the operations of the Federal Reserve banks in the following chapter. At this point, nevertheless, a brief description of the principal services made available to member banks and other attractions of membership should be worthwhile. The most valuable of the services are probably the clearing of checks, provided free of charge, and the collection of notes, drafts, and other maturing obligations, also largely free of charges. For their members, the Reserve banks make up packages of paper money and coins of the denominations desired, and dispatch them free of mailing and handling charges; likewise, they bear the costs of shipments of hand-to-hand money from the member banks. Other facilities make it possible for member banks to move funds speedily over the country, either by telegraphic transfers or by drafts.

The Federal Reserve banks undertake to grant loans to their member banks, usually at low or moderate rates of interest; because of their special powers as central banking institutions, they are able to lend liberally when all other sources of credit have evaporated. Member banks can call upon the Reserve banks for advice on their investment problems, and indeed, they may turn over all or portions of their investment portfolios to the Reserve banks for safekeeping. Finally, information and advice on other problems of banking, whether related to legal interpretations or practical bank operations, are readily supplied by the Reserve banks to their members.

Member banks enjoy considerable prestige by the mere fact of their membership. They undoubtedly have some advantage in competing with nonmembers for the business of discriminating customers who are likely to feel that federal banking standards make for safer banking than the standards of many of the states.

Even the members' obligation to own stock in the Federal Reserve banks is itself an advantage of membership. Rated very high in quality and paying an assured annual return of 6 percent, such stock is quite attractive at most times as an investment.

Objections to membership

Many reasons are offered to explain the failure or refusal of a large majority of state-chartered commercial banks to join the Federal Reserve System, as well as to account for withdrawals from membership. Undoubtedly the most important reason is that most of the nonjoiners and withdrawers are strongly convinced that they can operate more profitably as nonmembers than as members. This is obviously true for the banks that insist on deducting remittance charges when paying checks drawn on them; for these banks, the emphasis of the Federal Reserve on par collection is distasteful. In many states, moreover—and this is much more important—the reserve requirements prescribed by the state laws are lower than the customary requirements that apply to member banks, so that many bankers steer clear of membership to avoid tying up "excessive" amounts of their assets in "idle cash." Under some of the state laws, indeed, portions of the required reserves can be carried in interest-paying government securities rather than cash! Still further, many managements of state banks feel that they have more leeway for profitable investment under the state laws and regulations than they would have under the investment regulations of the Comptroller of the Currency which are made applicable to state member banks by federal law.

A second important reason why state-chartered banks stay out of the Federal Reserve System or leave it is that they can get interbank services as cheaply and as conveniently as do the member banks in using the Federal Reserve service facilities. The Reserve banks themselves provide some services to nonmembers as readily as to members and on the same terms. Nonmember banks can easily avail themselves of the clearing and collection facilities of the Reserve banks by keeping balances on deposit with them and agreeing to remit at par. Moreover, nonmember banks can borrow from the Federal Reserve banks, although in this they suffer a discrimination, since the rate of discount they pay is at least one percentage point higher than the rate charged member banks. But they may be able to avoid this penalty, or part of it, by borrowing instead from correspondent banks. And they are usually quite satisfied to depend upon correspondent banks for other desirable services, such as getting shipments of hand-to-hand money, having funds transferred telegraphically, depositing securities for safekeeping, and getting information and advice. As a rule, indeed, the correspondent banks provide a wider range of services than that of the Federal Reserve banks; and even when the services are the same in type, many nonmember banks are convinced that those of the correspondent banks are superior. This opinion is especially strong for check-clearing arrangements. The nonmember banks realize that, to qualify for the services of the correspondent banks, they must keep substantial demand deposit balances with them, but this simply makes them all the more inclined to shy away from keeping additional "idle cash" as reserves with the Federal Reserve banks.

Though attracted to membership, some state banks fail to apply in the expectation that, to qualify, they would be required to take certain actions they would like to avoid, such as to increase their capital, discontinue certain operating policies, cast off profitable affiliates, or divest themselves of some class or classes of investment securities. Some have withdrawn their applications for membership when actually told by the Federal Reserve authorities that one or more actions of these kinds would have to be taken before admission.

In a study of deterrents to membership published by the Board of Governors many years ago, the following additional reasons for nonmembership—most of them probably still pertinent—were listed:

> Unwillingness to be subject to both federal and state bank regulations, supervision, and examination; opinion that the Federal Reserve System's power to regulate is too broad; opposition to increasing governmental control; belief that the Federal Reserve examiners are too severe in their criticism; belief that the Federal Reserve System encourages branch banking, to which they are opposed; assumption that the Federal Reserve System is opposed to the dual banking system, which they wish to have continued; fear that their applications might be turned down because of the presence of undesirable assets; belief that membership would subject them to an excessive amount of inconvenience and red tape, and put them to extra work on account of the numerous reports to be filled out, etc.[15]

Proposed reforms

Among the recommendations that have been made in recent years for the reorganization and reform of the Federal Reserve System, membership has not been neglected. Some reformers, including the Commission on Money and Credit,[16] would answer the membership question neatly by requiring all commercial banks, or all insured commercial banks, to be members whether or not they like the idea Others, including the Board of Governors itself in an often-repeated recommendation to Congress, would eliminate a major reason for nonmembership by requiring all nonmember insured banks to hold reserves at the levels required of member banks.

---

[15]R. Magruder Wingfield, *Banking Studies*, Washington, D.C.: Board of Governors, 1941, pp. 289–290.
[16]*Op. cit.*, pp. 76–77.

In opposition, a large minority of the twenty-five–member Advisory Committee on Banking has proposed that membership in the Federal Reserve System be made optional *for national banks*.[17] Seeing an "urgent need for a thorough reexamination of the laws and regulations pertaining to the operations of national banks," Comptroller of the Currency James J. Saxon early in 1962 named this committee to study replies received from national banks to his inquiry to them about "needed changes," and to make its own conclusions and recommendations.

Another recommendation that, if adopted, might be a minor influence toward discouraging membership calls for the retirement of the stock of the Federal Reserve banks, or alternatively, its reduction to a nominal amount. For example, the Commission on Money and Credit suggested that each member bank simply hold a nonearning certificate of membership valued at $500.[18] Proposals of this kind envisage, of course, that the member banks would be paid for the amounts of stock cancelled.

FOR REVIEW

1. As background for the adoption of the Federal Reserve Act of 1913, what was the significance of the Currency Act of 1900 and the Aldrich-Vreeland Act of 1908?

2. Was not the Federal Reserve Act, as adopted in 1913, quite peculiar in providing for central banking on a regional basis? Discuss.

3. What is the composition of the Board of Governors of the Federal Reserve System? For what terms are the members appointed? What qualifications are required for appointment?

4. In the Federal Reserve structure, how important are the powers of the Board of Governors by comparison with the powers of the Reserve bank presidents?

5. What is the composition of the Federal Open Market Committee? What is its function? Does its power eclipse that of the Board of Governors? Explain.

6. Considering that the member banks own all the stock of the Reserve banks, what power do they have in determining the policies of the Reserve banks?

7. Over the years, what have the Federal Reserve banks done with their net earnings? What do they do currently with annual net earnings?

8. How can we account for the rather peculiar composition of the board of directors of each Federal Reserve bank? How much power do these boards have?

---

[17]Comptroller of the Currency, *Report of the Advisory Committee on Banking: National Banks and the Future*, Washington, D.C.: Government Printing Office, 1962, p. 114.
[18]*Op. cit.*, p. 91.

9. Explain the distinction between a branch of a Federal Reserve bank and a member of the Federal Reserve System.
10. What are the principal arguments in favor of the independence of the Federal Reserve? in opposition? Which side, in your opinion, has the stronger case? Discuss.
11. If you had the power to change the structure of the Federal Reserve System, what changes would you order? Explain your reasons.
12. What is the distinction between compulsory and voluntary membership in the Federal Reserve System? What are the chief qualifications for the voluntary membership of commercial banks?
13. Under what circumstances may members of the Federal Reserve System discontinue their membership?
14. How can one account for the fact that a large majority of state-chartered banks are not members of the Federal Reserve System?
15. Should all insured commercial banks be required to be members of the Federal Reserve System? Discuss.

CHAPTER 17

OPERATIONS OF THE FEDERAL
RESERVE BANKS

LOANS TO MEMBER BANKS

Although one of the principal reasons for the establishment of the Federal Reserve System in 1913 was to provide a new source of loan funds for the member banks, their dependence on the Federal Reserve banks for loans to augment their reserves has varied widely over the years. The loan volume of the Reserve banks was high during the period of World War I and for 3 years thereafter, but it then fell to moderate proportions until 1928 and 1929 when a big expansion occurred in connection with the stock market boom. After 1929, the volume remained moderate until and through the banking crisis of 1933, following which it fell to extremely low levels— a situation that continued well into the period of World War II. At no time in the entire period 1935–1942 did the monthly average of loans to member banks on the books of the Reserve banks exceed $24 million, and in many months of this period the volume was as low as $2 million or $3 million.

A slow expansion in lending activities began in 1943 and continued until the summer of 1945, reaching a high of $912 million in early June; but this figure was quite modest in relationship to the great expansion in commercial bank reserves that took place during the war years, because most of this expansion was effected by purchases of U.S. Treasury obligations by the Reserve banks. Thereafter, the loan volume of the Reserve banks continued in the moderate range until the fall of 1952 and the spring of 1953, when extraordinary pressures on the member banks forced them to greatly increase their borrowings, a new high since 1921 of slightly over $2 billion being reached in late December 1952. Many of the member banks were able to eliminate their debts to the Reserve banks or at least to substantially reduce their debts in the latter part of 1953. In the long period since then, as Table 17-1 shows, Federal Reserve lending operations have generally maintained positions in the lower and middle ranges—doubtless held down,

Table 17-1   **Outstanding Discounts and Advances of the Federal Reserve Banks, Selected Years, 1918–1970ᵃ (in millions of dollars)**

YEAR	HIGH	LOW	YEAR	HIGH	LOW
1918	1765	529	1950	306	43
1919	2140	1731	1952	1633	200
1921	2523	1180	1954	407	104
1923	873	547	1956	1060	706
1926	668	480	1958	564	109
1928	1090	465	1960	909	94
1930	501	189	1962	305	76
1933	999	114	1964	433	214
1935	10	6	1965	566	340
1938	11	7	1966	427	774
1941	12	2	1967	389	89
1943	90	8	1968	765	237
1945	633	118	1969	1407	697
1948	410	224	1970	1432	321

ᵃ Monthly averages of daily figures. The highs and lows are presented regardless of the months within each year in which they occurred. In 1970, for example, the high level of Federal Reserve lending of $1432 million occurred in July and the low level of $321 million in December.

Sources: *Banking and Monetary Statistics*, pp. 369–372, and *Federal Reserve Bulletin*.

in the later 1960s especially—by the smooth functioning of the federal funds market.[1]

Discounts and advances

When a Federal Reserve bank grants a loan to a member bank, the transaction may be either a *discount* or an *advance*. A discount or "rediscount" is a loan made to a member bank on "eligible paper"—on promissory notes, drafts, and other instruments on which it itself has already granted loans to its customers, provided that these instruments satisfy the "eligibility" requirements stated in the Federal Reserve Act. In effect, then, the member bank borrows on other people's obligations to pay, although it must "make good" on any on which the obligors default. On the other hand, an advance of a Reserve bank to a member bank is a loan whose repayment is solely the obligation of the member bank, as provided for in a "continuing lending agreement" it enters into with the Reserve bank. On advances, however, the member bank must pledge collateral that may be "eligible paper," Treasury obligations, securities of federal agencies, or other assets that the Reserve bank is willing to accept.

Although a member bank may have an abundant supply of Treasury obligations and securities of federal agencies to offer as collateral for Re-

---

[1]See Chapter 13.

serve bank advances (or, for that matter, an abundant supply of customers' paper "eligible" for rediscount), it has no right to demand an extension of credit. Its relationships with the Reserve bank in this regard are similar to those of a businessman and his bank. The Reserve bank has full discretion in deciding whether or not to grant loans applied for by member banks. The lending officers of the Reserve bank may decide that a member bank applying for an advance is overextending itself in its own loan and investment operations and reject the application for that reason.

Actually, the customary procedure of the Federal Reserve banks, in the first instance, is to grant without question and without delay member bank requests for advances. The reason for this is that the banks that apply for advances have deficiencies in their reserves—they wish to borrow at once to avoid the penalties for deficiencies.[2] If, then, the officers of a Reserve bank feel that a borrowing member bank is overextending itself or that it has been borrowing too frequently to offset deficiencies, they will notify the member bank *after the advance has been granted* that it must be rapidly reduced, that it must be fully repaid within a given period of time, or that further requests for advances will not be honored unless they are presented much less frequently.

Advances secured by treasury and federal agency obligations

Subject to whatever regulations the Board of Governors may prescribe, the Federal Reserve banks have general authority to grant advances to member banks secured by pledges of Treasury obligations, obligations of federal agencies, and obligations guaranteed as to principal and interest by the Treasury or by federal agencies (hereafter referred to simply as "Treasury and federal agency obligations"). At the time granted, such advances are limited to periods not exceeding 90 days, but it is possible to have their maturities extended. However, many advances secured by Treasury and federal agency obligations have maturities of only 1 day or a few days, as is often appropriate when member banks borrow to avoid penalties for reserve deficiencies.

Because advances by the Reserve banks to member banks secured by Treasury or federal agency obligations are simple transactions, they have long since supplanted almost all transactions involving the use of eligible paper. When eligible paper was used, the credit departments of the Reserve banks investigated the credit worthiness of the persons and firms who were primarily liable on it. But no special investigation of the member bank that puts up Treasury or federal agency obligations as collateral for advances is ordinarily necessary. From reports of condition and examination reports, the credit department of the Reserve bank already knows the

---

[2]See Chapter 13 for a discussion of reports of deposits, the determination of required reserves, and the assessment of penalties for deficiencies.

degree of "soundness" of the borrowing bank. Moreover, the quality of the collateral is unimpeachable. Very often, indeed, the member bank does not even have to supply the Treasury or agency obligations to be pledged. All or most of its holdings of these obligations may already be held in the vaults of the Reserve banks for safekeeping on a custodial basis. To pledge some of these holdings, therefore, all the member bank needs to do is to direct the Reserve bank to make a transfer from its custodial account to a collateral account.

Advances "secured to the satisfaction of" the reserve banks

Although most of the loans that are granted by the Reserve banks to member banks are advances secured by pledges of Treasury and federal agency obligations, the broadest lending authority that the Reserve banks appear to have is the provisions of section 10(b) of the Federal Reserve Act that empowers them to grant advances to member banks for periods to 4 months on any acceptable collateral—advances "secured to the satisfaction of" the Reserve banks themselves, as the law puts it. But there is a restriction: on section 10(b) advances, each of the Reserve banks must charge interest at a rate at least one half of a percentage point above "the highest discount rate in effect at such Reserve bank" on the date such advances are granted. In current practice, this really means a rate one half of a percentage point above the rate on advances to member banks secured by Treasury or federal agency obligations.

The restriction was originally intended to hold section 10(b) advances in reserve for financial crises and emergencies. When the new lending power with its restrictions was added to the Federal Reserve Act on a temporary basis in 1932 and then made permanent in 1935, Congress was obviously thinking about financial crises. The idea was that, as long as member banks had eligible paper and Treasury obligations on which to borrow, they would be most unlikely to ask for section 10(b) advances on which they would have to pay interest at the higher rate. But in a time of crisis when holdings of eligible paper and Treasury obligations might be scanty, the member banks would surely not refuse to pay a slightly higher rate in order to protect their solvency, and the Federal Reserve banks as "lenders of last resort" would surely come to their rescue by granting loans on the security of municipal securities, consumer notes, real-estate mortgage notes, and other kinds of assets not otherwise "eligible."

But the Board of Governors has long been saying that the "penalty rate" applicable to section 10(b) advances is far out-of-date, and it has repeatedly recommended its elimination by Congress. And doubtless most students of money and banking fully agree with its position—a position stated in part in its *Annual Report* for 1968 as follows:

> The need for enactment of such legislation has increased as member banks have reduced their holdings of U.S. Government securities and

broadened the scope of their lending in order to meet the expanding credit demands of their customers. Many of these loans cannot qualify as security for Federal Reserve advances except at the "penalty" rate of interest, although their quality may be equal to that of presently "eligible" paper.[3]

Loans on eligible paper

Although "eligible paper" is now of minor significance in the lending operations of the Federal Reserve banks, and although it would have no significance at all if the recommendation of the Board of Governors, as just mentioned, were adopted, its definition and description have held an important place in the literature of the Federal Reserve System. The founders of the system believed that the Reserve banks should grant loans to member banks only for short-term productive purposes. They envisaged that manufacturers, merchants, farmers, and other enterprisers would borrow from the member banks for working capital and that the member banks, should they find themselves short in lending capacity, would in turn rediscount the enterprisers' paper at the Reserve banks. In this way, every loan granted by the Reserve banks would be matched by an increased supply of goods coming to the market—goods produced with the aid of the borrowed funds. Accordingly, the legislation of 1913 authorized the Reserve banks to discount "notes, drafts, and bills of exchange arising out of actual commercial transactions; that is, notes, drafts, and bills of exchange issued or drawn for agricultural, industrial, or commercial purposes, or the proceeds of which have been used, or are to be used, for such purposes." To avoid the possibility that Federal Reserve credit might be used for speculation in securities, the original legislation further provided that the definition of eligibility "shall not include notes, drafts, or bills covering merely investments or issued or drawn for the purpose of carrying or trading in stocks, bonds, or other investment securities, except bonds and notes of the Government of the United States." To promote the use of loan instruments that member banks could readily transfer to the Reserve banks, there were stipulations that the latter could rediscount only *negotiable* "notes, drafts, and bills of exchange." And to fit Federal Reserve lending to the production cycles of enterprisers, there were provisions that, in general, the Reserve banks could rediscount business paper only when within 90 days of maturity, but farm paper when within 9 months of maturity.

The objective of establishing a direct relationship between lending by the Federal Reserve banks and the expansion of production began to break down as early as 1916, and this meant, of course, an immediate decline in the significance of eligible paper. The act of September 7, 1916, authorized the Reserve banks to make direct loans to member banks for 15-day periods on their own promissory notes secured by bonds and notes of the United

---

[3]P. 337.

States government. After the adoption of this legislation, the member banks had less occasion to be concerned about the "eligibility" of their customers' notes and bills of exchange for rediscounting or as collateral for advances, for they had every reason to believe that they could obtain ample advances from the Reserve banks as long as they had Treasury obligations to offer as collateral. And further blows were dealt to the "productive credit theory" and eligible paper by legislation adopted in the period 1932–1935 providing for section 10(b) advances, as already discussed, and raising to 90 days the permissible period for advances on Treasury obligations, as well as by legislation adopted in 1968 that authorizes advances to 90 days secured by obligations of federal agencies and obligations they guarantee, as also already mentioned.

Nevertheless, provisions for the rediscounting of eligible paper and for its acceptance as collateral on advances remain in the Federal Reserve Act, and its definition is still essentially as originally stated: notes and other loan instruments the proceeds of which have been used or are to be used for productive purposes, discountable at the Reserve banks if within 90 days of maturity, or within 9 months of maturity if farm paper, and acceptable by the Reserve banks as collateral for advances if within 90 days of maturity. Hence it is still possible for member banks to have eligible paper rediscounted at the Reserve banks or accepted as collateral for advances, but most of them choose to bypass this means of borrowing.

LOANS TO NONMEMBERS

Nonmember banks

The capacity of the Federal Reserve banks to provide advances secured by pledges of Treasury and federal agency obligations for periods to 90 days is not limited to member banks. Indeed, member banks are simply included in a general class of "individuals, partnerships, and corporations" to which such advances may be granted. Subject to whatever restrictions may be made by the Board of Governors, and provided that the Reserve banks are willing to accept their applications, therefore, nonmember banks can apply for advances to be secured by Treasury or federal agency obligations as freely as the member banks. For such advances to nonmember banks, however, the Reserve banks post a discount rate at least one percentage point greater than that charged member banks—a spread clearly designed to promote membership.

In "unusual and exigent circumstances," moreover, the Board of Governors may permit nonmember banks to borrow from the Reserve banks by having eligible paper rediscounted. For such loans, however, the board's action must have the affirmative vote of five of its seven members, and the Reserve banks must assure themselves that the applicants for rediscounting privileges are unable to secure "adequate credit accommodations" from other banking institutions, such as their correspondent banks.

Another means by which nonmember banks can gain access to the Reserve banks for rediscounting is to employ member banks as agents in offering their eligible paper. A member bank, however, must have the specific permission of the Board of Governors to act as agent in such a transaction. In any event, nonmember banks are generally as little interested in using eligible paper for borrowing as are the member banks.

Other nonmembers

On the face of it, wage earners, farmers, businessmen, industrial corporations, and other individuals and organizations may obtain advances from the Federal Reserve banks secured by Treasury and federal agency obligations on the same basis as nonmember banks; they are necessarily included among the "individuals, partnerships, and corporations" to which the Federal Reserve Act permits such loans to be granted. What is more, rediscounts of eligible paper in "unusual and exigent circumstances," as referred to above, are also available for "individuals, partnerships, and corporations." Clearly, however, these lending powers of the Federal Reserve banks are designed for emergencies, so that, in untroubled times, the wage earner, farmer, or businessman would surely be refused were he to apply directly to a Reserve bank for a loan.

DISCOUNT RATES

The discount rates of the Federal Reserve banks are the per annum rates of interest that they charge on loans—loans granted primarily, of course, to member banks but occasionally also to nonmember banks. There is no bargaining over the rate of discount that a borrowing bank must pay. For each class of loans it grants, a Federal Reserve bank has a published rate that it applies as a matter of course to each transaction of that class. However, the published rates are changed from time to time in keeping with changes in market rates of interest or as a means of influencing business activity—a matter to be discussed in Chapter 20. The various discount rates in effect at all the Reserve banks are usually identical; sometimes, however, there are disparities for a few days or weeks when one or two of the Reserve banks have put changes into effect, and the others delay for a short time before falling into line.

For most of their careers, the Reserve banks applied their discount rates —as the term itself implies—by subtracting the amount of the computed interest from the principal of loans, advancing the difference as "proceeds," and then requiring the borrowing banks to pay the principal at maturity. The present practice, however, is for the borrowing bank to pay at maturity both the principal and interest, with the interest computed on the basis of a 365-day year. On an advance of, say, $730,000 for 7 days at a "discount" rate of 6 percent, the interest would total $730,000 × 7/365 × 0.06, or $840, and the repayment obligation 7 days later would be $730,840. When, however, a borrowing bank pays its loan before maturity, its liability for interest is cut proportionally; in other words, it pays interest only for the period that the loan was outstanding. On the other hand, changes in discount rates announced by a Reserve bank apply from the date of change to all loans of the respective classes already outstanding.

Although, at any time, each Federal Reserve bank has several discount rates in effect, as illustrated in Table 17.2, the rate charged on advances to

Table 17-2 **Discount Rates in Effect at the Federal Reserve Banks on January 31, 1971 (percent per annum)**

CLASS OF TRANSACTION	RATE
Advances to member banks secured by Treasury or federal agency obligations	5
Rediscounts of eligible paper for member banks and advances to member banks secured by eligible paper	5
Other secured advances to member banks [sec. 10(b)]	5½
Advances to individuals, partnerships, nonmember banks, and nonbank corporations secured by Treasury or federal agency obligations	7

Source: Federal Reserve Bulletin, February, 1971, p. A9.

member banks secured by Treasury or federal agency obligations is often referred to as *the* discount rate. In view of the preponderance of this kind of advance in the lending operations of the Reserve banks, it is unquestionably the key rate in the Federal Reserve rate structure.

OPEN-MARKET OPERATIONS

The most important power possessed by the Federal Reserve in its role as central bank is that of buying and selling Treasury obligations in the open market. Such transactions are the principal means by which the volume of commercial bank primary reserves and therefore the total quantity of money in circulation are controlled. In Chapter 20, more will be said about open-market operations as a control instrument; for the moment, therefore, attention will be confined to some organizational and procedural details concerning these operations.

Open-market procedure

A basic fact that we should remember about the open-market operations of the Federal Reserve banks is that these banks do not individually buy and sell Treasury obligations or any other kind of security in the open market or anywhere else. As pointed out in the preceding chapter, the power to determine the volume and timing of the open-market transactions of the Reserve banks collectively is held by the Federal Open Market Committee (FOMC) that is composed of the members of the Board of Governors and five Reserve bank presidents. The directives of the FOMC go to the Federal Reserve Bank of New York that has long had responsibility for carrying them out. Its transactions in the open market are said to be transactions for the "System Open Market Account" (SOMA) in which all the Reserve banks share, as it were, by a continuing unanimous consent. A vice-president of the New York Reserve Bank is designated as the manager of SOMA, and a second vice-president acts as its "special manager." The special manager makes decisions continually about buying and selling foreign currencies; and the manager, continual decisions about buying and selling everything else that the law permits the Reserve banks to invest in, with the manager constantly trying, through his transactions, to produce effects on the domestic monetary situation as wanted by the FOMC; and the special manager doing the same for wanted balance-of-payments effects.

The responsibility of the manager of SOMA is especially great, because, as we shall see, the policy directives of the FOMC are not stated in a way to indicate precisely what he should do—nor presumably can they be. While, moreover, he must make decisions from hour to hour whether SOMA should be buying or selling and what and how much, he cannot know in any precise way what effects on the monetary situation a given amount of buying and selling will have nor how quickly the effects will show. He must constantly take many kinds of developments into consideration, especially the changes currently taking place and projected to take place in the many "factors supplying and absorbing reserves"[4] over which he has no direct control. He must continually judge whether these changes will have the effects that the FOMC wants or the effects that he must offset by SOMA transactions.

Scope of open-market operations

Despite the importance of open-market operations, the *kinds* of securities that SOMA, acting for the FOMC and all the Reserve banks, is authorized to buy and sell are few in number: direct and guaranteed obligations of the Treasury; direct and guaranteed obligations of all other federal agencies (a new authorization given on a temporary basis in 1966 and made permanent in 1968); obligations of state and local governments maturing in not more 6 months and issued in anticipation of tax receipts or other assured revenues; cable transfers, bankers' acceptances, and bills of exchange that would be eligible for rediscount; and foreign currencies.

---

[4]See Chapter 7.

It thus lacks authority to buy such additional classes of securities as issues of state and local governments maturing after 6 months, corporation stocks and bonds, and even the securities of foreign governments for the temporary investment of holdings of foreign currencies.

Concentration on Treasury Obligations   Throughout their careers, however, the Federal Reserve banks originally and then SOMA have generally found their capacity to buy and sell Treasury obligations sufficient for their control objectives. The national debt has continuously been large enough to ensure the availability of many Treasury obligations. In some periods in the 1920s, it is true, Reserve bank holdings of bankers' acceptances exceeded their holdings of Treasury obligations, but since then bankers' acceptances have had only a minor position in their portfolios. At no time have the Reserve banks and SOMA displayed much interest in investing in short-term obligations of state and local governments, or in recent years, in exercising the new power to buy and sell direct and guaranteed issues of federal agencies other than the Treasury. Since early 1962, on the other hand, SOMA's market transactions in foreign currencies have often amounted to substantial volumes, but as already indicated, such transactions are directed to the solution of balance-of-payments problems rather than to the control of the quantity of money in circulation at home.

The concentration of SOMA's open-market operations on Treasury obligations is indicated by the Reserve banks' enormous holdings of these obligations at $62,142 million at the end of 1970, and their huge increase in the preceding decade—from $27,384 million held at the end of 1960. At the end of 1970, on the other hand, holdings of bankers' acceptances amounted to only $57 million and foreign currencies to $257 million, while holdings of federal agency obligations and short-term securities of state and local governments were nil.[5]

Inclusions and Exclusions   When the Federal Reserve Bank of New York, in conducting the operations of SOMA, buys Treasury obligations, foreign currencies, and other instruments in the open market, it allocates almost all among the Reserve banks, including itself, in proportion to their outstanding Federal Reserve note issues at the end of the preceding year. SOMA's acquisitions thus become assets of the Reserve banks individually although they continue to be held by the New York Reserve Bank, and the Reserve banks, like any investors, must pay for their respective allotments. The payment process is essentially conducted by the New York Reserve Bank's paying the sellers, and then by the other eleven Reserve banks' paying for their shares through transfers in their accounts in the Interdistrict Settlement Fund. On the other hand, sales by SOMA are made as proportional

---

[5]*Federal Reserve Bulletin,* February 1961, p. 176, and January 1971, p. A12.

sales out of the portfolios of all twelve Reserve banks, so that they are individually entitled to receive payment. And again, the payment process is essentially conducted by the New York Reserve Bank's receiving payment from the buyers and then distributing the shares of the other eleven Reserve banks through the accounts of the Interdistrict Settlement Fund.

Accordingly, Federal Reserve open-market operations *do not include* the buying and selling of Treasury obligations by the Reserve banks in agency capacities—a kind of activity in which each engages individually and extensively. It is pointed out later in this chapter that the Reserve banks take subscriptions to and payments for new issues of Treasury securities, arrange exchanges, pay the principal of maturing issues, and buy and sell for the Treasury's own trust funds—all of this in their roles as "fiscal agents of the United States"—and that other dealings in Treasury debt instruments are often undertaken for foreign governments and central banks. It is true that such transactions take place in the market, but they are excluded from the category of open-market operations because the Federal Reserve authorities are not in a position *to control* these transactions. Indeed, SOMA may have to enter the market at times to offset unwanted effects of some of these fiscal agency transactions.

Nor do open-market operations include direct sales of obligations by the Treasury to the Federal Reserve banks. Such sales—which are almost exclusively sales to the Federal Reserve Bank of New York for its own account, that is, without allocation to the other Reserve banks—were authorized by legislation originally adopted in 1942 and repeatedly extended by Congress so that it remains in effect at the present time.[6] However, Federal Reserve holdings at any time of Treasury obligations bought directly are limited to $5 billion. Direct sales are excluded from the open-market category because, again, the Federal Reserve authorities are hardly in a position to control them, and because they obviously do not take place in the "open market." At any rate, direct sales occur only infrequently—to enable the Treasury to cover temporary deficiencies in its deposit accounts at the Reserve banks. For this purpose, the Treasury issues to the Reserve banks "special certificates of indebtedness."

Within the scope of open-market operations, on the other hand, are SOMA's transactions in buying Treasury obligations from nonbank dealers on the basis of repurchase agreements. At times of tightness in the money market, SOMA's manager may decide to ease the situation somewhat by offering to buy on a repurchase basis from nonbank dealers rather than by buying outright. Such a decision is most likely to be made when the objective is to ease the market situation for only a few days, since the easing

---

[6]Direct purchases and sales between the Federal Reserve banks and the Treasury were permitted before 1935, but a provision of the Banking Act of that year stated that direct and guaranteed obligations of the federal government could be purchased "only in the open market."

will be reversed as soon as the dealer fulfills his obligation to repurchase. On their part, the nonbank dealers are usually happy to have the opportunity to sell to SOMA on a repurchase basis, since the tightness in the money market typically means that they are having difficulty borrowing elsewhere and that, possibly, they are paying higher rates of interest than SOMA will charge on the repurchase transaction. In such a transaction, then, the dealer sells some of his holdings of Treasury obligations to SOMA and assumes the obligations to buy them back at the selling price plus interest within a period that may not exceed 15 days. The interest rate charged the dealer is usually the same as the discount rate on advances to member banks secured by Treasury obligations.[7]

Objectives of open-market operations

In keeping with the responsibility of central banks to control the quantity of money in circulation in order to promote the general public welfare, the fundamental objective of the open-market operations of the Federal Reserve is precisely such control. If the open-market power is the most important held by the Federal Reserve authorities because it is the principal means of controlling the size of commercial bank primary reserves, the basic objective could hardly be otherwise. Except for transactions in foreign currencies, therefore, almost all present-day open-market transactions of the Federal Reserve are undertaken to control the volume of commercial bank reserves in order to encourage monetary expansion, to hold it in bounds, or to prevent undesirable effects on the quantity of money that would normally result from changes in other "factors supplying and absorbing reserves."

Occasionally, however, SOMA engages in open-market operations for a second reason: to correct "disorderly conditions" in the market for Treasury obligations. This market is said to be "disorderly" if sellers are unable to find buyers at prices near the prices that have been prevailing, and if, therefore, sharp drops in prices are occurring from transaction to transaction and are likely to continue. Treasury securities are so widely held as a means for the temporary investment of funds shortly to be needed elsewhere that an atmosphere of panic can spread quickly, with many holders being drawn into the market as sellers as they seek to avoid losses. And SOMA is in a position to restore order, of course, by doing an extraordinary amount of buying.

During the years of World War II and in the postwar period well into 1951, SOMA often bought Treasury obligations for still a third reason: to prevent their prices from falling below certain specified levels. As this is

---

[7]It will be remembered that the Federal Reserve Bank of New York has a similar capacity to enter into repurchase agreements with nonbank dealers in bankers' acceptances. See Chapter 11.

the same as preventing their market yields from rising above specified levels, the market-price support policy enabled the Treasury to finance its wartime borrowing and the refunding of this borrowing and of other debts at low rates of interest. The Federal Reserve authorities willingly agreed with this idea during the war years, but they became increasingly unhappy about it in the postwar period, arguing with perfect logic that the support policy crippled the money-control function of open-market operations. At length, in March 1951, an "accord" was reached by which the Treasury stopped its demands for price supports.

As a final point, it must be especially emphasized that SOMA does not buy Treasury obligations, bankers' acceptances, and foreign currencies in the open market and allocate them to the Reserve banks to expand their earnings. Additional earnings are of negligible concern to the Federal Reserve authorities, for, as we saw in the preceding chapter, the Reserve banks' annual net income is so lush that they are able to pay expenses, distribute dividends to the stockholding member banks, provide certain credits to surplus, and still have hundreds of millions of dollars to give to the Treasury as a kind of voluntary contribution—technically as a self-imposed tax on their issues of Federal Reserve notes. It was not always so. Early in the 1920s, when loans to member banks fell sharply, the Reserve banks bought government securities as a source of income. But that was long ago.

Role of the Federal Open Market Committee

In order to decide what are to be the objectives of open-market operations in the immediate future, the Federal Open Market Committee meets in Washington at intervals generally ranging from 3 to 4 weeks. Usually all the Reserve bank presidents attend these meetings, although only five of them are officially members of the committee for the current year. The manager and special manager of the System Open Market Account also attend, as do various staff members of the Board of Governors and of the Reserve banks who are brought along in advisory capacities. Quite a gathering! When advice or action is needed quickly, additional conferences are held by telephone.

At each meeting of the committee, the course of business developments is discussed, with particular attention to the prospects for the next few weeks. On the basis of this discussion, a new "current economic policy directive" is given to the Federal Reserve Bank of New York or one given at an earlier meeting is simply continued in effect, while the committee's "continuing authority directive" may or may not be amended. The nature and flavor of the committee's directives can best be appreciated by direct quotations. The principal provisions of its "continuing authority directive with respect to domestic open-market operations" that was in effect at the beginning of the year 1969 were as follows:

1. The Federal Open Market Committee authorizes and directs the Federal Reserve Bank of New York, to the extent necessary to carry out the most recent current economic policy directive adopted at a meeting of the Committee:

   (a) To buy or sell U.S. Government securities in the open market, from or to government securities dealers and foreign and international accounts maintained at the Federal Reserve Bank of New York, on a cash, regular, or deferred delivery basis, for the System Open Market Account at market prices and, for such Account, to exchange maturing U.S. Government securities with the Treasury or allow them to mature without replacement; provided that the aggregate amount of such securities held in such Account at the close of business on the day of a meeting of the Committee at which action is taken with respect to a current economic policy directive shall not be increased or decreased by more than $2.0 billion during the period commencing with the opening of business on the day following such meeting and ending with the close of business on the day of the next such meeting; . . .

   (c) To buy U.S. Government securities, obligations that are direct obligations of, or fully guaranteed as to principal and interest by, any agency of the United States, and prime bankers' acceptances with maturities of 6 months or less at the time of purchase, from nonbank dealers for the account of the Federal Reserve Bank of New York under agreements for repurchase of such securities, obligations, or acceptances in 15 calendar days or less, at rates not less than (1) the discount rate of the Federal Reserve Bank of New York at the time such agreement is entered into, or (2) the average issuing rate on the most recent issue of 3-month Treasury bills, whichever is lower. . . .

2. The Federal Open Market Committee authorizes and directs the Federal Reserve Bank of New York to purchase directly from the Treasury for the account of the Federal Reserve Bank of New York (with discretion, in cases where it seems desirable, to issue participations to one or more Federal Reserve Banks) such amounts of special short-term certificates of indebtedness as may be necessary from time to time for the temporary accommodation of the Treasury; provided that the rate charged on such certificates shall be a rate $\frac{1}{4}$ of 1 percent below the discount rate of the Federal Reserve Bank of New York at the time of such purchases, and provided further that the total amount of such certificates held at any time by the Federal Reserve banks shall not exceed $1 billion.[8]

---

[8]Board of Governors, *Annual Report,* 1969, pp. 96, 97.

Illustrative of the committee's "current economic policy directives" is the following adopted at its meeting of November 25, 1969:

> . . . In light of the foregoing developments, it is the policy of the Federal Open Market Committee to foster financial conditions conducive to the reduction of inflationary pressures, with a view to encouraging sustainable economic growth and attaining reasonable equilibrium in the country's balance of payments.
>
> To implement this policy, System open market operations until the next meeting of the Committee shall be conducted with a view to maintaining the prevailing firm conditions in money and short-term credit markets; provided, however, that operations shall be modified if bank credit appears to be deviating significantly from current projections or if pressures arise in connection with possible bank regulatory changes.[9]

FISCAL AGENCY FUNCTIONS

As fiscal agents of the United States

The Federal Reserve banks are the chief fiscal agents of the federal government. Their services to the Treasury include the holding of its deposit balances; the payment of checks drawn on these balances; the transfer of funds throughout the country and abroad in its behalf; the collection of payments due it, as the clearing of checks received from the public for taxes and other obligations; assistance in the sale of its debt instruments; the exchange of such instruments; the payment of interest and principal on them; and the purchase of securities for its trust funds, such as the social security and civil service retirement funds.

Cash Transactions   The mere handling of the Treasury's deposit balances is a huge task. The balances are increased by deposits of gold certificates, SDR certificates, newly minted coins, and paper money and coins received by the Treasury in various transactions with the public; by transfers of Treasury deposits from tax and loan accounts at the commercial banks;[10] and by deposits at the Reserve banks of checks drawn on commercial banks received from taxpayers, buyers of government securities, and others.

Against the Treasury balances, many millions of checks are drawn each year for the payment of government employees and the personnel of the armed forces; the purchase of supplies and equipment; the payment of subsidies; the meeting of interest, pension, and other obligations; and the redemption of maturing debt instruments. During the year 1969, for example, the Reserve banks cashed a total of 575 million checks amounting to $208 billion drawn on the Treasury.[11] Virtually all the services of the Federal

---

[9]*Ibid.*, p. 202.
[10]See Chapter 7.
[11]*Ibid.*, p. 340.

Reserve banks as depositaries of the Treasury are provided free of charge, for the Treasury undertakes to compensate the Reserve banks for only a few services of a special character.

Assistance with Treasury Financing   Another important area of service of the Federal Reserve banks as fiscal agents of the federal government is their assistance in the issuance, exchange, and retirement of its bills, notes, and bonds. When the Treasury decides to float new issues of marketable securities, the Reserve banks prepare descriptive announcements that are sent to all banking institutions as well as to other prospective investors. They receive the subscriptions of investors, make allotments, deliver the securities to the buyers, and collect payment. They also supervise the sale of savings bonds and keep the records of the holders of these bonds.

Work related to transfers and exchanges of Treasury obligations already outstanding is also performed by the Reserve banks. The sale of unregistered obligations, including all issues of bills, requires no negotiations with the Treasury or with the Reserve banks since they pass by delivery, but the transfer of title to registered notes and bonds must be entered on the books. Again, investors sometimes want to switch the denominations of their security holdings, as when a person wants five $1000 bonds in place of a $5000 one. Often subscribers to new issues of Treasury securities are permitted to pay for them by merely turning in maturing issues they hold, and such exchanges entail clerical work of a somewhat different kind for the Reserve banks. Finally, the Reserve banks take care of interest payments on outstanding Treasury obligations and their redemption at maturity or when otherwise properly tendered for redemption, as in the case of savings bonds.

In the year 1969, the Reserve banks received for payment about 13 million interest coupons on Treasury obligations amounting to $6849 million, and issued, redeemed, and exchanged such obligations in the total amount of $1152 billion.[12]

Other fiscal agency functions

Departments of the federal government other than the Treasury and many of the federal agencies often ask the Federal Reserve banks for various kinds of services. In recent years, the Reserve banks have acted in capacities as fiscal agents, custodians, and depositaries for the federal land banks, the federal intermediate credit banks, the federal home loan banks, the Federal Deposit Insurance Corporation, and many other federal agencies. All these agencies reimburse the Reserve banks for the expenses entailed in the performance of their services, except for services as depositaries.

During the years of World War II, the Federal Reserve banks served in a special capacity as fiscal agents of the War and Navy Departments and the Maritime Commission in guaranteeing loans granted by financial insti-

---

[12]*Ibid.,* p. 340.

tutions to provide business firms with money to complete government contracts. Guaranteed loans were designated "V-loans" because they were subject to the provisions of Regulation V as issued by the Board of Governors. In September 1950, Regulation V was restored, and the Reserve banks once again set up procedures for V-loan guarantees—procedures still available at the present time. Loans to finance the production of equipment and supplies for "national defense" may be guaranteed by the Reserve banks on behalf of the Army, Navy, Air Force, Commerce, Interior, and Agriculture Departments, the Defense Supply Agency of the U.S. Department of Defense, the National Aeronautical and Space Administration, and the Atomic Energy Commission.

Services for foreign and international institutions

The Federal Reserve banks—especially the New York Reserve Bank—provide services ranging from simple depositary functions to extensive fiscal agency work for many foreign governments, foreign central banks, and international institutions, such as the International Monetary Fund, the International Bank for Reconstruction and Development, the Inter-American Development Bank, and the Asian Development Bank. The services of the Reserve banks on behalf of such institutions are often supplemented, however, by services of American commercial banks.

In this area, the role of the Federal Reserve Bank of New York as correspondent of foreign central banks is especially noteworthy. Its work in this capacity includes the holding of deposits, the safekeeping of gold shipped to the United States or obtained at the Treasury and placed under earmark, the investment of deposit balances in American securities at the direction of the foreign banks, the payment of interest and principal on foreign securities owned by American investors, and in certain circumstances, the granting of loans.

OTHER OPERATIONS OF THE FEDERAL RESERVE BANKS

Distribution of paper money and coins

The Federal Reserve banks are the channels through which supplies of paper money and coins flow to the general public, chiefly by way of the member banks. In dollar amounts, a very large proportion of the supplies available for delivery by the Reserve banks—the Federal Reserve notes—originate with them,[13] while other portions are accumulated through deliveries of new coins from the mints—for which the Treasury receives credit in its deposit accounts—and return flows of paper money and coins from

---

[13]For a description of the note-issue operations of the Federal Reserve banks, see Chapter 4.

the member banks, the Treasury, other governmental agencies, foreign governments and central banks, and international financial institutions.

Most of the flows of paper money and coins from the Federal Reserve banks toward the general public are initiated by member banks. To build up their vault cash in anticipation of large withdrawals, as before the Christmas shopping season, or replenish it when it has already been drawn down, they call on the Reserve banks for shipments of paper money and coins in whatever denominations they want. In making such shipments, the Reserve banks also stand ready to make deliveries to nonmember banks in response to requests of member banks. On these shipments, however, the expenses are charged against the member banks and they are expected to pass them on to the nonmembers.

Clearings and collections

The work performed by the Reserve banks in clearing checks drawn on bank demand deposits was described at some length in Chapter 6, but some additional services of a similar character may be mentioned here. Not only do the Reserve banks supply facilities for intradistrict and interdistrict clearing of checks, they perform an excellent service in collecting time items arriving at maturity. Promissory notes, commercial drafts, bankers' acceptances, bond coupons, and securities are all handled by the Reserve banks.

A member bank or a nonmember clearing bank can send such items to the Reserve bank in its district, and the latter obtains payment by presenting them directly to the person, firm, or corporation obligated; by sending them to other Reserve banks or branches; or by collecting them through other banking institutions. Ordinarily no charge is made for this service other than telephone and telegraph expenses, postage, express charges, and insurance and registry fees. Commercial banks that are requested by the Reserve banks to assist in collecting items of the kinds mentioned may levy reasonable charges for their services, and these are passed on to the banks for which collections are made.

Telegraphic and mail transfers

The Reserve banks provide facilities to member banks for the transfer of funds to all parts of the country. Their private wires are available to member banks without charge for transferring sums of $1000 or multiples of $1000 for their own benefit to other member banks. Should a member bank in South Bend, Indiana, for example, want to make an immediate payment in New York City for some securities purchased, it could request the Federal Reserve Bank of Chicago to wire the necessary funds to the Federal Reserve Bank of New York, where they would be placed to the credit of the New York correspondent of the South Bend bank. The reserve account of the South Bend bank at the Reserve Bank of Chicago would be reduced by the amount involved.

The Reserve banks also stand ready to arrange telegraphic transfers between member banks on behalf of their customers. Should a South Bend firm, for example, want to make an immediate payment to a San Francisco firm, a South Bend member bank could arrange for the payment through the Federal Reserve Banks of Chicago and San Francisco. For operations of this variety, the Reserve banks may use the commercial telegraph facilities and assess the costs of the telegrams against the member banks.

If speed is not essential for a given transfer of funds, a member bank can arrange with its Reserve bank for a mail transfer to any other member or nonmember clearing bank, whether the transfer is made for its own benefit or for the benefit of a customer. Alternatively, the member bank can simply draw a check upon its reserve account at the Reserve bank payable to the bank to which it wants to make the transfer. However, the latter procedure is somewhat more cumbersome than the former, since it requires the return of the check for payment to the drawee Reserve bank.

Net amounts payable to and by the Reserve banks because of interdistrict telegraphic and mail transfers are taken care of by means of debits and credits to their accounts in the Interdistrict Settlement Fund.

Miscellaneous activities

In addition to the operations already mentioned in this chapter, the Reserve banks have other tasks, some of which have been discussed elsewhere in this text. Among these are the following: (1) the examination of state-chartered banks that apply for admission to the Federal Reserve System, and the regular examination of state member banks; (2) the analysis of reports of condition filed by state member banks; (3) the dissemination and interpretation of the regulations of the Board of Governors; (4) the gathering and analysis of economic data of many kinds and the publication of analytical articles and reports, such as the generally excellent monthly and bimonthly "reviews" of business conditions and developments of eleven of the Reserve banks; and (5) the holding of securities for safekeeping for out-of-town member banks.

FEDERAL RESERVE BANK STATEMENTS

The Federal Reserve authorities publish a weekly statement of condition for each Reserve bank as well as a statement for the twelve banks combined; these are invaluable sources of information bearing on banking conditions and trends. Table 17-3 reproduces a recent combined statement and separate data for the Federal Reserve Bank of New York. The latter are included to show the dominant position of this bank, which, it will be noticed, accounted for approximately 25 percent of the combined resources of the Reserve banks at the date for which the figures were published.

Table 17-3   **Statements of Condition of the Federal Reserve Banks, December 31, 1970 (in millions of dollars)**

	TWELVE FEDERAL RESERVE BANKS COMBINED	FEDERAL RESERVE BANK OF NEW YORK
ASSETS		
Gold certificate account	10,457	1,942
SDR certificate account	400	93
Cash	221	20
Federal Reserve notes of other banks		187
Discounts and advances	334	104
Acceptances:		
Bought outright	57	57
Held under repurchase agreements	0	0
United States government securities:		
Bought outright	62,142	15,844
Held under repurchase agreements	0	0
Cash items in process of collection	11,081	2,805
Bank premises	128	8
Other assets:		
Denominated in foreign currencies	257	68[a]
All other	738	311
Total assets	85,815	21,439
LIABILITIES		
Federal Reserve notes	50,323	12,196
Deposits:		
Member bank reserves	24,052	6,157
U.S. Treasurer—general account	1,156	337
Foreign	148	56[a]
Other	1,233	737
Total deposits	26,589	7,287
Deferred availability cash items	6,917	1,439
Other liabilities and accrued dividends	582	147
Total liabilities	84,411	21,069
CAPITAL ACCOUNTS		
Capital paid in	702	185
Surplus	702	185
Other capital accounts	0	0
Total capital accounts	1,404	370
Total liabilities and capital accounts	85,815	21,439

[a] After deducting participations of other Federal Reserve banks.
Source: Federal Reserve Bulletin, January 1971, pp. A12, A13.

To grasp the information "buried" in the Federal Reserve statements, we should understand the nature of the various accounts listed as well as the more important relationships that exist among them. For that reason, it should be advantageous to devote brief attention to analysis, although many of the accounts should be quite familiar by reason of the exposition presented in the foregoing divisions of this chapter and in earlier chapters —and especially by reason of the extensive discussion in Chapter 7 of the factors supplying and absorbing reserves.

Asset accounts

In substance, the "gold certificate account" represents the claim that the Federal Reserve banks have against the physical gold stock held by the Treasury. Actually, however, this "claim" is of negligible significance to the Reserve banks, since the account varies in response to transactions initiated by the Treasury rather than by them. It typically increases by amounts equal to the value of gold bought by the Treasury, and decreases by amounts equal to the value of gold that the Treasury sells to foreign central banks. Much the same may be said for the "SDR certificate account," since changes in it are also initiated by the Treasury, as, for example, increases when the Treasury wants to get dollars with which to buy SDRs tendered by other members of the International Monetary Fund.

"Cash" consists of all the Treasury-issued money held by the Federal Reserve banks, and it is nowadays almost exclusively coins. In making shipments of coins to its member banks, the individual Reserve bank draws on its holdings of "cash," and for shipments of paper money, it can send "Federal Reserve notes of other banks," that is, of the other eleven Reserve banks, that it happens to be holding, or its own Federal Reserve notes. "Cash" never includes any of the notes that a Reserve bank itself has issued and then reacquired. Because the notes of each Reserve bank are classified as liabilities while outstanding, they can hardly be classified as "cash" when in its own possession. The *net* liability of all the Reserve banks to the public on Federal Reserve notes is obviously the difference between the total amounts issued by them collectively and the sum of "Federal Reserve notes of other banks" as reported by each bank separately as an asset; accordingly, "Federal Reserve notes of other banks" does not appear in the statement of the twelve banks combined.

In ordinary circumstances, "discounts and advances" stand exclusively or almost so for loans granted to member banks—the means of supplying them with reserves at their own requests—and increases and decreases in holdings of United States government securities are the principal means whereby the Federal Reserve authorities put into effect their own decisions to expand and contract reserves. In view of the extended discussion of Federal Reserve lending and open-market operations earlier in this chapter, a further explanation here should hardly be necessary.

The Federal Reserve Bank of New York acquires bankers' acceptances "outright" from time to time chiefly to promote the use of acceptances as a means of private financing rather than to create reserves for the commercial banks, although reserve creation does result. On the other hand, reserve creation, rather than assisting acceptance dealers, is said to be the objective when bankers' acceptances are bought "under repurchase agreements."

The asset "cash items in process of collection" must be considered in relation to "deferred availability cash items," which appears as a liability. These accounts originate in the check-clearing operations of the Reserve banks, the asset representing claims against drawee banks, and the liability standing for obligations to clearing or sending banks. The difference between the two accounts—the "float" that we discussed in Chapter 7—is the amount by which credits to the reserve accounts of sending banks, on the basis of Federal Reserve "time schedules," temporarily exceed charges against the reserve accounts of the drawee banks.

The entry "other assets" includes chiefly holdings of foreign currencies (ordinarily as deposits at foreign banks), accrued interest receivable on Treasury obligations, premiums paid on securities bought, claims against government agencies for expenses incurred in their behalf, and unused supplies.

Liability accounts

Further analysis at this point of "Federal Reserve notes" and "deferred availability cash" items should hardly be necessary. The importance of the reserve accounts of the member banks must be stressed because they are the principal component of the primary reserves of the commercial banking system. The "general account" of the U.S. Treasurer is highly significant as the reservoir into which flow sooner or later all of the many kinds of payments that the federal government collects and from which virtually all the payments that it makes both at home and abroad flow. The account "foreign deposits" consists principally of the balances held by foreign governments and their central banks with the Reserve banks for correspondent and related purposes. Finally, the account "other deposits" includes the clearing accounts of nonmember banks, the accounts of federal agencies, the deposit balances of international organizations, such as the International Monetary Fund, outstanding officers' (cashiers') checks issued by the Reserve banks, and other miscellaneous deposits.

Besides accrued dividends, the total for "other liabilities" is chiefly made up of unearned discount on securities bought and expenses incurred but not yet paid.

Capital accounts

"Capital paid in" is the par value of all the stock of the Reserve banks owned by the member banks. *Surplus* consists of accumulated net earnings of the Reserve banks remaining after the payment of dividends, the payment of franchise taxes and other contributions to the federal government, and the subscription to the stock of the FDIC. Earnings that accrue during the year in excess of amounts needed for dividends are carried in "other capital accounts."

FOR REVIEW

1. What is the distinction between the discounts of Federal Reserve banks and their advances?
2. What is eligible paper? Of what importance did the founders of the Federal Reserve System expect it to be in connection with the lending operations of the Federal Reserve banks? Why did they so expect? How important is eligible paper today?
3. What is the role of Treasury obligations and the obligations of federal agencies in the lending operations of the Federal Reserve banks?
4. For what amounts, if any, can member banks require the Reserve banks to grant them loans? Explain.
5. What is peculiar about loans to member banks "secured to the satisfaction of" the Reserve banks? Why does the Board of Governors want to remove the penalty rate on this class of loans?
6. To what extent do the Federal Reserve banks have authority to grant loans to borrowers other than the member banks?
7. To what kinds of transactions are Federal Reserve discount rates applied? What are the rules for their application?
8. What is the function of the System Open Market Account? What are the responsibilities of its manager? its special manager?
9. In what kinds of securities or instruments does the Federal Reserve carry on its open-market operations?
10. What kinds of Federal Reserve transactions in Treasury obligations are regarded as being outside the scope of open-market operations?
11. Are there any reasons for present-day Federal Reserve open-market operations other than monetary control? Explain.
12. What is the scope of a continuing authority directive of the Federal Open Market Committee? of a current economic policy directive?
13. What kinds of work do the Federal Reserve banks perform as fiscal agents for the Treasury? for foreign governments and central banks?
14. In statements of condition of the Federal Reserve banks, what is the nature of the following accounts: cash, Federal Reserve notes of other banks, deferred availability cash items, other capital accounts?

V

MONETARY THEORY

CHAPTER 18

VERSIONS OF THE QUANTITY THEORY

MONETARY THEORY IN GENERAL

Although many aspects of the study of money and banking, such as trying to define precisely what money is and to distinguish among its functions, could be said to be "monetary theory," the term is customarily reserved for doctrines that purport to explain how the very use of money affects the aggregate demand for goods, their output, employment, income, and price levels. Does the use of money in an economy exert influences of its own on these things, or is the outcome in a money economy much the same as it would be in a barter economy? Was John Stuart Mill right in his *Principles of Political Economy*, published in the year of revolutions, 1848, when he wrote:

> There cannot, in short, be intrinsically a more insignificant thing, in the economy of society, than money; except in the character of a contrivance for sparing time and labor. It is a machine for doing quickly and commodiously, what would be done, though less quickly and commodiously, without it: and like many other kinds of machinery, it only exerts a distinct and independent influence of its own when it gets out of order.[1]

Isolation of monetary theory

Until well into the 1930s, the prevailing body of neoclassical economic theory generally held that money was influential in itself only in determining the price level. The widely accepted doctrines of economic theorists included propositions that output is determined by the supply of the factors of production and the state of technology, that the supply of goods "creates its own demand" (Say's law of markets) and that, accordingly, the economy always tends to reach and remain at a level of full employment. Such doctrines concerning the behavior of the economy were developed and

---

[1]Rev. ed., New York: The Colonial Press, 1900, vol. 2, p. 11.

refined in "real" terms, and this seemed to leave to monetary theory only the task of explaining what causes the price level to be as it is at given times and what causes it to change—what, in other words, determines the value of money. And for a long time, monetary theorists were largely content to confine their attentions to this task, as they did in the formulation of the several versions of the "quantity theory" as described in this chapter.

However, monetary theorists often went off by themselves, as it were, and reached conclusions that money was often "out of order," and in its state of disorder, exerted a "distinct and independent influence of its own" on demand for goods, output, employment, and income, as in analyzing and describing the economic effects of inflation and deflation as discussed in Chapter 2 of this textbook. And other economists made further observations that the economy often does not tend to a level of full employment and that, in periods of full employment, destabilizing forces are at work that will cause the economy to fall from that level. Such observations were undeniable, since it was obvious that all industrial economies repeatedly experienced long periods of recession and depression with widespread unemployment. These economists were "business cycle theorists," and some of them developed "monetary theories" of the business cycle. But the trouble was that monetary theory and business cycle theory were not integrated with the main body of economic doctrine.

The Keynesian revolution

Then came the "Keynesian revolution," which is usually dated from 1936 with the publication of *The General Theory of Employment, Interest, and Money* by John Maynard Keynes.[2] The neoclassical theorists, of whom Keynes was one, realized that their theory was inadequate to account for the Great Depression, and especially for its persistence—its failure as a "temporary disturbance" to yield to forces that should have been working to push the economy back toward full employment. So Keynes, in his celebrated book, tried to integrate neoclassical theory with monetary theory and business cycle theory in a way that would surely be adequate, at least, to account for the extraordinary economic conditions of the 1930s. Most economists have long since agreed that Keynes succeeded very well in accounting for these conditions with his new theory of "underemployment equilibrium"—a doctrine based on short-run demand considerations rather than on long-run supply factors as emphasized in neoclassical theory and holding that forces tending to push the economy toward full employment and to keep it there are often weak and often absent. And it is hardly necessary to add that most economists have also agreed that many other Keynesian concepts and doctrines have been important contributions to

---

[2]New York: Harcourt Brace Jovanovich, 1936.

economic thought, and that his efforts to integrate monetary and business cycle theory with the general body of economic theory have been especially fruitful.

At the same time, it must be recognized that there is difficulty today in trying to define precisely the content of "Keynesian economics." In his later writings, Keynes himself modified some of the positions he had taken in the *General Theory,* and he accepted some modifications suggested by others; and present-day expressions, such as "neo-Keynesian" and "post-Keynesian" economics, indicate that there has been widespread acceptance of emendations to and refinements of Keynes's doctrines in the formulation of which he had no personal participation.

Resurgence of the quantity theory

Nevertheless, the quantity theorists have not given up. They have developed still another version of the quantity theory that they think to be at least as well-integrated with general economic theory and business cycle theory as Keynesian theory is said to be. This newest version is chiefly attributed to the "Chicago school" of economists, and justifiable so because it has been principally developed by economists at the University of Chicago, and for a long time now, under the leadership of Professor Milton Friedman. We shall study it later in this chapter, but for the moment, it is pertinent to say that the "Chicago" version of the quantity theory, as we may call it, assigns a much greater role to the quantity of money as a determinant of the demand for goods, output, employment, and income than does the "income-expenditure theory" that is the designation commonly accepted for the Keynesian line of thought.

So great, indeed, is the emphasis on the role of the quantity of money in the Chicago version of the quantity theory that its proponents are often called, sometimes derisively, "monetarists," as if to distinguish them sharply from the income-expenditure theorists who are dubbed, in turn, as "non-monetarists." In any event, there has been much controversy between the two groups—a controversy that has been especially significant in emphasizing the long-held, lukewarm attitude of the income-expenditure theorists toward monetary control as a means of promoting full employment, stable price levels, and good rates of economic growth. The income-expenditure theorists do not deny that they have generally espoused fiscal policy, that is, control by way of variations in government taxing and spending policies, as the means likely to be eminently effective in pushing the economy toward the three goals. Nor do they deny that they have had little faith in the effectiveness of monetary control. But the attacks of the "monetarists" on these views have increasingly brought concessions from the income-expenditure theorists in the direction of an agreement that, while fiscal policy remains important for control, the quantity of money and therefore monetary control are also important—that *money does count.*

This chapter and the next four

In the present chapter, then, we shall examine the several versions of the quantity theory, including the "Chicago" version, as we may continue to call it, and in Chapter 19, we shall turn our attention to the income-expenditure theory. In Chapter 19, however, we shall preface the analysis of the income-expenditure theory with a rather lengthy survey of the national product-national income accounts as published by the U.S. Department of Commerce—a survey especially designed to reveal why there is so much emphasis in the income-expenditure theory on the relationship between saving and investment. Then, with this background of theory, we shall be prepared to move on to a consideration of monetary policy in Chapter 20 and of fiscal policy in Chapter 21. Finally in this group of chapters, it should be advantageous in Chapter 22 to look at the major developments since 1950 in employment, output, and price levels, to review how the instruments of monetary and fiscal policy have been applied, and to try to decide how wisely they have been applied and how effective they have been.

THE TRANSACTIONS AND CASH-BALANCES VERSIONS

The several versions of the "quantity theory" to be discussed in the following pages are so called not because the quantity of money in circulation is accorded a position of special importance in them—except in the case of the Chicago version—but because their ancestry is traced to an original "crude" doctrine that, in the long run, the quantity of money is truly the sole determinant of the price level. As a matter of fact, until the proponents of the Chicago version accepted the appellation *quantity theory* for their version, the proponents of the other versions generally avoided it to emphasize the sophistication of their versions by comparison with the crudeness of the original quantity theory.

As indicated previously, all the pre-Chicago versions have been primarily aimed at explaining why the price level—or the value of money, as the reciprocal of the price level—is what it is at a given time and why it changes.[3] All, too, were formulated on the basis of supply and demand analysis.

Transactions version

Immediate Determinants of the Price Level Transactions-version theorists prefer to think of the value of money as being determined by the forces

---

[3]Thus Professor Irving Fisher, the principal architect of the transactions version, presented his formulation in a book titled *The Purchasing Power of Money*, New York: Crowell Collier and Macmillan, 1926.

of supply and demand over a period of time, rather than at a given time in a given market, as for the determination of the value of an economic good. Thus, the supply of money is its average quantity available during the period multiplied by the average number of times this average quantity turns over during the period, that is, its *velocity*. The demand for money is the *volume of trade*, or total sales during the period of commodities, services, and property rights. Accordingly, there are three immediate determinants of the value of money, which is to say, the "general" price level: the average quantity of money, its average velocity, and the volume of trade. At the same time, there are many remote determinants that influence the price level but always through their effects on the immediate determinants and not directly.

Among the immediate determinants, the transactions velocity or turnover of money deserves special consideration, although not necessarily a greater emphasis than is given the other immediate determinants. Whatever may be our judgment about the superior logic of one version of the quantity theory as against the others, transactions velocity is universally accepted as an important concept, and much attention is given to velocity data— specifically, the comprehensive Federal Reserve reports on the turnover of demand deposits—as indicators of current and probable developments in the economy, and possibly, depending upon the point of view, indicators of the influence of money itself on these developments. The concept of transactions velocity should not offend our sense of logic. Money is peculiar in not being consumed. After its use in innumerable transactions, it still retains full capacity to fulfill its functions. A dollar bill that changes hands twenty times in the course of a month clearly does the work of a single $20 bill that changes hands only once, so that, when velocity has been taken into account, the dollar bill proves to be as important as the $20 bill in the month's transactions.

Remote Determinants   Remote determinants of the price level include such things as gold production, importation, and exportation, the regulations that govern the issuance of bank notes by the central bank, and the organization of the commercial banking system and the reserve requirements that apply to it. Remote determinants of the velocity of money include the frequency with which payrolls are paid, business policies of selling on account as against selling for cash, the length of deferred-payment periods in credit selling, opportunities for investment as against holding money as a store of purchasing power, and anticipations of future business conditions and job prospects and their likely effects on the flow of income receipts. And remote determinants of the volume of trade comprise such factors as the organization of industry and markets, the size and skills of the labor force, a country's natural resources and accumulated capital equipment, and the state of its technology.

Statement of the Theory   Whatever the effects of all such remote determinants may be on the three immediate determinants, the latter, as supply and demand, determine the general price level and changes in it. Accordingly, it is appropriate to state as a fundamental conclusion that: *Other things remaining equal, the general price level varies in direct proportion to the supply of money, and in inverse proportion to the demand for money.* The "other things" of this statement refer only to the three immediate determinants, and not to outside forces or factors. If one of the immediate determinants changes, and the other two do not change—if they "remain equal"—then the general price level *must* react in a precise mathematical way.

Transactions Equation of Exchange   To clarify this fundamental conclusion and to demonstrate its logic, an "equation or exchange" of the following form is used:

$$PT = MV$$

Having the character of an index number, P stands for the general price level. It represents the average price paid for cotton, wheat, iron ore, lumber, and other commodities; for the services of skilled and unskilled labor and of people in the professions; and for land, buildings, machinery, stocks, bonds, and other kinds of property and property rights. Because P is the reciprocal of the value of money, it is the focus of principal interest—the transactions version seeks to explain why changes in P take place.

M is the average quantity of money available throughout a year or other period, and V is the average velocity of this money in the same period, so that MV is the supply of money.

T is the volume of trade, or the demand for money in a year or other period. It is not a summation of the ounces, pounds, tons, gallons, man-hours, and other quantities of all the things sold, since such a summation would be meaningless. Rather, T is also an index number—an index number of quantities of things sold as measured by a *dollar's worth* of each included item in a base year. Thus if 100,000 loaves of bread were sold in the base year at 30 cents a loaf, 30,000 units of bread would be included in T for that year; and if in another year, 120,000 loaves of bread were sold at 35 cents a loaf, 36,000 units of bread—$36,000 worth at the base-year price—would be included in T, with the new price per loaf ignored.

Significance of the Equation   As written above, the transactions equation of exchange, like all equations, is a truism—as when we say that "three plus four equals seven." It simply states that there is equality, on one side, between the quantities of all commodities, services, and property rights sold during a period multiplied by the prices paid for them, and on the other side, the total quantity of money given in exchange. The equation is merely a summation of millions of similar equations for individual transactions.

If a person pays $20 for 50 gallons of gasoline at 40 cents a gallon, the transaction can be expressed in the same way: 40 cents $\times$ 50 = $20. In the equation of exchange, instead of 40 cents, a composite price of all commodities, services, and property rights, P, appears; instead of 50 gallons of gasoline, a composite total of the bushels of wheat, the barrels of oil, the bales of cotton, and so on, sold in the course of the year, T, is entered; and instead of $20, the money paid for gasoline, MV is entered as the total amount of money paid for all things sold.

As a truism, the equation of exchange proves nothing, nor is anything proved by dividing by T, as is the usual procedure, to get P standing by itself on the left-hand side and to get MV as the numerator and T as the denominator of a fraction on the right-hand side, as follows:

$$P = \frac{MV}{T}$$

But the transposed equation, though proving nothing, does seem to demonstrate the logic of the transactions version. As a matter of simple arithmetic, it is clear that if MV rises by, say, 25 percent, and if there is no change in T—"other things remaining equal"—P must also rise by 25 percent; and that if T rises by 25 percent with MV remaining unchanged, P must fall in inverse proportion, that is, by 20 percent. In the matter of logic, we should recognize that MV, as the supply of money, can also be thought of as the over-all demand for commodities, services, and property rights; and that T, as the demand for money, can be thought of as the over-all supply of these things, both in terms of a given period of time. Is it not logical to conclude that if the over-all demand for commodities, services, and property rights increases by a certain percentage and there is no increase in quantities offered for sale, prices must rise by the same percentage, and that if the over-all quantities offered for sale increase in a certain proportion and there is no increase in demand, prices must fall in inverse proportion?

Moreover, the transposed equation can easily be made to express a theory by stating as an additional proposition that P is always passive—that M, V, and T are independent variables whose separate changes, to the extent that they do not offset one another, will have proportional effects on P, but that P itself is a dependent variable. This has generally been the doctrine of transactions-version theorists, but it is a doctrine that is hardly provable. Indeed, we may well have doubts about it, considering the apparent capacity of great corporations and powerful labor unions to set prices to effect changes in P that would necessarily *cause* compensating changes in M, V, or T or in some combination of these three determinants.

Cash-balances version

Different View of the Demand for Money   In the cash-balances version of the quantity theory, the demand for money is selected, as it were, as being peculiarly important among the determinants of the general price level. But the demand for money of the cash-balances version is not the "volume of trade" of the transactions version; instead, it is the amount of purchasing power that people wish to retain in the form of money at any given time. In relationship to *what*, do people wish to retain purchasing power? The theorists differ about this. In their several opinions, people are said to wish to retain purchasing power in some proportion to things they plan to buy within a given period of time, or to their total wealth, or to their income, or to a combination of these.

Relationship to the Transactions Version   If it is posited that people wish to hold purchasing power solely in proportion to things they plan to buy— and this is the variant of the cash-balances version that has been most commonly cited and explicated—then the volume of trade comes back into the picture, since it consists of the commodities, services, and property rights people plan to buy (and in terms of the transactions version, what they *will* buy) in a given period of time. This variant, therefore, gives us an equation of exchange that must be a variant of the transactions equation:

$$M = KTP$$

where M, T, and P have the same meanings as in the transactions equation, and K is the portion or percentage of, say, a year's expected purchases of commodities, services, and property rights over which people decide at a given time to hold purchasing power in the form of money. A transposition of the equation by dividing by KT puts it into a form directly comparable with the transposed transactions equation:

$$P = \frac{M}{KT}$$

Thus, we get another demonstration that, other things being equal, the general price level must vary in direct proportion to the supply of money and in inverse proportion to the demand for money.

That the transactions and cash-balances equations are essentially identical—when the assumption is that people decide to hold purchasing power *only* in relationship to the things they plan to buy—can easily be shown mathematically: If $PT = MV$, then $V = PT/M$, and if $M = KTP$, then $K = M/TP$, so that $K = 1/V$, and $V = 1/K$. If $1/K$ is substituted for V in the transactions equation, the cash-balances equation is produced; and if $1/V$ is substituted for K in the cash-balances equation, the transactions equation is produced. While, therefore, the determination of the value of money according to the postulates of the cash-balances version has often been said to be directly comparable with the determination of the value of any good by supply and demand forces, the period-of-time element of the transactions version is not really avoided. Velocity returns, as it were, "by the back door."

Money in Circulation and the Purchasing Power of Cash Balances   With M defined as the quantity of money in circulation and KT as the amount of purchasing power that people decide to hold, the cash-balances version may seem to be engaging in double talk. If a given number of dollars are in circulation, how can the people possibly hold more or fewer dollars? But that is the point! The given number of dollars can have more or less purchasing power *depending upon what the price level is.*

If the people are not satisfied with the purchasing power of the number of dollars they hold, the actions they will take will result in changes in this purchasing power without a change in the number of dollars. If they want to hold more purchasing power than before—which is to say, if their demand for money increases—they cut down, as buyers, their current spending, and as sellers, become more anxious to convert their goods into money. With the assumption that there are many buyers and many sellers in the various sectors of the market, such a decrease in the demand for goods and increase in their supply must cause the price level to fall. Thus the people achieve their objective: with the fall in the price level, the unchanged number of dollars they hold now have the power to purchase a greater quantity of commodities, services, and property rights than before.

INCOME VERSIONS

The income versions of the quantity theory are latter-day restatements of the transactions and cash-balances versions to make them theories—or at least, demonstrable explanations—of how the price level of current output is determined and what causes changes in it. Accordingly, T of the transactions version is replaced by Y as gross national product, or total current output in a given period of time valued at base-year prices, that is, in "constant dollars," and V is replaced by V_y, which is the *income velocity* of available money as spent for newly produced goods. Similarly, but with the assumption that people wish to hold purchasing power in their cash balances only in relationship to new goods they plan to buy, T of the cash-balances version is also replaced by Y. In both versions, P is replaced by P_y as the price level of current output, while M remains in its role as the quantity of money in circulation. The restated equation of the transactions version is, therefore, as follows:

$$P_y = \frac{MV_y}{Y}$$

and for the cash-balances version (with the limiting assumption stated above):

$$P_y = \frac{M}{KY}$$

The income-version theorists hold that, in the matter of price levels, what is really significant are the prices at which new goods can be sold and are sold, and that the prices of other things, such as secondhand goods of all kinds and even real property and corporate stocks, are hardly important separately, since they are largely determined in relationship to the prices of new goods. These theorists claim, moreover, that their versions are more useful for analyses that go beyond questions of price-level determination, as, for example, inquiries about the kinds of decisions that business firms are likely to make in response to increased prices for their current output that result from increases in the quantity of money or in income velocity.

The least that can be said for the income versions is that they have given us a highly useful tool in the concept of the income velocity of money —a tool that is widely used in attempting to judge the direction of recent developments in the economy as well as prospects for further developments in the same direction. And a nice thing about income velocity is that it is easily computed. It is found by dividing gross national product, as reported by the Department of Commerce for a quarter or year, by the average quantity of money in circulation in the same period, as reported by the Federal Reserve. However, a disadvantage is that the GNP figures are reported only quarterly, so that computed income velocities are not quite so up-to-date as we would wish.

THE CHICAGO VERSION

The Chicago version of the quantity theory is more clearly related to the cash-balances versions than to the transactions versions. In line with the traditional cash-balances version, it emphasizes the role of the demand for money. In fact, it has been described as "a theory of the demand for money."[4] And in line with the restatement of the cash-balances version in terms of income, it posits that the demand for money is primarily determined by the level of income—which means the level of GNP, since GNP is always matched by a level of money income of equal amount, as will be shown in Chapter 19. Unlike all other versions of the quantity theory, however, the current version is not aimed at price-level determination. Such an aim is specifically denied.[5]

Demand for money in relationship to income

People wish to hold money in proportions closely related to their incomes —although not necessarily in fixed proportions—rather than as purchasing power directly related to the cost of things to be bought. If, then, people have more money in their possession than they wish to hold in relationship to their incomes, they will spend the excess for goods or for securities.

---

[4]Milton Friedman, *The Optimum Quantity of Money*, Chicago: Aldine, 1969, p. 52.
[5]*Ibid.*

Increased spending for goods is increased demand, and assuming idle factors of production to be available, business firms will expand their outputs. Increased spending for securities will drive up their prices, and this is equivalent to a fall in interest rates. Lower interest rates will encourage people to borrow to spend for goods, thereby further increasing demand and leading to a further expansion of output provided that idle factors are available. Expanding the output of goods results in an expanded flow of money income to all who participate in productive operations, so that eventually people come to the collective decision that their money holdings are no longer excessive in relationship to their incomes. If idle factors of production are not available, efforts of the people to spend money holdings regarded as excessive, by way of the two routes mentioned, will simply have the effect of driving up prices. But higher prices mean higher money incomes to participants in productive operations (or at least, to some of them), so that, again, the decision is eventually reached that money holdings are no longer excessive.

If, on the other hand, people decide that their money holdings are inadequate in relationship to their money incomes, they will try to retain as much of these holdings as possible by curtailing their spending for goods, and to add to them by selling some of their security holdings. The selling of securities, by driving up interest rates, will discourage borrowing by (some) people who otherwise would have borrowed to spend for goods. Thus demand for goods, actual and potential, is cut, and business firms reduce their output. But cutbacks in output result in diminished levels of money income, so that the people eventually decide that, in relationship to these reduced levels of money income, their money holdings are no longer inadequate.

Implications for monetary control

Although the foregoing summary of the principal postulates of the Chicago version of the quantity theory hardly does justice to it—as is typically the fault of any summary designed to be brief—it should suffice to reveal why the Chicago-version theorists so strongly fix upon monetary control as the best possible means of promoting full employment, good rates of economic growth, and indeed, stability in the price level (this last-named goal, despite their denial of theorizing about price-level determination). Should employment be beyond "tolerable" limits and should other idle factors of production be available, the monetary authorities should surely pump additional money into the economy, giving the people, as it were, more money than they wish to hold in relationship to existing levels of income, and prompting them therefore to increase their spending for goods either directly or indirectly via the securities markets and borrowing. Likewise, is the doctrine that the monetary authorities *must* increase the quantity of money continuously at an appropriate annual rate to ensure that persons joining the labor force and added productive factors of other kinds will be promptly put to work. Assuming that people's money holdings are not regarded by them as excessive, larger quantities will be needed to "support" higher levels of GNP; and if the monetary authorities want GNP to move to higher levels, they must supply additional money.

FOR REVIEW

1. Explain what was revolutionary about the Keynesian revolution.
2. What is meant by the designation "monetarists" as ascribed to some present-day economists?
3. Why are the quantity versions of monetary theory so called?
4. In the transactions version of the quantity theory, what are the three immediate determinants of the price level? What influence do remote determinants have?
5. Why is it said that, in the transactions version, a precise mathematical relationship is held to exist between monetary supply and demand and the price level?
6. What is the transactions equation of exchange? the cash-balances equation? To say that the two equations mean the same thing, what assumption is needed?
7. Does the transactions equation of exchange prove the validity of the transactions theory? Explain why or why not.
8. In terms of the cash-balances version, how can the demand for money be other than the actual quantity of money that people hold?
9. How does the income version of the transactions theory differ in its approach from that of the original version of this theory?
10. What is meant by the transactions velocity of money? its income velocity? Are these concepts logical? Are they useful? Discuss.
11. Why is the Chicago version of the quantity theory said to be quite different from the earlier versions?
12. What is the general conclusion of the Chicago version about the influence of the quantity of money on employment, output, and income? By what process is the influence supposed to be exerted?

PROBLEMS

1. According to the transactions version of the quantity theory, what would be the resulting percentage increase or decrease in the price level in a given period of time if

   A. the quantity of money increased by 10 percent, and the velocity of money and the volume of trade remained unchanged?
   B. the quantity of money increased by 10 percent, its velocity increased by 10 percent, and the volume of trade remained unchanged?

C. the quantity of money, its velocity, and the volume of trade each increased by 10 percent?

D. the volume of trade increased by 10 percent, and the quantity of money and its velocity remained unchanged?

2. According to the cash-balances version of the quantity theory, what would be the resulting percentage increase or decrease in the price level if

A. the quantity of money increased by 10 percent, and the demand for purchasing power with respect to things to be bought remained unchanged?

B. the people sought to hold the power to purchase 1½ months' supply of things to be bought in a year rather than 1 month's supply as formerly, and the quantity of money and the volume of trade remained unchanged?

C. the people sought to hold the power to purchase a 1 month's supply of things to be bought in a year rather a 1½ months' supply as formerly, and the quantity of money and the volume of trade remained unchanged?

3. In terms of the transactions version of the quantity theory (a) what would be the percentage changes in the velocity of money as a result of the developments described in 2B and 2C, and (b) what would be the resulting percentage changes in the price level?

4. Determine the income velocity of money in 1969 and 1970, given the following data as reported by the Federal Reserve and the Department of Commerce (in billions of dollars):

	1969	1970
Federal Reserve:		
Average quantity of money in circulation	201.8	209.2
Department of Commerce:		
GNP in current dollars	931.4	976.5
GNP in constant dollars (1967 = 100)	855.3	851.3

CHAPTER 19

THE INCOME-EXPENDITURE THEORY

NATIONAL PRODUCT-NATIONAL INCOME ACCOUNTS

The best way to approach the income-expenditure theory of the influence of money on employment, output, income, and prices is by way of the national product-national income accounts of the Office of Business Economics (OBE) of the federal Department of Commerce. And it should be especially helpful to cite specific figures for the principal components of these accounts, in this instance for the year 1969.[1] The terminology of the accounts and of the theory is much the same.

GNP and its components

Gross national product (GNP) is the total output of all kinds of goods (including intangible services) in a year or other period of time valued at current market prices—output coming from factories, farms, mines, stores, offices, governments, households, and so on. In 1969, GNP amounted to $931,403 million, and its principal components (in millions of dollars) were the following:

Personal consumption expenditures	577,458
Gross private domestic investment	139,819
Net exports of goods and services	1,949
Government purchases of goods and services	212,177

Personal Consumption Expenditures Personal consumption expenditures measure the portion of output that is acquired by consumers for their

---

[1]The student should know that, from time to time, the OBE revises its figures for past periods, so that he may find national product-national income data for 1969 somewhat different from the figures cited in the text. Accordingly, it is worth mentioning that the figures presented in the following discussion come from the "National Income Issue," *Survey of Current Business*, July 1970.

own use, regardless of the survival of some of these goods in their hands at the end of a given period of time. It stands for total consumption in the sense of acquisition of consumer goods by ultimate users, and the word *personal* is used to emphasize that goods acquired by business firms and governments are not "consumed" in the consumer-goods sense.

Gross Private Domestic Investment Gross private domestic investment measures the portion of output that goes to business enterprises in the form of new plants, machinery, equipment, and additions to inventories, and to acquirers of new office and store buildings, homes, and other residential properties—all the additions to capital to be used as tools for further production, including, to repeat, new residential properties that are regarded as being capital equipment rather than consumer goods. Private domestic investment is labeled "gross" because no deductions are taken for capital used in producing GNP, destroyed in fires and floods and other disasters, and so on.

Net Exports of Goods and Services Net exports of goods and services measure the excess of output sold to the "rest of the world"—foreign countries and overseas territories and possessions of the United States— over the value of goods acquired from it. Our output flows to markets for sale, but the rest of the world comes into our markets, as it were, to buy some of this output; at the same time, goods flows to our markets from our own productive facilities are augmented by imports from the rest of the world.

Government Purchases of Goods and Services Finally, government purchases of goods and services measure the portion of output that is bought by (domestic) governments at all levels for their own use. The most important component of government purchases is the total of government payrolls and supplementary compensation to personnel, because governments are regarded as buying the output of this personnel, military and civilian, from the President to, shall we say, the dog catcher. Governments are productive, their output being measured by the compensation they pay to their personnel, but governments themselves buy this output. But governments also buy some of the output of private enterprises—military hardware and supplies, office equipment, mountains of paper, and so on— and this buying is included in the over-all figure for government purchases of goods and services.

Flows of money income

As output is produced, dispatched to markets, and sold, there are incurred many costs that are, at the same time, sources of money income that flow, as it were, in three streams, two of which flow to individuals, business corporations, nonprofit institutions, and other nongovernmental organizations that may be labeled collectively as "private income receivers," and the third of which flows to governments.

National Income The most important of the two flows of money income that go to the collective class of private receivers is called "national income." It consists of all the rewards to the factors of production for their contributions to output. In 1969, national income amounted to $769,505 million, and its components (in millions of dollars) were the following:

Compensation of employees	564,162
Proprietors' income	66,846
Rental income of persons	21,989
Corporate profits	85,797
Net interest	30,711

Listed here, then, we have rewards to labor, to proprietors of unincorporated business firms (including wages of management and returns on capital equipment employed as well as profits), to capitalists in rents and interest for the use of capital equipment (including, of course, interest on money invested in capital equipment), and to business corporations in the form of profits.

Other Nongovernmental Money Income The second stream of money income going to private income receivers originates in certain costs of production that are not rewards to the factors of production. But this second stream must be adjusted for a "statistical discrepancy." The OBE makes separate estimates of the value of output as it is sold in the markets and of the costs of producing this output, and in view of the huge magnitudes involved, it is not surprising that the two estimates never come out equally. At the same time, the OBE realizes that the costs of production, including profits, must be equal to the sales proceeds of what is produced. Accordingly, an adjustment, or "correction," to bring the two estimates to equality must be made somewhere, and it is made here. With such an adjustment, the second stream of money income amounted to $77,711 million in 1969, and its composition (in millions of dollars) was as follows:

Capital consumption allowances	78,858
Business transfer payments	3,523
Statistical discrepancy	−4,670[2]

Capital Consumption Allowances Capital consumption allowances are very largely depreciation charges that are universally recognized as costs of

---

[2]Since the adjustment is negative at this point, its effect is to reduce the OBE's estimate of costs of output to make it equal to its estimate of the sales proceeds of output.

production measuring the using up, so to say, of capital facilities in turning out goods, but they also include such additional capital costs as the destruction of productive facilities through fires and natural disasters.

But depreciation charges, for example, are often said to be simply "book costs"—how can they generate a flow of money income? The answer is that depreciation charges result in "cash throw-offs," as is emphasized in studies in business finance. For illustration, assume that a business firm's out-of-pocket money costs of producing a certain output amount to $90,000, that depreciation charges attributed as "book costs" to this output are $30,000, and that the output is sold for $135,000. The firm's income statement would look like this:

Sales		$135,000
Cost of goods sold:		
Out-of-pocket costs	$90,000	
Depreciation	30,000	120,000
Net profit (before income taxes)		$ 15,000

Of the sales proceeds, $90,000 simply reimburses the firm for its out-of-pocket costs that entered the streams of money income as it carried on its productive operations; but the sales proceeds exceed these out-of-pocket costs by $45,000. Thus the firm has *net* money income of $45,000, of which $15,000 comes to it in the national income stream as profit, and the balance of $30,000 in the "other" stream as a "cash throw-off" from depreciation.

Business Transfer Payments Business transfer payments chiefly comprise corporate gifts to religious, educational, charitable, and other nonprofit institutions and book charges for consumer bad debts. The business transfer payments obviously supply money income to the nonprofit institutions that are included among private income receivers; at the same time, they are regarded by the corporate donors as costs to be recovered, if possible, in the sales proceeds of their output. And book charges for consumer bad debts behave as book charges for depreciation, increasing costs but also resulting in cash throw-offs. If we add $5000 of corporate donations to the out-of-pocket costs, in the foregoing illustration, and $3000 as a book charge for bad debts, the profit is reduced to $7000. But $135,000 of money income is still generated in the firm's productive operations, with $95,000 going to suppliers of labor and other productive services and to the nonprofit institutions and the firm ending with $40,000 of added spending capacity, of which $30,000 and $3000 respectively come to it as cash throw-offs from the charges for depreciation and bad debts, and the balance of $7000 as net profit.

Money Income Flow to Governments The third stream of money income generated by costs in the course of productive operations flows to governments. It primarily consists of "indirect" business taxes and certain "nontax" obligations payable by business firms to governments. But it also includes "current surplus" of government enterprises that means, at least roughly, the net profits they earn collectively. However, the OBE combines "current surplus" with subsidies paid by governments to business, and when subsidies exceed current surplus, as they usually do, the result is a money flow away from governments rather than toward them. In 1969, "indirect business tax and nontax liability" amounted to $85,193 million, and "subsidies less current surplus of government enterprises" amounted to a positive $1006, indicating a net outflow from governments.

Indirect business tax and nontax liability includes virtually all taxes and government-imposed fees that are closely related to productive operations (including selling operations) and that are universally recognized, therefore, as additional costs of production. Included are corporation capital stock taxes, franchise taxes, taxes on business properties, excise taxes, sales taxes, and many others, as well as nontax-liability payments, such as license fees and fines and penalties. However, the OBE excludes at this point social security taxes and taxes on the net income of business enterprises, even the social security levies that employers are required to pay.

The reason for combining current surplus of government enterprises with government subsidies to business is that it is quite difficult, in an aggregative sense, to make meaningful distinctions between the two. If the profits of state liquor stores are subtracted from the deficits of the Postal Service, is it reasonable to say that the resulting large negative figure is a net deficit, or loss on the operations of these enterprises collectively, or a net subsidy to business enterprises? Probably most people would say it is primarily a subsidy to newspapers and magazines that have the second-class mailing privilege, to mailers of "junk mail," and so on. At any rate, when the combination item "subsidies less current surplus of government enterprises" is positive, it may best be regarded as a flow of money income from government into the national income stream, since subsidies, as the dominant element, go chiefly to pay wages that business enterprises could not otherwise afford and to give them profits they would not otherwise earn. Such wages and profits (and possibly other factor rewards) that are covered by subsidies are costs of production, but they do not get into the selling prices of goods. These costs are accepted and borne by governments whose objective is to hold down selling prices.[3]

---

[3]Although the OBE combines subsidies with "current surplus," it is possible to illustrate how they work separately as well as in combination. Suppose that a government enterprise incurs out-of-pocket costs of production of $50,000 and sells its output in the market at $60,000. It therefore pours $50,000 into the flow of money income to private receivers, and has left-over money income for itself equal to its profit of $10,000. But the same government now gives a subsidy of $25,000 to a business firm whose out-of-pocket costs of production are $150,000. The business firm sells its output for $150,000 since the purpose of the subsidy is to hold down prices. But

Relationship of GNP and national income

Although the concepts of GNP as the total output of goods and services valued at current market prices and of national income as the total rewards to the factors of production for their contributions to this output are not at all difficult to grasp, the relationship between the two magnitudes may not be so readily apparent. However, in view of the foregoing descriptions of the meaning and roles of capital consumption allowances, business transfer payments, indirect business taxes, and so on, an understanding of this relationship should not be too elusive. For the year 1969, it was as follows (with the figures, as usual, in millions of dollars):

Gross national product			931,403
Less:	Capital consumption allowances		78,858
Equals:	Net national product		852,545
Less:	Indirect business tax and nontax		
	liability	85,193	
	Business transfer payments	3,523	
	Statistical discrepancy	−4,670	84,046
			768,499
Plus:	Subsidies less current surplus		
	of government enterprises		1,006
Equals:	National income		769,505

Disposal of money income of private receivers

Before wage earners, capitalists, and other private income receivers get opportunities to decide what to do with their money income, governments make some important decisions for them by levying and collecting taxes. But governments are not entirely greedy, for they return substantial amounts of their revenues in pensions and the like to the private income receivers. To determine the *disposable income* of these receivers, therefore, it is necessary to deduct all kinds of taxes classified by the OBE as being paid from money income and to add the return flow of money from governments in pensions and comparable kinds of payments. Thus, dispos-

---

assuming that the business firm pays no indirect business taxes, $175,000 goes to private income receivers—$150,000 as the firm meets its costs of production plus the subsidy of $25,000. With the two transactions combined, the result would be market sales of $210,000 ($60,000 + $150,000) and money income received by private receivers of $225,000 ($50,000 + $175,000), and the government would have a deficit of $15,000 that it would presumably make up by increasing its tax levies or by borrowing. Total costs of production, including profits, could realistically be said to be $60,000 for the government enterprise and $175,000 for the business firm, for a total of $235,000, but sales amount to only $210,000, indicating that the subsidies, while getting into the national income stream, do not get into selling prices, as is their purpose.

able income is the net amount of money income over which the private receivers have choices as to use.

Taxes Paid from Income   In the national product-national income accounts, many different kinds of taxes and certain "nontax" payments to governments are classified as being paid from money income: taxes on net income itself, both individual and corporate; social security taxes as paid by both employers and employees; the many levies that are not related to business operations, such as annual taxes on personal property and taxes on inheritances, estates, and gifts; and among the "nontax" payments, automobile and drivers' license fees, fines, and tuition fees paid to state colleges and universities. The inclusions are not affected by government policy of collecting some taxes before the income on which they are levied reaches income receivers, as by the withholding from paychecks of income and social security taxes, and regardless of the contentions of some economists—in criticism of current classifications—that the shares of social security taxes that are borne by employers and probably corporation income taxes would be better classified as "indirect business taxes."

Government Transfer and Net Interest Payments   Payments of pensions and the like by governments are called "government transfer payments" —a category designed to clearly distinguish them from subsidy payments and "exhaustive" payments for purchases of goods and services. The transfer payments include, most importantly, social security benefits paid to the elderly and disabled and their dependents, hospital and medical insurance benefits, unemployment compensation benefits, welfare payments, pensions and disability allowances paid to veterans, and interest payments on government debts. Although economists usually classify government interest payments as a kind of transfer payment, the OBE prefers to list them separately; and while it treats interest paid by business firms as a productive expenditure—as a reward to capitalists for their contribution to output —it prefers to treat government interest as being nonproductive. Its argument for this position is that, because most of the interest paid by governments is paid on war debts, the payments would seem to have no significant relationship to current output and costs.

Disposable Income in 1969   In 1969, tax and nontax levies payable out of income amounted to $213,540 million, broken down (in millions of dollars) as follows:

Personal tax and nontax payments	117,305
Corporate profits tax liability	42,679
Contributions for social insurance	53,556

Government transfer payments "to persons" in 1969 amounted to $61,561 million, and net interest paid totaled $13,285 million, giving an over-all total for these transfer payments of $74,846 million. Accordingly, disposable

income in the hands of private income receivers in 1969 amounted to
$708,522 million, determined (in millions of dollars) as follows:

National income	769,505
Other private money income	77,711
	847,216
Less: Tax and nontax payments out of income	213,540
	633,676
Plus: Government transfer payments to persons and net interest paid	74,846
Equals: Disposable money income	708,522

Choices about Use of Disposable Money Income   All private holders of
disposable money income have only three choices concerning disposal:
(1) they may spend it for consumer goods, (2) they may give it to
foreigners ("rest of the world"), or (3) they may save it. The choices are
necessarily limited to these three because, in terms of both the national
product-national income accounts and the income-expenditure theory,
private saving is definable as disposable money income that remains unspent for consumer goods and as gifts to foreigners[4] in the year or other
period in which it becomes available for spending. As things always turn
out, a very large proportion of disposable money income is spent for
consumer goods and only a slight proportion is given to foreigners. The
amount of "personal consumption expenditures" in 1969, as shown at
the beginning of this chapter, was $577,458 million, and the amount of
"personal transfer payments to foreigners" was only $784 million. Accord-
ingly, with figures in millions of dollars, private saving in 1969 must have
resulted, so to say, as follows:

Disposable money income		708,522
Less: Personal consumption expenditures	577,458	
Personal transfer payments to foreigners	784	578,242
Equals: Saving of private income receivers		130,280

Other spending and saving

But spending in our markets in 1969 was not limited to consumer
spending, nor was saving restricted to that of private income receivers.
As indicated on the first page of this chapter, business enterprises, home
buyers, and other spent $139,819 million in buying new plant and equip-
ment, building inventories, acquiring new houses and other new residential
property, and acquiring all the other kinds of capital facilities called

---

[4]If disposable money income is given to people and organizations at home, then the
making of choices among the three is simply shifted to them, and the available amount
of disposable money income is not affected.

collectively "gross private domestic investment"; foreigners spent for our goods $1949 million in excess of the amount we spent for theirs ("net exports of goods and services"), and governments at all levels spent $212,177 in buying the services of their own personnel and other goods and services.

Spending for Domestic Investment   Where did business firms, home buyers, and others get the money with which to buy new capital facilities of many kinds in 1969? They must have received it from the sources depicted in Figure 9-1—some of it as their own savings, including the plowed-under profits of business corporations; some acquired directly from savers through the flotation of security issues; some from financial institutions out of their accumulations of savings from the public; and some money newly created by the commercial banks as made possible by reserves supplied to them by the Federal Reserve.

Spending on Imports and Exports   In any year, some of the goods that pour into our markets from foreign sources are bought by consumers for their own use, some are bought by business firms to expand their inventories or as capital facilities of other kinds, and some are bought by our governments. They thus disappear, as it were, into the categories of personal consumption expenditures, gross private domestic investment, and government purchases of goods and services, but we record them collectively as "imports of goods and services," as, in 1969, when they amounted to $53,564 million. In any year, too, some of the output of our own productive facilities is taken from our markets by foreigners as "exports of goods and services." These exports are a part of our GNP, but they are obviously not in the three categories just mentioned. Accordingly, to get the correct total for GNP, it is necessary to add to the three categories the excess of exports over imports (or to subtract the excess of imports over exports, should that be the situation). In 1969, our exports of goods and services amounted to $55,514 million, and since this exceeded imports, the difference of $1949 million (allowing for a slight rounding error) is entered as the net export component of GNP.[5]

On a net basis, we pay for all imports from foreign countries, but we donate to foreigners some of the money needed to pay for our exports.[6] In 1969, foreigners did not have to make a net payment to us of $1949 million, because, as we have already seen, private income receivers donated $784 million to foreigners, and in addition, the federal government made

[5]In 1969, our GNP of $931,403 million was equal to the sum of the three major categories, or components ($577,458 million + $139,819 million + $212,177 million, or $929,454 million) minus imports of $53,564 million and plus exports of $55,514 million, or alternatively, it was equal to $929,454 million plus net exports of $1949 million (allowing for slight rounding errors in the figures in both summations).

[6]This does not mean that nobody in the United States receives gifts or other donations from foreigners. The "net" basis of reporting means that incoming gifts and donations are subtracted from outgoing gifts and grants, and only the net result is entered in the accounts.

grants of $2050 million to foreigners. Thus, instead of increasing our outstanding claims on foreigners as a result of our excess of exports over imports, we reduced these claims because our grants and gifts exceeded the export surplus. In the national product-national income accounts, changes in claims on foreigners resulting from exports and imports of goods and services and gifts and grants are called "net foreign investment." Stated in this terminology, therefore, we had a negative net foreign investment in 1969 of $885 million, that is, $1949 million − $784 million − $2050 million,[7] or as we could also say, a disinvestment of $885 million.

Spending by Governments Governments spend chiefly for goods and services, but as we have seen, they also spend in granting subsidies, making transfer payments domestically and to foreigners, and paying interest. And of course, their spending capacity comes chiefly from the taxes and nontax revenues that they collect from the public. If their spending exceeds their revenues, they have deficits that are customarily financed by borrowing;[8] and if their revenues exceed their expenditures, they have surpluses. Government surpluses are a kind of saving, since, comparable to private saving, they are equal to the governments' disposable money income (revenues) that remain unspent for goods and services, subsidies, and interest and transfer payments. Thus total saving in the economy is equal to disposable money income, both governmental and private, that remains, in the year or other period in which this income becomes available, after private spending for consumer goods and as gifts to foreigners and after government spending for the purposes listed in the preceding sentence.

In the year 1969, our federal, state, and local governments had a collective surplus of $8654 million, computed (with all figures in millions of dollars) as follows:

Revenues:

Indirect business tax and nontax liability		85,193
Personal tax and nontax payments		117,305
Corporate profits tax liability		42,679
Contributions for social insurance		53,556
		298,733
Less: Expenditures:		
Purchases of goods and services	212,177	
Transfer payments:		
To persons	61,561	
To foreigners	2,050	
Net interest	13,285	
Subsidies less current surplus of government enterprises	1,006	290,079
Equals: Government surplus		8,654

---

[7]After adjustment for the rounding error mentioned previously.

[8]As possessor of the power to create money, the federal government could meet its deficits by starting the printing press, but it typically refrains from doing this.

Saving and Investment   When the government surplus of $8654 million in 1969 is added to the saving of private income receivers of $130,280 million in that year, as determined earlier, we get total saving for the economy of $138,934 million. For the same year, gross private domestic investment amounted to $139,819 million, while our foreign investment amounted to a negative $885 million, so that our net total investment was $139,819 million − $885 million, or $138,934 million. In 1969, therefore, saving and investment were equal. Saving and investment are always equal in any period that has ended. They are always equal *ex post,* as we say, because whatever goods were produced and were not sold to ultimate buyers in any past period must have remained in somebody's inventory, and an amount of money income equal to that generated in the production of these goods must have remained unspent for consumer goods and government goods and must therefore have been saved.

At this point, the income-expenditure theory takes off, as it were, from the national product-national income accounts. It is a major proposition of the theory that saving and investment are rarely equal, that there is little reason for expecting them to be equal, and that their inequality causes changes in employment, output, money income, and prices. Before we discuss that, however, it should be helpful to attempt to picture the goods flows and money flows that have been described. Such an attempt is presented as Figure 19-1.

Charting Goods Flows and Money Flows   In Figure 19-1, goods flows are shown as solid lines, and money flows as dashed lines, with arrows and arrow points indicating the directions of these flows. "Productive facilities" include all the people who participate in productive operations as well as plant, machinery and equipment, and so on. The investors are labeled "private," because, in the national product-national income accounts, government spending for facilities, such as schools, hospitals, and highways, is simply included in government purchases of goods and services, and is not therefore classified as "investment." Otherwise, the chart should be self-explanatory in view of the description of goods flows and money flows to this point, and the insertion of the dollar figures for 1969 (in billions) as already presented and analyzed should make its interpretation all the easier.

Figure 19-1 is obviously incomplete because it shows no interconnections between savers and investors, direct or indirect. There must have been many such interconnections in 1969 to account for the huge amount of spending by investors for capital facilities. Accordingly, a dashed line needs to be inserted from savers to investors in order to account for investment spending that was made possible by investors' own savings and by their direct acquisitions of money from savers by sales of new security issues; another dashed line, from savers to a box for financial institutions placed above private investors for savings they accumulated; and a dashed

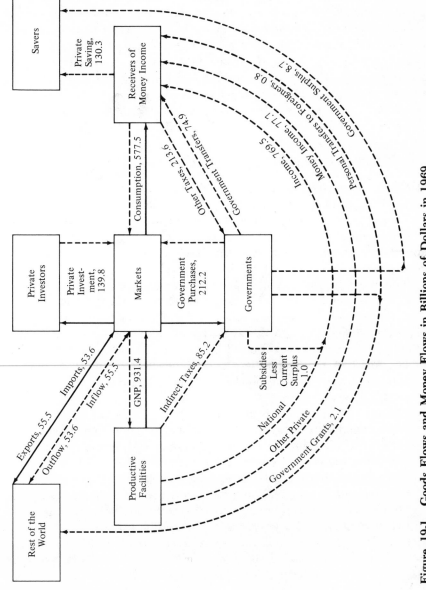

Figure 19-1 Goods Flows and Money Flows in Billions of Dollars in 1969

line, from the financial institutions to investors for the flow of money by way of loans and security purchases. But Figure 9-1, as presented in Chapter 9, shows such interconnections, so that the two charts should be studied simultaneously for a reasonably complete picture of what happens.

The whole idea is that, for saving and investment to be equal *ex post*, an amount of money equal to saved money income must be invested in new capital facilities (combined with net foreign investment or disinvestment). This does not mean that every dollar saved must somehow find its way into investment. Dollars saved may be hoarded or extinguished by repaying commercial bank loans. But dollars for investment must come from somewhere to equal the dollars hoarded or extinguished, and of course, the most likely sources are other people's dishoarding and especially the creation of new money by the commercial banks as permitted by the Federal Reserve. That is why, in Figure 9-1 the commercial banks are given a special position among the financial institutions, and the Federal Reserve is given a separate box above that for the financial institutions.

MAJOR PROPOSITIONS OF THE
INCOME-EXPENDITURE THEORY

Unlike the transactions and cash-balances theories and their income versions, the income-expenditure theory is not primarily a monetary theory. Instead, it is a theory of how the whole economic system works—a theory of the behavior of all the major forces that determine total demand, output, employment, money income, and the price level, so that the role that money plays as a determinant receives no special emphasis. Because of its sweeping purview, the income-expenditure theory cannot be stated as a single "fundamental conclusion," as in the case of the transactions and cash-balances theories. Many fundamental propositions are needed, and their listing should be a good way to begin our inquiry into the theory. In light of the lengthy discussion of the national product-national income accounts, most of the propositions should be clear in meaning and the soundness of many readily acknowledged. The listing follows:

1. The money income received by the people of a country in a year or other period of time is equal to the money costs of production of that period, including profits realized on sales at various stages of production. Thus the economic system generates sufficient purchasing power to make possible the sale of all goods currently produced at prices high enough to cover all costs of production, including such profits. (Profits, however, can be negative, that is to say, losses may occur in the production and sale of goods. But the occurrence of losses does not negate the necessary equality between money income on the one hand and total money costs of production on the other. If goods are sold at any stage at a profit, the profit itself gives the business firm purchasing power—money costs of production and money income are

increased simultaneously by an equal amount; if goods are sold at a loss, the loss reduces the business firm's purchasing power—money costs of production and money income are decreased simultaneously by an equal amount.)

2. Total output, or gross national product, is determined by the productive facilities of a country and especially by the decisions of enterprisers to employ them. Total money income is determined by the rates or prices that enterprisers pay for the use of productive factors and by their incurring certain nonfactor costs, such as depreciation charges, indirect business taxes, and donations to charitable institutions.

3. The decisions of enterprisers to employ productive facilities are based on their profit expectations, and these expectations are based, in turn, on their estimates of "effective demand"—the total sales proceeds they will receive for output at varying levels of employment. They select the level of employment at which they expect their profits to be maximized or their losses minimized.

4. Effective demand is total spending in any period of time for consumer goods, new capital or investment goods, government goods and services, and net exports of goods and services (which may be negative).

5. Spending for consumer goods is determined by the level of GNP and by the propensity to consume of private receivers of money income. The propensity to consume is stable.

6. Money income that is not spent for consumer goods, not paid *net* to governments as taxes and nontax obligations, and not donated *net* to foreigners (the "net" allowing for government transfer payments, including interest, returned to income receivers, and for donations from foreigners) is saved. Because the propensity to consume is stable, the propensity to save is also stable.

7. Domestic investment is spending for new capital goods. It is determined by the marginal efficiency of capital (the anticipated rate of net return to be earned by the use of new capital goods) and prevailing market rates of interest. Marginal efficiency is highly erratic. Foreign investment (or disinvestment) is the positive (or negative) difference between exports of goods and services and imports of goods and services, as adjusted for net private gifts and government grants to foreigners. Total investment is domestic investment plus foreign investment or minus foreign disinvestment.

8. If planned money saving including government surpluses, if any, is equal to planned total investment plus government deficits, if any,[9]

[9]In the remainder of this chapter, such references to government surpluses and deficits will be repeated only occasionally, but we should remember that government surpluses and deficits must always be accounted for in all analyses of saving-investment relationships. Government deficits, like investment spending, are an "offset to saving," whereas government surpluses are a kind of saving, and therefore something to be offset by investment if equilibrium is to prevail.

the economy is in equilibrium. Such an equilibrium means that total spending for newly produced goods is equal to the money income generated in their production including the profits that enterprisers *expected* to earn. Such an outcome of productive activity will, in turn, give the enterprisers no reason to change the volume of employment, whether or not idle productive factors are available. Thus it is always possible to have an "underemployment equilibrium."

The equilibrium may be indicated by formula as follows:

$$S + G_s = I + G_d$$

with S standing for private money saving, I for investment, G_s for government surpluses, and G_d for government deficits.

9. But because the bulk of savings decisions and investment decisions are made by different groups of people, these separate decisions can involve different sums of money. Planned saving and planned investment are not brought into equilibrium by shifts in market rates of interest, as the classical and neoclassical economists taught; rather *they are brought into equilibrium by shifts in the level of employment and therefore in the level of total output and money income.*

10. Thus an excess of planned saving over planned investment means that total spending for newly produced goods begins to fall below money income generated in their production, including the profits enterprisers *expected* to earn. As enterprisers realize that they will not receive the profits they anticipated when they decided upon a given volume of employment, they lower the level of employment to try to improve their position; by such action, however, they also reduce output and flows of money income. Successive reductions in employment, output, and money income continue until a level is reached at which planned saving and planned investment come into equilibrium. The reduction in employment, output, and money income diminishes the capacity of the people to save, and they must, accordingly, revise their plans downward. Thus the successive reductions in planned saving sooner or later bring it to a level where it no longer exceeds the volume of planned investment. At such a level, planned saving and planned investment may still be relatively large money amounts or they may be meager; in other words, the over-all downward movement in economic activity can be anything from a mild recession to a severe depression.

Expressed as a formula, an excess of planned saving over planned investment is as follows:

$$S + G_s > I + G_d$$

11. Thus also an excess of planned investment over planned saving means that total spending for newly produced goods exceeds the money income generated in their production, including the profits enterprisers *expected* to earn. The fact that enterprisers enjoy "windfall profits"

leads them to expand the level of employment, provided that idle factors are available; by such action, they also expand output and flows of money income. Successive additions to employment, output, and money income continue until a level is reached at which planned saving and planned investment come into equilibrium. The expansion in employment, output, and money income increases the capacity of the people to save, and they, accordingly, revise their saving plans upward. Thus the successive additions to planned savings sooner or later bring it to a level where it no longer falls short of planned investment. At such a level, both planned saving and planned investment may still be moderate in amounts or they may be greatly swollen; in other words, the over-all upward movement in economic activity may be anything from a modest recovery from depressed levels to a wild boom.

Expressed as a formula, an excess of planned investment over planned saving is as follows:

$$S + G_s < I + G_d$$

12. From all the foregoing propositions, the conclusion follows that planned saving and planned investment are in equilibrium only as business activity levels off at the end of periods of expansion and periods of contraction, so that, in terms of the saving-investment relationship, business expansions, contractions, and levelings may be pictured as in Figure 19-2 (with the government surpluses included as a component of S, and government deficits as a component of I).

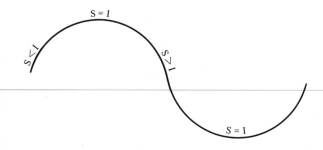

Figure 19-2   Saving and Investment in the Business Cycle

FOCUSES OF THE MAJOR PROPOSITIONS

All the major propositions of the income-expenditure theory as presented in the foregoing list are focused, we may say, on three things: (1) the decisions that business firms make from time to time about the quantities of the productive factors they will employ and put to work; (2) the planned investment of these firms in new capital equipment, including expanded inventories; and (3) the *resulting* relationship of planned saving and planned investment.

Profit expectations and effective demand

As for the first of these focuses, it is held that business firms make their decisions about employment of productive factors on the basis of their profit expectations, and that these profit expectations are based, in turn, on their anticipations of the *effective demand* for their outputs. It is demand as anticipated that is important for decision making about employment, and not the supply of productive factors. Supply of factors, no less than the supply of goods, does not create its own demand. Business firms want to maximize their profits or to minimize their losses, and they will not hire additional productive factors should they think that a worsening of their profit-loss outcome would result, but they will surely expand their employment of these factors if they anticipate a favorable result.

It is true, of course, that employment and output are necessarily limited in any country by the availability of productive resources and their quality. If a country is poorly endowed, its output must necessarily be small, no matter how anxious enterprisers may be to expand output; and if it is richly endowed, it can maintain a high level of output year after year, provided that enterprisers find it to their advantage to keep most of the resources employed. For the most part, this becomes a question of how much employment enterprisers will offer to labor, for all the other productive resources can be used only to the extent that labor is available and is put to work on them. It is also true that governments, households, and nonprofit institutions make decisions about the employment of productive factors, chiefly labor. Nevertheless, the total quantity of factors employed by these entities is usually only a small proportion of the available supply, so that the decisions of business firms predominate by a very wide margin.

In decision making about the arrays of productive factors they will put to work, business firms also play the predominant role in determining the level of money income. The total of money income will depend, of course, on prevailing wage and interest rates, rentals, taxes, and other costs; it may be small relatively to the volume of output, so that money costs and selling prices are low, or it may be high relatively to the volume of output, so that money costs and selling prices are high. Many costs, such as taxes, will be accepted by enterprisers as being largely beyond their control, while others, such as wages, will be recognized to be subject to change through bargaining processes. At any rate, once the enterprisers come to the decision to pay specific rates of wages and to meet other costs at a chosen level of employment, the decision necessarily governs the total of such outlays and therefore the total flow of money income.

As for the second and third focuses, as listed above, they can best be treated jointly under the subhead that follows.

Saving and investment *ex ante*

The reason why the income-expenditure theorists come to a conclusion about the saving-investment relationship that is different from that of the national product-national income accounts is because they look at saving and investment *ex ante*—in terms of the decisions that business firms, home buyers, and others are *now* making about investment, and the decisions that income receivers are *now* making to save some of the money income they expect to be getting, or in other words, in terms of planned investment and planned saving. Because the people who are planning to invest and the people who are planning to save are largely separate groups, why should we expect the amount of planned investment and the amount of planned saving to be equal?

According to the income-expenditure theory, such an expectation would be erroneous at most times for two reasons: (1) because spending for consumer goods is stable in relationship to the level of GNP, so that planned saving is also stable, and (2) because planned investment is erratic.

Stability of the Propensity to Consume   In the income-expenditure theory, the stability of the propensity to consume means two things: (1) that expenditures for consumption vary from period to period according to a pattern closely related to the varying levels of *real* GNP, that is, GNP adjusted for price changes; and (2) that consumption expenditure increase as real GNP increases but at a constantly diminishing rate.

These propositions can probably be best explained by means of an illustration. Let use assume that over a period of years in a certain country whose monetary unit is the dollar, GNP in dollar terms (but at stable prices) has varied between $400 billion and $500 billion, and that in these years consumption spending, also in billions of dollars, has been as indicated in the following table:

GNP	CONSUMPTION	MPC
400	260	
		0.9
420	278	
		0.8
440	294	
		0.7
460	308	
		0.6
480	320	
		0.5
500	330	

Now, the income-expenditure theorists hold that the relationship shown here between spending for consumption and real GNP would most likely prevail in further shifts of real GNP. If real GNP were to fall from $500 billion to $480 billion, consumption would be likely to fall, at least approximately, from $330 billion to $320 billion; if it were to fall further from $480 billion to $460 billion, consumption spending would be likely to fall to $308 billion; and if real GNP were to rise again to $500 billion, consumption would be likely to rise again to approximately $330 billion. This is what is meant by the *stability of the propensity to consume.*

Likewise, the illustration shows what is meant by the proposition that consumption spending rises with real GNP but at a constantly diminishing rate. As real GNP goes up from $400 billion in $20 billion increments, consumption spending increases at first by $18 billion, then by $16 billion, then by $14 billion, and so on. The same idea is indicated by the figures for the *marginal propensity to consume* (MPC) given in the last column of the table, for a steadily declining MPC means that consumption spending itself is expanding at a diminishing rate. The MPC between any two levels of real GNP is found by dividing the increment in consumption by the increment in GNP—often written

$$\frac{\Delta C}{\Delta GNP} \quad \text{or} \quad \frac{\Delta C}{\Delta Y}$$

with the Greek letter Δ meaning finite changes, C standing for consumption spending, and Y standing simply as a substitute symbol for GNP. Thus MPC is $12/20$, or 0.6, in the range of GNP between $460 and $480 billion, as is shown in the table.

Stability of the Propensity to Save   If consumption spending varies according to a particular pattern of relationship with real GNP, then saving must behave in a similar manner, since saving is disposable money income not spent for consumer goods (ignoring usually inconsequential government surpluses and personal gifts to foreigners). If consumption is stable, saving must also be stable. And if consumption spending increases with expanding real GNP at constantly diminishing rates, then saving must grow with expanding real GNP at constantly increasing rates. If the marginal propensity to consume within a given range of real GNP is $12/20$, or 0.6, then the marginal propensity to save is $8/20$, or 0.4.

Determinants of Investment   According to the income-expenditure theory, the volume of investment spending in any period has two determinants: (1) the marginal efficiency of capital (MEC), and (2) market rates of interest. MEC is the rate of profit that acquirers of new productive facilities —primarily business firms, of course—expect to earn from such acquisitions. MEC depends upon the prices of additional facilities, the probable expenses of their maintenance, and the prospective markets for, and selling prices of, the increased output they will make possible. In some field of enterprise at given times, MEC may be very high, particularly where inventions and innovations promise huge returns; and in others, where there is already much idle equipment, it will be nil or even negative. In general, MEC tends to decline as the accumulation of capital equipment increases. In a poor country, the addition of a few machines may promise handsome profits; but in a rich country, already well supplied with plants and equipment, the addition of further facilities may not be particularly attractive. Likewise, even in a rich country, the addition of new machines to replace obsolete ones in the early phase of a period of cyclical expansion will generally be more attractive than in a later period of the expansion when most plants have been well modernized.

Investment in new capital facilities will not take place in any firm or industry where MEC—as an anticipated *rate* of profit—is less than current rates of interest. No business firm will borrow to invest if it anticipates that the net earnings on the equipment to be acquired would be insufficient to cover the interest payments it will have to make; nor will it spend its own money for capital goods if it can derive a greater return by simply lending the money to somebody else. If, on the other hand, the MEC is higher than prevailing rates of interest, money will be spent for new capital goods in anticipation of the profits to be realized after interest and all other costs have been paid.

According to the income-expenditure theory, MEC, unlike the propensity to save, is highly erratic. The spread of labor disputes, the enactment of regulatory legislation that businessmen regard as unduly restrictive, the winning of a national election by a political party supposed to be prejudiced against business interests, the imposition of new taxes—such events can cause MEC to fall abruptly and drastically, while national and international events that businessmen hail as likely to be beneficial can cause MEC to rise as abruptly and as decisively.

But if MEC is erratic, if investment decisions are determined from day to day by MEC and market rates of interest, if planned saving is stable in relationship to the level of real GNP, and if equilibrium requires that planned investment be equal to planned saving, how can equilibrium ever be attained, or if attained, how can it be restored if disturbed by shifts in the erratic MEC? The classical and neoclassical economists taught that market rates of interest always prevail at levels at which saving and investment will be kept equal and the economy will be kept in equilibrium. But the income-expenditure theorists do not agree with this doctrine.

Views of Income-Expenditure Theorists on Interest Rates Some income-expenditure theorists hold that market rates of interest are determined by the supply of and demand for loanable funds, and others, by the demand for liquidity, or "liquidity preference," and the quantity of money available. However, most agree that the two viewpoints are much the same—that they are simply alternative ways of looking at the same phenomena—and all agree that both viewpoints lead to the conclusion that interest rates do not function in a manner to keep planned saving and planned investment equal.

According to the loanable-funds view, saved money income may be hoarded or extinguished by its use in repaying commercial bank loans or in retiring securities held by the commercial banks. It is therefore obvious that the total amount of saving is not necessarily offered as loans for investment spending. It is also obvious that the amount of money offered as loanable funds may exceed the amount wanted for investment spending because loanable funds coming from current saving may be augmented by the dishoarding of money previously hoarded and especially by the creation of new demand deposits by the commercial banks as permitted by the Federal Reserve. And on the demand side, there are outlets for saving and other loanable funds in addition to that for investment spending as for consumer spending and government deficit financing, so that it can hardly be said that, on the demand side, MEC is the sole determinant of the level of interest rates.

The liquidity-preference viewpoint regards the quantity of money as being fixed by the monetary authorities, and holds that, given this fixed quantity, market rates of interest are determined by varying degrees of preference people have for holding money as an asset rather than other assets and especially securities. If people are satisfied with their present money holdings, and if the quantity of money is reduced, interest rates will rise, and if the quantity of money is increased, interest rates will fall. Similarly, if people's liquidity preference increases with the quantity of money unchanged, interest rates will rise, and if liquidity preference declines, interest rates will fall. But if interest rates are so determined, they would appear to have no dependable relationship to planned saving and planned investment, such as would keep them in equilibrium.

In the liquidity-preference theory, there is always the implication that people's decisions about the amount of money they wish to hold as an asset depends upon the level of interest rates that already prevails. If prevailing rates are low, liquidity preference will be high because the cost of holding idle money—interest income forgone—will also be low; and if interest rates are high, liquidity preference will be low because holding money means forgoing relatively large amounts of interest income. As interest rates rise, therefore, people will be more and more willing to part with liquidity. But this means that they will be willing to make more money available as loanable funds—and thus the essential sameness of the loanable-funds and the liquidity-preference points of view is disclosed.

CONSEQUENCES OF SAVING-INVESTMENT DISEQUILIBRIUM

Although the income-expenditure theorists conclude that market rates of interest can hardly be depended upon to vary in a manner to keep planned saving and planned investment in equilibrium, they hold that *shifts in the over-all levels of employment, output, and money income* will eventually bring about such an equilibrium. If planned saving and planned investment are not in equilibrium, they will be brought to this state, not as a result of a few fluctuations in interest rates, but by changes in the whole tempo of business activity—changes that may be, indeed, sweeping and violent.

It is the position of the income-expenditure theorists that if planned saving exceeds planned investment, the levels of employment, output, and money income will fall, and continue to fall until equilibrium is established. The fall may by moderate or it may be long-continued and very sharp; there may be anything from a mild recession to a long and severe depression. In any case, the reduction in employment, output, and money income will curtail the capacity of the people to save, and it is this frustration of people's decisions to save that will have the effect, sooner or later, of bringing planned saving to a level where it will no longer exceed planned investment—reduced even when planned investment, too, may be reduced as a result of the general contraction of business activity. Likewise, the income-expenditure theorists hold that if planned investment exceeds planned saving, the levels of employment and output—assuming idle factors of production to be available—and money income will rise, and continue to rise, until an equilibrium is reached between planned saving and planned investment. The rise may be moderate or it may be long-continued and very strong; there may be anything from a modest recovery in business activity from a condition of severe depression to a wild boom with soaring prices. Whatever it may be, the expansion in employment, output, and money income will increase the capacity of the people to save, and planned saving will therefore move progressively toward the current level of planned investment. With increased money income and stable savings propensities, the people have no choice but to increase saving, and if investment spending does not continue to expand at an equal or more rapid pace, saving must eventually match it.

According to the view of the income-expenditure theorists, therefore, there is no force in the economic system that inevitably tends to cause investment spending to "fill the gap" created by saving at high levels of employment, output, and money income. If such a gap is not filled by investment spending, the simple fact is that the high levels of employment, output, and income will not continue to prevail. And there is also no force tending to cause employment, output, and money income to expand from low levels if planned saving and planned investment come into equilibrium at such levels, so that a condition of chronic *underemployment equilibrium* may obtain.

Further observations about the saving-investment relationship

It is the position of the income-expenditure theorists that, at any level of employment other than one approaching full employment, consumption spending and investment spending tend to vary in the same direction at the same time. The classical and neoclassical economists generally thought of them as moving in opposite directions. As they believed that the forces of competition constantly tend to bring about full employment, it was logical for them to hold that consumption could increase only if investment decreased and vice versa. As the output at full employment is limited, it must be shared between consumption and investment—one cannot expand unless the other releases productive factors. Accordingly, increased abstention from consumption was thought to be necessary for increased investment.

But the income-expenditure theorists hold that in an economy in which the forces of competition are not particularly effective, there is no inherent tendency toward full employment, so that investment can hardly be said to take place at the expense of consumption or consumption at the expense of investment. At the lower turning point of the business cycle, as business firms decide that their depleted inventories must be at least moderately replenished and that some of their broken-down and obsolete machines may well be replaced at the comparatively low prices then prevailing, their investment spending provides new jobs as well as expanded employment for those still working, and the increased flow of money income into the hands of the people gives them the long-wished-for opportunity to increase their consumption spending. The increase in consumption spending, in turn, makes further investment all the more attractive. At the upper turning point of the business cycle, on the other hand, the decisions of business firms to avoid further inventory accumulation and to defer other projects for capital expansion causes some people to lose their jobs and others to be reduced to shorter hours, with the result that consumption spending is cut. The curtailment of consumption spending, in turn, seems to prove to the business firms that they were right in deciding to reduce their investment outlays—so much so, in fact, that further cuts in these outlays now appear to be the most reasonable action they can take.

In effect, therefore, the income-expenditure theorists say that we can "save ourselves" into contraction and depression and that we can "spend ourselves" into expansion and prosperity. In periods of declining business activity, although saving may be most attractive to the individual who anticipates lower prices, it is suicidal for the people of a country collectively, since their efforts to save bring reduced employment and output, and investment simply does not take place. The people collectively are impoverished in that both consumption and investment goods that the economy is equipped to produce are just not being produced. Likewise, though frugality in spending for consumption goods in a period of revival of business activity may appeal to the individual, it can have the effect, if indulged in by the people generally, of bringing an incipient expansion to a very quick stop.

Implications for monetary and fiscal policy

Emphasis on Fiscal Policy The linking of government surpluses with private saving and of government deficits with private investment in the income-expenditure theory suggests why the theorists have generally chosen fiscal policy as the most likely means of achieving full employment, good rates of economic growth, and stability in the price level, and have usually displayed little confidence in the effectiveness of monetary policy. If the economy is at a level of full employment but with private investment opportunities diminishing in attractiveness—with MEC falling—it would seem logical that the federal government should cut taxes in order to reduce or eliminate the revenue surplus it would presumably be acquiring at such a time. Such a reduction in total saving would require less investment than before to maintain stability at the level of full employment. And if the reduction or elimination of the government's surplus were not enough for this objective, the government could reduce taxes further or increase its own spending, in either way accepting deficits to be financed by borrowing private savings, and thus further reducing the amount of private investment needed for equilibrium at the level of full employment.

Since the origins of the income-expenditure theory came chiefly in the period of the Great Depression of the 1930s, the inclination of the theorists to emphasize the likely effectiveness of fiscal policy by contrast with monetary policy also had its origins at that time. The problem was one of pushing the economy upward from the underemployment equilibriums that prevailed throughout much of the period. Yet, increasing the quantity of money did not appear to be the solution. After the banking crisis of 1932–1933 had been quieted, the commercial banks began to accumulate excess reserves at a rapid rate, so that there appeared to be no shortage of money —or at least, no shortage in the capacity of the commercial banks to create demand deposits should they be willing to lend and should people wish to borrow. Despite this big buildup in lending capacity, the banks (and other lenders) did not reduce their interest rates to zero or to negative levels, as would have been necessary to encourage borrowing for spending for many kinds of investment projects in relationship to which MEC must have been at negative levels. From this experience emerged the idea of a "liquidity trap"—the idea that when interest rates are at very low positive levels, people will simply hold as idle balances whatever additional money the monetary authorities choose to supply, as by buying securities in the open market. Thus adding to the quantity of money will have no effect toward promoting investment spending.

Concessions toward Monetary Policy But many income-expenditure theorists have conceded that monetary control should also be effective, with at least some of their concessions apparently resulting from the onslaughts of the "monetarists," as referred to in the preceding chapter. They have increasingly yielded to the argument that fiscal policy can be effective in a really significant way only if the quantity of money in circulation is expanded to "accommodate" it. If the government increases its spending as a direct means of increasing effective demand, it will have little success if it finances its expanded spending by increasing taxes or by borrowing private savings. The government's increased spending will "crowd out" an approximately equal amount of private spending that would otherwise have been effected; in other words, government spending will simply be substituted for private spending. But if the government finances its additional spending by means of newly created money—primarily, of course, by selling new debt instruments to the commercial banks for demand deposit balances—this spending will truly be increased effective demand. It should stimulate private spending instead of substituting for some of it. Accordingly, the Federal Reserve would have to "accommodate" such fiscal policy by supplying the commercial banks with sufficient reserves to enable them to buy the government securities.[10]

Price-Level Determination   In view of their orientation toward fiscal policy, the income-expenditure theorists have given relatively little attention to price-level determination. Their thinking in this area may be described as follows: if planned saving and planned investment are in equilibrium, the price level is likely to be stable; if planned saving exceeds planned investment, a downward pressure is exerted on prices; and if planned investment exceeds planned saving, an upward pressure is exerted on prices. However, the actual movement of prices depends not only upon changes in the saving-investment relationship but also on the availability of idle factors of production and the degree of market control exercised by enterprisers in various industrial fields. If idle factors are available, the stimulus exerted by an excess of planned investment over planned saving may have little effect on the price level but greater effect on employment and output. Or again, such a stimulus may result in immediate increases in prices in highly competitive fields of enterprise with little or no effect on output and employment. In industrial areas in which competition is strong among many sellers, sharp drops in aggregate demand are generally accompanied by sharp drops in prices with output and employment only slightly curtailed, and sharp advances in demand bring equally sharp advances in prices with output and employment little affected. In industries in which competitive forces are weak, on the other hand, substantial decreases in demand generally result in severe contractions in employment and output with only moderate price drops, if any, while substantial expansions in aggregate demand generally result in large expansions in employment and output with only moderate price hikes, if any.

FOR REVIEW

1.   Explain the nature of the four principal components of GNP.
2.   What is national income? What are its components?

---

[10]For a further discussion of the probable effects of varying policies of deficit financing, see Chapter 21.

3. What are capital consumption allowances? How do they contribute to income flows?

4. What are the effects of each of the following on costs of production, money income, and selling prices: business transfer payments, indirect business taxes, and "subsidies less current surplus of government enterprises"?

5. What is the nature of the statistical discrepancy that is incorporated in the national product-national income data?

6. As determinants of disposable money income, what are the roles of personal tax and nontax payments and government transfer payments? What is included in each of these items?

7. What are the three choices for the disposal of disposable money income that the holders of this income have?

8. In the national product-national income accounts, how is net foreign investment determined?

9. What is meant by the conclusion that saving and investment are always equal *ex post*? Is this an acceptable conclusion? Discuss.

10. Do you see any flaw in the argument of the income-expenditure theorists that the economic system generates sufficient purchasing power to make possible the sale of all goods produced at prices high enough to cover all costs of production including profits? Explain.

11. What is meant by the stability of the propensity to consume as this term is used in the income-expenditure theory? the stability of the propensity to save?

12. According to the income-expenditure theory, what are the determinants of investment spending?

13. In relationship to saving and investment, how are government surpluses and deficits treated in the income-expenditure theory?

14. What is the distinction between the concept of saving and investment *ex ante* in the income-expenditure theory and that of saving and investment *ex post* in the national product-national income accounts.

15. According to the income-expenditure theory, is there ever an equilibrium in the economy? If so, is this an equilibrium at full employment? Explain.

16. According to the income-expenditure theory, what are the economic consequences if, in any period, planned saving exceeds planned investment? if planned investment exceeds planned saving?

17. In the income-expenditure theory, what is the role of market rates of interest as determinants of employment, output, and money income?

18. Why have income-expenditure theorists generally favored fiscal policy rather than monetary policy for attempting to achieve full employment and good economic growth rates? Why have they given relatively little attention to price-level stability?

PROBLEM

Using the following national product-national income data for the year 1970 (in billions of dollars) published by the Department of Commerce (*Survey of Current Business,* May 1971, pp. 11–14), construct a table for each of the following to show its composition or determination:

A.   Total gross national product.
B.   Total national income.
C.   Other nongovernmental money income.
D.   Disposable money income of private receivers.
E.   Government surplus or deficit.
F.   Net foreign investment.
G.   Total investment.
H.   Total saving.

Personal consumption expenditure	616.7
Personal transfer payments to foreigners	.9
Government transfer payments to foreigners	2.0
Government transfer payments to persons	73.9
Government net interest payments	14.8
Business transfer payments	3.6
Gross private domestic investment	135.7
Net exports of goods and services	3.6
Indirect business tax and nontax liabilities	92.1
Tax and nontax payments out of income	210.7
Government purchases of goods and services	220.5
Subsidies in excess of current surplus of government enterprises	1.8
Capital consumption allowances	84.3
Statistical discrepancy (to be added in going from gross national product to national income)	−1.8
Capital grants received by the United States—SDRs (to be treated as adding to foreign investment and as a component of saving)	.9

MONETARY AND FISCAL POLICY

CHAPTER 20

INSTRUMENTS OF MONETARY POLICY

To introduce the discussion of the instruments of monetary policy in this chapter and the principles and procedures of fiscal policy in Chapter 21, it should be advantageous to state what monetary policy and fiscal policy are, to point to distinctions between them, and to indicate the lines or responsibility for the formulation and execution of both kinds of policy.

THE NATURE OF MONETARY AND FISCAL POLICY

Monetary policy

Monetary policy is the management of the expansion and contraction of the quantity of money in circulation in order to achieve specific economic objectives. There is virtually unanimous agreement that the objectives are full employment of labor (as defined in Chapter 2), a high degree of stability in price levels, and the promotion of economic growth from year to year at optimum rates. However, it is recognized that the monetary authorities may have in mind at times less comprehensive objectives such as seeking to improve our balance-of-payments position, to assist the U.S. Treasury in its debt management operations, and to eliminate "disorderly" conditions in the money market. At the same time, the general consensus surely is that giving attention to the less-comprehensive objectives must not be permitted at any time to seriously divert or weaken the main drive toward the comprehensive objectives themselves.

Quantitative and Selective Instruments Some instruments of monetary policy are described as "quantitative," and others are said to be "selective," or "qualitative." The chief quantitative instruments that are employed in the United States are changes in discount rates at the Federal Reserve banks, their open-market buying and selling of Treasury obligations, changes in reserve requirements applicable to the deposits of member banks of the Federal Reserve System, the setting of maximum interest rates that insured commercial banks may pay on savings and other time deposits, shifts in Treasury balances between the commercial and Federal Reserve banks, and management of the national debt by the Treasury in such a manner as to shift holdings of its obligations among the Federal Reserve banks, the commercial banks, and the nonbank public. The chief selective instruments are changes by the Federal Reserve in margin requirements applicable to loans for the purchasing and carrying of securities, certain kinds of "direct action" that the Federal Reserve may take in its supervision of member banks, the granting of loans by government agencies, and the guaranteeing by government agencies of loans granted by private financial institutions. During World War II and in the early 1950s, the Federal Reserve imposed regulation on consumer loans and credits as specially authorized by Congress, and in the early 1950s also, on loans for the construction of real property.

Differing Effects of Instruments   The quantitative instruments are so called because they are employed to control the total quantity of money available for all purposes, and the selective instruments, because they are employed to limit the availability of money for certain specific purposes. Because the commercial banks are the principal creators of money, and because their money-creating capacities depend on the amount of their primary reserves, the quantitative instruments of monetary policy generally have their effect on the quantity of money by way of the changes they cause in the primary reserve positions of these banks. The selective instruments, on the other hand, may be employed effectively even when the commercial banks have plentiful supplies of excess reserves. They achieve their peculiar effectiveness because they primarily limit the capacity of people to borrow rather than the capacity of banks to lend. A selective instrument employed restrictively can have the effect of freezing out many prospective borrowers of high credit standing to whom the banks would be eager to grant loans.

Fiscal policy

Fiscal policy is the shaping of the tax structure and the determination of the volume of tax revenues and the volume and direction of government spending in order to achieve specific economic objectives—objectives that are generally recognized to be primarily the three major objectives of monetary policy. The instruments of fiscal policy include the multitude of different kinds of taxes that are and that may be levied, as well as the detailed features of these taxes, such as inclusions and exclusions, allowable deductions, exemptions, and particularly rates, whether progressive, proportional, or regressive; and all the amounts and directions of government spending, including the granting of subsidies to private business, price-support programs, the allocation of contracts for military supplies to particular firms or geographical areas, insurance and welfare payments to the unemployed, and the implementation of work-relief and public-works programs.

Fiscal policy aimed at the three major objectives envisages the erection of a tax structure, not with primary emphasis on the raising of a given amount of revenue in the easiest way, but on the effects that specific kinds of taxes and different schedules of rates will have on consumption spending, saving, domestic and foreign investment, and prices; and the determination of the volume and direction of government spending, not with primary emphasis on what is necessary to provide certain services, but with major attention to how government spending will fit into the pattern of private spending currently taking place and projected.

Monetary and fiscal policy distinguished

Although monetary policy and fiscal policy are closely related in their objectives, we ordinarily should have little difficulty in distinguishing between them. Let us consider two examples.

A businessman has almost arrived at a decision to go ahead with plans to install new machinery in his factory, because a commercial bank having excess reserves has promised him a large loan at a moderate rate of interest; but at the last minute, as it were, he changes his mind because an announcement comes from Washington that Congress has passed and the President has signed a bill raising income tax rates. Thus monetary policy could be favorable for domestic investment, and fiscal policy unfavorable because of the weight of taxes on profits.

The Treasury sells new debt instruments to the commercial banks and gives the proceeds as grants to the states for the construction of schools, with the objective of stimulating activity in the construction industry as well as in industries that supply construction materials and consumer goods to construction workers and their families. Here we have applications of both monetary and fiscal policy. The Treasury's decision to borrow new money from the commercial banks rather than private savings is a matter of monetary policy, while its decision to spend to stimulate employment is a matter of fiscal policy. Were the Treasury to use the proceeds of its borrowing at the commercial banks to pay off some of its obligations held by the nonbank public, its action, as classified in this chapter, would be exclusively one of monetary policy.

Concerning the classification just mentioned, however, there are some differences of opinion. The point of view in this chapter is that, while the size of the national debt is a resultant of decisions concerning taxation and government spending that are clearly within the realm of fiscal policy, decisions concerning the composition of the debt and the sources of its financing fall within the realm of monetary policy. Some authorities treat debt management as a phase of fiscal policy, and some classify it as a third area of economic control and therefore distinct from both monetary and fiscal policy.

AGENCIES OF MONETARY AND FISCAL POLICY

Coordination in the use of the instruments of monetary and fiscal policy is essential if they are to be used with maximum effectiveness. A concentration of the instruments in the care of a single administrative agency would seem to be the best means of getting coordination; yet we quickly find that such a concentration does not obtain. It is true that all governmental powers of monetary and fiscal policy are entrusted under the Constitution to Congress, and we have concentration in that respect; but when Congress undertakes to delegate the powers to administrative agencies, it tends to follow no particular rule of concentration. Traditionally, the central bank has been thought to be the ideal agency for the exercise of powers of monetary control, and the national treasury for the formulation and execution of fiscal policy; and traditionally, too, it has been generally accepted doctrine that the policy decisions of the central bank should be free of domination or control by the chief executive officer of the government, whether persident or prime minister, or by the officials of the treasury. More by accident than by design has it been that, because of the tremendous growth of taxation and government borrowing and spending, the treasury has acquired important powers of monetary control in addition to the fiscal powers specifically delegated to it. In the United States, when Congress has thought it desirable to set up new programs of subsidies, price supports, government loans, and government guaranty of loans, it has generally preferred to establish separate new agencies to administer the programs rather than to delegate their administration to the Federal Reserve or the Treasury.

But such a scattering of authority does not go unchallenged. Many students of public affairs hold that the President should be fully and solely responsible for all the powers of monetary and fiscal policy that Congress chooses to delegate to the executive branch of the government. He should have, it is said, as much power to control the decisions of the Federal Reserve as he has to control those of the Secretary of the Treasury whose tenure is at his discretion;[1] likewise, he should have direct and immediate control over all government lending, guaranteeing, and subsidy-paying agencies—an area in which his authority, at the present time, is at best unclear and uncertain. The argument is that the President is chosen by the people to carry into effect the programs proclaimed in his campaign speeches and in his party's platform, and that he and his party are held accountable by the people for what the government does or does not do during his term of office and, even more importantly, for what actually happens

---

[1]In this connection, a review of the controversy about Federal Reserve "independence," as discussed in Chapter 16, should be instructive.

to the economy in that period. But if responsibility in the tremendously important area of monetary and fiscal policy is divided and diffused, how can he logically be held accountable?

Federal Reserve powers of monetary control

Despite some possibilities of division and diffusion, the powers of the Federal Reserve authorities to control the quantity of money in circulation are sufficiently strong to be fully effective in most instances. This is especially so because the Treasury almost always exercises its own money-control powers to support Federal Reserve policy—yielding decision making in this area, as it were, to the Federal Reserve and trying to avoid conflict.

Within the Federal Reserve structure, powers are concentrated in the Board of Governors. While discount rates are apparently "fixed" by the directors of the Reserve banks individually, the Federal Reserve Act gives the Board of Governors the authority "to review and determine" these rates. And this is unanimously understood to mean that the board may reject discount rates proposed by the Reserve bank directors and substitute rates of its own choice.

The board's power to direct the open-market operations of the Reserve banks through the System Open Market Account is obviously shared with them, since it is joined by five Reserve bank presidents on the twelve-member Federal Open Market Committee. While it is also obvious that the board can still have its judgments followed if its members stand together in voting on open-market decisions, it is also apparent that a majority of the board can be overruled if at least two of its members vote with the Reserve bank presidents in opposition to this majority.

The powers to change the reserve requirements that apply to the deposits of member banks, to set maximum interest rates that member banks may pay on time deposits, to change the margin requirements that apply to lending for the purchasing and carrying of securities, and to initiate "direct action" to curb member bank lending for speculative purposes are all held exclusively by the Board of Governors. In the matter of maximum interest rates prescribed for time deposits, the board's power is broader than it at first appears to be. This is because of the cooperation of the Federal Deposit Insurance Corporation. The FDIC has the power to set maximum rates payable by insured nonmember banks, but it invariably sets the same maximum rates as are set by the board for member banks.

With respect to all the board's exclusive powers, other officials in the Federal Reserve structure are not excluded from giving advice and offering criticism. This is especially true of the Reserve bank presidents, all of whom attend the frequent meetings of the Federal Open Market Committee although only five are members at any given time. At these meetings, all aspects of Federal Reserve policy are typically discussed, including questions about what the board should do in the exercise of its exclusive powers.

A final point is that some of the board's exclusive powers may be exercised only with the cooperation and assistance of the Reserve banks. For example, it is they that decide about lending to member banks even when they must charge the discount rates as "reviewed and determined" by the board.

Monetary and fiscal powers of the Treasury

As already listed, the Treasury's principal money-control powers are its capacity to shift its own cash balances between the Federal Reserve banks and the commercial banks and to manage the national debt in ways designed to affect its distribution among the Federal Reserve banks, the commercial banks, and the nonbank public. But, as already stated, the Treasury almost always exercises these powers in conformity with Federal Reserve policy—to support that policy, one may say, rather than to obstruct it.

But what about coinage policy, gold policy, and policy relative to acceptance of SDRs from other member countries of the International Monetary Fund? Could not the Treasury vary these policies in ways to exert important influences on the domestic monetary situation? In some respects it could although it chooses not to do so, and in other respects its powers in these categories are quite limited. As for coinage policy, it can hardly put more coins in circulation than the commercial banks ask for and the people want, and it would be unwise not to supply the quantity that people want. As for policies about gold, SDRs, and relationships with the IMF and its members, the specific directions of federal law and the statutes of the IMF largely limit its discretion. It can exchange dollars for foreign currencies by arrangements with foreign governments and central banks, decide whether or not to accept SDRs directly tendered by other IMF members, and try to persuade foreign governments to invest their excess supplies of dollars in special issues of Treasury obligations rather than to ask for gold. But the Treasury's discretionary actions in these areas are almost always aimed at improving our balance-of-payments position—a goal that is generally in close accord with Federal Reserve objectives.

Even in the area of fiscal policy in which the Treasury is usually thought to play the leading role, its powers are by no means comprehensive. It may hold back on spending or speed it up, change its direction in some instances, and in many instances, refuse to spend as much as Congress appropriates. It can change some of the myriad of rules that are applied in federal taxation in such manner as to increase or reduce revenues. But for the most part, its "fiscal policy" depends upon its powers of persuasion rather than upon fiscal powers already in hand—its powers to persuade Congress to enact the changes in tax and spending legislation that it recommends. And of course, this typically means the President's powers of persuasion and the legislation he recommends, since the Treasury wishes only that which the President wishes or that which he, in turn, has been persuaded to seek.

Powers of other federal agencies

A detailed enumeration at this point of all the agencies of the federal government that have authority to grant loans, to guarantee loans granted by private institutions, and to provide subsidies would not be particularly meaningful. The work of many of them is described elsewhere in this textbook in sufficient detail to be illustrative. Suffice it to say here that their collective powers—most of them having both monetary and fiscal policy aspects—are important, although certainly far less significant than those of the Federal Reserve and the Treasury; and that there is far less assurance, in most instances, that they will be used in concord with Federal Reserve and Treasury policies, as there is that Federal Reserve and Treasury policies themselves will be in harmony with each other.

FEDERAL RESERVE QUANTITATIVE INSTRUMENTS

The quantitative instruments of monetary policy exert their influence on the over-all quantity of money chiefly by way of bringing about changes in the volume of primary reserves held by the commercial banking system or in the "excess," or "free," portions of these reserves. As we well know,[2] the commercial banks can expand their loans and investment—and therefore, the volume of money in the form of demand deposits—only if they have excess primary reserves; and as a rule, they must contract the volume of their loans and investments and the volume of demand deposits if they have deficiencies in their primary reserves. In considering the use of the quantitative instruments, we must also keep in mind that an increase in excess reserves permits an expansion in demand deposits several times the amount of the increase and that a deficiency that cannot otherwise be corrected requires a several-fold contraction in demand deposits.

Changes in discount rates

Older Theory Concerning Discount Rates For many decades before the establishment of the Federal Reserve System, students of banking theory and practice looked on changes in discount rates as the most effective instrument that a central bank could have for controlling monetary expansion and contraction. The manipulation of discount rates had long been the principal means used by the Bank of England and other central banks to control the general credit situation. Accordingly, the framers of the Federal Reserve Act, in giving a similar instrument to the Federal Reserve authorities, anticipated that it could be used effectively in "credit control" in the United States.

---

[2]For assistance in understanding the workings of the instruments of monetary policy, a review of Chapter 7 and especially its treatment of the factors supplying and absorbing reserves should be most useful at this time.

As conceived by the founders of the Federal Reserve System, a discount rate was not to be a *penalty rate,* that is, a rate placed so high as to discourage borrowing at the Reserve banks except in times of emergency. Instead, the rate, as the act itself said, was to be set "with the view of accommodating commerce and business." Member banks were expected to go to the Reserve banks frequently to get the wherewithal to expand loans to their customers. Any member bank that had only sufficient reserves to satisfy the legal requirements could meet requests for additional loans by rediscounting its customers' notes with the Reserve bank in its district.

In these circumstances, the magnitude of the discount rates charged by the Federal Reserve banks might either encourage or discourage member banks' borrowing. Should the Reserve authorities believe the outstanding volume of money to be excessive, they might attempt to correct the situation by raising the rates. Since the member bank would have to pay a higher rate in borrowing, it would surely charge its customers higher rates in order to preserve its customary profit margin. The general effect would thus be to discourage borrowing by the public. On the other hand, should the Reserve authorities want to encourage credit expansion, they could reduce the discount rates, making the cost of new reserves lower to the member banks, so that, in turn, they could lend to their customers at lower rates.

Present-Day Significance   But changes in Federal Reserve discount rates have long since lost much of their importance as a control device. This is apparent in the fact that increases in the discount rates in recent years have generally been effected *after* rises in the whole array of market rates of interest, and decreases have been put into effect *after* drops in market rates. Moreover, changes in discount rates have often been accounted for as steps to keep them "in line with" or "in proper relationship with" the market rates.

Nevertheless, changes in Federal Reserve discount rates are often said to be psychologically important as a means by which the Federal Reserve reveals to the financial community and the public in general its attitude concerning current business developments. Should prices start upward in a period of full employment, the Reserve authorities may test the strength of the inflationary pressures by moderate sales of Treasury obligations in the open market; but should they become convinced after a time that the inflationary pressures are strong, they can well raise the discount rate by one fourth or one half of a point as notice that they intend to use all their *other* powers to curb further expansion in the outstanding volume of money. Likewise, should a decline in employment and output get under way, the Reserve authorities may take a mild step in the direction of monetary ease, such as buying a moderate quantity of Treasury obligations in the market; but, when convinced of the increasing gravity of the recession, they can well reduce the discount rate to indicate that they intend to use their other powers to provide favorable borrowing opportunities throughout the financial system. It is argued that, even if changes in discount rates follow changes in market rates of interest, their psychological significance is not lost. A decline in market rates, for example, typically indicates a weakening in the demand for loans—a weakening in expansive forces in the economy. If this decline is followed by a drop in Federal Reserve discount rates, the Reserve authorities thereby endorse, as it were, the market opinion that contractive forces are growing in strength; if it is not followed by a lowering of discount rates, the Reserve authorities indicate their conviction that market developments are of a seasonal or random nature.

Open-market operations

Potency The capacity of the Federal Reserve banks to buy and sell Treasury obligations in the open market for their own account can be aptly described as the most important power of monetary control available in the United States at the present time. Although the effects of open-market operations and the setup for decision making about them and their execution were discussed at some length in Chapters 7 and 17,[3] it is important to repeat at this time that open-market sales by the Federal Reserve banks of a given amount of Treasury obligations (in the absence of offsetting changes in other factors supplying and absorbing reserves) cause a reduction of the same amount in the primary reserves of the commercial banking system; and that their open-market buying of a given amount (in the absence of offsetting changes) provides the commercial banks with new primary reserves of the same amount.

That the open-market instrument is a very potent one is indicated by Federal Reserve holdings of Treasury obligations of approximately $68 billion at the end of November 1971 when total member bank reserves on deposit at the Reserve banks amounted to only approximately $24 billion. Clearly, therefore, the capacity of the Federal Reserve to reduce commercial bank reserves through open-market sales is far beyond what it will ever have to employ. And on the other hand, the capacity of the Federal Reserve to supply reserves through open-market buying is limited only by the availability of marketable Treasury obligations and other securities it is authorized to buy, such as issues of federal agencies.

Flexibility The open-market instrument is, moreover very flexible. It can be brought into action quietly and inconspicuously—without the fanfare that accompanies announcements of changes in discount rates and reserve requirements. As said previously, it can be used moderately to test the strength of an inflationary or deflationary development, and it can be used

---

[3] A rereading at this time of these earlier analyses is strongly recommended. See also Chapter 16 for some background details about the Federal Open Market Committee.

vigorously when the Federal Reserve officials are persuaded that expansionary or contractive pressures in the economy are indeed strong. An especially advantageous aspect is that it can be employed in one direction this week and in the opposite direction next week, without giving rise to misgivings about whether the "Fed" really knows what it is trying to do.

Procedure   The effectiveness of the open-market power, it is important to recall,[4] is not weakened by any uncoordinated action of the twelve Reserve banks separately, since the volume and timing of transactions are decided by the Federal Open Market Committee and the transactions are handled exclusively through the Federal Reserve Bank of New York. Moreover, its use does not depend on the cooperation or consent of the commercial banks. The manager of the System Open Market Account (SOMA) at the Federal Reserve Bank of New York makes his transactions with a small number of recognized dealers in government securities and so-called dealer banks, these dealers and dealer banks being "recognized" for the reason that they undertake at all times to quote prices to SOMA at which they will buy and sell for their own accounts large blocks of any outstanding issue of Treasury marketable obligations. Thus, the recognized dealers and dealer banks can be relied on to buy *at some price* when SOMA wants to sell and to sell *at some price* when it wants to buy.

This does not mean, however, that changes in primary reserves brought about by Federal Reserve open-market transactions affect only the dealers, their banks, and the dealer banks. If that were so, such transactions would scarcely be a good instrument of *national* monetary policy. On the contrary, the dealers and dealer banks maintain a market in government securities for institutions and individuals located in all parts of the country and abroad. A bank located in Dallas may sell securities to a New York dealer, and the latter, in turn, may sell the same securities to SOMA because it wishes to buy at that time. As a result, the Federal Reserve payment for the securities would be quickly passed to the Dallas bank, so that it, and not a New York institution, would get the reserves created by SOMA's purchase. Similarly, an individual investor dwelling in Seattle may buy some securities from a New York dealer just acquired from SOMA, so that the Seattle bank on which the investor's check was drawn, rather than a New York bank, would lose reserves.

Minor Limitations   The only significant limitations on the open-market operations of the Federal Reserve originate in the responsibility that it freely accepts to prevent and dispel "disorderly conditions" in the market for Treasury obligations. Conditions are disorderly if substantial variations in market prices occur from transaction to transaction, if prices gyrate aimlessly, or—most disorderly of all—if buyers of Treasury obligations *at any*

---

[4]See Chapter 17.

prices are difficult to find. Accordingly, SOMA must not permit its own transactions to cause disorderly conditions, as is most unlikely anyway, and beyond this, it may have to buy at times to correct disorderly conditions originating elsewhere even when it would prefer to stay out of the market or to sell, or to sell when it would prefer to stay out or to buy. Fortunately, however, SOMA's market interventions for this reason are required only rarely.

Changes in reserve requirements

Scope of Power Details concerning the authority of the Board of Governors to change the reserve requirements applicable to the deposits of member banks, the classification of banks on the basis of location, the classification and reporting of deposits, the computation of required reserves, and so on, were presented in Chapter 13. At the moment, it is sufficient to recall that the board can vary the requirements applicable to the demand deposits of reserve city banks between 10 and 22 percent; the demand deposits of country banks, between 7 and 14 percent; and the time deposits of all member banks, between 3 and 10 percent; and that the board itself determines which member banks are to be classed as reserve city banks and which as country banks.

Effectiveness of Changes Changes in reserve requirements do not cause changes in the *amount* of primary reserves held by the commercial banks; rather, they cause shifts in reserves between the "required" and the "excess" categories. An increase in requirements has the effect of reducing excess, or free, reserves by transferring some or all of them to the category of "required reserves," and a decrease in requirements brings a freeing of some reserves that were formerly required.

It is often said that variations in reserve requirements are doubly effective in changing both the amount of excess reserves and the degree of expansibility of demand deposits based on them. Assume that the member banks hold $126 billion of demand deposits, that they have $22 billion of primary reserves, and that the average legal requirement is $14\frac{2}{7}$ percent, or one seventh of the amount of demand deposits. Disregarding time deposits and the reserves required for them, excess reserves would be $4 billion, and this amount could "support" an expansion in demand deposits of $28 million. Now assume that the average legal requirement is raised to $16\frac{2}{3}$ percent, or one sixth of the amount of demand deposits. Immediately the required reserves become $21 billion, leaving only $1 billion of excess reserves—an amount that can "support" added demand deposits of only $6 billion instead of the $7 billion possible with a $14\frac{2}{7}$ percent requirement.

As the net demand deposits against which the member banks were actually holding required reserves in the late months of 1971 averaged about $146 billion, we can readily see that a change in requirements of only one or two percentage points can produce a substantial change in the loan and investment capacities of the commercial banking system. Changes at any one time of more than that amount are ordinarily not to be expected.

Limitations on Changes   Changes in reserve requirements can hardly be classified as a flexible instrument like open-market operations. Even more than changes in discount rates, changes in reserve requirements are generally understood by the financial community and by businessmen collectively to indicate a Federal Reserve conviction that an inflationary, or a contractive, development is strong, and that restrictive, or easing, actions will be pushed with vigor. Accordingly, a change in requirements in one direction cannot be quickly reversed without public suspicion that the Federal Reserve itself is rather confused. Even when made in the same direction, frequent changes in reserve requirements have often been condemned as complicating unduly the asset-management problems of member banks.

Because the law places upper limits beyond which the Board of Governors may not go in imposing reserve requirements, the instrument necessarily loses further restrictive potency when such limits are reached. On the other hand, the lower limits stipulated in the law, except that for time deposits, appear to have no practical significance for the foreseeable future.

Legislative Recommendations of the Board   Since the end of World War II, the Board of Governors has made a series of recommendations to Congress for new legislation in order to expand and modify its power to set and vary reserve requirements. In some instances, Congress has passed legislation as asked by the board; in some, it has enacted part of the requests; and in others, it has ignored the recommendations.

Pending at the present time are two recommendations that the board has repeated for several years: (1) that the "reserve city" and "country" classifications of member banks by their locations be discontinued, and that it be authorized to set reserve requirements for all member banks on graduated scales based on the respective amounts of their deposits; and (2) that nonmember insured banks be required to hold reserves at the same levels as required of member banks.

About the first of these recommendations, the board says that differences "in both size and function" between member banks now classified as "reserve city" banks and those now classified as "country" banks have become much less significant than they used to be, so that inequities in requirements result from the classification on the basis of location. Its principal argument in support of the second recommendation is that demand deposits of nonmember insured banks are no less a part of the quantity of money in circulation than are the demand deposits of member banks, so that they should be treated alike in the setting of reserve requirements.[5] It surely also has in mind that reserve requirements imposed on member banks, which have often been much higher than requirements imposed by the laws of many states, have been a major reason for the refusal of many state banks to join the Federal Reserve System and for quite a few to withdraw.

Other Recommendations   Several recommendations for reform in the reserve-requirement instrument of monetary control have come from sources other than the Board of Governors, particularly from scholars in monetary economics. Two of these recommendations are worthy of brief descriptions as being especially attractive.

One recommendation would add elements to the reserve-requirement power to make it a selective instrument as well as a quantitative one. This would be done by having reserve requirements apply against the earning assets of banks—against their various kinds of loans and security holdings— rather than against their deposit liabilities, as at the present time. If it were desired to encourage business loans and to discourage consumer loans, the requirement applicable to the former could be lowered and that applicable to the latter raised; likewise, variable changes could be made in requirements applicable to holdings of, say, Treasury obligations and holdings of municipal securities. The quantitative element would be retained, since uniform changes all along the line could also be prescribed.

The second recommendation is that, in periods of inflation, very high requirements, perhaps as high as 60, 70, or 80 percent, could be applied to *increases* in deposits occurring after a stipulated date. Such an arrangement, it is argued, would not greatly burden the commercial banks, as is possible when a sizable increase in requirements is made applicable to all deposits already on the books; yet it would be most effective in curbing the further expansion of bank loans and investments.

Setting interest rates on time deposits—Regulation Q

In 1933 the Federal Reserve authorities received the power to set maximum interest rates payable by member banks on savings and other time deposits, and in 1935 the Federal Deposit Insurance Corporation received a similar power pertaining to the time deposits of insured nonmember banks. But these powers were not designed as a new instrument of monetary control. Instead, they were aimed at holding down payments of interest on time deposits so that the banks would not be tempted, as in the 1920s, to seek high-yielding loans and investments that would also necessarily be high in risks. For many years, therefore, nobody gave much thought to the potentialities of interest-rate setting on time deposits as a means of monetary control.

---

[5]See, for example, the Board of Governor's *Annual Report*, 1968, pp. 338–339.

Recognition as Money-Control Instrument In late 1955, however, restrictive monetary actions of the Federal Reserve caused interest rates in the money market to rise above the "Regulation Q ceilings"—so called because the decrees of the Federal Reserve concerning maximum rates are contained in its Regulation Q, and because the FDIC always prescribes for nonmember banks the same maximums as are prescribed for member banks in Regulation Q. The result was an immediate slowdown in the growth of time deposits at the commercial banks but not at competing institutions not subject to interest-rate ceilings—institutions then including savings and loan associations and mutual savings banks. It was thus seen that Regulation G could serve handily in restricting commercial bank lending and investing, much in the manner of increases in reserve requirements. To explain: The commercial banking *system* does not ordinarily lose deposits when time depositors make withdrawals to invest in Treasury bills, commercial paper, or other money market instruments, or to open accounts at, say, savings and loan associations. Assuming that the time depositors make their withdrawals by asking for cashiers' checks, as is likely, the time deposits are at once converted into demand deposits, since cashiers' checks are a subclass of demand deposits. But demand deposits are subject to higher reserve requirements than time deposits, so that some of the formerly free reserves of the banks at which the withdrawals take place are now required reserves, or deficiencies result. Of course, the withdrawing time depositors will turn the cashiers' checks over to the people from whom they are buying money market securities or to the savings and loan association to which they want to "transfer" their deposits. But the security sellers or savings and loan associations will be most likely to deposit the cashier's checks in their own demand deposits at commercial banks. In this way, commercial banks somewhere in the system will have additional demand deposits equal to the withdrawn time deposits—deposits subject to higher reserve requirements. Only if the commercial banks find it necessary to curtail their loans and investments because of reserve deficiencies that result from such conversions of time deposits into demand deposits can it be said that the *system* can lose deposits to nonbank financial institutions and to the money (and capital) markets.

Experience in 1966 and 1969 Regardless of the 1955 experience, however, the Federal Reserve showed no significant inclination to use interest-rate regulation for monetary control until about mid-1966. Between January 1, 1957, and that time, it rather consistently raised the Q ceilings whenever money market rates moved above the ceilings already in effect. But the story was different in 1966 and again in 1969, when the Federal Reserve depended on the Q ceilings for restrictive effects as if they were a full-fledged instrument of monetary control. In those years, the Q ceilings were especially effective in limiting the lending and investing capacities of the large metropolitan banks and, indeed, in forcing them to scramble madly for reserves as never before to fulfill commitments to customers on outstanding lines of credit. As mentioned in Chapter 11, these banks had become aggressive bidders in the early 1960s for time deposits, especially the type evidenced by negotiable certificates of deposit (CDs). When, therefore, money market rates rose in 1966 and 1969 above the Q ceilings, many holders of CDs decided to let them "run off," that is, to take the proceeds at their maturities for investment in higher-yielding money market securities; and this meant for the commercial banking system, and especially for the big banks, large transfers from time deposits to demand deposits with higher reserve requirements.

Uncertain Status   Whether or not the Federal Reserve will continue from time to time to employ Regulation Q as a restrictive device is a debatable question. Its rigorous application in 1966 and 1969 has been widely criticized as having caused severe distortions in money flows and as having been particularly injurious to the market for the securities of state and local governments and particularly disrupting to international money flows, as evidenced by gyrations in the Eurodollar market. However, it has been most strongly condemned as being, unlike the other quantitative instruments, a kind of price-fixing in markets that are much more competitive— that is, the financial markets—than are many commodity markets where the thought of price-fixing by government is abhorrent.

QUANTITATIVE INSTRUMENTS OF THE U.S. TREASURY

The principal means at the disposal of the U.S. Treasury for influencing the quantity of money are its capacity to shift the cash balances of its own "general fund" between the Federal Reserve banks and the commercial banks and its authority to manage the national debt.

Management of the general fund

The general fund consists of money balances held by the Treasury at any time for meeting the many kinds of payments that the federal government customarily makes. It includes a relatively small amount of money in the Treasury's own vaults, its checking account balances at the Federal Reserve banks, and its "tax and loan account" balances at the thousands of commercial banks that are qualified as "special depositaries of public moneys."

As a potential influence on the quantity of money in circulation, the Treasury's "vault cash" is of little importance. The principal items constituting the vault cash are idle gold, that is, gold against which the Treasury has not given gold credits to the Federal Reserve banks, and Federal Reserve notes and coins received for taxes and the like and temporarily held pending deposit at the Reserve banks.

Much more important, then, is the division that the Treasury decides to make between its checking account balances at the Federal Reserve banks and at the commercial banks. When the Treasury deposits at the commercial banks the checks drawn by taxpayers and buyers of its debt instruments, the reserves and demand deposits of the commercial banks are not affected, for the transaction simply requires them to reduce the deposit accounts of the drawers of the checks and increase the tax and loan accounts of the Treasury. But when the Treasury deposits such checks at the Federal Reserve banks, the latter present them to the commercial banks for payment, reducing commercial bank reserves and increasing the "general account" of the Treasury. The commercial banks, in turn, charge the checks against the deposit accounts of the drawers. Thus both primary reserves and demand deposits are reduced. The Treasury does not spend its balances at the commercial banks by drawing checks on them; instead, when it wants to use these balances, it orders their transfer to the Federal Reserve banks, and the transfer has the same effect as would have been the deposit of taxpayers' and security buyers' checks at the Federal Reserve banks in the first place, that is, a reduction in both the reserves and demand deposits of the commercial banks.

As the Treasury ordinarily wants its general-fund transactions to have minimal effects on the volume of commercial bank reserves and demand deposits, it tries to pace transfers from them in amounts sufficient only to meet its current expenditures for a few days; in this way, the reserves and deposits lost in the transfers are quickly regained as the payees of Treasury checks deposit them at the commercial banks. But it is interesting to observe that the Treasury *could* affect commercial bank reserves and demand deposits by large amounts if it so chose. If it wanted to expand the volume of reserves and deposits, it would withdraw from the commercial banks less than the amount of its current expenditures, making up the difference by drawing down its balances at the Federal Reserve banks, and similarly, if it wanted to contract reserves and deposits, it would require the commercial banks to transfer more than the amount of its current expenditures, thereby building up its balances at the Reserve banks.

Management of the national debt

In the management of the national debt, the Treasury can importantly affect commercial bank reserves and demand deposits by differing decisions about the kinds of securities it will issue, to whom it will offer them, their maturities, the rates of interest they will bear, and so on.

Effects of Treasury Borrowing   When the Treasury borrows by the sale of its bills, notes, and marketable bonds and spends the money borrowed, (1) there may be no lasting effects on commercial bank reserves and deposits; or (2) demand deposits may be increased with no effects on the amount of primary reserves, although excess reserves are reduced; or (3) primary reserves and demand deposits may both be increased.

No lasting effects on the volume of commercial bank reserves and deposits result when the Treasury spends the proceeds of securities sold to the "nonbank public," that is, individuals, industrial corporations, savings banks, and all other kinds of institutions except the commercial and Federal Reserve banks. The nonbank individuals and institutions ordinarily pay for the securities by drawing checks on their deposit accounts at the commercial banks, and when the checks are cleared, balances in these deposit accounts are reduced. Temporarily, the Treasury may keep the payments as deposits at the same commercial banks in its "tax and loan accounts," but sooner or later, they will be transferred from the commercial banks to the Federal Reserve banks, and such transfers cause a reduction in the reserve accounts of the commercial banks at the Reserve banks as the Treasury balances there are increased. As soon, however, as the Treasury spends the borrowed money by drawing checks against its deposits at the Reserve banks, the payees deposit the checks at the commercial banks, and the latter collect by having their reserve balances increased. Hence both the reserves and the demand deposits of the commercial banks are restored to the level that obtained before the borrowing and the spending of proceeds took place.

When the Treasury borrows by selling its securities to the commercial banks, an expansion in their demand deposits takes place at once, assuming that they are permitted to "pay" by simply crediting the Treasury's tax and loan accounts on their own books. Such accounts are demand deposits, and they increase. In time, however, the Treasury orders the depositary banks to transfer its credit balances to the Federal Reserve banks. This is done at the Reserve banks by shifting balances from the commercial banks' reserve accounts to the Treasury's deposit accounts. But as the Treasury spends the money borrowed, the primary reserves of the commercial banks are restored to their former level, for the payees of the government checks deposit them at the banks. But these deposits at the commercial banks are new deposits, as they were created through the government's act of borrowing. Such new deposits—or rather, an equivalent amount—will remain on the books of the banks until the securities acquired from the Treasury are redeemed or until they are sold outside the commercial banking system. But the reserve requirements that apply to the new deposits reduce previously existing excess, or free, reserves.

Should the Treasury sell some of its debt instruments directly to the Federal Reserve banks and then spend the proceeds of these sales, the effect would be to increase both the primary reserves and the demand deposits of the commercial banks. The payees of the Treasury checks would deposit them at the commercial banks, and these banks would send them to the Reserve banks for credit in their reserve accounts. Actually, however, it does not work out precisely in that way, because the spending comes first! As we saw in Chapter 17, the Treasury uses its privilege of selling its security issues directly to the Reserve banks only to cover temporary overdrafts on its deposit balances there—so that, as one may say facetiously, its checks will not "bounce." Accordingly, the commercial banks' gains in reserves and demand deposits can better be said to come by way of the Treasury's management of its cash balances rather than by way of its debt management— by its drawing down its balances at the Reserve banks to negative levels. Moreover, the reserve and deposit gains of the commercial banks will typically be quickly canceled as the Treasury uses inflowing revenues (or proceeds of security sales elsewhere) directly deposited at the Reserve banks, or transferred from tax and loan accounts at the commercial banks, to retire the "special certificates of indebtedness" previously sold to the Reserve banks.

Retirement and Refunding When the Treasury retires some of its outstanding obligations by the use of surplus tax revenues, the effects on commercial bank reserves and demand deposits are exactly the converse of the effects of its borrowing and spending of the proceeds, that is to say, they depend upon the ownership of the securities called for redemption. As the money to be used for redemption is raised by taxation and accumulated as deposits at the Federal Reserve banks, there is an initial decrease in both commercial bank reserves and demand deposits, for the taxpayers draw checks against the commercial banks payable to the Treasury. When the Treasury, in turn, draws on its deposit accounts at the Reserve banks to redeem its outstanding obligations, (1) the primary reserves and demand deposits of the commercial banks are restored to the level that obtained before the taxes were collected if the security holders are nonbank individuals and institutions, for they will surely deposit the Treasury checks at the commercial banks; (2) the primary reserves of the commercial banks are restored if they are the holders of the securities, but the reduction in demand deposits because of the tax payments is final, since the redemption transaction as it affects the commercial banks is merely one of switching assets—Treasury securities for primary reserves—and (3) the reduction in the primary reserves and the demand deposits of the commercial banks occasioned by the tax payments is final in the event that the Treasury securities are held by the Federal Reserve banks, for the redemption in no way affects the commercial banks—the Federal Reserve banks merely cancel on their books equal amounts of assets and liabilities, that is, Treasury securities and Treasury deposits.

If, however, the Treasury merely refunds some of its outstanding obligations, that is, sells new securities and uses the proceeds to retire others previously issued, the over-all effects on bank reserves and demand deposits depend jointly on who holds the securities being redeemed and who buys the new securities. The sale has one of the "effects of Treasury borrowing," and the redemption, one of the effects of "retirement," both as described in the foregoing paragraphs. The separate effects of a refunding may cancel each other, as when the commercial banks buy new Treasury securities at the same time that some of their other holdings are being retired; the refunding may cause a contraction in reserves and deposits, as when the proceeds of Treasury securities sold to nonbank investors are used to retire some held by the Federal Reserve banks; or the refunding may result in an expansion of demand deposits without effects on the amount of reserves, as when the proceeds of Treasury securities sold to the commercial banks are used to retire some held by nonbank investors. And of course, other combinations are possible. Indeed, all the possible refunding combinations are significant as indicating that the Treasury's capacity to influence reserves and demand deposits—and possibly, therefore, spending, employment, output, and income—does not vanish because its budget is in balance. Maturities among its outstanding securities are continually occurring, so that it must continually make decisions concerning the classes of prospective buyers toward whom it should aim its refunding issues.

FEDERAL RESERVE SELECTIVE POWERS

Selective instruments of monetary policy are designed to regulate the availability of money in specific sectors of the economy or for specific uses rather than its over-all availability. They are especially noteworthy in directly affecting the demand for loans as well as the capacity of financial institutions to lend—they reach out, as it were, to the borrower as well as to the lender. Financial institutions may be eager to lend, but many loans may be precluded because many would-be borrowers cannot satisfy the margin requirements, the down-payment requirements, the installment-payment provisions, or some other restrictive stipulations of selective instruments currently in effect.

Margin requirements

The statutory power of the Board of Governors to set margin requirements is aimed at limiting the use of loan funds and particularly bank loans for speculation in securities. In setting margin requirements in recent years, however, the board has limited their application to loans for the purchase and carrying of "equity securities"—stocks, bonds convertible into stocks, bonds with stock-purchase warrants attached, and stock-purchase warrants themselves—traded on stock exchanges registered with the U.S. Securities and Exchange Commission, and comparable equity securities of about 300 corporations that are widely bought and sold in the over-the-counter market. For the latter, the board specifies the corporations by name and, from time to time, adds to and deletes from its list.

As set by the board, a margin requirement is the percentage of the purchase price of stocks and other equity securities that banks, brokers, dealers, and others in the business of lending *may not* lend. Accordingly, the *maximum loan value* of a security is the purchase price minus the margin requirement. For the purchase of common stock at a cost of $10,000 subject to a margin requirement of, say, 65 percent, therefore, any of the regulated lenders could not lend more than $3500.

The board's margin regulations apply to loans by banks, both member and nonmember, for the purchase and carrying of equity securities, whether granted to brokers and dealers or to other customers (Regulation U); similar loans granted by brokers and dealers to their customers (Regulation T); and similar loans granted by any other lender—any individual or enterprise—if, in any calendar quarter, its loans secured by equity securities amount to $50,000 or more or if its outstanding amount of such loans at any time in the quarter is $100,000 or more (Regulation G). In addition, the board has long had in effect margin requirements on short sales arranged by brokers and dealers for their customers.[6] On the other hand, the board has not set in recent years any margin requirements for the purchase and carrying of bonds that lack equity features, such as convertibility, and indeed, the law exempts all loans for the purchase and carrying of Treasury obligations and obligations of state and local governments, while indirectly providing an exemption also for the securities of federal agencies. Also exempt are loans whose proceeds are to be used for business, consumer, and other purposes unrelated to the buying and holding of securities, even when equity securities are pledged for their safety.

Direct action

A second selective instrument of monetary policy possessed by the Board of Governors is known as "direct action." It may be described as the specific approval or disapproval of the loan and investment policies of the commercial banking system in general and of individual member banks specifically, and the assessment of penalties against member banks that refuse to discontinue practices judged unsound. Before 1933, the board and the Reserve banks adopted various procedures of direct action on their own volition, but the Banking Act of 1933 gave the sanction of law to some procedures of this character. Nevertheless, the instrument of direct action is not an important one. General warnings to the whole commercial banking community about the inadvisability of certain loan and investment policies are likely to be ignored by the banks furthest out-of-line, and sitting in judgment upon the policies of individual member banks is a slow and cumbersome process.

---

[6]A *short sale* is a transaction in which a speculator sells securities he does not own. His broker borrows securities to make delivery to the buyer, and the speculator must at some time "cover" the transaction by buying identical securities so that they may be returned to the lender. The reason for the transaction is that the speculator hopes to be able to cover at a price lower than that at which the short sale was made.

Under the Banking Act of 1933, the Board of Governors is empowered, in the first place, to deny to any member bank its privilege of borrowing from the Reserve bank in its district, if it is found to be lending excessively "for the speculative carrying of or trading in securities, real estate, or commodities, or for any other purpose inconsistent with the maintenance of sound credit conditions." Second, the Board can restrict member lending on stock and bond collateral in any Federal Reserve district by setting a limit to such loans as a percentage of the member banks' capital stock and surplus. Third, the Board can order any member bank not to increase the volume of its loans on stock and bond collateral and can suspend its privileges of borrowing from its Reserve bank if it disobeys. Finally, the Board can remove officers and directors of member banks found guilty of "unsafe and unsound" banking practices—a term presumably broad enough to cover excessive lending for speculative purposes. Before exercising its power of removal, however, the board must warn the accused officers and directors and give them an opportunity to put an end to the "unsafe and unsound" practices; moreover, it must give them a reasonable opportunity to defend themselves.

Control of consumer and real-estate credit

The Board of Governors has had experience with two additional selective instruments of monetary policy: its regulation of consumer credit during the period of World War II and for a brief period in the early 1950s, and its regulation of real-estate construction credit, also in the early 1950s. Although the board itself has no standing authority to reimpose controls in these areas, the Credit Control Act of December 23, 1969, gave the President the continuing authority to empower the board to impose controls *on all kinds* of lending, selling on account, and financing by means of security issues should he decide controls to be "necessary or appropriate for the purpose of preventing or controlling inflation generated by the extension of credit in an excessive volume." Accordingly, a brief statement about the scope of the board's controls of consumer and real-estate construction credit in the 1940s and 1950s should be of interest.

The essential features of the board's regulations of consumer and real-estate credit (Regulations W and X) were twofold: requirements for minimum down payments to be made by buyers of designated consumer goods and real property, and the designation of maximum periods for the installment repayment of loans. Both kinds of regulations had the effect of reducing the demand for credit. People who could not make the prescribed down payments were directly and immediately excluded as applicants for loans. Likewise, people who might have enough to meet the down-payment requirements might, nevertheless, be excluded simply because the prescribed maximum maturity made the monthly installment payments too high for their budgets. The down-payment requirements were similar in character to the margin requirement on loans for the purchase and carrying of securities, as discussed above; but the maximum-maturity stipulation was something new, since the regulations concerning security loans do not require their repayment within a specified period of time.

FOR REVIEW

1. What is the nature of monetary policy? Explain the distinction between quantitative and selective instruments of monetary policy.

2. How important are the Treasury's powers of monetary policy by comparison with those of the Federal Reserve?

3. What is the nature of fiscal policy? Why is it said that the Treasury's fiscal powers depend upon its powers of persuasion?

4. To what extent are the Federal Reserve powers of monetary policy concentrated in the Board of Governors? the Federal Open Market Committee? the boards of directors of the Reserve banks?

5. How should the Treasury's debt management policies be classified—as monetary policies, as fiscal policies, or as a separate category? Discuss.

6. Is it your impression that Federal Reserve discount rates are set "with a view of accommodating commerce and business"? Discuss.

7. Why is it said that Federal Reserve open-market operations are much more flexible as an instrument of monetary policy than are changes in discount rates? changes in reserve requirements?

8. What is the basis for describing changes in reserve requirements as a doubly effective instrument of monetary policy?

9. What is your judgment about the proposal to have reserve requirements made applicable to bank assets rather than to deposits? Discuss.

10. Explain how it was possible for the Federal Reserve to use the regulation of interest rates on time deposits as a highly restrictive instrument of monetary policy in 1966 and 1969. Do you think that this was a proper exercise of power? Discuss.

11. Why is the Treasury's management of its own general fund described as a potential instrument of monetary policy rather than one actually employed?

12. Why may the Treasury design issues of its debt instruments to make them especially attractive to commercial banks? to the nonbank public?

13. Explain how the Treasury can employ debt management to influence economic developments even when its budget is balanced.

14. What are margin requirements as set by the Federal Reserve? On what kinds of transactions do they apply? How do they affect commercial banks? other classes of financial institutions?

15. What is meant by direct action as a selective instrument of monetary policy?

CHAPTER 21

PRINCIPLES AND PROCEDURES
OF FISCAL POLICY

TWO KINDS OF FISCAL POLICY

Fiscal policy may be said to be of two kinds: the kind that is specifically aimed at full employment, stable price levels, and an optimum rate of economic growth, and the kind that has goals that are not clearly related to these three. The first kind, with which we shall be exclusively concerned in this chapter, is often described as "compensatory" fiscal policy; the second has many names, depending upon the goals toward which it is directed. Examples of the latter are the enactment of tariff legislation to "protect" domestic industry; the imposition of heavy taxes on alcoholic beverages to discourage consumption; the use of tax measures for regulatory purposes, as to eliminate the manufacture of poisonous matches; the grant of subsidies to promote domestic shipbuilding; and the institution of programs of loans and grants to help other countries build their military facilities. Fiscal policy actions of these kinds undoubtedly have effects on output, employment, and income, but their relationship to goals like full employment is, at best, indirect and uncertain; some of them may, indeed, push the economy away from full employment, stable price levels, and good growth rates.

Compensatory fiscal policy, on the other hand, calls for direct and immediate changes in the flow of tax revenues and in spending programs to "compensate" for shortages and excesses in private sectors of the economy—shortages that, if not compensated for, will surely lead to a widening pool of unemployment; and excesses that, in the absence of appropriate monetary and fiscal action, will certainly result in inflation. Compensatory fiscal policy is not synonymous with compensatory spending, although the two are very closely related; at any rate, we must always remember that compensatory policy is concerned with changes in the tax structure and in tax revenues as well as with spending programs. Moreover, plenty of room for compensatory actions exists even when the government's cash income and outgo are in balance.

APPLICATION OF COMPENSATORY FISCAL POLICY

While it is possible to suggest fiscal policy actions that should be helpful in many different kinds of economic circumstances, a discussion at some length of two kinds of situations that frequently recur should be adequate: (1) a condition of spreading unemployment and (2) a situation of strong inflationary developments.

Fiscal policy to reduce unemployment

Inadequate Private Spending The growth of unemployment beyond the "tolerable" limit is unmistakable evidence that total spending for goods currently being produced is inadequate. Assuming that the government has not been reducing its expenditures, the conclusion is inescapable that spending in the private sectors of the economy has fallen short of what it should be. Therefore, the remedy is to build total spending to a higher level—to whatever level is necessary to cause employers to rehire idle workers, so that unemployment will be pushed back within the "tolerable" limit. The use of instruments of monetary policy may restimulate private spending—and if so, all to the good; but here we must concentrate our attention upon what appropriate fiscal policy would be.

From this point of view, the first question to confront the fiscal authorities is this: Shall tax revenues be reduced, shall government spending be increased, or is some combination of tax and spending procedures to be preferred? When this question has been answered, a second question, equally comprehensive, arises: What taxes shall be reduced or eliminated or substituted, and what shall we spend for, and when and where and how?

Four Compensatory Alternatives The first question has four possible answers:

1. To reduce tax revenues, leaving government expenditures unchanged.
2. To increase government spending, leaving tax revenues unchanged.
3. Both to reduce tax revenues and to increase government spending.
4. To increase both tax revenues and government spending.

Assume, for example, that the fiscal authorities decide, as a first approximation, that a change in the government's tax and spending programs of a magnitude of about $10 billion will be needed in the coming year to push total demand to the level needed to bring or keep employment within the "tolerable" limit. This is a "first approximation" because the authorities will surely conclude that a change of $10 billion may be more than enough or less than enough, depending upon which of the four alternative courses is chosen; it may be necessary to adjust the figure upward, or it may be possible to adjust it downward, on the basis of further study and analysis of the probably stimulating effects of the respective courses. The fiscal authorities anticipate, of course, that *private* spending in the coming year will fall short by much more than $10 billion in the absence of government compensatory action, but they conclude that the change in the government's programs, as finally decided upon, will so stimulate private spending as to bring it, together with government spending, to the desired total level. Stepped-up government spending for goods and services will presumably have certain "multiplier effects," as those who receive increased income from this source respend all or part of it, and as those who, in turn, benefit from the respending also step up their outlays. Likewise, increased spendings by taxpayers whose tax bills are reduced should also have "multiplier effects" as the beneficiaries of these and subsequent respendings increase their outlays all along the line. Let us suppose, also, that the fiscal authorities, in formulating their plans, are starting from a point at which the government's cash income and outgo have been in balance at a level of $200 billion.

By way of alternative 1, therefore, action would be taken to reduce tax revenues to $190 billion, and the government would need to borrow $10 billion to meet its expenditures at the continuing level of $200 billion. By way of alternative 2, government spending would be increased to $210 billion, and with tax revenues remaining at $200 billion, the government would have to borrow $10 billion. Alternative 3 would call for a reduction of taxes to, say, $195 billion, and an increase in expenditures to, say, $205 billion, and again the government would find it necessary to borrow $10 billion. On the other hand, the procedure of alternative 4 would call for the boosting of both tax revenues and government spending to a level of $210 billion, and no government borrowing would be necessary.

It is important to emphasize at this point that alternatives 2 and 4 fully and alternative 3 in part call for "compensatory spending"—for that term can most logically be used only to describe government spending *deliberately increased* to compensate for deficiencies in private spending—to help in "filling the gap," as we often say, caused by the falling short of private spending. Thus "deficit spending" and "compensatory spending" are not necessarily the same thing, as can readily be seen by the fact that in alternative 1 a deficit results but no compensatory spending is undertaken, and that in alternative 4 compensatory spending takes place without a deficit. In a similar way, the illustration shows that compensatory fiscal policy and compensatory spending are not necessarily identical, since alternative 1 can surely be described as a procedure of fiscal policy although it has nothing to do with compensatory spending.

Increased Spending versus Tax Reductions   However that may be, we must hasten on to the interesting question of which of the four alternatives is likely to be the most effective—effective in the sense of restoring the desired level of employment and rather quickly permitting the government to go back to a balanced cash position at the $200 billion level. Without doubt, alternative 2 is the most promising. Government spending for goods and services directly and immediately takes up some of the slack in private demand, helping to restore enterprisers' profits to reasonable levels and providing job opportunities for idle workers. Enterprisers are likely to be encouraged to increase their outlays for capital facilities, and wage earners, restored to their jobs, are likely to expand their spending for consumption. Alternative 4 might be equally effective, provided that the government, in increasing its tax revenues by $10 billion, found it possible to skim off private funds that would otherwise remain unspent—but it is rather difficult to devise tax measures with such precision that they will reach idle funds only.

The reductions in taxes proposed in alternatives 1 and 3 are also concerned with precision in tax management. The stimulus to employment by these routes (alternative 3, in part) is supposed to result from the willingness of people to spend their "tax savings." If, in alternative 1, the people have $10 billion less in taxes to pay than they paid in preceding years, will they promptly spend an additional $10 billion for consumption and investment goods? The answer depends upon who has been paying the taxes. If the taxpayers would surely spend whatever they did not have to pay in taxes, the tax reduction would be as stimulating as an equal increase in government spending; but if the taxpayers would hoard their tax savings, no stimulus at all would result from the tax reduction. In most circumstances, a reasonable assumption is that the result would be somewhere in between: if it is difficult to devise new taxes that will reach idle funds only, it is likewise difficult to manage a reduction in taxes that will favor only people who are anxious to spend.

Financing the Deficits   Whose money is to be borrowed is a matter of great importance when the government decides how it is to finance deficits, such as would be incurred by way of alternatives 1, 2, and 3. Let us look at alternative 2. It was stated that this would be likely to be the best route. Nevertheless, alternative 2 would not be stimulating to employment at all were the government to meet its stepped-up expenditures of $10 billion by borrowing from the people $10 billion that they would have spent for investment and consumption goods had the government not come along with its new offering of securities. The increase in government spending would be offset by a new reduction in private spending of the same amount. At least, the result would not be depressing, as might be the borrowing policy related to alternatives 1 and 3. In alternative 1, to take the extreme possibility, if the tax savings made possible by the reduction in taxes of $10 billion were hoarded, and if the government borrowed $10 billion from people who otherwise would have spent this money for goods, the result would be a further reduction in private spending of $10 billion, not offset in any way by government action, since alternative 1 does not envisage an increase in government spending.

All of which brings us back to the effects of government debt-management policies as discussed at length in the preceding chapter. Indeed, it should now be clear that the question of how the government should meet its deficits resulting from reducing taxes or stepping up expenditures tends to merge some aspects of monetary policy and fiscal policy. The decision to have a deficit cannot be separated from the decision of how it is to be financed.

But there is no need to repeat the detailed treatment of the preceding chapter. It should be apparent, on the basis of the principles there developed, that the most stimulating way to meet the deficits of alternatives 1, 2, and 3 would be for the Treasury to sell its new obligations to the Federal Reserve banks; that second in the order of stimulation would be sales to the commercial banks; that sales to nonbank investors who would otherwise hoard their money would come third; and that, as already specifically indicated, sales to nonbank investors who would otherwise spend their money for investment and consumption goods would have no rank at all in the order of desirability.

Further Compensatory Action The foregoing discussion does not necessarily lead to the conclusion that the government's compensatory action in a single year would be sufficient to restore a *stable* level of full employment. In the year of our illustration, unemployment should indeed be brought back within the "tolerable" limit as a result of the government's spending and taxing policies; but if the government were immediately to discontinue its compensatory activities, private spending plus ordinary government spending might still not be enough to hold the full-employment level. Private spending might tend to weaken in the second year if the government's compensatory action were stopped abruptly at the end of the first year. On the other hand, the second year would not be likely to require compensatory action as strong as that of the first year. Perhaps it would be possible to cut the dollar volume of the government's compensatory measures to, say, $5 billion. And in the third year, with private spending taking hold more firmly but with a few weak spots still obtaining, the government's measures might be sufficient at a magnitude of, say, $2 billion.

Assuming widespread public confidence in the wisdom of the government's policies, 3 or 4 years of gradually declining compensatory action ought to be enough, in most circumstances, to restore a full measure of private spending. The government would then be able to bring its cash budget into balance,[1] relying once again on private spending plus its own ordinary

---

[1]Not applicable, of course, to alternative 4, since it does not call for an unbalanced cash budget incidental to compensatory action. The appropriate action here would be the elimination of the increases in both spending and taxation.

outlays to provide a sufficient demand for goods to keep employment at the desired level.

Specific Tax and Spending Decisions   Not only must the fiscal authorities decide which of the four alternatives is the best one in the given situation, they must also face the much more complex problem of deciding what kinds of taxes to reduce (alternatives 1 and 3) or increase (alternative 4) and what kinds of spending to expand (alternatives 2, 3, and 4). Their specific decisions about the *kinds* of taxing and spending actions to take can have, in truth, more profound effects than the simpler decision to spend more or tax less. A poor selection of tax and spending policies might result in a need of government compensatory programs of a magnitude of, say, $8 billion in the second year instead of the $5 billion of the illustration; and surely it is possible that a very unpopular selection by the government would actually tend to cause unsupported private spending in the second year to fall below what it would have been in the first year without government stimulation. On the other hand, a wise selection could be so stimulating that the government would have to provide, say, only $3 billion of support in the second year and perhaps nothing at all in the third year.

Later in this chapter, we shall look into some of the problems involved in reaching decisions about the content of specific taxing and spending programs, but the treatment must be quite brief. The fiscal authorities ought to know how each kind of tax and each outlet for government spending affects private consumption and investment outlays, but the unfortunate fact is that our knowledge of effects is both cloudy and incomplete.

Fiscal policy to combat inflation

Monetary policy is generally recognized to be much more effective in combating inflation than in promoting an expansion in employment. But this does not mean that monetary control should take precedence over fiscal policy in inflationary periods, leaving the major use of the instruments of fiscal policy to periods of unemployment when monetary instruments are likely to be weak. Quite the contrary. If the instruments of fiscal policy are not used vigorously to combat inflation, they can scarcely be used at all, as major dependence upon them only in periods of unemployment would mean recurrent substantial increases in the national debt with little prospect of its ever being reduced—a result that could hardly be regarded as a reasonable long-range national policy. The people generally are likely to be convinced of the wisdom of fiscal policy, and to accept it with enthusiasm, only if there is assurance that the substantial deficits that are incurred in years of unemployment will be rather quickly offset, at least in part, by revenue surpluses, which inflationary pressures make equally wise.

Again—Four Alternatives   An inflationary development means that total spending in the economy, private and governmental, is excessive—that the demand for goods exceeds supply at current prices, so that prices are pushed upward. The remedy is obviously to reduce the amount of purchasing power available or, at least, to immobilize some of it if it is not to be drained off. In the matter of fiscal policy, the government again has four alternatives to choose from:

1. To increase tax revenues, leaving government spending unchanged.
2. To reduce government spending, leaving tax revenues unchanged.
3. Both to increase tax revenues and to reduce government spending.
4. To reduce both tax revenues and government spending.

Let us suppose that the fiscal authorities decide that, as a first approximation, changes in government spending and taxing programs of about $10 billion will be needed to overcome inflationary pressures expected to prevail in the coming year; and let us assume, as before, that the government starts its action from a position of balance in its cash income and outgo at $200 billion. Thus alternative 1 envisages the draining off of private purchasing power of $10 billion through an increase in tax revenues to $210 billion, giving the government a net revenue surplus of $10 billion; alternative 2 calls for the reduction of government spending from $200 billion to $190 billion, and again the government would have a net revenue surplus of $10 billion; alternative 3 would provide for a reduction in government spending of, say, $5 billion and an increase in tax revenues of the same amount, and the government likewise would have a cash surplus of $10 billion; and alternative 4, calling for reductions in both government spending and taxation of $10 billion, would leave the government with neither surplus nor deficit in its cash transactions.

Choosing from the Alternatives Since alternative 2 immediately lops off $10 billion of spending (plus, probably, a substantial proportion of what have been the "multiplier effects" of this spending in the past), it must be recognized as the most direct of the four routes. But as it does not reduce private purchasing power by way of increased taxation, care must be taken that private spending not be encouraged by the disposal of the revenue surplus. If the government were to return the surplus to the public by using it to retire some of its obligations held by nonbank investors, an increase in private spending would probably take place; hence the better policy would be to retire government securities held by the Federal Reserve and commercial banks in appropriate proportions.[2]

Alternative 2, nevertheless, requires reasonable judgments concerning the

---

[2]If it is the policy of the commercial banks to hold primary reserves equal to, say, 20 percent of their demand deposits, the Treasury could retire debt without adding to private purchasing power by redeeming $2 billion of its obligations held by the Federal Reserve banks and $8 billion held by the commercial banks. Assuming that the Treasury's surplus tax revenues had been collected in "tax and loan accounts," the effect

relative desirability of government spending and of private spending. Total spending is excessive, but that does not indicate in any way that the things the government spends for are less socially desirable and fruitful than are the things that the people in their private capacities choose or would choose to buy. If it is decided that all the existing spending programs of the government are essential for the general welfare, then the conclusion is inescapable that another alternative must be chosen. In such circumstances, alternative 1 would be the appropriate route—coupled with a decision not to return the purchasing power to the people by retiring government obligations held by them. In most instances, the most realistic decision would probably be that some kinds of government expenditures could be reduced, but not by such a large amount as $10 billion. Since we start with the assumption of a balanced cash budget, presumably including no provision for compensatory spending, the total amount of "unnecessary" or "deferrable" government spending to be squeezed out would probably be put at only a few billions, surely not exceeding $3 billion or $4 billion. Such a conclusion, therefore, would point to alternative 3 as the best route, with a reduction of, say, $3 billion in government spending, and adjustment in tax rates or the imposition of new taxes to bring in an additional $7 billion of revenue. And of course, alternative 3, like alternatives 1 and 2, would have to be buttressed by a decision to use the revenue surplus to retire debt held by the Federal Reserve and commercial banks in proper proportions.

Alternative 4 is, by all odds, the most unlikely route. Not only is it difficult to conceive of a situation where the sole impact of the cut in total spending should fall upon government outlays, but also the related reduction in tax revenues of $10 billion would presuppose that the tax cuts would reach only those who would be quite willing to hold their tax savings idle.

Other Considerations   The foregoing discussion has indicated that compensatory fiscal policy in periods of inflation must generally be matched with consistent debt-management policies, just as the two kinds of policy must be coordinated in periods of unemployment. Likewise, in the discussion of alternative 4, it was indicated that, where changes in tax revenues are involved, attention must be given to the sources of the revenues. In alternatives 1 and 3, no less than in alternative 4, changes in tax revenues may not bring about the desired result. If the increased tax payments called for in alternatives 1 and 3 were to come from people who would not have spent this money anyway, obviously no reduction in private expenditure for consumption and investment goods would result. We must also note that the

---

would be a reduction in commercial bank primary reserves of $2 billion and a reduction in demand deposits of $10 billion. Since the loss in reserves would be equal to 20 percent of the loss in deposits, the commercial banks would have no gain in excess reserves—no capacity resulting from the debt reduction to restore the lost deposits through their loan and investment operations.

kinds of government expenditures and taxes that are changed by any of the alternative courses tend to have varying influences on private spending, aside from the mere amount of money immediately involved—just as is true of compensatory actions to stimulate employment.

Finally, the continuation of a restrictive fiscal policy over a period of several years might be necessary, just as might be the continuation of a stimulating policy to restore and maintain a level of full employment. In terms of alternative 3, for example, should government spending be cut $3 billion and taxes increased by $7 billion in the first year, it might be desirable to restore not more than $2 billion of government spending and to cut taxes by not more than $3 billion in the second year, thus providing a revenue surplus of $5 billion; and in the third year, the revenue surplus might be held at, say, $2 billion by a further restoration of government spending of $1 billion and a further tax reduction of $2 billion.

Question of budget balancing

Compensatory fiscal policy by way of alternative 4 in each of the situations discussed envisages the annual balancing of the government's cash budget, but it was indicated that alternative 4, in both instances, is the least attractive and, therefore, the least likely to be selected. The other alternatives specifically call for cash deficits and surpluses, and as the preferred route of fiscal policy is apparently to be found among them, we conclude that compensatory fiscal policy and the annual balancing of the cash budget must generally be alien to each other. If the procedures of compensatory fiscal policy are to be used with maximum effectiveness, the older notion that the annual balancing of the budget is the first principle of "sound" government finance must be abandoned.

But rejecting the annual balancing of the cash budget as a "principle" of fiscal policy ought not to mean that the cash budget is never to be balanced —that the national debt must be expected to increase from year to year, with no reduction ever in sight. If business activity fluctuates cyclically in the future as it has in the past, there should be many years in which it would be the height of wisdom to have the budget in balance and, indeed, to have revenue surpluses to be used to retire debt. In years in which high-level employment at stable prices is assured without a need of added government spending or tax reductions for stimulation, the cash budget should surely be balanced; and in years of high-level employment with strong inflationary pressures, budgetary surpluses should surely be developed to curb the excessive spending that must be taking place. While restrictive monetary policy would probably suffice to curb excessive spending in periods of high-level employment and unneeded budgetary deficits, no responsible fiscal theorist would advocate or accept such a strange combination. There could be no better time for budget balancing and, with inflationary pressures, for revenue surpluses to be used to reduce the national debt. Thus we conclude that a confident, vigorous use of the instruments of fiscal policy to combat unemployment requires its vigorous use also in the opposite direction—to prevent and curb excessive spending—in periods of high-level employment and inflationary pressures. It might be possible, indeed, to achieve a "cyclically balanced budget," with the surpluses of the years of inflationary developments sufficient to offset the deficits incurred in years of underemployment, and with, therefore, no long-term increases in the national debt.

Many economists, however, see no reason for anxiety about continued increases in the national debt should the amounts of deficit spending needed to combat unemployment during some years of successive business cycles exceed the amounts of revenue surpluses appropriate to curb excessive spending in other years of these cycles. If the recurrent cyclical additions to the national debt so stimulate the economy that total output is substantially greater than it otherwise would be, then obviously the general welfare is advanced. There is no reason to fear increases in the national debt in themselves. The "burden" of the debt is not measured by its dollar amount alone, but by this amount as a ratio to gross national product. If this ratio does not rise despite rather steady increases in the dollar amount of the debt—or if it falls almost continuously, as in the post-World War II period —there would seem to be no cause for alarm. If we approve expansions in borrowing by business enterprises, consumers, and buyers of new residential property as stimulating to the economy and therefore promoting increases in output, why should we take a different attitude toward equally stimulating expansions in government debt? Especially is it argued that much government debt is really incurred for "capital expenditures" that surely increase productivity—expenditures for physical facilities, such as highways, improved harbors and waterways, and hydroelectric projects, and for "human capital," such as expenditures for education and health protection.

PROBLEMS OF FLEXIBILITY

The most serious difficulty encountered in gearing government spending and taxation to compensate for deficiencies and excesses in private spending is that of making the fiscal instruments flexible enough for prompt and effective use. The tempo of business activity may change abruptly, and following a change, it may proceed sharply in the new direction within a relatively short period of time. But Congress, which alone has the constitutional power to authorize changes in taxing and spending programs, moves rather slowly —often, indeed, with what may well be called extreme delays. Is there, then, any possibility that a system can be worked out for the quick application of the instruments of fiscal policy, even when Congress continues to be rather ponderous in its movements?

Indeed, there are possibilities, say the proponents of fiscal policy—not one possibility, but at least three: (1) devising a tax and spending structure having a great measure of "built-in flexibility"; (2) providing for changes in taxation and spending by means of "formula flexibility"; and (3) giving the President a large area of discretion in changing taxing and spending policies.

Built-in flexibility

A fiscal system with compensatory built-in flexibility is one in which changes in employment and output bring about, because of the very character of the spending and taxing programs already in effect, pronounced compensating changes in the government's fiscal position. If private consumption and investment spending were to fall by $20 billion, and if, as unemployment grew and output fell, revenues produced by taxes already in effect were to decline by, say, $8 billion and government spending, demanded by commitments already outstanding, were to increase by, say, $4 billion, we would have a very high degree of built-in flexibility. It is the "automatic" changes in government spending and taxing that results from changes in employment and output that distinguishes built-in flexibility from other arrangements for flexibility.

Though we may not be able to get built-in flexibility of the high degree just described, much can be done in this direction. Much has already been done. Our unemployment- and old-age insurance systems are especially notable in this regard because they have built-in flexibility on both the spending and taxing sides. In periods of unemployment, for example, the reduction in payrolls causes a reduction in revenue produced by the unemployment-insurance taxes, and simultaneously, the payment of unemployment benefits is stepped up sharply; likewise, tax collections in the old-age insurance system fall while, at the same time, elderly persons, losing their jobs, begin in increasing numbers to draw old-age insurance benefits. Additional built-in flexibility could readily be given to the unemployment- and old-age insurance systems, especially the former, and this is often advocated not only from the standpoint of its potential contribution to economic stability but also from the standpoint of equity. For the unemployment-insurance system, recommendations toward increased built-in flexibility include increasing the proportion of each employee's wage or salary upon which the tax is levied, modifying or eliminating "merit ratings" by which tax rates are often reduced for employers with good records of avoiding employee layoffs (since these good records are much more characteristic of periods of business expansion than of periods of recession), increasing the levels of unemployment-insurance benefits, and lengthening the periods during which the unemployed worker is eligible to receive these benefits.

Built-in flexibility in other spending programs of the federal government is rather hard to find, but the federal tax structure is well-supplied with such flexibility. This is so because of the prominent role assigned to income taxation. The fact that the individual income tax is rather steeply progressive causes the revenue it yields to vary more widely than do the percentage variations in employment. In periods of business recession, for example, a decline in a person's income results in a more than proportional reduction in his tax liability because the loss in income is subtracted, as it were, from the higher brackets where the higher rates prevail. Moreover, the pay-as-you-go method of collecting much of the individual income tax revenue means that the advantage of reduced tax liability is realized at just about the same time that income itself is reduced, rather than several months later. The take-home pay of workers is cut by something less than the amount by which wages have been reduced, because of the concurrent reduction in the amount of the withholding tax. Built-in flexibility in the corporation income tax is also due in part to its moderately progressive structure, but more particularly to the volatile character of corporate profits themselves. As profit margins tend to expand rapidly in periods of expanding activity and to narrow rapidly in periods of contracting activity, income tax revenues based on them necessarily vary just as sharply.

For increased built-in flexibility in income taxation, various methods of averaging incomes over several years have long been advocated. Recent federal tax legislation allows for some reduction in individuals' tax liability in the current year should the taxable income of that year substantially exceed the average taxable income of the preceding 4 years. But averaging aimed at built-in flexibility would chiefly work in the opposite direction by giving the taxpayer reduced tax liability in a year of *low* income, or even a claim for refund, *on account of taxes already paid* in a preceding series of years of higher income. Averaging the low-income year (surely a year of business recession for taxpayers collectively) with the preceding higher-income years would mean a reduced tax liability for these preceding years, so that there would be a "credit" to be applied against the tax liability of the low-income year or to be used as the basis of a claim for refund.

Some excise taxes, such as those levied on luxuries of highly elastic demand, also have the quality of built-in flexibility; but most excise taxes, tariff duties, retail sales taxes, and the like are quite weak in this respect. And it may be mentioned that property taxes—though they are a concern of state and local governments, rather than of the federal government—are especially lacking in built-in flexibility; tax levies on property holders may be just as high in depression as in prosperity, because of the slowness and inequities of reassessment procedures.

Formula flexibility

Many fiscal theorists hold the opinion that built-in flexibility, however much it may be extended and perfected, can be relied upon only to counteract relatively mild depressive and inflationary pressures—that it will always be inadequate to cope with strong and sustained pressures. Hence they argue that a further range of flexibility is essential, and they hope that either formula flexibility or flexibility by way of executive discretion will provide it.

A system of formula flexibility provides for specified changes in the tax structure and in the volume of government spending as determined by certain specified developments in business activity that can be easily identified and measured. It differs from built-in flexibility in *requiring changes* in the tax structure and in spending programs—in requiring decisions of administrative officials that the specified developments in business activity have taken place and that, therefore, the prescribed changes in taxing and spending must now go into effect.

To establish a system of formula flexibility, Congress would pass legislation stating precisely what tax and spending actions would be taken as the specified developments occurred, and of course, it would set standards for the measurement of these developments as indicators of when to initiate the authorized actions. It might stipulate that when unemployment reaches 5 percent of the labor force, the individual income tax rate for the current year in the lowest income bracket shall be reduced by 20 percent or that personal exemptions shall be increased by $100 and that when unemployment rises to 6 percent of the labor force, the cut in the income tax rate of the lowest bracket shall be increased to 30 percent or that personal exemptions shall rise by another $100. Similarly, the legislation might provide that a public works program of $5 billion shall be launched should unemployment reached 5 percent of the labor force and that an additional $5 billion shall be expended on the program should unemployment continue upward to the level of 6 percent of the labor force. The legislation would surely provide a standing appropriation for such a public works program so that delay in getting the necessary funds would be avoided.

Many other tax and spending measures might be included in a program of formula flexibility—the samples mentioned in the foregoing paragraph are merely intended to indicate how the details of the program would be set forth. Changes in corporation income tax rates and in excise taxes might be stipulated, and most certainly, we would expect the legislation to supply directives for additional tax and spending actions to be taken at a level of unemployment of 7 percent of the labor force and at higher levels. Likewise, the "formula" enacted by Congress would also have stipulations for changes in taxing and spending programs to combat inflationary developments, as well as specific instructions about when such changes should go into effect.

Although the foregoing description relates formula flexibility to employment data, Congress might prefer a different standard. It might authorize changes in taxing and spending to fight growing unemployment on the basis of changes in an index of industrial production or in an index of retail sales or in a combination of indexes. In any case, employment data would hardly be a good guide for action when the problem is one of combating inflation.

Since inflation is a persistent upward movement in the price level, formula action determined by changes in designated price indexes would certainly be much more realistic.

Formula flexibility has not yet been tried in the United States in any significant way, but it would seem to merit careful consideration by Congress.

Executive discretion

To establish a system of executive discretion, Congress would delegate authority to the President to make such changes in the volume of government spending and in the tax structure as he might deem necessary to maintain full employment, a stable price level, and an optimum rate of economic growth. Although Congress would surely set some limits to the range of the President's authority, as well as establish some standards for his guidance, it would not command him to take actions of designated scope on the occurrence of specified kinds of economic developments. With the Congressional standards in mind, the President and his advisers would doubtless give much attention to the statistics of employment and unemployment, as well as to many other data indicative of current business developments and tendencies, but he would still be quite free to decide whether or not to take action and when and how. The President would have leeway in shaping fiscal policy comparable to that which the Federal Reserve is supposed to have in shaping monetary policy.

At various times since the early 1930s, Congress has voted funds to the President and to some administrative agencies under his jurisdiction to be used at his discretion, and the same procedure can be repeated whenever Congress wishes to establish a system of "executive discretion" in the area of government spending.

From time to time, also, the President has received authority from Congress to change tariff duties within certain limits and in keeping with certain prescribed standards. But this has been a matter of relatively minor influence upon the economy. Much more could be tried. For example, the Commission on Money and Credit, in its report published in 1961, recommended that the President be given the power to vary the tax rate in the lowest bracket of the individual income tax by five percentage points upward and downward. It chose this bracket rate because it applies to all taxpayers "across the board" and is, accordingly, the principal determinant of the Treasury's individual income tax revenue.[3] In his economic report to Congress in January 1962, President John Kennedy endorsed, as it were, this recommendation of the commission. However, he asked for authority to reduce all individual income tax rates by as much as five percentage points and not sim-

---

[3]Commission on Money and Credit, *Money and Credit: Their Influence on Jobs, Prices, and Growth,* Englewood Cliffs, N.J.: Prentice-Hall, 1961, pp. 134–137. At the time of the commission's report, the lowest bracket rate was 20 percent, whereas it is now 14 percent.

ply the rate for the lowest bracket. But Congress failed to accede. Whether Congress has the constitutional authority to delegate to the President the power to change income tax rates or the rate of any other tax is a matter of grave doubt.[4] This doubt could be resolved, of course, by the adoption of an amendment to the Constitution specifically authorizing such a delegation of authority; but opposition to such a proposal would probably be great, because its adoption would mean an overthrow of one of the main pillars of the Anglo-Saxon legal tradition: that the "power of the purse" should forever be in the hands of the elected representatives of the people in the legislative body. Perhaps President Lyndon Johnson had such probable opposition in mind when, in his economic report to Congress of January 1965, he simply suggested that Congress could "reinforce confidence" by "insuring that its procedures will permit rapid action on temporary income tax cuts if recession threatens."[5]

PROBLEMS OF SPENDING

Spending is easy, but not so is wise spending. The federal government may pour great sums of money into the economy if it decides that this action is necessary to sustain full employment, and it may shut off the flow and even cut customary expenditures if it decides that too much spending is causing inflation. But wisdom in government spending requires emphasis on economy in government operations, precautions that spending will not be inimical to private enterprise, and a careful selection of spending programs that will be most stimulating to private outlays.

Economy in government operations

The stepping up and cutting down of government spending, as an instrument of compensatory fiscal policy, never imply a justification for waste and inefficiency in government. Even when unemployment is widespread, the government should strive to perform its services at the lowest reasonable cost—it should discharge employees who are providing no useful service, consolidate overlapping bureaus and offices, and eliminate wasteful duplicative functions. Taking action to greatly increase compensatory spending and continuing to search for economy in operations need never be regarded as contradictory.

The heart of the matter is that the need for new schools, hospitals, sewage disposal systems, and many other kinds of public facilities is so great in the United States that compensatory spending scarcely needs to be a

---

[4]In this connection, it is argued that the delegation of authority to the President to change tariff rates is justifiable because of *his* constitutional power to conduct foreign relations.

[5]*Economic Report of the President, January 1965*, Washington, D.C.: Government Printing Office, 1965, p. 11.

throwing-of-money-to-the-winds to be effective. The shabbiness and inadequacy of many of our public facilities are no less than shameful; surely, at any rate, reducing the backlog of needs in this area, as well as keeping up with ever-expanding requirements for additional facilities, should provide inexhaustible outlets for sane, carefully planned compensatory spending. And if a new spending program of, say, $20 billion is thought to be necessary in a certain year to sustain full employment, while, at the same time, $2 billion of wasteful government spending can be eliminated, what could be more pleasant than to increase to $22 billion the outlays for "cleaning up the environment" and for much-needed schools, hospitals, and other public facilities?

Government spending and private enterprise

If government compensatory spending is to be an instrument of the "middle course," whereby the government in its regulatory activities seeks to avoid the pitfalls of both *laissez faire* and regimentation, it should not seriously encroach upon the area of activity usually left to private enterprise. Nor need it do so. Compensatory spending to reduce unemployment does not require the enrollment of the unemployed on government payrolls or the taking over and operation of idle factories by the government. To the extent that the government spends for public facilities of the kinds mentioned above, it confines itself to functions long recognized as falling within its sphere of activity. There may be arguments pro and con on the question whether hydroelectric, slum-clearance, and other similar projects should be owned and operated by the government; but even should all such arguments be resolved in favor of the government, we can reasonably conclude that the result would not mean a very important stride in the direction of socialization.

Far from encroaching upon the area of activity of private enterprise, government compensatory spending should have the effect of revitalizing private activity at times when it is depressed through no fault of its own; after all, the immediate objective of compensatory spending is to stimulate *private* consumption and investment spending. Thus private industry should be expected to do the actual work of construction as the government undertakes public works programs. We expect the government to enter into contracts with private builders, and we expect the latter to hire employees, to buy materials and supplies, to sublet portions of the projects, and so on, all according to the customary procedures of private enterprise.

Selection of spending programs

Pros and Cons of "Heavy" Public Works   Although the building of important public facilities has been emphasized in the discussion of spending programs in the preceding paragraphs, opinion among fiscal theorists differs on the advisability of concentrating on what are often described as "heavy" public works. Critics of such a concentration say that long delays are involved in getting such public works projects launched and in cutting them off when and if they succeed in restoring full employment, that a shortage of skilled construction workers may obtain even when there is widespread unemployment elsewhere, and that the stimulus of spending for construction may be quite slow in reaching the mass of nonconstruction industries.

Such critics offer various alternatives. Some advocate spending for "light" public works, by which they mean the repair and modernization of schools, hopsitals, and other similar facilities, more extensive outlays for the upkeep of existing highways, parks, and playgrounds, the blacktopping of rural roads, the building of earth dams rather than great concrete monoliths, and so on. Others favor "make-work projects" that require much labor but little equipment to get purchasing power directly and quickly into the hands of the needy who will surely spend it quickly, and still others carry this idea a step further by advocating more generous direct payments to the unemployed—"relief," or "welfare," or whatever we may want to call it.

The difficulty with the alternatives is that their stimulating effects are most likely to be limited to the consumer-goods industries—not in the sense of causing them to expand facilities (for that would also stimulate the capital-goods industries) but in the sense of simply taking up some of the slack already developed there. Yet falls in investment spending are most likely to be the principal cause of spreading unemployment, so that a more or less direct stimulation of the private capital-goods industries would appear to be essential for the success of government compensatory spending. Government spending for heavy public works would surely supply such a stimulus.

Planning for Heavy Public Works   Not that the criticism of heavy public works programs is to be taken lightly. But surely delays in launching such programs can be greatly reduced by careful planning of projects long before they will be needed, including the drawing of detailed blueprints, the purchase of construction sites, and the anticipation of, and the finding of solutions for, whatever legal technicalities might threaten to delay action; and surely the planning can be such that parts of the over-all program can be completed within a limited period of time and other parts suspended from time to time, thus removing the threat that great outlays would still be necessary as full employment is reached and inflationary pressures grow. The training of additional construction workers should not be particularly difficult to accomplish, although some changes in union apprenticeship rules might be necessary. Finally, the argument that money spent for construction may be rather slow in carrying a stimulus to nonconstruction industries can be met, though not disposed of, by the argument that the proposed alternatives, similarly, would provide no immediate general stimulation to all industry.

In any case, a concentration on heavy public works does not rule out the use of the alternatives in a supplementary way. The unemployed in some sections of the country and in some occupations may have to be supported by way of light public works, make-work projects, and direct welfare payments until the stimulating effects of the heavy program are felt. But placing primary emphasis on any spending program other than that of providing important public facilities would appear to be most shortsighted—surely there could be no better time to clear up some of our woeful deficiencies in this area than when unemployment indicates that temporarily a surplus of productive facilities exists elsewhere.

PROBLEMS OF TAXATION

Changes in tax levies have effects, we have noted, depending upon the sources from which the revenues are derived—depending, that is to say, upon how people in their various capacities as wage earners, business managers, farmers, and so on, react to increases and decreases in the tax bills they must pay. A reduction in taxes will lose much of its potency in promoting an expansion in employment if the tax savings are hoarded, and an increase in taxes will be a weak measure for fighting inflation if the additional revenue comes from people who would not have spent this money anyway. This we have already decided.

But it is not enough to say that a change of this or that amount in revenues may have this or that effect on private spending. The fiscal planners must try to gauge the specific effects on spending of every kind of tax that may be levied—and not, indeed, spending in general, but precisely consumption spending, on the one hand, and investment spending on the other. If a growth in unemployment results from a decline in investment spending —with planned saving exceeding planned investment, in terms of the income-expenditure theory—it would surely be more logical to reduce taxes that burden investment rather than taxes that discourage saving. Perhaps, indeed, it would be desirable to increase taxes that discourage saving, so that consumption, thus stimulated, rather than government spending, would fill the gap caused by the deficiency in investment. Likewise, it might be most appropriate to encourage consumption directly by reducing taxes that tend to limit it. In times of peacetime inflation, on the other hand, the aim of the fiscal authorities may well be to hold consumption in check and to encourage saving, rather than to try to restrict investment spending.

A careful selection of taxes to be altered, as a procedure of fiscal policy, may be rewarded by effects more extensive than the effects that can be measured by the variation in revenues. In a period of business recession, a reduction in taxes that burden investment may result in an increase in investment spending of much more than the amount of the tax saving, with the more favorable tax situation encouraging additional investment spending from hoards and borrowing. Similarly, an imposition of a wide array of excise taxes on consumer goods in periods of inflation may not only cut consumer purchasing power by the amount of the additional tax payments but may also persuade many consumers to decide not to spend current money income or borrowed money for the taxed goods.

Even if the government's cash income and outgo are in balance in a period of full employment, certain changes in the tax structure may be advisable to preserve balance in the economy; they may be effective in checking developments likely to push the economy toward either unemployment or inflation. If it should appear, for example, that private outlets for savings are becoming difficult to find, immediate action could be taken by the tax route to discourage saving. This might be done by hikes in, say, the middle and upper brackets of the individual income tax, accompanied by offsetting reductions in taxes that bear directly on investment or, possibly, in those that directly burden consumption.

With these general observations as background, a brief analysis of some of the compensatory aspects of the three principal kinds of taxes that the federal government levies should be instructive.

Individual income taxes

Many fiscal theorists hold the opinion that the federal government must depend at all times very heavily on individual income taxes for its revenue if its tax policy is to make a lasting contribution to the goals of full employment and economic growth. Such a dependence is justified not only on the basis of equity, but also on the economic grounds that individual income taxes are likely to be less depressing to aggregate private spending than any other tax or combination of taxes. As long as moderate exemptions are granted, individual income taxes should not have the effect of seriously curbing spending for consumption. People of small means who, on account of the exemptions, have little or no income taxes to pay can be expected to spend most of their incomes for consumption goods; and people in the higher brackets can be expected to curtail their savings for reason of their tax obligations rather than their consumption expenditures.

If it is argued that heavy rates levied in the higher brackets of the individual income tax must inevitably discourage investment, the appropriate answer appears to be that such rates tend to discourage saving, which is quite a different thing. Opinion is strong that peacetime saving propensities tend to outrun investment opportunities and that, therefore, long-range adjustments in individual income taxation should emphasize, not a lowering of rates to encourage greater saving, but the removal of features of the tax legislation that seem to directly penalize investment. Recommendations often made in this direction include the full deduction of capital losses in the computation of taxable income, a more extensive system of income averaging than is at present provided for, since investment income often varies widely from year to year, and the elimination of the tax exemption for interest on securities of state and local governments to drive the savings of the wealthy into more venturesome channels.

Consumption taxes

If it is true that peacetime investment outlets tend to fall short of the propensity of economic society to save, a general rise in the propensity to consume would seem to be highly desirable, and a tax policy that heavily burdens consumption would seem to be unwise. Accordingly, criticism is often directed at the federal government for the prominent place given in its revenue system to excise taxes on alcoholic beverages, tobacco, gasoline, tires, tubes, air travel, and telephone service. Also originating here is the major objection to the adoption by the federal government of a manufacturers' or retailers' sales tax reaching all kinds of goods—with exceptions, possibly, for food and drugs—or a comparable "value-added" tax, such as has been adopted rather widely in recent years in Europe.

But such objections to consumption taxes are generally recognized to be invalid in war periods and in periods of massive preparation for war. Given the impossibility of having very high levels of production of both "guns and butter," stiff consumption taxes are hailed as an effective means toward allocating productive facilities to the guns at the expense of the butter.

Corporation income taxes

The corporation income taxes of the federal government are often condemned for the big bite they take out of corporate profits on grounds that they tend to choke off investment spending. Business corporations are the principal buyers of capital goods in our economy, and large proportions of their total buying power are derived, of course, from their retained after-tax earnings. Hence it is argued that corporation income taxes decisively reduce the amounts of funds available to corporate managements for investment and that they also make many projects for capital expansion unattractive by reducing the rate of after-tax net profit that can be anticipated from further investment.

The criticism of corporation income taxes does not appear to be weakened in any serious way if it is held that such taxes are wholly or largely shifted to the buyers of the output of corporate enterprises. For the taxes remain a burden on investment if the buyers of the goods are enterprisers who are going to use them in further productive operations, and they become a burden on consumption if the goods are sold to consumers.

Probably most fiscal theorists would welcome the elimination of corporation income taxes from the federal tax structure if a way could be found to include current corporate net income in the individual income tax returns of stockholders. Corporate net income should surely be taxed *somewhere*, as is the business income of proprietors and members of partnerships, but much of it would forever escape taxation if corporations were relieved of their tax liability and if stockholders had to pay only on the basis of dividends received, as at present. Various arrangements to solve this problem have been proposed from time to time, but none have so far gained strong support in Congress or elsewhere.

FOR REVIEW

1. What is compensatory fiscal policy? What other kinds of fiscal policy are there?
2. What is the relationship between compensatory fiscal policy and compensatory spending? and deficit financing?
3. In order to promote economic expansion, is reducing taxes by a given amount or stepping up government spending by the same amount likely to be more stimulating? Discuss.
4. What is likely to be the best way of financing deficits incurred as a result of fiscal policy aimed at stimulating economic expansion? Explain.
5. For tax increases to combat inflation, does it matter which taxes are increased? Discuss.
6. Does a continual program of compensatory fiscal policy mean that the government's budget will never be balanced? Discuss.
7. On what grounds do some fiscal theorists take the position that continued growth in the national debt need not be a matter of great concern?
8. What is built-in flexibility in fiscal policy? formula flexibility? To what extent is the fiscal policy of the United States characterized by flexibility of these two kinds?
9. In your judgment, would it be wise to give the President authority to change tax rates at his discretion? Discuss.
10. Why is it said that striving for economy in government is not incompatible with a compensatory spending policy?
11. What are the pros and cons of concentrating government compensatory spending on heavy public works?
12. Under what circumstances, if any, would you condemn the great dependence of the federal government on the individual income tax for revenue?

CHAPTER 22

RECENT DEVELOPMENTS IN MONETARY AND FISCAL POLICY

DEVELOPMENTS FROM 1950 TO FEBRUARY 1961

Background

For a survey of recent developments in monetary and fiscal policy, the spring of 1950 readily comes to mind as a good place to begin. By that time, most of the economic distortions and dislocations that had been caused by World War II had been cleared up. All the wartime direct controls of production, consumption, wages, and prices were off, and the reconversion of industry from wartime to peacetime production had been effected much more smoothly than had been anticipated. Returning soldiers had found peacetime jobs without prolonged delays, and great strides had been made in clearing up the huge backlog of deficiencies in consumer goods, especially durables, which had accumulated from the depressed 1930s as well as from the war years. Indeed, the occurrence of a brief recession from November 1948 to October 1949 had seemed to indicate that consumers by then were satisfied to reduce the pace of their goods accumulation, and business firms, the pace of their inventory buildups—the recession was generally described as an "inventory recession"—and of plant and equipment acquisitions.

But the period 1946–1948 had been characterized by an extraordinarily high rate of inflation, with the BLS index of wholesale prices, for example, rising by 50 percent between June 1946 and August 1948. However, the general attitude toward the inflation tended to be fatalistic. The inflation had to be. This was the "suppressed inflation" of the war years breaking out. During the war years, inflation had been largely curbed by means of wage and price controls, rationing, other controls, and by the sheer dearth of the kinds of goods on which spending concentrates in peacetime. It was impossible to drive up the prices of goods that were not being produced. But during the war years, saving increased enormously, made possible by the high levels of production of military goods and the drawing of many people, especially women, into the labor force at good wages, and roughly evidenced by an increase in paper money and coins in circulation outside banks between the end of 1940 and the end of 1945 of $19 billion, and, in the same period, increases in demand and time deposits at commercial banks (excluding Treasury deposits) of $55 billion and in the national debt of $233 billion.[1]

Even the Federal Reserve had a fatalistic attitude toward the powerful inflationary movement of 1946–1948. Immediately after the attack on Pearl Harbor, it had given assurances to the Treasury that its wartime borrowing would be financed at quite low rates of interest, and it had proceeded to make good on this commitment by a market-support policy aimed at keeping a "pattern of rates" on Treasury obligations ranging from $\frac{3}{8}$ of 1 percent per annum on bills to $2\frac{1}{2}$ percent on long-term bonds. But the Treasury was so pleased with this arrangement—this holding down of the interest cost on the tremendously increased national debt—that it insisted on a continuation of the market-support policy in the postwar years. It conceded that short-term rates could be permitted to rise, but it was adamant in wanting the line held on the long-term bond rate at $2\frac{1}{2}$ percent. This meant that the Federal Reserve had to buy in the market all $2\frac{1}{2}$ percent Treasury bonds offered by banks, insurance companies, and other investors whenever these offerings threatened to drive their market price below 100. Thus it lost control of bank reserves. As said by the then chairman of the Board of Governors, the Federal Reserve had become an "engine of inflation." The market-support policy was still in effect in the spring of 1950.

The Korean War and more inflation, 1950–1952

Following the invasion of South Korea in June 1950 and the prompt decision of the United States to intervene, a furious buying spree took hold here. Businessmen rushed to build their inventories, and consumers, remembering all the shortages of World War II and determined not to be caught short again, hurried into the markets to try to take care of all present and foreseeable needs. As a result, prices moved up rapidly. The rise in wholesale prices was, indeed, phenomenal, amounting to approximately 11 percent in the 6 months from June to December. Consumer prices, too, rose sharply, although by much less than wholesale prices, the rise for the 6 months amounting to about 5 percent. Nevertheless, the inflationary forces began to weaken in the spring of 1951. Wholesale prices reached a peak in February and March of that year and then began to slip downward slowly, with some interruptions, through the remainder of 1951 and all of 1952, reaching a low in December 1952. Consumer prices continued their upward movement through 1951, rising about 4 percent in the course of the year; but they then settled down to quite moderate fluctuations in 1952.

---

[1]*Federal Reserve Bulletin*, June 1946, pp. 631, 645, and May 1947, p 575.

Meanwhile, the Federal Reserve index of industrial production (on a 1957–1959 base of 100) reached a high of 82.5 in April 1951, fluctuated within a narrow range through July 1952 when it stood at 79.1, rose swiftly to a new high of 87.4 in September (the wartime peak having been 85.5 in November 1943), and continued on to a peak of 93.9 in July 1953. A highly favorable development of this period was a drop in unemployment to a level of only 2.6 percent of the labor force—a truly remarkable drop from the high of 7.7 percent in October 1949. The level of 2.6 percent, or a level only slightly higher, was maintained through August 1953, but thereafter unemployment rose sharply, reaching 4.5 percent of the labor force in December 1953.

New Federal Reserve Attitude   The buying spree of the fall of 1950 with its decisive effects on prices greatly disturbed the Federal Reserve. Here were the inflationary pressures of 1946–1948 in full force again, and here were the instruments of monetary policy still crippled by the market-support policy. But in this instance the Reserve officials decided to try to recapture an area for independent action. Their "declaration of independence" came on August 18, 1950, when the Board of Governors announced that it had approved a discount-rate hike at the Federal Reserve Bank of New York from 1½ to 1¾ percent—this on the very day that the Treasury announced a $13.5 billion refunding program, the largest in its history to that time, with no increase in interest rates.

Strong Federal Reserve support was given to the Treasury's huge refunding operation to see it through successfully, but this action did not indicate a retreat from the new stand taken by the Reserve officials. They tried to offset support transactions by sales of securities not immediately needing support; and at the close of 1950 they announced an increase in reserve requirements, to go into effect on various dates between January 11 and February 1, 1951,—an increase aimed at "freezing" about $2 billion of commercial bank reserves created by support operations. Other restrictive actions were also taken. Under authority of the Defense Production Act of September 8, 1950, they promptly imposed controls on consumer credit and credit for real-estate construction and, effective January 17, 1951, raised margin requirements on stock market loans from 50 to 75 percent. In sum, however, all these actions were only mildly restrictive.

In the meantime, many conferences were being held between Federal Reserve and Treasury officials to find a means of settling their differences, these continuing in January and February, including two at the White House in which President Harry Truman participated. At length, on March 4, announcement was made that a "full accord" had been reached "to assure the successful financing of the government's requirements and, at the same time, to minimize monetization of the public debt."[2] The Treasury offered

[2]*Ibid.*, March 1951, p. 267.

a new nonmarketable 2¾ percent bond in exchange for outstanding bonds maturing in 1972—bonds that had been particularly weak in market performance and for which much support had been provided by the Federal Open Market Committee. On March 5, Federal Reserve support was withdrawn from the market except for the bonds eligible for the exchange, and 3 days later support for these bonds, too, was withdrawn. By the end of March, many Treasury issues were selling below par.

Fiscal Developments   The federal government was rather slow in stepping up its expenditures following the Korean outbreak and our decision to resist aggression there, but it acted with reasonable promptness to increase tax revenues. As a result, a cash surplus of $482 million was realized in 1950 and one of $1304 million in 1951 (calendar years)—the latter in spite of a spurt in cash expenditures of $16 billion. The principal changes in tax legislation were increases in the rates of the individual and corporate income levies, the imposition of a new corporation excess-profits tax, and the addition of some new excises, the raising of the rates of others, and the lowering of the rates of still others.

The government's cash outlays took a further spurt of $15 billion in the calendar year 1952, but in this instance increases in revenues did not quite keep pace, with the result that a cash deficit of $1583 million occurred. This, however, had little effect toward weakening the restrictions of Federal Reserve policy which, by late 1952, had become quite tight.

Restrictive Monetary Policy   In the summer of 1952, the Federal Reserve began to intensify its restrictive policy, probably fearing the inflationary pressures that were likely to result from the huge increases that were taking place in government spending to rebuild our military strength. However, the index of industrial production was still fluctuating around the levels it had reached early in 1951, wholesale prices had been declining since April 1951, consumer prices had arisen only moderately in the same period, and sharp drops had taken place in private investment spending. But business activity moved upward rapidly in the late fall of 1952, and the Federal Reserve became more disturbed, being especially concerned about an extraordinary demand for loans that had developed. The expansion in business loans was well beyond the seasonal rate, consumer and mortgage loans were being granted in large volumes, and state and local governments and business corporations were adding to the big demands for loan funds by numerous security flotations. The commercial banks were anxious to meet these loan demands, and because they no longer had ready access to new supplies of reserves at the Federal Reserve banks by the sale of government securities, they rushed to the "discount window" to borrow. Thus on one December day the volume of outstanding Federal Reserve discounts and advances topped $2 billion—the highest level reached since 1921.

In these circumstances, the Federal Reserve thought it necessary to increase the pressure of its restrictive policy, and it set itself to this task early in 1953. In January, the discount rate was raised from 1¾ to 2 percent, and in that and the following months securities were sold in the open market and a direct approach was made to the member banks to impress upon them the need to reduce the amount of their borrowings at the Reserve banks. Conditions in the money market became increasingly tight, leading to a situation in April and early May described as the most "critical" since 1933. This development led the Federal Reserve to moderately relax its restrictive policy, chiefly through the purchase of government securities by the System Open Market Account and a reduction in reserve requirements.

Recession of 1953–1954 and recovery

In July 1953, business activity began to fall off, and the decline accelerated in the fall of that year and continued until August 1954. The index of industrial production fell from a high of 93.9 in July 1953 to a low of 84.5 in March and April 1954 and then fluctuated quite close to this level for several months. Wholesale and consumer prices continued their amazing record of stability, but unemployment rose sharply, especially after October 1953, reaching 5.2 percent of the labor force in February 1954 and a peak of 6.1 percent in September. As in 1948–1949, inventory disinvestment was a principal cause of the recession.

Although business expansion proceeded rather slowly for several months after the upturn of August 1954, it accelerated in November and December and in the early months of 1955. An extraordinary spurt in business spending for plant and equipment took hold in the first quarter of 1955 and continued to and even beyond the next downturn in total business activity in July 1957. The index of industrial production rose from 85.4 in August 1954 to 102.2 in July 1957. Wholesale and consumer prices, nevertheless, remained relatively stable until early 1956 when both series began to rise rapidly. From March 1956 to July 1957, the wholesale index rose by 4.8 percent, and the consumer index, by 5.3 percent. (It is important to emphasize that the only inflationary development of substantial proportions in the whole postwar period to the present time, *not connected with war and its direct results*, was this inflation of 1956–1957. From July 1957 well into 1965, the stability of the wholesale price index was no less than "phenomenal," and while the consumer index climbed almost without interruption, the long-range rate of rise was quite moderate and doubtless attributable in part to its upward bias mentioned in Chapter 2.) Another unfavorable aspect of the 1953–1957 period of expansion was that unemployment did not fall below 3.9 percent of the civilian labor force in any month.

Monetary Policy in the Recovery   The reduction in reserve requirements mentioned earlier became effective in the period July 1–9, 1953; it had the effect of releasing reserves of approximately $1.2 billion. Nevertheless, tightness in the reserve positions of the commercial banks occurred from time to time in the summer and fall, and it was not until December 1953 that Federal Reserve policy became specifically one of "active ease," as it was called.

In pursuit of the policy of active ease through most of the year 1954, the System Open Market Account bought securities in the open market, and the Board of Governors ordered another reduction in reserve requirements to go into effect in the period June 16–August 1; by these means, sufficient excess reserves were provided to enable most of the member banks to remain out of debt to the Reserve banks and at the same time to have a strong position for expansion of loans and investments. Moreover, two reductions in discount rates were put into effect, in February and April–May, bringing them down to 1½ percent at all the Reserve banks by May 15.

The spirited advance in business activity that began in late 1954 prompted the Federal Reserve authorities to switch from a policy of "active ease" to one simply of "ease." In the early months of 1955, with bank loans expanding once again at a rapid rate, and with industrial production approaching and then passing (in April) the earlier peak reached in July 1953, they became more and more restrictive. At first, the Board of Governors appeared to be especially apprehensive about the rapid rise in stock market prices and the accompanying marked expansion in security loans— developments that had continued through the year 1954 despite the slump in business activity. Accordingly, the Board ordered increases in margin requirements both in January and in April, bringing them in the latter month to 70 percent. By the late summer of 1955, however, it had moved to an over-all position of "firm restraint." From then to the downturn of July 1957—and beyond!—the reserve positions of the commercial banks were subjected to constant pressure, and many member banks found it necessary to substantially increase their borrowings at the Reserve banks. In the same period, borrowing to replenish reserves was made more and more burdensome by no less than six increases in the Federal Reserve discount rate, the last going into effect in August 1957 and bringing it to 3½ percent.

Fiscal Policy Although the recession beginning in July 1953 was largely attributed to inventory disinvestment, inept fiscal policy deserves a large share of the blame for delays in the recovery. A truce in the Korean fighting was reached in July 1953, and this was followed by large cutbacks in the government's military spending. Spending for "national security" in the fiscal year ending June 30, 1954, was approximately $3.5 billion less than in the preceding fiscal year. It is true that there was also a reduction in revenue brought about by the expiration of the corporate excess-profits tax at the end of 1953, a reduction in the rates of the individual income tax effective January 1, 1954, and reductions in the rates of many excise taxes effective April 1. However, these tax cuts were partially offset, in turn, by increases in social security levies effective January 1, 1954. Further reductions in both individual and corporate income taxes were provided for in the Revenue Code of 1954, but the immediate effects of these cuts were slight. At any rate, over-all changes in government revenues and spending in fiscal year 1954 resulted in a cash deficit of only $232 million in contrast with a cash deficit of $5274 million in the preceding fiscal year.

For the remainder of the period of the upswing to July 1957, the fiscal operations of the federal government tended to contribute to economic stability, not as a result of immediate planning but chiefly on account of built-in flexibility in revenue and spending programs, especially the former. In calendar year 1955, a modest cash deficit of $729 million helped to promote business expansion, while a big jump in revenues of almost $9 billion in calendar year 1956 resulting in a cash surplus of $5.5 billion, since cash spending was increased by only about $2.6 billion, made way, as it were, for the buoyant investment spending of that year. The Treasury was able to retire debt, thereby supplying funds to meet in part the great demand for loans and reducing the pressure on the Federal Reserve to create new reserves for the commercial banks. Chiefly accounting for the surplus was a very large increase in personal and corporate income tax revenues, as was to be expected of tax levies having a high degree of cyclical flexibility. A further increase in cash revenues of $4.2 billion occurred in 1957, but as cash expenditures rose by $8.5 billion—a rise chiefly attributable to military spending—the cash surplus was reduced to $1.2 billion. Because the increased revenue collections were concentrated rather heavily in the early part of the year, they may have added to the recessionary forces developing at that time; but the increase in expenditures doubtless tended to soften somewhat the decline in business activity.

Further fluctuations, 1957–1961

Some signs of weakness in the economy developed in the spring of 1957, but it was not until the late summer that business activity began to fall off decisively, the contraction continuing into April 1958. Between August 1957 and April 1958, the index of industrial production fell from 102.3 to 87.8, unemployment on a seasonably adjusted basis rose from 4.2 percent of the civilian labor force to 7.2 percent, and gross national product (at seasonally adjusted annual rates in constant dollars, that is, in this instance, in terms of the purchasing power of the dollar in 1958) fell from $455.2 billion in the third quarter of 1957 to $437.5 billion in the first quarter of 1958. The contraction was due chiefly to a sizable decline in investment outlays, amounting, in terms of constant dollars, to 18 percent between the second quarter of 1957 and the first quarter of 1958; but drop-offs in net exports throughout the period were also influential.

The recession of 1957–1958 was more severe than the earlier postwar recessions, but it was shorter lived. Beginning in May 1958, business activity moved up briskly and steadily for more than a year, the industrial production index rising from 89.5 in May 1958 to 109.9 in June 1959. The prolonged steel strike in the summer and fall of 1959—the longest on record —resulted in a setback in business activity; but the return of the steelworkers to their jobs early in November on the basis of a Taft-Hartley injunction quickly resulted in a further surge in activity, with the industrial production index reaching a new high of 111.7 in January 1960. Thereafter, business activity leveled off and then turned downward in May, the recession continuing until February 1961. Fortunately, however, the recession of 1960–1961 was not only short-lived but also relatively mild, with industrial production falling by only 5.7 percent and gross national product in constant dollars (on an annual-rate basis from the second quarter of 1960 to the first quarter of 1961) by only 1.4 percent.

On the other hand, a very unfavorable aspect of the whole period from 1957 to 1961 was the persistence of high levels of unemployment—higher in periods of contraction than the general decline in business activity seemed to warrant, and remaining high even in the long period of expansion continuing from April 1958 to May 1960. In this expansion period, it was truly discouraging that unemployment failed to fall below 4.9 percent of the civilian labor force in any month and that it fell as low as 4.9 percent in only 1 month.

Federal Reserve Policy   Despite the leveling off of business activity in the spring of 1957 and its downturn in July, the Federal Reserve was very slow in retreating from its policy of "firm restraint." It was not until November that a significant move was made in the direction of "ease" with a moderate amount of open-market purchases and a reduction in the discount rate from 3½ to 3 percent. Thereafter, however, easing operations were pursued with more vigor—by means of open-market purchases, three cuts in reserve requirements between February and May 1958, four cuts in the discount rate between January and May bringing it down to 1¾ percent, and a drop in margin requirements from 70 to 50 percent.

With business activity rising quite rapidly following its upturn in April 1958, the Federal Reserve moved rather quickly toward a policy of restraint. In August–September, the discount rate was raised to 2 percent, and in October–November, to 2½ percent, but these moves, especially the latter, were primarily designed to keep the rate in line with market rates. More deliberately in the direction of restraint were open-market sales undertaken in September to reduce quite sharply the volume of commercial bank excess reserves. Thereafter, the degree of restraint was gradually increased until it had become quite "firm" by June 1959—where it remained for the balance of the year. In 1959, three further increases in discount rates were effected, bringing them by September 18 to 4 percent at all the Reserve banks. Meanwhile, in view of the rapid rise in stock prices in 1958, margin requirements had been increased to 70 percent in August and to 90 percent in October. Nor was the Federal Reserve policy of restraint modified in any significant way on account of the prolonged strike in the steel industry beginning in July 1959 and extending into November, and even when the index of industrial production declined by 6.5 percent chiefly as a result of this strike.

As business activity again leveled off in the spring of 1960, Federal Reserve policy moved much more quickly toward "ease" than it had in 1957. By substantial open-market purchases, the Federal Reserve progressively reduced its pressure on the reserve positions of the commercial banks and by early fall had supplied them with relatively large amounts of excess reserves. In addition, cuts were made in the discount rate in June and August, in the margin requirement in July (from 90 to 70 percent), and in the reserve requirements applicable to what were then "central reserve city banks"—the principal commercial banks of New York City and Chicago—in September and December.

In the period 1957–1960, there was a steady increase in criticism of Federal Reserve policy as being much too restrictive. It was argued that the Federal Reserve authorities had apparently lost sight of the goals of full employment and economic growth in their anxiety to prevent inflation. This anxiety was said to be a blinding "obsession" in view of the fact that price levels had been remarkably stable since the beginning of 1952 except for the period from March 1956 to July 1957. However, the floodtide of criticism came only later when it was seen that the long period of expansion from February 1961 through 1965 was characterized by a monetary situation of almost continuous ease. The critics claimed that such an uninterrupted expansion might have been had from 1956, or even from 1952, had it not been for the Federal Reserve policy of monetary restraint. Particular emphasis was given by the critics to the slow rate of growth to which the outstanding quantity of money was held by Federal Reserve policy before 1961 in contrast to its much more rapid growth rate in the 1961–1965 period—an annual rate of growth of about 2 percent in the period 1951–1960 as against a rate of more than 3 percent in the period 1961–1965. The argument was that, in the earlier period, the growth rate of total economic activity was undoubtedly held down by deficiencies in the available quantity of money.

Fiscal Policy   The fiscal policy of the federal government in the years 1957–1960 has also been much criticized—to some extent in the course of these years, but especially in later years, with all the benefits of hindsight. It has been argued that the Treasury's cash deficits in this period came *too late* to be of maximum benefit—that, while they helped to get us out of the recessions of 1957–1958 and 1960–1961, they might have prevented the recessions from occurring had they come earlier. It has been argued that, had the government stepped up its spending or cut taxes in the fall of 1956 as business activity leveled off, or in the spring of 1957, the recession that began in July 1957 might have been avoided. As it was, the Treasury had a cash surplus in its fiscal year ending June 30, 1957, thereby adding to the forces of contraction. In the following fiscal year, the Treasury moved from a surplus to a deficit position. Nevertheless, the cash deficit amounted to only $1520 million, so that it failed to be a powerful force toward recovery. Again, it is argued that in the spring of 1960 when business activity was leveling off once more, a stepping up of government spending or a tax cut might have prevented the recession beginning in May. However, the Treasury's position moved from one of extraordinary cash deficit in its fiscal year 1959—the largest in peacetime history to that time, amounting to $13,144 million—to one of surplus in its fiscal year ending June 30, 1960, at $777 million.

Another line of criticism directed at the fiscal policy of the federal government on the basis of the developments in the period 1957–1960—really, in this instance, the period 1955–1960—has been that, in its revenue aspects, it tended to choke business expansions long before they could reach their full potential and cut the big backlog of chronic unemployment. The argument has been that, as business expanded, liabilities for taxes increased too rapidly and caused the Treasury to move too swiftly from a deficit position to a surplus position, thereby damping the forces of expansion in the economy. In support of this argument, it has been pointed out that, in the period of business expansion encompassing (roughly) the Treasury's fiscal years ending June 30, 1955, to June 30, 1957, its revenues expanded by more than $14 billion while its expenditures advanced by only about $9.5 billion; and that between the Treasury's fiscal years ending June 30, 1959 and June 30, 1960—also, for the most part, a period of business expansion— its revenues increased by approximately $13.4 billion while its spending fell by about $500 million. As no new taxes were levied in these two periods, and as only social security tax rates were raised, the revenue results appeared to signal *too much built-in flexibility* in the tax structures, chiefly a matter of excessive rates and too steep progression in the corporation and individual income taxes.

DEVELOPMENTS SINCE FEBRUARY 1961

The long period of business expansion that began in February 1961 seemed to be in a class by itself. By early 1965, it had already distinguished itself as the longest period of uninterrupted expansion in our peacetime experience, and it had already raised high hopes that the "business cycle" itself had become a thing of the past.

Business activity and new directions in policy

Business Developments Not that all was well in this period. The expansion itself was not smooth and steady, but came in fits and starts, with bursts of activity interspersed with months of "marking time." For example, business activity surged after the upturn of February 1961 until June, and then the rate of expansion slowed markedly through September, after which there was another rapid upward movement until May 1962 followed by a slowdown for the remainder of the year. In 1963, similarly, there was a fairly rapid expansion in the first 6 months, and then a slowdown during the summer, followed by expansion at a rather steady rate in the fall and continuing through 1964, but with hesitation here and there, and even a temporary downturn in October 1964, chiefly on account of strikes in the automobile industry. The periods of "marking time," as well as the relatively slow rate of the expansion in other periods, resulted in a continued availability of much idle productive capacity, especially unemployed labor. The acuteness of the unemployment problem was indicated by the failure of the rate of unemployment to fall below 6 percent of the civilian labor force in 1961, 5.3 percent in 1962, 5.5 percent in 1963, 4.9 percent in 1964, and 4.6 percent in the first half of 1965.

On the other hand, a very favorable aspect of the first 4 years of the long period of expansion beginning in 1961 was the remarkable stability in price levels. Even in early 1965, after some 50 months of expansion, the index of wholesale prices was virtually unchanged from its level at the start of the expansion. It is true that the consumer price index and the implicit price deflators of GNP rose rather steadily, but their rates of increase were quite moderate. Another significant stabilizing development was the absence of massive inventory build-ups and disinvestments, such as had characterized all preceding post-World War II periods of expansion and contraction. Throughout the period 1961–1965, on the average, inventory accumulation did not keep pace with rising sales, although some short-run feverish stocking of inventories took place, as in the early months of 1961, 1963, and 1965 because of threats of strikes in the steel industry.

New Directions in Monetary Policy   In the period 1961–1965, the Federal Reserve authorities seemed to take a new attitude toward the contribution they could make to economic welfare through the use of their instruments of monetary policy. No longer did they appear to think that the prevention of inflation was the best contribution they could make. Even by the end of December 1964, when the expansion had continued for 47 months, "ease" still prevailed for the reserve positions of the commercial banks—although industrial production had increased by 33 percent since February 1961 and gross national product in constant dollars had risen by 31 percent from the first quarter of 1961. It was quite remarkable, indeed, that in 1963 and 1964 Federal Reserve policy permitted increases in the outstanding quantity of money at rates substantially higher than the average rate of the first 2 years of the expansion, and much higher than the average annual rate of increase in the whole period 1951–1963.

The transformation in the outlook of the Federal Reserve authorities was all the more surprising because it occurred in a period of unprecedented difficulties in our international balance of payments. These difficulties were especially severe in 1961 and 1962, and there were rumors of an impending devaluation of the dollar. The difficulties were intensified by flows of short-term funds from the United States for investment in foreign money markets because of the attractions of higher interest rates there. The traditional way to arrest such flows would have been to tighten the monetary situation to cause domestic short-term rates to rise, but the Federal Reserve authorities took no strong moves in that direction. Although it is probable that they were somewhat less liberal in providing new reserves in 1961 and 1962 than they would have been had there been no outflows, their chief response was to shift their open-market purchases of Treasury obligations from short-term to intermediate-term issues as a means of avoiding downward pressure on short-term rates through their own transactions.

New Directions in Fiscal Policy If the change in Federal Reserve policy in the period 1961–1965 was remarkable, the change in direction in fiscal policy was even more so. But not at first. Its results in the period 1961–1963 were much the same as in earlier periods of recovery—quite stimulative in the early months of the expansion, but becoming progressively less so with increases in tax revenues on account of the growth of taxable incomes. Between the calendar years 1960 and 1961, the Treasury shifted from a cash surplus of $3593 million to a cash deficit of $6816 million—truly a very large shift and necessarily stimulating. But in calendar year 1962, as revenues increased more rapidly than spending, the cash deficit was reduced to $5668 million, and in calendar year 1963, for the same reason, the cash deficit was still further reduced to $4579 million.

In 1962, two special actions in the direction of stimulating the economy were taken—specifically to promote business spending for plant and equipment. Legislation was adopted to authorize business enterprises to take an "investment credit" against their income tax liabilities measured by their outlays for new machinery and equipment (basically, a credit equal to 7 percent of the cost of new depreciable personal property and certain classes of real property), and the Treasury issued new "guidelines" to permit more rapid write-offs of the costs of plant and equipment by way of depreciation deductions in income tax returns. But a really sweeping change in direction for fiscal policy was recommended to Congress by President John Kennedy in January 1963 when, despite the substantial cash deficits being experienced each year, he asked for tax-rate cuts and tax reforms expected to reduce the public's annual tax liabilities by $10.2 billion when fully effective. He argued that we had many deficits on account of "waste and weakness" in the use of our resources, that temporarily enlarged deficits, deliberately planned for and accepted, would push the economy toward full employment, and that, at full employment, tax revenues derived from greatly expanded individual and corporate incomes would permit budget balancing despite the reduction in rates.[3] For the first time, therefore, a President seemed to accept in full the tenets of compensatory fiscal policy as a means of promoting economic welfare.

Although Congress failed to enact President Kennedy's tax proposals, President Lyndon Johnson seemed to espouse the doctrines of compensatory fiscal policy with even greater enthusiasm than his predecessor. In January 1964, he asked for cuts in individual and corporate income tax rates that were expected to reduce the public's income tax liabilities within a 2-year period by $11.5 billion annually, with most of the reduction to go into effect immediately. In this instance, Congress responded quickly; in adopting the revenue Act of February 26, 1964, it gave the President almost exactly what he had asked. A very surprising aspect of this extraordinary change in the direction of fiscal policy was that it had the strong support of numerous leaders in the business community—apparently a large majority—as well as the support of substantial majorities of members of both political parties in Congress. There were some who said that the tax cuts should be matched more or less equally by cuts in government spending, but these pleas were muted. In the months following the adoption of the Revenue Act of 1964, indeed, there appeared to be an ever larger consensus that the tax cuts had been and were being most beneficial in accelerating economic expansion.

Escalation in Vietnam: economic effects

The decision of the Johnson administration early in 1965 to transform our military activities in Vietnam from advisory and supplier roles to roles as major combatants, and its subsequent decisions in that and the following years to rapidly and continually build up our participation as combatants seemed to have as consequences a progressive tearing apart of the fabric of American life. Not least among these consequences in the remainder of the decade were a multiplication of distortions in the American economy, an apparent ineptitude of monetary and fiscal policy in preventing these distortions and in reducing them when they were not prevented, a frequent lack of coordination in monetary and fiscal policy, a resulting allocation of blame to these policies for some of the distortions, and growing doubts, especially by 1970 and 1971, about the adequacy of monetary and fiscal policy to achieve the economic goals hitherto generally thought to be within their competence.

Decision for Guns and Butter   The principal initiating cause of the growth of distortions in the economy and the seeming ineptitude of monetary and

---

[3]*Economic Report of the President*, January 1963, Washington, D.C.: Government Printing Office, 1963, pp. xiv–xv.

fiscal policy in avoiding or coping with them appears to have been the decision of the Johnson administration, throughout the year 1965, that expansion in economic activity could be counted on to take care of growing domestic needs as well as escalation in Vietnam. We could have both guns and butter.

No doubt there were grave miscalculations concerning the length of our military involvement in Southeast Asia and the cost of escalation in men and military supplies and equipment. But at the start, it did not appear to be entirely fanciful to think that continued expansion in the economy, perhaps accelerated somewhat, would be sufficient to supply increased military requirements as well as growing domestic demands. The economy had been expanding since February 1961, but in the spring of 1965 we were far from full employment and high-level utilization of industrial capacity. The level of unemployment was still at 5 percent of the civilian labor force in February, and indeed, the economic planners were deciding that the economy needed further stimulation. As they later reported: "New stimulative policies were prepared in the spring of 1965 in order to complete the advance to full employment."[4] On the President's recommendation, Congress enacted legislation for a "major, phased reduction of excise taxes,"[5] the first phase of which went into effect in June. And there was a retroactive liberalization of social security benefits.

Move to Tight Money, 1965–1966   However, as the pace of military spending was accelerated, especially in the fall of 1965, private investment spending, especially for business plant and equipment, also expanded rapidly, and consumption spending also accelerated. By December, unemployment had fallen to 4.1 percent of the civilian labor force, and loan demands had reached huge proportions and were exerting strong upward pressures on interest rates. The Federal Reserve became alarmed. For quite some time its spokesmen had been calling for "fiscal restraint," but as no such restraint seemed to be forthcoming, it decided that restraint by way of monetary policy could hardly be avoided. It signaled its intention to move toward tight money by an increase in the discount rate at the Federal Reserve banks in early December from 4 to $4\frac{1}{2}$ percent. Thereafter, its restrictive actions became progressively more determined, and by the summer of 1966 an extraordinary degree of tightness had been achieved—one of almost panic proportions in August. In the whole period from April 1966 through January 1967 there was no net increase at all in the quantity of money in circulation.[6]

A peculiar aspect of Federal Reserve control at this time was the adop-

---

[4]*Economic Report of the President,* January 1968, Washington, D.C.: Government Printing Office, 1968, p. 67.

[5]*Ibid.*

[6]According to the revised money-in-circulation data of November 1970 as published in the *Federal Reserve Bulletin,* December 1970, p. 898.

tion of interest ceilings on time deposits as a major restrictive device—by way of "Regulation Q" as referred to in Chapter 20. In July 1966 the ceilings were lowered on "multiple-maturity" time deposits, except savings deposits, and the permitted rate on single-maturity certificates of deposit (CDs) was left unchanged although, at that time, some short-term market rates were above this permitted rate. Thus the failure of demand deposits to expand could not be attributed simply to shifts from demand deposits to time deposits. No significant shifts of that kind were taking place. In fact, the commercial banks were having great difficulties in holding their time deposits, and because of this, they found it necessary to borrow enormously in the Eurodollar market, to sell large amounts of portfolio securities, to increase their borrowings at the Federal Reserve banks, and to scramble elsewhere for cash assets—all this to enable them to meet outstanding loan commitments as well as to take care of additional loan demands of highly valued customers. The Federal Reserve's Regulation Q ceilings were principally designed to prevent commercial banks from competing too strenuously with "thrift institutions"—chiefly, in this instance, savings and loan associations and mutual savings banks—for the savings of individuals. But this objective was defeated by the rise in market rates of interest that was largely occasioned, on the supply side, by the tight money policy, including the impact of the Regulation Q ceilings themselves. Many individual savers decided to bypass both the commercial banks and the thrift institutions and invest directly in money and capital market securities to take advantage of the higher interest rates to be earned there, and many corporate and institutional holders of CDs decided likewise to invest in the open markets by refusing to renew these CDs at their maturities. The plight of the thrift institutions as primarily mortgage lenders on residential property was indicated by a drop in private housing starts from a seasonally adjusted annual rate of 1,769,000 in December 1965 to one of 848,000 in October 1966.[7] It was this kind of development, with accompanying difficulties that many state and local governments were experiencing in trying to borrow, that gave rise to charges, previously referred to, that monetary policy itself was the source of distortions in the economy.

Restrictive Moves in Fiscal Policy   Meanwhile, fiscal policy had also moved into the restrictive area. At the beginning of 1966, a scheduled rise in social security tax rates became effective, and in March, legislation was passed to cancel the "stimulative" reductions in excise taxes that had been scheduled in early 1965, to speed up the collection of corporation income taxes, and to introduce a system of graduated withholding for individual income taxes. These measures were followed by actions in September to cut back federal spending for domestic programs and, in view of the enormous

---

[7]*Federal Reserve Bulletin,* February 1967, p. 299.

demands for loan funds in both the money and capital markets, to restrict borrowing by federal agencies. Then in October, presumably to curb business borrowing to finance acquisitions of machinery and other productive equipment, Congress suspended the investment tax credit that had been adopted in 1962 as a stimulative device.

Lingering Effects of Tight Money in 1967   By November 1966, the Federal Reserve had begun to back away rather decisively from its policy of extreme tightness of the preceding summer, but the effects of the tightness were felt throughout the following year. From a high of 159.5 in December 1966, the seasonally adjusted index of industrial production fell to a low of 155.6 in May and June 1967, and the rate of expansion in GNP in constant dollars for the full year 1967 was only 2.6 percent, down from a rate of 6.5 percent in the preceding year. Despite this slowdown, the rate of inflation as measured by the BLS consumer price index amounted to 2.9 percent, a rate identical with that of 1966. At the same time, unemployment, which had fallen as low as 3.7 percent in November 1966 and 3.6 percent in March 1967, was back to a high of 4.3 percent in October 1967.

A peculiar aspect of the 1967 slowdown was that, although interest rates fell in the fall of 1966 and in the early months of 1967, they began to move up again in the spring and summer of 1967, with long-term rates in particular beginning to move up rapidly as early as April. Business corporations were floating great numbers of bond issues aggregating huge amounts. Remembering the extreme tightness of the monetary situation of the preceding summer, they had decided to tap the capital market to restore their liquidity and provide new spending capacity, and thus to cut down their dependence on the commercial banks for loans in time of need. As a result of this borrowing and other market developments, interest rates were driven to the highest levels they had reached in about 40 years.

Mixed Policy in 1968   In the late fall of 1967, business activity began to accelerate, and as new inflationary pressures were feared, the Federal Reserve turned again toward a restrictive policy. Once again, it signaled its move in this direction by an increase in the discount rate in November from 4 to 4½ percent (the rate had been cut from 4½ to 4 percent in April). It then proceeded to exert pressure on bank reserves by open-market operations in the first half of 1968, and in both March and April, it raised the discount rate, bringing it in the latter part of April to 5½ percent, its highest level since 1929. President Johnson had recommended to Congress the imposition of a surtax of 10 percent on individual and corporation income taxes, but there was much uncertainty about its adoption, and the Federal Reserve decided that it had to take on the principal burden of cooling an "overheating" economy. Nevertheless, it did not go nearly so far in the direction of tightness as in 1966, apparently thinking that continually rising interest rates were indicative of sufficient tightness. Indeed, the Federal Reserve began to relax its tight policy in June, when it became apparent that the tax surcharge proposal would pass in Congress, as it did on June 28, retroactively for corporations to January 1 and to April 1 for individuals.

Through the remainder of the year, Federal Reserve policy was generally one of providing reserves to the commercial banks to "accommodate" increasing loan demands. Some critics, in fact, accused it of being much too accommodating, basing their criticism on the high rate of growth in the quantity of money it was permitting and claiming that it was thus providing abundant fuel for more "overheating" and inflation. The rate for the full year at 7.8 percent was truly a large one. At that time, however, the Federal Reserve seemed still to be paying greater attention to market rates of interest than to the quantity of money, and as it turned out, most rates reached their highest levels "in modern times" by the end of the year. But, said the critics, the Federal Reserve should have realized that the continued rise in interest rates was not simply a response to the pressures of huge loan demands but, even more importantly, a response to inflationary developments and the prospects for more inflation. And they pointed to the price indexes for evidence of this inflationary influence on interest rates, as, for example, the rise in the consumer price index in the full year at 4.2 percent, the highest rate of rise since 1951.

Back to Extreme Tightness in 1969   In the area of monetary policy, Federal Reserve actions in 1969 can largely be described as a replay of those of 1966. In April, the discount rate went to 6 percent, and from June through September, the money supply was held virtually stationary, while in the same period the commercial banks actually lost time deposits, not to the thrift institutions, but to the open markets on account of Regulation Q. As in 1966, in fact, the thrift institutions also lost deposits in the same direction with a resulting severe curtailment of mortgage lending. As in 1966, too, the commercial banks had to sell securities from their portfolios, borrow heavily in the Eurodollar market and from the Federal Reserve banks, and use their inventive genius to devise other means of augmenting their capacity to satisfy their customers' loan demands, but falling far short of complete success.

Also following the 1966 pattern, fiscal policy in 1969 strongly buttressed restrictive monetary policy. Another increase in social security tax rates went into effect on January 1, the investment tax credit was repealed in April (it had been restored in the spring of 1967 after the October 1966 suspension), and in August, Congress voted an extension of the tax surcharge at 10 percent for the balance of the year, although it had been due to expire at the end of June. Although military spending continued to expand to the highest levels in the history of the country, the over-all result was a budget surplus of about $5.4 billion in 1969 in contrast to a deficit of about $16.1 billion in 1968. Despite all these restrictions of both monetary and fiscal policy—or perhaps because of them, at least in part, as some theorists hold —the rate of inflation in 1969 reached a new high for the 1960s at 5.4 percent as measured by the consumer price index.

Missed Targets in 1970   The restrictive policies of 1969 were undoubtedly overdone, if one judges that a recession is not a proper answer to a boom, even to one with strong inflationary developments—especially when the recession is characterized by an even higher rate of inflation and zooming unemployment. As measured by GNP in constant dollars, the recession from late 1969 to late 1970 was mild, with the output of the economy declining by only 0.4 percent in 1970. But inflation in that year of recession was especially disturbing at 5.9 percent as measured by the consumer price index, and even more so was the extraordinarily rapid rise in unemployment from a rate of 3.9 percent in January to one of 6.2 percent in December. In terms of the goals of full employment, stable prices, and good economic growth rates, all targets were missed in 1970.

The retreat of monetary and fiscal policy from their highly restrictive stance of 1969 came rather slowly in 1970, although we must make allowance for delayed responses to actions that were taken early in the year. As early as January, the Federal Reserve put the commercial banks in a better position to compete for time deposits by raising the Regulation Q interest-rate ceilings, but it was not until May that it moved decisively toward pumping reserves to them by means of open-market buying of Treasury obligations. Even as late as July, the average daily outstanding borrowings of the member banks at the Reserve banks were at the high level of $1432 million. Early easing actions in the area of fiscal policy were much more prominent, but also prominent were delayed responses because of the usual bunching of federal revenues in the first half of the year. Despite cuts in income tax liabilities provided in the Tax Reform Act adopted late in 1969 and by the reduction of the income tax surcharge to 5 percent for the first half of 1970, and despite boosts in spending on account of increased social security and veterans' benefits and a 6 percent hike in wages and salaries for federal employees (offset in part, after the first quarter, by cuts in military spending), there was a budget surplus of $5248 million in the first half of the year, followed by a swing to a huge deficit of $16,621 million in the second half.

However, the most important policy development in 1970 may have been the new attention given by the Federal Reserve to controlling the growth rate of the quantity of money as an intermediate[8] policy goal. The "mone-

---

[8]"Intermediate" in the sense of not being wanted for its own sake but as a means of achieving full employment, a stable price level, and good growth rates for the economy.

tarists" would surely be inclined to think so.[9] The new attitude was revealed in the published policy statements of the Federal Open Market Committee related to its directives to the manager of the System Open Market Account. All along students of money and banking had been taking it for granted that the FOMC must necessarily be giving much attention to the quantity of money, even when its earlier policy statements made few references to it while having many references to such "guidelines" or intermediate goals as levels of interest rates, conditions in the money market, and the volume of bank credit. Accordingly, the new references seemed to indicate enhanced respect for the doctrines of the "monetarists,"—beginning in January 1970 and continuing through 1970 and the following year —with their emphasis on the growth rate of the quantity of money as a preeminent determinant of employment, output, and income—but not a wholesale conversion, since the policy statements continued to include references to "guidelines" of the kinds just mentioned.

Move to Direct Controls in 1971

For monetary and fiscal policy, the most important development in 1971 was undoubtedly the display of shaken confidence indicated by President Nixon's action of August 15 in imposing on the economy a system of wage and price controls.

Developments in Monetary and Fiscal Policy   Until approximately the time of the President's action in August, both monetary and fiscal policy had been strongly stimulative. Between the middle of November 1970 and the middle of February 1971, the Federal Reserve banks have made five reductions in their discount rates, bringing them down from 6 percent to 4¾ percent, and the Federal Open Market Committee had been extraordinarily liberal in supplying reserves to the commercial banks as demonstrated by an expansion in the money stock in the period from December 1970 through July 1971 at an annual rate of 10 percent. Because this period of rapid monetary expansion was followed by a period of no expansion at all— from August 1971 to early December 1971—the Federal Reserve was widely criticized for having retreated from its apparent 1970 interest in a steady growth rate in the money stock to its traditional concern with the behavior of interest rates and conditions in the "credit markets."

In January 1971, President Nixon seemed to be making a strong commitment to a stimulative fiscal policy by his espousal of the theory of a "full-employment budget" in his message to Congress on the budget for the fiscal year ending June 30, 1972. This espousal promised, as it were, a level of government spending close to what total tax revenues would amount to

---

[9]See Chapter 18.

were the economy at full employment, given existing taxes and tax rates and allowing for probable price-level increases in a full-employment situation, and recognized substantial deficits as being necessary for stimulation as long as the economy continued to fall significantly short of full employment. In the same month, the President set the stage for reductions in tax payments for business enterprises by an authorization for increased charge-offs for depreciation in the determination of their taxable income. And in March, Congress passed legislation to increase social security benefits by 10 percent (retroactive to January but with the increases for January through June to be paid in June), and to defer to January 1, 1972 a previously scheduled increase in the wage-and-salary base on which social security taxes are levied. At least partially as a result of these actions, the budget deficit in the first half of 1971 was approximately $6620 million in contrast with a budgetary surplus of $5248 million in the first half of 1970.

Mixed Results   The monetary and fiscal policy actions of early 1971 appeared to have good results in restoring good rates of economic growth. On an annual basis, the growth rate from the fourth quarter of 1970 to the first quarter of 1971 was 7.7 percent, and from the first to the second quarter of 1971 was 4.8 percent. However, it was recognized that both these rates were rather seriously distorted on the high side as a result of the strike against General Motors in late 1970 and the consequent speedup in automobile production in the first quarter of 1971 following the settlement of the strike. Moreover, the Federal Reserve index of industrial production failed to show much buoyancy. Although it rose slowly from 105.3 in January to 107.2 in June (with 1967 = 100), it fell back in July to 106.1, at which point it was somewhat below the level of July 1970 at 107.5 and even further below that of July 1969 at 111.5.

Despite the stimulative character of monetary and fiscal policy in the first half of 1971, inflationary pressures appeared to be waning. On an annual basis, the rate of inflation between December 1970 and July 1971 was 3.9 percent, down from the December 1969–December 1970 rate of 5.7 percent. But the Nixon administration regarded the 3.9 percent rate as still much too high, and it was especially disturbed by the evidence that we were pricing ourselves out of foreign markets—evidence as particularly supplied by the Department of Commerce in its report that in the second quarter of 1971 our merchandise imports exceeded our exports by $1040 million. Moreover, our easy money policy caused interest rates to fall, so that there was a huge flow of dollars to Europe to take advantage of higher rates there. This flow due to interest-rate differentials was greatly augmented by large additional flows initiated by speculators who were convinced that, however it might be arranged, the dollar would have to be devalued. Partially as a result of such flows, our balance of payments on the basis of official re-

serve transactions reached negative levels of unprecedented proportions—
a level of −$5531 million in the first quarter, −$5725 million in the second
quarter, and −$12,108 million in the third quarter.

The employment situation, too, remained distressing. Although the seasonally adjusted rate of unemployment fell from 6.2 percent in December 1970
to 5.6 percent in June 1971, it mounted again in July and continued upward
in August to 6.1 percent.

Wage and Price Controls   It was against the background of developments
of the kinds described that President Nixon, on August 15, 1971, took the
dramatic action of imposing a system of wage and price controls on the
economy, as he had been empowered to do by the Economic Stabilization
Act passed by Congress in 1970. For a period of 90 days, wages and salaries
were not to be increased at all, and likewise for prices with some exceptions.
Subsequently, a Price Commission of seven members was chosen to police
sellers' pricing policies as well as to pass upon their applications and decisions for price increases after the 90-day "freeze" period in a second period
of indefinite duration to be known as "phase II." Likewise, a Pay Board of
15 members (with equal representation of labor, management, and the
"public") was set up to pass upon applications and decisions concerning
wage and salary hikes in the period of phase II. Shortly before the beginning
of the period of phase II, the Price Commission set 2.5 percent a year as
the "target" for maximum price increases but with the proviso that increases
within this range would be permitted only when justified by increased costs;
and the Pay Board set a "guideline" of 5.5 percent a year for maximum
wage and salary increases. The two agencies anticipated that the difference
of 3 percentage points between the "target" and the "guideline" would be
made up by growth in man-hour productivity.

In his program of August 15, President Nixon recommended further
stimulation to the economy by way of tax policy. He asked Congress to
restore a tax credit for investment by business in new capital facilities
such as had been adopted in 1962 and again in 1967; the repeal of the 7
percent excise tax on automobiles to be retroactive to August 15; and a
transfer from 1973 to 1972 of a scheduled rise of $50 in the personal ex-
emption under the individual income tax. In the opposite direction, however, the President revealed plans to cut spending by the federal government
in the current fiscal year (ending June 30, 1972) by $4.7 billion by means
chiefly of a postponement of a scheduled pay hike for its personnel, a 5
percent cut in this personnel, and a deferral of previously recommended
projects for welfare-system reforms and the sharing of federal revenues
with state and local governments. Most of the President's recommendations
were accepted by Congress in legislation passed in December, but a few,
such as that for the postponement of the pay hike for government personnel,
were rejected, and, as usual, Congress added a few ideas of its own, in-

cluding an advance to 1971 of the $50 increase in the personal exemption under the personal income tax.

Finally to be mentioned among the program of August 15, 1971 was the "temporary" suspension of the redeemability of foreign-held dollars and dollar claims in gold or other reserve assets and the imposition of a "temporary" surcharge of 10 percent on most categories of imports. The surcharge did, indeed, prove to be temporary, for it was removed in December immediately after an agreement had been reached on the devaluation of the dollar and the realignment of the pars of exchange among the "group of ten" leading industrial member countries of the International Monetary Fund, as discussed in Chapters 5, 25, and 26.

FOR REVIEW

1. Why was there generally a fatalistic attitude toward the inflation of 1946–1948? Was this attitude shared by the Federal Reserve?
2. What was the nature and consequences of the price-support policy that was ended with the "accord' of 1951?
3. Did the occurrence of three business recessions in the 1950s prove that monetary policy was too restrictive in that decade? fiscal policy? both monetary and fiscal policy? Discuss.
4. In your opinion, was the apparent concern of the Federal Reserve in the 1950s about the dangers of inflation justified by the events of that decade? Explain.
5. What is the basis of the argument that we had too much built-in flexibility in fiscal policy in the late 1950s? Did our experience in the period 1961–1965 appear to support or refute this argument?
6. After 4 years of business expansion, why were the economic planners still thinking in the spring of 1965 that further stimulative actions were needed?
7. What were the principal fiscal policy actions taken in the period 1961–1965? What was the stance of monetary policy in this period?
8. On the basis of what facts is it said that monetary policy was highly restrictive in 1966? in 1969?
9. How well was fiscal policy coordinated with monetary policy in 1966 and 1969?
10. Why is it said that all major targets of monetary and fiscal policy were missed in 1970? Do you agree with such an evaluation? Discuss.
11. What was the "new direction" in monetary policy that seemed to be indicated in 1970 in policy statements of the Federal Open Market Committee?
12. Describe the principal features of the actions taken and recommended by President Nixon in August 1971. For what reasons did he apparently think that these actions were necessary?

VII

INTERNATIONAL MONETARY TRANSACTIONS

CHAPTER 23

FOREIGN EXCHANGE AND THE
BALANCE OF PAYMENTS

In the money market of any country, *foreign exchange* consists of the moneys of other countries offered for sale. All the money supply outstanding in the United Kingdom at the present time is certainly not looked upon as "foreign exchange" by the British people or, indeed, by us; but the portions of that supply held as deposits with London banks by American banks and offered for sale by the latter in the New York market is surely "foreign exchange" from *our* point of view. In a similar way, dollar balances on the books of New York banks to the credit of banks in Canada, the United Kingdom, France, Switzerland, and other countries—balances that these banks are offering for sale in Toronto and Montreal, London, Paris, Zurich, and so on—are "foreign exchange" from the point of view of the countries named.

When, therefore, an American bank sells "exchange on London," it delivers an instrument payable in pounds and pence (or, as we say more simply, "in sterling") out of its deposit balance with a London bank. From the buyer of the sterling instrument, the American bank receives dollars— the number of dollars depending upon the "rate of exchange" at which the bank sells sterling. Similarly, a French bank buys "exchange on New York" when it pays francs at a certain rate in buying a dollar dividend check that a French investor has received from an American corporation.

THE FOREIGN EXCHANGE MARKET

New York is the center of the American foreign exchange market, although some less extensive market facilities for dealings in foreign money are available in other principal cities. In none of these locations, however, is the market formally organized in the sense of a stock or commodities exchange. Buyers and sellers carry on negotiations with one another chiefly by telephone and telegraph, but also to a smaller extent by use of the mails and personal contacts. Importers and exporters of merchandise, international travelers, capitalists interested in foreign investments, and many others come into the market from time to time because they want to buy instruments payable in foreign currencies to make payments abroad, or because they have received instruments payable in foreign currencies that they want to sell for dollars. But several classes of financial institutions are in the market at all times; it is their business to buy and sell foreign moneys or to assist in this function. As thus distinguished, the financal institutions include the foreign departments of our own commercial banks, American branches and agencies of foreign banks, and foreign exchange brokers.

Foreign departments of commercial banks

The large commercial banks of New York City and of a few other cities are the principal buyers and sellers in the foreign exchange market. They are merchants in foreign currencies. They are able to sell foreign currencies because they have deposits in these currencies with foreign banks, and they are willing to buy because they must constantly replenish their "stock in trade."

The foreign department of a bank can draw drafts against the deposits it maintains with correspondent banks located in foreign countries in the same way that an individual can draw checks on his bank in his home country. People who have payments to make in foreign countries can buy from a foreign department's supplies of foreign currencies, giving domestic money in payment, and the foreign department can continue to sell until its foreign deposits are exhausted. Indeed, it can sell beyond this point, "going short," but expecting to cover its excess sales before its drafts are presented to its foreign correspondents for payment.

A Foreign Department's Supply of Foreign Currencies   Several channels are open to the foreign departments of American commercial banks through which they can obtain or replenish the foreign deposits against which they make sales. The chief method is to purchase in the United States itself drafts and other instruments payable in foreign currencies, as well as foreign paper money and coins. Of outstanding importance is the purchase in the American market of instruments payable in foreign currencies. These instruments are received or are drawn by American exporters in payment for commodities, securities, and services supplied to foreign buyers, and they are sold to the American banks because the exporters want dollars rather than foreign funds. Foreign paper money and coins are brought into the country chiefly by tourists, either foreign tourists or American tourists returning from foreign countries; it is sold to American banks in exchange for dollars, and the American banks return it to the foreign countries for credit in their deposit accounts. American banks that are running short of a specific foreign currency may also be able to buy supplies from other American banks that have more than they require for their own current transactions.

An American bank can increase its deposits in one foreign country by transferring to it deposits that it has in other foreign countries. At a given time, for example, a bank that has deposits in Canada and England may find that there is only a small demand for sterling but a large demand for Canadian dollars; accordingly, it may sell a sterling cable to its Canadian correspondent, receiving the proceeds in Canadian dollars.

Again, an American bank may be able to buy supplies of foreign currencies from foreign banks, paying in American dollars. Should its supply of sterling run low, for example, it might be able to buy some from its British correspondent. The British correspondent would simply credit the deposit balance of the American bank in sterling, and the American bank would credit the account of the British bank in dollars at an agreed-upon rate of exchange. Likewise, the purchase might be made from a French bank that has an excess supply of sterling. The French bank would telegraph its London correspondent to debit its account and credit the account of the American bank, while the latter would credit the dollar account of the French bank—the size of the respective credits again depending upon the exchange rate that they may agree to.

Foreign and Domestic Correspondents The commercial banks that deal extensively in foreign exchanges typically have a broad network of correspondent institutions throughout the world. In many instances, banks operate branches in some foreign countries and are therefore often able to supply means of payment in those countries without outside assistance. Even more commonly, however, correspondent banks are employed. Generally speaking, the more branches and foreign correspondents a bank has, the better are the services it can provide its customers; but it is not necessary for each bank to maintain deposits in every country on which it sells exchange. In some cases, correspondents of correspondents are used. If an American bank has a correspondent in London and no others, it should ordinarily be able to sell exchange on Argentina, South Africa, Australia, and other countries by arrangement with the London bank. Were it to sell drafts in, say, South African rands, the South African bank upon which the drafts were drawn would charge the London bank, and it, in turn, would charge the account of the American bank. Also significant is the fact that, because of the great importance of the dollar as an international medium of exchange, at least one bank in almost every foreign country has dollar deposits in the United States. Although the American banks that hold these deposits may not have reciprocal deposits with the foreign banks, they can easily work arrangements with the foreign banks to increase their dollar credits in exchange for supplies of the foreign currencies wanted by business firms, other banks, tourists, and other customers.

Domestic correspondents are widely used to originate foreign exchange business. Connections with many domestic correspondents are particularly important in a country like the United States where the foreign exchange market is heavily concentrated in one city and where thousands of banks have no foreign correspondents of their own. Although many of the larger cities of the United States have at least one bank that has a foreign department with some correspondents abroad, people located in thousands of smaller communities would have poor access to the foreign exchange market were it not that banks in these communities can deal in foreign currencies by arrangements with the city banks. Thus, the nation's foreign exchange business is channeled to the big banks with many foreign connections.

Other institutions

Some foreign banks operate branches and agencies in the United States, principally in New York City, their foreign exchange business being much the same as that of the foreign departments of domestic banks. The banking laws of the state of New York permit the branches and agencies of foreign banks to buy and sell international bills of exchange of various kinds, to issue letters of credit, and to transfer funds by drafts, cables, and other means.

Acceptance dealers, as we saw in an earlier chapter,[1] buy acceptances outright and then resell them as short-term investment papers to other financial institutions. Because a large volume of international trade is financed by means of bankers' acceptances, the function of dealers in providing an orderly market for acceptances is an important one.

Foreign exchange brokers, all located in New York City, function principally as go-betweens for the foreign departments of the commercial banks. If, in the course of the day's business, a foreign department is buying much more of a given foreign currency than it is selling, it will normally want to move quickly toward a better balance in its "position." Perhaps the foreign departments of other banks need to replenish their supplies of the foreign currency on account of selling much more than they are buying. But the first bank does not get in touch with the other banks directly; it uses a foreign exchange broker to determine the prospects of selling its excess supply. It may tell the broker that it will sell at a stated rate, or it may ask the broker to find what the other banks will offer. The broker then "shops around" among the other banks to find buyers or to determine the rates prospective buyers are willing to bid. The brokers operate on a commission basis, the selling bank paying the commission.

THE SUPPLY OF AND DEMAND FOR FOREIGN EXCHANGE

In the preceding division of this chapter, it was explained that a bank is able to sell foreign currencies because it has deposits in foreign countries

---

[1]See Chapter 11.

against which it can draw drafts, and that it is able to replenish its deposits in several different ways. We were then considering the supply of and demand for foreign currencies from the point of view of the individual bank. But now it is desirable to look at the supply of and demand for foreign exchange from the standpoint of the United States as a whole. We must inquire about the kinds of international transactions that require payments by Americans to foreigners and payments by foreigners to Americans—all the kinds of transactions that generally result in purchases and sales of foreign currencies by American banks or in purchases and sales of dollars by foreign banks.

At the outset, a peculiarity of foreign exchange transactions, as indicated in the preceding sentence, deserves emphasis. Payments made by Americans to foreigners may not reduce the foreign balances of American banks, and payments made by foreigners to Americans may not increase them. The effect depends upon whose currency is used for making payments. Thus an American firm in buying goods from a British firm may pay in sterling or in dollars, whatever the terms of the contract may be. If payment is made in sterling, the normal effect is to reduce the balances held in London by American banks; but if payment is made in dollars, the effect is to increase the balances held by British banks in the United States. This example illustrates a general proposition: *Payments made abroad by Americans decrease the foreign balances of American banks or increase the American balances of foreign banks; and payments made by foreigners to Americans decrease the American balances of foreign banks or increase the foreign balances of American banks.*

At the outset, too, the terms *export* and *import* deserve special notice. From our point of view, our exports are all the kinds of international transactions in which we participate that require payments by foreigners to Americans; and our imports are all the kinds of transactions that require payments by Americans to foreigners. Thus it is customary to refer to sales of merchandise, services, real property, stocks, bonds, and so on by Americans to foreigners as exports because they require payments by foreigners to Americans; and also to refer to purchases by Americans of merchandise and services supplied by foreigners, real property, stocks, bonds, and so on as imports because they require payments by foreigners to Americans.

Imports and exports of merchandise

The most obvious kind of transaction that affects the supply of and demand for foreign exchange is the international sale of merchandise. When Americans import tangible goods from foreign countries, they must make payment either in dollars or in foreign currencies, and when they export tangible goods, they expect to be paid in dollars or in foreign currencies, depending upon the kind of payment agreed to. If American importers pay in dollars, the foreign exporters convert the dollar instruments into their domestic currencies by selling them to their banks. In this way, in accordance with the proposition stated in the second preceding paragraph, the dollar balances of foreign banks in the United States are increased. But if the American importers pay in foreign currencies, they must buy from American banks instruments payable in such currencies, and the sale of these instruments reduces American bank balances abroad.

Service transactions

A large array of transactions that require international payments are classified as service transactions. From the standpoint of any country, they include the purchase of services provided by foreign airlines, steamship companies, and other transportation companies; expenditures of residents of the country while traveling as tourists in other countries (except for purchases of merchandise that they bring back with them); hiring the services of foreign banks, securities dealers and brokers, selling agents, advertising agencies, and so on; expenditures by the country's government in foreign countries, as for the maintenance of its embassies and consulates and for military bases and military operations; and especially important for countries like the United States, interest, dividends, rents, and other earnings on investments made in foreign countries. Like merchandise, of course, services are both bought and sold by the people and government of the individual country, so that some service transactions require payments to foreigners while others require incoming payments.

From the standpoint of the United States, the principal kinds of service transactions in which we engage can be arranged as follows according to their effects on the supply of and demand for foreign exchange:

TRANSACTIONS THAT DECREASE AMERICAN BANK BALANCES ABROAD, OR INCREASE FOREIGN BANK BALANCES IN THE UNITED STATES.	TRANSACTIONS THAT INCREASE AMERICAN BANK BALANCES ABROAD, OR DECREASE FOREIGN BANK BALANCES IN THE UNITED STATES.
1. The purchase by Americans of the services of foreign enterprises—transportation companies, banks, insurance companies, and so on.	1. The purchase by foreigners of the services of American enterprises of comparable classes.
2. Expenditures by Americans traveling as tourists in foreign countries.	2. Expenditures of foreigners traveling as tourists in the United States.
3. Expenditures of the federal government in foreign countries on its embassies, consulates, troops, military bases, and military operations.	3. Expenditures by foreign governments in the United States, as on their embassies and consulates.
4. The payment of dividends, interest, rents, and so on upon investments of foreigners in the United States.	4. The payment of dividends, interest, rent, and so on upon investments of Americans in foreign countries.

Capital or investment transactions

Another large array of transactions that require international payments are classified as capital or investment transactions. They include the purchase in foreign countries of land, plant and equipment, and other fixed property—called "direct investment"—the purchase of securities issued by foreign corporations and governments; the granting of loans to foreign borrowers, including loans granted by governments, whether to private foreign borrowers or to foreign governments; and the making of deposits at foreign financial institutions. Also included among capital transactions are withdrawals of international investments previously made, as when a foreign owner of real property in a country sells it to a resident of that country, a corporation or government redeems bonds held by foreigners, and loan repayments are received from foreigners.

An American firm that is setting up a branch factory in France will very likely need francs to buy a site for the factory and materials for the buildings. If it undertakes no financing in France, it will have to acquire the francs through normal foreign exchange channels. Its purchases of raw materials and supplies and its payroll requirements will have to be met in the same way, at least until the sale of its products provide francs out of which current costs of operation can be met. In a similar way, a wealthy Canadian who decides to buy a winter home in Florida must acquire United States dollars with which to make the purchase; and an American who wants to buy British securities traded on the London Stock Exchange must buy sterling in order to make payment.

So it is, also, with all kinds of international lending, including transactions in bonds and money market instruments. The buying of bonds issued by foreign corporations and governments ordinarily requires the acquisition of the foreign currency so that payment can be made, and the same is true of the purchase of short-term debt instruments offered in foreign money markets. Likewise, the building of a deposit balance at a commercial bank of a foreign country in the currency of that country obviously requires an acquisition of that currency.

From the standpoint of the United States, the international capital transactions mentioned and illustrated in the preceding paragraphs can be classified as follows, according to their effects on the supply of and demand for foreign exchange.

TRANSACTIONS THAT DECREASE AMERICAN BANK BALANCES ABROAD, OR INCREASE FOREIGN BANK BALANCES IN THE UNITED STATES.	TRANSACTIONS THAT INCREASE AMERICAN BANK BALANCES ABROAD, OR DECREASE FOREIGN BANK BALANCES IN THE UNITED STATES.
1. The purchase by Americans of land, buildings, and other fixed property located in foreign countries.	1. The purchase by foreigners of land, buildings, and other fixed property located in the United States.

2. The purchase by Americans of securities of foreign corporations and governments.

3. The granting of loans by Americans to foreigners, including loans of the federal government to foreign governments.

4. The building of deposit balances by Americans at foreign banks.

5. The reacquisition by Americans from foreigners of American land and buildings and securities of American governments and corporations.

6. The repayment by Americans of loans previously obtained from foreigners.

2. The purchase by foreigners of securities of American corporations and governments.

3. The granting of loans by foreigners to Americans.

4. The building of deposit balances by foreigners at American banks.

5. The reacquisition by foreigners from Americans of foreign land and buildings and securities of foreign governments and corporations.

6. The repayment by foreigners of loans previously obtained from Americans.

Unilateral transfers

Unilateral transfers are peculiar kinds of transactions in that they typically require international payments without opposite flows of merchandise, services, investment instruments, or anything else, except possibly love, affection, and goodwill. They are gifts and other transactions that strongly resemble gifts and include "remittances" of residents of a country to families and relatives dwelling in other countries for living expenses and the like; private donations to religious missions in foreign countries, foreign charities, and foreign educational institutions; private and government donations for disaster relief in foreign countries; government grants to foreign countries for military purposes and economic development; and government disbursements of social security payments, veterans' pensions, and the like to beneficiaries dwelling in foreign countries.

In their typical effects on the supply of and demand for foreign exchange from the standpoint of the United States, unilateral transfers can be classified as follows:

TRANSACTIONS THAT DECREASE AMERICAN BANK BALANCES ABROAD, OR INCREASE FOREIGN BANK BALANCES IN THE UNITED STATES.

1. Remittances by residents of the United States to families and relatives dwelling in foreign countries.

2. Gifts by Americans to foreign religious, educational, and charitable institutions.

TRANSACTIONS THAT INCREASE AMERICAN BANK BALANCES ABROAD, OR DECREASE FOREIGN BANK BALANCES IN THE UNITED STATES.

1. Remittances by residents of foreign countries to families and relatives dwelling in the United States.

2. Gifts by foreigners to American religious, educational, and charitable institutions.

3. Donations by Americans for purposes such as disaster relief in
foreign countries.

4. Payments by the federal government of social security benefits,
veterans' pensions, and the like to
residents of foreign countries, and
its grants to foreign countries for
military purposes and economic
development.

3. Donations by foreigners for purposes such as disaster relief in the
United States.

4. Payments by foreign governments
of social security benefits, veterans' pensions, and the like to residents of the United States.

THE BALANCE OF INTERNATIONAL PAYMENTS

Summarized and combined in certain ways, all the merchandise, service, and capital transactions and unilateral transfers in which Americans participate in a quarter or a year and for which Americans incur obligations to pay foreigners and foreigners incur obligations to pay Americans constitute our "balance of international payments." As reported in statement form by the Office of Business Economics of the federal Department of Commerce, it gives us a picture of how we "made out" in the quarter or year in our total dealings with foreigners in which obligations to pay and rights to receive payments originated. In Chapter 2, we briefly considered the principal items in our balance of payments in 1970 and gave attention to achieving a "reasonable" balance as an objective of monetary and fiscal policy. But now it should be instructive to study in more detail the OBE report of the scope and outcome of our international transactions in that year, as presented in Table 23-1.

Preliminary observations

Exports and Imports   As was mentioned earlier in this chapter, all transactions that require payments by foreigners to Americans are classified by us as "exports," and all transactions that require payments by Americans to foreigners are classified as "imports." Exports are often also referred to as "credits" and are traditionally shown in tabular reports with plus signs, while imports are referred to as "debits" and are shown with minus signs. The terms *export* and *import* are well-understood in reference to movements of merchandise, but care must be exercised in extending their use to "invisible" items, that is, the service, capital, and unilateral transactions. For capital transactions, however, we can conveniently follow the movements of deeds to real property, stock certificates, debt instruments, and similar documents to determine whether or not they are imports or exports. Thus the receipt in the United States of stock certificates of foreign corporations is properly thought of as an import, or debit, since the transaction requires

Table 23-1   **Balance of International Payments of the United States in 1970 (in millions of dollars)**

	EXPORTS (CREDITS)	IMPORTS (DEBITS)	NET EXPORTS (+) OR NET IMPORTS (−)[a]
Merchandise, adjusted, excluding military[b]	+41,980	−39,870	+2110
Transfers under U.S. military sales contracts	+1,480		+1480
Direct U.S. military expenditures abroad		−4,851	−4851
Travel	+2,319	−3,953	−1634
Passenger fares	+553	−1,215	−662
Other transportation	+3,106	−2,789	+317
Income on investments:			
Private	+10,503	−4,143	+6360
Government	+906	−1,024	−116
Other services:			
Private	+1,669	−739	+930
Government	+387	−729	+342
	+62,903	−59,313	
Balance on merchandise and services			+3592
Unilateral transfers (net):			
U.S. government grants (excluding military)	−1739		
U.S. government pensions and other transfers	−462		
Private remittances and other transfers	−948		−3149
Balance on current account			+444
Long-term capital flows (net):			
From the United States to foreign countries:			
U.S. government	−2029		
Private	−5781		
	−7810		
From foreign countries to the United States	+4328		−3482
Balance on current account and long-term capital			−3038
Other transactions affecting the liquidity balance (net):			
Nonliquid short-term private capital flows	−548		
Allocation of special drawing rights (SDRs)	+867		
Errors and omissions	−1132		−813
Net liquidity balance			−3852

Table 23-1   (Continued)

	EXPORTS (CREDITS)	IMPORTS (DEBITS)	NET EXPORTS (+) OR NET IMPORTS (−)ᵃ
Liquid private capital flows (net)			—5969
Official reserve transactions balance			−9821
Means of financing:			
Nonliquid liabilities to foreign official agencies reported by:			
U.S. government			+535
U.S. banks			−810
Liquid liabilities to foreign official agencies			+7619
			+7344
U.S. official reserve assets (net)			
Gold	+787		
SDRs	−851		
Convertible currencies	+2152		
Gold-tranche position in IMF	+389		+2477
Total financing			+9821

ᵃ Some items do not add or subtract exactly to totals because of rounding.
ᵇ That is, excluding transfers under military grants, as well as transfers under military sales contracts entered on the next line.
Source: Survey of Current Business, June 1971, pp. 30, 32.

payments by Americans to foreigners.[2] Similarly, we can think of the "importation" of services, as when Americans must make payments for the transportation of merchandise in foreign ships and for tourist expenditures incurred in foreign countries.

Some Transactions on a Net Basis   In examining Table 23-1, we should observe that the headings for imports and exports apply only to the upper part of the table, that is, down to the double underlining, and that all the figures below this level are designated as being "net." Under unilateral

---

[2]Unfortunately, the common terminology here is much confused. Although the purchase of foreign stocks is labeled an "import," because, like the importation of merchandise, it requires a payment to foreigners, such a transaction is often also spoken of as a "capital export," because money is made available to foreigners as "capital." To avoid confusion, however, we must remember that the true "capital export" is really a merchandise export—the sending of machinery and equipment whose purchase by foreigners may have been made possible by the previous purchase of foreign securities by investors residing in the exporting country.

transfers, for example, the figures do not mean that no foreigners made remittances to relatives living in the United States and that no foreign governments paid pensions to residents here; they mean, rather, that our outgoing payments of these kinds exceeded incoming payments of the same kinds by the amounts of the negative figures shown. For another example, the negative figure of $5781 million for private long-term investment by Americans in foreign countries in 1970 does not mean that not a single American enterprise reduced its investment in foreign plant and equipment; it means, instead, that the negative figure resulted after deductions for such withdrawals.

Some Avoidance of Foreign Exchange Transactions　A further observation is that while the OBE seeks to account for all transactions that give rise to payment obligations between Americans and foreigners, some obligations originate and are discharged without the need for matching transactions in foreign exchange. For example, a Canadian manufacturer who sells merchandise in the United States for United States dollars may decide to invest the proceeds of his sales in the stock of an American corporation, so that the supply of Canadian dollars held by American banks and the supply of United States dollars held by Canadian banks would not be affected. Similarly, when an American corporation calls its bonds for redemption, the foreign holders of some of these may reinvest in other American securities; and again, a foreign holder of American securities may come to the United States as a tourist and spend here the dollars he receives as interest and dividends.

Balance in Individual Transactions　An equality between the total debits and the total credits in the balance of payments—or in other words, between the total of the minuses and the total of the pluses—is necessary because *each* international transaction results in equal debits and credits, so that the sums of these individual debits and credits must also be equal. If an American importer buys a shipment of British goods and pays immediately by obtaining a draft drawn by an American bank on its London correspondent, the merchandise import is exactly balanced by a capital movement, that is, the decrease in the balance of the American bank in London. The merchandise import is a debit item because it requires us to make a payment abroad, while the deposit withdrawal is a credit item, since it requires the London bank to make a payment to (for the account of) the American bank. Likewise, if an American manufacturer sells goods to a foreign buyer on 60-day credit terms, the merchandise export (credit) is exactly balanced by the temporary investment of the American manufacturer in "accounts receivable" due in 60 days from the foreign buyer (debit). When the foreign debtor makes payment at the end of 60 days by buying from his domestic bank a draft drawn on its American correspondent, two balancing capital transactions are effected, namely, the withdrawal of the American manufacturer's investment in the foreign country (credit) and the reduction of the foreign bank's deposit balance in the United States (debit).

Hence it is to be emphasized that we do not wait until the end of a year or other period of time to arrange for some kind of settlement for the net obligations that result from our international transactions. We do not say, for example, that we must surrender a certain amount of our reserve assets, such as gold, to foreign countries, because our purchases of merchandise, services, and securities in the course of a year exceeded our sales by the value of these reserve assets. The process of settlement goes on continuously, and as the foregoing illustrations show, it is really involved in each transaction.

Many Balances A final preliminary observation is that the word *balance* is much overworked in balance-of-payments statements and analyses. The comprehensive statement of a country's balance of payments is so called because it truly balances—the total of the debits or minuses is always equal to the total of the credits or pluses. But several subtotals in the comprehensive statement are also labeled as "balances"—the balance of trade, the balance on current account, and so on—and such subtotals carry plus or minus signs indicating that they are surpluses or deficits rather than equalities of some sort.

At this late date, however, little can be done to avoid use of the term *balance* in the two senses indicated, because the double use is so entrenched that attempts at substituting other terms would surely be fruitless. But confusion in analyzing the following description of the balance of payments of the United States in 1970 can be avoided if we keep in mind that it is the whole array of data presented in Table 23-1 that is in balance, and not partial groups of the data regardless of their labels.

Balance of payments of the United States in 1970

Balance on Merchandise and Services In 1970 we exported merchandise of a total value of $41,980 million and imported merchandise at a cost of $39,870 million, so that our *balance of trade* (not specifically labeled as such in Table 23-1) was the difference of $2110 million.[3] Much attention is given to our balance of trade as indicating the success of American business in finding foreign markets for its products by contrast, as it were, with the success of foreign producers in "penetrating" our domestic markets. Be-

---

[3]Although transfers under our military sales contracts could logically be included as merchandise exports, the OBE prefers to treat them as a service transaction—as a kind of offset to our direct military spending abroad which is more clearly of a service character.

cause our balance of trade in 1970 was "favorable" in that exports exceeded imports, we had reason to be pleased, although many critics were displeased because the surplus of exports was not greater. We also sold more services to foreigners in 1970 than we bought from them, so that the excess here plus the balance of trade gave us a surplus in our "balance on merchandise and services" of $3592 million.

Balance on Current Account　On all merchandise and service transactions, therefore, foreigners incurred obligations to us $3592 million in excess of the obligations we incurred to them. But we gave away a goodly amount of purchasing power in 1970 by way of grants of the federal government to less-developed countries for economic development, its payment of social security benefits and veterans' pensions to Americans living abroad, the sending of money by American residents to relatives dwelling in foreign countries, their donations to foreign charities, and so on. In effect, these "unilateral transfers" totaling $3149 million canceled an equal amount of our net claims on foreigners on merchandise and service transactions, reducing them to $444 million, the "balance on current account."

The balance on current account is always regarded as a key figure in a country's international transactions, since it is the direct result of its ordinary every-day buying and selling transactions with foreign countries—after allowance, of course, for the give-aways of purchasing power, that is, the unilateral transfers. It will be recalled, too, that the current account positions of member countries of the International Monetary Fund are greatly stressed in its operations, because one of its principal responsibilities is to help these countries to meet obligations on current account and especially to aid them to overcome "fundamental disequilibriums" in their current accounts.[4]

Balance on Current Account and Long-Term Capital　But if we accumulated net claims on foreigners of $444 million on current account, we used the amount of these claims and much more by adding to our investments in foreign countries much greater amounts than foreigners added to their investments in the United States. We added $7810 million to our long-term investments abroad, while foreigners added only $4328 million to their long-term investments here, so that the net difference of $3482 million offset the $444 million of our current-account claims and gave foreigners the resulting net claims against us of $3038 million labeled the "balance on current account and long-term capital." Considering the fact that we customarily invest more in foreign countries on a long-term basis from year to year than foreigners invest here, the OBE describes the balance on

---

[4]See Chapter 5.

current account and long-term capital as a "rough indicator of long-term trends in our balance-of-payments position."[5]

Net Liquidity Balance In addition, however, foreigners gained further liquid claims on us in 1970 of $548 million from nonliquid short-term private investments of Americans (nonliquid from the standpoint of the American investors) and $1132 million from sources that the OBE was unable to trace ("errors and omissions") but thought to be primarily additional outflows of short-term private investment funds. These gains in foreign claims on us were offset only to the extent of the allotment of $867 million in SDRs that we got from the International Monetary Fund in 1970,[6] so that the net gain to foreigners amounted to $813 million, bringing their total gain in liquid claims to $3852 million, the amount of the "net liquidity balance."

A net liquidity balance of −$3852 million for 1970 means that as an outcome of all our merchandise and service transactions with foreigners, all the unilateral transfers, and all our investment transactions with them in that year, *all* foreigners, including individuals, business enterprises, commercial banks, central banks, and governments, gained claims on us of that amount payable on demand or in short periods. The OBE describes the net liquidity balance as a "broad indicator of potential pressures on the dollar resulting from changes in our liquidity position."[7]

Official Reserve Transactions Balance Although the liquid claims of all foreigners on us increased by $3852 million in 1970, the claims of private foreigners actually decreased by $5969 million, as indicated by the minus figure of that amount for "liquid private capital flows (net)" in Table 23-1. As we did not pay off these claims, there was only one thing that the private foreigners could do with them. They sold them to their central banks or other "official agencies," as was surely possible in consideration of the responsibility of these agencies to buy excess dollar holdings when necessary to keep their exchange rates on the dollar from falling further than 1 percent of declared par values.

If total claims gained by all foreigners amounted to $3852 million and if private foreigners ended the year with a net reduction in their claims of $5969 million, then claims gained by the foreign official agencies must have totaled the sum of these two figures, or $9821 million, the amount of the "official reserve transactions balance."

The official reserve transactions balance has been described as indicating "the direct pressure that may be exerted by official agencies on United

---

[5]*Survey of Current Business*, June 1971, p. 24.
[6]See Chapter 5.
[7]*Ibid.*

States gold and other official reserves, or the foreign exchange rate."[8]
As events in 1971 were, indeed, to prove, foreign official agencies were
not at all pleased with their huge accumulations of dollar claims in 1970,
and even less with continued huge flows of dollars to them in the following
months—events that culminated in August 1971 in the suspension by
the United States of the redeemability of these foreign dollar holdings
in gold.

Means of Financing   What did the foreign official agencies do with the
dollar claims of $9821 million that they acquired in 1970? For the most
part, they simply continued to hold them at the end of the year. This
is shown in Table 23-1 under the heading "means of financing." They
continued to hold $7344 million in nonliquid dollar assets, such as United
States government securities, and in liquid dollar assets, such as deposit
balances with the Federal Reserve banks and commercial banks.

But we also used some of our official reserve assets to redeem, or
buy back, some of these dollar claims. On a net basis, we redeemed
$787 million of the claims by selling gold of that value to foreign official
agencies, and we bought back $2152 million in exchange for convertible
currencies that we already held and another $389 million in exchange
for currencies that we acquired by means of gold-tranche purchases from
the International Monetary Fund, for a total use of reserve assets of $3328
million. Nevertheless, our official reserve assets did not fall by as much
as $3328 million, because the use of reserve assets for settlement was
partially offset by the SDRs allotted to us by the IMF in 1970 and *still held*
by us at the end of that year in the amount of $851 million. Accordingly,
our reserve assets fell by the difference between $3328 million and $851
million, that is, by $2477 million, and this amount added to the $7344
million of dollar claims that foreign official agencies were still holding
at the end of the year gave an over-all financing or settlement of $9821
million carrying the plus sign and balancing, therefore, the official reserve
transactions balance of $9821 million carrying the minus sign. The balance
of payments must balance!

Errors and Omissions   Actually, the OBE was much more certain about
the "means of financing" in 1970 than about any of the other components
of its balance-of-payments report. It gets accurate data directly or indirectly from the U.S. Treasury, the Federal Reserve banks, and the
commercial banks concerning changes in our gold reserves, our gold-tranche
position in the IMF, deposit liabilities to foreign official institutions, and
so on. But its figures for the merchandise and service transactions, the
unilateral transfers, and the international investment transactions would

---

[8]Federal Reserve Bank of St. Louis, *Review*, August 1971, p. 9.

have resulted in an official reserve transactions balance of −$8689 million rather than −$9821 million had it not inserted "errors and omissions" at −$1132 million! It had various choices concerning the place to insert this figure to make the balance of payments truly balance, but it chose to put it in the place shown in Table 23-1 in the belief that the errors and omissions consisted chiefly of untraceable short-term investments by Americans in foreign money markets including the Eurodollar market.

Treatment of SDRs   How the 1970 allotment of SDRs to the United States by the IMF should be treated in our balance of payments was also a matter of choice for the OBE. Its manner of choosing is indicated in Table 23-1, with the total allotment of a declared value of $867 million entered as a plus item under "other transactions affecting the liquidity balance," and the unspent portion of the allotment in the amount of $851 million entered as a minus item among the means of financing. This was a logical position for the OBE to take on grounds that our SDR allotment gave us "out of the blue" a means of buying back excess dollars acquired by foreigners—a means that offset in part foreign acquisitions of liquid claims against us.

However, it can be reasonably argued that both of these figures could better be deleted, and that only the difference between them of $16 million should be entered as a plus item among the means of financing. Although SDRs allotted to us truly give us claims on foreigners, the SDRs that foreign countries get from the IMF give them claims on us. With SDRs treated in this alternative way, at any rate, our net liquidity balance in 1970 would have been −$3852 million plus −$867 million, or −$4719 million, the official reserve transactions balance would have been −$9821 million plus −$867 million, or −$10,688 million, and the means of financing would have been as follows (in millions of dollars):

Nonliquid and liquid liabilities to foreign official agencies (as detailed in Table 23-1)		+7344
U.S. official reserve assets (net)		
Gold	+787	
SDRs	+16	
Convertible currencies	+2152	
Gold-tranche position in IMF	+389	+3344
Total financing		+10,688

"Favorable" and "unfavorable" balances

A country is said to have a "favorable" balance of payments for a given period if, during the period, it acquired payment claims on foreigners because of its sales of merchandise, services, land, buildings, stocks, bonds, and other things in excess of payment claims acquired against it by foreigners because of their purchases of these kinds. Similarly, it is said to have an "unfavorable" balance if payment claims acquired by foreigners against it exceeded the payment claims it acquired against them. A country with a "favorable" balance is also said to have a balance-of-payments "surplus," while one with an "unfavorable" balance is said to have a balance-of-payments "deficit."

But all these descriptive terms can be quite misleading, because of their implication that certain over-all results of international transactions are good for a country, and that others are bad. A favorable balance or surplus is not necessarily good, nor is an unfavorable balance or deficit necessarily bad. For example, a rich country that has persistent balance-of-payments surpluses is likely to have its problems of combating inflation intensified, whereas one that has persistent balance-of-payment deficits as a result of adding to its foreign investments eases domestic inflationary pressures and, in addition, sets the stage for a future stream of income from these investments. Moreover, the goodness or badness of a country's over-all surpluses and deficits depends very importantly on the separate surpluses and deficits of the balance-of-payments components that, in combination, give the over-all net result—surpluses and deficits in its trade or merchandise accounts, in its service accounts, on current account, and so on. Suppose, for example, that a country has persistent deficits on current account but that these are offset by surpluses in its capital transactions. If the country is rich and if the deficits on current account result from imports of consumer goods, the country's international position would appear to be deteriorating, since it must be paying for the excess merchandise imports by reducing its net investment in foreign countries. But if the country is underdeveloped and if the deficits on current account result chiefly from imports of productive machinery and equipment— surely financed by foreign capitalists or governments or international institutions, as indicated by the surpluses on capital account—the country would stand to gain great benefits.

Causes and remedies

If a country decides that its balance-of-payments surpluses or deficits are not good for its welfare, however it may figure them, what can it do toward their elimination? Ordinarily, countries are much more anxious to eliminate deficits than surpluses, so that we may concentrate on that aspect of the question. Moreover, we can most advantageously direct our analysis to the situation of the United States, since we have reported deficits on the liquidity basis in every year from 1950 to the present time, except for 1957 and 1968. At the outset, it is pertinent to observe that our deficits were generally regarded as "good" by most countries, including ourselves, until about 1959, but that they have generally been looked upon as "bad" since about that year. In the earlier period, our deficits were "good" because they very largely resulted from the assistance we were giving to friendly foreign countries to expand their productive facilities and to build up their military forces. But the reasons for the "badness" of our recent deficits are not so easily stated, since they are seen in many different ways by many different authorities. Some, indeed, see very little in them that they regard as "bad."

In attempting to eliminate or reduce deficits, we should first look for causes. But causes are all over the place. Depending upon our viewpoint, they can be excessive imports of merchandise, insufficient exports of merchandise, too much spending by American tourists in foreign countries, too little spending by foreign tourists in the United States, too much dependence upon foreign airlines and steamship companies for transportation services, too little promotion of our transportation services for foreign use, too much spending by the federal government for the support of our military forces abroad, too little willingness of our major allies to relieve us of some of this burden by increasing their military spending, too many grants and loans of the federal government to underdeveloped countries for economic development, too little willingness of our major allies to accept larger responsibilities in this direction, too much direct investment by American firms in foreign plants and facilities, too much investment by Americans in securities issued by foreign governments and enterprises, and too little investment by foreigners in the United States in plants and equipment and stocks and bonds. A glance at Table 23-1 will indicate that this list of "causes" is by no means exhaustive. As for remedies, we could go through the list again, pointing out that our deficits could be eliminated or reduced by cutting merchandise imports, finding new markets for merchandise exports, cutting government spending abroad, reducing private investment in foreign plants and securities, and so on. But much of the list of possible remedies should be fairly obvious.

However all that may be, there is a concensus that the *principal* causes of our deficits have been two: government spending abroad for military purposes and by way of grants and loans for economic development— especially, of course, the spending for military purposes—and private investment by Americans in foreign countries. This consensus is reached because, in all our deficit years beginning with 1950 except 1959, 1968, and 1969, we have had surpluses on current account, some of them very large. While, therefore, we know that it would be helpful to expand our merchandise exports, to attract more foreign tourists to the United States, and so on, we conclude that the major remedy must be found in cutting government spending abroad, cutting private investment, or cutting both. But it is not easy to decide which should be cut, and by how much. Some say that private investment must not be sacrificed, since the income on this investment is a very important plus item in our balance of payments (as Table 23-1 reveals). But others say that the military and economic foreign policies of the federal government must not be sacrificed to private interests, beneficial though those interests may be to our economy.

The debate becomes more complex when ties between government spending and private investment, on the one hand, and other elements in the balance of payments, on the other, are recognized. For example, most of the grants and loans of the federal government to underdeveloped countries over the years have required these countries to spend all or most of the proceeds for American goods. Should the grants and loans have been reduced, therefore, our merchandise exports would surely have been cut, too, although probably by somewhat less than the cutbacks in grants and loans. But the same can be said for much of our private investment in foreign countries. If an American firm invests a certain number of dollars in a branch plant in a foreign country, but actually spends most of these dollars in buying machinery in the United States for equipping the branch plant, its investment (a minus item in the balance of payments) is matched by the machinery export (a plus item). The situation is similar for the dollar investment of an American capitalist in the stock of a foreign corporation that spends the dollars in buying equipment or raw materials in the United States. However, much government spending and private investment have no direct ties of these kinds. Spending by the federal government for supplies purchased in foreign countries for the provisioning of our troops stationed there have no such ties.[9] Nor is there such a tie when dollars invested by Americans in foreign plants and securities are spent in markets other than our own, although we expect that earnings on these investments, as a plus item, will eventually more than offset the investments themselves, as a minus item. We must be especially careful to avoid blanket claims that *all* private investment is beneficial or that it is harmful to our general welfare, as distinct from the welfare of the investors themselves. Suppose, for example, that an American firm establishes a branch plant in a foreign country, equips it with machinery bought in the United States, buys here most of the raw materials needed for production, and sells in a market that could not possibly have been reached from the firm's American plants. There could be few doubts about the balance-of-payments advantages of such a venture. But suppose that another American firm establishes a plant in a foreign country, purchases there most of the equipment needed, buys there or in other foreign countries most of the raw materials and supplies required for production, closes down its American plants, and then sells the products of the foreign plant in our market and in foreign markets—markets previously supplied with identical kinds of products from its American plants.

---

[9]However, some countries have bought military supplies in our market to balance in whole or in part our spendings in their domains for the maintenance of our military forces there.

In our balances of payments, as a result, we would have minuses for the original investment and for the continuing losses of merchandise exports and increases in merchandise imports, all of which would presumably be only gradually offset, and probably offset only in part, as earnings of the foreign plant were brought back—"repatriated" to the United States.[10]

FOR REVIEW

1. What is foreign exchange? At a given moment in the New York market, what does the supply of foreign exchange chiefly consist of? in the London market?
2. From what sources does the foreign department of a commercial bank ordinarily replenish its supplies of foreign currencies?
3. In foreign exchange markets, what is the function of a bank's foreign correspondents? acceptance dealers? foreign exchange brokers?
4. By what kinds of arrangements do smaller banks throughout the United States engage in foreign exchange transactions?
5. How do payments for our merchandise imports typically affect international bank balances?
6. What kinds of international transactions are called service transactions? How do payments by foreigners to Americans for services typically alter international bank balances?
7. What is the scope of international capital transactions? Why is there uncertainty about how short-term capital movements from the United States should be classified in our balance of payments?
8. What are unilateral transfers as recorded in the balance of payments? Do they result in equal debits and credits, as do other classes of transactions?
9. In a country's balance of payments, what items are classified as imports and exports? as debits and credits? as visible and invisible?
10. Why is it said that a country's balance of payments must always balance?
11. In our balance of payments, why are we inclined to give particular attention to the balance of trade? the balance on current account?
12. In a balance of payments, what items are included as "means of settlement" on the liquidity basis? on the official settlements basis?
13. Is it always advantageous to a country to have surpluses in its balance of payments year after year? Discuss.
14. Is it likely to be harmful to a country to have repeated deficits in its balance of payments? Discuss.

---

[10]As related to several other problems of continuing importance in international monetary affairs, the problem of our balance-of-payments deficits is further analyzed in Chapter 26.

CHAPTER 24

FOREIGN EXCHANGE INSTRUMENTS

Payments required for international merchandise, service, and capital transactions may be arranged in several ways, with the means selected in each instance depending upon the terms agreed to by buyer and seller, borrower and lender, or debtor and creditor. Let us first survey the means that are generally available for making immediate international cash payments: (1) bankers' sight drafts, cables and telegraphic transfers, (2) personal checks, (3) cash letters of credit, (4) travelers' letters of credit, (5) travelers' checks, (6) international money orders, and (7) paper money and coins.

MEANS OF INTERNATIONAL CASH PAYMENT

Bankers' sight drafts, cables, and telegraphic transfers

Bankers' sight, or demand, drafts, cables, and telegraphic transfers are the most important means of making international cash payments. A *sight draft* is of the nature of a check: a written order drawn by a domestic bank on its foreign correspondent[1] to pay to bearer or to the order of a designated payee a specific sum of money. A *cable* or a *telegraphic transfer* is an order transmitted by wire to the foreign correspondent to make payment to a designated payee. Except for the mode of transmission, therefore, bankers' sight drafts, cables, and telegraphic transfers are payment orders of quite similar character. As indicated in the preceding chapter, the

---

[1] As used frequently in this chapter, the term *correspondent* and its synonyms should be understood to be inclusive of banks' foreign branches. As a general rule, a domestic bank can supply through its foreign branches payment facilities and other services of the same kinds and qualities as it would otherwise be likely to supply by arrangements with independent foreign banks as correspondents.

domestic bank is able to issue (sell) such orders because it is simply drawing on its demand deposit balance with the foreign correspondent.

Instruments of these kinds are made available by domestic banks to their customers for any sums, regardless of size. The customer pays in domestic money at the agreed-upon rate of exchange, and the bank, of course, has its foreign balance reduced by the face amount of the instrument.

A cable is sent in code by the domestic bank to its foreign correspondent. Beside paying for the amount of the cable at the agreed-upon rate of exchange for cable transfers, the customer bears the cost of sending the cable. Between countries not separated by oceans, telegraphic transfers take the place of cables, with the customer also bearing the cost of transmission.

Personal checks

Personal checks are quite important as mediums of international cash payment. Here is meant, of course, ordinary checks, such as individuals and firms draw on their local banks in meeting domestic obligations. Between countries whose political and business relations are excellent, as the United States and Canada, personal checks are commonly accepted. An important business corporation that enjoys a world-wide reputation will ordinarily find its personal checks accepted without hesitation in all parts of the world. Corporations, in paying dividends on stock, and both corporations and governments, in paying interest on registered bonds, usually send checks to the foreign as well as to the domestic holders of these securities.

On receiving a personal check drawn on a bank located in a foreign country, an American would normally sell it to his own bank for dollars, and this bank would send it to its correspondent in the country where it originated. There it would be presented for payment to the drawee bank, and the correspondent would credit the account of the American bank.

Cash letters of credit

A *cash letter of credit* is an instrument issued by a bank to authorize a designated party to draw a check or draft on it for a specified sum of money payable on demand. It can be used as a means of international cash payment when, for example, an importer refuses to pay for merchandise until it has left the exporter's country, and at the same time, the exporter refuses to ship the merchandise until he is assured of immediate payment. To illustrate, let us suppose that an American importer is buying broadcloth from a British firm at a price of $10,000. The American importer could, of course, obtain a domestic instrument for that amount, but he does not want to make payment until the goods have left the hands of the British exporter; and the latter, in turn, is not willing to trust the American importer's unsupported promise to pay. In these circumstances, the American importer could obtain a cash letter of credit from his bank and send it to the British exporter, who should then be willing to ship the goods since, in effect, he has a deposit with an American bank against which he is authorized to draw. He would ship the goods, draw the draft, and sell it to his bank for sterling; and the British bank would send it to its American correspondent which would collect from the American issuing bank and credit the deposit balance of the British bank. The American importer would be protected by a stipulation in the letter of credit making the draft payable only if accompanied at the time of presentation by a bill of lading giving title to the broadcloth.

Travelers' letters of credit

A *traveler's letter of credit* is a variant of the cash letter. It authorizes the person to whom it is issued to draw demand drafts on the issuing bank by presenting it to the bank's correspondents in foreign countries. The total amount that may be drawn is specified, as well as the time limit within which the drafts will be acceptable. Travelers' letters of credit provide a convenient means of payment for those who must spend relatively large sums while traveling in foreign countries. Buyers for department stores, for example, may not know at the time of their departure the prices or the quantities of the goods that they will buy in various countries from individual sellers. As purchases are made, therefore, the drafts for the necessary payments can be drawn under a letter of credit.

The bank from which a traveler's letter of credit is obtained notifies its foreign correspondents of the issuance of the letter, giving its number, the date of issue, the amount involved, and the name of the purchaser, or "beneficiary." Travelers' letters issued by American banks authorize the drawing of dollar drafts.

The traveler carries with him a letter of identification bearing his signature, and he presents this together with the letter of credit to the foreign correspondents when he wants to draw drafts. The teller of a correspondent bank, after assuring himself of the genuineness of the letter of credit, requires the traveler to draw the draft in his presence and compares the signature on the draft with that in the letter of identification. If fully satisfied with evidence, the correspondent bank buys the draft, paying in its own currency at its buying rate for demand drafts on the country in which the letter was issued. Finally, the teller of the correspondent bank notes on the letter of credit the name of his bank, the amount of the draft it is purchasing, and the date, as notification to other correspondents that the full amount of the letter of credit is no longer available for drawing. A correspondent that buys a draft that exhausts the letter of credit returns the letter to the issuing bank.

In buying a traveler's letter of credit, the beneficiary may be required to pay for it immediately at full face value; if so, the issuing bank is fully protected. The bank, in this case, not only earns the commission charged but also has the use of the funds until the drafts come through from the foreign correspondents for payment. Sometimes the arrangement between the issuing bank and the beneficiary merely calls for the charging of the latter's deposit account as the drafts are presented for payment. Because the bank, in this instance, does not have temporary use of the funds involved, it is likely to charge a higher commission rate than it charges on cash contracts.

Travelers' checks

Most issues of travelers' checks are orders drawn by banks on themselves by which they obligate themselves to pay specific sums of money on demand to the order of the persons or firms whose names are subsequently written in as payees. Travelers' checks are intricately engraved and are printed on paper specially processed to prevent counterfeiting. In the United States, such checks are issued by many of the larger metropolitan banks and by the American Express Company in round amounts ranging upward from $10. The buyer of travelers' checks writes his name on the face at the time of purchase and then signs them again—"countersigns" them—when he uses them in making payments. Banks, transportation companies, hotel cashiers, and others who cash travelers' checks are usually satisfied with a comparison of the two signatures as a sufficient identification of the person who offers them.

A person who buys travelers' checks in the United States pays for them immediately at full face value, and adds a commission, which is usually 75 cents or $1 per $100. Thus the issuing bank not only earns the commission but also has the use of the principal from the time of issue until the time of redemption. The interest that the bank is able to earn on the principal may be substantial, for several weeks or months may elapse before many of the checks will be presented to the bank for payment.

Rarely do American buyers of dollar travelers' checks have difficulty in passing them as a means of payment, either in the United States or abroad. The checks are accepted not only by banks, but also by railroad companies, hotels, and merchants and other businessmen. In the United States, they are generally accepted at full face value; and in foreign countries, they are accepted by banks in exchange for their own currencies at their current buying rates for dollar instruments payable on demand. A foreign bank that buys travelers' checks from American tourists sends them to its American correspondent which, in turn, presents them to the drawee bank for payment. The payment is then credited by the American correspondent to the dollar deposit account of the foreign bank.

International money orders

Both the United States Postal Service and the American Express Company issue money orders[2] for use in making payments in foreign countries. Post offices in all parts of the country are authorized to sell international money orders payable in most of the countries with which we maintain diplomatic and commercial relations. The maximum allowed for each order is $100, but any number of orders can be bought at the same time. On orders up to $10, the buyer pays a fee of 45 cents; on those from $10.01 to $50, 65 cents; and on those from $50.01 to $100, 75 cents. For only a few countries are the orders issued in terms of their currencies; for all others, the orders are payable in dollars. International money orders payable in dollars are likely to be inconvenient for certain kinds of transactions, since the buyer does not know exactly the amount of foreign currency his dollar orders will bring, this depending upon the conversion rate used by the foreign post office or other foreign correspondent agency. In most instances, the international orders are transmitted directly by the Postal Service to the foreign post offices or agencies, and the latter notify the payees.

The services of the American Express Company in supplying international money orders are somewhat broader than those of the Postal Service. It usually makes available orders on more countries than does the Postal Service, as well as a larger number payable in foreign currencies.

Paper money and coins

Paper money and coins are used as a means of international cash payment chiefly by tourists and, even by them, only to a moderate extent. For example, American tourists are usually able to spend United States dollars with all-too-great ease in many parts of Canada, and Canadian tourists have comparable ease in spending Canadian money at least in American border cities. Tourists returning from foreign countries often bring substantial amounts of foreign paper money and coins with them. These they sell to domestic banks which then have these supplies, as well as foreign paper money and coin brought in by foreign tourists, to sell to people departing for foreign countries. When such supplies exceed the demand, the domestic banks ship the excess to their foreign correspondents for credit in their deposit accounts.

DEFERRED INTERNATIONAL PAYMENT

Not all international commercial transactions are settled by immediate cash payments. Although most of the service and capital transactions are

---

[2]It is worth mentioning that bankers' sight drafts are also often referred to as "money orders."

so completed, many international shipments of merchandise are arranged on terms that permit the postponement of payment for varying periods. Many exporters of goods to foreign countries are quite willing to sell "on time," but generally they demand special safeguards not required in domestic trade. Deferred payment can be arranged by the use of book accounts, promissory notes, commercial letters of credit, and trade drafts.

Book accounts and promissory notes give the exporter no special protection, for their status in international transactions is much the same as in domestic commerce. Only individuals and firms of the highest credit standing can expect, therefore, to be able to buy on the basis of book accounts and promissory notes. As a matter of fact, promissory notes are rarely used, but book accounts have a position of prominence, especially in transactions between firms located in countries having excellent commercial relations. Canadian firms often sell to American firms on book accounts, and American firms often so sell to Canadian firms.

The book account and the promissory note are not means of payment but means of deferring payment. When the credit period has elapsed, the importer must make payment by using one of the cash instruments already discussed. If a Canadian exporter sells a shipment of goods for $10,000 Canadian on a 60-day account to an American firm, the latter must arrange for a cash payment at the expiration of the 60 days—and for this purpose, it would very likely buy a banker's sight draft or telegraphic transfer payable to the Canadian exporter.

The commercial letter of credit and the trade draft, on the other hand, can be used simultaneously as a means of deferring payment and as a means of final payment. In other words, an importer or other debtor, at the expiration of an allowed credit period, may have no need to make further arrangements to pay the foreign exporter or creditor.

Commercial letters of credit

A *commercial letter of credit* may be defined as an instrument issued by a bank at the request of one party authorizing a second party to draw a draft against the bank for a designated sum payable at a specified time. It will be seen that this definition fits cash letters of credit and travelers' letters as already examined; they are, therefore, properly classified as types of commercial letters. At this time, however, attention will be confined to commercial letters that authorize second parties to draw drafts payable in the future rather than on demand.

The bank that grants a letter of credit is known as the "issuer"; the party who applies for the letter is called the "opener"; and the party to whom it is addressed is designated the "beneficiary." The issuing bank is said to "open an acceptance credit." In some instances, the opener is also the beneficiary; however, in the most common use of commercial letters of credit, whereby a bank in the importer's country underwrites the financing of an import transaction, the opener is the importer, and the beneficiary is the foreign exporter. Nevertheless, many variations in arrangement are possible, and some of these are discussed in the following pages.

Letter of Credit Issued by the Importer's Bank   For the sake of clarity, concrete illustrations will be employed to show some of the uses of commercial letters of credit. Let us suppose, first of all, that an American firm is buying $10,000 worth of goods from a British exporter, and that the terms of the contract require the American firm to obtain a commercial letter of credit from an American bank authorizing a draft at 60 days' sight. The procedure may be described as follows:

1. The American importer applies to his bank (American bank A) for the letter of credit in favor of the British exporter. In issuing the letter, American bank A requires the importer to sign a contract agreeing to provide it with the funds to meet at maturity the draft to be drawn.
2. The American importer sends the letter of credit to the British exporter. (Here the procedure may vary. American bank A may send the letter directly to the British exporter; or it may cable advice to its British correspondent bank that the letter of credit has been opened in favor of the British exporter.)
3. The arrival of the letter of credit assures the British exporter that he will be paid for his goods, since he is able to rely on the obligation of American bank A, which, we may presume, has an established international reputation. He therefore delivers the goods to the shipping company and obtains a bill of lading, which is a document of title. He draws the draft on American bank A and takes it, together with the bill of lading, the letter of credit, and other required documents, to his own bank. As the letter of credit informs the British bank that the exporter has the right to draw the draft, it will not hesitate to participate in the transaction. The exporter may ask the bank to send the draft to the United States for acceptance by American bank A and for collection 60 days later; but more likely, he will request the bank to buy the draft and give him the proceeds in sterling. We may, therefore, assume that the British bank buys the draft.
4. The British bank now sends the draft with all documents attached to its American correspondent bank (American bank B).
5. American bank B presents the draft and documents to American bank A, and the latter, if satisfied that the terms of the letter of credit have been fulfilled, writes its acceptance across the face of the draft and returns it to American bank B. In accepting the draft, American bank A detaches the documents. The letter of credit, having done its work, is filed away; and the bill of lading and other documents are likely to

be surrendered to the importer. Although the importer will have approximately 60 days in which to make payment, it is desirable that he be able to obtain the goods immediately from the shipping company —as he can if he has the bill of lading. The sale of the goods will presumably provide the funds for the importer's payment to the bank. To protect itself, American bank A requires the importer to sign a document by which it retains a "security interest" in the goods and by which the importer obligates himself to use the proceeds of their sale to make the payment owing to the bank.

6.   American bank B, meanwhile, may hold the accepted draft—now a *banker's acceptance*—until maturity or may sell it in the American money market, depending upon the instructions received from the British bank as the owner of the acceptance. If the British bank is in no immediate need of dollars, it may instruct American bank B to hold the draft until maturity, and it will then earn the full discount charged the British exporter, less whatever service fees it must pay American bank B. On the other hand, if it wants to build up its American dollar balance immediately, the British bank will order American bank B to sell the acceptance in the American money market and credit the proceeds to its account. In the money market, American bank C may buy the acceptance for inclusion among its secondary reserve assets.

7.   Before the maturity of the acceptance, the American importer pays $10,000 plus a commission to American bank A, which is thus supplied with funds to meet the acceptance when it is presented for payment by American bank B or American bank C, as the case may be.

Features of Acceptance Credits   Certain observations about the illustration detailed in the preceding paragraphs may be expressed. It is important to notice, in the first place, that American bank A, the issuer of the letter of credit, does not make a loan to the importer or to anyone else. At no time is it out of funds. It merely agrees to accept the draft in place of the American importer, and thus we say that it is *lending its good name.* Sometimes, it is true, accepting banks buy their own acceptances in the money market—in which case they are in all essential respects making loans to the openers of their letters of credit.

In accepting, American bank A makes itself primarily liable on the instrument, and would be required to meet it at maturity though the importer might default upon his obligation.

The importer is the recipient of a loan or credit, since he is able to obtain the goods approximately 60 days before he pays for them; yet the British exporter receives payment as soon as he sells the draft to his bank. Obviously, then, the British bank is granting the loan or credit to the American importer as long as it holds the draft and as long as American bank B holds the acceptance in its name. If the acceptance is sold in the

American money market, the buyer there (American bank C) becomes a lender to the importer.

Finally, no international payment is necessary at the maturity of the acceptance—a fact that justifies the earlier statement that the commercial letter of credit can be used simultaneously as a means of deferring payment and as a means of final payment. It is true that a conversion of currencies takes place at the time that the British bank buys the dollar draft for sterling, but the conversion is effected long before maturity.

Letter of Credit Issued by the Exporter's Bank   The exporter's bank can assist in financing the exportation of merchandise by issuing a commercial letter of credit directly to the exporter at his request. Such an arrangement is convenient when the exporter wants to have funds available while awaiting payment from the foreign importer. It may be that no bank in the importer's country issues letters of credit, or if they are obtainable, there may be some misgivings about their quality. At any rate, the foreign importer has no part in the contract between the exporter's bank and the exporter.

Suppose, for example, that an American exporter is sending a shipment of goods to a Colombian importer at a price of $5000. The terms of the contract call for the drawing of a trade draft at sight against the Colombian importer with bill of lading and other documents attached. This means that the Colombian importer must accept and pay the trade draft before the bill of lading will be surrendered to him. While awaiting payment for the goods shipped, the American exporter may need other funds immediately to carry on his customary operations. The procedure would be as follows:

1. The American exporter delivers the goods to the shipping company and obtains a bill of lading, after which he draws the trade draft on the Colombian importer. He attaches the bill of lading and other required documents to the draft, takes them to his bank, and asks it to send them to Colombia for collection. At the same time, he asks the bank to permit him to draw a draft against it for $5000 payable at the time that the payment from Colombia is expected to come through. The bill of lading, which is in the possession of the bank, is security for the transaction, but additional security may be required. If the letter of credit is issued, the American exporter draws the draft, and the bank accepts it, sells it in the American money market, and gives the exporter the proceeds.

2. The American bank sends the trade draft and documents to its Colombian correspondent, and the latter presents the draft to the Colombian importer for payment. If he pays, the bill of lading and other documents are released to him.

3. Since the trade draft is payable in dollars, the Colombian importer

would be likely to pay it by buying a banker's sight draft on a bank in the United States for $5000. When this is received from the Colombian correspondent of the American issuing bank, the latter has the funds with which to pay its acceptance at maturity.

Letter of Credit Obtained by the Importer from a Bank in the Exporter's Country In the foregoing illustration, the American exporter might have been willing to allow the Colombian importer 60 days or some other period of time in which to make payment had the latter been able to obtain a commercial letter of credit of satisfactory quality. Although the American exporter would probably not be willing to draw a draft against a Colombian bank payable in pesos, he would be willing to draw against an American bank at 60 days' sight if the draft were payable in dollars. Hence the Colombian importer might arrange the financing if his own bank in Colombia were able to obtain a letter of credit from an American bank. The procedure would be as follows:

1. The Colombian importer asks the Colombian bank to arrange for the issue of a letter of credit by an American bank (American bank A) to the American exporter. The Colombian importer, at the same time, enters into a contractual agreement with his bank to make payment within approximately 60 days.
2. The Colombian bank asks American bank A, its correspondent, to issue the letter of credit, at the same time agreeing to provide American bank A with $5000 plus a commission before the maturity of the draft to be drawn by the American exporter.
3. Assuming American bank A's willingness to participate in the transaction, it issues the letter of credit to the American exporter.
4. The American exporter, now having full assurance about payment, delivers the goods to the shipping company and obtains a bill of lading. He draws the draft, attaches the bill of lading, the letter of credit, and other documents, and let us say, discounts the draft at his bank (American bank B) and receives the proceeds.
5. American bank B, now the owner of the draft, presents it to American bank A for acceptance, at the same time surrendering the bill of lading and other documents. American bank B may hold the acceptance until maturity and thereby finance the export shipment or sell it in the American money market, in which case the buyer there would finance the transaction.
6. Meanwhile, American bank A sends the bill of lading and other documents to the Colombian bank; these are released to the Colombian importer in exchange for a document of title or security interest.
7. The Colombian importer is obligated to pay the Colombian bank (in pesos, it is likely) according to the terms of the original contract; and

the Colombian bank, in turn, must pay American bank A $5000 plus a commission before the maturity of the latter's acceptance.

Letter of Credit Issued by a Bank in a Third Country   Many shipments of goods between two countries are financed by means of acceptance credits opened by banks in third countries. To illustrate this arrangement, let us assume that a Colombian importer is buying a shipment of goods from a Canadian exporter. We may assume that the Canadian exporter would not be willing to draw a trade draft on the Colombian importer or to draw under a commercial letter of credit issued by a Colombian bank, and we may further assume that no Colombian bank has a correspondent in Canada and thus cannot easily have a Canadian letter of credit issued. Under the circumstances, the parties decide to draw the contract in terms of United States dollars, and the Colombian importer is required to obtain a letter of credit from an American bank in favor of the Canadian exporter. The steps by which the transaction would be completed are the following:

1. The Colombian importer requests the Colombian bank to have its American correspondent (American bank A) issue the letter of credit.
2. American bank A, in complying with the request of the Colombian bank, issues the letter of credit directly to the Canadian exporter.
3. On receiving the letter of credit, the Canadian exporter delivers the merchandise to the shipping company, obtains a bill of lading, draws the draft, and takes all documents to his Canadian bank. As the draft is drawn in terms of United States dollars, we may assume that the Canadian exporter sells it to his bank for Canadian dollars.
4. The Canadian bank sends the draft and documents to its American correspondent (American bank B).
5. American bank B presents the draft and documents to American bank A, and the latter accepts the draft and detaches the documents. American bank B may hold the acceptance until maturity or sell it in the American money market, depending upon the instructions of the Canadian bank, the owner of the acceptance. In either case, American bank B credits the deposit account of the Canadian bank when the proceeds are received.
6. American Bank A sends the bill of lading and other documents to the Colombian bank, and the latter surrenders them to the Colombian importer on immediate cash payment or against some document of title or security interest designed to ensure future payment, according to the terms of the original agreement between the bank and the importer.
7. The Colombian bank must remit payment to American bank A to provide it with funds to pay the acceptance at maturity.

If the Canadian bank were to authorize American bank B to sell the acceptance in the American money market, the buyer there would be financing the shipment of merchandise between Canada and Colombia. This possibility—really a probability—suggests why New York and London are recognized as leading international money markets, since it indicates how the banks of New York and London can (and do) finance many international transactions in which American and British firms are in no way involved as importers or exporters, in addition to most of those in which these firms do participate. The dollar and the pound are highly regarded in all parts of the world, and importers and exporters in most countries are generally willing to transact their business in terms of dollars or pounds when their own currencies cannot be used. Thus countries that have international commercial transactions of only meager volumes usually find it essential to maintain banking connections in New York or London or both.

Acceptance Credits to Create Dollar Exchange   All the uses of commercial letters of credit thus far illustrated involve the opening of acceptance credits for the movement of merchandise between countries. Banking authorities in the United States and elsewhere have generally insisted that bankers' acceptances be used only in self-liquidating transactions, whereby the sale of goods provides the funds with which the acceptances can be paid. But one use of acceptance credits not necessarily self-liquidating is sanctioned by law in the United States; this is their use "to create dollar exchange." Banks are permitted to grant acceptance credits to create dollar exchange, because such credits enhance the position of the dollar as an international medium of exchange by making it more readily accessible to banks in certain "less-developed" countries than it would otherwise be.

The major trading nations ordinarily need no special assistance in acquiring dollar balances; but smaller countries, whose exports to the United States are seasonal or otherwise sporadic, would be likely to find themselves without dollar balances from time to time should they not have access to acceptance credits. The republics of Central America typically build up sizable dollar balances at American banks during the seasons when they are selling sugar, coffee, and other commodities to us, but at other times, the dollar balances often tend to vanish. Hence, acceptance credits are supposed to take care of the off seasons for such countries. Member banks of the Federal Reserve System are permitted to create dollar exchange by means of acceptance credits only for the countries, territories, and dependencies of Latin America (except Haiti and the Dutch West Indies) and for Australia, its dependencies, New Zealand, and Indonesia.

To see how dollar exchange is created, let us suppose that a Nicaraguan firm has a payment of $20,000 to make in the United States but that its Nicaraguan bank has no dollar balance with its correspondent here against which it could issue a banker's sight draft. However, it has a standing arrangement with the American correspondent for the creation of dollar exchange. The procedure would be as follows:

1. The Nicaraguan bank gives the Nicaraguan firm a banker's sight draft on its American correspondent for $20,000. At the same time, it draws a time draft for approximately the same amount against the American bank.
2. The Nicaraguan firm sends the banker's draft to its American creditor, and the Nicaraguan bank sends the time draft directly to its American correspondent. Presumably, both instruments will go by the same mail and will arrive in the United States simultaneously.
3. The American correspondent bank accepts the time draft, sells it—now a banker's acceptance—in the American money market, and credits the proceeds to the account of the Nicaraguan bank. Whoever buys the acceptance, it is obvious, really makes a loan to the Nicaraguan bank. At any rate, when the banker's sight draft is presented for payment by the American payee, the Nicaraguan bank has a sufficient balance to meet it.
4. To complete the transaction, the Nicaraguan bank must supply its American correspondent with $20,000 before the maturity of the acceptance. If in the meantime, Nicaraguan exporters have been selling coffee, sugar, and other commodities in the United States, the task of providing dollar "cover" should not be difficult. The Nicaraguan exporters would be receiving payment in dollar instruments that they would sell to the Nicaraguan bank. And the Nicaraguan bank would send these to its American correspondent for collection and credit to its account.

Types of Letters of Credit A commercial letter of credit may be *revocable* or *irrevocable*. When a bank issues a revocable letter of credit, it can cancel the letter before the authorized draft is presented for acceptance. Thus if some event occurs that endangers the position of the bank, it can escape its obligation to accept. Because of their weakness, revocable letters may not be acceptable to foreign exporters, and foreign banks may refuse to buy drafts drawn under them. Irrevocable letters, on the other hand, obligate the issuing bank to accept the authorized draft as long as the terms of the letter are fulfilled. A beneficiary, however, can consent to the cancellation of an irrevocable letter.

Again, commercial letters of credit may be *confirmed* or *unconfirmed*. A confirmed letter is one whose terms are guaranteed by a bank other than the issuer. Confirmation is usually obtained upon the initiative of the beneficiary; it is desirable when there is some doubt about the credit position of the issuing bank. But confirmations also originate when banks ask their foreign correspondents to issue letters of credit in the requesting banks' names, since it is customary for the correspondents to add their confirmation. By confirming a letter of credit, a bank agrees to fulfill its terms if the opening bank defaults for any reason, and it also usually undertakes to buy without question the draft drawn under the letter. An unconfirmed letter is one that depends exclusively on the opening bank's obligation to accept.

Accordingly, it is possible to have an irrevocable confirmed letter of credit, likely to be an instrument of the highest quality; an irrevocable unconfirmed letter, likely to be adequate, although somewhat weaker than the irrevocable confirmed letter; and a revocable unconfirmed letter, an instrument of the weakest quality—a type rarely used. The fourth possible combination—a revocable confirmed letter—does not exist in practice, for no bank will guarantee a letter that the opening bank itself may cancel.

Commercial letters are also classified as *revolving* and *fixed*. The authorization to draw of a fixed letter is exhausted when a draft of the designated amount has been drawn and accepted; a revolving letter can be drawn on in part or in full repeatedly. For an illustration of a revolving letter, let us assume that an American firm expects to buy several shipments of coffee from a Brazilian exporter over a period of several months, and that the total cost of the shipments is not known when the letter is opened. It gets its bank to open a revolving letter for, say, $50,000 in favor of the Brazilian exporter and he makes several shipments and draws drafts totaling $35,000. In making further shipments, the Brazilian exporter would apparently be entitled to draw only to the amount of the remaining $15,000; but if the American importer pays the bank $35,000 to cover the drafts already drawn, the full authorization of the letter of credit is restored, and the Brazilian exporter would again be in a position to draw up to $50,000.

Trade drafts

The terms arranged between importers and exporters in international trade sometimes call for the use of trade drafts rather than drafts drawn on banks under commercial letters of credit. A *trade draft* is an order drawn by one party on a second party to pay a certain sum of money to bearer or to the order of a third party on demand or at a fixed or determinable future time. A trade draft is drawn by the exporter on the importer himself and not on the importer's bank. The first and third parties of a trade draft can be identical, that is, the exporter, although a bank is likely to be named as the third party if it buys the draft from the exporter or if it undertakes to make collection for him.

Trade drafts are classified as follows:

1. Sight or demand drafts.
   A. Clean.
   B. Documentary for payment.
2. Time drafts.
   A. Clean.
   B. Documentary.
      (1) Documentary for acceptance.
      (2) Documentary for payment.

Clean Trade Drafts A clean trade draft is unaccompanied by a bill of lading or other document of title. Whether payable at sight or at some future time, it is used only when the exporter has full confidence in the ability and willingness of the foreign importer to pay. The sale of goods on the basis of a clean trade draft is similar to a sale on book account, since the exporter has no special safeguards of any kind. As the bill of lading and other documents are sent to the importer directly, he can obtain the goods from the shipping company without reference to the draft. The trade draft itself is usually given to a bank in the exporter's country for collection. The exporter's bank forwards it to its correspondent in the importer's country, and the correspondent presents it. If it is a sight instrument, the importer is asked to pay at once; if a time instrument, he merely writes his acceptance across the face, and the correspondent bank then holds it until maturity, when it is again presented, this time for payment.

Documentary Trade Drafts A documentary trade draft is one to which is attached a bill of lading or other document of title, to be surrendered to the foreign importer only after he has paid the draft, if it is a sight or documentary-for-payment (D/P) bill, or only after he has accepted it, if it is a documentary-for-acceptance (D/A) bill. Documentary sight drafts and D/P time bills protect the exporter, since title to the goods does not pass to the importer until he has made payment. On the other hand, the D/A bill offers little protection, since the bill of lading is released to the importer upon his writing his acceptance. It would be possible for him to obtain the goods and sell them and then fail to make payment at maturity. Accordingly, D/A bills, like clean drafts, are used only in selling to foreign customers of good credit standing.

Documentary trade drafts may be sold by the exporter to his bank or merely turned over to it for presentation and collection. Banks do not usually buy clean bills and D/A bills because of the lack of protection; nor as a matter of fact, do they buy D/P bills unless the exporter's credit rating is sound. This means that, in buying trade drafts, the banks rely on the obligation of the exporter who is secondarily liable, rather than on that of the foreign importer who, upon acceptance, becomes primarily liable. While a bank in buying a D/P bill retains title to the goods until the foreign importer pays, the proceeds of the sale of the goods might not be sufficient to reimburse it should he fail to pay.

Whether a bank buys documentary trade drafts or merely undertakes their collection, it forwards them to its correspondent in the importer's country, and the latter presents them for payment or for acceptance, as the case may be. When payment is received, the correspondent credits the account of the exporter's bank, and the latter credits the account of the exporter (if it has not already done so in buying the bill). The foreign importer is usually given the right to inspect the goods before accepting a D/A bill or paying a D/P bill.

The arrangement may appear anomalous when a D/P bill payable at some future time is used. The goods arrive in the importer's country, but he is not able to take possession of them until he makes payment, and the terms of the bill may permit the deferment of payment for a considerable period of time. Such bills are therefore used chiefly for shipments of goods that can be stored in public warehouses in the importer's country until he can find a buyer or otherwise arrange payment. Sometimes, however, the correspondent bank in the importer's country takes the responsibility of releasing the bill of lading to the importer before the latter has paid the draft. In such instances, the importer typically gives the correspondent bank a document of title or of a security interest for its protection.

RELATED DOCUMENTS

In the foregoing pages, references have been made repeatedly to the bills of lading and "other documents" that are frequently attached to drafts when they are forwarded for collection or payment. By way of concluding the chapter, therefore, brief descriptions of the more important kinds of documents referred to should be appropriate.

Bill of lading

A *bill of lading* is a contract for the transportation of goods between the exporter and the transportation company. The bill of lading is made out in triplicate: the first or original copy, which is given to the exporter, is a document of title giving the party in whose favor it is issued the right to claim the goods at their destination; another copy is given to the exporter as his receipt; and the third copy is retained by the transportation company as its evidence of the transaction. The first or original copy—the document of title—is usually made "to the order of" the exporter, who is able to transfer title to the goods by endorsement; this is the "bill of lading" to which frequent reference has been made.

Certificate of marine insurance

Another document invariably required in shipments of goods by ocean carriers is a certificate of marine insurance. Rail carriers in the United States and in many other countries are made responsible by law for damages to goods during the course of transit, but this is not true of ocean steamship lines. Marine insurance is desirable not only to protect the exporter should the goods be lost at sea but also to protect whatever bank purchases his drafts; indeed, exporters would find it impossible to sell drafts to banks were the shipments uninsured.

An exporter can enter into separate negotiations with a marine insurance company every time a shipment is made, obtain a certificate covering the shipment, and pay the necessary premiums; but more commonly, he will obtain from the insurance company an "open policy" enabling him to prepare his own certificates of insurance as he forwards each shipment. He notifies the insurance company of the certificates he has filled out and pays the premiums.

Hypothecation certificate

A *hypothecation certificate* is a document required when an exporter sells to his bank drafts drawn on foreign importers and foreign banks. The certificate, however, remains with the buying bank and does not accompany the drafts on their journeys abroad. The bank requires the certificate to protect itself in the event that it is refused payment by the foreign banks or importers upon whom the drafts are drawn, for it is a guaranty of the seller of the drafts to reimburse the bank for any losses.

Suppose that an American importer who is buying a shipment of goods from a British exporter is required to obtain a commercial letter of credit from an American bank. The American bank, in opening the acceptance credit, requires the importer, as we have seen, to sign a contract to provide it with funds to meet the draft (acceptance) at maturity. If the importer defaults, the American bank can bring suit against him for breach of the contract. Now the British exporter draws the draft and sells it to his British bank—and that bank also demands protection. Hence the hypothecation certificate, as executed by the British exporter, authorizes the British bank, upon default of the American issuing bank, to sell the goods as well as to seize other property of the exporter to reimburse itself.

The exporter may sign a separate hypothecation certificate every time he sells a draft, or he may give the bank a "general letter of hypothecation" which guarantees it against loss on all drafts that he may sell it regardless of their number, the amounts involved, and the timing of these sales.

Other documents

Several other kinds of documents that are customarily attached to drafts moving in international mails remain to be mentioned. *Consular invoices* are required by the United States and by many of the countries of Latin America. The foreign exporter of goods to the United States must obtain such an invoice from the American consul located in his country. Merely a description of the merchandise being shipped, it is used by American customs officials in assessing tariff duties against the shipment. Some countries require *certificates of origin* and *antidumping certificates* to assure customs officials that the terms of trade and tariff treaties with other countries are being observed. *Inspection certificates* are often required for imports of meat, butter, and other foodstuffs, and *health certificates*, for imports of cattle, sheep, and other livestock.

A bank is likely to require the exporter to attach a copy of the *commercial invoice* to the draft that he turns over to it for sale or for collection, but there is no reason why this invoice cannot be sent directly to the importer, since it is simply the exporter's bill for the goods.

Finally, the exporter may include among the documents a *letter of instructions*. Such a letter is especially desirable if the exporter's bank and its foreign correspondent are merely acting as collection agents. It states what steps the banks are to take if the foreign importer of his bank, as the case may be, fails to accept the draft.

FOR REVIEW

1. How are bankers' sight drafts used in making international cash payments? cables? telegraphic transfers?
2. Describe the procedure of using a traveler's letter of credit for making payments in foreign countries.
3. What is a traveler's check? an international money order? What institutions provide these instruments? How are they used for payments abroad?
4. How is it possible for a banker's acceptance to be both a means of deferring payment and a means of final payment?
5. Describe the procedure by which a domestic bank finances merchandise imports by means of commercial letters of credit.
6. How can a bank in the exporter's country, by means of a commercial letter of credit, finance an export shipment as requested by the exporter? as requested by a bank in the importer's country?
7. How are bankers' acceptances used in the United States "to create dollar exchange"? Why are they so used? On whose behalf?
8. What is the distinction between revocable and irrevocable letters of credit? between confirmed and unconfirmed letters? between revolving and fixed letters?
9. What is a trade draft? What is the distinction between clean and documentary trade drafts? between D/A and D/P bills?
10. Why are bills of lading often attached to drafts that are to be presented for acceptance or payment?
11. What is a hypothecation certificate? How are such certificates used in foreign trade financing?

CHAPTER 25

FOREIGN EXCHANGE RATES

The foreign departments of commercial banks were described in Chapter 23 as merchants in foreign currencies whose "stock in trade" consists of demand deposit balances in these currencies on the books of banks in the foreign countries. Carrying forward this concept, we may say that foreign exchange rates are the *prices* at which the merchants are willing to buy and sell units of the foreign currencies. As in the purchase and sale of many commodities, many different prices or rates are quoted, and they vary from time to time, and sometimes, at least slightly, from bank to bank. In periods of brisk buying and selling, the whole array of rates on one or several of many foreign currencies may change hourly or even more frequently; and in other periods, rates may vary very little for several days or weeks. Banks set rates that vary according to whether they are buying or selling, the kinds of instruments they are dealing in, the face amounts of these instruments, the importance of the customers who are buying or selling, and whether the customers are buying or selling for immediate or future delivery.

CLASSIFICATION OF FOREIGN EXCHANGE RATES

As prices charged or paid in the different kinds of transactions in which foreign currencies are bought and sold, the principal classes of rates are the following: spot buying and selling rates, buying rates for time instruments, and forward buying and selling rates. However, for all these rates, a second round of classification is generally necessary: the making of a distinction between rates that are "free" and those that are "official."

Spot buying and selling rates

In rate designations, the terms *buying* and *selling* always refer to the position of banks—chiefly to that of the commercial banks as principal dealers in foreign currencies, but occasionally also to the position of central banks when they enter the market as buyers or sellers. A *buying rate* is, therefore, a price in domestic currency at which a bank will buy or will contract to buy each unit of a foreign currency; and a *selling rate* is a price in domestic currency at which it will sell or will contract to sell each unit of a foreign currency. A spot rate is a per-unit price paid or charged for a quantity of a foreign currency that is to be made available immediately and for which the payment or charge in domestic money must typically be made immediately also. Thus a *spot buying rate* is the amount of domestic money that a bank will pay at once for each unit of a foreign currency to be delivered to it at once by means of a banker's sight draft, a cable, or a telegraphic transfer; and a *spot selling rate* is the amount of domestic money that the bank demands as immediate payment per unit of a foreign currency that it makes immediately available by a sight draft, a cable, or a telegraphic transfer.

Among spot buying and selling rates, it is almost always necessary to draw additional distinctions based upon who the buyers and sellers of the foreign currencies are. In any foreign exchange market, spot rates of the central bank in transactions with the commercial banks will typically vary at least slightly from the spot rates that the commercial banks apply in transactions with one another, and the inter-commercial bank rates will typically, in turn, vary from the rates they pay and charge in transactions with nonbank customers—importers, exporters, international investors, tourists, and so on. For spot rates applied to transactions with nonbank customers, moreover, further small variations will most likely prevail based on the size of the individual transaction as well as the over-all importance of the customer as a user of the banks' services.

For transactions with given customers or given classes of customers, the banks' spot selling rates are always higher than their spot buying rates, the difference, or "spread," being the gross profit they expect to earn per unit on most of their transactions. Such spreads are generally quite small—even minute, some might say—since the banks seek large transactions and large volumes of transactions, rather than wide profit margins per unit, as the principal multiplier of profits. Not that the profit margin indicated by paired buying and selling quotations at a given hour are always exactly earned; when sales are made today of foreign currencies bought yesterday or the day before, the profit margin may be exceeded if rates have generally gone up, and it may be narrowed, eliminated, or made negative if rates have generally fallen.

Buying rates for time instruments

In selling foreign currencies, banks customarily sell only demand instruments—chiefly, of course, bankers' sight drafts, cables, and telegraphic transfers. They do not draw drafts on their deposit accounts with foreign correspondents payable in 30 or 60 days or at other future times; accordingly, they have no reason to quote selling rates for time instruments. But business corporations, individuals, and other entities draw many drafts on foreign banks payable at future times—in most instances, of course, as beneficiaries of commercial letters of credit opened by the foreign banks—and they usually wish to sell these immediately to their banks for domestic money. Hence the buying rates for time instruments or "bills."

Banks' buying rates for time instruments as quoted on any given day or at any given hour are always less than their spot buying rates quoted at the same time. The spreads increase with the lengths of the maturities of the time bills, since, as will be explained shortly, they are chiefly interest charges based on these maturities.

Forward rates

A *forward rate of exchange* is a rate quoted or agreed to by contract for the delivery of an amount of foreign currency at a designated future time, such as 30 or 60 days or 6 months. A forward selling rate quoted by a bank to a customer today is the rate at which it will immediately agree to deliver to him at the designated future time a banker's sight draft, cable, or telegraphic transfer payable in a foreign currency; and a forward buying rate is a rate at which it will contract at once with the customer to buy foreign currency instruments that he expects to have available for sale at the designated future time. In spot transactions, therefore, foreign currencies are transferred immediately for immediate cash payment in domestic money; while forward transactions are simply contracts for deliveries of foreign currency instruments and for payments at designated future times, but with the rates of exchange to be applied to these future deliveries and payments agreed to at once.

For some examples: If you sell a dollar traveler's check to a foreign bank, it will pay you a spot buying rate for a demand instrument. If you draw a 60-day draft on a foreign bank as authorized by a letter of credit it issued to you, and if you sell this draft to an American bank, it will pay you in dollars at a buying rate for time instruments. If you arrange with your bank for a telegraphic transfer payable at once in Montreal in Canadian dollars, you will pay your bank a spot selling rate for a demand instrument. If you expect to receive in 60 days a large dividend check from a foreign corporation payable in the foreign currency, and if you contract with your bank to sell this check to it *when you get it*, it will thus commit itself to pay in dollars at the forward buying rate it now quotes you. Finally, if you must make a large payment in a leading foreign country in 60 days, your bank will surely quote today a forward selling rate at which it would be willing to contract to deliver the foreign currency you will need to meet your obligation.

Free and official rates

The distinction between free and official rates of exchange always tends to be fuzzy, because *all* national governments intervene in their foreign exchange markets and because their intervention normally exerts important influences on rate levels. Indeed, it would be no exaggeration to say that all rates in all markets are unfree in varying degrees. Nevertheless, a useful distinction may be drawn, with *free rates* defined as rates arrived at without government dictation through bargaining among commercial banks and with their customers, and with *official rates* defined as rates set by government decree.

The principal reason for the fuzziness in the distinction is that two kinds of government-set rates of quite different character are called "official rates": (1) spot buying and selling rates at which the central bank of a country will intervene to prevent bargained rates from going beyond certain limits, and (2) rates at which buyers and sellers of foreign exchange instruments are required to do their buying and selling. Thus the spot rates in London on New York have recently stayed within the range $2.5471–$2.6643 for a pound, because tendencies of the rates to go outside these limits have been checked by actions of the Bank of England in the London market. As long as Britain honors its commitment of December 1971 to restrict rates to this range, we can thus say that $2.5471 is its "official" spot selling rate for dollars and that $2.6643 is its "official" spot buying rate. At the same time, however, we think of the exchange rates that prevail in the New York market as being freely bargained—as they surely are, but within the limits stated! On the other hand, some governments decree, for example, that proceeds from the sales of certain classes of exports must be sold to an officially designated institution at an officially designated rate— in which circumstance, the rate can hardly be said to be "free" in any sense.

Relationship among spot and time-bill rates

When exempt from fixing by government decree, all the exchange rates quoted at a given time in any country on a foreign currency tend to be closely related, and changes in these rates tend to occur, if at all, in unison in a manner such as will maintain their established relationship. Let us first consider relationships among spot buying and selling rates and time buying rates, leaving for later examination certain relationships between free and official rates and between spot and forward rates.

For the first type of relationship, as just mentioned, it should be helpful to refer to a typical array of spot buying and selling rates and buying rates for time instruments quoted in the New York market for large transactions in sterling, as follows:

SELLING		BUYING	
Cables	2.6050	Cables	2.6046
Demand	2.6050	Sight	2.6046
		30-day	2.5892
		60-day	2.5764
		90-day	2.5635

Spot Rates for Wire Transfers The selling rate for cable or telegraphic transfers in large transactions is the key rate quoted on any foreign currency—the rate on the basis of which all others are determined. The spread between this rate and the buying rate for wire transfers is the gross profit margin of the banks. In the rates on London listed above, the spread, it will be noticed, amounted to only ½₅ of a cent per pound.

When a bank sells a cable on London by drawing on its correspondent there, the payment is usually made by the correspondent on the following day, the selling bank's account being debited at that time. But when it buys a cable transfer in sterling, it will normally get credit in its London account on the following day. Hence interest or discount is not normally involved in the spread between the cable buying and selling rates—a circumstance justifying the description of the spread as purely profit margin. Indeed, a bank having no London balance could sell sterling cables of a given amount for delivery on the following day if at approximately the same time it could buy sterling cables of the same amount also for delivery on the following day. As its funds would not be "tied up" at all, it would have no reason to charge interest.

An American bank may buy cable transfers on London from other banks that have excess balances there or from American business firms and individuals that carry deposit balances at London banks.

Spot Rates for Sight Drafts The demand selling rate for sterling is the rate at which American banks are willing to sell sight drafts on their London balances; and the sight buying rate, that at which they are willing to buy paper instruments offered by American exporters and others payable on presentation at British banks.

Before airmail became widely available and fast, demand rates were usually lower than cable rates because of interest allowances. In selling a sterling draft, an American bank, though receiving payment in dollars at once, would not have its London balance charged for several days—for the time required for the steamship's crossing. In the meantime, it could use its London funds needed to meet the draft in short-term investments in the London money market. In fact, it might not have London funds at all at the time of selling the draft, expecting to meet it by cabling funds a few days later. In either event, as it could earn interest for the days involved, it could afford to sell the draft at a lower price than it would charge for a cable. Likewise, in buying demand instruments payable in London, it would pay in dollars at a lower rate than the cable buying rate to compensate for a loss of interest for the period from the time of the purchase of the instruments to the expected time of their presentation in London.

Because airmail nowadays makes it possible for payments on drafts to be made or received in London as quickly or almost as quickly as on cables, there is very often no difference between cable and demand rates, as in the rates listed above.

Time-Bill Buying Rates As mentioned previously, American banks do not sell drafts drawn on their foreign balances payable at future times—hence the absence from the list of any selling quotations of this kind. But they expect to have offered to them for purchase many bills drawn on foreign banks payable in the future, and they are quite willing to buy these as long as they can get them at rates that allow for the time differential. American exporters may be drawing drafts under letters of credit issued by British banks for the payment of sterling in 30, 60, and 90 days, and periods of other lengths, and they will want to sell these immediately for dollars; yet they can hardly expect to get the same dollar proceeds they would get if they had sight drafts to sell.

The time rates, however, are not fixed arbitrarily; they always bear a close arithmetical relationship to the selling rates for cables. The spread between any time buying rate for sterling and the cable selling rate consists, as it were, of three elements: the customary profit margin, discount from the date of purchase to the date of maturity (plus the 3 days of grace allowed in England), and the British stamp tax on time bills of one-twentieth of 1 percent of the face amount. The rate of discount used in computing the present value of a time bill payable in sterling is that prevailing in the British money market, since the buying bank will most probably sell the bill there as soon it has been accepted by the bank on which it is drawn. With the pertinent discount rate in the London market at 6 percent per annum, the computation of the 60-day buying rate listed above would be as follows:

Selling rate for cables		$2.6050
Less: Profit margin		0.0004
Sight buying rate		2.6046
Less:		
Discount for 63 days at 6%	$0.0269	
British stamp tax of ½₀ of 1%	0.0013	0.0282
Sixty-day buying rate		$2.5764

Small Transactions In handling small transactions in a foreign currency, banks usually pay a little less in buying and charge a little more in selling than they do in effecting larger transactions. Nevertheless, the differentials are usually quite moderate, except for transactions in foreign paper money and coin.

THE DETERMINATION OF RATE LEVELS

Supply and demand

As for prices in general, we may say that the levels of foreign exchange rates in the markets of countries that do not fix them by government decrees are determined by the interaction of the forces of supply and demand. In such a market, the supply of a given foreign currency is a schedule of the quantities that will be offered at various rates, and demand is a schedule of the quantities of the foreign currency that will be bought at various rates, so that market rates always tend to move to levels that will bring supply and demand into equilibrium.

But while ordinary supply and demand theory of this kind appears to be sufficient to explain why, for example, the New York cable selling rate on London may be $2.5875 at one time and $2.6212 at another time, it hardly suffices to explain why this rate is in close proximity to $2.6057 for quite lengthy periods of time. A crucial explanatory element is obviously missing, and this element is clearly the manipulation of supply and demand by governments and their central banks in their foreign exchange markets, even when their intervention may fall short of rate fixing by decree. Such intervention may range anywhere from a relatively simply altering of supply and demand schedules by a central bank's readiness to buy and sell foreign currencies at specified rates to the imposition of a great array of market regulations that have the effect, as it were, of making supply and demand whatever a government wishes them to be.

Exchange rates between Article VIII members of the International Monetary Fund

As we discussed in Chapter 5, each member country of the International Monetary Fund that has accepted responsibilities under Article VIII of the Bretton Woods Articles of Agreement—including all leading industrial countries that are members and many "less developed" members as well—has a commitment either (1) to redeem in gold quantities of its currency held by other members at its declared fixed gold value, or (2) to redeem these quantities in the currencies of the members requesting redemption if these members say that the currency to be redeemed was acquired in current account transactions or that their own currencies are needed for current account transactions. Also in Chapter 5 we learned that only the United States chose the first option but that in August 1971 it suspended the redeemability in gold of foreign-held dollars—thereby, in effect, switching to the second option at least temporarily; and that all other Article VIII members have all along chosen the second option. We saw that the second option amounts to the member's commitment to keep spot exchange rates in its market on all other currencies of Article VIII members within $2\frac{1}{4}$ percent of the pars of exchange as agreed to by the ten leading industrial member countries (the "group of ten") in December 1971 and as subsequently arranged among the currencies of other member countries.

Intervention by Central Banks   Accordingly, the commitments of all Article VIII members including the United States *require* their central banks to intervene in foreign exchange markets when spot exchange rates threaten to go beyond the permitted margin of $2\frac{1}{4}$ percent on either side of the pars of exchange. This amounts to saying that the central banks must take action to change supply and demand conditions in the exchange markets when supply and demand from other sources tend to push the exchange rates outside the permitted limits. Let us consider how all this works in relationship to spot rates for sterling in the New York market and in the spot rates for dollars in the London market. As set in the "realignment" of rates of December 1971, the permitted range for these rates became $2.5471–$2.6643. Such a range means that the Bank of England must stand ready to buy all dollars offered it at $2.6643 per pound, and to sell dollars without limit at $2.5471 per pound. To buy at $2.6643 and to sell at $2.5471 may sound like a losing proposition, but the Bank of England is smarter than that! The peculiar "sound" of the proposition originates because sterling rates in New York and dollar rates in London are both quoted in terms of dollars. In London, however, dollars are cheap at $2.6643, because the buyer gets $2.6643 for a pound instead of, say, $2.60 or $2.61, and obviously no commercial bank will sell dollars to the Bank of England at $2.6643 per pound if it can sell elsewhere at, say, $2.65 or even $2.6642. In the opposite direction, dollars in London are expensive at $2.5471, because that is all the buyer gets in exchange for his pound, whereas previously he may have gotten, say, $2.59 or $2.60; and obviously, again, no commercial bank will buy dollars from the Bank of England at $2.5471 if it can buy them elsewhere at, say, $2.55 or even $2.5472.

Sterling Rates in the New York Market   If a strong demand for sterling in the New York market threatens to exhaust the London deposits of New York banks, they will increase their spot selling rate. At the same time, they will try to buy additional supplies of sterling and will offer higher prices for it in view of the increase in the selling rate. But they will not pay more than $2.6643 for a spot pound since, in effect, they can buy any quantity of pounds from the Bank of England in exchange for dollars at that price.

If, on the other hand, American exporters are offering for sale in the New York market a large volume of sterling demand instruments, the New York banks will become more and more reluctant to buy. Accordingly, they will progressively decrease their spot buying rate, and because they are tending to accumulate more sterling than they want, their selling rate also. But they will not decrease their spot selling rate below $2.5471 since, in effect, they can sell any portion of their sterling holdings to the Bank of England at that price.

Dollar Rates in the London Market   When the demand for sterling in New York threatens to exhaust the London balances of the New York banks, they are likely to turn to the London banks with bids for additional supplies, offering dollars in payment. As the London banks buy more and more of the dollars thus offered, they will become increasingly reluctant to buy at the going rate; accordingly, they will reduce their spot buying rate on dollars. At the same time, therefore, that the spot selling rate on sterling in New York is being increased toward $2.6643, the spot buying rate on dollars in London is being *reduced toward $2.6643*. Pressures in one market are transmitted to the other, with the result that rates in the two markets tend always to vary in a "reciprocal" manner.

In a similar way, if the New York banks are accumulating more sterling than they want to hold, they most likely will offer the excess supplies to the London banks, asking for dollars in payment. This *new demand for dollars* in the London market will tend to drive the London spot buying rate on dollars *up* toward $2.5471. At the very time, therefore, that the excess supply of sterling instruments in the New York market is driving down the sterling rate toward $2.5471, the pressure of the increased demand for dollars in London will tend to drive the dollar rate there toward the same figure.

If spot rates in New York and London fail to move simultaneously in the reciprocal relationship just described, banks in either market will quickly effect transactions in both markets to earn a profit made possible by the discrepancy. Such "arbitrage" operations—to be discussed and illustrated a little later—will tend to restore the reciprocal relationship between the two sets of rates.

Sources of Dollars for England   Where does the United Kingdom get the dollars that the Bank of England sells when the London spot buying rate on New York approaches or reaches $2.5471? The question is obviously an important one for the proper functioning of the IMF system and specifically for the stability of exchange rates, since the Bank of England is supposed to be able to sell dollars "without limit" at $2.5471. It can create pounds without limit to buy dollars, but it cannot create dollars. If sales of whatever amount of dollars it happens to be holding are insufficient to prevent pressure on the London-New York rate toward $2.54, it surely must have ways of acquiring additional dollars. The major procedures by which it may acquire dollars are the following:

1. By buying them from the IMF or the U.S. Treasury for gold.
2. By activating its "swap lines" with the United States, ostensibly buying dollars in direct exchange for pounds, but essentially borrowing dollars with an obligation to repay in not more than 1 year.
3. By using its gold-tranche drawing rights to buy dollars from the IMF, assuming that it has not already exhausted these rights.
4. In the absence of gold-tranche drawing rights, by using its credit-tranche drawing rights at the IMF to buy dollars—but such "rights" are available only with the consent of the IMF and subject to whatever stipulations it may impose concerning Britain's internal monetary and fiscal policies; and in any case, their use typically requires "repurchases" within 3 to 5 years.
5. By offering SDRs to the United States for dollars but subject to our willingness to accept the SDRs.
6. By getting the IMF to designate one or more other member countries to accept its SDRs in exchange for dollars or other convertible currencies.
7. By using its holdings of convertible currencies other than the dollar (possibly acquired by step 6) to buy dollars in the New York market or in other foreign exchange markets—but an unlikely procedure, since buying dollars in any foreign exchange market, because of the reciprocity of rates among markets, would tend to increase the upward pressure on the dollar rate in London, instead of relieving this pressure.

Monetary Reserve Drains and Reactions   If the United Kingdom were to take step 1, 3, 5, 6, or 7, or some combination of these steps, it would be using its international monetary reserves, and it surely would not want to continue along this line for a prolonged period. If a substantial amount of these reserves were being lost without relieving the upward pressure on the dollar rate, it would surely seek diligently for other means of relief. At the least, it would probably try to attract an inflow of foreign investment funds by increasing interest rates, especially by increases in the "bank rate," that is, the discount rate of the Bank of England. It would be likely to be much concerned about the apparent unattractiveness of its export prices in relationship to comparable commodity prices in other markets and about the apparent attractiveness to its own people of import prices in relationship to the prices of comparable goods produced at home. Thus it might decide to promote exports by paying export subsidies to domestic producers, to curb imports by imposing or increasing tariff rates, and to try to hold down all prices by introducing or intensifying an "incomes policy," which is to say, by controlling wages and prices. And if the situation continued to worsen, it might even be tempted to impose restrictions on current account transactions in its foreign exchange market itself.

All this does not mean that every time the Bank of England or other central bank must intervene in the market to prevent rates on the dollar or on other currencies from rising above permitted limits, additional emergency measures of the kinds described are likely also to be necessary. Typically, the need for intervention by the central bank is occasioned by purely temporary developments that are soon reversed by developments in the opposite direction in the ordinary course of private international business transactions. But the description of possible emergency measures in the preceding paragraph was designed to lay a foundation, as the lawyers say, for two propositions: (1) that governments and central banks may and do take actions to alter supply and demand conditions in foreign exchange markets other than simple offers to buy and sell foreign currencies; and (2) that substantial losses from a country's international monetary reserves tend to force it to adopt restrictive policies, as was generally the result of substantial losses of gold in the functioning of the old gold standard.

Devaluation as a remedy   With respect to the second of these propositions, however, we should observe that the present international monetary system of the IMF and its members has an "out" for countries that continue to suffer serious drains from their monetary reserves without prospects for reversal through developments in the ordinary course of international business—an "out" that proponents of the old gold standard were inclined to abhor. In the IMF system, the remedy is devaluation. If, in terms of the illustration, England were to lose more and more of its monetary reserves, it could hardly avoid the realization that it had got itself into a state of "fundamental disequilibrium" in its balance-of-payments position. And surely it would conclude, however reluctantly and however embarrassing it might be, that an appropriate remedy would be a devaluation of the pound—a reduction in its par value in terms of the dollar to perhaps $2.40 or $2.20.

Despite reluctance and embarrassment, devaluation would surely have attractions as an appropriate remedy, since, at one stroke, England's export prices would become much cheaper to foreign buyers and the prices of foreign goods would become much more expensive for British buyers, so that a big improvement in current account could be anticipated. And prospects for a much improved British economic performance might also promote an inflow of foreign investment funds seeking a share in the enhanced prospects for profits and other kinds of income.

Transactions with the IMF   Still in terms of the illustration, we must inquire what would be likely to happen if England were to take steps 4 and 6 in the forgoing list of ways to acquire dollars—were it to go to the IMF to use its credit-tranche drawing rights to buy dollars or some of its SDRs to buy dollars or other convertible currencies. By either route, England would be likely to receive advice from the IMF to adopt or intensify restrictive monetary and fiscal policies and possibly to adopt or intensify an "incomes policy." By way of the credit-tranche route, moreover, the IMF might stipulate that England *must* tighten its policies of these kinds as a condition for the privilege of buying dollars. But England would hardly receive advice or stipulations from the IMF to adopt export subsidies and higher tariffs, since that would be quite contrary to the spirit of the Bretton Woods Agreement. And especially would it receive no advice or stipulations to impose restrictions on current account transactions in its foreign exchange market, because such impositions by leading member countries would threaten the breakdown of the whole IMF system. On the other hand, if Britain were continuing to lose large amounts of its international monetary reserves and, at the same time, drawing heavily on its credit tranches (with the IMF's consent, of course), the IMF might be earlier than the British monetary authorities in recognizing the need of a devaluation of the pound and in so recommending.

All of which means that a high degree of stability in exchange rates close to pars of exchange is a major objective of the IMF system but not an exclusive one. The economic welfare of member countries is not to be sacrificed by efforts to maintain such a degree of stability in the face of powerful forces of disequilibrium. That is why the Bretton Woods Agreement contains provisions for changes in par values and pars of exchange.

Central Bank Intervention on the Buying Side When the customers of a country's commercial banks offer them much larger quantities of a foreign currency than other customers want to buy from them, they lower their buying rates because of their increased reluctance to buy, and at the same time, they lower their selling rates because of their greater anxiety to sell. And further reductions in these rates will surely be made if the flood of the foreign currency continues—perhaps to or closely approaching the level at which the central bank must come into the market to buy excess supplies of the foreign currency in order to fulfill its government's commitment to keep the rate within $2\frac{1}{4}$ percent of the par of exchange.

Such buying by the central bank, if it becomes necessary, is not likely to be at all difficult, since central banks generally have very great capacities to create domestic money to be paid for that which they want to buy. Nor would it appear to be unpleasant for the country to increase its international monetary reserves by receiving a convertible foreign currency in exchange for domestic money. If it did not want to hold large supplies of the particular foreign currency that had been flooding its market, it could presumably exchange it for more acceptable forms of international reserve assets. Were the currency in question the United States dollar, for example, the foreign country might ask us to take back some of its excess accumulations of dollars in exchange for some of our SDR holdings, or use them to buy back its own currency from the IMF,[1] thereby reducing any credit-tranche re-purchase obligations it might have or expanding its gold-tranche position.

But monetary reserves are by no means unlimitedly desirable. According to the theory of the old gold standard, inflows of gold, by expanding bank reserves, were expected to lead to expansions in domestic money supplies with upward pressures on price levels resulting, and such an inflationary outcome remains possible in the IMF system. The central bank of the foreign country previously referred to would be creating reserves in domestic money for its commercial banks in buying their excess supplies of dollars, and it could anticipate more demand deposit creation by them with attendant inflationary pressures were it not to immobilize the increased reserves. Although its immobilization powers might be adequate, it would still have difficult problems to cope with, because of the usual uncertainties about how far it should go in using its money-control instruments and about the likely effects of any given money-control action.

Moreover, it would doubtless find it necessary to multiply its restrictive actions should a flood of dollars or other foreign currencies into its market continue, and after a time, indeed, it and its government would doubtless be forced to the conclusion that the country's balance-of-payments position was one of "fundamental disequilibrium." They would surely recognize that its export prices were too cheap and foreign goods too expensive at exchange rates within $2\frac{1}{4}$ percent of the existing pars, although they might reject the remedy that the IMF system envisages for such a situation, namely, a re-valuation of the country's monetary unit—an increase in its par value in terms of gold.

Exchange rates between other countries

Because the Article VIII members of the IMF bind themselves to avoid imposing "restrictions on the making of payments and transfers for current international transactions," except by special permission of the fund, their actions to influence exchange rates, as we have noted, are chiefly buying and selling interventions by their central banks to keep the rates within the permitted range. From time to time, and for considerable periods of time, some of the Article VIII members have obtained the IMF's permission for some restrictions on payments on current account, particularly limitations on spending by their peoples on travel in foreign countries; and almost all of these members have continuously imposed restrictions of varying scopes on the buying and selling of foreign currencies in their markets for international capital transactions—restrictions for which approval by the IMF is not required.

On the other hand, members of the IMF that have not made the

---

[1]Provided that the "buy-back" with dollars would not cause the fund's holdings of dollars to exceed 75 percent of the United States quota.

commitments of Article VIII in its Articles of Agreement reserve the right to impose many kinds of restrictions on current account transactions in their foreign exchange markets as well as on capital transactions. These are called Article XIV members, and they comprise a large majority of the IMF's membership, although none of these members is described as an "industrial country." And of course, nonmembers of the IMF, including Switzerland and all the "Iron Curtain" countries except Yugoslavia, are not bound at all by its rules.

Article XIV Members   In general, the Article XIV members of the IMF reserve rights to restrict current account transactions in their foreign exchange markets, because their international monetary reserves are slim and because they have considerable difficulties in getting sufficient proceeds from export sales and inflows of foreign investment funds to pay for that which they classify as "essential" imports and to meet obligations on outstanding external debts. Accordingly, their interventions in the foreign exchange markets, aside from controls on capital account transactions, are chiefly directed to the promotion of export sales and to reducing imports of "nonessential" goods.

But there is a wide range in the severity of the balance-of-payments difficulties with which the Article XIV members as a general class must grapple and, therefore, a wide range in the scope of their interventions in their foreign exchange markets. Many of these countries have set par values for their monetary units in terms of the United States dollar and generally succeed in keeping their exchange rates for current account transactions within the 2¼ percent range with the assistance of relatively mild measures, such as the payment of export subsidies and the imposition of import taxes, tariffs, and "surcharges." Others with declared par values are able to keep exchange rates for most current account transactions within the 2¼ percent limit by means of more elaborate systems of exchange control. Still others have been unable to make their declared par values very meaningful in relationship to the exchange rates prevailing in their markets, the severity of their balance-of-payments difficulties robbing them of the capacity to make these par values meaningful. Finally, some twenty members of the IMF have not bothered to set par values at all for their monetary units[2] in the realization that, given the breadth and tightness of their controls, such values would be fictitious.

Exchange Rationing   Aside from payments of export subsidies and imposition of import taxes, tariffs, and surcharges, "exchange rationing" is the most common procedure of exchange control. It is popular because it can be

---

[2]International Monetary Fund, *Twenty-first Annual Report on Exchange Restrictions,* Washington, D.C., 1970, pp. 568–572.

applied limitedly or extensively depending upon the gravity of the controlling country's balance-of-payments difficulties. In a system of exchange rationing, persons and organizations in the controlling country's jurisdiction are required to sell all or portions of the foreign currency proceeds of their international transactions to a designated agency, such as the central bank, specified commercial banks, or an exchange control board or commission. By government direction, then, the designated agency sells the foreign currencies thus accumulated according to a system of priorities, making them generously available to importers of "essential" goods and obligors on external debts on which the government wants no defaults to occur, and only sparingly, if at all, to other would-be spenders.

If a country's balance-of-payments difficulties are great, it will probably require that the foreign currency proceeds of all classes of international transactions be sold to the designated agency; if they are moderate, it may stipulate that only varying percentages of the proceeds of different classes of transactions be so allocated. In systems of partial rationing, the unrestricted proceeds of transactions may be sold in the "free market," so that a controlled market and a free market exist side by side. In a system in which rationing is complete, it is necessary for all prospective users of foreign currencies to apply to the designated agency for whatever supplies they need; but in a partial system, the designated agency normally undertakes to supply exchange only to people whose requirements are regarded as essential, leaving all other prospective users to buy their supplies, if possible, in the free market.

Official Rates   A system of rationing requires the setting of official rates of exchange at which the designated agency will buy and sell the foreign currencies that the regulations require to be turned over to it. There may be only one spot buying rate and one spot selling rate, with the selling rate at least slightly higher than the buying rate to cover the administrative expenses of directing the rationing system; but it is common practice for controlling countries to have several spot buying and selling rates in effect simultaneously. By setting different rates for various kinds of transactions, a country can produce extraordinary effects in its balance of payments —much the same kinds of effects that result from changes in tariff rates and the granting of export subsidies. It can strongly encourage the importation of essential commodities by selling the requisite exchange at rates substantially below the rates at which it sells for other purposes, and it can sharply discriminate against importers of nonessential goods and services by setting extraordinarily high rates for the exchange they would need. In a similar manner, it can promote the exportation of goods in plentiful supply by paying relatively high rates for the proceeds of such exports, or it can discourage exports of scarce goods by stipulating only a low buying rate for the proceeds of their sale abroad.

Even where a system of exchange rationing is only partial, a government can exercise major influence on the character and volume of international transactions by means of rate arrangements. This is so because rates in the controlling country's free market are almost invariably materially higher than the official rates designated by the government. If the government wants to encourage the exportation of certain kinds of goods, it simply rules that only a small percentage of the proceeds must be sold to the designated agency at the relatively low official rate, the remainder being disposable in the free market at the higher rate prevailing there; and for exports of goods in scarce supply, it stipulates that a large percentage of the proceeds must be allocated to the designated agency, leaving only a small proportion to be sold in the free market. Likewise, the importation of essential goods can be promoted by providing the full amount of exchange needed at the relatively low official rate, while the importation of non-essentials can be kept at a meager level simply by a refusal to allocate exchange at the official rate to their prospective importers—making it necessary for them to pay the higher rate of the free market.

A country that establishes—or, at least, countenances—a multiplicity of rates in its controlled and free markets is said to engage in "multiple currency practices." The situation is much as it would be if it had several different monetary units in use simultaneously—one unit to be used to buy goods of one classification, another those of a second, another those of a third, and so on.

Import Quotas and Licenses For maximum effectiveness, exchange rationing regulations are often coupled with systems of import quotas and licenses. Exchange rationing, as such, is concerned with means of payment, but import quotas and licenses reach directly, as it were, the goods to be transported. When a system of import quotas and licenses is in effect, a designated government department, board, or commission must decide what quantities of various kinds of commodities are to be imported over a period of time (the quotas being based closely on anticipated export sales of domestic products), what foreign services must be paid for (also depending upon projected export sales), what countries are to be favored when purchases are arranged (this depending very largely on the areas in which exported goods are being sold), and what importers at home are to do the buying abroad. Import licenses are then granted according to the established quotas, and goods are not permitted to enter the country unless they have been licensed, nor can the importers obtain the foreign currencies to make payment unless they have previously obtained licenses. In this way, people who want to import goods classified as nonessential can be frozen out, while in a system without import licensing, they might be able to get the foreign currencies they want in a "black market."

Blocked Accounts and Payments Agreements Although there are many other procedures of exchange control, brief descriptions here of "blocked accounts" and "bilateral payments agreements" should be sufficiently illustrative.

Blocked accounts are chiefly deposit accounts at banks in a controlling country in the names of nonresidents, and they are primarily employed to control international capital transactions. If you own real estate in the blocking country or securities issued by its governmental bodies or enterprises, you will generally be permitted to sell these assets there but not to convert the proceeds into the currency of your own country. The proceeds go into a blocked account on which you may draw to reinvest in other properties and securities in the blocking country, probably to meet your expenditures as a tourist there, and possibly, in relatively small amounts from year to year, to pay for goods imported from there. If you do not want to use your blocked balance to reinvest in the blocking country, travel as a tourist there, or import goods from there to the extent permitted, you will probably be allowed to sell it to other nonresidents for whatever kind and amount of money they are willing to pay; but these buyers of your blocked balance will be subject to the same restrictions in its use that previously applied to you. In some blocking systems, rent, interest, dividends, and other kinds of income earned on assets held in the blocking country must also be paid into the blocked accounts, with similar restrictions on spending. Thus current account payments of these kinds due from the blocking country as well as capital transactions are brought under control.

Payments agreements are "bilateral" because they are arrangements between two countries for the mutual control of trade and service transactions and related payments between them, and sometimes with certain kinds of capital transactions also arranged. Many payments agreements are essentially barter arrangements, with one country saying to the other, in effect, that in the course of a year we will buy such-and-such quantities of goods of such-and-such kinds from you if, in the same year, you will buy certain prescribed quantities of prescribed goods from us. For payments for the goods in both directions, a rate of exchange is arranged, but it may be quite artificial in the sense of having no close relationship to the rates quoted in the foreign exchange markets of the two countries on each other's currency. In some instances, indeed, payments between the two countries are not made physically, so to speak, across their boundary lines. Importers in country A make payment in A currency into an account at A's central bank for their imports from B, and A's exporters to B get payment out of this same account; and payments are made and received in country B in the same way. Such arrangements are often called "clearing agreements," although they are essentially only a variation of payments agreements.

Switzerland and the Iron Curtain Countries   Switzerland deserves special mention as the only major industrial country outside the Iron Curtain that is not a member of the IMF. Nevertheless, it cooperates rather closely with the IMF. It is especially celebrated as the haven of huge amounts of foreign funds that are placed with Swiss banks in secret accounts and that these banks invest for the account holders in securities issued, for the most part, in other countries—to a large extent, no doubt, in the countries from which the foreign funds originate. Switzerland has a declared gold value for its franc and therefore pars of exchange with the United States dollar and other currencies of IMF members that have established par values in terms of gold or of the dollar. For the most part, foreign exchange transactions in the Swiss market are uncontrolled, and the Swiss National Bank keeps spot exchange rates on currencies of Article VIII members of the IMF within a range of approximately 2 percent on either side of the pars of exchange.

Because trade, service, and capital transactions among Iron Curtain countries are closely controlled by the governments of these countries, and because, indeed, many of these transactions are directly undertaken or at least arranged by governments, declared values of currencies and posted exchange rates tend to have only minor significance. Many of the transactions of these countries with one another as well as with countries outside the Iron Curtain are arranged on the basis of payment agreements in which, as mentioned previously, agreed-upon exchange rates may be quite artificial. In other transactions with the "free world," the Iron Curtain countries generally sell for free-world currencies and then use these currencies to buy whatever they want to buy or are permitted to buy. In some instances, as in the cases of the Soviet Union and mainland China, gold is sold in European markets for additional supplies of free-world currencies needed for "essential" purchases.

EXCHANGE ARBITRAGE

The rates of exchange between any two currencies in which transactions are freely permitted always tend to be reciprocal. If the spot selling rate in New York on London is $2.60, the spot selling rate for dollars in London should be the same; that is, if a pound costs $2.60 in New York, a dollar in London should cost $100/260$ of a pound, or about 38.5 pence.

In the event that exchange rates between two money centers are sluggish in maintaining or regaining their reciprocal relationship, they are brought into line, in the normal operations of free exchange markets, as a result of the operations of arbitragers.

Arbitrage is a simultaneous operation in two or more markets to gain a profit made possible because of discrepancies in prices or rates. Most arbitrage transactions in foreign exchange are affected by the foreign departments of commercial banks with the assistance of their correspondents abroad. As speed is essential, only cable or other wire transfers are employed. In arbitrage operations, the banks are often content with profits as low as $\frac{1}{20}$ of 1 percent, for even a rate of profit of such a minute size can yield good returns on voluminous transactions.

Two-point arbitrage

To begin, let us say that at a given time the cable selling rate in New York on London and the cable selling rate in London and New York are both at $2.60. Then let us assume that, as a result of a sudden increase in demand for sterling, the New York rate on London goes to $2.6025, with the London rate of New York remaining at its former level. An American bank would immediately see an opportunity for a profit. It would sell, say, £100,000 of cables in New York at $2.6025, receiving in payment $260,250; and at the same time, it would instruct its correspondent in London to sell $260,000 of dollar cables at the current rate of $2.60, receiving in payment £100,000. The pounds received in London would cover those sold in New York, and $260,000 of the amount received in New York would cover the dollar cables sold in London. The bank would thus have a profit of $250 less the expenses of the transactions.

Were the London selling rate on New York to go to $2.6025, with the New York rate on London remaining unchanged, the bank would buy £100,000 in New York at a total cost of $260,000, at the same time instructing its London correspondent to buy $260,250 of cables in London. As the latter would cost £100,000, the arbitrage operation would yield, like the first, a gross profit of $250.

The opportunity to gain a profit by means of arbitrage operations does not remain available indefinitely; the operation itself tends to cause the original discrepancy to disappear. In reference to the first illustration, the sale of £100,000 in New York would tend to cause the New York rate on London to fall, and the sale of dollar cables in London would tend to cause the London rate on New York to fall also. Hence a new reciprocal rate, perhaps at about $2.6013, would quickly tend to result.

Three-point arbitrage

It is sometimes possible for arbitragers to gain a profit by operating simultaneously in three or more markets. Assume that, at a certain time, the cable and telegraphic selling rates quoted in New York, London, and Paris are as follows:

New York on London	$2.6057
London on New York	$2.6057
London on Paris	13.3308 francs
Paris on London	13.3308 francs
New York on Paris	19.5465 cents
Paris on New York	5.1160 francs

As the rates are in exact reciprocal relationship to one another, no opening for an arbitrage profit exists at the moment. But suppose that the rate in London on Paris—a "cross rate" from the standpoint of Americans —goes to 13.3315 francs. An American bank would buy, say, £100,000 of sterling cables for $260,570, and its correspondent in London would use the £100,000 to buy 1,333,150 francs. The American bank would sell 1,333,150 francs in New York at 19.5465 cents, receiving in payment $260,262. The sterling and franc transactions would obviously cancel out, and the dollars received in the sale of the francs would cover the cost of the pounds and leave a gross profit of $262 for the bank.

FORWARD CONTRACTS

The foreign departments of commercial banks generally stand ready to buy and sell the currencies of leading industrial countries, not only for immediate delivery and payment, but also for "forward" delivery and payment. A forward transaction is a contract by which a bank agrees to buy or sell, at a rate designated at once, a specified amount of a foreign currency to be delivered and paid for at a specified future time.

Forward contracts are sought by importers, exporters, and short-term investors in foreign securities as a means of avoiding the risks of fluctuations in exchange rates. For illustration, assume that an American importer is considering a purchase of merchandise in England at a cost of £30,000. The current rate of exchange in New York on London is, $2.5471, but the importer is to be allowed 60 days to pay, and he has no assurance that at the expiration of that period the rate will still be $2.5471. Should the rate have risen to $2.6643 by the end of the 60 days, the merchandise would cost $3516 more than originally anticipated. If, however, the importer gets a bank to agree to sell him £30,000 in 60 days at $2.5471, he need not worry about rate fluctuations.

Likewise, an American exporter who is to receive a payment of £30,000 from a British firm in 90 days would probably want to know immediately how many dollars he will get for the sterling. If the spot buying rate in the United States were now close to $2.6643, he might hope to get approximately $79,929. But fluctuations in rates in the 90-day period might cut that amount—and his gross profit—by as much as $3516. To avoid the risks of possible rate fluctuations, therefore, he would be likely to want his bank to agree to buy the £30,000 in 90 days at a rate set immediately.

The principal reason why people make short-term investments in foreign money markets is because interest rates there are higher than at home. But they realize that they may not earn this interest-rate differential—that, indeed, they may earn less than at home—should the rate of exchange at which they can sell the foreign currencies to be received at the maturity of their investments be materially less than the rate paid when the investments were made. Ordinarily, therefore, they will make such foreign investments only if, at the time of investment, they are able to make contracts with banks for the forward delivery of the foreign funds to be received at maturity *at rates that will not, in effect, erase the interest-rate differential.*

The risks of fluctuations in exchange rates against which forward contracts give protection are really much greater than indicated by the figures used in the two illustrations. The figures are perfectly valid for any period during which the United Kingdom continues its policy of keeping the sterling-dollar rate within the range $2.5471–$2.6643; but it is surely *possible* for that country, within any 60- or 90-day period, to discontinue its policy of pegging the rate. Moreover, it is *possible* for the United Kingdom to change the par value of the pound in terms of the United States dollar in such a period—as it did in September 1959 when the par, as measured in dollars, was reduced from $4.03 to $2.80, and as it did again in November 1967 when the par was further reduced to $2.40.

Position of the banks

In negotiating forward contracts, the banks would be assuming the risks of rate fluctuations if they, in turn, did not take steps to avoid or neutralize them. It is their customary practice to hedge their forward commitments, and their preferred method of hedging is to balance forward purchases and sales. A bank that sells £30,000 for delivery in 90 days at $2.60 can avoid the risks of rate fluctuations by negotiating, at the same time, a 90-day forward purchase of £30,000 at, say, $2.5996. If, at the expiration of 90 days, the spot selling rate is actually $2.61 and the spot buying rate is $2.6096, the bank "loses" 1 cent a pound on its forward selling contract, but "gains" 1 cent a pound on its forward buying contract. The loss and gain are, of course, purely theoretical, since the bank earns a gross profit at its usual rate of about $\frac{1}{25}$ of a cent per pound on the £30,000 bought and sold.

The banks may also protect themselves by matching their forward contracts with spot purchases and sales. A bank that contracts to deliver £10,000 in 60 days may find itself unable to hedge by negotiating a forward contract to buy an equal sum. But it can buy £10,000 in the spot market and perhaps "swap" this for a forward contract with another bank that is "short on spot" and "long on forward," or if a swap cannot be arranged, it can instruct its British correspondent to invest the sterling temporarily in British money market securities, thus ensuring its capacity to make delivery in 60 days. A temporary diversion of the funds to the British money market would avoid, of course, a loss of interest, such as would result were the sterling to be held idle.

In providing facilities by which importers, exporters, and short-term investors are enabled to avoid the risks of fluctuations in exchange rates, and in attempting to avoid the risks themselves, the banks are assisted, as it were, by speculators. Speculators in foreign exchange are not motivated by any altruistic regard for the banks, but they deliberately assume risks in the expectation of profiting from rate fluctuations. The "bull" in the foreign exchange market expects the rates on foreign money centers to rise, while the "bear" expects them to fall, and both are willing to risk their funds on the accuracy of their forecasts. Suppose, for example, that a speculator believes that he will be able to sell sterling in the spot market 60 days hence at $2.6050 per pound, and he finds a bank that is quoting a 60-day forward selling rate of $2.60. He is happy to contract with the bank for a forward delivery at $2.60, for he expects to be able to sell at a profit of ½ cent per pound the sterling to be delivered to him. The bank that agrees to make forward delivery may have just contracted with an exporter to buy the same amount of sterling at $2.5996 60 days hence, so that, by means of the forward sale to the speculator, it hedges its forward purchase. The exporter avoids the risks of rate fluctuations, as does the bank, but the speculator accepts them willingly.

Forward rates

The rates quoted for forward contracts may be the same as the spot rates, or they may be at "premiums" or at "discounts" in relationship to the spot rates, that is, higher or lower than the spot rates by margins so described. Just as the spot rates at any time vary according to the supply of and demand for foreign currencies for immediate delivery, so also do forward rates fluctuate with the volume of contracts calling for forward sales and the volume calling for forward purchases. If many American exporters are expecting to receive sterling payments in 60 days and are negotiating contracts with their banks to sell the sterling when received, and if many investors are in the market for similar contracts in connection with investments in the British money market that they are contemplating, the forward rates on sterling tend to go to discount levels. On the other hand, if many American importers must make payments in sterling in 60 days and are contracting to buy sterling for delivery at that time, the forward rates tend to go to premium levels.

Forward Premiums On the whole, however, the forces of supply and demand that determine spot rates are the same forces that determine forward rates (always allowing for central bank intervention to keep spot rates within certain limits), so that it is ordinarily impossible for one set of rates to vary greatly from the other. The extremely close relationship that exists between the spot and forward markets, and the choice many buyers and sellers have of negotiating their transactions in either market or of "playing" one market against the other, preclude extreme spreads between spot and forward rates—preclude, that is to say, excessive premiums and discounts in forward rates. An American importer who has a payment of £10,000 to make to a British creditor in 60 days can buy that sum in the spot market and hold it for 60 days or contract with his bank for a delivery of that amount in 60 days. If the bank's spot selling rate is $2.60, the importer knows that he can meet his obligation at a cost of $26,000 minus the interest to be earned on a £10,000 investment in the British money market for 60 days. Would he be willing to contract at $2.62 for a forward delivery? The forward contract would cost him $200 more than the spot purchase, but he would have the use of $26,000 as working capital in his business operations for 60 days. Accordingly, he would have to weigh his decision on the basis of his need for working capital, his capacity to borrow in the United States, the interest rate he would have to pay on such borrowings, the interest rate to be earned on British money market investments, and of course, the $200 premium for the forward contract. Should he decide to buy spot, his purchase would tend to drive up the spot rate, and his withdrawal as a demander in the forward market would tend to cause the forward rate to fall. Should many importers be making decisions of this kind, therefore, the spread between the spot and forward rates would very likely be narrowed.

A forward premium might also be regarded as excessive by speculators, so that they would hasten to sell the foreign currency for future delivery. In terms of the foregoing illustration, they might be willing to contract to sell large amounts of sterling at $2.62, expecting to be able to cover these forward sales by buying the sterling at a lower price in the spot market 60 days hence. Such forward sales of speculators would also tend to cause the forward premium to decline, thereby narrowing the gap between forward and spot rates.

Finally, the operations of the commercial banks generally contribute to the elimination of excessive premiums. Believing the forward premium to be excessive, banks would be inclined to sell liberal amounts of the foreign currency for forward delivery, and inasmuch as they would probably not be able to hedge their forward sales with forward purchases, they would very likely buy the foreign currency in the spot market to ensure their capacity to make delivery. The foreign currency bought in the spot market could be invested temporarily in the foreign money market, so that the willingness of the banks to undertake this kind of transaction would depend, as in the case of the importer mentioned above, upon prevailing rates of interest in the foreign money market by comparison with those obtaining at home. In any event, the purchases by the banks in the spot market and their sales in the forward market would also tend to narrow the spread between the two sets of rates.

Forward Discounts Excessive discounts in rates for forward contracts are also likely to set in motion various kinds of operations that will narrow them. Exporters who have accepted time bills in their possession have the choice of selling them immediately at the banks' buying rates for such bills or of holding them to maturity and contracting with the banks for the delivery of the foreign currency when it is received. If the forward discount should appear to the exporters to be excessive, they would very likely sell their bills at once, and the banks, in buying, would be inclined to reduce their spot rates because they would be likely to resell the bills immediately in the foreign money market and thus get an increased supply of the foreign currency. At the same time, the withdrawal of the exporters as suppliers from the forward market would tend to cause the forward rates to rise.

Should speculators believe forward discounts to be excessive, they would be anxious to buy foreign currencies for future delivery, expecting to be able to sell the currencies when delivered at better prices in the spot market. Their forward purchases would also tend to cause forward rates to rise.

Finally, the commercial banks would be encouraged to negotiate forward purchase contracts in liberal amounts, at the same time permitting their current foreign balances to fall below the customary levels, since they would anticipate replenishing these balances when taking delivery on the forward contracts. Their willingness to sell beyond normal limits in the spot market and to buy liberally in the forward market would exert a further influence toward causing spot rates to fall and forward rates to rise, thereby reducing the discount on the forward rates.

FOR REVIEW

1. What is the distinction between a spot buying rate for a foreign currency and a time-bill buying rate? Why are there no quotations for time-bill selling rates?
2. From whose standpoint are exchange rates said to be "buying rates" and "selling rates"?
3. What accounts for the spread between the cable buying rate and the cable selling rate for a foreign currency? between the cable selling rate and the buying rate for 60-day bills?
4. In what respect at the present time are quotations in the London market on the United States dollar "free"? In what respect can they be said to be "official"?
5. Why is it said that there is a great difference between official rates quoted in some countries and official rates quoted in others?
6. How realistic is it to say that the level of the dollar-sterling exchange rate is determined by the forces of supply and demand?
7. How does the Bank of England keep the sterling-dollar rate within the range $2.5471–$2.6643? Why does it want to do this?
8. What are the several ways that the Bank of England can get dollars needed to keep the sterling-dollar rate from fluctuating too widely?

9. Under what circumstances might the United Kingdom decide that it ought to reduce the par value of the pound from its present level of $2.6057?
10. Do all members of the IMF have commitments to keep their exchange rates from fluctuating beyond the 2¼ percent range? Explain.
11. What is the purpose of a system of exchange rationing? How does such a system operate?
12. As means of exchange control, what are blocked accounts? bilateral payments agreements?
13. What is exchange arbitrage? Why are arbitrage transaction effected? What influence do they tend to have on exchange rates?
14. What is the distinction between spot rates of exchange and forward rates?
15. What motives do people have for buying foreign exchange for forward delivery? selling for forward delivery?
16. What actions do banks take to avoid risks of loss when they buy and sell foreign currencies for forward delivery?

PROBLEMS

1. From January 1, 1960, to August 10, 1969, the official value of the French franc was 20.255 United States cents.

    A. In this period, what was the par of exchange in Paris on New York, that is, the official value of the dollar in terms of francs (to four decimal places)?
    B. On August 10, 1969, France devaluated the franc by 11.1111 percent. What was the resulting new official value of the franc in United States cents? the new official value of the dollar in terms of francs (to four decimal places)?
    C. Assume that at a certain time after August 10, 1969, the franc was selling in New York at 18 cents and the dollar was selling in Paris at 5.53 francs. Indicate how an arbitrage profit could have been made on a $180,000 transaction, and determine how much the gross profit would have amounted to, that is, the profit before expense deductions.
    D. Assume the same facts and instructions as for C except that the dollar was selling in Paris at 5.57 cents.

2. From March 6, 1961, to October 26, 1969, the official value of the West German mark was 25 United States cents, but on October 26, 1969, Germany revaluated the mark upward by 9.2896 percent.

    A. What was the resulting new official value of the mark in United

States cents (to four decimal places)? What was the official value of the dollar in Frankfort before and after the revaluation?

B. Assume that at a certain time shortly after the revaluation of October 26, 1969, the mark was selling in New York at 27.33 cents and that the dollar was selling in Frankfort at 3.67 marks. Indicate how an arbitrage profit could have been made on a $100,000 transaction, and determine how much the gross profit would have amounted to.

C. Assume the same facts and instructions as for B except that the mark was selling in New York at 27.22 cents.

3. Early in 1971, the pars of exchange between New York, Brussels, and Rome at exact reciprocal levels were as follows:

New York on Brussels	2 cents
Brussels on New York	50 francs
New York on Rome	0.16 francs
Rome on New York	625 lire
Brussels on Rome	0.08 franc
Rome on Brussels	12.5 lire

Assume that a given time in this period exchange rates in the three markets were actually at these levels but that, because of a sudden demand for Belgian francs in Rome, the rate on the franc there went to 12.6 lire. Indicate how an arbitrage profit could have been made on a series of transactions involving $100,000, and determine how much the gross profit would have amounted to.

CHAPTER 26

CURRENT INTERNATIONAL
MONETARY PROBLEMS

THE PROBLEM OF FIXED VERSUS
FLEXIBLE EXCHANGE RATES

Still with us is the age-old problem of trying to reconcile the keeping of exchange rates at fixed levels for long periods of time with divergent developments in the national economies whose moneys the exchange rates connect. Moreover, the action of the IMF in December 1971 in expanding the permissible range of fluctuations to 2¼ percent above and below the pars of exchange of its member countries hardly solved the problem. As the new range was described as a "temporary regime," its duration was left in doubt, and even as such, it was widely criticized as being inadequate.

Currency overvaluation and undervaluation

Although the member countries of the IMF, and particularly the Article VIII members, are expected to employ their tools of monetary and fiscal policy to achieve high degrees of stability in their domestic price levels, their aims in this direction are not always identical, and especially varied are the degrees of their success or failure in achieving their aims. Accordingly, the problem is essentially one of trying to carry on international transactions on the basis of fixed exchange rates among countries that are experiencing in their domestic economies many different rates of inflation and deflation—different rates of inflation almost exclusively, we may say, since but little deflation has occurred anytime during the whole post-World War II period.

The very fact that different rates of inflation are experienced means that the currencies of some countries at fixed rates become overvalued: their export prices become unattractive to foreign buyers, and the prices of foreign goods become increasingly attractive to their peoples; while the currencies of other countries become undervalued: their export prices become quite attractive to foreign buyers, and the prices of foreign goods become more and more expensive in terms of their domestic currencies. The countries whose currencies.become overvalued because of out-of-line rates of inflation on the high side soon experience deficits in their balances of payments that tend to become chronic, while those whose currencies become undervalued because of out-of-line rates of inflation on the low side experience surpluses in their balances of payments that also tend to become chronic. In the terminology of the Bretton Woods Agreement, both groups of countries move toward and into positions of "fundamental disequilibrium" in their balances of payments.

Devaluation and revaluation upward as remedies

But, as was pointed out in Chapter 25, the Bretton Woods Agreement has remedies for fundamental disequilibriums: devaluations in terms of gold or the United States dollar of the par values of overvalued currencies, and revaluations upward[1] in the par values of undervalued currencies. Nevertheless, countries are reluctant to devaluate, and they are even more reluctant to revaluate upward. Their delays in taking actions that speculators come to regard as inevitable permit crisis situations to develop in foreign exchange markets, and these are seriously disturbing not only to the countries that have the chronic balance-of-payments difficulties but also to the countries to which or from which the "hot money" of the speculators flow.

In the case of a country with an obviously overvalued currency, for example, the speculators use their bank balances in that country and liquidate their short-term investments there to buy the currencies of other countries, expecting to be able, after the devaluation has been effected, to buy at bargain rates that which they are now selling. If the speculators have no bank balances or liquid assets in the country with the overvalued currency, they sell the currency short, likewise expecting to be able to make delivery on their forward contracts at bargain rates. All this selling drives up the country's exchange rates on other currencies, and its central bank, to keep these exchange rates within the prescribed limit, must use some or much of its international monetary reserves to supply the wanted foreign currencies. And as a further result, there must obviously be disturbances and difficulties in monetary management for the countries to which the "hot money" flows.

Pros and Cons of Devaluation Although the devaluation of a country's monetary unit promises a quick improvement in its balance-of-payments position by making its export goods cheaper to foreign buyers and foreign

---

[1]Although the term *revaluation* is often used as an antonym of the word *devaluation*, it is probably safer to add the adjective *upward* to avoid uncertainty about direction. Another possibility is "upvaluation."

goods more expensive to its own people, countries are reluctant to devaluate. An important reason for this reluctance is prestige. If a country's currency has been widely used as an international medium of exchange and widely held by other countries as a reserve asset, its devaluation will surely be a blow to the confidence of foreign holders and users. If foreign holders of its currency and other assets denominated in its currency have been given guaranties against losses through devaluation, its obligations to these holders are automatically increased; if these holders have not been given such guaranties, it breaks faith with them, and they suffer losses in terms of their own currencies because they were not smart enough—or perhaps we should say, not ruthless enough—to get out when the speculators did.

Then there is the very difficult question of selecting the percentage by which the monetary unit should be devaluated. If the percentage selected is too small, there may be some relief, but the balance-of-payments deficits will continue because the currency remains overvalued. And it would be especially embarrassing to have to consider another devaluation within a relatively short period of time. If the percentage is too large, the currency becomes undervalued, with penalties, as it were, of a different kind—including, possibly, retaliatory actions by other countries aggrieved by the competition of export prices made "unfairly" cheap.

Even the purported advantage of curbing imports through devaluation can soon become illusory, especially if the devaluating country must import large quantities of raw materials and foodstuffs. Its importers will surely try to pass on their increased import costs; if they succeed in so doing, demands for increased wages will surely ensue. Then, if wage hikes are granted, the export industries, among others, will want to increase their prices to, at least, cover the increased costs of raw materials and labor—an action that, if taken, will diminish or perhaps cancel the original price advantage gained by the devaluation. By a system of wage and price controls, the country may be able to prevent wage hikes and the passing on of higher import prices, but the inauguration or expansion of such a system of internal control would doubtless be regarded as a highly disadvantageous consequence of devaluation.

Unattractiveness of Revaluation Upward Countries whose currencies become undervalued at existing exchange rates appear to have even stronger reasons to resist revaluations of their par values upward. The fact of undervaluation itself generally indicates that they have been highly prosperous with high levels of employment and output. Their export industries have been flourishing because of the attractiveness of their prices to foreign buyers, and their industries that produce for the home market have been free of strong competition from foreign producers. And it is likely that these advantages have been only moderately offset by high prices for needed imports of raw materials and foods—high in terms of their domestic currency. A revaluation upward of a significant percentage would mean, therefore, a sharp undercutting of such favorable conditions. It would mean for the export industries an immediate increase in the competition of foreign producers in external markets and increased competition from foreign goods in the home market for domestic producers, although prices in terms of domestic money for imported raw materials and foods would fall. It would surely be painful to contemplate eliminating previously enjoyed advantages in both foreign and domestic markets, as well as probable cuts in profits and employment—all this, as it were, simply to bring the par value of monetary units to levels more "realistic" in relationship to those of other countries.

Indeed, other to-be-expected consequences of devaluation would also be unattractive, including the prospects—in fact, the certainty—that the value of the devaluating country's foreign investments would be immediately cut in terms of domestic money and that the income on these investments, although continuing at the same rate in foreign currencies, would also be less in domestic money. However, a favorable result—probably slight—would be a decrease in the burden of external debts payable in foreign moneys.

Proposed alternative remedies

The best means to reconcile exchange rates held to narrow ranges with divergent developments in the countries whose currencies are connected by the exchange rates is doubtless to eliminate the divergencies—to have all these countries achieve stable prices or to, at least, manage to keep their inflationary developments proceeding at a uniform rate. Such appears to have been the hope of the Bretton Woods conferees when they decided that exchange rates should be fixed. But practical experience surely teaches that such a goal will prove to be illusory. So the next-best solution would appear to be to modify the emphasis on fixed exchange rates—to let them be more flexible, so that their fluctuations will more or less automatically reconcile or make "corrections" for disparate price-level movements from country to country. Not flexibility in the Bretton Woods sense of substantial changes at rare intervals, long-delayed and made effective reluctantly in circumstances of crisis, but frequent changes—even continuous ones— in exchange rates so that the process of adjustment to disparate rates of inflation will be constantly happening.

Remedies proposed along this line have generally been of four scopes, described as (1) wider bands, (2) crawling pegs, (3) moveable wider bands, and (4) freely floating exchange rates.

Wider Bands   The proposals for wider bands for exchange rates are predicated on the proposition that the long-held IMF rule for keeping exchange rates within 1 percent of the pars of exchange was simply too strict. Accordingly, the proposals are that the Articles of Agreement of the IMF should be amended to permit rate fluctuation ranges of 2 or 3 percent or of even as much as 5 percent on a permanent basis. It is argued that if the dollar-sterling rate, for example, were permitted to fluctuate between $2.5275 and $2.6839 (within a 3 percent band), between $2.5015 and $2.7099 (within a 4 percent band), or possibly between $2.4754 and $2.7360 (within a 5 percent band), movements of rates within such limits should "automatically" adjust for out-of-line developments in internal economies. They should compensate, as it were, for disparaties in short-term interest rates that, with a 1 percent band, have often resulted in huge inflows and outflows of "hot money," and for seasonal swings in trade and service transactions that, with a 1 percent band, have often had disruptive effects on holdings of monetary reserves and internal monetary conditions. It is argued that, with wider bands, central banks would not be constantly losing and gaining international monetary reserves because of developments in their foreign exchange markets that turn out to be short-lived—that their interventions in these markets would need to be far fewer than they have been with a narrow band. Another claim for wider bands is that, by increasing the risks of speculation in foreign currencies, they would reduce speculative raids on currencies. In the present system, it is said, speculators are *guaranteed* against losses beyond limited levels by the commitments of central banks to keep exchange rates within a narrow band. Any widening of the band, therefore, will reduce the protection speculators get from such a "guaranty."

Crawling Pegs   But wider bands would not be very helpful to a country whose price level continues to get further and further out of line with the price levels of other countries—a country whose progressive rate of inflation, in other words, is much greater than the inflation rates of other countries. In terms of the dollar-sterling rate again, and assuming England to be the country with the high rate of inflation, the exchange rate (with an allowable band of, say, 3 percent) would be likely to go to $2.5275 and stay there, so that the Bank of England would have to continue on and on using monetary reserves to prevent the dollar rate in London from going to still higher levels. Accordingly, as in the present system, England would still have to accept the conclusion that it had reached a state of fundamental disequilibrium, and to ask the question of when and to what extent it should devaluate the pound.

Hence the proposals for crawling pegs. It is argued that large price-level disparities do not develop overnight—that they develop gradually over considerable periods of time—and that it should be possible to adjust for them, also gradually, by frequent small changes in the official par values themselves. Assuming the 1 percent band rule of the IMF to be in effect, England ought to *reduce the par value* of the pound to, say $2.59 (from the 1971 par of $2.6057) if for many weeks the sterling-dollar rate in the market has been hovering around $2.58. Then, with the 1 percent rule now applying to the new par value of $2.59, England should make a further reduction in the pound's par value to, perhaps, $2.58 if market rates hover around, say, $2.575 for many weeks. And so on, for a gradual devaluation of the pound which might eventually total 8 or 10 percent or more—but a process of devaluation that would presumably preclude the crisis circumstances, as well as prospects for huge speculative profits, that occur in the present system when devaluations-at-one-stroke of large proportions appear to be unavoidable.

Some advocates of the crawling-peg solution have suggested that par values be automatically changed periodically on the basis of changes in some indicator, probably on the basis of an average of market rates of exchange as they have prevailed over a period of several months. However, others reject this idea on the grounds that governments want to take many developments into consideration to make decisions about changes in par values, and that they could hardly be expected to make commitments to slavishly obey the directions of an indicator. In any event, all the crawling-peg proponents appear to be virtually unanimous in holding that whatever changes in par values are made should be made promptly, probably as frequently as monthly, and that each change as a percentage should be quite small, probably not more than $\frac{1}{6}$ or $\frac{1}{4}$ of 1 percent a month.

Moveable Wider Bands   Proposals for moveable wider bands for par values are simply combinations of the separate proposals for wider bands and crawling pegs. The attitude of the proponents of moveable wider bands is that, if the present IMF rules are to be changed, they should be changed in a manner to gain the whole array of advantages claimed for wider bands and crawling pegs separately. With a wider band of, say, 3 percent, the sterling-dollar rate would be permitted to fluctuate within the range $2.5275–$2.6839, and that would have advantages as described earlier, but it might not assist for long if England were approaching a position of fundamental disequilibrium. The position of fundamental disequilibrium could probably be avoided if England changed its par value month after month at a rate of, say, $\frac{1}{6}$ of 1 percent a month upward or downward depending upon whether the disequilibrium were one of undervaluation or overvaluation. Whatever the distance the par value might "crawl" in a lengthy period of time, however, England would still be likely to have frequent drains from and accretions to its monetary reserves if it were still committed to keeping exchange rates within 1 or $2\frac{1}{4}$ percent of the shifting pars. Hence the idea of permitting both the frequent small changes in par values envisaged in the crawling-peg proposal and a wider range of rate fluctuations than the present "temporary" $2\frac{1}{4}$ percent around each new par-value level.

Freely Floating Exchange Rates   Proposals for freely floating exchange rates envisage a complete turnabout from the fixity of exchange rates as incorporated in IMF rules and as a prime feature of the old gold standard.

There would be no declared par values for currencies and no commitments of governments to intervene in foreign exchange markets to keep rates within prescribed limits. The determination of exchange rates would be fully surrendered to the interplay of the forces of supply and demand.

The principal argument offered in support of freely floating exchange rates has a firm foundation in capitalist economic theory: that welfare is optimized when markets are free—when economic decisions are made on the basis of market prices that are free to fluctuate with changing supply and demand. If economic decisions can best be made in individual economies internally in relationship to free market forces, why should not the same be true for international economic relationships and transactions? Considering the emphasis given to the desirability of governmental non-interference with price determination in domestic markets, why should there be a directly opposing doctrine concerning the determination of the market prices of foreign currencies? If a country's export prices rose out of line with the price levels of other countries, their exchange rates on it would fall so that its export goods would be no more expensive to foreign buyers than before; at the same time, the rise in its exchange rates on foreign currencies would keep the relationship between domestic prices and the costs of foreign goods in terms of domestic money the same as before.

Another argument in support of freely floating exchange rates is that a world-wide system of such rates would permit central banks to concentrate their control activities on domestic goals of full employment, stable price levels, and good rates of economic growth, without the need to cope with balance-of-payments difficulties simultaneously. Were central banks free from balance-of-payments concerns—free to concentrate on domestic goals —they would be likely to have greater success in achieving price-level stability at home, and success of this kind would also promote stability in exchange rates despite the absence of controls directly aimed at rate stability.

A similar argument holds that central banks would not have to struggle to accumulate large volumes of international reserve assets, nor would there be sizable losses of reserves because of exchange-rate management to put them under pressure to curb expansive domestic developments. Each country would still want some accumulation of monetary reserves to cover external buying needs in times of declining export sales or temporary interruptions in such sales, but their reserve needs would surely be much less than in the present system in which substantial drains frequently occur in a way wholly incidental to keeping exchange rates within narrow limits.

A final argument that may be mentioned here—without exhausting the subject—is that a system of freely floating exchange rates would tend to preclude the imposition of quantitative restrictions on international trade and service transactions. The point of this argument is that, for countries that are losing substantial amounts of their monetary reserves, quantitative restrictions, such as import quotas and tariffs and export subsidies, are all too tempting as alternatives to monetary devaluations.

Probably the strongest argument against freely floating exchange rates is one on the practical plane: that central bankers, commercial bankers, importers, exporters, international investors, and statesmen fear the consequences of floating rates, do not want them, and will surely oppose any proposed moves in that direction. But the attitude of the opponents is not purely psychological. They have other arguments. They emphasize the chaotic conditions in foreign exchange markets in the middle and late 1930s as historical evidence of the disastrous consequences of floating rates. They especially stress the argument that international selling on lengthy credit terms would probably fall enormously were investors and sellers not to have assurances of reasonable long-run stability in exchange rates. And they argue that central banks would surely engage in practices of "competitive currency depreciation"—of deliberately selling their currencies at lower and lower rates to make goods prices in their markets more and more attractive to foreign buyers. Indeed, some proponents of floating rates readily admit that central banks would be inclined so to act, and they therefore stipulate that, in their proposed floating-rate systems, the central banks would be required to stay out of the foreign exchange markets. In answer, the opponents of floating rates argue that getting central banks and their governments to accept restrictions of such an extraordinary kind would be impossible; but the proponents counterargue that commitments to nonintervention would hardly be more restrictive than present commitments to keep exchange rates within a narrow band.

THE PROBLEM OF INTERNATIONAL
MONETARY RESERVES

The validity of one of the propositions of the proponents of floating exchange rates appears to have been amply proved in the post-World War II period: the proposition that countries are likely to want to amass large volumes of international monetary reserves if they make commitments to keep exchange rates within narrow limits. The proof is shown in the refusal of all the leading industrial member countries of the IMF, except the United States and Canada, to accept the responsibilities of Article VIII of its Articles of Agreement until 1961—and a little later for some—when they had accumulated substantial amounts of reserves, in their scramble throughout the 1950s to amass this accumulation, and in their continued anxiety—shared by the United States—about where additional reserves were to come from to keep pace with expanding international trade and investment.

Reserve build-ups

The reserve build-ups of the industrial members of the IMF took the forms chiefly of gold and dollars—dollars spent by the United States by way of generous grant and loan programs of the federal government and huge foreign investment by American business enterprises and individuals, and gold drawn, to a large extent, from our monetary stock through the cashing of some of these dollars. Our balance-of-payments deficits (on the liquidity basis) in every year in the period 1950–1960, except 1957, were attributable chiefly to these programs of the federal government and to this private investment; and the reserve build-ups were reflected, of course, in a reported increase in our "liquid liabilities to foreigners" (excluding international and regional institutions, such as the IMF and the World Bank) from about $6 billion at the end of 1949 to approximately $18.7 billion at the end of 1960 and in a decline in our gold holdings in the same period from $24.4 billion to $17.8 billion.[2]

In this period, the industrial member nations gladly accepted United States dollars as an excellent monetary reserve asset, although, to the extent that they converted dollars into gold, they presumably indicated an even greater preference for gold. At the same time, the United States was pleased with the foreign build-up of dollar assets and gold, and even when the gold build-up meant a shrinkage in our own gold reserves. All along we wanted the industrial member nations to accumulate sufficient monetary reserves to make them feel safe enough to accept the responsibilities of Article VIII, so that we could all get the machinery of the IMF system to work fully in the manner it was originally intended to work.

Concern about size and quality

But acceptance of Article VIII responsibilities by the industrial members of the IMF, instead of quieting anxieties concerning monetary reserves, tended to increase them. From what source would come annual increases in reserves needed for expanding trade and investment? And there was new concern about the *quality* of these reserves, particularly the quality of the United States dollar that had so prominent a place in the reserves of many countries.

As for quantity, it was apparent that gold production could not be depended upon to supply annual additions to reserves in the proportions thought to be needed. Yet gold continued to be regarded as the best of all possible reserve assets, and this was precisely why there were growing doubts concerning the quality of the United States dollar as a reserve asset. Esteem for the dollar as being "as good as gold," which was the general attitude of the 1950s, was diminishing. Our continuing gold losses in the period 1961–1968 at an annual average exceeding that of the 1950–1960 period (including for both periods our gold-tranche position in the IMF) and our continuing balance-of-payments deficits (on the liquidity basis)

---

[2]Excluding changes in our IMF gold-tranche position. *Federal Reserve Bulletin,* May 1954, pp. 540, 547, and February 1971, pp. A75, A76.

also at an annual average exceeding that of the 1950–1960 period were sources of ever-increasing concern about dollar quality. And it was apparent to all that our remaining gold reserves, including our gold-tranche drawing rights, amounted, say at the end of 1968, to only a minor fraction of our reported liquid liabilities to foreigners—at about 36 percent, with liabilities to international and regional institutions included. More and more were foreign countries protesting that they were selling large numbers of their manufacturing plants and great arrays of other productive facilities to American corporations for dollars that we could create in unlimited amounts.

Accordingly, many proposals for augmenting world monetary reserves have been advanced in recent years, mostly in directions away from the United States dollar.

Proposals concerning reserves

Revaluation of Gold Prominent among the proposals has been the perennial one that gold reserves be increased and gold production stimulated by the simple procedure of raising the price of gold dramatically, as to a level of $70 an ounce. Until late 1971, however, the United States consistently refused to entertain this kind of proposal on the grounds that we would be breaking faith with the countries that, at our urging and sometimes in response to our "arm twisting," valiantly continued to hold dollar assets instead of demanding gold from our shrinking reserves. Even our concession of late 1971 to raise the price of gold from $35 to $38 an ounce was, of course, a small one. Aside from this concession, therefore, the only significant thing that had been done about gold was the decision of the "group of ten" countries of March 17, 1968 to discontinue pouring monetary gold into private hoards via the London market. Such pouring had continued for several years as a means of keeping the market price of gold from rising too far above $35 an ounce, so that the decision was, as it were, an acceptance of a "two-tier" price system for gold, that is, an official price of $35 an ounce, and market prices in London, Paris, Zurich, and other foreign centers fluctuating in response to supply and demand conditions.

Multiple Currency Reserves There have been proposals for "multiple currency reserves": that countries be persuaded to diversify their holdings of convertible currencies as carried among their reserve assets, presumably in the direction of holding fewer dollars and pounds and more deutsche marks, guilders, Swiss and French francs, and so on. Despite increased grumbling about "unwanted dollars," however, greatly expanded holdings of such other currencies have appeared to be even more unwanted.

Increased IMF Quotas Then there have been proposals for increased quotas in the IMF to give it greater capacities to assist member countries to cope with balance-of-payments difficulties in current account. As was pointed out in Chapter 5, two such proposals were accepted and were put into effect (after an earlier one of 50 percent in 1959); the general increase of 25 percent that became effective in 1966, and the general increase of about 35 percent that went into effect in 1970. But all the countries that consented to these increases realized that they did not thereby receive increased monetary reserves, since the added gold-tranche drawing rights that resulted from the quota increases simply replaced gold reserves previously owned outright in their own names. They also realized, of course, that their increased credit-tranche drawing rights could be helpful in times of difficulty, but they knew that these drawing rights were, in effect, a borrowing capacity rather than an addition to reserves.

Creation of SDRs   Finally, there have been proposals for the creation of a new kind of international reserve asset by the IMF itself. And as the student surely knows by now, these proposals have borne fruit in the creation of about 3.5 billion units of special drawing rights (SDRs) at the beginning of 1970, another of approximately 3.0 billion at the beginning of 1971, and still another of about 3.0 billion at the beginning of 1972, and in the prospects for additional creations in subsequent years.

SDRs and dollars

At the time in 1968 when the decision for SDRs was rapidly approaching adoption, the thought and hope were that by the time the first allocation was made in 1970 the United States would have largely succeeded in putting its balance of payments in order, that is, that it would no longer be running deficits of any significant size. From 1970 on, additions to international monetary reserves would come chiefly by way of SDR creation rather than from a continued flood of dollars. It was even pleasant to think that by 1970 the United States would be starting to have surpluses in its balance of payments and that annually thereafter it would be in a position to call back some of the dollars previously sent abroad as a result of earlier balance-of-payments deficits.

Thus it was rather shocking when our balance-of-payments deficit in 1970 on an official settlements basis was the greatest of all—on any basis —by a wide margin, at close to $10 billion. Anxiety concerning possible shortages in international monetary reserves quickly shifted to anxiety concerning excesses and the difficulties to be expected in attempting to curb the strong inflationary pressures that such excesses would be likely to generate. Increasingly, officials of foreign governments and their central banks turned to protesting that, by absorbing dollars in huge amounts, they were slavishly financing American takeovers of their manufacturing plants and other productive facilities and financing our military activities throughout the world, including our military adventures in Southeast Asia with which many have little sympathy and toward which others are distinctly hostile.

A straitjacket for our Article VIII partners

The new trend in the anxieties and misgivings of our Article VIII partners in the IMF indicated their growing conviction that they had put themselves in a kind of straitjacket by their commitments to keep exchange rates within 1 percent of parity—that they had to go on accepting dollars willy-nilly as long as they continued to honor this commitment. They had set the par values of their monetary units in terms of dollars and cents, but even more importantly, they used dollars—and apparently they had to continue to use dollars—as the principal "intervention currency" in the transactions of their central banks to keep exchange rates within the prescribed limits.

If a country's commercial banks resisted the flood of dollars by continually reducing their spot buying and selling rates on dollars, its central bank soon had to come into the market to buy the excess dollars to prevent the spot selling rate from falling below the 1 percent limit. And what could the central bank do with the excess dollars? It could keep them quite unprofitably as idle demand balances in American banks, or it could invest them in time deposits or in short-term U.S. Treasury obligations or even in intermediate-term Treasury obligations—perhaps the latter, in response to our "arm twisting." But it was not likely to ask for their redemption in gold in any sizable amounts, for fear that, if many central banks were to do this, the whole IMF system would collapse. Although the United States might refrain as long as possible from suspending redemption in gold, any substantial gold drains would make our promise of redemption less and less credible.

THE PROBLEM OF OUR BALANCE-OF-PAYMENTS DEFICITS

It is thus clear that the problem of fixed versus flexible exchange rates, the problem of adequacies, inadequacies, and excesses in international monetary reserves, the fate of SDRs, and indeed, the fate of the whole IMF system have all been closely related to or even dependent on actions of the United States to avoid continued balance-of-payments deficits.

On the whole, our attitude has been that we must reduce these deficits and if possible, eliminate them, but at times we have wavered in this attitude, and in the late 1960s we were asking ourselves whether we really had to do anything. In the early 1960s, at any rate, we had to accept the fact that foreign countries were no longer finding additional dollars eminently desirable, and through most of the decade, we adopted measure after measure aimed for the most part at reducing the deficits but with some designed to make dollars more palatable.

Palatability measures

Illustrative of measures to make additional dollars more welcome to foreign countries have been efforts of the Federal Reserve and the Treasury to "twist up" short-term interest rates—efforts that were especially stressed in the period 1961–1964. A major idea here was simply to improve the profitability of investments of foreign-held dollars in our money market securities.

Another measure of this kind has been persuading foreign central banks —and necessarily of course, their governments—to invest surplus dollars in intermediate-term Treasury obligations, given attractive interest rates, and guaranteed against devaluation, or denominated in the foreign currencies as an alternative way of guaranteeing against devaluation.

Measures to improve the trade and service balance

Concerning services, the principal focus of attention has been tourism, with campaigns to keep Americans at home—"See America First"—and to persuade foreigners to come here as tourists, the latter including advertising in foreign periodicals, efforts to ease the entry of foreigners through customs, and admonitions to our people to treat foreign tourists courteously. But the principal minus item in our international exchange of services, if service it can be called—"military expenditures abroad"—has been largely inviolable, except for agreements by some countries, such as West Germany, to spend here for military equipment and supplies amounts in relationship to our spending in these countries for our military installations and troops.

On the other hand, measures to improve our balance of trade have been numerous, particularly in the direction of attempting to expand exports. These measures have included generous lending by the Export-Import Bank to finance export shipments and generous guaranties of loans granted by private institutions, American and foreign, for such financing; the development of programs of insurance to protect exporters against losses due to both credit and "political" risks—the latter pertaining to such dangers as government seizure of exported goods without compensation—the adoption of the Trade Expansion Act of 1962 that gave the President extraordinary powers to reduce tariff rates for similar concessions by foreign countries— a measure aimed especially at the removal or reduction of tariffs of the Common Market countries alleged to be especially discriminatory against our exports of farm products—and even a cutback from $500 to $100 in the value of goods that returning American tourists may bring in duty-free and a change from wholesale to retail valuations for the $100 worth of goods.

Measures to reduce American private investment abroad

Measures aimed at reducing American private investment in foreign countries have been of two kinds: (1) behind-the-scenes actions designed to make foreign investment less attractive simply as a matter of investors' choices, and (2) direct controls.

The behind-the-scenes actions have included the following: elimination of the right of Americans to own gold abroad; removal of some tax advantages of American investment in foreign "tax havens," as provided for in the Revenue Act of 1962; the actions of the Treasury and the Federal Reserve to "twist up" short-term interest rates to encourage short-term investment at home; operations by the Treasury in forward exchange, also designed to reduce the attractions of higher interest rates on short-term investments in foreign markets; an exemption from interest rate ceilings for time deposits held in American banks by foreign governments and their "official" monetary institutions; and pressures on foreign governments to relax their restrictions on investment by their peoples in American securities and other assets.

The direct controls have been especially noteworthy as marking an extraordinary departure from our long-held dogma that, for the welfare of all mankind outside the Iron Curtain, international capital flows should be free of all impediments and obstacles. Three kinds of direct controls have been employed: (1) an "interest equalization tax," designed to make unattractive investment by Americans in foreign security issues; (2) specific restrictions on investment by American business enterprises in plant, equipment, and other productive facilities located in foreign countries; and (3) a "voluntary" system of restraint on foreign lending and investment by American commercial banks and other financial institutions.

An overvalued dollar?

Despite all the measures for the promotion of exports of merchandise and for curbing merchandise imports, as described in the preceding pages, our trade surplus in 1968 narrowed to $624 million, down from an average level of close to $5 billion in the preceding five years. Although there was a slight improvement in 1969 and a greater one in 1970, with the trade surpluses at $660 million and $2110 million, respectively,[3] these improvements were obviously not of sufficient proportions to be reassuring.

Accordingly, the claim was more and more frequently made that the dollar was overvalued. It was claimed that we had greater difficulty in selling in foreign markets because, *at existing exchange rates,* our export prices for many kinds of goods had become too high for foreign buyers; and that we had increased our buying abroad because, at these exchange rates, the prices of many kinds of foreign goods had become much more attractive to us. It was further claimed that prospects for a big growth in our trade surplus in the foreseeable future through the ordinary course of international business developments were not bright, and that we should admit, therefore, that we had gotten ourselves into a position of fundamental disequilibrium. And we were reminded that in the IMF system the remedy for a fundamental disequilibrium because of the overvaluation of a currency is its devaluation.

---

[3]Excluding exports under United States military agency sales contracts and imports of our military agencies. *Survey of Current Business,* June 1971, p. 30.

But it appeared that, as long as the United States continued to fulfill its commitments under the Bretton Woods Agreement, a devaluation of the dollar would have no effect in correcting an overvaluation, assuming that an overvaluation actually existed. A devaluation in terms of gold—like that of 1934—would, indeed, reduce the gold value of the dollar, but it would make no change in the values of the British pound, the French franc, the German mark, and other currencies in relation to the dollar. Because the par values of all these currencies were set in terms of dollars and cents, obviously these dollar-and-cents valuations would not be affected by anything we might do about a new gold weight for the dollar. In effect, a devaluation of the dollar in terms of gold of any percentage would result in an automatic equal devaluation in terms of gold of all other currencies with dollar-and-cents par values. Thus our export prices as measured in foreign currencies would be exactly the same as before, and likewise for import prices measured in dollars.

Nevertheless, the United States broke one of its major commitments under the Bretton Woods Agreement by President Nixon's action of August 15, 1971 in "temporarily" suspending the redeemability of foreign-held dollars in gold or in other monetary reserve assets. The effect of this suspension was to clear the way for a meaningful devaluation of the dollar and a "realignment" of pars of exchange as agreed to by representatives of the "group of ten" leading industrial countries and the IMF in December of that year. In the December action, the United States promised a devaluation of the dollar of 7.89 percent, and the other nine countries, in effect, shifted from dollar-and-cents valuations for their currencies to valuations in terms of gold. The United Kingdom and France simply retained the gold values of their monetary units that had been implied all along by their dollar-and-cents valuations, so that their pars of exchange shifted upward solely on account of our devaluation of the dollar; while the other seven agreed to shifts in pars that combined the effects of our devaluation with changes by them in the previously implied gold values of their currencies—a slight devaluation by Italy and revaluations upward by the remaining six.

However, the agreement of December 1971—including, additionally, the permission for rate fluctuations within a range of $2\frac{1}{4}$ percent above and below pars—was recognized to be an "interim" solution for difficulties that were especially pressing at that time. The realignment of pars of exchange would surely help the United States to improve its balance-of-payments performance, but many problems of obstacles to trade, capital flows, and other international transactions remained untouched. There were still many questions about what the long-run permissible range for rate fluctuations should be and about how it should be managed. Still untouched, too, was the very important question of the redeemability of foreign-held dollar deposits and other short-term dollar obligations owing to foreigners estimated to be around $50 to $60 billion. And perhaps most important of all, there remained for consideration many proposals for a thorough overhaul of the IMF machinery. Thus one must conclude this chapter on "current international monetary problems" by saying that most of the problems discussed here are still far from solution. But such a conclusion need not be entirely pessimistic; one can also say that here we have a great challenge and that we ought to have the intelligence and strength to meet it effectively.

FOR REVIEW

1. How is the problem of fixed versus flexible exchange rates related to the problem of controlling inflation?
2. Why are members of the IMF reluctant to devaluate their monetary units to escape from fundamental disequilibriums? to revaluate their monetary units upward?
3. What is the wider-band proposal for the management of exchange rates? the crawling-peg proposal?
4. Would wider bands for exchange rates keep countries from falling into fundamental disequilibriums? Would crawling pegs do so? Explain.
5. What are the principal arguments in favor of freely floating exchange rates? the principal opposing arguments?
6. Why is it said that, with freely floating exchange rates, international reserve needs would be much less than in the present IMF system?
7. Why are increased IMF quotas of minor importance as a solution to the problem of adequacy of international monetary reserves?
8. Has the problem of adequacy of international monetary reserves been solved by the creation of SDRs by the IMF? Discuss.
9. Why did the Article VIII members of the IMF other than the United States seem to be in a "straitjacket" in the decade of the 1960s with respect to their acceptance of United States dollars?
10. What actions has the United States taken in the service area to improve its balance-of-payments position? in the capital area?
11. What remedy is available to the United States for a clearly recognized overvaluation of the dollar?
12. How could other members of the IMF help the United States to pull out of a fundamental disequilibrium in its balance of payments? Would they have good reasons to give this help? Discuss.

RECOMMENDED SOURCES AND READINGS

MAJOR SOURCES OF CURRENT STATISTICS

Every student of money and banking should be thoroughly familiar with the content of the *Federal Reserve Bulletin* as published monthly by the Board of Governors of the Federal Reserve System. Early in a course in money and banking, the student should page through an issue of the *Bulletin* to savor the wealth of its current statistics on developments in virtually all the areas to which the monetary authorities must presumably give attention in working toward money-control decisions. The *Bulletin* is the primary source of many of the statistics it presents, including the factors supplying and absorbing reserve funds, the reserve positions of member banks, the operations of the Federal Reserve banks, estimates of money in circulation, the index of industrial production, consumer credit, and the flow-of-funds accounts; and it also presents a great array of data taken from other sources, as for wholesale and consumer prices, employment and unemployment, gross national product, the balance of payments, and our international financial assets and liabilities. Also reported in the *Bulletin* are the regulations of the Board of Governors currently in effect, the policy decisions of the Federal Open Market Committee adopted approximately 3 months earlier, new laws relating to money and banking passed by Congress, and new regulations adopted by the board as well as amendments to and interpretations of existing regulations. (The Board of Governors has two additional publications in which many of the statistical series reported in the *Federal Reserve Bulletin* are presented in graph form: its annual *Historical Chart Book* with the graphs tracing developments generally from about 1915–1920 to approximately the September of the year of publication; and its *Monthly Chart Book* with developments generally depicted from the early 1960s to close to the dates of monthly publication.)

Second in importance to the *Federal Reserve Bulletin* as a source of current data on development that the student of money and banking should be interested in is the *Survey of Current Business* published monthly by the Office of Business Economics of the federal Department of Commerce. While there is some duplication in its statistical coverage with that of the *Bulletin,* it is especially important as the primary source of data on gross national product and our balance of international payments—two kinds of data that it presents in massive detail, especially, for the data on gross national product, in its July "National Income Issue." It is also notable for the great mass of data it presents on production, sales, inventories, and prices in certain aggregates for the whole economy, as for manufacturers and retailers in general, as well as for many specific industries individually.

And third among major sources of data on current developments deserving the attention of students of money and banking are the monthly issues of *International Financial Statistics* published by the International Monetary Fund whose headquarters are in Washington. Each of these issues reports on the quotas of the IMF member countries, their gold-tranche and credit-tranche drawings, their resulting reserve positions, and their allocations, further acquisitions, and uses of SDRs. Additionally, each issue presents summary tables of gold and foreign currency holdings of the member countries, exchange rates among them, comparative price levels, and major flows of commodity imports and exports, and for each member country separately, an amazing amount of detail concerning its international monetary position, the major assets and liabilities of its central and commercial banks, its government finances, its internal price levels and interest rates, and major features of its balance of payments and national product-national income accounts.

ANNUAL REPORTS AND FACT BOOKS

In the areas of monetary and fiscal policy, the most comprehensive official descriptions of annual developments in the economy, judgments about the character and direction of these developments, actions taken, and actions recommended are undoubtedly those presented in the *Annual Report of the Board of Governors of the Federal Reserve System* and the *Annual Report of the Council of Economic Advisers.* The latter, supported by much statistical detail, is published by the Government Printing Office in a single volume with the *Economic Report of the President* shortly after the President's report is transmitted to Congress (almost always in January). For surveys of international monetary developments, the *Annual Report of the International Monetary Fund* is especially helpful; for interpretations, criticisms, and recommendations in this sphere, the *Annual Report of the Bank for International Settlements;* and for official American attitudes toward these developments, the *Annual Report of the Board of Governors of the Federal Reserve System,* the *Annual Report of the Federal Reserve Bank of New York,* the *Annual Report of the National Advisory Council on Inter-*

national Monetary and Financial Policies, and the semiannual reports of the special manager of the Federal Reserve's System Open Market Account published in both the *Monthly Review* of the Federal Reserve Bank of New York and the *Federal Reserve Bulletin.*

For massive arrays of data on the assets, liabilities, expense, and income of commercial banks, as well as other details concerning them, the annual reports of the Federal Deposit Insurance Corporation and of the Comptroller of the Currency are outstanding sources in addition to the Federal Reserve publications; and for the affairs of commercial banks in the individual states, the annual report of the bank supervisory agency in each particular state. For comprehensive details concerning the structure of individual classes of nonbank financial institutions, their activities, and developments concerning them, you can turn to the annual reports of government supervisory agencies, such as the Federal Home Loan Bank Board, the Farm Credit Administration, and the National Credit Union Administration, and to "fact books" published (typically) by trade associations, such as those of the Institute of Life Insurance, the United States Savings and Loan League, the National Association of Mutual Savings Banks, and the National Consumer Finance Association.

PERIODICALS

For students who have special interests in given classes of financial institutions, or who acquire such interests, there are numerous monthly magazines for keeping abreast with current developments, problems being faced, proposed solutions to problems, attitudes toward proposed legislation, and so on. Many of these magazines are published by trade associations, including *Banking* of the American Bankers Association, *Savings and Loan News* of the United States Savings and Loan League, and *Mutual Savings Banking* of the National Association of Mutual Savings Banks. Others are published by "regular" publishing houses, including *Best's Review,* with separate life-health insurance and property-liability insurance editions, *Finance: The Magazine of Money,* and *Bankers Monthly.*

FREE MATERIALS

Concerning the availability of publications in the field of money and banking, an aspect that especially deserves mention is that many are supplied free of charge. I do not refer here to "house organs" that report on the doings of the issuing enterprises, laud their accomplishments, and mention who has been promoted to this or that office, but to publications on current developments and current problems of excellent quality written by highly competent economists and other analysts. Outstanding in this classification are the "monthly reviews" of eleven of the twelve Federal Reserve banks (excluding the Federal Reserve Bank of Minneapolis which discontinued its publication of this type a few years ago) and the "monthly letters" of many of the larger commercial banks. You can simply write to the issuing institution to ask to have your name put on the mailing list to receive its monthly business review or letter. Among the Federal Reserve banks, the monthly reviews are specifically designated as follows:

Boston, *New England Business Review* (bimonthly).
New York, *Monthly Review.*
Philadelphia, *Business Review.*
Cleveland, *Economic Review.*
Richmond, *Monthly Review.*
Atlanta, *Monthly Review.*
Chicago, *Business Conditions.*
St. Louis, *Review.*
Kansas City, *Monthly Review.*
Dallas, *Business Review.*
San Francisco, *Monthly Review.*

Moreover, the Federal Reserve banks generally make available reprints of many of the articles carried in earlier issues of their reviews that someone may have overlooked at the time of original publication; additional weekly and monthly reports on specific kinds of developments; and some of them, collections of essays as well as collections of papers presented at conferences that they have sponsored.

The monthly letters of leading commercial banks are so numerous that mention of a few could well be regarded as unfair to those not mentioned. Nevertheless, we may venture to suggest that the most widely known of these letters are probably the *Monthly Economic Letter* of the First National City Bank, *The Morgan Guaranty Survey* of the Morgan Guaranty Trust Company, and *Business in Brief* of the Chase Manhattan Bank, all of New York City.

Among suppliers of free materials, the International Monetary Fund surely must be accorded special notice. By writing to it in Washington, you can have your name added to its mailing lists to receive its weekly *International Financial News Survey* and its quarterly magazine *Finance and Development* which carries articles on its own organization and operations and on international financial problems and developments of many kinds. It also makes available without charge its *Annual Report* as well as its *Annual Report on Exchange Restrictions.* In the matter of annual reports, I should mention that some such reports of government agencies are also supplied without charge, most notably those of the Board of Governors of the Federal Reserve System and the Federal Deposit Insurance Corporation.

BOOKS OF READINGS

For further reading on the many topics covered in this textbook, the most convenient sources—and often the sources of best quality—are the books of "readings" that several distinguished scholars have assembled and edited. So far as I am aware, the following is a complete listing of recently published books or editions of books of this type:

CARSON, C. D. (ed). *Money and Finance: Readings in Theory, Policy, and Institutions.* 2d ed. New York: John Wiley & Sons, Inc., 1970.

CRUTCHFIELD, JAMES A., CHARLES N. HENNING, AND WILLIAM PIGOTT (eds). *Money, Financial Institutions, and the Economy.* Englewood Cliffs, N.J.: Prentice-Hall, Inc., 1965.

FENSTERMAKER, J. VAN (ed). *Readings in Financial Markets and Institutions.* New York: Appleton-Century-Crofts, 1969.

RITTER, LAWRENCE S. (ed). *Money and Economic Activity.* 3d ed. Boston: Houghton Mifflin Company, 1967.

SMITH, WARREN L., AND RONALD L. TEIGEN (eds). *Readings in Money, National Income, and Stabilization Policy.* Rev. ed. Homewood, Ill.: Richard D. Irwin, Inc., 1970.

WARD, RICHARD A. (ed). *Monetary Theory and Policy.* Scranton, Pa.: INTEX, 1966.

WILLIAMS, HAROLD R., AND HENRY W. WOUDENBERG (eds). *Money, Banking, and Monetary Policy: Readings in Domestic and International Policy.* New York: Harper & Row, Publishers, Inc., 1970.

WOLF, HAROLD A., AND R. CONRAD DOENGES. *Readings in Money and Banking.* New York: Appleton-Century-Crofts, 1968.

BOOKS OF OTHER TYPES

For students who want to go beyond the textbook and the kinds of publications already described to study given topics more deeply, a great number of monographs, collections of essays, more specialized textbooks, reports of congressional hearings, and so on are available. A complete listing of such publications would be overwhelming to the student, while the selection of only a few as being "best" would be likely to be faulty. In the following listings, therefore, I present for each major division of the textbook a fairly large number of titles of books and comparable publications that I judge to be "good" on the topics discussed in that part, with choices falling chiefly on recently published works and with apologies to the authors of inadvertently overlooked books that deserve to be judged as good as or even better than some or all of the listed books.

Part 1: Money

BALL, R. J., AND PETER M. DOYLE (eds). *Inflation.* Baltimore: Penguin Books Inc., 1969.

DUNNE, GERALD T. *Monetary Decisions of the Supreme Court.* New Brunswick, N.J.: Rutgers University Press, 1960.

FRIEDMAN, MILTON, AND ANNA SCHWARTZ. *A Monetary History of the United States.* New York: Columbia University Press (for the National Bureau of Economic Research), 1963.

GOLD, JOSEPH. *The Stand-by Arrangements of the International Monetary Fund.* Washington: International Monetary Fund, 1970.

HAMMOND, BRAY. *Sovereignty and an Empty Purse: Banks and Politics in the Civil War.* Princeton, N.J.: Princeton University Press, 1970.

HENDRICKSON, ROBERT A. *The Future of Money.* Englewood Cliffs, N.J.: Prentice-Hall, Inc., 1970.

LESTER, RICHARD A. *Monetary Experiments.* Princeton, N.J.: Princeton University Press, 1929.

MASON, WILL. E. *Clarification of the Monetary Standard.* University Park, Pa.: Pennsylvania State University Press, 1963.

MYERS, MARGARET G. *A Financial History of the United States.* New York: Columbia University Press, 1970.

NUSSBAUM, ARTHUR. *A History of the Dollar.* New York: Columbia University Press, 1957.

RICHARDSON, DENNIS W. *Electric Money: Evolution of an Electronic Funds-Transfer System.* Cambridge, Mass.: MIT Press, 1970.

ROBERTSON, ROSS M. *History of the American Economy.* 2d ed. New York: Harcourt Brace Jovanovich, 1964.

STUDENSKI, PAUL, AND HERMAN E. KROOSS. *Financial History of the United States.* 3d ed. New York: McGraw-Hill Book Company, Inc., 1963.

WEIL, GORDON L., AND IAN DAVIDSON. *The Cold War: The Story of the World's Monetary Crisis.* New York: Holt, Rinehart and Winston, Inc., 1970.

Part 2: Financial Institutions and Markets

BLACK, ROBERT P., AND DORIS E. HARLESS. *Nonbank Financial Institutions.* 3d ed. Richmond, Va.: Federal Reserve Bank of Richmond, 1969.

CROTEAU, JOHN T. *Economics of the Credit Union.* Detroit: Wayne State University Press, 1963.

DOUGALL, HERBERT E. *Capital Markets and Institutions.* 2d ed. Englewoods Cliffs, N.J.: Prentice-Hall, Inc., 1970.

EINZIG, PAUL. *The Euro-Dollar System.* 4th ed. New York: St. Martin's Press, Inc., 1970.

FRIEND, IRWIN, MARSHALL BLUME, AND JEAN CROCKETT. *Mutual Funds and Other Institutional Investors: A New Perspective.* New York: McGraw-Hill Book Company, Inc. (for the Twentieth Century Fund), 1970.

FRIEND, IRWIN, and others. *Investment Banking and the New Issues Market.* New York: The World Publishing Company, 1967.

GOLDSMITH, RAYMOND W. *Financial Institutions.* New York: Random House, Inc., 1968.

HOAGLAND, HENRY E., AND LEO D. STONE. *Real Estate Finance.* 4th ed. Homewood, Ill.: Richard D. Irwin, Inc., 1969.

House Committee on Banking and Currency. *Comparative Regulations of Financial Institutions.* Washington, D.C.: Government Printing Office, 1963.

JACOBS, DONALD P., LORING C. FARWELL, AND EDWIN NEAVE. *Financial Institutions,* 5th ed. Homewood, Ill.: Richard D. Irwin, Inc., 1972.

KETCHUM, MARSHALL D., AND LEON T. KENDALL (eds). *Readings in Financial Institutions.* Boston: Houghton Mifflin Company, 1965.

KONSTAS, PANOS, and others. *Money Market Instruments.* 3d ed. Cleveland: Federal Reserve Bank of Cleveland, 1970.

KROOSS, HERMAN E., AND MARTIN R. BLYN. *A History of Financial Intermediaries.* New York: Random House, Inc., 1971.

LAZERE, MONROE E. (ed). *Commercial Financing.* New York: The Ronald Press Company, 1968.

MAISEL, SHERMAN J. *Financing Real Estate: Principles and Practices.* New York: McGraw-Hill Book Company, Inc., 1965.

MONHOLLEN, JIMMIE R. (ed). *Instruments of the Money Market.* 2d ed. Richmond, Va.: Federal Reserve Bank of Richmond, 1970.

PEASE, ROBERT H., AND LEWIS O. KERWOOD (eds). *Mortgage Banking.* 2d ed. New York: McGraw-Hill Book Company, Inc., 1965.

POLAKOFF, MURRAY E. (ed). *Financial Institutions and Markets.* Boston: Houghton Mifflin Company, 1970.

PROCHNOW, HERBERT V. (ed). *The Eurodollar.* Chicago: Rand-McNally & Co., 1970.

RABINOWITZ, ALAN. *Municipal Bond Finance and Administration: A Practical Guide to the Analysis of Tax Exempt Securities.* New York: John Wiley & Sons, Inc., 1969.

ROBINSON, ROLAND I. *Money and Capital Markets.* New York: McGraw-Hill Book Company, Inc., 1964.

Securities and Exchange Commission. *Report of Special Study of the Securities Market.* Washington, D.C.: Government Printing Office, 1963.

SWACKAMMER, GENE L., AND RAYMOND J. DOLL. *Financing Modern Agriculture: Banking's Problems and Challenges.* Kansas City, Mo.: Federal Reserve Bank of Kansas City, 1969.

WELFLING, WELDON. *Mutual Savings Banks: The Evolution of a Financial Intermediary.* Cleveland: Case Western Reserve University Press, 1968.

Part 3:   Commercial Banking

American Bankers Association. *The Commercial Banking Industry.* Englewood Cliffs, N.J.: Prentice-Hall, Inc., 1962.

CROSS, HOWARD. *Management Policies for Commercial Banks.* Englewood Cliffs, N.J.: Prentice-Hall, Inc., 1962.

FENSTERMAKER, J. VAN. *The Development of American Commercial Banking: 1782–1837.* Kent, Ohio: Kent State University Press, 1965.

FISCHER, GERALD C. *American Banking Structure.* New York: Columbia University Press, 1968.

GIES, THOMAS G., AND VINCENT P. APILADO. *Banking Markets and Financial Institutions.* Homewood, Ill.: Richard D. Irwin, Inc., 1971.

HAMMOND, BRAY. *Banks and Politics in America.* Princeton, N.J.: Princeton University Press, 1957.

HAYES, DOUGLAS A. *Bank Lending Policies: Issues and Practices.* Ann Arbor, Mich.: The University of Michigan Press, 1964.

HODGMAN, DONALD R. *Commercial Bank Loan and Investment Policy.* Champaign, Ill.: University of Illinois Press, 1963.

JESSUP, PAUL F. (ed). *Innovations in Bank Management: Selected Readings.* New York: Holt, Rinehart and Winston, Inc., 1969.

KOHN, ERNEST. *Branch Banking, Bank Mergers, and the Public Interest.* New York: New York State Banking Department, 1964.

———— AND CARMEN J. CARLO. *The Competitive Impact of New Branches.* New York: New York State Banking Department, 1969.

MCCARTHY, EDWARD J. *The Reserve Position: Methods of Adjustment.* Rev. ed. Boston: Federal Reserve Bank of Boston, 1970.

NADLER, PAUL. *Commercial Banking in the Economy.* New York: Random House, Inc., 1968.

PROCHNOW, HERBERT V. (ed). *The One-Bank Holding Company.* Chicago: Rand-McNally & Co., 1969.

REED, EDWARD R. *Commercial Bank Management.* New York: Harper & Row, Publishers, Inc., 1963.

ROBINSON, ROLAND I. *The Management of Bank Funds.* 2d ed. New York: McGraw-Hill Book Company, Inc., 1962.

Senate Commitee on Banking and Currency. *Federal Banking Laws and Reports: 1780–1912.* Washington, D.C.: Government Printing Office, 1963.

TRESCOTT, PAUL B. *Financing American Enterprise: The Story of Commercial Banking.* New York: Harper & Row, Publishers, Inc., 1963.

WILLIS, PARKER B. *Federal Funds Market: Its Origin and Development.* Rev. ed. Boston: Federal Reserve Bank of Boston, 1970.

Part 4: The Federal Reserve as Central Bank

BECKHART, BENJAMIN H. *The Federal Reserve System.* New York: Columbia University Press, 1971.

BOPP, KARL R. *Introduction to the Federal Reserve System.* Philadelphia: Federal Reserve Bank of Philadelphia.

CLIFFORD, A. JEROME. *The Independence of the Federal Reserve System.* Philadelphia: University of Pennsylvania Press, 1965.

EASTBURN, DAVID P. (ed.) *Men, Money, and Policy: Essays in Honor of Karl R. Bopp.* Philadelphia: Federal Reserve Bank of Philadelphia, 1970.

ECCLES, MARRINER. *Beckoning Frontiers.* New York: Alfred A. Knopf, Inc., 1951.

HARDING, W. P. G. *The Formative Period of the Federal Reserve System.* Boston: Houghton Mifflin Company, 1925.

House Committee on Banking and Currency. *Hearings on the Federal Reserve System after Fifty Years.* 3 vols. Washington, D.C.: Government Printing Office, 1964.

————. *Staff Report: The Federal Reserve System after Fifty Years.* Washington, D.C.: Government Printing Office, 1964.

WARBURG, PAUL M. *The Federal Reserve System.* 2 vols. New York: Crowell Collier and Macmillan, Inc., 1930.

WILLIS, H. PARKER. *The Federal Reserve System.* New York: The Ronald Press Company, 1923.

Part 5:   Monetary Theory

ABRAHAM, WILLIAM I. *National Income and Economic Accounting.* Englewood Cliffs, N.J.: Prentice-Hall, Inc., 1969.

CLOWER, R. W. (ed). *Monetary Theory: Selected Readings.* Baltimore: Penguin Books, Inc., 1969.

DEAN, EDWIN (ed). *The Controversy over the Quantity Theory of Money.* Boston: D.C. Heath & Company, 1965.

DILLARD, DUDLEY. *The Economics of John Maynard Keynes.* Englewood Cliffs, N.J.: Prentice-Hall, Inc., 1948.

FISHER, IRVING. *The Purchasing Power of Money.* Rev. ed. New York: Crowell Collier and Macmillan, Inc., 1926.

FRIEDMAN, MILTON. *The Counter-Revolution in Monetary Theory.* Occasional Paper #33. London: Institute of Economic Affairs, 1970.

GARVEY, GEORGE, and MARTIN R. BLYN. *The Velocity of Money.* New York: Federal Reserve Bank of New York, 1969.

HANSEN, ALVIN H. *A Guide to Keynes.* New York: McGraw-Hill Book Company, Inc., 1953.

JASZI, GEORGE, and others. *Readings in Concepts and Methods of National Income Statistics.* Washington, D.C.: U.S. Department of Commerce, Office of Business Economics, 1970.

JOHNSON, HARRY G. *Essays in Monetary Economics.* Cambridge, Mass.: Harvard University Press, 1969.

KLEIN, LAWRENCE R. *The Keynesian Revolution.* London: Macmillan & Co., Ltd., 1950.

LAIDER, DAVID E. W. *The Demand for Money: Theories and Evidence.* Scranton, Pa.: INTEX, 1969.

LECKACHMAN, ROBERT (ed). *Keynes and the Classics.* Boston: D. C. Heath & Company, 1964.

———— (ed). *Keynes' General Theory: Reports of Three Decades.* New York: St. Martin's Press, Inc., 1964.

MARSHALL, NATALIE (ed). *Keynes: Updated or Outdated?* Boston: D. C. Heath & Company, 1970.

PRAGER, JONAS (ed). *Monetary Economics: Controversies in Theory and Policy.* New York: Random House, Inc., 1971.

RUGGLES, NANCY and RICHARD. *The Design of Economic Accounts.* New York: Columbia University Press (for the National Bureau of Economic Research), 1970.

THORN, RICHARD S. (ed). *Monetary Theory and Policy.* New York: Random House, Inc., 1966.

WEINTRAUB, ROBERT E. *Introduction to Monetary Economics.* New York: The Ronald Press Company, 1969.

YEAGER, LELAND B. (ed). *In Search of a Monetary Constitution.* Cambridge, Mass.: Harvard University Press, 1962.

Part 6:   Monetary and Fiscal Policy

AHEARN, DANIEL S. *Federal Reserve Policy Reappraised: 1951–1959.* New York: Columbia University Press, 1963.

ANDERSON, CLAY J. *A Half-Century of Federal Reserve Policymaking:1914–1964.* Philadelphia: Federal Reserve Bank of Philadelphia, 1965.

ARROW, KENNETH J., and MORDECAI KURZ. *Public Investment, the Rate of Return, and Optimal Fiscal Policy.* Baltimore: The Johns Hopkins Press (for Resources of the Future, Inc.), 1970.

BACH, G. L. *Making Monetary and Fiscal Policy.* Washington, D.C.: Brookings Institution, 1971.

BRUNNER, KARL (ed). *Targets and Indicators of Monetary Policy.* San Francisco: Chandler Publishing Co., 1969.

CHANDLER, LESTER V. *American Monetary Policies: 1928–1941.* New York: Harper & Row, Publishers, Inc., 1971.

Commission on Money and Credit. *Money and Credit: Their Influence on Jobs, Prices, and Growth.* Englewood Cliffs, N.J.: Prentice-Hall, Inc., 1961.

Committee for Economic Development. *Fiscal and Monetary Policies for Steady Economic Growth.* New York: Committee for Economic Development, 1969.

EASTBURN, DAVID P. *The Federal Reserve on Record.* Philadelphia: Federal Reserve Bank of Philadelphia, 1965.

——— (ed). *Men, Money, and Policy: Essays in Honor of Karl R. Bopp.* Philadelphia: Federal Reserve Bank of Philadelphia, 1970.

Federal Reserve Bank of Boston. *Controlling Monetary Aggregates.* Boston: Federal Reserve Bank, 1969.

FRIEDMAN, MILTON. *A Program for Monetary Stability.* New York: Fordham University Press, 1960.

Joint Economic Committee. *Joint Economic Report* (annual). Washington: Government Printing Office.

LEWIS, WILFRED, JR. *Federal Fiscal Policy in the Postwar Recessions.* Washington: Brookings Institution, 1962.

MAYER, THOMAS. *Monetary Policy in the United States.* New York: Random House, Inc., 1968.

MEEK, PAUL. *Open Market Operations.* 2d ed. New York: Federal Reserve Bank of New York, 1969.

STEIN, HERBERT. *The Fiscal Revolution in America.* Chicago: University of Chicago Press, 1969.

WOODWORTH, G. WALTER. *The Money Market and Monetary Management.* New York: Harper & Row, Publishers, Inc., 1965.

Part 7: International Monetary Transactions

COHEN, BENJAMIN J. *Balance-of-Payments Policy.* Baltimore: Penguin Books, Inc., 1970.

COHEN, STEPHEN D. *International Monetary Reform: 1964–1969.* New York: Frederick A. Praeger, Inc., 1970.

COOPER, R. N. (ed). *International Finance: Selected Readings.* Baltimore: Penguin Books, Inc., 1969.

EGON, SOHMEN. *Flexible Exchange Rates.* Rev. ed. Chicago: University of Chicago Press, 1969.

Federal Reserve Bank of Boston. *The International Adjustment Mechanism.* Boston: Federal Reserve Bank, 1970.

GRUBEL, HERBERT G. *The International Monetary System: Efficiency and Practical Alternatives.* Baltimore: Penguin Books, Inc., 1970.

HALM, GEORGE N. (ed). *Approaches to Greater Flexibility in Exchange Rates.* Princeton, N.J.: Princeton University Press, 1970.

HANSEN, ALVIN H. *The Dollar and the International Monetary System.* New York: McGraw-Hill Book Company, Inc., 1965.

HORSEFIELD, J. KEITH, and others. *The International Monetary Fund, 1945–1965: Twenty Years of International Monetary Cooperation.* 3 vols. Washington, D.C.: International Monetary Fund, 1969.

International Finance Section, Department of Economics, Princeton University. A special recommendation must be accorded to its occasional publications of superb quality written by many authors and published in four series: Essays in International Finance, Princeton Studies in International Finance, Reprints in International Finance, and Special Papers in International Finance.

International Monetary Fund. *Role of Exchange Rates in the Adjustment of International Payments: Report by the Executive Directors.* Washington, D.C.: International Monetary Fund, 1970.

KINDLEBERGER, CHARLES P. *Europe and the Dollar.* Cambridge, Mass.: MIT Press, 1966.

MIKESELL, RAYMOND F. *Financing World Trade: An Appraisal of the International Monetary System and of Proposals for Reform.* New York: Thomas Y. Crowell Company, 1969.

———. *The U.S. Balance of Payments and the International Role of the Dollar.* Washington, D.C.: American Enterprise Institute for Public Policy Research, 1970.

YEAGER, LELAND B. *The International Monetary Mechanism.* New York: Holt, Rinehart and Winston, Inc., 1968.